The
Christ
of the
Prophets

The
Christ
of the
Prophets

O. Palmer Robertson

P U B L I S H I N G

P.O. BOX 817 • PHILLIPSBURG • NEW JERSEY 08865-0817

Page design and typesetting by Lakeside Design Plus

Printed in the United States of America

Library of Congress Cataloging-in-Publication Data

Robertson, O. Palmer.
    The Christ of the prophets / O. Palmer Robertson.
        p. cm.
    Include bibliographical references and index.
    ISBN 0-87552-564-4 (cloth)
    1. Bible. O.T. Prophets—Criticism, interpretation, etc. 2. Prophets—Biblical teaching. I. Title.

BS1505.52.R63 2004
224'.06—dc22

2004044156

To My Three Sons
John Murray Robertson
David Elliot Robertson
Daniel Isaac Robertson

"As for me, this is my covenant with them," says the Covenant
LORD. "My Spirit, who is on you, and my words that I have put in
your mouth will not depart from your mouth, or from the mouths
of your children, or from the mouths of your children's children
from this time on and forever," says the Covenant LORD.
—*Isaiah 59:21*

CONTENTS

ANALYTICAL OUTLINE

INTRODUCTION

Something started God's prophets to writing. By the time they were finished, they had produced a body of literature unparalleled in human history. Nothing before or since has equaled the corpus of literature produced by the prophets of Israel.[1] But what was it that moved the prophets to produce this unique body of writing?

For a good many years, the prevailing approach in biblical criticism asserted that the prophets originally delivered their messages only in oral form as short, abrupt declarations. These rather irrational, ecstatic utterances were later written down and then repeatedly revised by a series of subsequent editors.[2] More recently, greater credence has been given to the view that the original prophets themselves wrote

1. "Wholly unique" is the characterization of the prophetic material given by Clements. He continues: "Nowhere else from antiquity has there been preserved such a literary collection." Prophetic literature on the scale of the Old Testament "remains a wholly unique product" of ancient Israel; *Old Testament Prophecy*, 203.

2. See Mowinckel, *Prophecy and Tradition*; and Rowley, *Servant of the Lord*, 93. The earlier opinion of scholars was largely based on the then-prevailing perspective that viewed the prophetic materials as the product of an evolutionary process. On the basis of this philosophical presupposition, the early prophets of Israel were perceived as more or less primitives who uttered their prophecies in a state of ecstasy, while only later did the religion of the prophets evolve into a more coherent system of belief. Von Rad, *Old Testament Theology*, 2.6, categorizes the idea of a "straight line of development" from ecstatic bands of prophets to Isaiah and Jeremiah as an "inadmissible oversimplification."

more of their messages than was previously recognized.[3] Obviously, from any perspective it must be acknowledged that somebody at some time in Israel's history wrote a great deal of material that has come to be known as "prophetic."

Certainly its creation may be legitimately attributed to the movement of God's inspiring Holy Spirit. Isaiah's rapturous vision of "the Lord, high and lifted up" with cherubim covering face and feet as they flew; Joel's prediction that "in the last days" God would "pour out his Spirit on all flesh" so that men and women, young and old, would see visions and dream dreams; Ezekiel's imagery of the valley of dry bones, with the inquisitive challenge to his faith, "Son of Man, can these bones live?"—these words, these images, and hundreds of passages like them throughout the prophets—these are not the normal productions of human scribblings that can be easily duplicated. They impress any impartial reader with a sense that these words are indeed *extraordinaire*.

But again the question must be raised, What was it in time and history that spurred on this outpouring of inspired literature across decades, even through centuries of time, manifesting a form and substance that had never occurred before and has never been repeated since?

In the pattern of scripture, the great saving events in Israel's history that first brought the nation into being were recorded so that posterity could understand their significance. According to the Pentateuch,

---

3. See von Rad, *Old Testament Theology*, 2.40–45. Lindblom, *Prophecy in Ancient Israel*, 221, affirms that it is an "incontestable fact" that the prophets themselves "sometimes" wrote their oracles. According to Fohrer, *Introduction to the Old Testament*, 359, "most" of the prophetic sayings were written down "while the prophets were still alive." In analyzing God's command for Ezekiel to eat the scroll presented to him, Zimmerli, "From Prophetic Word to Prophetic Book," 430, concludes that "it is evident that the prophet was already familiar with scrolls of this kind, inscribed with the prophetic word." In a peculiar twist of recent scholarship, some now propose that in contradistinction to the procedures of the preexilic prophets, the post-exilic prophets exclusively wrote their messages without ever proclaiming them orally. It is rather interesting to find these recent perspectives anticipated by a scholar of the previous generation who took the witness of the prophetic material more seriously than is generally done: "In some cases the prophet, under the protecting inspiration of the Spirit of God, may have written down long sections of his messages shortly after having delivered them orally. On the other hand, it may be that some of the prophecies were never delivered orally, but were purely literary products" (Young, *Introduction to the Old Testament*, 157–58).

the exodus from Egypt did not occur merely as the dramatic deliverance of one more people from the bondage of enslavement. These great events were instead a redemptive action by God himself in which he delivered his chosen people from their sinful pollution through the blood of the Passover lamb. Likewise, the laws of Israel were not merely the refinements of an upward spiral of humanity's ascent to moral perfection. Instead, the "ten words," the Ten Commandments, came in the context of a divine covenant initiated at Mount Sinai, a solemn bond of a blood-sealed oath by which the self-revealing Covenant LORD committed himself and his people to one another for eternity.

These mighty, formative acts of God in behalf of his chosen covenant people were carefully recorded and their abiding significance preserved in writing for the generations to come. Consequently, every future age is able to confirm for itself the intent of God in forming this people in the processes of human history and to join with Israel in the covenant that was intended to make them a blessing to all the nations of the world.

A similar circumstance surrounded the peak, the climactic epoch of God's dealings with his people under the auspices of his covenant with Israel. The history of divine blessing in the covenant reached its pinnacle in the days of David and Solomon almost five hundred years after Israel's deliverance from the oppression of pharaoh. In this glorious era, God's binding oath of the kingdom covenant was confirmed specifically with David and his descendants. God would have a "house," a dwelling place, a temple for his worship that would remain located squarely in the midst of his people's land. There he would meet with them, bless them, and make them a blessing to all the nations. At the same time, David would have a "house," a dynasty, a line of descendants that would reign on the throne in Jerusalem forever (2 Sam. 7:10–16; Pss. 89:19–37; 132:1–18). The merger of these two "houses" in one place on Mount Zion established the reality of God's kingdom on earth. As a consequence, the messianic kingdom of righteousness, forgiveness, justice, and love would expand eventually to embrace all other kingdoms of the world. God's anointed messiah would rule from sea to sea and from the river to the ends of the earth (72:1–17). God would subdue all enemies of righteousness and justice under messiah's feet (Ps. 2). This simultaneous establishment of David's throne and God's throne in Jerusalem marked the highest point of the realization of God's purposes in the history of Israel. The messiah and his kingdom stood at the center of all other nations, positioned so that God's work of redemption from sin and its consequences could spread throughout all the peoples of the earth.

Understandably then, this climactic event in the movement of redemptive history was also recorded by inspired writings, this time by the poets of Israel. If the nation was to be properly led in worship, a body of literature must inspire the adoration of the people. So David, the "sweet psalmist of Israel," spoke of the heavens that declare the glory of God and the firmament that proclaims the work of his hands; he wrote of the exaltation of man in creation and redemption, man who was made "a little lower than the angels" but "crowned with glory and honor"; he described the blessedness of the man whose transgressions are forgiven and whose sins are covered; he praised the Lord who served as his light and his salvation, the strength of his life; and he paid homage to the appointed messiah as God's son installed on Zion's holy hill, who would inherit the nations and overrule the abuses of power by earth's selfish monarchs. These psalms of David's day celebrated the glories of the messiah and his kingdom that had come and were yet to come.

But what then in the movement of redemptive history was the role of the writings of the prophets? What distinctive developments in history brought forth this great and glorious body of prophetic literature? If the climax in Israelite history had been realized in the establishment of the messianic monarchy, what was left?

Vos is undoubtedly correct in his observation that "the new organization of the theocratic kingdom under a human ruler" brought forward the prophetic ministry in Israel's history.[4] This "epochal onward movement" of the establishment of an anointed king who ruled for God represented a dramatic step forward in the manifestation of the saving purposes of God. Fittingly, Samuel made his appearance in conjunction with the establishment of Saul and David as Israel's first kings.

4. Vos, *Biblical Theology*, 203.

Throughout the remainder of the history of Israel's kings, the prophets often addressed their messages particularly to the rulers of both Israel and Judah.

But clearly a difference existed between the ministry of the early prophets such as Elijah and Elisha and the later prophets as represented by Isaiah and Ezekiel. In the first case, the personal histories of the prophets themselves served as the focus of their ministries, while their recorded words are few. Elijah dramatically confronts King Ahab on Mount Carmel, but says very little, while the history of his protégé Elisha includes as many as eighteen miraculous actions. But while the lives of Isaiah, Jeremiah, and Ezekiel have some significance as an embodiment of their message, it is the record of their words, now in written form, that represents the distinctive core of their ministry.[5]

But once more the question may be asked, what was it in the processes of Israel's history that led to the creation of such a significant corpus of written materials as the focus of the prophetic ministry?[6] If the establishment of the monarchy represented the apex of redemptive history in its progress under the old covenant, what was left?

The tragic was the thing that was left. This chosen, favored people of God's covenant would fail in their commitments. Rather than serving as God's light to the nations, this chosen people would display more depravity than the peoples surrounding them. As a consequence, they must be rejected by God, exiled, returned to their place of origin beyond the river. This nation that had been highly favored for fourteen hundred years since the time that their father Abraham left Ur of the Chaldees must now be forcibly returned to the land of the Chaldeans as God's righteous judgment for their persistence in rebellion.

But what in the purposes of God could this tragic development mean? How could the banishment of God's elect nation aid the progress

5. For the development of this distinction, see von Rad, *Old Testament Theology*, 2.33.

6. Fohrer, *Introduction to the Old Testament*, 360, reasons that "the spoken word [of the prophet] had to be recorded quickly so as to preserve its effectiveness." Only if it were written down could the power of the prophetic word be released again. While some truth may reside in this observation, it appears to attribute mantic power to the word itself rather than to the working of the sovereign Lord in the confirmation and enforcement of the truth of his word.

of God's plan for redeeming a people from fallen humanity? How would it all conclude? If God's people became "not my people," what could the future hold for a divine working that would revitalize a universe groaning in travail, waiting for redemption?

It was Israel's exile, and the future beyond the exile, that the literary prophets of Israel were called and commissioned to explain. They were prophets because their calling was to speak more than to act. They would not lead the nation into actions of a redemptive nature comparable to the deliverance from Egypt under Moses or the consolidation of the kingdom under David. As prophets, they were called first and foremost to speak, and by their speaking to demand repentance from the transgression of God's law and faith in God's word of grace.

But this group of God's servants was also commissioned to write. They were called to write because of the very nature of the historical moment in which they lived. The nation would be devastated, destroyed, annihilated. First the northern kingdom would be overrun by the Assyrians, carried into captivity far beyond its own bounds. But then the absolutely unthinkable would occur. The kingdom of Judah, harboring the hallowed place of God's dwelling, would disappear from the face of the earth. How then would even a thread of hope regarding God's redemptive purposes be maintained? What was left for Israel and consequently for all the nations that they were to bless with the good news of redemption? Where now was God's great work of revitalizing a corrupted earth?

Into this vacuum of apparent hopelessness the prophets were called to speak and to write. They must write as well as speak so that the continuity of hope could be maintained across the generations. As the period dawned in which arose "the great Asiatic universal monarchies" that were destined by God to be the instruments for the chastisement of his chosen nation, some affirmation of the unthreatened sovereignty of their God must be provided.[7] If nothing remained of the institutional activities of temple life in Jerusalem that were so perfectly designed to pass on the expectations of redemption to the

7. Keil, *Introduction to the Old Testament*, 1.279.

generations to come, something else must arise to fire a flame of hope in the hearts of future sons and daughters. That something else would be the inspired writings, the preserved predictions not only of exile but also of restoration after devastation. If the exile itself were anticipated in the written records of the prophets, then when that awful moment came, its place in the purposes of God could be comprehended. Instead of creating an atmosphere of unbelief, the exile as anticipated by the prophets would challenge the remnant of God's people to a faith that would see the Covenant LORD's just, purposeful hand in it all. At this critical juncture, it became necessary to establish the omniscience and omnipotence of the one true living God over the "apparent superiority of the gods of the heathen, as this became prominent in the victory of the worldly powers over the theocracy."[8]

Simultaneously, prophetic predictions of a restoration even after the devastations of exile could only have the effect of moving the people to a faith that looked to the future. For if God were true to his word in the message about the exile, he could be expected to be true to his word in the message about restoration.

And this restoration, what would it be? Would it mean simply a return to the old state of things that prevailed before exile? Would it anticipate a cycle of decline into sin followed inevitably by repeated divine judgments? Would the future kings of a restored Israel be no better than the kings of the past that were so roundly condemned by the prophets?

Not according to the writings of these same prophets. Preserved for posterity was the hope of a restoration far more glorious than the days before exile. A new covenant, a new Zion, a new temple, a new messiah, a new relation to the nations of the world—these were the expectations designed to create future hope for the people who would have to endure the trauma of deportation from their land. But not only for their own generation were these inspired writings divinely designed. They were meant for all future generations, until the time of the tri-

8. Ibid.

umphant coming of the expected messiah, which would eventually bring about the creation of a new heaven and a new earth.

So for all generations even until today the inspired writings of the prophets speak. Without the turning to God in faith and repentance that they demand, their words will not be rightly heard. But for all generations and peoples who will read and hear with the understanding that only faith can give, they will forever bring the message of hope and restoration.

It is for this reason that the writings of these prophets of old must be heard anew. They speak today just as clearly as they spoke at the time of their inspiration. With renewed faith let the generation of today hear this prophetic message, which centers on the coming messiah and his glorious kingdom once more.

1

The Origin
of Prophetism in Israel

"Of the beginnings of prophecy in Israel we know nothing."
—Johannes Lindblom, *Prophecy in Ancient Israel*

"The beginnings of Israelite prophecy remain obscure."
—Walther Zimmerli, *The Law and the Prophets*

"[Scripture] does not supply the information which is needed for
a solution [regarding the origin of prophetism in Israel]."
—Brevard S. Childs, *Biblical Theology
of the Old and New Testaments*

"Prophecy in Israel . . . begins in the inexplicable appearance of
individual persons who claim to speak Yahweh's revelatory word. . . .
The emergence of [these people] . . . is indeed an odd, inexplicable,
originary happening in Israel. . . . These originary individuals
are odd and cannot be explained by any antecedent."
—Walter Brueggemann, *Theology of the Old Testament*

In this fashion, leading biblical critics express their united, agnostic
viewpoint concerning the origin of prophetism in Israel. They simply
do not know how the phenomenon arose. For them, its origin is an
unsolved mystery. How a two-hundred-year-long stream of individuals who were convinced that God had communicated directly to them

could have originated is for them a puzzle without solution. Yet certain sources continue to be proposed for the origin of prophetism in Israel. Before considering the biblical testimony concerning the origin of prophetism in Israel, these alternative explanations for prophecy's origin in Israel must be examined.

I. Alternative explanations for the origin of prophetism in Israel

A. Ecstatic behavior

Biblical evidence indicates that some form of ecstatic experience was occasionally associated with prophetism in Israel. This element in the prophetic experience extends from early manifestations in the behavior of Saul (eleventh century B.C.) to the stunned response of Ezekiel to his visionary experience (sixth century B.C.). The Spirit of God came on Saul, who stripped himself of his robes and "prophesied" in the presence of Samuel (1 Sam. 19:23–24). After receiving his vision, Ezekiel sat overwhelmed for seven days (Ezek. 3:15). Centuries later, it is said of even the apostle Peter (first century A.D.) that "ecstasy" (*ekstasis*) fell on him in connection with the vision that launched his ministry to the vast world of Gentile nations (Acts 10:10). In view of this evidence, it is proposed that prophetism in Israel followed a developmental pattern similar to the phenomenon among the Canaanites and in other religions, evolving in a naturalistic manner from its primitive ecstatic beginnings to the more sophisticated utterances of Israel's later prophets.

It is quite difficult to provide convincing evidence that the commonplace human experience of ecstasy answers the question of the origin of biblical prophecy. The previously held opinion that Israelite prophecy originated in the merger of a nomadic element that Israel brought into Palestine and a native brand of Canaanite prophecy "is largely hypothetical and raises a number of problems."[1] This theory is based on "unexamined evolutionistic assumptions which cannot be supported by the evidence of the texts themselves."[2] Childs notes that

1. Porter, "Origins of Prophecy in Israel," 13.
2. Ibid., 14.

"increasingly a consensus has arisen that there is no way of correlating specific terminology [for prophetism] with historical growth."[3]

In addition, not all ecstasy is of the same character. Experiences of ecstatics can range from mindless mantic behavior to intensified spiritual insight. In the many reported instances of prophetic dreams and visions in scripture, little support may be found for the idea that the biblical prophet lost anything in terms of mental acumen in the process of his prophesying. To the contrary, the ecstasy associated with biblical prophecy is better understood as an experience that "lifts the human mind to the highest plane of intercourse with God."[4] The evidence of scripture indicates that as the biblical prophet came out of his visionary experience, he had full remembrance of what he had seen and heard. Even though transported into the presence of the cherubim-encircled God, the prophet Isaiah remains fully self-conscious, even to the point of developing a painful awareness of his personal sinfulness (Isa. 6:5). It is thus appropriately suggested that ecstasy in the sense of a mindless mantic behavior "was never an element of genuine and original Israelite prophecy."[5]

If, therefore, the origin of prophecy in Israel cannot be found in a developmental process from a mindless ecstasy to rational speech, what then brought about this widespread, persistent phenomenon in Israel? A second proposal is that prophetism in Israel arose in association with the cultic practices of the nation.

B. Cultic practice

Gone are the days in which it was seriously proposed that the prophet in Israel stood as the critical antithesis to Israel's priesthood. Passages in which the prophets critique Israel's ritual system are now rightly understood as judgment on the heartless manner rather than the outward mode of worship. The simple observation that the prophets critiqued the prayers of the nation just as vigorously as they condemned their sacrifices supports this conclusion.[6] But was the prophet, like the priest, attached professionally to the worship centers

3. Childs, *Biblical Theology of the Old and New Testaments*, 168.
4. Vos, *Biblical Theology*, 245.
5. Ibid., 14.
6. Harrison, *Introduction to the Old Testament*, 746–47.

of Israel? Could the cult be understood as the legitimate originator of prophetism in Israel?

The most straightforward answer to this question is simply that there is little evidence that the prophetic movement got its start from association with the cultic practices of Israel. Clearly, the prophets participated in Israel's worship practices as a normal part of their life. Some few scripture passages suggest the possibility of a residential role of prophets in relation to the temple and its cultic activities.[7] But as Vawter observes, though there may be some ground for connection with the cult in a few cases, "there is simply no probability in favor of the 'cultic' hypothesis."[8] The assessment of Rowley that "we must beware of outrunning the evidence"[9] regarding the role of cultic prophets in Israel continues to provide a sensible perspective on the subject. The relation of the prophets in Israel to

7. Jer. 35:4 refers to the "chamber" of the sons of Hanan son of Igdaliah the "man of God" that was located in the house of the Lord. This statement could be interpreted to mean that descendants of a prophetic figure had a permanent locale in the temple. Yet the assertion is far from establishing the role of cultic prophets in Israel. Bright, *Jeremiah*, 189, notes that the term *man of God* "occurs only here in Jeremiah, and we do not know if by the late seventh century it had acquired a special connotation distinct from *nābīʾ* (prophet)." Bright does allow for the possibility that Hanan was "a cultic functionary of some sort." In referring to the same passage in Jeremiah, Johnson, *Cultic Prophet in Ancient Israel*, 62, notes evidence that "the prophets had special quarters (but not necessarily a permanent residence) within the Temple itself." On this basis he affirms that "one can hardly do other than infer that the reference is to a particular school or guild of prophets forming part of the Temple personnel." While the inference is possible from the text, it certainly is not compelling, particularly in view of its heavy dependence on the assumption that "man of God" must mean prophet at this time and not merely a pious person in this single use of the term in Jeremiah, who by contrast uses the term *prophet* numerous times. A more significant potential source for references to a cultic-type prophet in Israel is the books of Chronicles. At some points in Chronicles, prophesying is best understood as having "its wider signification of the singing and playing to the praise of God performed in the power of the Divine Spirit" (Keil, *Chronicles*, 270; see 1 Chron. 25:1, 3; 2 Chron. 29:30; 35:15). In other cases, the priests are used of God to communicate a divinely revealed prophetic message in response to a particular situation (20:14; 24:20). In neither of these cases, however, does the text give adequate evidence to support the idea that these priests were empowered to speak forth on demand the very word of God as a cultic celebration might require.

8. Vawter, "Introduction to Prophetic Literature," 193.

9. Rowley, *Servant of the Lord*, 105.

12

the cult does not encourage the idea that prophetism grew out of the nation's worship practices.[10]

C. Ancient Near Eastern prophecy

A phenomenon that may be called prophecy clearly existed among the various nations of the ancient Near East.[11] Jeremiah himself recognizes the activity of prophets among the nations surrounding Judah (Jer. 27:2–4, 9–10). Many ancient texts have come to light that may be designated as prophetic in nature, particularly material from eighteenth-century B.C. Mari of the middle Euphrates and from the seventh-century B.C. Neo-Assyrian Empire.[12]

1. Mari

The eighteenth-century materials from mid-Euphrates Mari that might compare with biblical prophecy include two ritual texts, about fifty out of eight thousand letters and about twelve economic or administrative texts out of a total of twelve thousand.[13] These prophetic texts are preserved in the form of secondhand references to prophecies, pri-

10. See the review of the evidence in Harrison, *Introduction to the Old Testament*, 746–47. For a full development of the cultic hypothesis, see Johnson, *Cultic Prophet in Ancient Israel*. After his review of the biblical materials, Johnson concludes by stating that "it is difficult to see how one can resist the conclusion that the prophets, quite as much as the priests, were officially connected with the temple cultus" (61). In his preface, however, he distances himself from the "complicated question as to whether or not any of the canonical prophets are to be regarded as cultic prophets" (v). He states: "The fact is that we are not yet at the stage where this question can be discussed in anything like a satisfactory way." That the prophets often functioned in connection with the temple at Jerusalem cannot be denied. But this assumption can hardly establish that they held the position of cultic functionaries.

11. Vawter, "Introduction to Prophetic Literature," 186–87, notes that most, if not all religions, "have produced the phenomenon of prophecy." Huffmon, "Origins of Prophecy," 176, states that prophecy as defined in the Bible is "not a unique or isolated happening in the world of the ancient Near East." Yet as will be argued, certain distinctives clearly mark the biblical phenomenon as unique.

12. According to the analysis of Nissinen, "Socioreligious Role of the Neo-Assyrian Prophets," 89, more than 130 ancient Near Eastern texts concerning prophetic phenomena have been identified. He indicates that about half of these texts come from Mari, and a little less than half from Assyria.

13. For a full presentation of the texts at Mari, see Durand, *Archives epistolaires de Mari*, 377–452. See also Huffmon, "Company of Prophets," 48–49.

marily presented to the king as letters from various officials, informing him of the basic substance of certain oracles that have been brought to their attention.[14] The texts mention various individuals who claim to have received messages that originated with the deity. This material has some similarity to prophecy in the Old Testament. Yet its substance is quite different, as the following particulars indicate:

- Scope of concerns: The biblical prophets manifest a breadth of concern over social, ethical, and religious matters, while the texts of Mari are more narrowly concerned with matters primarily related to the welfare of the king.[15]
- Centrality of the prophetic ministry: Prophecy in the Bible plays a center-stage role in Israelite society. But the occasional oracle of a prophet in Mari makes only a minor contribution in the life of the community.[16]
- Critique of king and people: "In contrast with Mari, the Bible is replete with prophecies unfavorable to the king and to the people."[17] While the Mari texts have as their intention the support and encouragement of the king, the prophetic declarations in the Old Testament more often condemn rather than commend the highest authorities of their society.
- Verification of prophetic oracles by cultic means: If the validity of the prophetic message in Mari was questionable, the correspondent with the king would recommend that a further ora-

14. Malamat, "Forerunner of Biblical Prophecy," 37.

15. Malamat, ibid., 36, observes that the many references to military affairs and the concern for the welfare of the king "is significantly distinct from biblical prophecy, which presents a full-fledged religious ideology, a socioethical manifest, and a national purpose alongside the universal vision." For a somewhat different perspective, see Parker, "Official Attitudes toward Prophecy," 67–68.

16. Huffmon, "Company of Prophets," 49, notes that "prophetic messages [in Mari] are clearly subordinate to other, more common means of divine communication."

17. Malamat, "Forerunner of Biblical Prophecy," 42. Huffmon, "Origins of Prophecy," 173–74, notes that the Mari oracles are often critical of the king for failing in his duties to various gods and temples; and on one occasion the king is even reminded of his obligation to promote justice. Yet Huffmon indicates that the Mari texts are mostly favorable to the king. In sum, the Mari texts cannot compare with the thoroughgoing rebuke of king and people found in Israel's prophets.

14

cle be sought to confirm the prophetic word. No such cultic means was employed in Israel to verify the prophet's message, whether believed or not.[18]

- Crudity of prophetic action: In Mari, a prophet devours a raw lamb and then announces the "devouring" of the country. While this passage is described as the "most illuminating text" among the prophetic oracles of Mari, it is also noted that "the crudity of the action exceeds anything attributed to the Israelite prophets."[19] Actions of the biblical prophets may be characterized as unusual, but not crude.

- Material support from the royal court: On occasion a prophet in Mari received gifts and material support from the royal court, such as a garment, a silver ring, a donkey. At other times the prophet might even go so far as to directly request a gift.[20] Except for the aberrant covetousness of Elisha's servant Gehazi, the prophets of Israel did not seek or receive support from the court of Israel's king. This factor indicates a wholly different role in society for Israel's prophets in contrast with their counterparts at Mari.

- Prophets speaking in the name of a variety of gods: In Israel the true prophet speaks exclusively in the name of the one and only God, the creator of all things, the Covenant LORD of Israel. But in Mari the prophets promote the different interests of various gods.[21]

So how is prophecy at Mari related to the origin of prophetism in Israel? It cannot be said that the two realms of prophecy are "in no

18. Malamat, "Forerunner of Biblical Prophecy," 47, indicates that, in contrast with Mari, the prophetic word in Israel "is never subjected to corroboration by cultic means; it is simply vindicated by the test of fulfillment (cf. Deut. 18:22; Jer. 28:9; Ezek. 33:33)." Parker, "Official Attitudes toward Prophecy," 68, finds that prophecy, in the basic sense of a person bringing a message from the gods, is "essentially the same" at Mari and in Israel. But he further notes that omens were not used in Israel to check the prophet's words, as in Mari.

19. Gordon, "From Mari to Moses," 69.

20. Huffmon, "Company of Prophets," 54; Malamat, "Forerunner of Biblical Prophecy," 39.

21. Huffmon, "Company of Prophets," 56, cites an example from Mari to this effect.

way comparable."[22] On a most basic level, both groups of prophets intend to present a message from God (or the gods).

Yet the differences are quite basic, so that it would be very difficult to support the idea that the origin of Israelite prophecy may be found in the institution of prophetism as manifested a thousand years earlier at Mari. After a full review of the materials, one recent critic notes: "It therefore seems safest to conclude that, in its earliest manifestation, Israelite prophecy was essentially an indigenous phenomenon with a character of its own dictated by the unique situation in which Israelites found themselves."[23] In the light of the available evidence, the least that should be said is that it is premature to suggest that Mari presents the "prototype of prophecy in Israel."[24]

2. Neo-Assyria

The seventh-century Neo-Assyrian prophetic texts are called "the closest historical and phenomenological analogy to ancient Israelite/Judean prophecy."[25] These texts were first made publicly known in 1875 when George Smith published an unusual cuneiform tablet from Nineveh that he labeled "Addresses of Encouragement to [the Assyrian king] Esarhaddon," whose reign may be dated approximately 680–669 B.C.[26] By 1915, most of the currently known corpus was published in English, French, or German. After World War I, little interest was shown in the texts virtually to the end of the twentieth century. Although the texts were available, they did not receive the examination they deserved.

But in 1997, the complete text of the tablets was published, with extensive notes and translation.[27] These seventh-century texts were written during the same time span as several of Israel's literary prophets and in a period when Assyria had extensive contact with its vassal-state Israel. For these reasons alone, this extrabiblical prophetic mate-

22. As pointed out by Gordon, "From Mari to Moses," 76.
23. Blenkinsopp, *History of Prophecy in Israel*, 48.
24. Malamat, "Forerunner of Biblical Prophecy," 36.
25. Nissinen, "Socioreligious Role of the Neo-Assyrian Prophets," 114.
26. Parpola, *Assyrian Prophecies*, ix.
27. Parpola's *Assyrian Prophecies* should spark extensive research into the materials. The tablets themselves are currently located in the British Museum.

rial stands much closer to the biblical material than do the Mari texts, which date a thousand years earlier.

This collection of Assyrian texts consists of twenty-eight oracles by thirteen prophets, four male and nine female.[28] As a rough estimate, the actual words of the texts equal about one percent of the biblical prophetic texts. Rather than consisting of indirect reports of prophecies contained in correspondence addressed to the king as found at Mari, many of these Assyrian texts preserve the actual wording of prophetic utterances on "collection tablets" containing five to ten short oracles on a single tablet. Only in a very limited sense is a context provided for the utterances, and no response to the prophecies is indicated.

With only a few exceptions, these prophetic declarations focus on a word of reassurance for the king or his royal family. King Esarhaddon is assured that he will overcome all his opposition and that his sons will succeed him.[29] According to one analysis, "the king's self-interest determines truth or falsehood" in any particular utterance of a prophet.[30]

The worship of the goddess Ishtar "was the primary setting for the Assyrian prophets' socioreligious role."[31] As devotees of Ishtar, most of the prophets, the majority of them being women, "represent the motherly aspect of the divine, manifested as nursing the king and as fighting for him."[32] At the same time, these prophets and prophetesses could also proclaim words that came from other deities besides Ishtar.

So how does this prophetic material compare with the phenomenon of prophecy in Israel, much of which was being produced in the same time period? Because they are indeed "the closest historical and phenomenological analogy to ancient Israelite/Judean prophecy" (Nissinen's assessment, quoted above), a broad similarity may be seen in these prophets' claim to declare words of the deity

28. Ibid., xlviii.
29. Ibid., 4–11.
30. Huffmon, "Company of Prophets," 62.
31. Nissinen, "Socioreligious Role of the Neo-Assyrian Prophets," 104; see also 95.
32. Ibid., 99.

to their contemporaries. The value placed on these oracles is indicated by their being collected and recorded on tablets preserved in the royal scriptorium. But more particularly, what connection may be made between Assyrian and Israelite prophecy? Could it be that prophecy in Assyria served as the source of the similar phenomenon in Israel?

Parpola proposes that the similarities between Assyrian and biblical prophecy can be explained by "conceptual and doctrinal similarities of the underlying religions, without having to resort to the implausible hypothesis of direct loans or influences one way or the other."[33] In considering this analysis, it may be noted first that "direct loans or influences" are discounted as an "implausible hypothesis," which means that in Parpola's opinion Assyrian prophecy should not be regarded as the source of Israelite prophecy. Further, Parpola concludes that Assyrian prophecy should not be considered as directly influencing the prophetic material of the Bible.

Yet Parpola proposes that similarities of religion explain the comparable features between Assyrian and Israelite prophecy. For example, in oracle 1.4, the deity speaks first as Bel, then as Ishtar of Arbela, and finally as Nabu, son of Bel—leading Parpola to conclude that "one cannot help being reminded of the holy trinity of Christianity."[34] The concept of God as the "sum total of gods" in the ancient Near East "certainly also was part and parcel of first-millennial B.C. Jewish monotheism."[35] For Parpola this is enough to confirm "that both Judaism and Christianity share many apparently polytheistic concepts and features with Assyrian religion."[36] For example, because the goddess Ishtar is the god Assur revealed in his mother-aspect, "she is the functional equivalent of the biblical Spirit of God."[37] In summarizing the significance of these proposed parallels, Parpola affirms: "All things considered, the conceptual frame-

---

33. Parpola, *Assyrian Prophecies*, xvi.
34. Ibid., xviii.
35. Ibid., xxi.
36. Ibid., xxii.
37. Ibid., xxvi.

work of Assyrian prophecy emerges as largely identical with that of ancient Israelite prophecy."[38]

Each of these proposed parallels might be discussed at length to display the erroneous comprehension of basic biblical testimony concerning the absolute oneness of the God of the Bible in contradistinction to all polytheistic concepts. Hopefully, evidence for this basic truth of the Judeo-Christian heritage need not be marshaled once more. But if these kinds of spurious comparisons lie at the root of the supposed connection between prophetism in Assyria and Israel, then the uniqueness of biblical prophecy is all the more strongly enforced. This uniqueness is even doubly accented if these Assyrian prophetic texts are judged to be the closest parallel to biblical prophecy in the ancient Near East.

In this regard, the whole concept of seeking the origin of biblical prophecy in foreign contexts needs to be placed under the severest scrutiny. Why, in principle, should a foreign origin for Israelite prophecy be more favorable for the development of the phenomenon than an indigenous development?[39] What in the history or society of Mari or Assyria makes these nations more amenable to the origination of the idea of prophetism than the nation of Israel? To the contrary, if any credence is given to the biblical testimony regarding the experience of the exodus, Sinai, conquest, and kingship in Israel, then every reason existed for prophetism as a movement to arise in Israel. Similar kinds of reasons would be difficult to find in the historical records of other nations.

More convincing parallels may be discovered in the material that is designated Collection Three of the Assyrian prophetic texts, which

38. Ibid., xxiv. While the academic community is greatly indebted to Parpola in making available this edition of the prophetic texts from Assyria, the philosophical basis for comparisons with the biblical text must be weighed with a critical eye. Parpola explicitly describes his method in finding parallels: "The 'cover picture' used as an aid in analyzing, interpreting and piecing together these disconnected fragmentary bits of evidence was the comparative evidence provided by related religious and philosophical systems" (xvii). His misappropriation and misapplication of the basic biblical witness concerning the essential nature of God makes it doubly necessary to exercise discretion in drawing conclusions based on Parpola's personal analysis, particularly in his editorial notes.

39. Vos, *Biblical Theology*, 224.

contains five brief oracles. The second oracle, entitled "The Covenant of Assur," includes the following lines:

> [You]r [king] has put his enemy [under] his foot.

> From sunrise to sunset there is no king equal to him.

> This covenant tablet of Assur enters the king's presence on a cushion. Fragrant oil is sprinkled, sacrifices are made, incense is burnt, and they read it out in the king's presence.[40]

The parallels to expressions in Psalms 2 and 72 are quite striking and deserve further analysis. But it must be noted that these biblical passages have been dated much earlier than the seventh-century Assyrian texts.[41] It is therefore difficult to argue that these later Assyrian texts served as the source of the ideas found in the psalms.

The third oracle of Collection Three refers to the "covenant tablet of Assur" and indicates that it was "read out in the king's presence."[42] The fourth oracle, entitled "The Meal of the Covenant," contains the phrase "[enter] the cove[nant]."[43] The text further refers to eating bread and drinking water and states that after forgetting the covenant, a person will be reminded of his obligation to keep the covenant made in behalf of Esarhaddon by drinking this water. The goddess that uttered this oracle then complains that she has no food for her banquet.[44]

Once more, these materials need to be considered carefully in terms of the light they might shed on the biblical texts, particularly as they relate to the making of a covenant. Many parallels instantly suggest themselves, but must be weighed carefully before conclusions

---

40. Parpola, *Assyrian Prophecies*, 23, 25.

41. Dahood, *Psalms*, 1.7, says of Ps. 2: "The genuinely archaic flavor of the language suggests a very early date (probably tenth century)." Concerning Ps. 72, Kraus says, "The song is undoubtedly preexilic and could be assigned to a relatively early time" (*Psalms*, 2.77). Commenting generally on the dating of the Psalter, Weiser says: "The majority of the psalms came into existence in the pre-exilic period of Israel's history" (*Psalms*, 91).

42. Parpola, *Assyrian Prophecies*, 25.

43. Ibid.

44. Ibid., 25–26.

about precise relationships may be offered. Among other things, it must be considered that the covenant-making procedure appears among some of the oldest traditions in Israel and thus predates this Assyrian material by several centuries.[45]

II. Biblical testimony regarding the origin of prophetism in Israel

Since the various alternative explanations for the origin of prophetism in Israel prove unsatisfactory, the testimony of scripture itself, an often overlooked and strangely minimized source, may be considered with even greater care. In this record may be found a coherent and cogent explanation for the origin of this amazing and unique phenomenon of prophetism in Israel. This source provides needed information concerning the origin of prophetism in the flow of Israel's history, while also defining the leading aspects of this unique phenomenon.

Prophetism according to scripture finds its remotest origin in the purposeful creation of all things by the one and only God of the universe. Several passages in the writings of the prophets bind together the one God's creative activity with his word of purpose as revealed through his servants the prophets:

> He who
> > forms the mountains,
> > creates the wind,
> > and *declares his thoughts to man,* . . .
> the Covenant LORD, God Almighty is his name. (Amos 4:13)[46]

45. See the comments of von Rad that the narrative concerning the covenant in Gen. 15 "is probably one of the oldest narratives in the tradition about the patriarchs" (*Genesis*, 189).

46. The precise meaning of the passage is disputed. The problem in interpretation arises with the ambiguous character of the pronoun *his*. Does this refer to God's thoughts or to man's thoughts? Anderson and Freedman, *Amos*, 456, conclude that it is God's own thoughts that he is revealing to man: "It is his secret thought, his inner musing, that he reveals," which is indeed a most amazing affirmation in the scriptures. Wolff, *Joel and Amos*, 224, says that both the *hapax legomenon shekho* (his plan) and the participle *maggid* (who declares) support the idea that it is God's plan that is being revealed. It would indeed seem rather superfluous for God to declare a person's own thoughts to him, even in a context of divine judgment. For an alternative viewpoint, see Niehaus, "Amos," 407.

And again:

> This is what *God the Covenant* LORD *says*—
>> he who created the heavens and stretched them out,
>> who spread out earth and all that comes out of it, . . .
> I, the Covenant LORD, have called you in righteousness. (Isa. 42:5 NIV)

And yet again:

> This is the word of the Covenant LORD concerning Israel.
>> The Covenant LORD,
>>> who stretches out the heavens,
>>> who lays the foundation of the earth,
>>> and who forms the spirit of man within him, declares:
>> "I am going to make Jerusalem a cup
>>> that sends all the surrounding peoples reeling."
>>>> (Zech. 12:1–2 NIV)

The climax of this binding of the creative purposes of God to prophecy appears in a context of extensive ridicule of the heathen idols that cannot speak (Isa. 44:9–20). In vivid contrast with the muteness of the idolatrous gods, Israel's God declares even future events before they occur:

> This is what the Covenant LORD says,
>> your redeemer,
>> and the one who formed you in the womb:
> I am the Covenant LORD,
>> the maker of all things,
>> the one who stretched out the heavens by myself alone,
>> who spread out the earth, even I alone,
>> who foils the signs of the pretenders,
>> who makes fools of prognosticators,
>> who overturns the wise,
>> and makes their knowledge look foolish,
>> who brings to pass the word of his servant,
>> and confirms the anticipations of his messengers. (Isa. 44:24–26)

This broader context of a purposeful creation and a planned redemption alone provides an adequate explanation for the emergence of prophetism in Israel. This one and only God, standing in stark contrast to all other "nothing-gods," confirms his plan through his prophetic spokesmen to his chosen people. Through a series of self-initiated covenantal bonds, revealed and sealed in the processes of human history, God makes known his person, his purpose, and his will for his people and for the nations of the world.

Israel's prophets thus saw themselves as raised up to be the living line of covenantal mediators between God and his people. Their solemn position involved being brought into the counsels of the Covenant LORD. Because of this privileged position, the prophet could declare authoritatively both the moral will and the redemptive purpose of the sovereign Covenant LORD of creation. In this role, the prophet could announce the consequences of blessing or cursing that would attend the chosen lifestyle of the people. In addition, by divine revelation, he was enabled to anticipate the history of God's judgment and blessing in both its short-term and long-term eventualities, making known to the people the plans of the Lord by which he would accomplish his redemptive purposes.

So the prophetic movement of Israel had its ultimate origin in the divine purposes of creation and redemption. But when in time and history did prophetism arise within the nation of Israel?

It might be assumed that the prophetic movement had its origin in Israel about the time of the great eighth-century prophets such as Isaiah, Micah, Hosea, and Amos. In many ways this period represents the high-water mark in the history of prophetism in Israel. But both Hosea (6:5; 9:7–8; 12:10, 13) and Amos (2:11–12) attest to the activity of prophets before their time. Alternatively, it could be proposed that prophetism in Israel originated with the earlier ministries of Elijah and Elisha[47] or even with the ministry of Samuel at the time of the establishment of the monarchy.[48] But the notation that "the word of the Covenant LORD was rare [during Samuel's boyhood]; there were

47. See von Rad, *Old Testament Theology*, 2.6.
48. Huffmon, "Origins of Prophecy," 177, says that this is the picture presented in the text of scripture, which in his opinion "seems to be essentially correct."

not many visions" presumes that a prophetic ministry had been in place for some time prior to the days of Samuel (1 Sam. 3:1 NIV).

According to scripture's self-testimony, prophetism's origins go back much further than the time of the monarchy in the history of God's redemptive activity among Israel. The early words of the prophet Hosea indicate the actual origin of prophetism in Israel: "By a prophet the Covenant LORD brought Israel from Egypt, and by a prophet he was kept" (Hos. 12:13 NASB). In this passage, the term *prophet* is chosen to best characterize the ministry of Moses. He was not king in Israel, though he exercised extensive powers in the nation. Though from a priestly family, he did not function primarily as a priest. He was a prophet, communicating God's revelatory word to his people. Prior to the days of Moses, God communicated directly with the head of individual families by vision, dream, or theophany. The patriarchs Abraham, Isaac, Jacob, and Joseph all received personal revelations. Rather than having another person bring the word of God to them, the Lord himself appeared in a variety of ways. Hosea speaks of this more ancient mode of divine revelation in the same passage:

> [Jacob] struggled with the angel and overcame him;
>> he wept and begged for his favor.
> He found him at Bethel
>> and talked with him there—
> the Covenant LORD God Almighty,
>> the Covenant LORD is his name of renown! (Hos. 12:4–5 NIV)

In Moses' day, however, the nation consisted of a massive population of 600,000 families. How was God to make known his will to this numerous nation? Rather than cause the same dream, vision, or theophany to occur simultaneously to 600,000 heads of families, God would speak to the whole nation through a single human, designated as his prophet. Rather than addressing all the people individually, the Lord would communicate his will, his message, through this single designated person, not normally through a supernatural manifestation of the divine nature or through an angelic being.

24

Scripture attests that by the prophet Moses the Lord accomplished the great saving event of bringing his people out of Egypt. In addition, it affirms that the formal establishment of the ongoing office of prophet occurred in connection with the events at Sinai. At that time, the people themselves requested a mediator (Exod. 20:18–21; Deut. 5:22–27). Because they were terrified by the manifestations of God's presence on the mountain, they asked Moses to go up and meet the Lord on their behalf. This request of the people became the occasion for the establishment of the office of prophet in Israel. As the event is later reported:

> A prophet from your midst, from among your brothers, like [Moses] the Covenant LORD your God will raise up for you. You must listen to him. [It will be] exactly according to all you asked of the Covenant LORD your God in Horeb on the day of the assembly when you said, "Do not make me hear the voice of the Covenant LORD my God again, and do not make me see this awesome fire again, or I will die." (Deut. 18:15–16)

According to the testimony of scripture, this request of the people at the time of the assembly at Sinai explains the origin of the office of prophet in Israel. The people were terrified at the manifestation of the presence of God, so the Lord appointed a prophetic mediator to separate the people from the awesome occurrences associated with the revelation of his will. As a consequence, the prophet in scripture takes on the role of gracious mediator. He stands between God and the people to deliver the word of the Lord. At the same time, the humanly fragile character of the prophet makes him much more subject to rejection and abuse by the people than the Lord himself in all his splendor would have been. No one dared abuse God at Sinai, for the glories of the deity were manifested with great awesomeness. But the gentleness of God's grace now makes his personal spokesman subject to their victimizing. Yet even by this position of vulnerability, the appointed prophet of the Lord embodies the principal message of God in his gracious covenant. Sinners at their worst, abusing the high privilege of receiving a word from the Lord, may still be redeemed from their self-destructive ways because of the long-suffering of the Lord as displayed in the abuses endured by his servants the prophets.

25

Several insights into the nature of prophecy may be derived from this biblical testimony concerning the origin of prophetism.

First, the awesomeness of the role being fulfilled by the bearers of this office deserves special notice. The person of the prophet substitutes for the presence of almighty God himself. This small, single voice replaces all the fearsome signs that accompanied the theophany at Sinai. The smoking, shaking mountain, animated by intense fire and blasting trumpet, now finds its equivalent in the gentle voice of a brother speaking among brothers.

Second, the origin of the truly prophetic word must not be sought in the subjective experience of the prophet. Even in cases in which the word of the Lord is transmitted to the prophet through an internal experience, the word itself originates with God and substitutes for his presence.

The absolute independence of the prophetic word from the person of the prophet is underscored by the fact that the office of prophet was not transmitted by natural generation, contrary to the pattern established for the offices of priest and king in Israel. The son of the king or of the priest normally succeeded his father in their respective offices. But no example in scripture suggests that the son of the prophet ever succeeded his father. Only by the direct calling and commissioning of the Lord could a person enter legitimately into the office of prophet. Even then, the prophet had to wait on God to reveal his word to him. He could not by his own initiative create a legitimate word of prophecy, even though he might earnestly ask the Lord to speak to him on a particular issue.[49]

Third, the word of the prophet does not primarily involve predictions regarding future events. Moses' main task in delivering the law at Sinai was not to predict the future, but to declare God's will as it was revealed to him. Not a single prediction is found in the Ten Commandments, the heart of the revelation communicated through Moses.

In this regard, the common distinction between the forth-telling of the prophetic word and the foretelling of the future by the prophet

49. Even the prophet Nathan's well-meaning response to David's desire to build a house for the Lord had to be corrected by a subsequent word that came directly from the Lord himself (2 Sam. 7:1–5).

must be carefully analyzed. From the beginning, the "telling forth" of the prophet was just as much a revelation of the word of God as was his foretelling of the future. It simply is not the case that the speaking forth of the prophet on various issues of the day was a kind of preaching with diminished authority, while his foretelling of the future was inspired in a higher sense.

The essence of prophetism is best defined in terms of this speaking forth of the word of God, not in terms of whether it involves a foretelling of the future. Given certain specific circumstances, the prophet would predict a future event. Obviously this kind of insight could occur only by divine revelation. Yet the essence of prophecy was not determined by the predictive element, but by the nature of the prophet's utterance as a revelation from God.

This perspective on the essence of prophecy is important for evaluating the question of the continuation of prophecy today. Clearly no one can infallibly foretell the specifics of the future, as was the case in biblical prophecy, apart from a direct revelation from the sovereign God who controls the future. But it is just as true that no one can "tell forth" the word of God in the prophetic sense apart from experiencing a revelation from God. Whether as foreteller or forth-teller, the prophet communicated revelation from God. If a person affirms that biblical prophecy continues today in either of its basic forms, it should be clear that he is expressing belief that revelation continues today. While a contemporary preacher may be "prophetic" in his pulpit ministry, he is not prophesying in the biblical sense of the word. Just as a preacher today may be apostolic but not an apostle, so he may be prophetic without being a prophet.

Fourth, as a consequence of the uniqueness of the prophetic ministry, the nation of Israel must be seen as having a distinctive role among the peoples of the earth. The book of Deuteronomy reflects on the privileged position of the Israelite nation by pointing out their uniqueness as recipients of the revelation of God's law to them: "What other nation is so great as to have such righteous decrees and laws as this body of laws I am setting before you today?" (Deut. 4:8 NIV). Because of the special revelation of God's will communicated through Moses in his prophetic role at Sinai, Israel stood out distinctly among the

nations of the world. This uniqueness of Israel in the plans and purposes of God indicates among other things that a full understanding
of prophetism in Israel can never be achieved by comparison with similar phenomena among other nations of the world. The previously
noted agnosticism of modern critics with respect to the origin of
prophetism in Israel should not be surprising, for Israel as recipient
of God's revelation is indeed unique. The distinctiveness of the body
of Israelite prophetic materials speaks for itself. According to the apostle Paul, Israel is unique "first of all" in that "they have been entrusted
with the very words of God" (Rom. 3:2 NIV).

From this uniqueness of Israel, it should not be concluded that
God had no concern for the other nations of the world. Rather, from
the beginning it was explained to Abraham that his descendants would
be a blessing to all nations (Gen. 12:3). When God first set apart Abraham and his descendants, he made it plain that any foreigner could
become a full participant in all the privileges of the sons of Abraham,
an equal heir of the same blessings (17:12–13). Interestingly, the first
use of the term *prophet* in scripture refers to Abraham's intercession
as the key to blessing for the nations of the world (20:7).

Fifth, as great as the office of prophetic mediator may appear in
the context of its origins, it cannot represent the manner in which the
ultimate purpose of God's covenant will be realized. The essence of the
covenant speaks of an intimacy of union between God and his people.
"I shall be your God and you shall be my people" summarizes the closeness of the relationship established by the covenant. Yet it was out of
terror in the presence of the Covenant LORD that the people asked for
someone to mediate God's word to them. So long as the people felt they
must have an intermediary between themselves and God, the ultimate
purpose of the covenant could not be fulfilled. This point is emphasized by Paul's statement that "a mediator does not speak of one" (Gal.
3:20). The presence of a mediator implicitly suggests a separation of
people from one another. For example, if husband and wife can communicate only through a mediator, then obviously they have not experienced the oneness intended in the marriage relationship.

In the processes of redemptive history, it becomes plain that only
if God himself should become the one who mediates the divine word

could the oneness of fellowship intended by the covenant be fulfilled. Once God himself became the mediator, the need for the intermediary work of the prophetic figure would come to an end. The new covenant confirms this perspective on the final goal of prophetism. The writer to the Hebrews speaks of the finality of prophetic revelation as found in the person of Jesus. Previously God spoke in many different ways through many different prophetic mediators. But now he has spoken with finality in his Son (Heb. 1:1–2). When the prophetic revelation comes directly through Jesus Christ the Son of God, then the ultimate goal of the covenant has been realized. He is the one mediator between God and men (1 Tim. 2:5). Experiencing the revelation of God through the Son means being one with God himself.

So according to the biblical testimony, prophetism in Israel had its origin with the establishment of the theocratic nation in the Mosaic period. As the foundational law of the covenant was being revealed, the prophetic office came into being. As a consequence, in stark contrast with a long history of negatively critical reconstruction, law and prophecy do not stand over against one another. Instead, prophetism originates with the mediation of God's law.

2

PROMINENT ASPECTS
OF PROPHETISM RELATED
TO ITS ORIGIN

Several passages in the Pentateuch closely connected with the origin of prophetism in Israel provide significant insight into a number of prominent aspects of the phenomenon at the point of its first appearance. Among these passages are Exodus 4:14–16; 7:1–5; Numbers 11:21–30; 12:1–8; Deuteronomy 13:1–5; 18:9–22. First among these prominent aspects is the priority of Moses.

I. The priority of Moses in relation to all other prophets

Since the days of Wellhausen at the end of the nineteenth century, the legal portions of the Pentateuch that scripture attributes to the prophetic gift granted to Moses have been regarded as belonging to a much later stage in the so-called evolutionary development of Israel's religion (see chap. 5 §I.B). While the scriptures present the law of Moses as providing the foundation for the ministry of Israel's prophets, this alternative viewpoint reverses the order and contends that the prophets of Israel came first and were subsequently followed by the institutions of law in Israel. In the opinion of Wellhausen, the book of Deuteronomy was a pious fraud that originated at the time of its discovery during the reform of King Josiah of Judah in about 627 B.C. Well-meaning officials composed the book in a way that made it appear to be Mosaic in origin, buried it in the neglected rubble of the temple in Jerusalem, and then supposedly discovered it again—all as a means of aiding Josiah in his reforming efforts.

If it is legitimate to inquire into the origins of the book of Deuteronomy, it should be equally legitimate to inquire into the origins of Wellhausen's theory. To his credit, Wellhausen resigned from a theological faculty out of conscience, feeling uneasy about preparing students for the gospel ministry. According to his own testimony, as a young student he found himself questioning the origins of the legal portions of the Pentateuch. He felt that the law of Moses was "like a ghost" that makes a noise but has no real substance in the writings of the prophets of Israel. Then at the age of twenty-three he heard for the first time the theory of Graf that the law actually followed rather than preceded the ministry of Israel's prophets. "Almost without knowing the reasons for his hypothesis, I was won over to it," attests Wellhausen.[1]

For more than one hundred years the academic world has largely taken its signals from Wellhausen, who was convinced of a theory about the origins of the Pentateuch almost without knowing the reasons for the proposal. In subsequent research, portions of the legal sections of the Pentateuch have been acknowledged as being more ancient than the latter part of the seventh century B.C. But the dating of the core of Deuteronomy in connection with the discovery of the lawbook during the reign of Josiah (640–609 B.C.) continues essentially as the unmovable anchor of the dominant schools of biblical criticism. As a consequence, the historical Moses along with his prophetic ministry as mediator of God's revealed law to Israel has been turned into a ghost, while some unknown person designated as the Deuteronomist, along with his Deuteronomistic school, has risen to unparalleled heights of glory. This truly ghostly figure is credited by various scholars not only with the composition of the book of Deuteronomy, but also with the shaping of the books of Joshua, Judges, Samuel, and Kings. Even further, this unknown and unknowable figure, along with his unat-

1. For this account of the origins of Wellhausen's hypothesis, see Zimmerli, *Law and the Prophets*, 23.

tested school, is credited with the rewriting of a significant portion of the prophetic books, particularly Hosea and Jeremiah.

In the end, scripture itself offers a more convincing testimony concerning the relation of law and prophet in Israel. Moses stands at the apex of prophetic activity in Israel. At the beginning of Israel's experience of prophetism, the peak is reached. Other prophets labor in the shadow of Moses. In his role as prophet par excellence, Moses delivered the law to God's people, which became the basis for their whole national (and personal) weal and woe.

This perspective of Moses as head of the prophetic movement in Israel does not deny progress in revelation. A prophet like Isaiah has a much richer appreciation of the work of the coming messiah and his kingdom than did Moses. Clearly Isaiah's picture of the suffering servant who was wounded for our transgressions stands closer to the consummating work of the Christ than the image of the Passover lamb as revealed through Moses. Yet Moses still fulfills the role of primal fountainhead of the revelation of God's law to his people, which contradicts the idea of a naturalistic evolution of prophetism in relation to law in Israel's experience. If the fountainhead of all prophetism appears at its beginning in the person of Moses, then revelation from God rather than religion concocted by men must be the origin of the truth he declares.

Two passages from the Pentateuch underscore the supremacy of Moses in old covenant revelation: Numbers 12 and Deuteronomy 18. These two passages indicate the priority of Moses by noting God's response to opposition to Moses in his prophetic role and the uniqueness of Moses in relation to all other prophetic figures.

A. Opposition to Moses

Who would oppose Moses, and why? Had he not been the instrument used by God to bring Israel out of Egypt? Was he not the mediator of God's law at Sinai? Why should he be opposed? The self-centeredness of the human heart explains the opposition to Moses. Both pretense and pride play a role in this opposition.

This opposition comes from within Moses' own family. Miriam (his sister) and Aaron (his brother) object to the role of Moses as leader of the nation (Num. 12:1). Scripture makes it plain that Miriam was the ringleader of this opposition. She is mentioned prior to Aaron, and the verb that describes the opposition to Moses is feminine singular: "Now Miriam and Aaron, she spoke [*wattedabber*] against Moses." This perspective on the matter is confirmed by the fact that Miriam alone was struck with leprosy at the end of the episode (12:10).

Calvin suggests that the complaint of Miriam and Aaron against their own brother indirectly serves a good purpose by indicating that nepotism did not play a part in Moses' prominence within the nation.[2] His role as mediator of God's word to his people was altogether a matter of divine appointment. More significantly, this incident provides an opportunity for making plain the uniqueness of Moses in the history of prophetism within Israel.

The initial accusation leveled against Moses is that he married a Cushite woman (Num. 12:1). Does this charge mean that Moses is guilty of polygamy? Or is the complaint against Moses based on his marriage to a foreign woman not of Israelite origin?

Most likely Moses is not guilty of polygamy, since the Lord himself defends Moses against his accusers. Furthermore, the fact that he married a foreigner was not in itself wrong, so long as the non-Israelite woman had professed the God of Israel for herself. Possibly this Cushite woman is none other than Moses' wife, Zipporah the Midianite. Some evidence indicates that Cushite and Midianite are overlapping terms.[3] Yet this marriage of Moses to Zipporah had occurred so many years earlier that it does not seem likely that a complaint would have been registered at this late date.

In the end, the objection to Moses' marriage seems to be based on a pretense. The real reason for the opposition emerges in the second complaint: "Has the Covenant LORD spoken only by Moses? Has he not also spoken by us?" (Num. 12:2). Miriam and Aaron are jealous of Moses' office as prophetic mediator for God's people. They object to the prominence given to this one person, even though he is their

2. Calvin, *Four Last Books of Moses*, 4.41.

3. In poetic parallelism, Habakkuk declares: "I saw the tents of Cushan in distress, the dwellings of Midian in anguish" (Hab. 3:7 NIV).

brother. By criticizing his marriage, they attempt to bring Moses down so that they can exalt themselves to a position of greater prominence.

The insatiability of the human spirit for position and power becomes even more apparent when it is realized that envy burns in the souls of Miriam and Aaron even though they both have their own positions of prominence. Since the time of the exodus from Egypt, Miriam had been known as a prophetess in Israel (Exod. 15:20), and the word of the Lord had come through her. In addition, Aaron had been divinely appointed as high priest in Israel. He alone had access to the Urim and Thummim in determining the will of God for the people (Exod. 28:30; Lev. 8:8; see also Num. 27:21; Deut. 33:8; Ezra 2:63; Neh. 7:65). Furthermore, Moses had no expectation that his office as covenantal mediator would pass through his family line. But God had determined that Aaron's sons would succeed him in his office as high priest. Neither Miriam nor Aaron had reason to complain that God was unwilling to work through them. In fact, later scripture indicates that both Aaron and Miriam were of crucial importance in God's salvation of Israel. They were sent along with Moses to lead the nation (Mic. 6:4). Aaron and Miriam should have been humbled because of their privilege of being the instruments of God's revelation. But only Moses manifests the kind of humility that they should have displayed.

In commenting on this failure of Miriam and Aaron, Calvin says: "When the lust for rule takes possession of men's hearts, not only do they abandon the love of justice, but . . . humanity becomes altogether extinct in them since brothers thus contend with each other and rage, as it were, against their own bowels. Ambition has been and still is, the mother of all errors, of all disturbances and sects."[4]

Sad to say, the sin of jealousy over positions of prominence in God's service continues into the new covenant era. More than enough work in the ministry of the Christian gospel exists for all, and yet members, elders, and ministers of Christ's church bite and devour one another because of jealousy. Instead of this self-centered approach, servants of the Lord Jesus should rejoice in the many gifts that have been given to the various members of his body.

4. Calvin, *Four Last Books of Moses*, 4.42.

In this situation, Moses could not speak in self-defense without opening himself to the insinuation that his prominence had come from his own self-assertiveness. As unusual as it might first appear, Moses' statement about himself that he was the "meekest man on the face of the earth" should be regarded as a true representation of the nature of the man (Num. 12:3). His retiring nature confirms that he did not place himself in this office.[5]

But the Lord would not allow his servant to be abused by his brash relatives. He "heard it" and "spoke suddenly" in response to the situation (Num. 12:3–4). The Lord summoned Miriam, Aaron, and Moses before the tabernacle, where he reminded them of the ultimate source of every gift for ministry. In particular, he made it completely clear that the Lord himself would sovereignly determine who would speak for him, what his chosen prophets would say, and what position they would hold as instruments of his word.

B. Uniqueness of Moses

Moses is not the only person who will be entrusted with divine revelations, as Miriam and Aaron wrongly assert (Num. 12:2). The Lord responds to their complaint by making plain that other prophets will arise in Israel after Moses. God will reveal himself to these various prophets.[6] Their prophetic word will not be of their own making,

5. Contrary to negatively critical opinions, this statement should not be regarded as an *a-Mosaica*, a statement that could not have been made by Moses himself, thereby proving that Moses could not have written the Pentateuch. Instead, it presents a true representation of the man Moses, as confirmed by his earlier reticence to take on the leadership role in bringing Israel out of Egypt (Exod. 4:10–13).

6. The precise reading of the critical phrase in Num. 12:6 has caused extensive discussion, with three basic options. (1) The Hebrew text is corrupt and in need of modification (Gesenius, *Hebrew Grammar* §128d; McNeile, *Numbers*, 66). The most common alteration reads, "If there is a prophet among you [*nabi bakem*], I, *yhwh*, will speak to him." Others propose the omission of *yhwh*. (2) The phrase is an example of a broken construct chain: "If there is among you a prophet of *yhwh*" (Freedman, *Pottery, Poetry, and Prophecy*, 237; Wenham, *Numbers*, 112). Ashley, *Numbers*, 220 n. 7, says that the Masoretic Text "may be retained once it is recognized that this construction is the so-called broken construct chain, with a pronominal suffix intervening between the construct and its genitive." (3) The Masoretic Text should be understood in its more common sense. Says Johnson, *Cultic Prophet in Ancient Israel*, 46 n. 7: "It is generally agreed, of course, that the Hebrew can only mean, 'If

but will come through dreams and visions (12:6). Yet over against this twofold mode of communication with all other prophets, an emphatic negative introduces the manner in which God will speak to Moses: "Not so" (*lo-ken*) (12:7).

By this distinction, God places Moses in an entirely different category from all the other prophets in Israel's history. Moses stands alone in his distinctive role as recipient of divine revelation. The jealousy of Miriam and Aaron became the opportunity for God to underscore Moses' uniqueness. In effect the Lord says, "You think Moses holds too exalted a position? Let me explain to you just how exalted he is! He stands not only higher than the two of you; he stands in an entirely different category from all other prophets that ever will arise in Israel's history. He is unique. He functions as the fountainhead of all Old Testament prophetism. All subsequent prophets shall be overshadowed by Moses. The validity of all later prophecy shall be determined by comparison with the prophetic utterances of Moses."

The distinctiveness of Moses as God's premier prophet is underscored by the Lord's speaking to him "mouth to mouth" (Num. 12:8). This assertion is not intended to deny the reality or accuracy of the revelation that other prophets shall receive. But Moses will stand in a category wholly different than all other prophets in Israel.

God says concerning Moses: "In all my house he is trusted" (Num. 12:7b). This phrase apparently refers to Moses' being proven trustworthy as a faithful bearer of the message that God had given him. But what is this "house" of God? Does the word allude to the tabernacle in the wilderness, as it does in subsequent passages (Judg. 18:31; 19:18; 1 Sam. 1:7, 24; 2 Sam. 12:20)? This interpretation appears to be too limiting, for the service of Moses as prophetic spokesman for God went well beyond the cultic activities associated with the tabernacle. Occasionally in the Old Testament the term *house* refers to a

---

your prophet be *yhwh*.'" Johnson comments: "This is regularly dismissed as nonsense; but is it quite so nonsensical as it appears?" He proceeds to affirm that the true prophet, in delivering his message, could be regarded, like the "angel of *yhwh*," as virtually *yhwh* in person. He further indicates that the oscillation between first person and third person "is a characteristic feature of prophetic utterances." See Young, *My Servants the Prophets*, 47–49, for a helpful discussion of the options.

family unit, such as the house of Abraham (Gen. 18:19; Deut. 25:9). But in addition it is used frequently in the Pentateuch to designate the people of Israel (Gen. 46:27; Exod. 16:31; 19:3; 40:38; Lev. 10:6; 17:3, 8, 10; 22:18; Num. 20:29). In this context, it appears that "house" refers to the people of Israel. This passage is distinctive in referring to Israel as "*my* [God's] house." The nation of Israel serves as the place of God's own dwelling, and Moses has been entrusted with a most responsible position in this "house."

In addition, it is said of Moses: "And the likeness [or form] of the Covenant LORD he will see." Scripture says elsewhere that no man can see God and live (Exod. 33:18–19). Yet Moses as prophet shall see the form of God. These statements are not contradictory. Moses will not see the essential nature of God. Yet he will see a form that shall manifest the nature of the invisible God to the understanding of mortal man. This experience by Moses places him in a category distinct from all the other prophets. He is unique in the history of prophetism in Israel, and by God's appointment he holds a position of priority that will belong to no one else.

In a second passage asserting his uniqueness, Deuteronomy 18:9–22, Moses appears as the first of Israel's prophets as well as the paradigm for all others who will fulfill this office. At Sinai, Moses and Moses alone was commissioned by God to be his mediator of revelation in response to the plea of the people. Terrified at the foot of the mountain, they pleaded with Moses to go up on the mountain in order to receive the revelation of God's law. Moses thus functions as the divine prophet, bringing the word of the Lord to the people, and as a consequence he played a unique role as the paradigm of all subsequent prophets in Israel. The later prophets would be "like Moses." Neither Aaron nor any other individual in the nation would provide the pattern for the long history of prophetism in Israel. Moses and only Moses fulfilled this role. In this sense, Moses was a distinctive figure, unique in Israel's history. None other in Israel was like him. As Deuteronomy later indicates: "No prophet has risen in Israel like Moses, whom the Covenant LORD knew face to face. . . . For no one has ever shown the mighty power or performed the awesome deeds that Moses did in the sight of all Israel" (34:10, 12 NIV).

In summary, Numbers 12 and Deuteronomy 18 establish the priority of Moses in the prophetic line, providing a key to the entire subsequent history of prophetism in Israel. Later prophets never rise above Moses in their position or experience. The bulk of subsequent prophetic literature essentially expands on what Moses already had declared to God's people. The Pentateuch as revealed through Moses functions as the foundational document for the entirety of revelation that comes to the theocracy. Much of the work of subsequent prophets builds on the foundation of revelation laid by Moses as the fountainhead for the old covenant people of God.

It should not be surprising, then, that a modern critical consensus declares that it knows nothing of the beginnings of prophecy in Israel, for no naturalistic developments can explain its origin. If the scriptural testimony concerning the unique role of Moses in Israelite prophecy is denied, then the whole key to its unfolding in redemptive history is lost. The negatively critical rearrangement of the Mosaic material decimates the coherent structure inherent in scripture. Mosaic materials cannot be resettled later in history to accommodate a naturalistic view of Israel's religion without obscuring the divine origin of the biblical revelation. That revelation reaches an initial peak in the man Moses and finds its consummation in the man Christ Jesus, the one and only mediator between God and men.

II. God's initiative in bringing forth a prophetic word

Before Israel entered the promised land, the Lord warned them that they would be bombarded by various Canaanite devices for determining the will of God (Deut. 18:9–11). The nation would be continually tempted to resort to these other methods of determining the future. But the Lord's people must recognize the abominable character of these practices. The ongoing ministry of the prophets would be essential in restraining the people from resorting to these forbidden methods of determining his will. A proper response to this ongoing threat required a constant manifestation of the prophetic office in Israel.

But what could insure the presence of a continuous prophetic ministry among the people? What provision could be made for maintaining an unbroken line of prophetic figures? The offices of priest and king in Israel were formally established by Mosaic legislation (Deut. 17:14–20; 18:1–8). These offices were perpetual in nature, being passed on by natural generation from father to son. But how would the corresponding office of prophet be sustained on a long-term basis? Should a particular tribe in Israel be designated as the source of the prophetic line, just as Levi supplied Israel's priests and Judah its kings? Would the various prophets be enabled to pass on their prophetic powers to selected successors? Or should a "career training center" be established for equipping potential prophets in Israel?

From the beginning it was made clear that multiple appearances of a "prophet like Moses" were to be expected. The constant presence of Canaanite options for determining the will of God would demand a regular presence of prophets in Israel. Yet none of these suggested methods of sustaining the prophetic office could guarantee the continuation of a line of true prophets in Israel.

Only one provision is made for this need of a continuous line of prophets in Israel. God himself would take the initiative. He alone could "raise up" a prophet in Israel like Moses. The phrase *I shall raise up a prophet* (Deut. 18:18) places strong emphasis on the necessity of the divine initiative in the maintenance of the prophetic office. Any further revelation that might supplement the words communicated by God through Moses must wait on the divine initiative. God alone shall determine when his people need additional revelations of his will. If Israel desired revelation beyond the words found in the law of Moses or beyond the knowledge that would be available to them in the Urim and Thummim, they must wait on the initiative of God. The subsequent history of the prophetic movement that stretched across the centuries confirms this understanding of the divine source of prophetism in Israel.

A further indication of the necessity of the divine initiative in raising up a prophet may be seen in the Lord's response to the frustration of Moses regarding his inability to govern the vast population of the nation of Israel (Num. 11:11–12). The Lord, by his own personal initiative, takes from the Spirit that was on Moses and places it on the seventy elders, so that they prophesy (11:25). As great as was his position in the history of prophetism, even Moses did not have the power to invest others with the prophetic gift. God alone controlled the various manifestations of his Spirit among the people. A person could not on his own decide that he would utter a prophecy wherever and whenever he wished. Neither could one person legitimately establish another in the prophetic office. Only God the sovereign Covenant LORD could initiate the truly prophetic word.

An event that occurs just at this point underscores the fact that only God exercised control over the prophetic spirit. While Moses and the seventy elders are assembled at the tent of meeting, two men prophesy in the camp (Num. 11:26). Out of zeal for the one he serves, Joshua urges Moses to restrain them (11:28). In Joshua's opinion, no prophetic activity should occur outside the supervision of Moses.

But Moses' greatness is seen in his knowing his place as servant in God's house, not as lord over God's house. Instead of complying with the urgings of Joshua that he silence these two who are prophesying, Moses expresses the longing of his heart that all God's people would be prophets and that God would put his Spirit on them all (Num. 11:29). Moses understands that the Spirit that empowered him to prophesy was not his own to control. It came to him as a gift from God. Furthermore, he has no concern for maintaining his own prominence. Instead, he longs to see the broadest possible extension of the Spirit of prophecy. This Spirit was not of human origin and could not be controlled by even the greatest of God's servants. Only the Lord himself is capable of originating the truly prophetic word.

Remarkably in some circles today, there are those who assume to themselves the power to communicate the gifts of the Spirit to others. By the application of baptismal waters, by the laying on of hands, or by the offering of specific prayers, some people presume they can do what Moses readily acknowledged he had no power to perform. It is assumed that the various gifts of the Spirit, including the ability to prophesy, are placed in the hands of some to dispense as they will. Yet outward symbols such as baptism and laying on of hands are intended in scripture as signs and seals of the realities of the Spirit, not as originators of the Spirit's gifts.

The prayerful longing of Moses that the Spirit of God come down on all God's people finds its realization some fourteen hundred years later when the Spirit was poured out on all flesh on the day of Pentecost (Acts 2:17). At that point the distribution of the prophetic gift anticipated the spread of the gospel to all nations as the assembled multitude heard the apostles speak in various languages under the influence of the Holy Spirit. In this climactic case, as in the days of Moses, the Spirit of prophecy originated with the action of God alone. Clearly no human being could initiate the experiences of the day of Pentecost.

III. The words of the prophet as the very word of God

From early on, scripture stresses that the prophet in Israel would minister a word of revelation from the Lord and not merely his own personal observations. The phrases "I will make myself known" to him and "I will speak" to him characterized the revelatory experience of the prophet (Num. 12:6c). His message was not a thing of his own creation. He did not speak out of his own personal insight. Instead, God made known both himself and his will as he spoke to the prophet.

One frequently misinterpreted passage underscores the fact that the prophet had personal knowledge of the revelatory character of the word that came from the Lord. In the report of the Spirit's coming on the seventy elders, it is stated that they prophesied "but they did not add!" (Num. 11:25c). Some interpreters suggest that this disclaimer means that the seventy elders never again prophesied. They did it once on this occasion of the initial distribution of the Spirit, but never did it again.[7] A more convincing analysis understands the phrase to mean that the seventy elders added nothing of their own to their prophetic utterances that had been inspired by the Holy Spirit. God communicated with and through them by putting words in their mouths, and

---

7. For this interpretation, see Young, *My Servants the Prophets*, 69.

they did not presume to append any statement that might be confused with the very word of God.[8]

This understanding of the statement that the elders "did not add" finds support in the threefold appearance of virtually the same phrase in the book of Deuteronomy. In each case, the affirmation concerning "not adding" indicates the finality of God's revelatory word. After reiterating the Ten Commandments (Deut. 5:6–21), Moses notes that even God himself "did not add" any further words to the Decalogue (5:22). Instead, the Ten Commandments were engraved on two tablets of stone as a permanent record of the Lord's will for his people. In the second occurrence of this phrase, Moses admonishes the people regarding God's laws as they had been revealed to him: "Do not any of you add to the word that I am commanding you" (4:2). A third notation appears in Deuteronomy when the subject of false prophecy is being discussed. Rather than listening to false prophets who urge them to follow other gods, the Israelites are warned that they must not add to the commandments of the Lord that were delivered through Moses their appointed prophet (12:32).

In the same way, the seventy elders who prophesied did not append their own reflections to the word of God that had come to them through revelation. Recipients of the prophetic word were fully capable of discerning the difference between the divine revelation that came to them and their own personal reflections. In their experience, prophecy clearly fell in the category of direct revelation from God, which must be distinguished from merely human utterances.

Further confirmation of the revelatory character of the prophetic word may be seen in the self-awareness of the prophet that he had indeed received a revelatory word from the Lord. This is implied by the pronouncement of the death penalty for false prophecy (Deut. 13:5). It would hardly be appropriate to execute a person for uttering a word that had not actually come from God if the prophet himself had no ability to distinguish between a word revealed to him by the Lord and his own inner impulses. This revelatory character of the

---

8. The Septuagint's *kai ouketi prosethento* (and yet they did not add) supports this understanding of the Masoretic Text. As the elders prophesied, they added nothing of their own thinking to the formation of the words.

prophet's word is underscored by the description of both the mode of reception and the mode of delivery of the prophetic message.

A. Mode of reception

In anticipating the ministry of Israel's prophets, the Covenant LORD declares that he will communicate his word in two ways: in visions and in dreams (Num. 12:6). These modes of divine communication will characterize the experience of the prophets throughout the ages. Receiving a message through visions and dreams clearly indicates that the prophet's message originated with revelation from God, not with the insight of man. Although the Lord will communicate with Moses in a distinctive manner (12:7), there can be no discounting the fact that all the prophets will receive their message by revelatory experiences.

The idea that the prophetic message came through divinely inspired dreams and visions is subsequently confirmed by the fact that even written prophecy in the Old Testament is represented as a thing seen. The "writings" of Isaiah the prophet are described as a "vision" that he "saw" (Isa. 1:1). The "word" that Isaiah "saw" describes a particular message that he received (2:1; see also 13:1). Amos and Micah also "saw" their word from the Lord (Amos 1:1; Mic. 1:1). Habakkuk speaks of his entire book as a "burden" that he "saw" (Hab. 1:1). Rather than implying an origin in the human subconscious for these prophetic experiences, these terms stress that visions and dreams were revelatory communications of truth that had their origin in God alone.

B. Mode of delivery

The relationship between Aaron and Moses at the time of their mission to the pharaoh of Egypt epitomizes the essential idea of the prophet in Israel. God graciously concedes to the weakness of Moses. Because of his timidity, Aaron his brother will speak for him: "You will speak to [Aaron] and will set the words in his mouth. I myself will be with your mouth and with his mouth. I will teach both of you what you shall do. He will speak for you to the people. So he, even he, will be for you as a mouth, and you will be for him as God" (Exod. 4:15–16).

As prophetic spokesman for Moses, Aaron must not innovate. He must not attempt to communicate his own ideas. The precise words that he shall speak to pharaoh will be placed in his mouth. Only those words given directly to him by the originator of the prophetic word may be spoken. The descriptive phrases used by God underscore the immediacy of the relationship between God's word and the prophetic word. The divine revelation goes directly from God into the mouth of the prophet. Consequently, the word of the prophet is the very word of God. God does not communicate his revelation to the prophet "thought to thought" or "mind to mind," but "mouth to mouth."

By this emphasis it becomes clear that prophecy is concerned not merely with the reception of the word of God by the prophet, but with its delivery to the people as well.[9] In one sense, the reception and the delivery of the prophetic word cannot be easily separated from one another. The whole prophetic experience is presented as a unified event. The function of the prophet was never complete apart from the delivery of his message precisely as it had been received.

This early description of the mode of communication of the prophetic word underscores the absolute perfections of the prophet's speech in its representation of God's word. By the Lord's placing his words in the mouth of the prophet, the divine revelation is sure to be preserved in its integrity as it passes through the vehicle of the prophet to the people.

C. Consequences of the revelatory character of the prophetic word

Two immediate consequences of the revelatory character of the prophetic word may be noted. Both the authority and the unity of the

9. The concept that the new covenant prophetic word begins as the inspired, infallible, and inerrant word of God when received by the prophet, but then loses its full divine authority at the point of its delivery contradicts this basic principle of prophecy even in its old covenant form (Grudem, *Gift of Prophecy*, 135, 137, 139; see also 110–11). It would certainly be surprising if new covenant prophecy were of an inferior quality to its old covenant counterpart at this critical point. In addition, it might be asked, what would be the point of God's infallibly communicating his word for the people to the prophet if in the end the revelation loses its infallible character when delivered? For a more extensive analysis and critique of this perspective on new covenant prophecy, see Robertson, *Final Word*, 85–126.

message of the prophets may be regarded as inevitable results of their words coming as verbatim revelations from God.

1. Authority

An early passage referring to the role of prophetism in Israel emphasizes that the authority of God's word is in no way diminished by passing through the Lord's prophet. In his commission to Moses, the Lord declares: "See, I have made you as God to pharaoh, and Aaron your brother will be your prophet. You shall declare all that I command you, and Aaron your brother shall declare to pharaoh that he send the sons of Israel from his land" (Exod. 7:1–2).

In this situation, Moses functions as God to pharaoh, Aaron is prophet for Moses, and pharaoh is recipient of the prophetic word. Moses as God mediates his word to pharaoh through Aaron, who serves as his prophet. Yet the word passing through Aaron comes to pharaoh with the full authority of God himself. Pharaoh may attempt to compromise the authority of the word of the Lord because it comes to him through a rather unimpressive human instrument. He may presume to suggest that the people sacrifice in the land or that they not go too far into the wilderness (Exod. 8:25–28). He may propose that only the men go for worship, leaving families and flocks behind (10:11, 24). But Moses' revelatory word as mediated to him through Aaron is not any less authoritative. It is the very word of God. As the divine word passes through the prophet, its integrity is preserved so that its original authority as the word of God is not diminished in any way.

From the beginning of the institution of prophecy in Israel, the word of the prophet came with the full authority of God's word. Prophetic mediatorship in no way minimizes the authority of the divine word. From this perspective, it should be anticipated that the word of the prophets as ultimately preserved in the inspired scriptures should be treated with the same respect required of the authoritative word of God.

2. Unity

A second characteristic of the prophetic word arising out of its revelatory character is its unity. Because the various words of the prophets all originate with the one and only creator God, no one word of a prophet can contradict another. This unity of the prophetic word may be seen in the passage of Scripture that first describes the distribution of the Spirit of prophecy among the elders of Israel:

> So Moses went forth and spoke to the people the words of the Covenant LORD. Then he gathered seventy men from the elders of the people and made them stand around the tent. Then the Covenant LORD came down in the cloud and spoke with him. He took from the Spirit that was on him and set it on the seventy elders. Then as the Spirit rested on them, they prophesied. But they did not add. (Num. 11:24–25)

Moses had indicated that he could not bear the burden of this large community of people alone (Num. 11:13–14). So the Lord provides a solution by distributing among the seventy elders the Spirit that had rested on Moses. Nothing in the context suggests that the Spirit on Moses was reduced by this process. The rabbis compared the sharing of the Spirit on Moses to the lighting of many candles from a single candle. The flame of the original candle is in no way diminished by the lighting of any number of other candles. So the Lord takes from the Spirit on Moses and places it on the seventy elders without diminishing Moses' experience of the Spirit.

The redistribution of the Spirit on Moses indicates that all along the Spirit was sufficient for the crisis currently being faced. No new or additional Spirit came on the seventy elders. All along the deficiency resided in the man Moses. He himself was not sufficient to serve as the single instrument of the Spirit's work, even though the Spirit that had been placed on him was completely adequate for the task.

The method by which the Spirit was dispersed among the elders emphasizes the unity of the Spirit of prophecy. All true prophecy originates in a single source. At this crucial point of its initial dispersal among many individuals, the oneness of the Spirit of prophecy is underscored. As a consequence, one prophetic utterance will never contradict another.

IV. Wholesale rejection of alternative ways of determining the word of the Lord

Moses functioned as prophet in bringing the nation out of Egypt by speaking as God's prophet to pharaoh. He continued in this role as prophet by communicating God's sustaining word to the people during their wilderness wanderings. But if Israel were to be preserved throughout the time they were in the land, the will of God must be revealed to them through a series of prophets raised up by the Lord. So as a countermeasure to the abominable ways of the Canaanites, the Lord will raise up a "prophet like Moses" to mediate his revealed will. Because the threat of the Canaanite alternative will appear consistently across the centuries, a series of prophets will have to be raised up to counterbalance their erroneous words and ways. In this regard, a total lack of tolerance toward any rival to Israel's prophets is demanded of the nation in anticipation of their coming into the land (Deut. 18:9).

Alternative ways for determining the will of the gods were already being employed by the Canaanites. These various practices had the potential of undermining the effectiveness of the prophetic office in Israel. No less than nine Canaanite practices are characterized as "abominations" to the Lord (Deut. 18:10–11). These abominations represent methods by which the Canaanites sought to determine the will of their gods. Calvin says: "Let us learn from this passage with how many monstrous and ridiculous fascinations Satan, whenever God loosens the chain by which he is bound, is able to bewitch unhappy men, and how great power to deceive the father of lies obtains from the just vengeance of God for the purpose of blinding unbelievers."[10]

As previously noted, prophets in Mari and Assyria were free to serve as spokesmen for more than one god. Both the moral standards of these various gods as well as their long-term interests would be promoted by the utterances of their diviners. But the claim of the God of Israel to be the one and only God, the sole creator and Lord of heaven and earth, could not allow recognition of a multiplicity of gods. The root reason for this condemnation of other gods and their divinations

10. Calvin, *Four Last Books of Moses*, 1.429.

rests on the foundation that a person comes to be like the thing he worships. As the prophet Hosea declares,

> They consecrated themselves
>> to that shameful idol
> and became as vile
>> as the thing they loved. (Hos. 9:10b NIV; see also Ps. 115:4–8)

A multiplicity of other gods inevitably promotes greed rather than generosity, lying rather than telling the truth, sexual immorality rather than purity, rebellion rather than submission to authority, death rather than life.

The first abomination in the list in Deuteronomy indicates the despicable character of the religion of these other gods: "Never shall there be found among you one who causes his son or his daughter to pass through the fire" (18:10). By offering human sacrifice, the Canaanite worshiper attempted to convince the gods of the depth of his devotion and to coerce them to fulfill his personal desires. The worshiper actually expected to determine the course of the future through this repulsive practice of offering human sacrifice to the gods.

Scripture does not provide a great amount of detail about this practice of causing a son or daughter to "pass through the fire." But the procedure was followed widely among ancient peoples. The Carthaginian god Moloch took the form of a human figure with a bull's head. His arms were outstretched to receive children offered in sacrifice. This metal image was heated red hot by a fire kindled inside the idol. Children were laid on the idol's arms and rolled into the fiery belly of the god. Flutes and drums drowned out the cries of the victims. Mothers stood by without shedding a tear to display their willingness to make these offerings.[11] This abominable practice shows the extent to which humanity will go in attempting to determine the course of the future.

It might be assumed that modern man has gotten well beyond those ancient brutalities. Yet the modern practice of abortion, particularly partial-birth abortion, is often not far from those earlier ways

---

11. Nicol, "Molech, Moloch," 2075.

of sacrificing children in order to satisfy personal desires. An effort to determine the course of the future by abominable actions contrary to the will of God may lie at the root of a great deal of the modern practice, just as much as it did in ancient days.

The other eight abominations listed in Deuteronomy 18:10–11 indicate various ways by which a person might attempt to know or influence the future. The specific outworking of these ancient practices is somewhat uncertain.[12] But they involved various forms of divination through analyzing the shapes of clouds, charming snakes, reading herbs shredded into a special brew, casting a spell, consulting the spirit world, and communicating with the dead. Since this broad spectrum of practices current in the ancient world would rival the institution of prophecy in Israel, not a single exception is to be allowed to this prohibition. All these practices are labeled as abominations in the sight of the Lord. The people redeemed by the Lord must have nothing to do with any of these methods of attempting to determine the future.

Not all these ancient practices may be dismissed as bygone superstitions. For with all the refinements of modern civilization, many current divinatory devices fill the same role as these ancient abominations. The horoscope, fortune teller, witchdoctor, and shaman all seek to determine the future in supernatural ways. An ineradicable compulsion exists in humanity that moves people to aspire to be like God by knowing the future. Yet all these modern divinatory practices fall under the same condemnation as their ancient counterparts. They are abominable to the Lord. The people who claim to know the one and only God are admonished to turn aside from consulting any source other than the inspired revelation mediated through his servants the prophets.

The serious consequences of following these ways of seeking to know the will of God are declared in no uncertain terms: "For all who do these things are an abomination to the Covenant LORD, and because of these abominations the Covenant LORD your God shall drive them out before you" (Deut. 18:12). Not only the practices but equally those

12. For an analysis of the various terms, see Young, *My Servants the Prophets*, 22–23.

who use these methods are abominable before the Lord. As a consequence, God will drive out the people who had occupied Palestine since before the time of Abraham. Even the heathen could not engage in these practices without incurring God's wrath.

It is instructive to note that the basic evil that caused the expulsion of the Canaanites was not the sin of idolatry, immorality, or brutality. It was not gluttony, lying, or covetousness. The abominable sin that brought God's judgment on the Canaanite civilization was their seeking to determine God's will through their own devices. Their condemning sin was a religious sin, the sin of seeking to know God's purposes in some way other than the way appointed by God himself.

So it is today, as in every generation. The god of modernity is the god of tolerance, demanding that every religion be regarded as having equal value in everyone's eyes. Yet as a basic truth it must be recognized that if there is only one God, he alone must be acknowledged as the only source of ultimate truth.

In contrast with the religions of Canaan, Israel's undivided commitment to the Lord must be displayed concretely in their unquestioning loyalty to God's servants the prophets. They must firmly reject all rival efforts to know the will of God: "But you! Not so! The Covenant LORD your God has not permitted you!" (Deut. 18:14). The Lord's word of prohibition excludes all other ways of attempting to know the will of God. Recognition of the unique nature of prophetism in Israel means the wholesale rejection of all alternative ways of determining the will, the purpose, the mind of the one and only creator God.

In summary, rivals to the prophetic office have been numerous throughout the ages. These human substitutions for the divinely established office of prophet shall continue to manifest themselves in countless ways. Though sometimes taken lightly, God's word says they are abominations that bring down divine judgment.

V. The danger of departing from the Lord's prophet

Departure from the Lord's appointed prophet is envisioned as a serious offense, bringing devastating consequences on both the individual and the nation. This departure from the prophet could occur in one of two ways: by disobedience or by pseudoprophetism.

A. Departure by disobedience

Disobedience to the message of the prophet is described as "not listening" to the words that the prophet speaks in God's name (Deut. 18:19). This deficiency in listening does not mean simply failing to give full attention at the time the prophet delivered his revelation to the people. As a matter of fact, the word of the prophet generally was delivered so vividly that it is difficult to imagine someone failing to pay attention to what was being said. Instead, this not listening refers to a refusal to obey, a failure to heed, a determination to go in the opposite direction than the way directed by the prophet.

It should be remembered that the core of prophecy originally delivered by Moses was summarized in the Ten Commandments. These directions for the life of God's people provide the essence of the message of the prophets that was to be obeyed. It was, as a matter of fact, disobedience to these basic commandments that ultimately brought disaster on the nation of Israel.

God will not leave it in the hands of human judges to see that the person who rejects his prophet is brought to account. Neither will he simply assume that the circumstances of life will bring about justice. Instead, he himself will call the person to account. Earlier in scripture, during the days of Noah, God personally held a murderer responsible for his crime (Gen. 9:5). The same word ("require") is now applied to the person who fails to listen to God's word (Deut. 18:19). Not heeding the word of God's prophet means that God himself will initiate judicial process against that person.

This ancient accountability specified at the time of prophetism's origins is transferred ultimately by Jesus to his own contemporaries. In issuing a solemn warning, he echoes the consequences of failing to heed the word of God's prophets found in the old covenant scriptures:

> For this reason also the wisdom of God said, "I will send to them prophets and apostles, and some of them they will kill and some they will persecute, so that the blood of all the prophets, shed since the foun-

dation of the world, may be charged against this generation, from the blood of Abel to the blood of Zechariah, who was killed between the altar and the house of God; yes, I tell you, it shall be charged against this generation." (Luke 11:49–51 NASB)

God shall require an accounting from those who abuse his prophetic men. To enforce this fact, our Lord Jesus repeats the principle: "Yes, I tell you, it shall be charged against this generation." Climactically, the generation that rejects *the* prophet, the unique prophet like Moses, will be as guilty as though it had rejected the whole line of prophets from Abel to Zechariah.

At another point Jesus underscores the solemn responsibility laid on people who have the opportunity of hearing the word of the Lord: "He who rejects me and receives not my word has one that judges him. The word that I have spoken, the same shall judge him in the last day, for I have not spoken of myself but the Father who sent me, he gave me a commandment what I should say and what I should speak" (John 12:48–49). Jesus indicates that his words originate with the Father. As a consequence, whoever rejects him and does not receive his word rejects God himself and shall be judged by him. The very words of the prophet that a person dares to reject shall become the basis of his judgment. Awesome consequences shall follow any failing to heed the prophetic word.

B. Departure by pseudoprophetism

The second way of departure from the prophet is described as pseudoprophetism. A person may presume to declare a word in God's name when the Lord has not commanded him to speak. The seriousness of this offense is seen in the required death of the person who prophesies falsely (Deut. 18:20–22). This anticipation of false prophecy among God's people eventually was confirmed by the long history of prophetic conflict within Israel (see chap. 4 §IV). In the end, the failure to follow the Lord's directives in distinguishing between true and false prophets resulted in the exile of the entire nation.

In view of an anticipated conflict among voices equally claiming to be prophetic, criteria distinguishing the false prophet from the true are provided by the Lord. The simplest test centers on whether a person speaks in the name of another god (Deut. 18:20). Whenever the name of another god is invoked, the speaker must be regarded as a false prophet. No syncretism may be allowed, for only one true and living God exists. As a second test, a person must be judged to be a false prophet if his word does not come to pass (18:22). The pseudo-prophet may speak in the name of the true God. But if his prediction does not come to fulfillment, he must be put to death.

A third criterion for distinguishing between the true and the false prophet underscores the foundational character of the prophetic utterances of Moses: "You shall keep his commandments and obey his voice, serve and seek him. That prophet or dreamer of dreams [who contradicts these commands] must die, for he speaks rebellion against the Covenant LORD your God" (Deut. 13:4b–5a). The truly prophetic word always will harmonize with the words previously spoken by Moses. Anyone who contradicts the laws of Moses cannot be a true prophet.

So from the beginning of prophetism in Israel, the contrast was made between true and false prophets. God's people were duly warned that they would have to exercise discernment in detecting the word that came from the true prophets of the Lord.

VI. Jesus as the consummation of prophetism

The tension created by the establishment of a prophetic mediator at Sinai pointed to the need for ending this separation between God and his people at some point in the future. God appeared at the top of the shaking, smoking mountain, displaying his awesome glory as he spoke by the trumpet sound of his voice. The people trembled in fear at the bottom of the mountain and pled with Moses to mediate the words of this awesome God. While the role of prophetic mediator was essential for the communication of the divine word, this very arrangement made impossible the realization of the central purpose of the covenant, which was to establish an intimacy of fellowship between God and his people. Somehow this circumstance had to be altered.

This entire scenario encourages the expectation that some resolution of the problem would appear in the future. God's purpose in the covenant will not be frustrated. Unity between the Covenant LORD and his people must be realized. Indeed, the Lord will not minimize his greatness and his glory as the Almighty. But somehow the deficiency represented by the mediatorial role of Moses must be overcome. In this context, the claims of the new covenant scriptures concerning Jesus of Nazareth may be fully appreciated, for at many points the presentation of Jesus as prophet supplies an answer to this limitation of the prophetic office of the old covenant.

A. Jesus as originator of the prophetic word

Moses did not originate the prophetic word. He served only as a conduit, as a mediator of the word from God to the people. All the prophets of the old covenant functioned in this limited capacity. "Thus says the Lord" was the normal formula used by the prophets in declaring their message to the people. They could speak only what the Lord communicated to them.

In contrast with the mediatorial role of Moses and all subsequent prophets, Jesus is presented as the originator of the prophetic word and not merely its mediator. The gospel records never report Jesus as introducing any of his statements by the common prophetic formula, "Thus says the Lord." This formula, as significant as it might be, also indicates that the spokesman has not originated the word he declares to the people. In sharp contrast, Jesus regularly introduces his prophetic statements by, "Truly, truly I say to you." The authority with which he speaks comes from himself. As a consequence, all the limitations associated with prophetic mediatorship as originally instituted in Israel are altogether removed. By hearing the words of Jesus, God's people hear the words of God, for he is in himself the originator of the divine word.

B. Jesus as distributor of the Spirit's gifts

At the time of the initial distribution of the Spirit of prophecy, Moses clearly exercised no control over the manifestations of the prophetic gift. God took the initiative in taking from the Spirit that was on Moses and placing it on the seventy elders so that they prophesied (Num. 11:25). At the same time, Eldad and Medad prophesied totally out from under the supervision of Moses (11:26–27). Clearly the distribution of gifts for ministry was not under Moses' direction.

An instructive passage from the new covenant scriptures closely parallels this incident from the days of Moses and establishes Jesus as distributor of the Spirit's gifts. In this case, John the disciple plays a similar role as Joshua in his zeal for his mentor. John reports that the disciples had seen someone casting out demons in Jesus' name, but they were forbidding him because he was not with them (Mark 9:38). Jesus' response was not what John might have expected: "Do not hinder him, for no one has the power to do a wonder in my name and then is able quickly to speak evil against me" (9:39).

Comparison of this narrative with the incident recorded in Numbers 11 illuminates the progress of revelation with respect to the prophetic office. Both passages concern the gifts of God's Spirit, although the Old Testament text centers on the gift of prophecy while the New Testament text is concerned with the gift of healing. Both incidents report a manifestation of the Spirit's gifts outside the immediate circle of the prophetic head of the day. In the old covenant situation, Moses gathers the seventy elders to himself at the tent of meeting outside the camp of Israel. But beyond the sphere of Moses' control, the prophetic Spirit manifests himself. In the case of Mark's narrative, Jesus gathers his disciples about him. But once again the Spirit works outside the immediate circle of the prophetic head of the day.

More significant than the parallels is the substantial difference between these two cases. In the first case, Moses appears as needy servant to the prophetic word. He cannot bear the burden of the people alone. The manifestation of the gift of prophecy outside the immediate sphere of Moses' influence underscores Moses' limitations. He forever remains a servant to the prophetic word, exercising no control over the spontaneous phenomenon that occurs outside his realm of control. Moses may be appreciated for his greatness in the context of the old covenant. He alone is the giver of God's law to the people. He towers above all others as the appointed mediator of the covenantal documents. Yet his limitations are immediately apparent.

In dramatic contrast, Jesus functions as Lord over the prophetic word. Twice reference is made to this individual who was not directly attached to the disciples of Jesus as performing his ministry *in Jesus' name* (Mark 9:38–39).

Comparison of these two passages establishes the superiority of Jesus over Moses. At the consummation of redemptive history, a prophet greater than Moses arose who himself directed the distribution of the prophetic gift. Moses had no control over the prophesying of Eldad and Medad. But clearly Jesus ruled over those who worked miracles in his name. They could do nothing apart from his personal release of power.

This authority over the prophetic word is further underscored in connection with the kingly role of Jesus in his exalted state. According to the New Testament, Jesus as the exalted Christ "ascended on high" to the right hand of God (Eph. 4:8; Ps. 68:18). By defeating Satan on behalf of God's people, he "led captivity captive," freeing men from sin's bondage and initiating them into the "glorious liberty of the children of God" (Rom. 8:21). From an old covenant perspective, the conquering Lord *received* gifts (Ps. 68:18 [= 67:19 Septuagint]) in anticipation of a future day of their distribution. But in his exalted position as God's anointed, Jesus Christ now pours forth his own Spirit, *distributing* gifts of ministry as he will (Eph. 4:8). Comparison of Psalm 68 with its citation in Ephesians 4 underscores the different perspective about the messiah's distribution of gifts. Psalm 68:18 may be translated, "You *received* gifts from [or for] men" (*laqakhtah mattanot baadam*). In similar fashion, the Septuagint states, "You *received* gifts among men" (*elabes domata en anthrōpō*). In significant contrast, Ephesians 4:8 reads, "He *gave* gifts to men" (*edōken domata tois anthrōpois*).

It is legitimate to ask about the citation methodology of the new covenant scriptures at this point. Has the apostle Paul acted properly by modifying the wording of this psalm so that it reads "gave gifts" instead of "received gifts"? In view of the developments in redemptive history between the age of the psalmist and the era of new covenant fulfillment, this treatment of the old covenant text is perfectly legitimate. Because the great day of the consummate exaltation of the anointed king has arrived, this old covenant truth may be legitimately inverted so that it reflects the new circumstances of the new day of messiah's exaltation. Today the conquering messiah has "given gifts to men" rather than "receiving gifts for men." From the perspective of the old covenant, the coming messiah was yet to receive the gifts he would distribute to the members of his kingdom. But from the perspective of the new covenant, by his baptism and resurrection in the power of the Spirit, Jesus received the gift of the Spirit without measure so that he could distribute the gifts of the Spirit to the subjects of his kingdom. By this distribution of the gifts of the Spirit he established in the church first apostles, then prophets, then pastors and teachers (Eph. 4:11).

Clearly Jesus Christ in his exalted position is greater than either Moses the prophet or David the king. He is like Moses as prophetic spokesman who delivers the inerrant word of God. But he is greater than Moses in that he distributes the gift for speaking a prophetic word as he will. He is like David in that he deserves the homage that all nations can bring. But he is greater than David in that he sovereignly and graciously distributes far more gifts than he ever will receive.

C. Jesus as Lord over the prophetic word

When Miriam and Aaron challenged the exalted position of Moses as God's spokesman, the Lord himself spoke in defense of Moses' unique role as prophet par excellence (Num. 12:4). They must not oppose Moses, for in all God's house he was faithful (12:7–8). Among the community of people where the Lord dwells, Moses distinguished himself for his trustworthiness.

The new covenant scriptures indicate that Jesus also "was faithful to the one who appointed him, just as Moses was faithful in all God's house" (Heb. 3:2 NIV). For a very significant reason, however, Jesus is worthy of greater honor than Moses. Both men proved faithful to the task given them in relation to God's people, his "house." But at that point the comparison ceases, for in developing his house imagery, the writer to the Hebrews indicates a startling thing. Clearly every house has to be built by someone, and ultimately God is the builder of everything. But while Moses functioned as a servant within this house, Jesus as God's unique Son stood beside God as builder of the house (3:3–6).

Moses held the highest possible position in relation to his contemporaries. In his unique role as the preeminent individual of the entire prophetic movement, he was of an entirely different category than all other prophets that would arise in Israel. All subsequent prophets of the old covenant era were less than he. In a similar fashion, Jesus is presented in the new covenant scriptures as being in an entirely different category than Moses. As the Son of God, one with the creator of all things, he is the originator of the prophetic word. He is the word (John 1:1). He does not fall on the side of those who are part of the house. He falls instead on the side of God the builder of the house. As creator of all things, Jesus the Son is of a totally different essence than Moses the servant: "If the word spoken by old covenant messengers was steadfast, and every transgression and disobedience received a just recompense of reward, how shall we escape if we neglect so great a salvation, which at the first began to be spoken by the Lord and then was confirmed to us by those that heard him?" (Heb. 2:1–2). Christ is unique as prophet by reason of the very essence of his nature. As son over the house and standing alongside God as the builder of the house, his word must be recognized as nothing less than the very word of God.

D. Jesus as the consummative prophet

The reference to the Lord's raising up a prophet like Moses anticipated the long line of prophets that would serve as Israel's alternative to the abominations of the Canaanites. But a strong case may be made that this anticipation also intends to look forward to a single individual:

- The use of singular "prophet," while not in itself sufficient for expecting one prophetic figure uniquely like Moses, allows this possibility much more than would a plural form, in which it would be difficult to suppose a reference to a singular prophetic figure that God would raise up in the future.

59

- Moses played a distinctive role in comparison with all other prophets (Num. 12:1–8). Consequently, this announcement concerning the expectation of a prophet like Moses raises a significant question. Does this "likeness" protect Moses' uniqueness in that some might be similar but none ever equal to him? Or might it point to the appearance of a single individual who would correspond consummately to the first of the prophets in his unique prominence? In particular, Moses was distinguished as one who would receive revelation from God in a manner that was distinctly different than the other prophets. So if a prophet was to arise like Moses in the fullest sense, he would have to be "one who received his revelations like Moses."[13]

According to Driver, the possibility of a reference to an individual who would be distinctively like Moses is inherent in the text: "The terms of the description are such that it may be reasonably understood as *including* a reference to the ideal prophet, Who should be 'like' Moses in a pre-eminent degree, in Whom the line of individual prophets should culminate, and Who should exhibit the characteristics of the prophet in their fullest perfection."[14] Von Rad also finds reference to a single prophet par excellence. He interprets the passage as describing the coming of an eschatological prophetic mediator who shall be like Moses not in the sense of being a prophet of judgment and doom. Instead, he shall be like Moses as one interceding, suffering, and even dying in behalf of the people. In this experience, the life of the prophet shall embody his message. According to von Rad, this portrait of a prophet is "in harmony with that of the suffering servant of God in Deutero-Isaiah."[15]

These observations deserve careful consideration. In terms of his role as a suffering prophet, Moses anticipates the servant of Isaiah. The servant of the Lord concept in Isaiah demonstrates the interaction of the "many" and the "one" in a way similar to the movement

13. Fairbairn, *Interpretation of Prophecy*, 498.
14. Driver, *Deuteronomy*, 229 (emphasis original).
15. Von Rad, *Deuteronomy*, 124.

between a singular prophet and the entire prophetic movement as anticipated in Deuteronomy 18.

God's raising up a prophet like Moses includes the idea of a single prophetic person who would suffer uniquely in behalf of God's people. The long line of prophets in Israel resembles Moses in many ways. Yet none of them can be regarded as like Moses in the fullest sense: "No prophet has risen in Israel like Moses, whom the Covenant LORD knew face to face" (Deut. 34:10 NIV). Not a single one of the prophets functioned like Moses as the unique lawgiver for God's people, whose revelation was confirmed by many miraculous signs (34:12). This limitation in the long line of prophets leaves open the prospect of a prophetic figure in the future that will be like Moses in the fullest sense. One of Israel's distinctive hopes crystallizes in the expectation of a final prophet with whom the Lord will speak "mouth to mouth" and who will manifest the power of God in himself, even as did Moses.

On several occasions, the new covenant scriptures refer to a popular expectation regarding the appearance of a prophet like Moses. The people query John the Baptist, "Are you the Prophet?" (John 1:21 NIV). They cannot understand why John presumes to lead the people into the wilderness and to initiate a baptism unto repentance if he is not the Christ, Elijah, or the prophet (1:25). When Jesus later satisfies the multitude with bread and fish in the wilderness, the people quickly conclude, "Surely this is the Prophet who is to come into the world" (6:14 NIV). As Moses provided bread for their fathers, so Jesus miraculously provided bread in the wilderness. Having made this identification, the people determine to make Jesus their king (6:15). Since Moses had united prophetic and regal roles in himself, they may have anticipated that the coming prophet like Moses would be identified with their regal messiah.[16] At a later time, Jesus dramatically offers life-giving water for all who will come to him, just as Moses provided water in the wilderness. On the last day of the Feast of Tabernacles, which reminded the people of the days of their wandering in the wilderness under the leadership of Moses, Jesus loudly declares, "If anyone is thirsty, let him come to me and drink" (7:37 NIV). When the people

16. See Cullmann, *Christology of the New Testament*, 23.

heard these words, many of them concluded, "Surely this man is the Prophet'" (7:40 NIV). These people saw in Jesus the "prophet like Moses" that had been promised, and Jesus encouraged them in this identification.

Jesus is specifically identified as the promised prophet in Peter's sermon occasioned by the healing of a lame man in the Jerusalem temple (Acts 3:19–26).[17] According to Peter, the message of prophetism across the centuries finds its major summation in the prediction concerning the coming of the prophet like Moses: "For Moses on the one hand [*men*] said, 'A prophet for you the Lord your God will raise up from your brothers like me'" (3:22). But Peter indicates that Moses was not the only one who anticipated a consummation of the history of prophetism in the last days: "On the other hand [*de*] all the prophets from Samuel and those who followed him spoke about these days," the days of the life, death, and resurrection of Jesus the consummate prophet (3:24).

Earlier in his message Peter indicated that by his healing miracle God glorified Jesus his *pais* (Acts 3:13). This term possesses an inherent ambiguity, meaning either "son" or "servant." Contrary to the normal rule of hermeneutics that a word must have a single significance in a particular context, this term appears to carry both meanings in this passage.[18] Peter declares that by this miracle of healing "God . . . has glorified his son/servant," who is identified as Jesus (3:13). But just as the prophetic servants of the Lord experienced constant Israelite rejection of their ministry, so Jesus as God's son/servant was betrayed by God's people before Pilate, even though the Roman governor had declared him innocent (3:13b).

Comparing the phraseology of Acts 3:22 and 3:26 shows that Peter intends to interchange the prophet anticipated by Moses with Jesus as the servant/son:

17. The identification of Jesus with the promised prophet as reflected in the early proclamation of the newly formed Christian church is also seen in its appearance in the final testimony of Stephen (Acts 7:37–38).

18. For a similar use of a double entendre in scripture, note the use of *ben* in Ps. 80:15. The Hebrew term can mean either "son" or "vine," and the context of the psalm suggests that the psalmist intended to communicate both significances in this particular verse.

God shall raise up a prophet [*prophētēs*]. (Acts 3:22, quoting Deut. 18:15)

God has raised up his servant/son [*pais*]. (Acts 3:26, providing a running commentary on Deut. 18:15)

Peter presents a profound Christology by this biblical-theological exposition of Deuteronomy 18:15. Very likely his hearers, who were steeped in the scriptures, would have related the term *pais* to Isaiah's suffering servant, for this term is used of the servant of the Lord in the Septuagint version of Isaiah 42:1; 52:13; 53:2. These verses describe the suffering servant who proclaims truth to the nations as he discharges his prophetic role.

The constant resistance to the prophetic word in Israel's history did not manifest itself merely as a passive rejection of the message of the prophets. Instead, it eventuated in active persecution of the prophets by the people. The prophet took the brunt of the ire of the people in their rejection of the word of God and thus became a suffering figure. A part of his office involved receiving in himself the rebuff of the people of God, suffering at their hands as he declared God's word to them.

With this background in mind, a fuller appreciation of Peter's interchange of servant/son with a prophet like Moses may be realized. The suffering prophet and the suffering servant of the Lord merge in Peter's interchange of *pais* with prophet. Jesus as the prophet is also the son/servant, epitomizing in himself the prophetic office as it merges with the suffering servant concept in Isaiah's thought. At the same time, as son (*pais*) he fills the office of royal messianic ruler. From Peter's perspective, Jesus is the prophet like Moses. He fulfills all the expectations developed by the long line of prophets that preceded him. He is the prophet who would consummate God's purpose as it was indicated from the time of the origination of the prophetic office.

In this context, the apostle demands a response typical of the ministry of Israel's prophets: "Repent therefore and turn, that your sins may be wiped away, in order that times of refreshing from the presence of the Lord may come" (Acts 3:19). Jesus had ascended to heaven only forty days previously. Yet Peter tells the people to repent so that the Lord "may send the Christ" who had been appointed for them

63

(3:20). Already he looks forward to the glorious return of Christ and its associated "time of restoration of all things . . . declared by God's holy prophets" (3:21).[19]

Although God intends to bless his people through raising up this prophet like Moses, the alternative potential for greater judgment also must be recognized: "And it shall be that every person who does not listen to that prophet shall be utterly destroyed from his people" (Acts 3:23).[20] In this manner Peter underscores the severity of the consequences of rejection of this prophet like Moses, whom he now identifies as Jesus. Anyone rejecting Jesus, the prophet like Moses, will be utterly destroyed, cut off forever from the people of God. This reality should not catch Peter's hearers by surprise, since "all the prophets . . . foretold these days" (3:24 NIV).

Peter concludes his message by developing a second quotation from the old covenant scriptures: "Through your seed all the nations of the earth shall be *blessed*" (Acts 3:25, quoting Gen. 22:18). In explaining the significance of this covenantal promise given to Abraham, Peter declares, "To you first, God having raised up his son, sent him that he might *bless* you in turning each of you from his evil ways" (Acts 3:26). The blessing of the covenant made with Abraham finally comes to its fullest realization by God's sending his son/servant Jesus. Jesus consequently fulfills the role of this prophet like Moses. The long line of abused prophets originates with Moses and finds its consum-

19. The noun *apokatastaseōs*, which in Acts 3:21 refers to the restoration of all things as promised by the prophets, should be compared with the verb *apokathistaneis* in 1:6. Because of this connection between the two verses, the restoration of all things in 3:21 may be regarded as providing an explanation for the restoration of the kingdom to Israel in 1:6. The restoration of Israel in the prophets is equivalent in its new covenant context to the renewal of the whole earth, not merely the reestablishment of the state of Israel. See Robertson, *Israel of God*, 141–42.

20. The latter half of Acts 3:23 combines a phrase from Lev. 23:29 (describing the fate of the man who profanes the Day of Atonement) with the quotation from Deut. 18:19. That Peter refers to Lev. 23:29 is substantiated by his use of the rather unusual Greek word *exolethreuthēsetai* (shall be utterly destroyed), a term found in the Septuagint version of this verse, but not in Deut. 18:19. In accord with customary New Testament quotation methodology, Peter has conjoined into a single quotation two Old Testament passages dealing with a similar theme.

mation in Jesus Christ. As a result, all the blessings intended in God's covenant flow through him.

VII. Conclusion

At the time of prophetism's origin, strong emphasis is placed on the exclusiveness of the prophetic word as the only way for God's people to receive his revelation. An abomination in the sight of God is any effort that seeks to determine the will of God in any way other than through the inspired office of prophet.

At the consummate fulfillment of the long history of prophetism in Israel, it is expected that a single prophet like Moses will appear. This consummate prophet will embody all the principles of prophetic activity, including the suffering and rejection that invariably come to God's prophets. The threat of divine judgment hangs over all who reject the messenger sent from the Lord. Yet in the end, the purpose of God in establishing his covenant will be realized. His people shall be brought into a permanent oneness with him. This final prophet will be God himself with his people, declaring his word to his people.

3

THE PROPHET'S CALL
AND COMMISSION

In seeking to understand the role of prophet in the plan and purpose of God, an analysis of the prophet's call and commission will provide distinctive insights. Analyzing the induction of individuals into this sacred office aids in understanding the role that the prophet was expected to play. Just as a marriage ceremony or an ordination service anticipates the basic relationships that will follow, so the call of the prophet helps in providing a clear definition of his responsibilities, for the prophets came to their work with "a profound sense of divine vocation."[1] This sense of calling from God dramatically affected their work. They had no doubt that they had been commissioned by the Lord to be his messengers. "A prophet knows that he has never chosen his way himself: he has been chosen by the deity."[2] As a consequence, the prophet lived with a sense of compulsion to speak, and to speak only what God had revealed to him. Without any doubt the ministry of the prophets of Israel would have been totally different apart from this consciousness of being called and commissioned directly by God. Because of this sense of direct divine calling, the prophet functioned as a totally independent religious figure in the history of Israel.

Scripture records the calling and commissioning of various individuals as spokesmen for the Lord. Apart from Israel's writing prophets, prominent figures called to a prophetic ministry include Moses (Exod.

1. Bright, *Jeremiah*, xxiv.
2. Lindblom, *Prophecy in Ancient Israel*, 6.

3–4), Samuel (1 Sam. 3:1–4:1a), and the Isaianic servant of the Lord (Isa. 49:1–6; 50:4–9).[3] The call of Gideon (Judg. 6:11b–17) and the divine commissioning of the prophet Micaiah (1 Kings 22:19–22) may also be instructive in analyzing the significance of the prophetic call.[4] In terms of the writing prophets of Israel, four instances of divine calling to a prophetic ministry are recorded: Isaiah (Isa. 6), Amos (Amos 7:10–17), Jeremiah (Jer. 1:4–10), and Ezekiel (Ezek. 1:4–3:11). Isaiah and Amos lived in the eighth century B.C. near the beginning of the history of Israel's writing prophets. In contrast, Jeremiah and Ezekiel ministered toward the end of old covenant prophetic history, in the latter part of the seventh century and continuing into the sixth century. While the period of time in which these particular prophets labored spans more than 150 years, the circumstances associated with their call and commission remain essentially the same.

The call of God might come as a general summons to the office of prophet or as a commissioning to carry out a specific mission in a concrete historical circumstance. In either case, the report of the divine call to his servants the prophets regularly includes a vision of God, introductory word, divine commission, prophetic expression of reluctance, divine reassurance, and confirming sign.[5] The various accounts of calls to the prophetic office display too much variety to establish the existence of a preset form for recording a prophetic call.[6] Yet certain dominant aspects of the prophet's call deserve further consideration.

3. Habel, "Form and Significance of the Call Narratives," 314–16, attempts to find the elements of a prophetic call in Isa. 40 by a comparison with Isa. 6. But Isa. 40 has little in common with Isa. 6 "and does not look anything like a call to a prophetic ministry," as noted by Blenkinsopp, *Isaiah*, 1.226. Isaiah 40 is not addressed to an individual and includes none of the normal elements of a prophetic call such as the vision of God, the reaction of inadequacy, and the anticipation of rejection by the people.

4. It should be noted, however, that the narrative of 1 Kings 22, which is regularly cited as a prime example of a prophetic call, can be termed a call narrative "only with difficulty" (Seitz, *Isaiah 1–39*, 54).

5. Note essentially these elements indicated in Habel, "Form and Significance of the Call Narratives," 298. Most of these elements appear quite naturally in the outline of Ezekiel's call, as indicated in Clements, *Ezekiel*, 9–10.

6. Contra Habel, "Form and Significance of the Call Narratives," 305. Zimmerli, *Ezekiel*, 1.97–98, detects two basic forms for the prophetic calls. The first form, found in the calls of Moses, Gideon, Saul, and Jeremiah, reports a divine overcoming of the

I. The historical context of the prophet's call

Since the ultimate origin of prophetism in Israel finds its roots in a purposeful creation (see chap. 1 §II), it should not be surprising to find scripture tracing the roots of the call of the prophet to the eternal purposes of the creator. As the Covenant LORD says specifically to Jeremiah:

> Before I formed you in the womb
>   I knew you,
> before you were born
>   I set you apart;
>   I appointed you
>   as a prophet to the nations. (Jer. 1:5 NIV)

Consistently in scripture, the Covenant LORD of Israel appears not only as king in Israel, but also as lord of the universe.[7] From his sovereign heavenly throne he rules over the rise and fall of nations. From this domain of authority he calls and commissions certain people of his choosing to be the bearers of his revealed word. As a consequence, the person that God determines to call as his prophet is appointed "over nations and kingdoms to uproot and tear down, to destroy and overthrow, to build and to plant" (Jer. 1:10 NIV).

This long-standing divine purpose regarding the role of prophetism indicates that the appointment of a specific prophet by the Lord does not rest on previous faith or personal endowment.[8] Neither can the task of the prophet be treated as a vocation to be studied and learned by an aspiring individual. Instead, a person must be compelled to fulfill this critical role by the summons of the sovereign Lord.

In accord with this principle, only slight information is given about the personal life of the prophet, particularly prior to his call.

---

sense of inadequacy. The second form, represented by the calls of Isaiah, Micaiah, and Ezekiel, involves an entering into the divine council. Zimmerli indicates that it is pressing the evidence to speak of a "fixed formula" for recording the prophetic call (99).

7. Baltzer, "Office and Calling of the Prophets," 569.
8. See von Rad, *Old Testament Theology*, 2.57.

After surveying the scant evidence in scripture concerning the background of the biblical prophets, one commentator observes: "It begins to look as if little importance was attached to the prophet's life, activity, and social status."[9] As in the case of the person who stood as the transitional figure between the old covenant and the new covenant eras, the prophet of God is nothing more than a "voice" (John 1:23). But the voice is the voice of God.

Yet unquestionably the prophet's call came in the context of a specific historical situation. The circumstances surrounding the prophet's call often combined factors of crisis in the nation with normal routine activities on the part of the prophet. Moses receives his call while shepherding his flock in the Sinai desert at the very time in which the Israelite people were groaning under the burdens of their enslavement in Egypt (Exod. 2:23–3:1).[10] Gideon is ironically summoned as a mighty warrior while covertly threshing wheat in the bottom of a winepress, even as Israel suffers under the oppression of the Midianites (Judg. 6:11–12; see also 6:2, 6). Amos is busily employed in his role as farmer in the southern part of Judea when the Lord calls him to prophesy against the depraved worship practices of the northern kingdom that ultimately led to their exile (Amos 7:14). This combining of the commonplace character of the prophet's life with circumstances of national and international crisis underscores the insignificance of the person called to the prophetic office.

In each of the four records of a call that came to Israel's literary prophets, specifics of the historical circumstance surrounding the divine summons to service are noted, which indicates that the prophets are not abstract philosophers dealing with nebulous ideas about God. They are men involved in the flow of time and history, demonstrating the purposeful involvement of their God in the course of human history. In particular, their ministries regularly relate to the circumstances of

9. Blenkinsopp, *History of Prophecy in Israel*, 34. He notes elsewhere that the prophet Ezekiel "has disappeared almost completely behind the book that bears his name" (Blenkinsopp, *Ezekiel*, 15).

10. See the comments of Habel, "Form and Significance of the Call Narratives," 298.

the people of Israel, God's chosen instrument for communicating the divine plan of redemption to the world.

Each of the recorded cases of the prophetic calls to Isaiah, Amos, Jeremiah, and Ezekiel is reported in the first person by the prophet himself. No one could attest to their calls to the prophetic office except the prophet himself. Yet these reports must not be seen merely as interesting autobiographical notations. They function in the prophetic literature as authentications, as "public proclamations" in which the person "announces his divine commission and thereby commits himself openly to the secret, inner compulsion from God."[11] While these solemn attestations of the prophets to their experience of a divine call could not be objectively verified, neither could their authenticity be denied. But they served to alert the community to the solemnity of the claim that was being made.

More specifically, a commission came to Isaiah "in the year that King Uzziah died," about 740 B.C. (Isa. 6:1 NIV).[12] Uzziah had been a good king in Judah until his heart was lifted up in pride because of his successes. When in presumption he entered the temple to offer sacrifice in contradiction to the law of Moses, he was struck with leprosy on his forehead. Precisely at the place where the golden plate of the high priest bearing the inscription HOLINESS TO THE LORD should have been dangling (Exod. 28:36–38), the king was struck by this singular act of divine judgment. King Uzziah ultimately died a leper "in a sep-

---

11. Ibid., 306.

12. It is difficult to determine whether the call in Isa. 6 came at the beginning of Isaiah's ministry or subsequently. Young, *Isaiah*, 1.232, concludes that Isa. 6 records Isaiah's initial call and that the earlier chapters of the book begin by setting forth the major themes of his prophecy. Seitz, *Isaiah 1–39*, 55, notes that it is impossible to say whether the passage records the inaugural episode setting apart the prophet. He observes, however, that the time of the vision is identified as "the year that King Uzziah died," while the opening verse of the book states that Isaiah ministered "in the days of Uzziah" (Isa. 1:1). It might, however, be noted that the text does not say that Isaiah had his vision on the day that Uzziah died, leaving open the possibility that Isa. 6 occurred sometime prior to Uzziah's death but during the year in which he died. As an alternative possibility, it may be that Isaiah ministered as a prophet for some period prior to experiencing this particular vision, which then served as confirmation of his call to the prophetic office.

arate house, for he was excluded from the house of the Covenant LORD" (2 Chron. 26:16–21 English Standard Version).

Against this sobering backdrop Isaiah received his commission. In the year that King Uzziah died, Isaiah heard the seraphim repeating "holy, holy, holy" and was commanded to continue in the prophetic office through many purging judgments until the Lord had raised up a holy seed in the land (Isa. 6:3, 13). Uzziah's severe judgment foreshadowed the devastation that would come to the disobedient nation, and Isaiah's commission at this precise point essentially determined the course of his prophetic ministry for the years to come.

The exact time of Amos's call is not indicated in scripture, but he recounted the call during the reign of King Jeroboam II of Israel in the middle of the eighth century B.C. (Amos 7:10–15). Amaziah the priest of the false worship center at Bethel admonished Amos to "go home" to the southern kingdom of Judah, where he could freely prophesy and earn his bread. This false priest had already presented an alarming report to the king concerning the prophecies of Amos. He leveled the charge of conspiracy against the prophet (7:10a). He inadvertently acknowledged the powerful effect of Amos's ministry by indicating that the land was "unable to endure all his words" (7:10b NASB). Amos would be allowed to return and prophesy in his own home territory, but his condemnatory prophecies directed at the ruler of the northern kingdom and the "holy place of the king" at Bethel would be tolerated no longer (7:11, 13). Amos responded by indicating that his role as prophet was not something of his own making. By using the emphatic form of the first-person pronoun, three consecutive clauses underscore that he personally had nothing to do with his call to the task of the prophet:

> I was not a prophet,
> and I was not the son of a prophet,
> but I was a shepherd, and one who took care of sycamore-fig trees.
> (Amos 7:14)

Then in marked contrast, he asserts the Lord's initiative in his calling as a prophet:

72

But the *Covenant* LORD
    took me from following the flock
and the *Covenant* LORD
    said to me, "Go prophesy to My people Israel."
Now hear the word of the *Covenant* LORD. (Amos 7:15–16a NASB)[13]

Amos did not become a prophet by virtue of his own decision. Neither was he the son of a prophet, which might indicate some form of subordination in his role as prophet.[14] Instead, he was a shepherd, a farmer tending sycamore trees. God was the one who told him to go and prophesy to his people Israel (7:10–15). His presence in the northern kingdom of Israel was not his own personal choice. It was God's determination. Clearly this recounting of Amos's call underscores the fact that the prophetic office was not something a person might choose to fulfill on his own.[15] Divine initiative communicated by direct revelation alone had the power to establish a person as a true prophet of the Lord.

Jeremiah's call is specifically dated in the thirteenth year of King Josiah, about 627 B.C. (Jer. 1:2). This date was very close to the time that Josiah began his first public reform aimed at purging Israel of its corrupted worship practices (2 Chron. 34:3–7). Because he would be living through a tumultuous period in the nation's history, the prophet was commanded not to marry (Jer. 16:2).[16] By the time of his call, the northern kingdom had been in exile for almost one hun-

---

13. For the development of these contrasting assertions, see Wolff, *Joel and Amos*, 312–13.

14. Ibid., 314.

15. The statement of Amos 7:14 has been heavily discussed as to whether the text says, "I *am* not a prophet" or "I *was* not a prophet." Wolff states: "Ordinarily the rule holds that a nominal clause describes a state of affairs contemporary with the time span defined by the verbal clause with which it is associated. Since the verbal clause in question, 7:15, reports events in the past, many have thus decided in favor of a preterite translation of 7:14 as well" (*Joel and Amos*, 312). Wolff then offers "reasons to the contrary" and concludes (312–13) that Amos intended to deny he was a prophet in the sense that he did not hold the permanent office of prophet, even though he had been commissioned by God to speak as a prophet. Wolff's contrary reasons are not as strong as his initial grammatical observations.

16. This circumstance anticipates the directions of Paul respecting marriage in view of the present distress that prevailed in his own day (1 Cor. 7:25–27).

dred years. Jeremiah's difficult task would involve standing for God's truth as the recalcitrant southern kingdom experienced a similar national trauma.

Ezekiel's summons to divine service was distinctive in that it occurred outside the land of Palestine. In the fifth year of King Jehoiachin's exile, about 593 B.C., the call came to this descendant of the priestly line of Israel to serve as the Lord's prophet (Ezek. 1:2–3; see also 33:21–22).[17] He was commissioned as Israel's watchman, being given the responsibility of sounding the first alarm in warning the wicked of the consequences of his way. In this critical position as watchman, the prophet would forfeit his own life if he failed to fulfill his mission.[18]

While continuing to live in the land of Babylon, Ezekiel was given unique visions of the departure of God's glory from the temple in Jerusalem and the consequent destruction of this once-holy place. But in the end he also was given visions of a restored temple of greater proportions and with a fuller glory.

From these varied historical circumstances of the Lord's calling and commissioning of his prophets, we see that these spokesmen for God were summoned in response to particular historical situations. The prophets were not called as abstract philosophers detached from the sometimes hard, cold realities of history. Instead, the Lord spoke directly to concrete historical situations confronted by his people through these various individuals commissioned as his messengers. But these historical roots of the prophetic office never isolated the prophetic message to a single era. The word of the prophet frequently anticipated the future, while also communicating God's message to the present generation. His inspired words addressed his own age quite specifically, but in a way that speaks pointedly across the centuries.

17. The opening reference to the thirtieth year (Ezek. 1:1) is variously interpreted. The simplest understanding is to see a reference to the age of the prophet. Thirty was the minimum age for assuming the role of priest in Israel (Num. 4:3). See VanGemeren, *Interpreting the Prophetic Word*, 323; Blenkinsopp, *Ezekiel*, 16.

18. Brownlee, *Ezekiel*, 50.

II. The vision of God

Inadequate evidence makes it impossible to affirm that a vision of the Almighty was essential to every call of a prophet. But in the cases of Isaiah and Ezekiel, the manifestation of God in his glory formed an integral part of their call and commission as prophets of the Lord. Jeremiah asserts that the false prophets have not "stood in the council of the Covenant LORD" (Jer. 23:18 NIV), implying that he had undergone that awesome qualifying experience (see also 1 Kings 22:19–23).[19] The exalted vision of divine majesty played a vital role in the summons of many of the nation's prophets, and this visionary experience could not fail to have strong impact on the prophet.

The word of God comes "with the strength of [God's] hand" upon him (Isa. 8:11). Cramps seize the loins of the prophet like those of a woman in labor, and twilight becomes a horror to him (21:3–4). After receiving his vision, the prophet was exhausted, lay sick for several days (Dan. 8:27), and his "natural color turned to a deathly pallor" (10:8 NASB). When he heard the message from the Lord, the prophet's heart pounded, his lips quivered, decay crept into his bones, and his legs trembled (Hab. 3:16). On receiving his call, the prophet sat overwhelmed by his vision for seven days (Ezek. 3:15). These words do not describe merely hyperpsychic experiences, for they consistently result in the most exalted of human utterances that give all glory to one and the same creator God.

In the case of Isaiah, the Lord appears seated on his throne in the temple (Isa. 6:1). It should not be regarded as incidental that this vision occurs in God's temple in the chosen city of Jerusalem, for central to God's covenant with David was the merger of the king's throne with the very throne of God (2 Sam. 7:25–29; 1 Chron. 29:22–23). David

---

19. Blenkinsopp, *History of Prophecy in Israel*, 34, says that the recurring "thus says the Lord" of the prophets presupposes a scene of the divine court in session, presided over by the Lord as ruler of the heavenly council. The prophet has been brought into the meeting of this council and is then designated as a messenger with a mission. Blenkinsopp may be reading too much in the phrase, and he errs when he implies a mythological framework for the scene. The imagery of the prophet being brought into the divine council serves to represent the awesome responsibility of the prophet.

insisted on locating the place of the temple, representing God's throne on earth, alongside his own palace and throne. This permanent locale for the throne of God served as a symbolic reminder that Israel's kings ruled only by virtue of the Lord's sovereignty manifested in Jerusalem. The earthly successors of David might fail in their responsibilities as rulers, but the Lord in his sovereignty never would fail.

Isaiah's vision demonstrated that heavenly holiness had come to earth. The seraphim perpetually covered themselves as they stood before the Lord crying "holy, holy, holy." This manifestation of God's holiness on earth caused the doorposts and thresholds of the temple to shake, which provided a foreboding of the destruction of this majestic structure that eventually occurred because of its impurities. After experiencing a purification from the altar, the prophet responds to the query issued from the throne: "Whom shall I send? And who will go for us?" (Isa. 6:8 NIV). The assertion that this account "assumes a polytheism that peoples the heavens with many gods"[20] totally ignores Isaiah's vivid picture of the universal sovereignty of the one God over all the nations and his mockery of their meaningless idols. Although the seraphim are present in Isaiah's vision as creaturely worshipers, neither they nor any other creature ever appears as the person for whom and by whom a prophet receives his commission. God and only God sends forth his prophetic spokesmen. He alone is the "I" who commissions his spokesmen, and he alone is the "us" for whom the prophet goes.

Whose glory then did Isaiah see in the temple as the holy one of Israel? In the immediately following context, the prophet Isaiah anticipates the appearance of a virgin-born descendant from the line of David whose name-essence will be "God-with-us" (Isa. 7:14). This stem of Jesse will reign on David's throne forever as the "mighty God" who has been "Father from eternity" (11:1; 9:6–7; see chap. 8 §IV.A.1). While downgrading interpretations seek to muffle the testimony of these passages, their full significance in context provides the proper framework for the startling witness of the new covenant scriptures that Isaiah "saw Jesus' glory and spoke about him" (John 12:41 NIV). When the oneness of God is joined to the concept of a divine messiah, a proper

---

20. Brueggemann, *Isaiah*, 1.58.

framework is provided for acknowledging the multiple personhood of the one and only God.[21] Only this understanding of the old covenant scriptures provides an adequate explanation for the ease with which Jewish believers in Jesus the Christ could affirm his full deity equally alongside their long-established faith in the oneness of God.

This initial vision of God's holiness had a profound impact on Isaiah's ministry. To him, God was distinctively the "holy one of Israel." This designation of God appears twenty-five times in the book of Isaiah, twelve times in Isaiah 1–39, and thirteen times in Isaiah 40–66. This unique description of God is used only two other times in the whole prophetic corpus (Jer. 50:29; 51:5).[22] Clearly Isaiah's concept of God was significantly impacted by the vision that initiated his prophetic call. This God was "exalted by his justice," for "the holy God will show himself holy by his righteousness" (Isa. 5:16 NIV).

Ezekiel had an elaborate vision of the glory of the Lord at the time of his call to the office of prophet. Consequently his whole book may be summarized as a description of "the departing and returning glory." In successive stages through the first portion of Ezekiel's prophecy, the Shekinah rises from its dwelling place in Jerusalem and departs from the temple mount (Ezek. 9:3; 10:13, 18–19; 11:22–23). But the latter portion of the book centers on the reconstruction of a greater temple with greater glory than ever could have been imagined in association with the earlier temple complex (42:15–20; 43:2, 5).

In his vision, Ezekiel sees four living creatures positioned beneath the throne of the Almighty. Wheels interlace wheels covered with embedded eyes, conveying a sense of readiness for instant movement in any direction by the almighty, all-knowing God. The vision communicates the basic idea of mobility inherent in a "wheeled chariot throne." Wheels inside wheels simultaneously allow forward and lat-

21. Childs, *Isaiah*, 59, echoes with approval the analysis of Calvin, who said: "God never revealed himself to the Fathers but in his eternal Word and only begotten Son," and so the gospel of John is quite correct in affirming that Isaiah saw Jesus and spoke of his glory, even though it would be wrong to limit Isaiah's vision to only the glory of Christ (Calvin, *Isaiah*, 201).

22. The phrase is found one time in the historical books (2 Kings 19:22) and three times in the psalms (Pss. 71:22; 78:41; 89:18).

eral movements.[23] The brilliance of flashing lightning and the sound of expansive rushing waters provide sight and sound for the vision. Above the expanse was the form of a man whose person glowed like heated metal. This man was seated on a throne of sapphire surrounded by darkened clouds and a rainbow. Out of this vivid manifestation of the glory of the Lord, Ezekiel heard a voice commissioning him to go as a prophet charged with delivering God's words to the people (Ezek. 1:4–2:8).

The vision of God granted to Ezekiel is intimately connected to his call to service. The task was so great that nothing less than a spectacular vision of God's glory could sustain the prophet. This chosen servant forever after must evaluate his work in terms of the originating vision, never in terms of the response of men. It was ultimately this great and glorious God that he served, not the people who were the recipients of his message. The vision enforced the importance of his role as a prophet and the necessity of faithfulness to the task to which he was called.

In the context of the new covenant, similar visions were associated with the call of God's spokesmen. Jesus received his commission for ministry in connection with the vision of heaven opened and the descent of the dove (Matt. 3:16). Simultaneously, the voice from heaven declared him to be God's beloved son (3:17). In response to this authenticating vision, Jesus began to announce the coming of the kingdom of God. The apostle Paul also explains that he was "lifted up to the third heaven" in preparation for his ministry (2 Cor. 12:2–4). His exalted vision culminated in the union of Jews and Gentiles as one new man in Christ. The largeness of his task was matched by the greatness of his vision.

So in both old covenant and new covenant contexts, the vision of God was a vital part of the prophet's call. This vision communicated to the prospective prophet something of the awesomeness of the one with whom he had to deal. More than words could convey, the glimpse of God's glory experienced by the prophet made him aware of the greatness of the person for whom he would speak. Never could

23. Blenkinsopp, *Ezekiel*, 21–22.

he forget the moment of confrontation with the incomprehensible divine one. Never could the face of man, however embellished with temporal glories, ever compare with the overwhelming presence of the almighty God who had called and commissioned him. Clearly this office could not be properly filled simply on the basis of human decision. But the vision of God's glory could well prepare these men for the highest of human callings.

III. Commission from the Almighty

The call of Jeremiah indicates that the prophet first was consecrated to the Lord and then commissioned with his message: "Before I formed you in the womb I knew you, before you were born I set you apart . . . as a prophet to the nations" (Jer. 1:5 NIV). The prophet was not his own. Before birth, by the divine creator's autonomous action, he was consecrated, dedicated in body and soul to the Covenant LORD of Israel. Just as God had taken the Levites as his own at the time of the formation of the nation at Sinai and then given them to Aaron to do the work of the tabernacle, so the Lord now claimed the prophet to be his own and then commissioned him as his spokesman (Num. 8:16, 19).[24] The prophet is solemnly commanded, "Go!" (Isa. 6:9; Jer. 1:7; Ezek. 2:3; 3:4; Amos 7:15; see also Judg. 6:14). He cannot wait until people come to him when he has received a word from God. He must be bold in taking the initiative, even if he knows the people will not respond favorably to his message.

To whom is the prophet of God sent? First and primarily, the Lord commissions his prophets to deliver the message to his own covenant people, to those who have been bound to him for blessing and curse, for life and death, by the sovereignly administered bonds previously made with Adam, Noah, Abraham, Moses, and David. Sometimes the prophet was commissioned specifically to the apostate kingdom of the north (Amos 7:15). At other times he was sent exclusively to the kingdom of the south, as in the cases of Habakkuk, Zephaniah, and Jeremiah. On some occasions the prophet received his com-

---

24. For the comparison, see Kidner, *Message of Jeremiah*, 25.

mission specifically for an exiled people, uprooted from the land that gave them national coherence, as with Ezekiel and Daniel. But in each of these cases, the message and ministry of the prophets was directed to the small, seemingly insignificant community known as Israel. This people had been chosen and favored by God to receive the rich ministry of God's choicest servants among humanity. Even until today they are marked off as favored first of all because to them were committed the oracles of God (Rom. 3:2).

The commission of the prophets encompassed a far wider community as well. "A prophet to the nations" is the awesome description of the task given to Jeremiah (Jer. 1:5). At just the time when the great oriental empires were emerging, God sent his lonely prophets to confront them with his word. More powerful than the armies of men would be this word delivered by the prophets. Because they spoke the very word of the one who created and sustained all things by his word, the prophets were appointed "over nations and kingdoms" (1:10). The Lord was "watching" over his word (1:12). Just as a leopard intently watches his prey, crouching in the grass until the right moment to spring into action (5:6), so the Lord watches over the word of his prophet to see that all he says will come to pass.[25] It was this determined commitment of the Lord to fulfill every word of his prophets that the kings of Jerusalem failed to consider adequately. They should have paid close attention to the precise wording of the prophet's message in view of its expressing the predetermined plan of God. But instead, the kings of Jerusalem "took their own decisions too seriously. They imagined they were unfettered to do whatever they pleased as long as it worked. But this 'watching' of Yahweh asserts that there is a shape, a flow, an intentionality to history that cannot be nullified or evaded."[26]

The Lord's prophet thus labors with the responsibility of a watchman (Ezek. 3:17). He must not fail to sound the alarm, warning the people of the coming judgment of the Lord. He is sent to a rebellious house. But whether they choose to hear or disregard, he must warn them of the judgment that will come if they fail to heed the word of the Lord.

25. Since the leopard hunts alone in contrast with the lion, he is extremely intent in watching every movement of his prey.
26. Brueggemann, *Jeremiah*, 27.

This powerful word coming forth from the Lord by the instrumentality of the prophet inherently had the capacity "to uproot and tear down, to destroy and overthrow, to build and to plant" (Jer. 1:10 NIV). Four words of judgment and two words of blessing characterize the message delivered by the prophets of the Lord according to Jeremiah's commission. As a consequence, the rise and fall of even Jerusalem was "not according to its own capacity for life and survival, but only according to the sovereign inclination of Yahweh."[27] Even the sacred temple complex, housing as it did the ever-present glory of the Covenant LORD, was not exempt from the prophetic word that brought about its uprooting and tearing down, its destroying and overthrowing, for "no historical structure, political policy, or defense scheme can secure a community against Yahweh."[28] Nations rise and nations fall according to the all-encompassing purposes of the one and only Lord of creation and providence.

Quite interestingly, this prophetic language of destroying and raising the temple of God is used by Jesus as he begins his prophetic ministry (John 2:19). In this instance, however, he refers to the temple of his body (2:21). After his resurrection from the dead the disciples recalled what he had said, and as a consequence "they believed the Scripture and the words that Jesus had spoken" (2:22 NIV). In this instance, the scripture that the disciples believed could very well have included the reference to the ministry of the prophets in terms of destroying and raising.[29]

The prophets thus received a solemn commission from the Lord. Their words went forth with history-shaping power. Nothing could

27. Ibid., 26.
28. Ibid., 25.
29. Brueggemann (ibid., 26) offers stimulating comments along these lines. But unfortunately his wording creates a serious ambiguity: "In John 2:19 the verbs 'destroy' and 'raise up' appear. They are used with reference to the Jerusalem establishment, specifically the temple." If Brueggemann intends to state that the original intent of Jesus was to refer to the destruction of the Jerusalem establishment and the temple, he misdirects the words of Jesus, who, according to his closest disciple, "spoke of the temple of his body" (John 2:21). It was the false witnesses at Jesus' trial who referred Jesus' words to the destruction of the temple (Matt. 26:61). Despite the ambiguity, it may be best to assume that Brueggemann intends to refer to the intent of the words of Jeremiah, who indeed was speaking of the destruction of the Jerusalem establishment and the temple.

stop their fulfillment once the words had been uttered, for the prophets' declarations were identical with the determining word of God himself.

IV. Response of inadequacy

It should not be surprising that once the experience of beholding his initiating vision was over, the prophet Ezekiel sat numbed among the exiles in Babylon, overwhelmed for seven days (Ezek. 3:15). What earthly mortal could absorb the glory of the eternal God without being dramatically affected? Who could prove sufficient to the task of communicating the awesome message of divine judgment inherent in his vision?

Jeremiah's response to the vision that initiated him into the office of prophet was essentially the same. Obviously he had not sought the office to which the Lord called him. Having been summoned to divine service in a way similar to Moses, he offered an excuse similar to Moses'.[30] He was a mere child. He had no capacity to speak. How could he serve as God's appointed prophet to the nations of the world (Jer. 1:6)?

Isaiah's vision of God's holiness drives the prospective prophet to the brink of despair: "Woe is me . . . for I am a man of unclean lips, and I dwell among a people of unclean lips" (Isa. 6:5). Later he would pronounce the divine woe over sinful nations, but now he pronounces woe on himself. His impure lips could not possibly serve as instruments of the divine word. Rather than preparing him for service, this vision of God's glory at first leaves him with the impression that he has been ruined once and for all.

Yet this deep conviction of sin was a common element of the prophetic call. Only when a person became fully aware of his own sinfulness and the grace of God that was capable of restoring him could he take on the role of God's spokesman to a sinful humanity. The psalmist expresses the concept vividly:

30. Habel, "Form and Significance of the Call Narratives," 308.

Cleanse me with hyssop,
    and I will be clean;
wash me,
    and I will be whiter than snow. . . .
Then I will teach transgressors
    your ways,
And sinners
    will turn back to you. (Ps. 51:7, 13 NIV)

This reaction of a sense of total inadequacy for service as God's prophet must be only the intermediate stage of response. A live coal from the altar purges Isaiah's lips of their impurity. In a distinctive play on words, Jeremiah is told that he cannot remain terrified of the people to whom he must deliver God's message, or the Lord will terrify him before them (*al-tekhat mippenehem pen-akhitteka lipnehem*; Jer. 1:17). After remaining for seven days in a stupor, Ezekiel receives his charge as a watchman for the nation. The glorious Lord of the vision will hold him personally accountable if he does not warn the wicked of the consequence of his ways (Ezek. 3:18).

It was appropriate that the persons called to the office of prophet understood from the beginning the solemnity of their task and the glories of the one they were to serve. A sense of inadequacy and unworthiness was quite appropriate—so long as the prophet was not crippled by the awesomeness of the position he must fill.

V. Reaction of the people

It might be expected that the people to whom a prophet was sent would react with delight and humble submission to the Lord's sending a chosen messenger to reveal his truth to them. After all, it was in response to the original plea of the people at Sinai that the Covenant LORD first established the mediatorial office of prophet in the days of Moses. But generally speaking the people would not respond in this receptive manner, and the prophet must have a realistic understanding of the reaction he could expect from the beginning.

It was explained to Ezekiel that as a general rule the house of Israel would not listen to his words (Ezek. 3:7). Since he was not being sent to a people of obscure speech, the only obstacle to their accepting the prophet's words would be their own hardened hearts. Even though they would set their faces against God's prophet "with determined and insolent effrontery,"[31] the prophet's responsibility remained undiminished. Whether they listened to him must not be the determining factor in fulfilling his calling (3:16–21). If the prophet failed to deliver his message from the Lord, he would be held personally accountable for the perishing sinner's blood.

Jeremiah could expect much opposition to the message he must deliver. And in preparation for the rejection that Jeremiah would face, God declares on the day of his calling that he made the prophet "a fortified city, an iron pillar, and a bronze wall to stand against the whole land" (Jer. 1:18 NIV). Kings, priests, and people would combine their forces to fight against Jeremiah, but the Lord would uphold him so that they could not overcome him.

Isaiah willingly volunteers as one to be sent with the message (Isa. 6:8), but his enthusiasm is immediately dampened when he is told the kind of response he may expect (6:9–11). In fact, God's intent from the beginning is to let the prophet serve as his instrument of judgment on a people who have already rejected him through centuries long past. Isaiah is charged to harden the people's hearts and to blind their eyes. The radical element in the commissioning of Isaiah is not that the people will reject his message, but that his preaching will be God's instrument of hardening them.[32] One commentator proposes that these statements are best understood in terms of the "extravagant uses of language typical of Hebrew poetry."[33] But instead, the hardening predicted is properly understood as a "judicial blindness, as the natural result and righteous retribution of the national depravity."[34] The hearts of this calloused people will be hardened even more by the message of grace and forgiveness.

31. Fairbairn, *Ezekiel*, 36.
32. Lindblom, *Prophecy in Ancient Israel*, 188.
33. Gowan, *Theology of the Prophetic Books*, 63.
34. Alexander, *Isaiah*, 1.91.

This aspect of the prophetic ministry is indeed a difficult one to comprehend. Until the land has been utterly devastated, Isaiah must continue in this solemn prophetic role of hardening the people's hearts according to the purposes of God (Isa. 6:9–13a). The Septuagint translators seem to have felt the theological difficulty of the assertion, in view of their rendering of the passage: "The heart of this people were made fat and their ears heard with difficulty and their eyes closed."[35] But the passage must be given the full weight of its implications. The prophetic word serves clearly as a manifestation of God's grace in that the Lord continues to present his word to the people. At the same time, the word of the prophet serves as a very real manifestation of the judgment of God on a recalcitrant people, for "those dulled and numbed are headed toward termination."[36]

It is well worth noting that the new covenant scriptures repeatedly quote this more difficult section of the record of Isaiah's call. The classic "whom shall I send and who will go for us?" followed by the prophet's exclamatory "here am I; send me!" (Isa. 6:8) never finds its way into the scriptures of the new covenant. But the declaration that by the prophetic word people's hearts will be hardened is quoted in all three synoptic gospels as well as in the gospel of John (Matt. 13:13–15; Mark 4:10–12; Luke 8:9–10; John 12:39–41). It appears in the writings of Luke (Acts 28:25–29) and in the works of Paul (Rom. 11:7–8). By the intention of the Lord, old covenant history anticipated these new covenant counterparts.

Yet in the end, there will be a holy seed in the land. The sovereignty of God's grace assures it. Just as a shoot sprouts from a tree that has been cut down, so a remnant shall remain in the land (Isa. 6:13). Although the prophet must live with many rejections, he may be assured that his message will not be delivered in vain. Both in its rejection and its acceptance, God will be glorified.

The message of the prophets also guarantees that "in the present day," even as throughout the days of the prophets, "there remains a remnant according to the election of grace" (Rom. 11:5). A remnant

35. See Seitz, *Isaiah 1–39*, 55.
36. Brueggemann, *Isaiah*, 63.

will be gathered despite the continual hardening of hearts against the gospel of God's grace.

This perspective on the response of the people to the ministry of the prophets ultimately prepares the way for an understanding of the reaction to the ministry of Jesus. The rejection of Jesus and his teaching as recorded in the gospels should not be read as a "redactional coloring" of Jesus' life designed to explain a failed ministry. Instead it represents "an integral part of the selfsame struggle" of God with his people that had been going on throughout the history of the prophetic ministry.[37] This rejection of the prophetic word of Jesus was "the ultimate climax" to the "hardening" of Israel by the ministry of the prophets.[38] The exile of Israel as God's people had to come as an act of divine judgment before the gracious provisions of the restoration after exile could be experienced: "The prophetic drama does not permit a rush to [the restoration of] postexile, even as the gospel does not permit a rush past Friday to arrive too early and too easily at Sunday."[39] These historical realities about the way of God's working redemption in the world find their consummate realization in the rejection and restoration of Jesus the Christ, the embodiment of the Israel of God. He must first undergo the judgmental rejection of God and men that he might be the innocent sin-bearer of his people. Only then will he enter into his glory and move human history along toward the restoration of all things by his resurrection from the dead and his renewal of a fallen universe.

VI. Conclusion

The record of the calling and commissioning of these prophets provides significant insight into the responsibility they were given by the Lord. Inadequate evidence makes it impossible to assume that each and every prophet of the Lord had the kind of vision experienced by Isaiah and Ezekiel. But the trust of the prophetic office always had the

37. Childs, *Isaiah*, 59.
38. Ibid.
39. Brueggemann, *Isaiah*, 63.

implicit assumptions that were made so explicit by these glorious occasions. Several key factors may be noted regarding the prophet's call.

First, the prophets did not function as religious philosophers. They did not spend their days speculating about the nature of God and his relation to the world. Instead, they were people called and commissioned with a divinely revealed message that was pertinent to a specific historical circumstance. It is not that their prophecies were time bound and therefore irrelevant for today. Since their message originated in the eternal God, their words always will have significant application to every age. But the prophet was not called to deal in philosophical abstractions. Instead, he spoke God's concrete word to the people of his own time in a way that continues to speak concretely today.

Second, the prophets were not called to office by virtue of their religious piety or personal qualifications. Amos was nothing more than a shepherd, a tender of sycamore trees. Ezekiel lived among the exiles, the chastened people of the Lord. He may not have been as wicked as his contemporaries, but nonetheless he was a sinner speaking to sinners. Jeremiah fully recognized that he did not possess natural gifts of elocution that would qualify him as spokesman for the Lord. Only because the Lord put words in his mouth could he fulfill the office of prophet. Isaiah confessed that he was a man of unclean lips, indicating his understanding that his heart also disqualified him from fulfilling the role of spokesman for the Lord. In a day in which so many people step forward eagerly to speak for the Lord, it is good to be reminded of the basic disqualification that belongs to every sinner.

Third, the divine call of the prophets indicates that they were independent religious agents.[40] They owed the origin and continuation of their office to no one but God himself. Neither king nor priest nor another prophet was the source of their authority, and none of these people could take their office from them. Their accountability was only to the majestic God who had called them.

Fourth, the divine call to office explains the compulsion under which the prophets labored. As Amos attests:

40. See von Rad, *Old Testament Theology*, 2.53.

> The lion has roared—
> > who will not fear?
> The Sovereign Covenant LORD has spoken—
> > who can but prophesy? (Amos 3:8 NIV)

In similar fashion, Jeremiah declares;

> So the word of the Covenant LORD has brought me
> > insult and reproach all day long.
> But if I say, "I will not mention him
> > or speak any more in his name,"
> his word is in my heart like a fire,
> > a fire shut up in my bones.
> I am weary of holding it in;
> > indeed, I cannot. (Jer. 20:8b–9 NIV)

The distinctive, unmistakable, call of the Lord to the prophet served as the sure foundation for his proclamation of the divine word. "It was in virtue of such assurance that the call he had received was from God, that he condemned the pretensions of false prophets."[41]

Fifth, the divine call established the legitimacy of the office of the prophet. In this regard, the Lord contrasts the propriety of Jeremiah's place as a prophet with the illegitimacy of the false prophets by virtue of their having never received the commission given to him:

> I did not send these prophets,
> > yet they have run with their message;
> I did not speak to them,
> > yet they have prophesied.
> But if they had stood in my council,
> > they would have proclaimed my words to the people
> and would have turned them from their evil ways
> > and from their evil deeds. (Jer. 23:21–22 NIV)

The clear implication is that in contrast with these false prophets, Jeremiah experienced his commissioning vision from the Lord and was

41. Oehler, *Theology of the Old Testament*, 2.316.

brought into the inner circle of his secret council. In addition, the written record of the prophet's call provides a permanent authentication for his assumption of the prophetic office.[42] The real point of the written record of the prophetic call is "the vindication and legitimization of the prophet as a spokesman for God."[43]

Sixth, the call of the prophet is never success oriented. Because the Lord's hand rests on Jeremiah, he can fulfill his prophetic role without human approbation (Jer. 15:17). From the beginning he understands that he must expect rejection, opposition, and failure if measured by human standards. His essential responsibility is to remain faithful in declaring the word of God exactly as it is delivered to him. By his call, the prophet is prepared for the failure he will face in his effort to persuade the people to believe and respond positively to his message.[44] In applying this principle to God's servants throughout the ages, Calvin says: "Sometimes God wants his servants to rest in his authority so as to labor even with no hope of success. . . . Although our labor may be useless, it is enough that it pleases God. When we are ordered to do something, let us learn to leave the outcome in God's hand."[45]

Seventh, the call to office issued to the various prophets of the old covenant prepares the way for a unique prophet in the future, who will issue the call to others as well as being called himself. With the exception of Elijah's call to Elisha and Moses' laying hands on Joshua, the prophets of the old covenant did not have the capacity to issue a prophetic call to others. But when Jesus came as the prophet without equal, he experienced the heavenly vision that certified him as God's son and servant (Matt. 3:17). In a unique way, his calling to office could be attested by others who saw the descending dove and heard the heavenly voice (John 1:32–34). From that point on, Jesus demonstrated his own unique power to call and commission spokesmen for the Lord (Matt. 4:18–22; 28:18–20; John 1:33–50). Even further, he

42. Von Rad, *Old Testament Theology*, 2.55; Bright, *Jeremiah*, 6; Lindblom, *Prophecy in Ancient Israel*, 182.
43. Baltzer, "Office and Calling of the Prophets," 568.
44. Von Rad, *Old Testament Theology*, 2.65.
45. Calvin, *Ezekiel*, 1.62.

himself became the central object of the heavenly vision that commissioned major prophetic figures of the new covenant era (Acts 9:1–9; Rev. 1:9–20). In these regards, no other can compare with him. He is the supreme prophet among the prophets.

With the completion of Christ's work of redemption by his death and resurrection, and with the provision of an inspired interpretation of his finished work in the new covenant scriptures, the extraordinary office of prophet as the very mouthpiece of God came to its conclusion. Because prophetic visions of the Almighty along with new revelations ceased with the end of the apostolic age, the church should not expect a continuation of the prophetic office as such in the present era. Yet ministers of Christ today must take seriously their responsibility of being prophetic in their declaration of the word of the Lord. In this regard, many lessons may be learned from the initial calling and commissioning of the prophets of old. May the Lord show favor to his church in every age by continuing the blessings of a prophetic ministry until he returns in glory.

4

PROPHETS TRUE
AND FALSE

The greatest threat to the well-being of God's people throughout the ages has come from those who present themselves as prophetic spokesmen of the Lord but actually are not. Instead of communicating the revealed truth originating in God, these people speak a deceptive lie.

The very presence of two kinds of prophets among God's people must invariably have a significant impact on the life of the community. Often two respected figures would confront one another, each claiming divine authority for his message. Who were the people to follow? How were they to distinguish the true prophet from the false? Because the destiny of the nation hinged on the words spoken by these opposing personages, it was vitally important that the people understand the differences that characterized these prophetic figures and their ministries. In considering prophets true and false, several matters deserve consideration.[1]

I. The ultimate source of true and false prophecy

True prophecy found its ultimate origin in a purposeful creation by the one and only God. By revelation coming through dream and

1. A brief but helpful summary of the discussion regarding true and false prophecy may be found in VanGemeren, *Interpreting the Prophetic Word*, 61–67. See also Sanders, "Hermeneutics in True and False Prophecy," 21–29.

vision the creator would communicate his purpose, his will, to his people. Both his moral will and his consummative purpose would be revealed to his people through his servants the prophets. The words of the true prophet were not his own. They came directly by revelation from God as he spoke "mouth to mouth" through his prophetic instrument.

Although scripture provides little explanation of the ultimate origin of evil, it clearly indicates the instrument by which falsehood and evil made its way into this world. Scripture gives no suggestion of an evil being that had an equally ultimate existence alongside God. But immediately upon man's creation in innocency, the serpent introduced the first lie that contradicted the truth of God (Gen. 3:1, 4–5).[2] From that point on, the voice of the speaking serpent resonated in the utterances of the false prophets. If the intent of Satan is to oppose the purposes of God with respect to the redemption of his people, then it is understandable that he would seek to misrepresent the truth in a way that would contradict the revelation given through the Lord's prophets. By this method he would strike at the root of the means by which God had determined to direct the faith and life of his people. Sometimes more subtly, sometimes more boldly, that same voice has continued to speak through the ages even until today. According to the Apocalypse, "that old serpent, the devil, or Satan" will be actively contradicting God's truth until the end of the age (Rev. 12:9).

In this regard, to state that the existence of false prophecy indicates something "sinister" about God and that false prophecy manifests God's own "demonic activity" represents the height of blasphemy.[3] It is certainly legitimate to affirm that the holy one of Israel orders the evil purposes of men and Satan to achieve his own ends.

---

2. Crenshaw, *Prophetic Conflict*, 78, presumes to attribute moral wrongdoing to God, making him the author of evil by creating the serpent. He asserts that the declaration that all that God created was very good is "something of a shallow mockery." In presuming to make these accusations against God, he goes well beyond the witness of scripture concerning the origin of evil. A significant, guarded silence separates the record of God's creating all things "very good" from the appearance of the tempting serpent.

3. Ibid., 78–79.

It is even appropriate to state that the sovereign Lord ordained all things, even the wicked actions of men and Satan, to serve his ultimate purposes. But to suggest that in order to understand the existence of false prophecy the "dark side of God, the 'demonic,' must be taken into consideration"[4] is to pervert the true nature of the holy one of Israel. A pernicious error that twists the essential nature of God lies at the root of the statement that the false prophets "are indeed true prophets while speaking an untrue message."[5] In actuality, this statement makes truth into falsehood and falsehood into truth and so falls into the same category as the utterances of the false prophets of Israel who made good evil and evil good (Isa. 5:20). It is not God who lies, but the false prophet. That God in his providential ordering makes use of the false prophets for his own purposes does not in any way make the Lord culpable or blameworthy for the lies they utter. When the prophet Micaiah reports that a spirit from the heavenly council would "go out and be a lying spirit" in the mouths of all Ahab's prophets (1 Kings 22:22 NIV), it must be remembered that this lying spirit goes to prophets already committed to speak for the false god Baal. These false prophets, whether self-consciously or otherwise, are already dedicated to communicating untruth in their prophesying. The Covenant LORD of Israel simply employs the evil practices of these evil prophets to accomplish his righteous purposes. Far from being the blameworthy source of lies, the Lord directs these lies so that they serve the truth. False prophets forever must be held responsible for the lies they have spoken in the name of the Lord. Nothing that God has done has ever forced a person to lie.

The ultimate origins of true prophecy and false prophecy are quite distinct from one another. True prophecy comes directly from the one true and living God as his means of communicating his will to his people. But false prophecy has its origins in the wicked purposes of the evil one who seeks to mislead and bring devastation to the world that God made.

4. Ibid., 77.
5. Ibid., 76.

II. The motivations of prophets true and false

Something drives a prophet. No one assumes the role of speaking to men for God without a strong inner impulse. But the driving motive of true and false prophets is radically different. The true prophet sent from the Lord spoke out of a sense of necessity similar to the compulsion expressed by the apostle Paul: "For necessity is laid upon me; yea, woe is me if I preach not the gospel" (1 Cor. 9:16). According to Jeremiah, God's word was like fire in his mouth (Jer. 5:14). He lived under compulsion to speak in order to be relieved from the burning sensation caused by the Lord's word.

In addition to the prophets' own desire for relief from the weighty presence of the Lord's word, a further motivation was the sense of the people's need. The prophet understood that living in sin invariably brought calamity into the lives of God's nation. As difficult as it might be, the true prophet must declare as clearly as possible the sin of the people with the hope that they would hear and repent. Then perhaps the Lord would turn away from his intent to bring judgment on them for their sin. The Lord himself expresses this understanding of the prophet's responsibility: "Tell them everything I command you; do not omit a word. Perhaps they will listen and each will turn from his evil way. Then I will relent and not bring on them the disaster I was planning because of the evil they have done" (Jer. 26:2b–3 NIV).

Not so for the motivating force of the false prophets. They were driven men, but not because the word of the Lord compelled them to speak. Two motives in particular kept them at the task of assuming the role of spokesmen for God: personal gain and acceptance by men.

The eighth-century prophet Micah declares the Lord's word about the thing that motivates false prophets: "As for the prophets who lead my people astray, if one feeds them, then they proclaim 'peace'; if he does not, they prepare to wage war against him" (Mic. 3:5 NIV). In this case, the motivation for prophesying clearly was personal provision and comfort. If a person seeking a word from the Lord did not pay an amount that the prophet regarded as adequate

94

remuneration, he could expect stringent opposition by the prophet, opposition so stringent that it could be called war. People who have not experienced the wrath of the hypocritically pious might tend to discount this dramatic figure of speech. But the wrath of the self-righteous exceeds all others, since they are convinced that they represent the cause of God.

The prophet Ezekiel is instructed by the Lord to "set his face" against the women who were prophesying falsely among the people of Israel. In bringing disaster on the people of God by leading them astray, their motivation has been "a few handfuls of barley and scraps of bread" (Ezek. 13:19 NIV). Disregarding altogether the well-being of the people whom they should be serving, these false prophetesses had personal gain as their principal motive. Throughout the ages prophets have spoken for the sake of their own advantage. At great cost to the people of God, the false prophet concerns himself only with his own personal advancement.

The other driving motive of the false prophets was personal acceptance of themselves and their ministries by the people. Sadly, it was just this kind of prophet that the people themselves desired. They would be very happy with a prophet who would tell them what they wanted to hear. Micah describes the prevailing situation in his day: "If a liar and deceiver comes and says, 'I will prophesy for you plenty of wine and beer,' he would be just the prophet for this people" (Mic. 2:11 NIV). Nothing would suit them more than to have a prophet in tow who would follow behind and meekly offer as a word from the Lord just the things the people wanted to hear. The situation is the same in all ages. Always people will assert that they wish to hear a true word from the Lord. But actually they desire an authoritative reflection of their own ideas that will promote their own good.

The thing that drove the prophet had a significant effect on the message he delivered. If the word of the Lord truly had come to him, the prophet must deliver that word exactly as it came, whatever the consequences. But the false prophet moved by concern for personal gain or acceptance with the people would speak whatever he determined the crowd wanted to hear.

III. The character of the person and work of prophets

The principal characterization of the false prophet's person and work is not very nice. He is a liar, and his message is a lie. He lives a lie, and he tells lies (Mic. 2:11; Jer. 23:14, 26). The false prophet is described in this blunt way because lying is his principal characteristic. He says that he has received a word from the Lord, but the Lord has not spoken to him. That he speaks as though his words were from God intensifies the damage done to the lives of others. The recipients of his message are placed under the burden of either heeding the word of the prophet because it comes to them as the word of God or of ignoring that word and running the risk of disobedience to their creator.

Behind the sin of lying in the name of God is a heart attitude of presumption and stubbornness. The false prophet "has not stood in the council of the Covenant LORD," and yet he presumes to speak as though he understood the mysteries of God that would not be available to the common man (Jer. 23:16, 22). These false prophets claim that God has come to them in a special way when they declare, "I had a dream! I had a dream!" (23:25). But actually they declare only the delusions of their own heart (23:26). God has not commissioned them as his messengers, and yet they run as though they have been sent by the sovereign Lord himself (23:21). The false prophet abuses the trust associated with his office (23:10c). He uses his power to strengthen the hand of the wicked and to intimidate the true prophet even to the point of threatening death (23:14).

One assumption basic to the distinction between true and false prophets is that all people, even the finest of God's own people, regularly need rebuke for their sinful ways. In contrast with the false prophets who speak soothing, agreeable words because they themselves benefit by the positive response of the people, Micah describes his own state as a true prophet of the Lord: "But as for me, I am filled with power, with the Spirit of the Covenant LORD, and with justice and might, to declare to Jacob his transgression, to Israel his sin" (Mic. 3:8 NIV).

Consider the distinctiveness of the experience of this true prophet of the Lord. He has strong confidence of God's being with him, which no circumstance can destroy. He possesses a power that goes beyond his own person. The Spirit of the Lord, the Spirit of all truth, fills him so that he lives out of a consciousness that God is guiding the path of his life. The moral might of the Lord's own just cause undergirds him, not with a sense of false presumption but with the confidence that he does not speak out of his own head and heart but from the counsel of the Lord. All this inner strength comes to focus in the empowerment of the prophet "to declare to Jacob his transgression, to Israel his sin." What false prophet would find meaningful purpose and fulfillment in exposing the wrongdoing of the people toward whom he is attempting to ingratiate himself? How could he expect that publicly denouncing the evil, depraved heart of his hearers would lead them to pay him a more substantial salary? Moved by an inner compulsion and provided with a depth of insight into the twisted motivations of men's hearts, the true prophet of the Lord speaks out because he understands that his revelation from God represents the only hope for his hearers.

At regular intervals the true prophets of the Lord experienced confrontations with false prophets. But the great struggle between true and false prophets reached its climax in the days of Jeremiah. The situation may be compared to the days of Jesus' ministry on earth, when Satan responded to the presence of the incarnate Christ by a greater display of his powers than at any other time in human history. Demon-possessed people came forth as clear indicators of the strength of Satan's hold on humanity. In a sense, it may be said that Satan determined at the time of the incarnation to defy the powers of the Son of God.

In a similar way, Satan's lying prophets manifested themselves in a more determined fashion during the days of Jeremiah than during any other period of history in the old covenant. The prophet was declaring to the people of Jerusalem the destruction of their beloved city even while the Babylonian forces were descending upon them. It seemed as though the Lord's prophet was the worst of traitors, calling for surrender to the enemy with all the humiliations that submission would bring. As a consequence, many passages in the prophecy of Jeremiah vividly depict the contradictory stance of the false prophets, often including the threats they directed against the Lord's true servant:

- The false prophets have lied by saying that no harm will come to the people; but God will make his words as fire in Jeremiah's mouth to consume the wicked (5:12–14).
- The plots against Jeremiah's life make him think of himself as "a gentle lamb led to the slaughter"; but God will punish the false prophets (11:18–23).
- The false prophets are declaring "the delusions of their own mind"; and as a consequence they will suffer the most severe of the curses of the covenant (14:13–16).
- Pashhur the priestly rival to Jeremiah has God's prophet beaten and put in the stocks. Jeremiah responds by announcing that Pashhur will be carried away into Babylon with all his house, never to return (20:1–18).
- The false prophets are godless people, spreading wickedness in the Lord's holy temple. God has not sent them, they have not stood in his council, so because of their presumption their path will become slippery and they will be banished into darkness (23:9–40).
- Jeremiah prophesies that Jerusalem will become like Shiloh in its devastation if the people refuse to listen to his prophetic word. But instead of submitting, the people along with their false prophets determine to put Jeremiah to death (26:1–24).

The pungent message delivered specifically to Jeremiah's assistant, Baruch, also underscores the threats regularly directed against the life and well-being of the Lord's prophets. The Lord asks Baruch: "Do you seek great things for yourself?" Are you in quest for comforts in life? "Do not seek them." God will see to it that your life is preserved as you are tossed about from one nation to another. That is his gift to you. But do not make the mistake of looking for all the pleasurable things that life can afford, because these things are not the assigned lot of the man called to be the Lord's prophet (Jer. 45).

This contrast between true and false prophet finds its most vivid expression in the face-to-face confrontation between Jeremiah and Hananiah the false prophet (Jer. 28). In the days of Zedekiah, the last king of Judah, the Lord commanded Jeremiah to strap a yoke about his neck, symbolizing the sure bondage to the king of Babylon that the nation would experience. Judah and all the surrounding nations were advised to submit to this yoke if they wished to continue in their own land despite their servitude to Babylon (27:1–15).

But Hananiah presumed to offer a contrary prophecy. Not only would these countries be spared the domination of Babylon, but within two years all the treasures taken from the Lord's house by Nebuchadnezzar would be returned to Jerusalem. Exiled King Jehoiachin would be released and would return to the land. To dramatize his prediction, Hananiah confronted Jeremiah before all the people and broke apart the symbolic yoke about his neck. The Lord could not tolerate this overt contradiction of his true word. Jeremiah must declare to Hananiah that he had acted presumptuously in prophesying lies. As a consequence of his preaching rebellion against the Lord, Hananiah would die within the year. And so it was. Within two months, Hananiah the false prophet was dead (28:17; see also 28:1).

The lesson is driven home in a most forceful way. The false prophet presumes to make up in his own imagination a word from the Lord. He declares what he knows the people will want to hear. But because this lie has the disastrous effect of leading the people from trusting in the true word of the Lord and acting accordingly, the false prophet stands under the curse of God and sooner or later will receive a just recompense for the wrong he has done to the Lord's people.

The contrast could not be more dramatic. In one case, the prophet of God speaks the truth of the Lord's word, however saddening the message may appear to God's people. But in the other case, the false prophet presumes to create a supposed word from the Lord that actually is a figment of his own imagination. The false prophet is motivated by covetousness and a desire to be liked by the people, while the true prophet speaks things that the people will not want to hear because of a compulsion from the Lord and out of unselfish concern for the good of the people.

IV. Criteria for distinguishing between true and false prophecy

How was the nation to distinguish between the utterances of the true and the false prophets? The patriarchal records show no concern for such a problem. Abraham, Isaac, and Jacob clearly knew when God spoke to them, even though through a lapse of faith they might doubt that the Lord's word would come to full realization. The problem came with the institution of the prophetic office in Israel. Now, even though the very word of God was being delivered, it came through the instrumentality of a brother speaking to brothers. The simple, humble voice of a man became the instrument of the revelation from God. As a consequence, some criteria were needed to confirm that this prophet was actually sent from God and that his words were God's words. The people themselves initially framed the question when the office of prophet was first established in Israel (Deut. 18:21). In that context, certain criteria for identifying the truly prophetic word were provided by the Lord himself. By the application of these criteria, the people could distinguish the true word of the true prophet from the pretended word of the lying prophet.

A. Biblical criteria for distinguishing between true and false prophecy

Essentially, three bases for making the critical judgment between true and false prophecy were provided. First, if a prophet ever spoke in the name of another god, he must be regarded as a false prophet, despite any other characteristics that might mark him out as a person worthy of being heard: "If a prophet or a dreamer of dreams should arise in your midst and give you a sign or a wonder, and the sign or wonder happens exactly as he has declared it to you; if at the same time he says, 'Let us go after other gods that you have not known, and let us serve them'; then you must not listen to the words of that prophet or dreamer of dreams" (Deut. 13:1–3a).

A prophet whether true or false might display an ability to perform signs or wonders. Israel had already witnessed a rivalry to their premier prophet Moses while they were still in Egypt. The magicians of the pharaoh performed their false wonders.[6] The ability to mock Moses' genuine powers by the hypnotism of snakes, by the illusion of turning water into blood, and by the multiplication of frogs quickly ran its course, and the so-called magicians were forced to admit that Moses' greater powers had to be attributed to "the finger of God" (Exod. 8:18–19).

The new covenant scriptures also attest to the "signs and false wonders" that might be performed by a false prophet (2 Thess. 2:9).[7] Even Jesus affirmed the possibility of signs and wonders being performed by false prophets: "Pseudochrists and pseudoprophets shall arise with all power, and they shall give great signs and wonders" (Matt. 24:24). For this reason, the significance of this test of true prophecy stretches into the present day. In the current climate, many people demand the manifestation of the spectacular to confirm a person's ministry. But according to the test of scripture, even working wonders is not the final criterion that establishes a person as a true prophet of the Lord.

In conjunction with his performance of signs and wonders, the false prophet shows his true colors by encouraging his devotees to follow other gods. Having established a position of trust, he declares, "Let us go after other gods that you have not known, and let us serve them" (Deut. 13:2b). Now it becomes clear that this prophet has not received his message from the God who delivered Israel from Egypt. Instead, he promotes a god that Israel has never known. But the Israelites must not hearken to the words of that prophet or dreamer of dreams. No matter how spectacular the sign or wonder that he performs, the person who speaks in the name of another god must be regarded as a false prophet.

This test of true and false prophecy is variously evaluated. One critic acknowledges that this criterion would be valid if a false prophet belonged to the Baal cult, even though he regards the biblical tests in general to be "impossible of application or impractical."[8] According

---

6. It seems best to regard these mimicries of Moses' miracles as tricks or illusions, not as genuine transformations of the natural orders of God's creation.

7. The terms used in the New Testament for signs and wonders are identical to those found in the Septuagint version of Deut. 13:1.

8. Crenshaw, *Prophetic Conflict*, 55–56.

to this view, the inadequacy of this criterion becomes manifest when the prophet swore allegiance to the Covenant LORD although continuing to prophesy in the name of Baal.[9]

From a more radical perspective, it is asserted that this basic test of loyalty to the one true God was doomed to failure. For even though the "fundamental canonical thrust of the Bible is the struggle to monotheize," it is doubted that any large unit of the Bible is "thoroughly monotheistic."[10] If it actually is the case that no major section of scripture is altogether monotheistic, then obviously the proposal that a true prophet would speak only in the name of the one Covenant LORD would have to be regarded as fallacious.

But the self-testimony of scripture warrants a much stronger position with respect to this test for true and false prophecy. The prohibition against speaking in the name of another god made no allowances for a syncretistic approach that would permit a person to be a worshiper of the Covenant LORD while prophesying in the name of Baal. The prophets themselves roundly condemned this type of syncretism. Zephaniah declares in no uncertain terms:

> I will cut off . . .
> > those who swear to the Covenant LORD
> > and [at the same time] swear by Molech. (Zeph. 1:4b–5)[11]

If Israel's Covenant LORD created all things visible and invisible, then the self-revelation of his distinctive name may legitimately become the foundation for testing the truth or falsehood of all prophecy. As Childs observes, "In a real sense the whole issue of false prophecy turns on the abuse of God's name."[12] With this understanding in mind, it simply would not be possible for a person to be recognized as a true prophet if he were a devotee of Baal even though prophesying in the name of the Covenant LORD. This first test would clearly differentiate between the true and the false prophet whenever a person attempted syncretism.

9. Ibid., 55.
10. Ibid., 40–41.
11. See Robertson, *Nahum, Habakkuk, and Zephaniah*, 264–65.
12. Childs, *Old Testament Theology in a Canonical Context*, 69.

Second, a clear distinction between true and false prophets hinged on whether the predictive words of a prophet were fulfilled. If the prophet's predictions did not come to pass, he would be discredited and must not be believed (Deut. 18:22). This test of the prophetic word clearly rested on its origin in God, for no human being can have clear and concrete knowledge of the future apart from a revelation from the God who determines the course of the future.

The thoroughgoing nature of this criterion is seen in that not merely a specific prophecy, but the person of the prophet himself is discredited by an unfulfilled prediction. As a consequence, a particular individual could "predict" correctly any number of events. But if he failed once in his prophecies, from that point on he was to be regarded as a false prophet whose words were not to be regarded as coming from God. This second test of fulfilled predictions made no allowance for a "percentage count." Any failed prophecy meant that the person was branded a false prophet.

The true prophets of Israel were quite comfortable with this test of their ministries, as indicated on several occasions. When challenged concerning his prophecy about the death of Ahab, Micaiah publicly put his prophetic ministry on the line: "If you ever return safely, the Covenant LORD has not spoken through me." Then turning to the people, he underscored his own self-challenge: "Mark my words, all you people!" (1 Kings 22:28 NIV). The entirety of the books of Kings may be read as confirmation of the predictions of God's servants the prophets, for as many as twenty confirmations of prophecies are recorded in the two books.[13]

The writing prophets of Israel regularly subjected themselves (and contemporary prophetic pretenders) to the scrutiny of fulfilled or unfulfilled predictions. The prophet Isaiah reports that the people were attempting to silence the Lord's prophets (Isa. 30:10). The Lord responds by commanding that Isaiah put his word in permanent form. He must write his message so it can be an everlasting witness for the

13. See Robertson, *Christ of the Covenants*, 252–69; von Rad, *Old Testament Theology*, 2.342–56.

days to come (30:8). Future generations will see clearly the truthfulness of the prophet's words.

In a context of continual confrontation with false prophets, Jeremiah reiterates the Lord's criterion for separating the true prophet from the false: "The prophet who predicts prosperity [*shalom*]—when the word of the prophet comes to pass, then that prophet will be confirmed as one who was actually sent by the Covenant LORD" (Jer. 28:9). Apart from the confirmation of fulfilled predictions, a person could not be established as a true prophet from the Lord. Once again it becomes clear that confirmation relates to the person of the prophet and not merely to a specific message.

In Ezekiel's day, the Lord expresses his displeasure over a people who treat his prophet as though he were a beautiful singer even as he pronounces the most severe of judgments (Ezek. 33:32). Vindication of the prophet's predictions will establish that he was not merely another dramatic actor: "So when these [judgmental declarations] come to pass—and be sure that they will come to pass!—then they will be forced to recognize that a prophet has been in their midst" (33:33). The prophet has no doubt that his predictions will be fulfilled.[14] This confidence arises only because he knows that his words are not his own, but have originated with the Lord himself. The fulfillment of predictive prophecies was the sure test to be applied to every person claiming to be a prophet.

Many objections are raised against this criterion in an effort to demonstrate its ineffectiveness. It is objected that this criterion would be effective only in retrospect.[15] Only after the prophecy was fulfilled could it be affirmed with confidence that the word was from the Lord. But this objection overlooks many factors. On the one hand, it may be observed that the biblical prophecies are peppered with short-term as well as long-term predictions. It would not take long for contemporaries of a prophet to verify the truthfulness of his message. In addition, as previously noted, prophetic confirmation related not merely to specific predictions, but to the person of the prophet. Once a per-

14. Crenshaw, *Prophetic Conflict*, 14, suggests that the prophet may have had to "walk the razor's edge between certitude and doubt all his days."
15. Ibid., 50.

son was confirmed as a true prophet of the Lord by the fulfillment of short-term predictions, the people could generally trust in his long-term prophecies.

Some interpreters go to great lengths to show the hopelessness of Jeremiah's dilemma in his confrontation with Hananiah.[16] The true prophet of the Lord is presented as a dejected wimp because Hananiah's prophecy sounds as good as his own. Perhaps Jeremiah even begins to doubt his own prediction.

But this perspective on the encounter of the two claimants totally ignores the subsequent developments. The Lord will not allow his faithful servant to be left in this kind of embarrassing situation. Jeremiah returns with a short-term prediction that all the people will be able to confirm. Hananiah the false prophet will die within the year (Jer. 28:16). No more than two months later, Hananiah dies (28:17; see also 28:1). What more dramatic way could be imagined for the confirmation of the true prophet and his word from the Lord? To suggest, as some commentators do, that these two prophetic figures were at a stalemate totally ignores the conclusion of the confrontation. By the fulfillment of his solemn short-term prediction, Jeremiah's long-term prediction is verified. He is God's true prophet.

At the same time, the significance of long-term predictions for the people may be made evident by comparison with new covenant counterparts. According to the apostle Peter, the promise of the coming of the Lord naturally raises the question, "What manner of people ought you to be?" (2 Pet. 3:11). The certain return of the Lord should spur God's people to sober and righteous behavior. If the long-term predictions regarding the return of the Lord have significant effect on the total lifestyle of the people of the new covenant era, the same principle would apply to long-term predictions of the old covenant scriptures.

The assertion that many predictions of the true prophets failed to find fulfillment represents a serious obstacle to the effective use of this criterion.[17] One critic asserts that the "most notable failure of

16. See Brueggemann, *Theology of the Old Testament*, 631, who says that "scholars are agreed" that "no objective criteria" exist for deciding between the claims of Jeremiah and Hananiah.

17. Crenshaw, *Prophetic Conflict*, 51–52.

105

prophetic promise" is found in the book of Isaiah, "for this poetic masterpiece is permeated with unfulfilled predictions."[18] In noting Isaiah's repeated claim that the God of Israel had the ability to predict the future, it is judged to be "ironical" that the "grandiose predictions by this author failed to materialize at all."[19] The prediction of Isaiah that the desert would blossom like a garden is cited as one instance of this failure of the prophet, along with his assertions that Babylon would be destroyed and Cyrus would worship the God of Israel.[20]

Each of the various illustrations intended to establish the failure of biblical predictions could be considered on an individual basis.[21] But the reference to the prophecy concerning the blooming desert as an instance of failed prophecy makes it plain that a very wooden, literalistic concept of fulfillment is being employed as the measuring line for prophetic fulfillment. Admittedly, difficulties will continue to exist in coming to a proper understanding of all the predictions of the prophets. But when recognition is given to the biblical principle of ultimate fulfillment in a new covenant consummation, few serious problems remain.

Furthermore, the suggestion that the predictions of the prophets were "collected and edited" after the fact of their fulfillment[22] under-

18. Ibid., 51 n. 39. "Damning with faint praise" rightly describes this commendation of the book of Isaiah as a "poetic masterpiece" that is nonetheless "permeated with unfulfilled predictions." In support of his judgment that the prophets' writings are permeated with unfulfilled prophecies, Crenshaw quotes E. Osswald, who states that in view of the abundance of unfulfilled prophetic words, the faith of the prophets "was erring faith."

19. Ibid., 52 n. 41.

20. Ibid., 51 n. 39.

21. Crenshaw lists twelve passages that supposedly demonstrate the failure of predictions by various prophets (ibid., 51 n. 39). His insistence on a literal view of fulfillment is seen in his including Ezek. 40–48 in his list of unfulfilled prophecies. He also faults the prophecy of Huldah (2 Kings 22:18–20), stating that Huldah predicted that King Josiah would be gathered to his fathers in peace, which he was not. But in looking at the actual prophecy of Huldah, it becomes apparent that the prophetess in fact predicted something quite different. Josiah would be gathered to his fathers (true), he would be buried in peace (also quite true), and his eyes would not see the disaster that God would bring on Jerusalem (true as well). It might further be noted that, with all the editorializing supposedly going on, it would be strange indeed if some redactor along the way would not have caught and corrected the supposed error in the record of Kings.

22. Childs, *Old Testament Theology in a Canonical Context*, 140.

cuts the whole point of recording these prophecies in writing. A written prophecy that has been tampered with after the fact of fulfillment has lost its significance as a divinely revealed anticipation of the future. A modification in substance subsequent to the event anticipated in the prediction makes the whole prophecy suspect. Strange indeed is the reasoning that starts with the assumption that the prophet had to be consistent in his prophecies if he were to maintain credibility, but then asserts that the composing of prophecies after the event (which pretended to be recorded before the event) made it possible for the various utterances to be harmonized.[23] It is noted, and correctly so, that a prophet "could not be constantly changing his message and its implications" if he were to be accepted as a true prophet.[24] But how then could a prophet's words be regarded as valid if the writing down of his speeches provided the opportunity for harmonization of his presumably divergent utterances?

It seems highly unlikely that the earlier writings of the classical prophets of Israel were kept secret from the public eye, so that any necessary alterations for the sake of harmonizing divergent statements could be made without affecting the respect in which the prophet had been held. By the very nature of the case, written records of prophetic utterances could not be conveniently modified for purposes of harmonization without discrediting their predictions. If the very purpose of the original recording of the prophet's words in writing was to extend the authority of his spoken word into the future, then the initial record of the prophet's utterances would have to be regarded as sacrosanct from the beginning and therefore necessarily preserved from alteration or modification.

Retained in its integrity in written form, a truly prophetic word serves as an ongoing wonder that confirms the claim of the prophet that he speaks only by direct revelation from God. Only the sovereign God who has a purpose for his creation can know for certain the course of future events.

As a third criterion for distinguishing between the true and the false prophet, it was early indicated and subsequently reiterated that

23. Clements, *Old Testament Prophecy*, 210–11.
24. Ibid., 210.

a prophet should be regarded as true only if he spoke in conformity with God's previous revelations, particularly as they came through Moses as the fountainhead of biblical prophecy. Instead of listening to the multiple voices that might come through various sources, Israel must keep the commands of its Covenant LORD and obey his voice (Deut. 13:4; see also Isa. 8:20).

The reference to keeping God's commands refers to the ministry of Moses in particular, for he was Israel's lawgiver.[25] His priority over subsequent prophetism is established by his commands becoming the criterion for judging between true and false prophecy. His recorded law must take precedence over later prophetic utterances. The prophet was not expected to be constantly introducing something previously unknown to the people. Instead, he was to make it plain that he stood on the old foundations established by Moses.[26] Although living on the basis of old commands, statutes, and ordinances may never appear so exciting as listening to fresh, new prophetic utterances accompanied by startling signs and wonders, the words spoken by Moses must be given preeminence. They provide the basis for testing all subsequent words of prophecy.

It goes without saying that the prophet's lifestyle as well as his verbalizing were expected to conform to the law established by Moses. It would be unthinkable that a prophet would live immorally and still be judged as a true prophet of the Lord. So the greed of the false prophets is roundly condemned by the true prophets of Israel (Mic. 3:5, 11; Jer. 6:13). Their immoral behavior desecrates the most holy place of the Lord (23:10–11, 13–14; 29:21, 23). This third test, the test of prophesying in accord with the commandments of Moses, stood as a guard to protect the people from the promotion of immorality, idolatry, greed, injustice, and violence.

For this reason, the contemporary accusation of moral misbehavior on the part of Israel's classical prophets must be seen as a critique of their role as true prophets of the Lord. It is insinuated that Isaiah was guilty of immoral actions by having sexual relations with

25. Clements, *Prophecy and Tradition*, 52, indicates that being like Moses meant that the true prophet conformed his teaching to the torah delivered by Moses.
26. Fairbairn, *Interpretation of Prophecy*, 14–15.

"the prophetess," on the assumption that this woman was not his legitimate wife.[27] According to one analysis, either Hosea acted immorally in marrying a prostitute or God acted immorally in failing to inform the prophet of his prospective wife's inclinations.[28] The circumstance of Hosea's marriage is judged to be "offensive to one's moral sensitivity."[29] In response, some protest must be registered against these accusations against God and his prophetic servants.

The significance of moral law to truth in prophecy has particular relevance in the modern circumstance. Situations constantly arise in which a supposed word from the Lord contradicts the revelation of God's moral law that came through Moses. So-called Christian counselors have been known to advise extramarital relationships as a way of relieving marital tensions. On the basis of claims that prophecy is currently being fulfilled by Israel's national reconstitution in the land of the Bible, the basic restrictions of the Ten Commandments regarding the claiming of another person's property have been largely ignored. But the prophecies, promises, and fulfillments of God's word as communicated through his prophets cannot and will not contradict the Mosaic revelation of the moral law of God.

God continually tests the loyalty of his people on the basis of their commitment to this earlier prophetic word. As a matter of fact, the reason that false prophets arise is because "the Covenant LORD your God is testing you to find out if you love the Covenant LORD your God with all your heart and with all your soul" (Deut. 13:3 NASB). Precisely in contrast to an evolutionary concept of prophetic activity, the earliest word of God becomes the testing point for all subsequent prophecy.

These three criteria were provided as the bases for distinguishing between the true and the false prophet in Israel. Contradicting any one of these criteria would prove sufficient to brand a person once and for all as a false prophet. If he advocated following another god other than the God of their fathers, if any of his prophecies did not come to pass, if by word or by life he contradicted the moral standard established by the law of Moses, he must be regarded as a false prophet.

27. Crenshaw, *Prophetic Conflict*, 58.
28. Ibid., 57.
29. Ibid., 58.

B. Modern criteria for distinguishing between true and false prophecy

Modern negative criticism judges these biblical criteria to be wholly inadequate. "What is clear," says Brueggemann, is that the prophets of Israel make "a claim of authority that is impossible to verify."[30] Crenshaw concludes that "all [the biblical criteria for distinguishing between true and false prophecy] are inadequate."[31] Even the collapse of prophecy in Israel is blamed on the nation's failure to develop valid criteria for distinguishing between true and false prophecy. According to this perspective, the "essential weakness of prophecy" was its lack of "any means of validating a message claimed to be of divine origin."[32] Because of the conclusion that the biblically prescribed tests of true and false prophecy were ineffective, certain other imaginative criteria are proposed:

- It is proposed that a prophet who receives his message through dreams "is by that very fact a false prophet."[33] But this conclusion is based on a false analysis of the passage that depicts the false prophet as exclaiming "I had a dream, I had a dream" (Jer. 23:25–28). Dreams and visions were the standard manner of receiving prophetic messages (Num. 12:6). In the passage from Jeremiah, God's prophet is mimicking the exaggerated claims of prophetic pretenders, not setting up a criterion for judging between true and false prophets.

- It is proposed that the false prophet declared "weal" while the true prophet announced "woe."[34] But these two elements of

30. Brueggemann, *Theology of the Old Testament*, 631.
31. Crenshaw, *Prophetic Conflict*, 61.
32. Ibid., 103.
33. Ibid., 54. Crenshaw appropriately proceeds to qualify this statement in view of the extensive presence of dreams and visions among the true prophets as represented in the prophetic literature.
34. A remarkable development based on this proposed distinction between true and false prophets is seen in the treatment of Mic. 4:9–5:1 by van der Woude, "Micah in Dispute," 255. Though the text in Micah contains no formal indicators of a dialogue between speakers, van der Woude assigns the blessings to the false prophets and the cursings to the true prophets. In his judgment, this analysis justifies regard-

blessing and curse arise naturally out of the application of the basic principles of God's covenants made with Israel (see chap. 5). The more carefully the contexts of the various prophetic utterances are considered, the clearer it becomes that the true prophets of the Lord offered prophecies of both blessing and cursing.

- It is proposed that the false prophet could be identified as a cultic prophet, while the true prophet would offer severe criticisms of the cult. But although the level of prophetic involvement in the cult is unclear, the true prophets certainly participated in the established worship practices of Israel. A similar conclusion may be reached regarding the supposition that the true prophets were nonecstatic, while the false prophets were ecstatic.[35] Biblical evidence is lacking that would identify all false prophets as ecstatics and all ecstatics as false prophets.[36]

- It is proposed that the distinction between true and false prophets arose from different hermeneutical approaches to Israel's ancient traditions.[37] Both groups of prophets appealed to the same traditions. Yet the true prophet saw God not only as redeemer but also as creator, so that God was presented as the potter while the people were the clay. But the false prophet treated God as though he were clay in fulfilling his service of redemption, while the people were the potters who shaped God however they would. This analysis may aid in understanding how false prophets developed their perspectives on God as someone who existed exclusively for the purpose of bringing redemptive blessing to the people. But it ignores the consistent biblical witness that the true prophets of God based their affir-

---

ing the entire passage as preexilic. Such suppositions are hardly necessary for establishing a preexilic date of the prophecy in view of the assured blessings and threatened curses found in Israel's covenants, which were well known in Israel long before the time of Micah.

35. See Mowinckel, "'Spirit' and the 'Word.'"

36. Wilson, *Prophecy and Society*, 49.

37. Sanders, "Hermeneutics in True and False Prophecy," 37. Sanders shows his Barthian hermeneutics when he states that the Reformers taught that "the Bible became the Word of God in new contexts only when interpreted dynamically by the Holy Spirit" (29).

mations on fresh revelations received directly from the Lord, not on conclusions reached as a consequence of certain hermeneutical principles by which they applied earlier words from the Lord to their own day.

- It is proposed that the false prophet could be identified as the person who showed inadequacy in handling the job of the prophet, while the true prophet coped successfully with the pressures of his vocation.[38] But this basis for distinguishing the false prophet from the true only imposes a modern criterion into an ancient context.

- It is proposed that sociological factors explain the difference between true and false prophets. Different groups in Israelite society had differing ideas as to how prophets should act. As a consequence, "decisions about true and false prophecy were essentially made by applying sociological criteria to determine which prophetic claims were valid and which were not."[39] So Jeremiah appears as a "peripheral prophet," critiquing the social establishment of his day, while Hananiah was a "central prophet" speaking in support of people in power (Jer. 28).[40]

38. Coggins, "Prophecy—True and False," 80–82.
39. Wilson, *Sociological Approaches*, 77.
40. Wilson analyzes the prophet as a human figure intimately related to a specific social setting (*Prophecy and Society*, 3). In considering the social location of prophecy, Wilson notes that "intermediaries" in every society are related to some sort of "support group" that enables them to function in the society (87). He develops his treatment of biblical prophecy largely based on the idea of an "Ephraimite" tradition of prophecy as the only variety of prophecy that can be clearly identified in the biblical texts. He connects this Ephraimite tradition with the Deuteronomistic history, the Elohistic layer of the Pentateuch, and the writings of Hosea and Jeremiah, since all these works share common traditions and theological perspectives. He identifies this common tradition as a "northern Israelite perspective" (17), but offers virtually no proof of this united view of prophecy and its Ephraimite origin, except to footnote certain sources that on examination appear to offer little support to his hypothesis. As one argument for the idea of an Ephraimite prophetic community, he asserts that the title *nabi* "is a characteristic of the Ephraimite tradition" (256). But he readily admits that the title was also occasionally used of "Judahite" authors as well, and then proceeds to enumerate over seventy of these Judahite exceptions (63). Having presupposed an Ephraimite tradition of prophecy, Wilson then speaks of this northern tradition as generally peripheral to the main line of the Israelite establishment. Yet because the tradition is identified with its own social grouping, it retains the capac-

But the contest between true and false prophet in Israel did not center on the horizontal level of relationships between social groupings, even though the prophets had obvious concerns regarding the social realm. The contest focused instead on the vertical relation of God to people as this more principled relationship would affect the sociological realm. The true prophet in Israel based his ministry on a relationship to the self-revealing God of the covenant as the only proper way to define a legitimate relationship among various groups of people.

The contemporary multiplication of hypothetical distinctions between true and false prophecy falls short of developing convincing criteria. If it be assumed that the prophetic presence in Israel was a purely naturalistic phenomenon, then the search for naturalistic explanations to distinguish between true and false prophecy must continue. But if, as scripture claims, actual revelations from God were occurring through Israel's true prophets, then the biblical criteria for distinguishing between true and false would prove to be quite adequate.

In sum, the negatively critical perspective fails to appreciate the effective manner in which the biblical criteria operated in Israel's corporate life. These criteria, rightly applied, would have been altogether adequate for separating the false prophets from the true. In short, it is simply not accurate to speak of the collapse of prophecy in Israel because no adequate criteria existed to resolve the conflict between true and false prophecy. God never lost his ability to communicate his

---

ity to function in society (17). Hosea is identified as an Ephraimite peripheral prophet, influenced by Deuteronomy, and presumably supported by the group that carried on the Ephraimite tradition (230). Isaiah, on the other hand, is presented as a leading example of the Judean group of prophets. In this capacity, he appears as a central prophet, encouraging stability on the basis of the old traditions. Yet Isaiah also appears at points as a peripheral prophet, severely criticizing the cult. To explain this rather "ambiguous picture," Wilson assumes that Isaiah may have moved about among various support groups (272–73). Simply reading the biblical account of the role of Israel's prophets uncovers the basic problem associated with this sociological explanation of their ministry. These men faced down kings, prophets, and people without giving any evidence of dependence on a support group. Because they were convinced that they came with a word from the sovereign Lord of heaven and earth, they found their support outside the realm of normal social groupings.

revelatory word whenever he chose to do so. Indeed, prophecy in its old covenant form came to an end approximately four hundred years before the birth of Jesus Christ. But that termination was not because of failed criteria for distinguishing between true and false prophecy. As the progress of redemptive history terminated in terms of old covenant redemptive events at Israel's return from exile, the interpretive words of the prophets came to their conclusion. But throughout the era of the old covenant, the original criteria for testing prophecy were completely adequate.

Beyond providing criteria for distinguishing between true and false prophets, the Lord also instituted a penalty for false prophecy in Israel. The assignment of the death penalty underscores the seriousness of the lying prophet's offense (Deut. 13:5). Because the prophet in Israel held such a significant position, death had to be the penalty for those who would presume to fill this office without a legitimate call from God. The king or the priest might not necessarily die for abuse of his office in Israel. But the false prophet must die. The reason for the severity of the punishment corresponds to the damage that could be done to God's people through the false prophet. As Calvin said of a critical moment in the history of the church: "When liberty is taken to teach anything that may please men, the whole of religion must necessarily be corrupted . . . so that there is no difference between light and darkness . . . the church cannot stand except false teachers be prevented from turning truth into falsehood."[41]

Civil governments today should not attempt to fulfill the same role as the theocratic government of the nation of Israel as it was administered under the shadowy form of the old covenant. As a consequence, modern governments representing various religious traditions should not be expected to make judgments regarding which persons claiming to be prophets are true and which are false. Neither should modern governments execute the death penalty on people who might be judged to be false prophets. The church, however, under the new covenant should exercise the oversight of its members in a responsible way by protecting them from people falsely presuming to have an inspired,

41. Calvin, *Twelve Minor Prophets*, 5.380.

infallible word from the Lord. Discipline by the church should include exhortation, admonition, and, if necessary, excommunication for the person who falsely presumes to speak a word from the Lord.

V. The consequences of the ministries of true and false prophets

"Talk is cheap" is a truism underscoring the fact that words come easier than deeds. But talk is never cheap for the person who stands in the position of prophet for the Lord. For both the hearer and the speaker, the words of the prophet bring with them large consequences.

A. For the people at large

False prophecy has an immediate effect on both good and bad people: "You disheartened the righteous with your lies, when I had brought them no grief, and . . . you encouraged the wicked not to turn from their evil ways and so save their lives" (Ezek. 13:22 NIV).

It is sad to think that someone trying to do God's will would be disheartened by a person supposedly representing the Lord himself. Yet the power of the prophetic office allows a person to foster just that kind of discouragement. At the same time, the prophet can interfere with people's sense of sin by encouraging them not to turn from their wicked ways, and thus these people may miss an opportunity to be delivered from sin and its consequences. Still further, false prophecy has the effect of sparing those who should have died for their sin and killing those who should not have died (Ezek. 13:19). An awesome responsibility rests with the prophet. With his words he exercises the power of life and death.

The prophet Jeremiah saw the outworking of these effects on the people as a result of the words of the false prophets. The prophets of Samaria led the Lord's people astray, and the prophets of Jerusalem "strengthen[ed] the hands of evildoers, so that no one turns from his wickedness" (Jer. 23:13–14 NIV). As a consequence, "ungodliness has spread throughout the land" (23:15). The work of the prophet is not a matter of incidental significance in the life of the nation. It has a profound effect for good or for evil. By refusing to confront the people about their sin, the prophet can fill the people with false hopes of peace and security that never will be realized (23:16–17).

The consequences of false prophecy for the nation go far beyond the encouragement of the wicked and the disheartening of the righteous. It is not simply that here and there a good man will die in his stand for the truth because the false prophets use their influence against him. No, the future of the whole nation hinges on the words of the prophets true and false. If the false prophets are allowed to continue, the majority of the people eventually will believe them and the whole nation will suffer calamity: "Therefore because of you, Zion will be plowed like a field, Jerusalem will become a heap of rubble, the temple hill a mound overgrown with thickets" (Mic. 3:12 NIV). Even the most sacred of divine institutions will be devastated because of the unfaithfulness of the false prophets. They cannot live without men's approbation, and so they will not live. But sadly, the nation as a whole will suffer total devastation along with them. God will forget about his people, cast them out of his presence, and bring on them everlasting disgrace that never will be forgotten (Jer. 23:39–40).

This curse because of the deception of the false prophets found concrete realization through the exile of Israel. According to the lamentations of Jeremiah,

> The visions of your prophets
> were false and worthless;
> they did not expose your sin
> to ward off your captivity.
> The oracles they gave you
> were false and misleading. (Lam. 2:14 NIV)

But the true word of prophecy has the capacity to nourish, to feed, to refresh the soul of the sinner. In contrast with the powerless, ineffective word of the false prophet, the word of the Lord spoken ever so softly by the true prophet is like fire and a hammer (Jer. 23:29). Inherent in the true word of the Lord is the power to consume the wicked just as a flame ignites stubble. As a hammer shatters solid rock, so the word of the true prophet cracks the heart of the most hardened sinner.

116

The church today needs to be fully aware of the perils associated with a ministry whose motivation is for personal approval by peers and people. Pastors, preachers, and elders should consider the devastating effect on their churches of unfaithfulness to the word of God. Toleration in oneself or in others of infidelity to the word of the Lord means ruin for God's people.

B. For the false prophet

God has his special appointments for the false prophets who presume to speak in his name. He will make their path slippery and will banish them to darkness (Jer. 23:12a). The sun will set for the false prophets, and they will be overcome with darkness (Mic. 3:6). They will be ashamed, disgraced, and go about with their faces covered (3:7). God stands against them. They will be excluded from the council of God's people and will not be listed in the records of the house of Israel. Like the unbelieving generation of Moses' day, the false prophets will not be allowed to enter the promised land and shall not participate in the blessings of the Lord (Ezek. 13:8–9). In the end, God will expend his wrath on those prophets who whitewashed the walls of Jerusalem, covering up the people's sins rather than confronting them (13:15–16). Just like Hananiah the false prophet who dared to contradict Jeremiah, they shall die an untimely death. Shemaiah and his descendants will be punished so that he will have no one left among his people (Jer. 29:32).

It should not be forgotten that false prophecy invariably has its effect on the moral character of the false prophet himself. The Lord reveals that the false prophets Ahab and Zedekiah "have done outrageous things in Israel." They "have committed adultery with their neighbors' wives" and in God's name "have spoken lies" (29:23 NIV). As a consequence, they will be burned in the fire by King Nebuchadnezzar, and their names will become a mocking byword among the people (29:21–22).

So the warning from God's word goes out to all those who would prophesy falsely in the name of the Lord. This warning is directed specifically to those who would be tempted by personal gain to declare certain things as the word of the Lord that have not originated in divine revelation.

C. For the true prophet

But what about the true prophet? What may he expect as a consequence of his faithfulness to the word of the Lord? What does straw have to do with grain? asks the Lord (Jer. 23:28c). The straw of false prophecy has no substance. It cannot nourish the soul of man. To substitute the straw of false prophecy for the grain of the true word of God is to starve the famished people of the Lord. In contrast, the true prophet can expect some degree of satisfaction from his ministry. Through his words the hungry people of God will be fed.

Yet the true prophet also must expect other things for himself. The true prophet can expect trembling bones and a broken heart because of the Lord and his holy word (Jer. 23:9). He can expect to be challenged, told to shut up and go home (Amos 7:12–13). He will be accused publicly by authorities before authorities (Jer. 26:11). He must undergo false accusation and threats against his life (Amos 7:10; Jer. 26:11). Sometimes he can expect physical abuse and possibly even death. On occasion he might be delivered from the death threat, as were Jeremiah and Micah (Jer. 26:17–19, 24). But on other occasions he may flee for his life to foreign countries and still be pursued to the death, as was the prophet Uriah (26:20–23). All these things the prophet of the Lord may expect.

But he also will have the daily joy of fellowship with the Lord and his true people. He will have the word of the Lord as a fire in his belly, stirring his soul and giving him a sense of mission. He may see God's people heed his word, repent of their sins, and go forward with the work of the Lord (Hag. 1:12). In those cases, he will have the privilege of delivering a message of encouragement and blessing to the people (1:13–14). All these things will come as a consequence of his filling the office of true prophet of the Lord.

VI. Conclusion

The people of God through the ages have lived with prophets true and false. One company of prophetic voices speaks severely to them, but blesses them in the end. The other company flatters and coddles them, but eventually serves as the cause of their destruction.

Clearly the role of the prophet in speaking forth the very word of God is not to be seen as merely another job. The words of prophets true and false would be the crucial point at which the battle would be joined between Satan and Christ. The apex of controversy and contention would center on the ministry of the prophetic word and the response of the people to that word, for the battle between God and Satan on its most basic level centers on the proclamation of the truth. In this battle, the priority of Moses above all subsequent prophets must be maintained. His lawgiving becomes the ultimate test of what is true and what is false. So the true prophet of the Lord fills a position of critical significance for the people of God.

5

Covenant and Law
in the Proclamation
of the Prophets

The prophets of Israel had the responsibility of denouncing their contemporaries for their sins and calling them to a life of faith and holiness. It was the solemn duty of the prophet to critique the life of God's people, while also issuing words of hope. God's judgment and God's blessing were the great themes of the prophets.

But on what basis did the prophets denounce the cultural patterns of their day? What gave them the idea that at some time in the future the blessing of God would return? Were their condemnations based on their own personal conceptions of right and wrong? Did their predictions about the future rest on their own political acumen? Were the prophets aligned with a certain social community that determined their outlook? These matters raise the question of the basic foundation of the ministry of the prophets and, more particularly, the role of law and covenant in the message of Israel's prophets. In this regard, three elements deserve specific consideration.

I. The relation of covenant and law to the prophets

A. The biblical testimony

The question of the relation of covenant and law to the prophets would not appear to be a difficult one. As the scriptures themselves testify, law and covenant undergirded the whole perspective of the prophets in analyzing the past, present, and future of the people to whom they spoke. The law revealed by God at Sinai and the covenant with his people that dated back to the time of the patriarchs provided for the prophets the standard by which they presumed to condemn sin and to promise redemption for the nation of Israel. Without the foundational concepts of God's law and God's covenant, the prophets would have been totally awash in a sea of relativism. No other basis can adequately explain the manner in which the prophets so confidently and consistently joined messages of judgment and blessing to one another.

This simple though not simplistic answer to the question of the relation of covenant and law to the prophets has a venerated place in the history of interpretation. According to a Jewish tradition summarizing the ministry of the prophets: "Neither have [the prophets] diminished anything nor have they added anything to what is written in the torah except the recital of the roll of Esther" (Babylonian Talmud, tractate *Megillah* 14a); "Moses had already spoken all the words of the prophets, and 'all that was prophesied afterward comes from the prophecy of Moses'" (Midrash Exodus Rabbah 42.8 on 32:7).[1]

In many respects Calvin's five-page introduction to Isaiah offers more insight into the ministry of Israel's prophets than the hundreds of pages of modern disputations regarding the sources of the prophetic messages: "It is customary to make a great number of statements and dissertations about the office of the Prophets. But, in my opinion, the shortest way of treating this subject is to trace the Prophets to the Law, from which they derived their doctrine. . . . [For the prophets] utter nothing but what is connected with the law."[2] Calvin proceeds in brief compass to line out the heart of the prophetic ministry in three categories. In each area he points out the sources in the law of the prophetic ministry: (1) the prophets explain more fully in terms of commands what was briefly stated in the two tables of the law; (2) the prophets develop in particular the threats and promises that Moses proclaimed in general terms;

1. Cited in Zimmerli, *Law and the Prophets*, 14.
2. Calvin, *Twelve Minor Prophets*, 5.xxvi.

and (3) the prophets "express more clearly what Moses says more obscurely about Christ and his grace."[3]

Thus, when the prophets explain to Israel its moral duties, they introduce nothing new but rather explain the portions of the law that had been misunderstood. In terms of threats of judgment, the prophets describe in detail what the law had spoken of in general terms. For example, Leviticus 26 speaks of the coming day when the life of the disobedient nation will hang on a thread, while the prophets go beyond the law and specify Assyria and Babylon as the divine agents of judgment.[4] In terms of promised blessings, the law declares that God will bring Israel back to their land even though he has scattered them (Deut. 30:4), but the prophets are more specific in announcing that the return will occur within seventy years.[5]

Though furiously disputed, this dependence of the prophets on the prior ministry of the law finds repeated affirmation from many divergent quarters. Warfield asserts that "from Sinai, and from the revelation-act at Sinai alone," could the expectation be created of the coming of God, who will fill the world with his glory as he once did at Sinai.[6] Bright sees a reflection of the most ancient traditions of Israel in the binding of the lawgiving experience to Israel's covenantal relationship. He notes that the Israelite son is envisioned as asking, "What is the meaning of the stipulations, decrees and law the Covenant LORD . . .

3. Ibid., xxvii.

4. Unknowingly, Calvin touched on the passage in Leviticus that forces modern critics who do not believe in predictive prophecy to insist that this material must be dated at the time of Israel's exile. The passage anticipates the day in which Israel will be scattered among the nations, the land will enjoy its neglected Sabbaths, and the Lord will ultimately remember his covenant with them (Lev. 26:33–34, 40–42). The passage so clearly anticipates Israel's future that it must be understood, as Calvin proposes, to provide the basis for the subsequent denunciations and encouragements of the prophets. If not, it will have to be treated as having been written after the fact, despite its self-representation as originating in Moses' day. Only then can it be affirmed that the prophets developed their message apart from the law.

5. Von Rad, *Old Testament Theology*, 2.4 n. 2 quotes Martin Luther to the same effect: "Prophetia enim nihil aliud quam expositio et . . . praxis et applicatio legis fuit" ("for prophecy was nothing other than exposition and . . . practice and application of law").

6. Warfield, *Christology and Criticism*, 22.

123

has commanded?" The response must be, "We were slaves . . . in Egypt, but the Covenant LORD brought us out. . . . [He] commanded us to obey all these decrees . . . so that we might always prosper and be kept alive" (Deut. 6:20–24 NIV). Bright asks, "What could be clearer?" God's covenant provides the historical context for lawgiving and becomes the basis for the ministry of the prophets. They appeal to both covenant and law in explaining to Israel the alternatives of blessing and cursing that face them.[7] Clements says: "The institution of the covenant by Yahweh, from its inception, contained a basic code of law which expressed the obligations imposed upon each Israelite."[8] Clements affirms that the prophets did not create a new religion or introduce a new morality: "Without the prior fact of the covenant the prophets would not be intelligible to us."[9] In similar fashion, von Rad notes that "time and again" the prophets can be seen "applying provisions of the old divine law to the situation."[10] Childs, though at one point speaking of the "lengthy development which both expanded and contracted the commandments" of the Decalogue,[11] argues vigorously for the "traditional sequence" of law preceding prophets, stating that it is "inconceivable" to reverse the canonical order.[12] Brueggemann affirms that "a case can be made . . . that the indictments [directed against Israel by the prophets] grow out of the old commands of Sinai."[13]

7. Bright, *Covenant and Promise*, 29. Bright proceeds to note that Josh. 24 is perhaps the clearest example of the way in which the Covenant LORD's saving acts provided the basis for law and covenant in Israel. Joshua cut a covenant for the people, drew up for them decrees and laws, and wrote these words in the book of the law of God. This representation clearly presents law and covenant as established in Israel long before the ministry of the nation's literary prophets.

8. Clements, *Prophecy and Covenant*, 71.

9. Ibid., 125–26. A significant shift in Clements's perspective may be seen by comparing *Prophecy and Covenant* and his later *Prophecy and Tradition*. In the later work, Clements says that he wishes "to modify the tendency" in his earlier study to present a relatively uniform covenant theology. He can no longer see the covenant, particularly as it is expressed in the Deuteronomic code, as necessarily existing prior to the eighth-century prophets (22–23).

10. Von Rad, *Old Testament Theology*, 2.179–80.

11. Childs, *Old Testament Theology in a Canonical Context*, 63.

12. Childs, *Biblical Theology of the Old and New Testaments*, 174.

13. Brueggemann, *Theology of the Old Testament*, 374. Brueggemann later stresses the role of the historical Moses as Israel's lawgiver: "Torah-addressed Israel is indeed

So it might appear that the question is clearly resolved. According to Alt, the only existing tradition of the origins of Israelite law is found in the canonical books of the Old Testament. The account that they provide "seems at first sight consistent and unambiguous": "According to this tradition, every legal ordinance observed in Israel was laid down by the divine will of Yahweh, and had been revealed by him in the last generation before the tribes came out of the desert to settle in Palestine . . . in the covenant delivered through Moses."[14] So it is broadly recognized that according to the biblical self-testimony, the ministry of the prophets rested firmly on the revelation of law at Sinai and the covenant made with the fathers. These previous histor-

---

Moses-addressed Israel, so that it is the historical, nameable person of Moses who convenes and constitutes Israel as the peculiar partner of Yahweh" (579). Yet later, he displays the internal tension in critical reconstructions of Israel's history by asserting that both the priestly and the Deuteronomistic theologies are exilic and assigned to Moses only in the canonical process (673). As a consequence, the Mosaic legal material of the Pentateuch is severely reduced and does not constitute an adequate basis for the condemnations found in the prophets.

14. Alt, *Essays on Old Testament History and Religion*, 81. Alt then proceeds to argue against the representation of the origin of law found in scripture. In his epoch-making article that set the stage for the treatment of Israelite law for the next seventy years, Alt employed form-critical analysis to reveal two types of laws with two differing origins: casuistic law (case law) was Canaanite in origin, while apodictic law (declarative law) came from Israel itself. The process by which Alt reached this influential conclusion is quite remarkable. He notes that "we have at present no original sources for the study of Canaanite law" and that even "the process by which the Israelites took it over remains unknown" (98–99). Yet having affirmed that the casuistic law is purely secularistic since it has no mention of God, Alt reaches two conclusions: (1) because it has no mention of God, it must not have originated with Israel; and (2) because it has no religious orientation, it must have a polytheistic base, so that it can suit many groups with different gods (98). Alt thus concludes that because the casuistic laws of Israel do not mention God, they must be based on a concept of many gods! As a consequence, they must be Canaanite and not Israelite in origin. With respect to apodictic law, Alt chooses Exod. 21:12 as his first example (104). In this passage, the form is not case law but declarative law. Every killing is a crime punishable by death. Absolutely no exceptions are allowed for manslaughter or other contingent circumstances. Yet Alt can make this assertion only by totally ignoring the following two verses, which (in casuistic form) discuss the specific exceptions. At least two kinds of law may be identified in the Pentateuch, but Alt's effort to establish two separate origins for these two kinds of law can be maintained only by wrenching the various laws from their context and by resorting to an argument from silence.

ical experiences set the stage for the condemnations and the encouragements issued subsequently by the various prophets of Israel.

B. Reconstructed tradition history

However, in the arena of scholarly debate the relation of law to prophet is not as clear as might be supposed from the biblical testimony. The reconstructed tradition history has gone through a long process of debate that has defined the framework of the present state of the discussion.

Recognition must be given to Wellhausen for popularizing at the end of the nineteenth century a reconstructed history of prophet in relation to law. Wellhausen adopted Graf's theory that the prophets actually preceded law in Israel's religion, and he made some startling statements in his summary of the effect of law on the elevated view of God as originally found in the prophets: "Prophecy died when its precepts attained to the force of laws; the prophetic ideas lost their purity when they became practical"; "the Creator of heaven and earth becomes the manager of a petty scheme of salvation; the living God descends from His throne to make way for the law"; "the law thrusts itself in everywhere; it commands and blocks up the access to heaven."[15] From these remarks, it becomes apparent that Wellhausen was not dispassionately interested in the academic question of the relation of law to prophet. Instead, he saw law in scripture as a totally negative thing, threatening the very essence of pure religion. Though his motives are not altogether clear, it may be noted that Wellhausen eventually resigned from theological teaching because his role in providing training for the gospel ministry "weighed heavily" on his conscience.[16]

Wellhausen's wholesale isolation of law from the prophets could not stand the test of time. Subsequent critics analyzed his thesis that the prophets were creative religious geniuses who worked altogether apart from a prior law as overly simplistic. Even if it should be granted that cultic material and the substance of the book of Deuteronomy must be dated much later than the time of Moses, a

15. Wellhausen, *Prolegomena to the History of Israel*, 488, 509.
16. Zimmerli, *Law and the Prophets*, 22, citing Wellhausen.

large amount of legal material in the Pentateuch could go back to the Mosaic period.[17]

The fulcrum for Wellhausen's whole hypothesis was the connection of the origin of the book of Deuteronomy with the discovery of the "book of the law" among the temple rubble in the days of King Josiah around 621 B.C. Wellhausen's thesis was that the reform of Josiah concentrated on laws concerning a centralized sanctuary that had not been present in earlier legislation. In sweeping terms, Wellhausen flatly declared: "About the origin of Deuteronomy there is still less dispute; in all circles where appreciation of scientific results can be looked for at all, it is recognised that it was composed in the same age as that in which it was discovered."[18] With that firm assertion lifted above and beyond the realm of dispute, the remainder of the materials of the Pentateuch could be handily arranged in a logical, developmental sequence.

One analysis of this all-inclusive hypothesis states quite bluntly that the discovery of the lawbook in the days of Josiah in actuality never could have settled the issue of the dating of the Deuteronomic lawbook, "since it leaves unclear how much older the law book was at the time when it was rediscovered."[19] This obvious conclusion should have been acknowledged long decades ago. The simple report of the discovery of a lawbook hardly suffices to indicate the book's age or content. A more straightforward statement of an underlying but often unspoken reason for the dating of Deuteronomy well after the ministries of the great eighth-century prophets is offered by the same author: "Some parts of Deuteronomy cannot have been written as early as King Josiah's reign, *since they make allusion to the disasters that befell Jerusalem in the sixth century* BCE (e.g., Deut. 29:21–28)."[20] Implicit in this conclusion are a large number of unproven assumptions. The statement directly contradicts the larger perspective of the prophetic movement in Israel to the effect that the God who created this world with a purpose also wills to direct events so that they real-

17. Ibid., 30, 42.
18. Wellhausen, *Prolegomena to the History of Israel*, 9.
19. Clements, "Book of Deuteronomy," 278 (emphasis added).
20. Ibid.

ize his purpose. This God determined to reveal certain aspects of his plan and purpose to individuals chosen by him so that they might be his witnesses in this world.

Essentially two alternatives have been proposed in substitution for Wellhausen's overly simplistic restructuring of the relation of law to prophets. Neither of these two options, working in directions somewhat counter to one another, have won universal support in the arena of biblical criticism.

On the one hand, it is proposed that the lawbook of Deuteronomy represents the foundational document of an overarching philosophy of history that finds expression in the unified books of Joshua through 2 Kings. The single author of these historical books had as his intent "to teach the true meaning of the history of Israel from the occupation [under Joshua] to the destruction of the old order [in the exile]. The meaning which he discovered was that God was recognisably at work in this history, continuously meeting the accelerating moral decline with warnings and punishments and, finally, when these proved fruitless, with total annihilation."[21] In proposing this hypothesis, Noth appropriately indicates that this perspective on Israel's history as presented in the books of Joshua–2 Kings is established by countless specific details, not merely by vague generalities. Not occasionally but repeatedly the point is driven home. The Lord of Israel enforces the law of his covenant throughout this history of his chosen people.

It would seem quite obvious that the book of 2 Kings was composed after the exile of the kingdom of Judah in 586 B.C., since it records the events of Israel's history up to that point. But when it is proposed that the book of Deuteronomy belongs to this general period or shortly before Israel's exile, the whole point of the "countless specific details" that permeate the books of Kings is flatly contradicted. Over and over again the God of this history is presented as not only planning the future, but predicting very specific events by the mouths of his servants the prophets. Von Rad calls attention to this "system of prophetic predictions and exactly noted fulfil-

21. Noth, *Deuteronomistic History*, 89.

ments," identifying eleven different specific instances of prediction and fulfillment.[22]

How then does the book of Deuteronomy fit into this historical scheme of God's predictive word of prophecy determining the course of history? Unless the whole theology being propagated by these books is denied, Deuteronomy serves as the grand promoter of these principles, laying the foundation that shall control the entire subsequent history. Deuteronomy's word is the Covenant LORD's word that sets the stage for the unfolding history that follows. The whole book presents itself as a document of covenant renewal initiated by God through Moses just before this grand history is about to begin. In this declaration, the Covenant LORD promises blessings and threatens curses on his people on the basis of their response to the law of the covenant as it is now being propounded to them just before they enter the promised land.

Building on this foundation, the books of Joshua–2 Kings analyze the subsequent history of the next eight hundred years. As the ongoing drama of the history unfolds, the prophets of Israel provide the living testimony of the Covenant LORD to his people based on this covenantal law, which had been declared to them at their beginning. In this context alone can the full significance of the opening words of the book of Deuteronomy be properly appreciated: "These are the words that Moses spoke to all Israel in the wilderness east of Jordan. . . . Moses proclaimed to the Israelites all that the Covenant LORD had commanded him. . . . East of the Jordan in the territory of Moab, Moses began to expound this law, saying . . ." (Deut. 1:1, 3, 5).

God honored the Israelite people with a special role and so "placed them under a special obligation, which was formulated in the Deuteronomic law."[23] But the whole reality of this developed theology of history is contradicted when the book of Deuteronomy is denied its proper place at the beginning of the history. Apart from the historical moment when the Covenant LORD propounds his covenantal

22. Von Rad, *Studies in Deuteronomy*, 78. As a matter of fact, as many as twenty instances of specific prediction and fulfillment may be noted in 1–2 Kings. See Robertson, *Christ of the Covenants*, 252–67.
23. Noth, *Deuteronomistic History*, 89.

law that will determine the events that follow, the whole historical record becomes a mockery of the God who declares that he will direct the course of the future on the basis of the principles revealed in his covenant. In the developed theology of the book of Deuteronomy, covenant law must come before the ministry of Israel's prophets. This law of the covenant provides the basis for the message and ministry of all the prophets that follow.

The second major development concerning the relation of law to prophets since Wellhausen has to do with the covenantal form of the book of Deuteronomy. For decades people puzzled over the form of Deuteronomy, with its unique blending of legal stipulations, historical recollections, curses, and blessings. Halfway through the twentieth century it was discovered that many of the formal elements in the legal portions of the Pentateuch paralleled ancient Near Eastern treaty forms dated to the fourteenth to the twelfth centuries B.C.[24] Even the order of elements in the book of Deuteronomy has been seen as corresponding to the pattern found repeatedly in the treaty forms of the ancient Hittite Empire.[25] While some studies attempt to relate these elements to Assyrian documents from the eighth and seventh centuries B.C., the biblical materials correspond much more convincingly to the more ancient documents of the Hittite Empire.[26]

The implications for the question of the relation of law and covenant to the prophets of Israel should be immediately apparent. If the structure of the book of Deuteronomy as a whole corresponds to ancient Near Eastern treaty forms that existed five hundred or more years before Israel's literary prophets, then the discussion of the priority of law to prophet can no longer be pursued in piecemeal fashion. Instead, the whole corpus of the covenantal document of Deuteronomy is confirmed as being Mosaic in origin. In this more comprehensive

24. See the classic statement in Mendenhall, "Ancient Oriental and Biblical Law."
25. See Kline, *Treaty of the Great King*, 27–44.
26. Weinfeld, "Deuteronomy," 27. For an earlier refutation of the view that the biblical materials fit more appropriately the covenant forms of the first millennium B.C., see Kitchen, *Ancient Orient and the Old Testament*, 90–102. Weinfeld acknowledges that Deuteronomy "surely preserves motives of the old covenant tradition," although he contends that they were reworked according to the later forms.

130

way, law and covenant must be seen as laying the foundation for the ministry and message of Israel's prophets.[27]

These two roughly simultaneous tendencies in the analysis of Deuteronomy pull the book in two different directions. On the one hand, a unified perspective on the relation of Deuteronomy to the books of Joshua–2 Kings leads to placing the final edited form of Deuteronomy in the postexilic period, in accord with the last events recorded in 2 Kings. While debate continues over precisely which legislation in the Pentateuch preceded the prophets, the unifying argument of Deuteronomy is regarded as having developed in the last stages of the prophetic ministry in Israel. On the other hand, when parallels with the Hittite treaties are taken seriously, the very form of the book of Deuteronomy argues for an origin roughly corresponding to the time of Moses himself. In this case, the theological perspective of Deuteronomy is vindicated by the whole subsequent history of the nation of Israel.

Perhaps it is too much to hope that modern critical scholarship will acknowledge that the final form of Deuteronomy dates to the age of Moses, as supported by parallels with the Hittite treaty forms, while at the same time recognizing the remarkable oneness of the biblical message displayed by the connection of Joshua–2 Kings to the theology of Deuteronomy. Even on the basis of modest conclusions regarding these proposals, the priority of covenant and law to the ministry of the prophets in the theology of scripture should be clearly established.

Two further currents concerning the relation of the lawbook of Deuteronomy to the prophets deserve consideration. One of these currents flows directly from Wellhausen into contemporary studies and has to do with the hypothesis of the centralized sanctuary. According to this theory, the worship of Israel changed drastically through the reform of King Josiah of Judah by his demand for a centralization of worship (2 Kings 23:1–15, 19–20). From this perspective, Israel's older laws as found in the "book of the covenant" (Exod. 20–24) would have allowed for many locales for worship in Israel. But the law of Deuteronomy, it is posited, introduces the idea of centralized worship, which allows only one place for the people to assemble for offering their sacrifices (Deut.

27. Note the conclusion in this direction by McConville, *Law and Theology in Deuteronomy*, 159.

12:1–7, 13–14). This hypothesis compares these two sources of law for Israel and concludes that the Deuteronomic legislation must have actually originated centuries after the time of Moses, contrary to the way in which the book of Deuteronomy presents itself. Building on this basic premise, it is even proposed that the standard of judgment for the kings of Israel did not rest on a basis of good and evil works according to God's law. Instead, it was, according to von Rad, "the insistence on centralised worship" that served as the basis for the judgment by the Deuteronomist regarding the behavior of the kings of Israel and Judah.[28]

Suffice it to say in response to these propositions that the two lawbooks are not contrary to one another in their regulations, even though a distinction may be noted.[29] There had always been centralization about the tabernacle from the earliest traditions of Israel in the wilderness, even though allowance was made for altars to be erected wherever God chose to reveal his name (Exod. 20:24).[30] But when the nation was on the verge of entering the territory of the Canaanites, the issue of foreign altars came dramatically into the picture. All the altars of the Canaanites must be destroyed (Deut. 12:2–3). At the same time, the nation must centralize its worship "to avoid the contamination of the pure worship of Yahweh by idolatrous practices."[31] For that reason, the legislation of Deuteronomy speaks of "the place" where worship was to be permanently located (12:4–7). While centralization is clearly a factor in this legislation, the word-

28. Von Rad, *Studies in Deuteronomy*, 76.

29. Noth, *Deuteronomistic History*, 95–96, attempts to explain away all instances of sacrifice at places other than the central sanctuary found in the books of Joshua–2 Kings, such as the reference to the multiple altars in the days of Elijah (1 Kings 19:10). But their manifold presence in these historical books either severely weakens his case for the unifying relation of Deuteronomy to the books of history or destroys the idea of an exclusively central sanctuary.

30. Von Rad, *Deuteronomy*, 16, finds it necessary to modify his assertion that the most important distinctive of Deuteronomy was its "demand to centralize the cult": "Yet, on the other hand, we do not find that all the parts of the book express, or even assume, this demand which was revolutionary for its time. There are not a few laws in Deuteronomy which do not seem to know anything about this demand for centralization." At the same time, von Rad regularly dismisses as pre-Deuteronomic or un-Deuteronomic any material that does not fit his theory. See *Deuteronomy*, 115, 165; *Studies in Deuteronomy*, 86.

31. Kline, *Treaty of the Great King*, 80.

ing of the biblical text itself indicates that a matter of equal significance was *permanency* of locale. Specifically, it is "the *place* the
Covenant LORD your God will choose . . . to put his Name there for
his dwelling [or place of abode]" (12:5 NIV).[32] The permanent location of the sanctuary would mean that God had taken up a single
place for his abiding residence within the domain of Israel's territory.
By this action, it would become clear that the kingdom of God had
finally come for the nation in an abiding form.

In terms of the legal basis for God's judgment of the kings of
Israel and Judah, von Rad denigrates the repeated statement in
Deuteronomy (fifteen times) and Kings (eleven times) that the "ordinances, statutes, and commandments of Yahweh" serve as the basis
for divine judgment. Von Rad refers to the "awkwardly redundant
statement that a king had not followed the 'ordinances, commandments and statutes of Jahweh.'" Rather than acknowledging the obvious fact that a standard other than centralization of worship is repeatedly communicated by these phrases, von Rad attempts to minimize
their significance by caricaturing them as manifesting "a very decided
flagging of descriptive power."[33] To the contrary, these repetitions
only underscore the central role of the law of God in the judgments
of the kings.

A second current development in the analysis of law in relation
to the prophets is the discovery of the stellar, novalike character of
Deuteronomy. Now it suddenly appears that Deuteronomy has
expanded to the point that it fills virtually the entire universe of biblical documents. The Deuteronomistic corpus is currently seen as consisting of the book of Deuteronomy, the Deuteronomistic history
recorded in Joshua–2 Kings, editorial modifications of several prophetic

32. Von Rad, *Studies in Deuteronomy*, 38, at one point comes close to recognizing that the greater emphasis in Deuteronomy is on permanence of locale rather than
centralization. He states that the element that is "decidedly new" in Deuteronomy in
contrast with Exodus is "the assumption of a constant and almost material presence
at the shrine."

33. Ibid., 77. It should be noted that these same expressions are also found in the
legislation of other portions of the Pentateuch (Exod. 15:26; Lev. 26:3, 15; see also
Gen. 26:5, summarizing the lifestyle of Abraham, the father of the faithful).

books such as Hosea and Jeremiah, and numerous additions to the narrative of Genesis–Numbers![34]

So what has happened? Wellhausen got the parade going by placing Deuteronomy in the seventh century B.C. at the time of Josiah's discovery of a lawbook in the temple rubble, well after the great eighth-century prophets Hosea, Isaiah, Amos, and Micah. With this chronology of Deuteronomy firmly fixed, the J and E elements of Genesis–Numbers could be placed in the preceding centuries, while the detail-conscious cultic P document, a creation of the exile, would naturally follow the work of Deuteronomy. But now so many Deuteronomistic elements are being discovered among these other so-called sources of the Pentateuch that the whole corpus of Genesis–Numbers is taking on a Deuteronomistic air. Something of a unifying purpose binds the tetrateuch of Genesis–Numbers to the book of Deuteronomy.

In the halls of academia, these matters are still open to debate. It is not surprising to hear affirmation that the Wellhausen construct is "in serious and possibly terminal crisis" and that if these newer perspectives are sustained "it is difficult to see how the documentary hypothesis can survive in anything like its classical form."[35] At the same time, Wellhausen's infamous characterization of Deuteronomy as a "pious fraud" lives on in the expressions of contemporary scholarship. Von Rad feels the necessity of repeating himself to make his point regarding Deuteronomy's representation of itself as being of Mosaic origin: "This fiction is maintained consistently throughout the whole of Deuteronomy. But it really is a fiction."[36]

The assertion that Deuteronomy is fictional in its self-representation as a covenantal document originating at the beginning of Israel's history has significant consequences. Assuming that the various statements found in the other lawcodes of the Pentateuch specifically anticipating exile and restoration must be dated, along

34. Blenkinsopp, "Introduction to the Pentateuch," 317. Blenkinsopp speaks of "a significant D component in Gen–Num" and "the absorption of J into the D school" (313).

35. Ibid., 312–13.

36. Von Rad, *Deuteronomy*, 28.

with Deuteronomy, very near or even after Israel's exile, certain conclusions naturally follow:

- This reconstruction means that the covenantal standard found in Deuteronomy was raised only in the form of a pretense that it was made known to Israel's ancestors when in actuality this basis of the nation's accountability was not revealed to them until they were on the verge of exile or even in a state of exile. Why then should Israel's God be regarded as having greater integrity than the gods of the Philistines or the Egyptians?
- This reconstruction means that the God of Israel had not given adequate warning to the nation of Israel regarding the stipulations of its covenant relationship and the dire consequences of covenant violation. Why then should Israel's God be regarded as more just in his dealings with his people than the gods of Edom or Moab?
- This reconstruction means that without having made known the full basis of its covenantal accountability, Israel's God would not or could not spare them from the calamities of the exile. Why then should this God be regarded as being either more powerful or more gracious than the gods of the Assyrian or Babylonian conquerors?

If as a matter of fact this Covenant LORD of Israel actually appears to be no more powerful, no more gracious, no more truthful, no more just than any other god of human imagination, then why should people from the various nations of the twenty-first century place their hope and trust in him? Though he presents himself as the one and only creator, sustainer, and redeemer of this world, why would he merit the faith of the nations when he shows himself to be impotent, untruthful, unjust, and unmerciful in relation to his own covenant people?

When the book that claims to be a revelation from the God of Israel is openly represented as a fiction, it is no wonder that the world of biblical academics today is rife with unbelief. Since the teachers of the teachers are characterized by unbelief regarding the divine source of moral law, it should not be surprising that the professing church is permeated with nominalism and immorality.

Having considered the relation of covenant and law to the prophets, it is possible now to turn to the treatment of these two great themes in the writings of the prophets themselves. First it will be helpful to note the central factor of both law and covenant in the prophets. Then in the next chapter, the concrete application of covenant and law by the prophets may be considered.

II. The central factor in law

Israel is declared to be distinctive among all the nations of the world because no other nation is so great "as to have such righteous decrees and laws as this body of laws" that God set before them (Deut. 4:8 NIV). Yet with all the breadth of law made available to the prophets, one particular prohibition surfaces as the major focus of their denunciations. The central factor in law as applied by the prophets to the people of their day is the prohibition against idolatry.[37] Over and over the people are condemned by the prophets for their worship of idols. The condemnation of idolatry stands first among the prohibitions of the book of Deuteronomy, which serves as the most powerful application of the law in the context of the Mosaic covenant. In rehearsing the revelatory process at Sinai forty years earlier, Moses indicates the reason that his people never should resort to idols:

> You saw no form of any kind the day the Covenant LORD spoke to you at Horeb out of the fire. Therefore watch yourselves very carefully, so that you do not become corrupt and make for yourselves an idol, an image of any shape, whether formed like a man or a woman, or like any animal on earth or any bird that flies in the air, or like any creature that moves along the ground or any fish in the waters below. (Deut. 4:15–18 NIV)

37. Clements, *Old Testament Prophecy*, 111, introduces one section of his book with the heading "Idolatry—The Worst of Sins."

136

Because of their unique experience, Israel must not be enticed to worship "things the Covenant LORD your God has apportioned to all the nations under heaven" (4:19 NIV). Distinctive to Israel was the invisible God who delivered them from the furnace of Egypt and claimed them as his own people (4:20). For this reason, the nation must never stoop to worship idols that can be seen. Their God made himself known to them as the unseen one who delivers them from every situation of distress. He is the living God who has power to act on behalf of his people. Therefore they must not insult him by depicting him in the shape of anything that may be seen.

This early exposition of the centrality of the law prohibiting idolatry provides a natural bridge to the concept of covetousness as the root of idolatry, for the desire for more things is essential to the idea of idolatry. The things that God made must never be substituted for the God who made them. The connection between covetousness and idolatry is made explicitly when the new covenant scriptures speak of "covetousness, which is idolatry" (Col. 3:5). This turning to things as a substitute for knowing, loving, and serving God is the central sin of mankind in every generation. So it should not be surprising to find the prohibition against all forms of idolatry as the central focus of the law of God.

It might have been thought that the first commandment, forbidding the people from having any god other than the Lord of their redemption, would have been the central point of concern for the prophets. But the prohibition against idolatry serves more effectively in establishing the uniqueness of Israel's God because of its concreteness in terms of application. "Idols of the heart" are indeed denounced by the prophets (Ezek. 14:3–4, 7). But the very concreteness of the prohibition against idolatry enables it to serve most effectively as the linchpin of the law. This principle applies just as effectively in a postmodern world as it did in the days of Israel's occupation of the promised land. Ralph Waldo Emerson expresses it well in his "Ode," dedicated to W. H. Channing (1847): "Things are in the saddle and ride mankind." The degrading consequence of idolatry, whether of the ancient or the more modern variety, is often overlooked. But the prophet Hosea spells out the inevitable effect of idolatry:

137

When they came to Baal Peor,
they consecrated themselves to that shameful idol
and became as vile as the thing they loved. (Hos. 9:10b NIV)

According to Hosea, the idol-worshiper experiences a peculiar judgment. He is doomed to become nothing more than a "thing" resembling the thing he worships.

III. The central factor in covenant

Law in the proclamation of the prophets never functions independently as an abstract standard defining right and wrong, good and evil. Instead, law functions in relation to the covenant and its administration of a personal relation to God. As one commentator summarizes the relationship: "The prophets must consequently be regarded, not simply as teachers of morality, but as spokesmen of the covenant. For the morality which they taught implied the existence of a unique bond between Yahweh and Israel."[38]

A. The unity of the covenants

The larger role played by covenant in relation to law underscores the centrality of the personal dimension in all the commands of God. Central to all the covenants is the "Immanuel" principle. "I shall be your God and you shall be my people" formulates the heart of God's covenantal relationships.[39] The Mosaic covenant of law emphasizes that the Immanuel principle may communicate either blessing or cursing. The law of this covenant provides abundantly for the reconciliation of the transgressor. But apart from a proper repentance joined to faith in the reconciling sacrifices, the intimacy of relationship estab-

38. Clements, *Prophecy and Covenant*, 80. Clements minimizes the significance of the covenant in his later work, finding no references to covenant and law in the original materials of Hosea and Amos. But he then discovers strong Deuteronomic-covenantal redaction in these same books. He provides no criterion for distinguishing between what was original to these prophets and the redactional elements. See *Prophecy and Tradition*, 42.

39. See Robertson, *Christ of the Covenants*, 45–52.

138

lished in the covenant will bring only curse in the lives of the people. Yet the whole purpose of the law's revelation is not ultimately to condemn, but to serve God's grace as it operates for man's redemption.

The revelation of grace even in law undergirds the message of hope in the ministry of the prophets. These spokesmen for God may anticipate devastation as a consequence of the violation of the law. Yet beyond Israel's destruction is the prophetic assurance of restoration. This restoration is possible only because covenant supersedes law. Not because the chastened nation achieves meritorious righteousness that earns restoration to God's favor, but only because of the priority of grace in the covenant may the nation expect fulfillment of the promise that they shall return to the land they have lost. Indeed, in the process of restoration they will be given a new heart that will incline them to walk in all the commandments of the Lord. But the grace of the covenant forever remains supreme. Never may the nation demand blessing because of their lawkeeping. Instead, the people must always plead humbly on the basis of the unmerited promises given graciously in the covenant.

B. Diversity within the covenants

A recurring tendency in the analysis of the various covenants recorded in scripture is to characterize some covenants as conditional and others as unconditional. This tendency naturally spills over into various contemporary treatments of the message of the prophets. A thoroughgoing advocacy of this duality in the divine covenants may be seen in the analysis of Bright, who extensively develops the idea of covenants that alternate between unconditional and conditional promises. The Abrahamic covenant is presented as unconditional, followed by the clearly conditional Mosaic covenant, which in turn is superseded by God's unconditional bond with David.[40]

This alternation between two kinds of covenants is then employed by Bright to explain the differing messages of the prophets. To Hosea, covenant meant the conditional covenant made by God with Israel through Moses at Sinai. Concerning Hosea, Bright says: "The theol-

40. Bright, *Covenant and Promise*, 26, 28, 142.

ogy of Yahweh's eternal covenant with David meant nothing to him."[41] On the other hand, the prophet Isaiah saw everything through the eyes of the unconditional Davidic covenant. From this prophet's perspective, God "bound himself for all the future through his unconditional promises to David."[42]

This differentiation, according to Bright, explains the struggle between true and false prophets in the days of Jeremiah. Jeremiah's entire thinking was oriented toward a Deuteronomistic perspective, which rested firmly on the ideas of the conditional, Mosaic covenant. From Bright's perspective, the concept of the covenant found in the book of Deuteronomy stood in direct conflict with the unconditional character of the covenant made with David: "One might, indeed, go so far as to say that Deuteronomy undermines the Davidic covenant altogether. It renders the position of the monarchy insecure by placing it under conditions."[43] Bright's tour de force is encapsulated in his statement that Josiah's reform might be called "the victory of the Mosaic covenant over the Davidic."[44] In a similar vein, he argues that Jeremiah's greatest struggle was with the false prophets who held to the unconditional sustaining of Zion along with David's line of successors on the basis of the Davidic covenant. As Bright summarizes the issue: "On the one side stood men who apparently believed that the nation's survival was unconditionally assured by the promises of God; against them stood a prophet who was clearly convinced that it was not."[45]

While this basis for a distinction between true and false prophets has the appeal of simplicity, it simultaneously threatens the reliability of either one set of biblical prophets or the other. If Isaiah, for example, is responsible for promoting a theology of unconditional covenant, he must bear the blame for the erroneous teachings of the false prophets

41. Ibid., 87; see also 112.
42. Ibid., 113.
43. Ibid., 131.
44. Ibid., 135. It would be strange indeed for Josiah as a successor to David to cut his own throat by working diligently to replace a covenant that assured the unbroken reign of himself and his sons with a covenant that would imperil his own life as well as the life of his descendants.
45. Ibid., 17; see also 142.

in Jeremiah's day. On the other hand, if Hosea and Jeremiah erred in declaring a conditional covenant, some explanation must be provided for the actuality of Israel's exile.

To create this dichotomy between covenant and covenant, between prophet and prophet, Bright must eliminate from the various prophets those elements that contradict his hypothesis. So the reference to a restored Israel's seeking "David their king" in Hosea 3:5 must be excised from the original text of the prophecy and be regarded as probably having been added at a later date when Hosea's words were transmitted to a Judean context.[46] More radically, every allusion to a coming Davidic king must be eliminated or explained away. What, according to Bright, was the future hope of Israel after the exile? "Certainly," he says, "it would not take the form . . . of the coming of a 'messianic' deliverer of the house of David." Concerning any expectation related to the Davidic line, there was "no positive role in Jeremiah's thinking at all."[47] The reference in Jeremiah to raising up "a righteous Branch to David, a king who will reign wisely" (Jer. 23:5) is discarded as an "oblique allusion" to hope centered in the Davidic covenant. The parallel passage in 33:14–16 is lacking in the Septuagint and so "probably represents a later addition to Jeremiah's words." The description of a restored Israel serving "David their king, whom I will raise up for them" (30:9 NASB) is "probably not original with Jeremiah."

And so it goes. With all due respect, it seems quite apparent that the presupposed theology of a dualism in Israel's covenants dictates exactly which passages in the prophets may be regarded as genuine and which passages must be regarded as secondary additions. In the end, Bright's effort to unite in the new covenant these two covenantal streams, the unconditional and the conditional, lacks the coherence necessary to be convincing.[48] A covenantal promise from God cannot be conditional and unconditional at the same time. Either the promises have conditions, or they do not.

46. Ibid., 87 n. 16.
47. All of the following quotations by Bright in this paragraph are from ibid., 193.
48. Ibid., 197–98.

The resolution to this problem must begin by noting that *certainty of fulfillment is not the same thing as absence of conditions*. To assert that the Davidic covenant had no conditions is to ignore the bulk of the prophetic ministry in both the former and the latter prophets. David charges Solomon to keep the decrees, commands, laws, and requirements of the law of Moses so that the Lord may keep his promise to him (1 Kings 2:3–4). These covenantal promises shall realize their fulfillment, not because they are given without conditions, but because the Lord himself in his grace will see to the fulfillment of all conditions. As Vos properly observes, in Isaiah the emphasis lies on the "absolute sureness of the divine promise,"[49] which does not at all require absence of conditions. Certainly it should be recognized that the various covenants to which the prophets allude have their own distinctive emphases. The covenant with the fathers is the simplest in terms of its promises, but it is not without stipulations that threaten death and promise life. The Mosaic covenant concentrates on the obligations of the covenant participant, but is hardly lacking in gracious promises of restoration and forgiveness. The Davidic covenant centers on the establishment of the theocratic kingdom with the arrival of the designated king, building on the foundation of the promises made to the fathers, but never without the conditions associated with the covenant established through Moses.

The various prophets of Israel thus move with ease from one aspect of the various covenants to another, from threat of judgment to promise of blessing. Only a recognition of both the unity and the diversity of the covenants on which they based their ministries can explain the richness and the unceasing relevance of their ministries throughout the different ages of Israel's history.

---

49. Vos, *Biblical Theology*, 277.

6

Prophetic Application
of Law and Covenant

Having considered the central factors of both law and covenant in the understanding of the prophets, it is possible to look more closely at the concrete application that the prophets made of these principles. The usage of law and covenant takes on a general form as well as a more specific application.

I. The application of law by the prophets

Some effort has been made to establish natural law as the root of the ethics of Israel's prophets.[1] But the consistent appeal of the prophets to the law as mediated through Moses undercuts this premise. In judging the lifestyle of their contemporaries, the prophets consistently appeal to the legal materials of the covenant documents. This appeal relates to the law in general and in its specifics.

1. See Barton, "Ethics in Isaiah of Jerusalem," 80, 85–86. In his effort to establish the role of natural law in Isaiah, Barton inadvertently echoes eight of the Ten Commandments of Sinai. He is correct in developing pride and idolatry as the principal sins of the people. But his case for natural law actually serves better to underscore the role of God's revealed law. Von Rad says that the condemnation of the people by the prophets is not based merely on general ethical principles, but is founded "on the older tradition of sacral law, especially in the Book of the Covenant" (*Old Testament Theology*, 2.136). Clements, *Prophecy and Tradition*, 44, says a "revealed torah" is a fundamental basis of Israel's life, so that the detailed denunciations of the prophets can be called a forsaking of the torah revealed at Sinai.

A. General application of law by the prophets

From the earliest era of prophetism to the last, the law is applied to the people as an explanation for the judgment or blessing they may expect. According to eighth-century Hosea, God declares that he wrote for them the myriad things of his law, but they regarded them as something alien. As a consequence they are condemned to return to Egypt (Hos. 8:12–13).[2] Because they rejected the knowledge that God gave them, the Lord will reject them as his priests; because they ignored God's law, the Lord will ignore their children (4:6). Israel is guilty of wholesale sinning. From God's perspective, there is only cursing, lying, murder, stealing, and adultery; and as a consequence the whole land is in mourning (4:2–3).[3] The five specific sins enumerated by Hosea, all indicated grammatically in the form of absolute infinitives, clearly refer to the third, ninth, sixth, eighth, and seventh commandments.[4]

At the other end of Israel's history, the same disregard for God's law prevails. The Lord will come quickly to give his testimony in court against the people for their sin. He will speak against them because they are sorcerers, adulterers, and perjurers. They defraud laborers of their wages, they oppress the widow and the orphan, and they deprive the alien of his justice. Ever since the time of their forefathers they have turned away from the Lord's decrees and have not kept them (Mal. 3:5–7). Israel is no better at the end of its history than it was at its beginning.

Isaiah is known generally for his exalted depiction of God in his glory. But he also is noteworthy for his elevated view of the law

2. Phillips, "Prophecy and Law," 223, observes that Hos. 8:12 indicates that there was already in Hosea's day "a clear complex of written law accredited to Yahweh, to which appeal could be made."

3. The *rib* (controversy) that the Lord has with his people may be properly characterized as a "covenant lawsuit." On the basis of violation of stipulations of the covenant, the Lord has a case against his people. Other passages in Hosea apply the law to his people: 7:1b–7 (deceit, robbery, lies, and adultery) and 9:5 (appointed feasts).

4. Phillips, "Prophecy and Law," 225, says there can be "no doubt" that these five absolute infinitives refer to five of the Ten Commandments. He then asserts that there is "strong presumption" that they are due to a "Deuteronomic redaction" of Hosea, but he provides no basis for this presumption.

of God.[5] At one point the prophet asks the question, "Who of us can dwell with the consuming fire [of God's judgments]?" (Isa. 33:14 NIV). He answers his own rhetorical question: "He who walks righteously and speaks what is right, who rejects gain from extortion and keeps his hand from accepting bribes, who stops his ears against plots of murder and shuts his eyes against contemplating evil—this is the man who will dwell on the heights, whose refuge will be the mountain fortress. . . . Your eyes will see the king in his beauty and view a land that stretches afar" (33:15–17 NIV). Clearly from Isaiah's perspective the blessing of life for God's people hinges on their sensitivity to the law of the Lord.

This exalted view of God's law becomes even more explicit when the prophet reflects on the character of the law itself: "It pleased the Covenant LORD for the sake of his righteousness to make his law great and glorious" (Isa. 42:21 NIV). But Israel would not obey his law, and so he poured on them his burning anger (42:24–25). Again, the Lord identifies himself in relation to his law: "I am the Covenant LORD your God, who teaches you what is best for you, who directs you in the way you should go. If only you had paid attention to my commands, your peace would have been like a river, your righteousness like the waves of the sea. Your descendants would have been like the sand, your children like its numberless grains; their name would never be cut off nor destroyed from before me" (48:17–19 NIV). All the blessings of the covenant would have come to Israel if only they had been willing to live according to the law of the Lord. Ultimately the people will discover that their only hope lies in the law promulgated by the Lord's chosen servant (42:4c).

When Israel was on the verge of its captivity, the prophet Jeremiah pointed to the crucial role that the law of God played in Israel's weal and woe. Though the knowledge of the will of God should have

5. Says von Rad: "Isaiah's concern for the divine law cannot be stressed too strongly" (*Old Testament Theology*, 2.149). This observation may be contrasted with the proposal by Bright (*Covenant and Promise*, 113) that Isaiah's ministry should be understood in terms of the unconditional promises found in the Davidic covenant. Isaiah clearly stresses the Davidic covenant, but he could hardly be characterized as a prophet that ministered promises without conditions.

been instinctive to the nation, they have been led astray by their scribes and scholars. In vivid imagery, the prophet declares: "Even the stork in the sky knows her appointed seasons, and the dove, the swift and the thrush observe the time of their migration. But my people do not know the requirements of the Covenant LORD" (Jer. 8:7 NIV). The fixed orders of the creator are understood by the lower level of creatures, but God's own chosen people have lost contact with the will of the Lord. Yet the nation keeps on boasting of their privileged position as recipients of the revelation of God: "How can you say, 'We are wise, for we have the law of the Covenant LORD,' when actually the lying pen of the scribes has handled it falsely?" (8:8 NIV).

If they have rejected the word of the Lord, what kind of wisdom could they have (8:9)? They have lost all their bearings and must wander in the darkness of their own self-appointed counselors. The wise men of the day may puzzle over the reason for the devastation of the land. But to the Lord the answer is obvious: "It is because they have forsaken my law, which I set before them; they have not obeyed me or followed my law. Instead, they have followed the stubbornness of their hearts" (9:13–14a NIV). The root of Israel's problem is that they are circumcised only in the flesh. Without showing favoritism among the peoples of the world, the Lord has made a determination: "'The days are coming,' declares the Covenant LORD, 'when I will punish all who are circumcised only in the flesh—Egypt, Judah, Edom, Ammon, Moab and all who live in the desert in distant places. For all these nations are really uncircumcised, and even the whole house of Israel is uncircumcised in heart'" (9:25–26 NIV).

The intimate connection between the true prophet and the law of God is seen in the plots of Jeremiah's contemporaries to discredit him and therefore to nullify his words. In making their plans, the evil schemers assure themselves they still retain the teaching of the law: "They said, 'Come, let's make plans against Jeremiah; for the teaching of the law by the priest will not be lost, nor will counsel from the wise, nor the word from the prophets. So come, let's attack him with our tongues and pay no attention to anything he says'" (18:18 NIV). In other words, they have prophets and priests of their own liking who will declare to them exactly what they want to hear, just as though it

146

were the word of the Lord. By discrediting pesky Jeremiah they will silence the source of the word that displeases them.

This principle is true in every age. Men will do what is necessary to silence the word of the true prophet sent by God and substitute words that please themselves. One sign of the end of the present era will be that "the time will come when men will not put up with sound doctrine. Instead, to suit their own desires, they will gather around them a great number of teachers to say what their itching ears want to hear" (2 Tim. 4:3 NIV).

In his famous temple sermon in which Jeremiah exposes the false trust in the temple, the prophet specifically rehearses violations of the first, second, third, sixth, seventh, eighth, and ninth commandments (Jer. 7:5–10). But even after the chastened people were carried into exile into Egypt, "to this day" they have not followed the law of the Lord, the decrees he set before their fathers (44:10).

The prophet Ezekiel indicates that Israel rejected God's laws as early as the wilderness experience, "even though if a man should keep them he will live" (Ezek. 20:13, 16). Because they would not observe these life-giving laws, the Lord gave them over to statutes that were not good and to laws they could not live by, laws that even went so far as to require that they sacrifice their firstborn (20:25). The prophet details the sins of which the nation is guilty: they have shed blood, made idols, treated father and mother with contempt, oppressed the alien, mistreated the fatherless and the widow, desecrated the Sabbath, harbored slanderers, committed lewd acts, dishonored their father's bed, defiled their daughters-in-law, accepted bribes, taken excessive interest—and have forgotten the sovereign Lord (22:3–12). In this prophetic catalog of the people's sins, the role of the Ten Commandments delivered at Sinai and renewed in the plains of Moab is quite evident. The standard by which Israel is being judged is the law delivered through Moses.[6] But even after the chastening judgment of the exile, they continue to violate all the commandments of the law (33:23–29).

6. "The standard by which Ezekiel measures Israel's conduct are the 'ordinances' . . . , the 'judgments' . . . , which Jahweh gave to his people (Ezek. v.6, etc.)" (von Rad, *Old Testament Theology*, 2.224).

In comparison with other nations, God showed special favors to Israel. As a matter of fact, he set Jerusalem as the center of the nations, with the other countries organized around her. Yet Israel rebelled against the Lord's laws and decrees more than all the countries around her. She had not even conformed to the lesser standards of the nations next door (Ezek. 5:5–7). It is for this reason that the Lord will inflict punishment on Israel in the presence of the other nations (5:8). His righteous standards must be upheld, and Israel's favored position in possessing the Lord's law has only brought greater condemnation on her. Israel must experience divine judgment, for they "have not followed my decrees or kept my laws but have conformed to the standards of the nations" that surround them (11:12 NIV). As a consequence, the prophet Ezekiel is given a vision of the glory of the Lord departing from the temple in Jerusalem and moving away toward the mountain east of it (11:23). Because they had lost their distinctiveness as the people of the Lord through failing to conform to the requirements of the law that made them different from the other nations of the world, they no longer could retain the special blessing of the Lord's glory dwelling among them.

At the eve of the manifestation of God's grace in restoring Israel, the prophet Daniel humbly confesses the sin of the people, noting that it was because of their violation of the law that the curses of the covenant came on the nation. In his prayer he acknowledges:

> We have been wicked and have rebelled; we have turned away from your commands and laws. We have not listened to your servants the prophets, who spoke in your name to our kings, our princes and our fathers, and to all the people of the land. . . .
>
> We have not obeyed the Covenant LORD our God or kept the laws he gave us through his servants the prophets. All Israel has transgressed your law and turned away, refusing to obey you.
>
> Therefore the curses and sworn judgments written in the Law of Moses, the servant of God, have been poured out on us, because we have sinned against you. . . . Just as it is written in the Law of Moses, all this disaster has come upon us, yet we have not sought the favor of

the Covenant LORD our God by turning from our sins and giving attention to your truth. (Dan. 9:5–6, 10–11, 13 NIV)

Noteworthy in this passage is the fact that the ministry of the prophets
is identified closely with the message delivered by Moses.[7] The prophets
of Israel had done no more than apply the law revealed through Moses
to the lives of their contemporaries. The reason for the deportation of
the nation needs no further explanation than the curses written in
God's covenant with Moses almost a thousand years earlier. The task
of the prophets was no more creative than to apply the law of Moses
to the nation to which they ministered.

So far as the law of Moses and the future expectation of Israel
from an old covenant perspective is concerned, virtually the last words
spoken by a prophet make the relationship clear. Malachi declares:
"Remember the law of my servant Moses, the decrees and laws I gave
him at Horeb for all Israel" (Mal. 4:4 NIV). According to the expectations of the last old covenant prophet, Elijah would return one day to
call the people to repentance. Either they would properly respond to
this call, or the Lord would come and strike the land with a curse
(4:5–6). The old covenant scriptures thus conclude by establishing the
abiding role of the law in the life of God's people. At every phase of
the ministry of the prophets to the nation, the law of God continues
as the objective basis of God's judgment.

B. Specific application of law by the prophets

The prophets of Israel did not appeal to the law of Moses in only
general terms. More specifically, each of the original Ten Commandments that summarize God's law are applied to their contemporaries.
Samples of these applications may serve to reinforce the role played
by these specific commandments in the ministry of the prophets across
the centuries.[8]

---

7. "Even for Daniel the ground of Israel's well-being is loyalty to the traditional
commandments, and her greatest danger anything which prevents this loyalty" (ibid.,
2.309).

8. Phillips, "Prophecy and Law," 230, proposes that the Ten Commandments
should be traced back to "local indigenous legal practice, long administered by the
elders in the gate." But is it actually supposed that the law of the Sabbath, the law

1. You shall have no other gods beside me (Exodus 20:3)

"See if there has ever been anything like this," asks the Lord through Jeremiah. "Has a nation ever changed its gods?" Yet the Lord declares: "My people have committed two sins: They have forsaken me, the spring of living water, and have dug their own cisterns, broken cisterns that cannot hold water" (Jer. 2:10–11, 13 NIV). How foolish Israel has been, how absurd in light of their own experience and in view of the behavior pattern followed by all other nations of the world. Changing gods is like attempting to rewrite history. It would be like trying to eliminate Shakespeare from the history of English literature or George Washington from the origins of the United States of America. Israel was delivered under the leadership of Moses, who revealed the name of the Covenant Lord to the people. But now shall they replace their Covenant Lord with some other god to explain their origins? Israel's folly in choosing another god beside the one that delivered them is almost incomprehensible.[9]

2. You shall not make any graven image (Exodus 20:4)

Principal among Israel's graven images were the calves formed for the worship of the northern kingdom. The Lord declares through Hosea: "With their silver and gold they make idols for themselves to their own destruction. . . . This calf—a craftsman has made it; it is not

---

against covetousness, the law against idolatry simply arose spontaneously at the various Israelite gates in the land? Any effort to get behind the Ten Commandments as they now appear in the scriptures appears to be an extremely vain pursuit. The perfection of these ten words, the manner in which they summarize the whole human moral obligation, the uniqueness of their role as a standard in Israel—all these factors speak not of human but of divine origin. Where did Israel get the idea of one day in seven for rest and worship? How did they come across the concept that their God was not to be worshiped by idols? In the context of Canaanite immorality, where did Israel get the idea of a prohibition against adultery? The first command to have no other gods and the last command not to covet another person's possessions are indeed distinctive to this nation.

9. Violations of this first prohibition are cited by the prophets at various stages of the nation's history. Hosea 13:4 specifically alludes to this command in the charge to Israel: "I am the Covenant Lord your God, who brought you out of Egypt. You shall acknowledge no God but me" (NIV). Zephaniah 1:4b–5 condemns the syncretism that joins Baal to the Covenant Lord. After the exile, Jer. 44:15 makes accusation against the wives in Egypt who burn incense to other gods.

God. It will be broken in pieces, that calf of Samaria" (Hos. 8:4, 6 NIV). Idol worship eventually will bring about the devastation of the northern kingdom. According to Hosea, the worship of idols leads people to treat one another as less than human. Because the Israelites consecrated themselves to their idols, they became as vile as the idolatrous things they loved (9:10). As a consequence, their daughters turned to prostitution and their daughters-in-law to adultery (4:13).

These references to the origins of idolatry in Hosea represent only the beginning point of an extensive history in which the people insisted on representing God by idols. Of the fifteen prophetic books, all except Joel, Haggai, and Malachi refer to the worship of idols. Nine different terms for idol are used for an aggregate total of approximately two hundred occurrences. The folly of worshiping idols is emphasized particularly in Isaiah 40–48, where the vivid contrast is drawn between mute idols that cannot speak and the Covenant LORD who has the power to determine the future and therefore to predict its outcome. The sin of representing the invisible creator God by some man-made form was indeed the persistent sin of Israel that ultimately brought about its corruption, condemnation, and captivity. People today should not congratulate themselves as being superior to their forefathers by having no physical idols, when the equally idolatrous practice of retaining an insatiable desire to possess more and more things clearly dominates modern society.

3. You shall not take the name of the Lord your God in vain (Exodus 20:7)

Classic among the denunciations of the prophets regarding Israel's empty worship practices are the words of the Lord through Amos: "I hate, I despise your religious feasts; I cannot stand your assemblies. . . . Away with the noise of your songs! I will not listen to the music of your harps. But let justice roll on like a river, righteousness like a never-failing stream!" (Amos 5:21, 23–24 NIV).

The prophetic denunciation of Israel's sacrifices led earlier critics to conclude that a great rift divided prophet from priest in Israel. But the division was never between priests and prophets as such. Instead, the absence of a true-heart loyalty to the one true living God was the focus of the prophetic condemnation. Amos exposes this divided loyalty to the Covenant LORD even in the process of worship when he notes that in their hearts the people are longing for the end of the Sabbath day's worship so they can carry on with their business (8:5).

One of the greatest blasphemies against God was regarding him as having no more power to act than the Egyptian god whom Isaiah characterized as "Rahab the Do-Nothing" (Isa. 30:7 NIV). According to Zephaniah, the people were thinking, "The Covenant LORD will do nothing, either good or bad" (Zeph. 1:12 NIV). The prophet Jeremiah accuses the people of lying when they say concerning the Lord, "He will do nothing! No harm will come to us" (Jer. 5:12 NIV). Eventually the people had to "eat their words," for the God of Israel is anything but a do-nothing god. He proved his reality by bringing the righteous judgment of the exile on the people who persisted in their sin.[10]

4. Remember the Sabbath day to keep it holy (Exodus 20:8)

A distinctive mark that set apart Israel as a people belonging to the Covenant LORD was their observance of the Sabbath. This day was called a sign given by God for his people (Exod. 31:13). If the people would only restrain themselves from doing their own pleasures on the Lord's holy day and would call the Sabbath a delight; if they would honor the day by not going their own way, by not doing their own thing, and by not speaking their own words, then they would find their joy in the Lord and would feast richly on the inheritance promised their father Jacob (Isa. 58:13–14). According to the prophet Ezekiel, the Lord gave Israel not only his decrees and commandments; he also gave them the Sabbath as a sign that they might know that the Lord had made them holy (Ezek. 20:12). Yet this blessing was not intended only for Israel. Foreigners as well could experience this blessing: "Foreigners who bind themselves to the Covenant LORD . . . all who keep the Sabbath without desecrating it . . . these I will bring to my holy mountain and give them joy in my house of prayer" (Isa. 56:6–7 NIV).

10. Other instances in which the prophets expose the sin of the people for "taking his name in vain" are the taking of oaths in the name of the Lord, but not in righteousness (Isa. 48:1b), fasting but not with a true concern for the welfare of God's people (58:3–12), going to the idolatrous worship center of Bethel (Amos 4:4), swearing falsely (Zech. 5:1–4; 8:17), showing contempt for the name of the Lord (Mal. 1:6).

But instead of allowing the holy day of the Lord to mark them off as his distinctive people, the nation manifested its avarice by treating the Sabbath as though it were a burden to them. An attitude of impatience toward the Sabbath was part of their trampling the poor and cheating with dishonest scales. "When will the Sabbath end," they said, "that we may market wheat?" (Amos 8:5). A century after Amos, the prophet Jeremiah was told by the Lord to stand at the gate where kings entered the city of Jerusalem, as well as at all the other gates. At those prominent places he was to command the people to not engage in trafficking on the Sabbath day, but to keep the Sabbath holy. Their forefathers failed to pay attention to this command. If they would only restrain themselves from bringing their loads through these gates on the Sabbath, they would see kings who sat on David's throne with their entourage marching through these very gates. But if they failed to obey the Lord with respect to the law of the Sabbath, he would kindle an unquenchable fire in these very same gates (Jer. 17:19–27). The promise that was so distinctly attached to the Sabbath command continued to be offered even to the point of Israel's termination at the conclusion of their years of incessant rebellion against the law of their God.

The same circumstance prevails today. God's people continue to forfeit the Lord's richest blessings, founded in the Sabbath ordinance of creation, repeated in the perfect summary of God's law, vivified in the accomplishment of redemption by Christ's resurrection.[11] By endless processes of human rationalization, the effort is made to overthrow the sure promises of the word of the living God.[12] But for all

11. For a treatment of the abiding value of the Sabbath ordinance in a new covenant context, see Murray, *Principles of Conduct*, 30–44; Robertson, *Christ of the Covenants*, 68–74.

12. In Carson's *From Sabbath to Lord's Day*, an impressive array of international evangelical scholarship makes a strong effort to overthrow the role of the Sabbath as a creational ordinance. In the final essay of this collection, Lincoln readily acknowledges the effect of establishing that the Sabbath was a creational ordinance: "If the hypothesis of the Sabbath as a creation ordinance could be established, then, whatever the temporary nature of the Sabbath as part of the Mosaic covenant, the appeal could still be made to the permanence of the mandate for one day of rest as inherent to humanity made in the image of God" (346). He then refers to Carson's essay in the same volume for a "detailed refutation" of the claim that Jesus established the creational-ordinance character of the Sabbath when he said, "The Sabbath was made [*egeneto*] for man [*dia*

who accept the gracious provision of a Sabbath rest that still remains for the people of God, the richness of the heights of the earth and the heritage of Jacob is theirs.

5. Honor your father and your mother (Exodus 20:12)

According to the prophet Micah, the breakdown of proper respect for authority brought with it untold calamity within the social structures of Israel: "Do not trust a neighbor; put no confidence in a friend. Even with her who lies in your embrace be careful of your words. For a son dishonors his father, a daughter rises up against her mother, a daughter-in-law against her mother-in-law—a man's enemies are the members of his own household" (Mic. 7:5–6 NIV).

The commandment to honor parents would seem at first sight to be a matter of small significance for the larger movements of human history. But breaking the law of respect for God-ordained order invariably devastates an entire society. When the structures of the family are violated, the foundational stability of a community erodes.[13] In describ-

---

ton anthrōpon]" (Mark 2:27 NIV). This passage is noteworthy not only for what it says, but for what it does not say. According to Mark's testimony, Jesus did not say, "The Sabbath was *commanded* for *Israel*." He said instead, "The Sabbath was *made* [i.e., came into being] for *man*." Though Carson's discussion is quite extensive (62–66), it fails to supply the promised refutation regarding a reference to a creational ordinance in these words of Jesus. Carson acknowledges that the statement that the Sabbath "was made" refers to God's action. But *when* was the Sabbath "made" by God? Since the Sabbath was not "made" but "commanded" at Sinai with the giving of the law, the phrase most naturally should be taken as referring to his creative activity. Carson finds four uses of the term *anthrōpos* in Mark (89 n. 56). The use in 2:27 does not fall in either of the first two categories ("sons of men" [used one time] and "Son of Man" as a messianic title). Carson acknowledges that the distinction between his last two categories "may be artificial," since both refer to *men in general* or *generic man* (humanity), though one of these categories occasionally refers to a particular man. Yet Carson insists that Mark 2:27 "cannot refer to 'mankind' merely on the basis of the word *anthrōpos*." To what, then, does the word *anthrōpos* refer? The term must mean either man in general (i.e., generic man, mankind) or a particular man (and clearly Jesus does not say that the Sabbath was made for one particular man). It thus seems clear that Mark 2:27 refers to God's action of "making" the Sabbath for the sake of "mankind" in general, which is the same thing as saying that the Sabbath is a creation ordinance.

13. The command concerning respect for parents finds repeated emphasis in the legal portions of the Pentateuch (Exod. 20:12; 21:17; Lev. 19:3; 20:9; Deut. 27:16). Specific references to this command are also found in the writings of the preexilic (Mic. 7:5–6), exilic (Ezek. 22:7), and postexilic (Mal. 1:6) prophets.

ing the corruptions of the city of Jerusalem that sealed its fate, the prophet Ezekiel mentions the crimes of violence, idolatry, slander, adultery, and bribery (Ezek. 22:1–12). But right in the middle of this listing of heinous sins is the sin of "treat[ing] father and mother with contempt" (22:7 NIV).

A similar listing is found in the new covenant catalog of human acts of depravity. Among the sins of homosexuality, murder, and hating God is found also the sin of being disobedient to parents (Rom. 1:24–32, esp. 1:30). It is against this kind of unrighteousness that the wrath of God is revealed from heaven. At the same time, God still offers the promise of long life to all people who will honor their father and their mother (Eph. 6:1–3).

6. You shall not kill (Exodus 20:13)

It was not only the brutal conquerors who stood condemned for the acts of violence committed against the weaker nations. Habakkuk opens his prophecy with a complaint against the Lord because of the unchecked violence that characterized the lives of God's own people: "How long . . . must I . . . cry out to you, 'Violence!' but you do not save? . . . Destruction and violence are before me; there is strife, and conflict abounds. Therefore the law is paralyzed, and justice never prevails" (Hab. 1:2–4 NIV).

A century earlier, the prophets Amos and Micah chastised the people for the brutal ways in which they had treated one another. The needy are trampled under foot, and the poor of the land remain marginalized (Amos 8:4). The rich who hold the reins of wealth, position, and power are especially guilty of crimes of violence (Mic. 6:12). This unrestrained assault on people makes the law useless. Violence destroys society's reasons for coherence.

7. You shall not commit adultery (Exodus 20:14)

King David's act of adultery was especially heinous in the eyes of God because it was committed despite all the provisions that the Lord had made for his sexual desires (2 Sam. 12:7–8). In a similar way, the people of Israel en masse turned to a life of lust despite all the blessings of the Lord: "I supplied all their needs, yet they committed adultery and thronged to the houses of prostitutes. They are well-fed, lusty stallions, each neighing for another man's wife" (Jer. 5:7b–8 NIV). The prophet Amos also condemns the adulterous actions of his contemporaries. Both a father and a son are guilty of resorting to the same girl (Amos 2:7).

Though the Lord showed great patience with the immorality of the nations of Israel and Judah, the consequences of their corrupt lifestyle was certain. The Lord would avenge himself for the shame that such a nation brought on his name. In vivid treatment of idolatry combined with adultery, Ezekiel declares the end that must eventually come. Both Israel and Judah are characterized as lewd prostitutes. As a consequence, a mob will stone them, cut them down with their swords, kill their sons and daughters, and burn down their houses (Ezek. 23:47). The Lord will terminate the lewdness of the land, so that all women may take warning and not imitate the immoral behavior of these two nations (23:48).

The devastation of Israel and Judah is recorded in the annals of human history. Events transpired just as the prophets of the Lord anticipated. The lesson to be learned from the lewdness of both nations should be clearly understood by all people. Yet sadly, one civilization after another has sunk into sexual immorality and suffered the inevitable consequences of devastation.

8. You shall not steal (Exodus 20:15)

Stealing may be committed not merely by breaking in and taking another person's possessions. Robbery also may be committed by taking advantage of a position of authority and withholding what rightly belongs to others. Isaiah the prophet pronounces God's woe over all such activity: "Woe to those who make unjust laws, to those who issue oppressive decrees, to deprive the poor of their rights and withhold justice from the oppressed of my people, making widows their prey and robbing the fatherless" (Isa. 10:1–2 NIV). When the truth is finally told, it may be expected that a large number of officials and rulers in the various countries of the world today will fall under Isaiah's indictment: "Your rulers are rebels, companions of thieves; they all love bribes and chase after gifts" (1:23 NIV).

The various professions of the people proved to be a constant source of dishonesty. One prophet speaks of unjust scales (Hos. 12:7). Another describes the common practice of the merchants: skimping the measure, boosting the price, selling the sweepings with the wheat (Amos 8:5–6). This kind of dishonesty is not confined to biblical times. Recent years have witnessed the wholesale abuse of traders taking advantage of people in distress. In North America, hurricane victims in Florida were charged exorbitant prices for desperately needed drinking water. In Africa, impoverished women in a time of drought had to go down on their knees to sweep the floor of granaries, having no choice but to include the chaff with the wheat.

Let all peoples of all nations beware, for even the mighty nation of Babylon did not escape God's judgment on thievery forever: "Woe to him who piles up stolen goods and makes himself wealthy by extortion! How long must this go on? Will not your creditors suddenly arise? Will they not wake up and make you tremble? Then you will become their victim" (Hab. 2:6–7 NIV). Even the remnant of Israel who returned to the land after exile continued to sin against their brothers by thievery. God shows the prophet Zechariah a vision of a flying scroll representing the written law of God. This flying scroll, taking on the attitude of a modern attack helicopter, entered into the house of every thief, consuming its timbers and stones (Zech. 5:3–4).

Clearly the worst thievery that a man can commit is robbing God. The Israelites continually dared to steal from their gracious redeemer by withholding the tithe (Mal. 3:6–9). If only they would return to him and keep his law, they would see the windows of heaven opened and the blessings of the Lord outpoured, blessings too massive to comprehend (3:10). But the reluctance of even the wealthiest people to part with the precious tithe testifies to the hardness of the human heart even in the context of an affluent society.

9. You shall not lie (Exodus 20:16)

Both the northern and the southern kingdoms of Israel were marred by the profuse lying of the people. One evidence of the prevalence of lying according to Hosea is the abundance of lawsuits. The prophet declares: "They make many promises, take false oaths, and make agreements; therefore lawsuits spring up like poisonous weeds in a plowed field" (Hos. 10:4 NIV). As a consequence of lying even under legal oath, the people may expect that their false gods will be carried into Assyria as tribute for the great king (10:6).

Having had many bitter experiences himself, Jeremiah knew what he was talking about when he issued his warning:

> "They make ready their tongue
>   like a bow, to shoot lies;
> it is not by truth
>   that they triumph in the land. . . .
> Beware of your friends;
>   do not trust your brothers.
> For every brother is a deceiver,
>   and every friend a slanderer.
> Friend deceives friend,
>   and no one speaks the truth.
> They have taught their tongues to lie;
>   they weary themselves with sinning.
> You live in the midst of deception;
>   in their deceit they refuse to acknowledge me. . . .
> Their tongue is a deadly arrow;
>   it speaks with deceit.
> With his mouth each speaks cordially to his neighbor,
>   but in his heart he sets a trap for him.
> Should I not punish them for this?"
>   declares the Covenant LORD.
> "Should I not avenge myself
>   on such a nation as this? . . .
> I will make Jerusalem a heap of ruins,
>   a haunt of jackals;
> and I will lay waste the towns of Judah
>   so no one can live there." (Jer. 9:3–6, 8–9, 11 NIV)

By the time of the exile of the southern kingdom, the sin of lying had pervaded the nation to the degree that not a single honest person could be found among them. Jeremiah receives a challenge reminiscent of the plea offered by Abraham concerning the destruction of Sodom and Gomorrah. At that time, the Lord agreed that if ten righteous people could be found in the populous valley, he would spare it. But now without even the pleading of the prophet, the Lord lowers the quota of righteous people that will be required for the sparing of Jerusalem: "Go up and down the streets of Jerusalem, look around and consider, search through her squares. If you can find but one person who deals honestly and seeks the truth, I will forgive this city. Although they say, 'As surely as the Covenant LORD lives,' still they are swearing falsely" (Jer. 5:1–2 NIV). Lacking even one person who would speak the truth in all Jerusalem, the Lord could do no other than destroy the city.

The "spin culture" of today will do no better than Jeremiah's Jerusalem when brought before the bar of God's justice. Is there to be found one person who always speaks only the truth? Yet the final hope of the prophet remains: "The remnant of Israel . . . will speak no lies, nor will deceit be found in their mouths" (Zeph. 3:13 NIV). At least one person is known to have fulfilled this aspect of God's holy law (Isa. 53:9; 1 Pet. 2:22).

10. You shall not covet (Exodus 20:17)

It might be assumed that God would not have much concern over covetous attitudes in the human heart. But Isaiah indicates that the Lord is enraged because of the nation's sinful greed (Isa. 57:17). Even the prophets of the people are "dogs with mighty appetites" who "never have enough" (56:11 NIV).

Perhaps the most thoroughgoing condemnation of covetousness among the prophets is found in the words of Amos, spoken in the days of national expansionism and prosperity on the part of both the northern and the southern kingdoms during the eighth century B.C. Amos repeatedly condemns his contemporaries for their luxuriant living at the expense of others:[14]

> They sell the righteous for silver,
>   and the needy for a pair of sandals. (2:6b)

14. The following quotations are from the NIV.

[Salvation cannot come to] those who sit in Samaria
    on the edge of their beds
    and in Damascus on their couches. (3:12)

I will tear down the winter house
    along with the summer house;
the houses adorned with ivory will be destroyed
    and the mansions will be demolished. (3:15)

Hear this word, you cows of Bashan on Mount Samaria,
    you women who oppress the poor and crush the needy
    and say to your husbands, "Bring us some drinks!" (4:1)

You trample on the poor
    and force him to give you grain.
Therefore, though you have built stone mansions,
    you will not live in them;
though you have planted lush vineyards,
    you will not drink their wine. (5:11)

You lie on beds inlaid with ivory
    and lounge on your couches.
You dine on choice lambs
    and fattened calves.
You strum away on your harps like David
    and improvise on musical instruments.
You drink wine by the bowlful
    and use the finest lotions,
    but you do not grieve over the ruin of Joseph.
Therefore you will be among the first to go into exile;
    your feasting and lounging will end. (6:4–7)

Hear this, you who trample the needy
    and do away with the poor of the land, . . .
skimping the measure,
    boosting the price
    and cheating with dishonest scales,
buying the poor with silver
    and the needy for a pair of sandals,
    selling even the sweepings with the wheat.

The Covenant LORD has sworn by the Pride of Jacob: "I will never forget anything they have done." (8:4–7)

The constant coveting for more and more items of luxury leads the people to take advantage of the poor and to oppress the needy. In the end, they shall possess nothing. The era of prosperity and expansionism under Jeroboam II of Israel and Uzziah of Judah came to a rapid end. Within twenty-five years of these prophecies, the northern kingdom was no more.

The prophets of Israel thus made extensive application of the Ten Commandments to the lives of their contemporaries. Both individually and socially these laws of the Lord were the standard by which he judged his people. It is quite remarkable to note the thoroughgoing manner in which these commandments permeate the message of the prophets. Perhaps the greatest need of church and society today is a thoroughgoing, searching application of these same Ten Commandments. If God expects people to repent of their sin, then the requirements of his righteous law must be fully understood.[15]

C. Beyond the specifics: the broader implications of lawkeeping

Even in reviewing this thoroughgoing application of the Ten Commandments to the life of God's people, it should be obvious that the prophets were not legalists. They understood the law of God as teaching the way to a full life, not as a rigid code of restrictions that would rob people of their joys. As the book of Deuteronomy itself indicated, these laws were to be understood as "your life" (Deut. 32:45–47). Looking beyond the specifics in the application of God's law by the prophets, it becomes obvious that these messengers of the Lord expected more than formal observance of the Ten Commandments. They aimed their comments at the heart of their hearers. Particularly they were concerned in two areas: care for the needy, the orphan, the widow, and the stranger; and love for God and man.

15. The best detailed explanation and application of the Ten Commandments can still be found in the Larger Catechism of the Westminster Standards, QQ. 98–152.

161

1. Care for the orphan, widow, and stranger

The concern of the prophets for caring for the needy was written in large letters in the law as recorded in the Pentateuch:

- The stranger was to enjoy the Sabbath rest (Exod. 20:10).
- Israel must not vex strangers, since they themselves were strangers in Egypt (Exod. 22:21; 23:9).
- Some fruit must be left for the poor and the stranger (Lev. 19:10; 23:22).
- The Israelite must love the stranger even as he loves himself (Lev. 19:34).
- God loves the fatherless, widow, and stranger, so Israel must also love them (Deut. 10:18–19).
- Along with the Levite, the stranger, fatherless, and widow shall share in the third-year tithe (Deut. 14:28–29; 26:12).
- The stranger, fatherless, and widow shall rejoice with the Israelite at the feasts of weeks and of tabernacles (Deut. 16:11, 14).
- The justice of the stranger, fatherless, and widow must not be perverted (Deut. 24:17).
- Gleanings of fields, trees, and vineyards shall belong to the stranger, fatherless, and widow (Deut. 24:19–21).
- A curse is pronounced on those who deny justice to the stranger, fatherless, and widow (Deut. 27:19).

According to these references, the people of God had a special responsibility to care for the orphan, widow, and stranger. Because of their failure in these areas, the prophets spoke serious words of condemnation. Especially odious to the Lord were people who showed great zeal for religious rituals but had no heart for those assigned to them by the Lord for special concern. The people of Isaiah's day gave every indicator that they were a deeply committed people. On a daily basis they sought the Lord and seemed eager to know his ways. They viewed themselves as a nation that did what was right, not forsaking the commands of their God. They were perpetually fasting and humbling themselves before the Lord (Isa. 58:2–5). Yet none of these activities gave

162

any pleasure to the Lord. He looked for a different kind of devotion. As Isaiah describes it: "Is not this the kind of fasting I have chosen: to loose the chains of injustice and untie the cords of the yoke, to set the oppressed free and break every yoke? Is it not to share your food with the hungry and to provide the poor wanderer with shelter?" (Isa. 58:6–7 NIV).

In a passage made famous by modern efforts to set prophet against priest, Micah denounces the empty formalism of his day:

> With what shall I come before the Covenant LORD
>   and bow down before the exalted God?
> Shall I come before him with burnt offerings,
>   with calves a year old?
> Will the Covenant LORD be pleased with thousands of rams,
>   with ten thousand rivers of oil?
> Shall I offer my firstborn for my transgression,
>   the fruit of my body for the sin of my soul?
> He has showed you, O man, what is good.
>   And what does the Covenant LORD require of you?
> To act justly and to love mercy
>   and to walk humbly with your God. (Mic. 6:6–8 NIV)

In detailing the particulars of the kind of religion that the Lord loves, the prophets regularly echoed the requirements of the Mosaic law. Isaiah urges his contemporaries to "judge the fatherless and plead for the widow" (Isa. 1:17). Hosea, his contemporary to the north, pointed out that in the Lord the fatherless find mercy, which should provide the pattern of life for God's people (Hos. 14:3). A century later Jeremiah stands in the gate of the Lord's house and declares: "If you do not oppress the alien, the fatherless or the widow and do not shed innocent blood in this place, . . . then I will let you live in this place, in the land I gave your forefathers for ever and ever" (Jer. 7:6–7 NIV). Because Israel failed in these areas, they were carried away into captivity.

Even after the severest chastening through the exile, the people of the postexilic period had to be reminded of their obligation to the orphan, widow, and stranger. Zechariah finds the people complaining because of the fasting they had done for the past seventy years as they mourned the fall of Jerusalem. But had they learned the lesson regarding the importance of caring for the needy? He admonishes them: "This is what the Covenant LORD Almighty says: 'Administer true justice; show mercy and compassion to one another. Do not oppress the widow or the fatherless, the alien or the poor'" (Zech. 7:9–10 NIV).

At the end of the ministry of the old covenant prophets, the same reminder and rebuke had to be issued by Malachi. The Lord declares: "I will come near to you for judgment. I will be quick to testify against . . . those . . . who oppress the widows and the fatherless, and deprive aliens of justice" (Mal. 3:5 NIV).

If this neglect of their special charge characterized the people of God over so many centuries, then obviously it may be expected that this error will recur just as frequently in the present day. It might be rightly observed that the evangelical and reformed churches of today have great guilt for negligence in these areas. While insisting on sound doctrine as they should, they frequently bypass the essential elements of true religion. As James says, "Pure religion and undefiled before God and the Father is this: to visit the fatherless and widows in their affliction, and to keep oneself undefiled by the world" (James 1:27).

2. Love to God and man

A second central factor that went far beyond the formalities of lawkeeping was the requirement to love God and man—expectations that arose out of the Mosaic law itself. They were not stipulations first proposed by the prophets that might foster a legalistic perspective on life. Neither were these requirements of love introduced only under the greater light of the new covenant. Instead, the larger law of love came at the time of the initial giving of the law through Moses. God's people must love the Lord with all their heart, mind, and soul and their neighbor as themselves.

The law of love to neighbor is expressed explicitly for the first time in the book of Leviticus. God's law warns against seeking revenge or harboring a grudge against anyone. Instead, the people of God are admonished: "Love your neighbor as yourself" (Lev. 19:18 NIV). This directive is enforced all the more strongly by the reason that is immediately appended: "I am the Covenant LORD." This particular formula serves regularly in Leviticus as an abbreviation for the longer: "I am the Covenant LORD your God who brought you out of the land of Egypt, out of the house of bondage." Because the Lord had been gracious in delivering the Israelites from their oppression despite their continuing sinfulness, they must not retain a resentful spirit against their brother. Instead, they must love him with the intensity and the concreteness with which they love themselves.

This requirement of love is not limited to Israelite brothers. All aliens who live in the land must be treated exactly as native-born persons. No excuse exists for mistreating the foreigner. Instead, the Lord commands: "Love him as yourself, for you were aliens in Egypt" (Lev. 19:34 NIV; see also Deut. 10:19). The Lord's reasoning is compelling: for four hundred years Israel had been forced to live as strangers in Egypt; certainly they could understand the importance of loving the stranger.

In addition, the law specifies that wholehearted love to God must characterize the Lord's people. The great Shema of Israel is followed immediately by the first and greatest command of the Lord: "Hear, O Israel: The Covenant LORD our God, the Covenant LORD is one. Love the Covenant LORD your God with all your heart and with all your soul and with all your strength" (Deut. 6:4–5 NIV). This specific command is followed by the admonition that these laws must be on their hearts and must be impressed on the hearts of their children as they talk of them while sitting at home, walking in the way, lying down, and rising up. As symbols on their hands and foreheads, as laws inscribed on the doorposts of their houses, these laws are to be remembered at all times (6:6–8).

Concrete evidence of true respect for these laws will be seen as the people walk according to all the commandments that the Lord has given them (Deut. 11:1). As a consequence of living in accord with this wholehearted love of the Lord, the people may expect that the Lord will drive out all the nations before them and give them the land he has promised (11:22–25). Repeatedly the law emphasizes the central significance of loving the Lord:

- God shows love across a thousand generations toward those who love him (Exod. 20:6).

- God keeps covenant with those who love him (Deut. 7:9).
- What does the Lord require except that you love him (Deut. 10:12)?
- Because the Lord multiplied his people, they must love him (Deut. 11:1).
- If you love the Lord, he will bless you (Deut. 11:13).
- If you love the Lord, he will drive out your enemies (Deut. 11:22–23).
- God will test you to see if you love him (Deut. 13:3).
- If you love the Lord, he will add more cities of refuge (Deut. 19:9).
- The Lord will circumcise your heart so you will love him (Deut. 30:6).
- Life and good, death and evil, hinge on loving the Lord (Deut. 30:15–16).
- Choose life by loving the Lord (Deut. 30:19–20).

It should be clear, then, that in the Mosaic lawcode, love to God and neighbor played a vital role in Israel's maintaining a right relationship with the Lord. Essential to their whole religious commitment must be this unswerving loyalty to the Lord.

Surprisingly the prophets of Israel make only limited use of these commandments of love. Isaiah refers to the foreigners who bind themselves "to love the name of the Covenant LORD and to worship him" (Isa. 56:6).[16] Hosea complains that there is "no faithfulness, no love, no knowledge of God in the land" (Hos. 4:1). He urges his contemporaries: "Sow for yourselves righteousness, reap the fruit of unfailing love, . . . for it is time to seek the Covenant LORD" (10:12). He calls on the people to "maintain love and justice," referring to their obligation to love their neighbors (12:6). In his great prayer of confession at the time of the return from exile, Daniel addresses the Lord as "the great and awesome God, who keeps his covenant of love with all who love him and obey his commands" (Dan. 9:4). Zechariah admonishes the people of the postexilic era to "love truth and peace" (Zech. 8:19). But

16. All biblical quotations in this paragraph are from the NIV.

these few references are quite limited when compared to the centrality of the command to love in the Mosaic lawbooks.

Clearly the prophets had not forgotten the place of love in the bonds of the covenant. But apparently they saw little that would be gained by a general admonition to love directed toward a corrupted people. It may be that the prophets felt that appeal to the generally stated law of love would not serve adequately to quicken the consciences of their contemporaries. Instead, they pointed out the twisted character of the love of their contemporaries:

- They all love bribes (Isa. 1:23).
- Their prophets love to sleep, neglecting their role as watchmen for Israel (Isa. 56:10).
- Having forsaken the Lord, they perfumed themselves and climbed into the beds of Moloch and other gods they love (Isa. 57:8–9).
- They love foreign gods (Jer. 2:25).
- They are so skilled at pursuing their love of other gods that even the worst of women could learn from them (Jer. 2:33).
- They love for their prophets to prophesy lies (Jer. 5:31).
- They greatly love to wander (Jer. 14:10).
- They love playing the prostitute with the handsome Babylonian men (Ezek. 23:14, 17).
- They love the sacred raisin cakes of other gods (Hos. 3:1).
- Their rulers love shameful ways (Hos. 4:18).
- They have been unfaithful to the Lord and love the wages of a prostitute (Hos. 9:1).
- They love to bring their offerings to Bethel and Gilgal, the centers of false worship (Amos 4:4–5).
- They hate good and love evil (Mic. 3:2).

If the prophets say little about the first and great command—the command to love the Lord their God with all their heart, soul, mind, and strength—it may be in part because they saw the need for their contemporaries first to purge themselves of the idolatrous loves that filled their lives. Ultimately the only cure for this wholehearted departure into sin lay in their return to an all-consuming love for the Lord who had redeemed them and formed them into a people for his own possession.

D. The relation of the law to the condemnation of the nations

Another question may be posed concerning the role of God's law in the ministry of the prophets. How do the prophets make judgments about the nations of the world that surround God's covenant people? What is the standard by which curse or blessing is pronounced over them?

Interestingly, the nations are not brought to judgment very often on the basis of their conformity to the Ten Commandments.[17] The fullest single application of the moral law to the nations is found in Habakkuk's condemnation of Babylon for plundering, killing, seeking unjust gain, shedding blood, forcing others to drink, and worshiping idols (Hab. 2:6–20). Otherwise, in enumerating specific sins, the prophets generally refer to three realms of moral misbehavior: pride, idolatry, and violence. Perhaps even more strikingly, their mistreatment of God's own people explains the Lord's condemning judgment of the nations. Note the particulars of these two bases for God's condemnation of the nations.

1. Pride, idolatry, and violence

Self-exaltation in particular is mentioned repeatedly as the sin of the heathen nations.[18] The prosperous Mediterranean port city of Tyre

17. Phillips, "Prophecy and Law," 220, surely got things backward when he says that Amos condemns foreign nations on the basis of rulings found in the Pentateuch, while the indictment of Israel displays a "total lack of reference" to sanctions of law. His condemnation of Judah specifically notes that the nation had "rejected the torah of the Covenant LORD" (Amos 2:4), while no mention of torah is found in the judgments pronounced over the six foreign nations. With respect to the nation of Israel, in three verses reference is made to the first, third, seventh, ninth, and tenth commandments (2:6–8). Elsewhere, Amos calls Israel to account for violation of the first and second commandments (5:5, 26), third commandment (8:14), and quite strikingly the fourth commandment regarding the Sabbath (8:5). He also finds Israel guilty of transgressing the sixth (8:4), eighth (8:5b), ninth (5:10), and tenth (4:1; 5:12) commandments. Contrariwise, the nations are condemned for violence (1:3), enslavement (1:6, 9), brutality (1:11, 13), and vengeance (2:1).

18. Clements, *Prophecy and Tradition*, 65, observes that pride is the main basis of the prophetic condemnation of the nations. This pride manifests itself in a determination to dominate in trade and military splendor and in the desire to rule over others.

said in the pride of her heart, "I am a god" (Ezek. 28:2 NIV). Therefore Tyre must be plundered "to bring low the pride of all glory" (Isa. 23:9 NIV). Babylon is doomed because the nation presumes to say, "I am, and there is no other," an affirmation that should be made only by almighty God himself (47:8). The arrogance of Babylon is seen clearly in its haughty assertion, "I will ascend to heaven . . . I will make myself like the Most High" (14:13–14 NIV). Nebuchadnezzar is literally humbled to the dust and feeds among the wild beasts because he took pride in the buildings of Babylon (Dan. 4:29–30, 33). Nebuchadnezzar's son Belshazzar learns nothing about the pitfalls of pride from the experience of his father, and so the hand writing on the wall announces that the Lord has numbered his days. Because he did not humble himself even though he knew all that had happened to his father, but set himself up against the Lord of heaven, refusing to honor the one who held his life in his hand, he must perish that very night (Dan. 5:22–23, 30). Notoriety characterizes Moab's pride—"her overweening pride and conceit, her pride and her insolence"—therefore she will be trampled down (Isa. 16:6, 8 NIV). A hundred years later, Moab's pride is still just as notorious, and so the nation will be devastated like Sodom by divine judgment (Zeph. 2:8–10). Because Egypt said, "The Nile is mine; I made it," the Lord is against the Egyptians (Ezek. 29:9 NIV). Assyria's carefree capitol city of Nineveh boldly proclaims, "I am, and there is none besides me." As a consequence, "all who pass by her scoff and shake their fists" (Zeph. 2:15 NIV). The pride of the Philistines the Lord will cut off (Zech. 9:6).

The nations are also regularly condemned for their acts of violence and their idolatry (Amos 2:1; Jon. 3:8c; Nah. 3:1, 4; Isa. 17:8; 19:1, 3; 47:12). But the crime most often emphasized by the prophets is this sin of pride. The nations of the world substitute themselves for God. This single sin that serves as the source of so many other evils brings the nations under the condemnation of the Lord.

It is difficult not to recall the new covenant context in which King Herod, wearing his royal robes, made his famous speech in the city of Caesarea by the sea. Because he did not give praise to God, an angel of the Lord struck him dead (Acts 12:21–23).

169

2. Mistreatment of God's people

Alongside the prominence of pride as a cause for God's judgment on the nations, another reason is given repeatedly by the prophets. Because of their mistreatment of the people of God's covenant, the nations stand under the Lord's judgment. Even a mocking attitude can bring the wrath of God on a neighbor of the Lord's people. This theme finds repeated emphasis in the prophets. Over a thousand years before Israel's first writing prophets began their ministry, God made a promise to Abraham concerning the effect of the attitude of the nations of the world to him and his descendants. Any nation who cursed God's covenant people, the Lord himself would curse; and any nation who blessed God's covenant people, the Lord himself would bless (Gen. 12:3; 27:29).

Because of the widespread misapplication of these words across the ages, this cursing and blessing of the nations on the basis of their relation to the patriarch and his descendants must be analyzed with care. It is not that the fate of the nations hinges on their treatment of people who are Jewish in a formalistic, nationalistic sense, although the mistreatment of any people eventually will bring down the judgment of God. Instead, treatment of the true Israel of God by the world's nations will determine their fate in this world and the next.[19] Paul the apostle states quite plainly that "he is not a Jew who is one outwardly" (Rom. 2:28–29 NASB) and that any Gentile may become a full-fledged Jew by being engrafted into the stock of God's elect people by faith (Rom. 11:17, 19; Eph. 3:6; Gal. 3:26). Indeed, any Jew who comes to believe that Jesus is their promised Christ will be grafted back into the community of God's people (Rom. 11:23). But apart from specific faith in Jesus as their messiah, people who are Jews outwardly no longer function as the covenantal basis for God's blessing and cursing of the nations of the world. It is not the treatment of Jews as such that determines the well-being of various peoples of the world. Instead, it is the attitude of nations and individuals to the true "Israel of God," consisting of believing Jews and Gentiles scattered among the peoples of

19. For a fuller discussion of the identity of the "Israel of God," see Robertson, *Israel of God*, 33–46.

the world, that determines the curse or blessing that comes from the hand of the Lord.

This curse/blessing relation of all nations to the Israel of God receives widespread application by the prophets of old. In declaring his coming judgment on Babylon, Isaiah acknowledges that the Lord was angry with his own people and gave them into the hands of the Babylonians. But this heathen nation in their turn showed God's people no mercy (Isa. 47:6). As a consequence, they should not be surprised if they receive no mercy from the Lord. As the Day of the Lord's vengeance on Babylon draws nearer, Jeremiah declares that the Lord will punish Babylon "for crushing Israel's bones" (Jer. 50:17–18 NIV). The Lord summons troops to encamp against Babylon and "repay her for her deeds" (50:29 NIV). He assures his people that he will "repay Babylon and all who live in Babylonia for all the wrong they have done in Zion" (51:24 NIV).

The prophet Amos repeatedly returns to this theme as he announces the coming judgment of the Lord on the various nations surrounding Israel. Edom was merciless in pursuing his brother Israel with the sword, hacking away at his own blood relative, and so shall be cursed (Amos 1:11). Both Damascus and Ammon stand condemned for brutally assaulting the neighboring Israelite community of Gilead. Damascus threshed Gilead's inhabitants with heavy farming equipment, and Ammon attempted to subdue Israel's future generations by ripping open pregnant women (1:3, 13). Both Gaza and Tyre sold whole communities, most likely Israelite in origin, into slavery (1:6, 9). Because of this abuse of the Lord's people, Israel's immediate neighbors all stand condemned.

In similar fashion, the prophet Obadiah condemns Israel's Edomite neighbors to the east for "the violence against your brother Jacob" (Obad. 10 NIV). Nahum in his turn vividly depicts the destruction of Nineveh to the north for plotting evil against the Lord by afflicting Judah (Nah. 1:11–12). Along the same lines, Ezekiel declares the Lord's judgment on Ammon for their mockery of Israel at the time of their fall: "Because you have clapped your hands and stamped your feet, rejoicing with all the malice of your heart against the land of

Israel, therefore I will stretch out my hand against you and give you as plunder to the nations" (Ezek. 25:6b–7a NIV).

According to Ezekiel, Edom also will suffer judgment from the hand of the Lord because they "took revenge on the house of Judah and became very guilty by doing so" (Ezek. 25:12 NIV). The law of absolute justice will prevail in Edom. Because Edom harbored an ancient hostility and delivered Israel over to the sword at the time of their calamity, those killed by the sword will be scattered throughout Edom (35:5, 8). Because the Edomites planned to seize the two nations of Judah and Israel after their defeat, the Lord will deal with them in the fury of his jealousy (35:10–11). Because they rejoiced in the devastation of Israel, all Edom will be devastated (35:15). Philistia also must undergo the Lord's judgment because they "acted in vengeance and took revenge with malice in their hearts, and with ancient hostility sought to destroy Judah" (25:15 NIV). Because Egypt was a splintering staff that tore open Israel's shoulders and wrenched their backs when they leaned on her, the land of Egypt will become a desolate wasteland (29:6–9). Ezekiel declares that when the Lord returns his people they will have no more malicious neighbors, for he will inflict punishment on all their neighbors who have maligned them (28:24, 26).

Perhaps the most dramatic picture of the nations being brought to judgment because of their mistreatment of God's people is found in the prophecy of Joel. All the nations of the world shall be gathered in the "Valley of Jehoshaphat." This descriptive phrase (Joel 3:2) may allude to the incident in which Israel's invading enemies destroyed one another in the days of Jehoshaphat (2 Chron. 20:1–30). In the coming day of judgment depicted by Joel, multitudes will be assembled in the valley of decision. But the decision will not be men's prerogative. Instead, God shall make a determination (Joel 3:12–14).[20] The Lord will enter into judgment against all the nations "concerning my inheritance, my people Israel, for they scattered my people among the nations and divided up my land" (3:2 NIV). "Egypt will be desolate, Edom a desert waste, because of violence done to the people of Judah, in whose land they shed innocent blood" (3:19 NIV). In this last great

20. See Robertson, *Prophet of the Coming Day of the Lord*, 110.

day of judgment by the Lord, all nations will be judged on the basis of their treatment of God's people.

Once more it must be remembered that the people of God cannot be identified with Israel "according to the flesh." It is the treatment of the *true* people of God, whether Jewish or Gentile in origin, that will be the basis for God's decision concerning the multitudes from all nations in the day of judgment. The nations of the world should thus be alerted. Their response to the people of God scattered across the earth will be the basis for their eternal judgment. While violation of all the Ten Commandments has universal application, it is distinctively the treatment of God's people by the unbelieving world that will serve as the basis for their curse or blessing.

II. The application of covenant by the prophets

Paralleling the role of law in the ministry of the prophets is the central place given to the covenants that God made with men. Both the general concept of the covenant and the specifics of the various covenants established by the Lord in the processes of history may be seen as playing a vital role in the lives of the people.

In some cases, many of the divine covenants are collected in a single prophetic pronouncement. In anticipating the future for a restored Israel, Ezekiel depicts the nation's hope by alluding to a series of covenants: "My servant David will be king over them, and they will all have one shepherd [allusion to the Davidic covenant]. They will follow my laws and be careful to keep my decrees [Mosaic covenant]. They will live in the land I gave to my servant Jacob, the land where your fathers lived [Abrahamic covenant]. . . . I will make a covenant of peace with them; it will be an everlasting covenant [new covenant]" (Ezek. 37:24–26 NIV). The prophet found that a single covenant was not adequate for depicting the future expectations of the people in their restored land. Clearly he sees each of the successive covenants building on the Lord's previous commitments to his people. The various covenants have not replaced one another in the processes of history. The legal requirements of the Mosaic covenant have not interfered with the promises of the Abrahamic covenant. Instead, each successive covenant contributes to God's entire purposes for his people.

A passage in Jeremiah's prophecy underscores this principle of the unity of the covenants. In reassuring the people of the Lord's faithfulness to his covenantal commitments just before the devastation of the exile, Jeremiah declares that the Lord will make the descendants of David and the Levites "as countless as the stars of the sky and as measureless as the sand on the seashore" (Jer. 33:22 NIV). By this obvious allusion to the promises of the Abrahamic covenant and to the Lord's commitments in the Davidic and the Mosaic covenants, the prophet binds these three great covenantal administrations together as a firm basis for the anticipation of the future beyond exile.[21]

In a similar fashion, the prophet Isaiah weaves together the Abrahamic and Davidic covenants in anticipation of a return to the original state of things in the garden of Eden. Israel must look to Abraham their father and be confident that the Lord will surely comfort Zion, for he will transform her desert so that it takes on the character of a restored garden of Eden (Isa. 51:2–3). The two covenants ultimately will merge in this one great consummation.

This comfortableness of the prophets with a merger of the various covenants displays itself again in the message of the postexilic prophets. According to the eschatological expectations of Zechariah, foreign nations who do not go up with Israel to celebrate the feast of tabernacles will be cursed with plagues just as was Egypt of old as a consequence of their mistreatment of the seed of Abraham (Zech. 14:16–19). This prophet joins elements of the Abrahamic, Mosaic, and new covenants and so creates a montage of eschatological expectation.

This repeated merger of the various covenants as a basis for understanding the future hope of God's people should provide a warning against any effort to separate too rigidly these differing administrations of God's grace across the ages from one another. Although distinctive in their differing contexts, the covenantal commitments of the Lord manifest an essential oneness.

21. The effort to restrict Jeremiah to a Deuteronomistic outlook that conforms only to the Mosaic covenant can overturn the clear testimony of this passage, among others, only by presupposing what is intended to be proven.

174

In looking more closely at specific covenants as they appear in the ministry of the various prophets, special emphases emerge. The covenants do not play equal roles in the messages of the prophets. Certain covenants clearly maintained a priority in their thinking. Yet each of the various divine covenants finds representation in the various messages of the prophets.

A. God's covenant with Adam

Some people deny any mention of a divine covenant with Adam in the scripture. It must be acknowledged that the early chapters of Genesis do not use the term *covenant* to describe this epoch in the history of humanity. Yet Hosea indicates that Israel and Judah are no better than other peoples, for "like Adam, they have broken the covenant" (Hos. 6:7 NIV). Whether Hebrew *adam* in this text refers to man(kind) in general or to the first man, the implication is the same. God established a covenant with humanity that could be distinguished from the covenant made with Israel.[22] Jeremiah refers to the unchangeable character of God's "covenant with the day" and his "covenant with the night," which uses covenant terminology to refer to the orders established at creation (Jer. 33:20 NIV).[23] In the minds of these prophets, the bond established by creation provides the foundation for God's ongoing work in redeeming his people from their fallen condition.

Accordingly, the prophet Isaiah declares that God's judgment on Israel for the violation of its covenant will result in a curse of the ground that compares with the original curse. Several times he refers to the "thorns and thistles" that will choke out the productivity of the Lord's vineyard (Isa. 5:6; 7:24–25; 32:13). While the Hebrew terms for thorns and thistles in most of these cases are not the same words found in Genesis 3:18, the likelihood is that Isaiah intends to depict the original curse of the ground being repeated because of Israel's disobedience. In a parallel passage, the prophet Hosea uses the same words for thorns and thistles as found in Genesis 3:18 (Hos. 10:8). In Isaiah, this

22. For further consideration of the optional ways of interpreting *keadam*, see Robertson, *Christ of the Covenants*, 22–24.

23. For an analysis of these phrases in terms of their reference to creation's order, see ibid., 19–21.

175

connection to the curse of the original covenant is supported by the imagery of a return to paradisiacal circumstances on the other side of Israel's chastisement (Isa. 32:15–20).

The references by the prophets to God's original relationship to humanity in a covenantal framework are not large, but they are significant. The work of redemption assumes the covenantal structures of creation as the point from which man deviated by sin and as the basis for an expectation of the earth's renewal.

B. God's covenant with Noah

In confirming his unchanging love toward his people, the Lord indicates that as he swore that the waters of Noah would never again cover the earth, so now he swears never again to rebuke his people (Isa. 54:9–10). The covenant with Noah that had continued in effect for unknown ages in the past now provides the pattern for God's preservation of his people throughout the ages to come. The integrity of the almighty God that had held true to its oath to the patriarch Noah guarantees the blessing of God through unending years of the future.

In a passage from his "little apocalypse" (chaps. 24–27), Isaiah echoes the language that originally described the unleashing of the flood waters in the days of Noah: the "windows of heaven were opened," and water deluged the earth (Gen. 7:11). In similar fashion, Isaiah anticipates the coming day in which the "windows of the heights will be opened," and a second universal judgment will be the consequence (Isa. 24:18). The prophet anticipates that final day in which the earth as it is now known will come to an end. To vivify his message, he resorts to the old flood language regarding the opening of the windows of heaven. Just as in the days of Noah the wickedness of man became so great that a cataclysmic judgment from the Lord was inevitable, so in the future the same circumstance will bring about a similar cataclysmic judgment. The prophet says: "So heavy upon it is the guilt of its rebellion that it falls—never to rise again" (24:20 NIV).[24]

24. Is the prophet anticipating a day in which the Lord will negate his commitments in the Noahic covenant that he would never again destroy the earth with a flood

From a different perspective, the prophet Hosea recalls the gracious side of the covenant with Noah in his anticipation of a consummative covenant with the universe. The gods of Baal promised fertility for the earth, but did not have the power to carry out their word. But the Covenant LORD will "cut a covenant" with the beasts of the field, the birds of the air, and the creatures that move along the ground (Hos. 2:18). The enumeration of living beings echoes exactly the language of Genesis in its repeated listing of the creatures involved in the flood incident (Gen. 6:7; 8:17, 19; 9:2). The multiplied productivity of the earth anticipated by Hosea stands in deliberate contrast with the judgments of the flood and anticipates the blessedness of the people in a restored land (Hos. 2:21–23).[25]

One further allusion to God's covenant with Noah in the prophetic writings may be found in the reference to the fixed order of day and night, which may refer to the reestablishment of these creational ordinances as confirmed in the covenant with Noah (Jer. 33:20). In any case, the order established by God's commitment to Noah provides the basis for assurance concerning God's faithfulness in the future. In the mind of the prophets, the covenantal bond made with Noah continued to maintain its significance.

C. God's covenant with Abraham

The prophets repeatedly assure Israel of their future blessing on the basis of God's covenantal commitments to Abraham. The Lord who "redeemed Abraham" tells the house of Jacob that they shall not be ashamed (Isa. 29:22). Israel as "descendant of Abraham" is God's chosen servant (41:8). The nation must "look to Abraham [their] father," who was called into covenant relationship (51:2). The "unchanging love" of the Lord is still directed to Israel as "Abraham"

(Gen. 9:11)? Not quite, for the original promise was that "so long as the earth remains" it would be preserved from a universal judgment as was the case with the flood (8:22). Furthermore, Isaiah uses the destruction of the earth by flood only as an illustration of the type of universal judgment that can be expected in the future.

25. One of the primary criteria for identifying the priestly document of the Pentateuch is this supposed interest in listings found in Genesis. Yet while the P document is generally dated in the sixth century B.C., this identical listing of creatures in eighth-century Hosea appears as a reflection of an even older tradition.

in accordance with the oath of the covenant (Mic. 7:20). The prophets repeatedly refer to the blessing of the seed originally given to Abraham (Isa. 6:13; 41:8–10; 43:5; 44:3; 45:19, 25; 48:19; 53:10; 54:3; 59:21; 61:9; 65:9, 23; 66:22; Jer. 30:10; 31:36–37; 33:22; 46:27; Ezek. 20:5; Zech. 10:9). In a similar fashion, the promise made to Abraham concerning the land finds a constant emphasis in the prophets, particularly as it relates to the theme of restoration after exile. The promise to Abraham that he would be a "blessing to the nations" may be regarded as one of the key platforms of the message of the prophets, dominating their expectation of the future.

The single fullest treatment of the covenant with Abraham among the prophets is found in the dramatic rehearsal of the covenant-renewal ceremony enacted in the days of Zedekiah, the last king of Judah (Jer. 34). With the king of Babylon pounding against the gates of Jerusalem, Zedekiah orders a covenant-renewal ceremony involving a "passing between the pieces" (34:18–19). This procedure echoes exactly the pattern of covenant making followed by Abraham (Gen. 15:10, 17–18). Alongside this allusion to the covenant-making ceremony that inaugurated God's covenant with Abraham, the covenant-making procedure followed by King Zedekiah equally reflected the pattern of Mosaic covenant renewal, involving the reading of the law and the pledge of obedience by the people. The judgment pronounced on Zedekiah and his contemporaries arises from their violation of the first of the specific laws enumerated in the "book of the covenant" regarding the sabbatical release of Israelite slaves (Exod. 21:1–3; see also Jer. 34:12–17).[26]

The binding together of these two covenants explains how the prophets of Israel could anticipate both disaster and blessing for Israel. Disaster must come because of violations of covenant law. But blessing can be promised as the final end because of the sovereign commitment on the part of God to bless his people despite their deserving nothing. It is only in this fuller context of the merger of multiple covenants that the ministry of the prophets can be properly understood.

26. For a fuller discussion of this blending of the Abrahamic and Mosaic covenant-making procedures in Jer. 34, see Robertson, *Christ of the Covenants*, 131–37.

D. The Mosaic covenant

The whole basis for the pronouncement of imminent judgment against the nation rests on the place of Mosaic law in the divine covenant. The prophets had no firm foundation for denouncing violation of the Sabbath, worshiping of idols, giving of recognition to other gods, sexual relations outside the marriage union, if no law existed that condemned these practices, particularly in view of their directly contradicting the accepted cultural practices of the peoples surrounding them.[27] In a statement introducing a major portion of his prophecy, Jeremiah sums up the role of Mosaic law for the life of God's covenant people:

> This is what the Covenant LORD, the God of Israel, says: "Cursed is the man who does not obey the terms of this covenant—the terms I commanded your forefathers when I brought them out of Egypt. . . ." I said, "Obey me and do everything I command you, and you will be my people, and I will be your God. Then I will fulfill the oath I swore to your forefathers, to give them a land flowing with milk and honey." (Jer. 11:3–5 NIV)

The commandments of the covenant made through Moses served as the basis for the ministry of the prophets. Essentially everything they said was "all founded on the Mosaic inheritance."[28] At the same time, in the minds of the prophets the covenant with Moses must be seen as inseparable from the Davidic covenant that followed. Israel's literary prophets functioned during the specific period of Israel's history in which the covenant with David was in effect. This historic context makes the central role of the older Mosaic covenant in the ministry of the prophets even more striking. The covenant made through Moses lost none of its significance by the introduction of the covenant with David.

E. God's covenant with David

It is understandable that the Davidic covenant would play a significant role in the ministry of the prophets. This covenant was the

27. See Bright, *Covenant and Promise*, 84 n. 6.
28. Lindblom, *Prophecy in Ancient Israel*, 314.

last and most developed covenant in the historical experience of the nation. In addition, the prophets addressed themselves primarily to the kings of Israel and the nation of Judah with its center in Jerusalem, and these two elements define the heart of the Davidic covenant. This covenant clearly plays a central role in the ministry of the prophets of Israel from the eighth to the fifth centuries B.C. All the prophetic expectations concerning a future for Israel derive from the two central promises of this covenant: (1) the preservation of a descendant of David on the throne and (2) the divine defense of the city of Jerusalem.[29]

The northern monarchy originally established its independence from the rule of David's line under the cry:

> What share do we have in David,
>> what part in Jesse's son?
> To your tents, O Israel!
>> Look after your own house, O David. (1 Kings 12:16 NIV)

Despite these deep-rooted alienations, Hosea makes no apologies for his setting forth of the only long-term hope for this rebellious kingdom. Because of its sin, Israel will become "not my people." But "afterward the Israelites will return and seek the Covenant LORD their God and David their king" (Hos. 3:5 NIV).[30]

The plot of Syria and Ephraim to replace the descendant of David with the "son of Tabeel" in Isaiah's day cannot succeed. If necessary God will cause even a virgin to conceive and bear a son (Isa. 7:6–7, 14). God's covenant commitment to David will not be broken. Pre-exilic, exilic, and postexilic prophets all echo the covenant commitment made to David regarding the perpetual line of his descendants on the throne of Israel. This promise provides the strongest basis for

29. See Clements, *Prophecy and Covenant*, 56; Bright, *Covenant and Promise*, 55, 70. Bright's extended treatment of these twin themes of the Davidic covenant as found in the psalms is especially illuminating (58–72). Concerning the declaration that the Davidic line would endure forever, that his throne would be like the sun and moon, standing firm while the skies endure, Bright says: "Those are strong words. Nor are they to be dismissed as mere hyperbole, for they were believed" (60).

30. Clements, *Prophecy and Tradition*, 30, states that Hos. 3:5 "must certainly be a redactional addition." But he provides no rationale for his conclusion.

hope in a future messianic king beyond the judgments of exile (Isa. 9:6–7; 11:1–10; 16:5; 22:20–25; 25:6–12; 33:20–21; 37:31–32; 55:3b–4; Jer. 23:5–6; 33:14–26; Ezek. 34:23–24; Hos. 3:5; Amos 9:11–12; Mic. 5:2; Zech. 6:9–15).

At the same time, the whole prophetic message concerning the uniqueness of Jerusalem/Zion and its temple complex depends on the initiating word of the Davidic covenant. As Nathan the prophet indicated, David's son will build *a house* for the Lord at *the place* selected by King David, though this place ultimately had been determined by the Lord (2 Sam. 7:13; see also Ps. 78:67–72). These covenantal assurances provided the foundation for the continual emphasis of the prophets on the role of the Zion/Jerusalem complex.

Amos the prophet-farmer from the southern kingdom stresses the unbroken role of Zion and Jerusalem in his message to the inhabitants of the north: "The Covenant LORD roars *from Zion* and thunders *from Jerusalem*" (Amos 1:2 NIV). He ends his extended word of judgment on the northern kingdom of Israel by pointing them to the hope of the restoration of the fallen booth of David and the rebuilding of the walls of Jerusalem (9:11–12).

Isaiah's entire message of hope centers on this promise to David regarding the exaltation of the Zion/Jerusalem complex: "In the last days the mountain of the Covenant LORD's temple will be established. . . . The law will go out *from Zion*, the word of the Covenant LORD *from Jerusalem*" (Isa. 2:2–3).[31] In the final day, the remnant of Jerusalem/Zion "will be called holy," and the Lord will create all over Mount Zion "a cloud of smoke by day and a glow of flaming fire by night" (4:3–5). Kings of the earth and powers of heaven will be punished, for the Covenant LORD will reign on Mount Zion and in Jerusalem (24:21, 23). Like birds hovering overhead, so the Covenant LORD of hosts will shield Jerusalem (31:5). The fire and the furnace of God's judgments that will consume Assyria are located in Zion and Jerusalem (31:8–9). No one living in Zion will say, "I am sick," and all "the sins of those who live there will be forgiven" (33:24). It is to Jerusalem that the message of comfort and glad tidings must be delivered (40:2, 9). Jerusalem is the city about which

31. All biblical quotations in this paragraph are from the NIV.

Cyrus declares, "Let it be rebuilt" (44:28; see also 45:13). "The ransomed of the Covenant LORD will return" to Zion with their singing, and "sorrow and sighing will flee away" (51:11). Jerusalem the holy city will be adorned with "garments of splendor" (52:1). The afflicted city will be rebuilt with sapphires, rubies, and sparkling jewels (54:11–12). All the "sons [of Jerusalem] will be taught by the Covenant LORD, and great will be [her] children's peace" (54:13). The Lord's holy mountain will be "a house of prayer for all nations" (56:7). "The Redeemer will come to Zion, to those in Jacob who repent of their sins" (59:20). Foreigners will rebuild the walls of Zion, the glory of Lebanon will adorn Zion's sanctuary, and all Israel's enemies will call Zion "the City of the Covenant LORD" (60:10–14). Those who grieve in Zion will wear "a crown of beauty instead of ashes" (61:3). For the sake of Zion and Jerusalem, the prophet "will not keep silent, till her righteousness shines out like the dawn" (62:1). Zion will be called "the City No Longer Deserted" (62:12). The Lord "will create Jerusalem to be a delight and its people a joy" (65:18). The "wealth of the nations" will flow to Jerusalem, and foreign peoples will be brought as "an offering to the Covenant LORD," with some of them serving as priests and Levites (66:12, 20–21).

While the presence of this "Zion theology" is not unique to the prophecy of Isaiah, the manner in which it permeates his whole book is overwhelming.[32] Yet it must be remembered that the whole imagery derives directly from the covenant made with David. Without question the Davidic covenant played a prominent role in the ministry of the prophets.[33]

F. The new covenant

The new covenant in the prophetic writings provides the necessary transition into an entirely different era that was to supersede the

32. Other prophetic passages containing a theology of Zion are Amos 9:11; Mic. 4:1–5; Obad. 21; Jon. 2:4; Zeph. 3:14–17; Jer. 33:6–9; Hag. 2:6–9; Zech. 2:1–13; 4:1–14; 12:1–9; 13:1; 14:1–21.

33. For the realization of this aspect of the Davidic covenant in terms of its new covenant fulfillment, see Gal. 4:24–26 and Heb. 12:22–24. Fairbairn, *Interpretation of Prophecy*, 285, says that in the eyes of the new covenant apostles, the old Zion of Palestine is gone. The only Zion that remains is the place of Christ's rule at the right hand of the Father.

imperfections of the old covenant forms. After a succession of covenants stretching over fourteen hundred years and encompassing the lives of Abraham, Moses, and David, the chosen nation of God still was not fulfilling its mission of being a blessing to all the nations of the world. The old covenant forms and shadows simply were not capable of bringing God's people to their consummate state.[34] So on the horizon of the future arises the divine provision of a different kind of covenant. This new covenant will not be isolated from all the previous dealings of the Lord with his people,[35] but it shall be totally different in that its essence will rest on the renewal of all things, including the hearts of God's covenant people.[36] Even the lawbook of Deuteronomy had called for the obedience of the heart, and the new covenant now shows how it can happen. The Lord will take the initiative and write his law in the hearts of the people.[37]

G. Summary

For the prophets the series of covenantal bonds that the Lord sovereignly established with Israel explains the origin of the nation in the past, speaks to the dealings of the Lord with his people in the present, and anticipates the experiences of weal and woe in the future. The true religion of Israel does not have its origin in the imaginations

34. Von Rad, *Old Testament Theology*, 2.398–99, says that Ezekiel and Jeremiah indicate that Israel is "inherently . . . unable" to obey the Lord. With the new covenant, the Lord will bring obedience to the torah within the people's power. Gowan, *Theology of the Prophetic Books*, 105, misreads the scriptures when he states: "Most OT writers assume that humans have the ability to obey if they only try." This interpretation of scripture has been a standard error of all works-righteousness schemes. The permeating call to repentance (which Gowan, p. 7, denies to the preexilic prophets) accompanied by the offer of reconciliation and forgiveness shows the inability of the human to obey.

35. VanGemeren, *Interpreting the Prophetic Word*, 332, says it well: God's new acts of redemption according to Ezekiel are "in grand fulfillment of the creation, Abrahamic, Mosaic, and Davidic covenants."

36. The prophets anticipated the new covenant in Hos. 2:18–23; Isa. 54:5–10; 59:21; Jer. 31:31–34; 32:40; 50:4–5; Ezek. 16:59–63; 36:24–38; 37:12; 37:18–28.

37. Von Rad, *Old Testament Theology*, 2.213, says the Lord will bypass the process of speaking and listening, which is not quite correct. Even in the context of the new covenant, the word will still go forth. Only now it will penetrate the stony heart of the hearer and bring it to life.

of men, but in the initiatives of God. All the ministries of the prophets may be explained in terms of their application of the various covenants to the people.

III. Interconnection of covenant and law in the prophets

These two large factors, law and covenant, provide the foundation for understanding the ministry of the prophets. But how do these two factors relate to one another?

- The law has its origin in the covenant. Israel's special relation to the Lord as a consequence of the covenant leads to his revelation to them of the law. Because of the covenant, Israel is introduced into a fuller understanding of God's will than had ever been enjoyed by any other nation.
- The covenant of redemption, arising out of a principle of grace, makes blessing possible despite death-deserving transgression of the law. Prophecies of exile and restoration may be understood only in the context of the gracious provisions in God's covenants.
- The perfected merger of law and covenant is found in the provisions of the new covenant. No longer will the statutes, ordinances, and commandments of the Lord remain outside the life of the people. Instead, the administration of the new covenant will create a heart that delights in doing the law of the Lord. In this final covenantal context, all the blessings of the covenant will be experienced by God's people.

Because of the union of law and covenant in the prophets, the expected response to both these dimensions of God's relation to his people is the same: repentance and faith followed by a life of obedience to the Covenant LORD. The significance of these concepts is seen in the rich variety of ways in which they come to expression in the prophets.

The prophets may join their call to repentance with a sure promise of blessing. Or they may offer only the limited possibility of restoration in the event of a return to the Lord. Both kinds of call to repentance occur in the same chapter in Amos. In addressing the word of the Lord to the northern kingdom, Amos declares, "Seek me and live" (Amos 5:4); "seek the Covenant LORD and live" (5:6); "seek good, not evil, that you may live" (5:14). But then he immediately adds, "Hate evil, love good. . . . *Perhaps* the Covenant LORD God Almighty will have mercy" (5:15).[38]

It is argued by some that the call to repentance has no place whatsoever in the genuine message of the prophets.[39] Others propose that a conditional "perhaps" attached to the message of repentance is incompatible with the declarative "thus says the Covenant LORD" of the prophets.[40] But both forms of the call to repentance suit well the ministry of the prophets. The Lord would have never initiated a covenant to redeem a rebellious people if he had not been open to the prospect of their returning to him. So Hosea places a prayer of repentance on the lips of the people: "Come, let us return to the Covenant LORD. He has torn us to pieces but he will heal us" (Hos. 6:1 NIV). Joel instructs priests and people to put on sackcloth and declare a holy fast (Joel 1:13–14). Micah directs the people: "Heed the rod and the One who appointed it" (Mic. 6:9 NIV). And Isaiah admonishes the nation, "Stop doing wrong, learn to do right! . . . If you are willing and obedient, you will eat the best from the land" (Isa. 1:16–17, 19 NIV).[41]

At the same time, the sinner can never boast that he has the key that controls God, so that if a person repents he should have no fear whatsoever of God's judgment falling on him. No, the Almighty alone determines when he shall inflict his chastening judgments on his people.

38. All biblical quotations in this paragraph are from the NIV.

39. Gowan, *Theology of the Prophetic Books*, 7. In contrast, Childs strongly asserts that the prophets consistently brought the message of repentance to the nation. He notes that prior to the exile Jeremiah preached "Turn" for twenty-three years (*Old Testament Theology in a Canonical Context*, 141).

40. Westermann, *Prophetic Oracles of Salvation*, 238. Westermann regards the unconditional oracle a feature of the "charismatic" presence of a prophet. He states that a conditional message provides "unanimous testimony" to the Deuteronomist redaction. No proof is provided for this rather sweeping assertion.

41. Lindblom, *Prophecy in Ancient Israel*, 350, strongly affirms that the call to repentance is a legitimate part of the message of Israel's prophets.

His actions are not thereby to be viewed as arbitrary, for inherent in the nature of God abides a sense of justice and restorative mercy that is anything but arbitrary. It is, however, simply a fact that people do not control God. Acts of repentance do not have the power to manipulate him.

Yet the repeated "perhaps" of the prophets provides ample reason for people to repent: "Perhaps the Covenant LORD God Almighty will have mercy" (Amos 5:15 NIV). "Perhaps you may be hidden on the day of wrath" (Zeph. 2:3). "Who knows? He may turn . . . and leave behind a blessing" (Joel 2:14 NIV). For this reason, the people should return to the Lord who has warned and even chastened them.

The other side of a proper response to law and covenant according to the prophets is faith. In view of the condescension on the part of God in establishing the intimacy of a covenantal relationship, the great sin of Israel was failure to trust him for everything necessary for life and salvation.[42] In confronting Ahaz at the time of the Syro-Ephraimite invasion, Isaiah plays on the Hebrew word for "faith" (*amen*): "If you do not stand firm in your faith, you will not stand at all" (Isa. 7:9 NIV). Motyer says: "Faith is the central reality of the Lord's people, not just their distinctiveness but their ground of existence. No faith, no people."[43]

The numerous ways in which the concept of faith comes to expression in the prophets is just one indicator of the central role of this response to the covenant and the law given to Israel. A sample of expressions, taken primarily from Isaiah, provides some idea of the breadth of terminology used to communicate the idea of faith by the prophets:

- trust the Lord (Isa. 26:3–4; 28:16; 50:10; Jer. 39:18; Nah. 1:7; Zeph. 3:2, 12)
- call on the name of the Lord (Zeph. 3:9)
- rely on the Lord (Isa. 10:20)
- look to the Lord (Isa. 22:11; 31:1; 51:1, 5)
- have regard for the Lord (Isa. 22:11b)
- rest and be quiet (Isa. 30:15)
- wait for the Lord (Isa. 30:18)

42. Ibid., 342.
43. *Motyer*, Isaiah, 83.

186

- listen to the word of the Covenant LORD (Isa. 51:4; Jer. 26:3)
- give ear (Isa. 55:3)
- seek the Lord (Isa. 51:1; 55:6)
- call on the Lord (Isa. 55:6)
- wait in hope (Isa. 51:5)
- have God's law in the heart (Isa. 51:7)
- make God your refuge (Isa. 57:13)

Entrustment of the whole person to the God of the covenant is the key to a proper response to the message of the prophets. God's people must stop placing their trust in men and put their whole reliance on the one true and living God.

Out of this repentance and trust will flow the life of obedience. Having received the blessings of redemption, a person rejoices to walk in the ways of the Lord. The obedience that flows from faith seals the possession of the promises found in God's covenants. The Lord's servant shows his readiness to serve by obeying the voice of the Lord (Isa. 50:4–5). The Lord will be their God, and they will be his people, but only if they obey his voice (Jer. 7:23). The people must reform their ways and actions and obey the Covenant LORD their God (26:13). Only if the people diligently obey will they have the privilege of intimate communion with the Lord and his heavenly hosts (Zech. 6:15).

The desired response to his covenant and his law is clearly laid out by the Lord. The people must register their sorrow and their repentance for their sin, and they must express their complete trust in the Lord alone for their salvation. Then they will be enabled to live a life pleasing to him.

Law and covenant must be seen as major defining factors in the ministry of the prophets of Israel. Virtually all the problems related to understanding the ministry of the prophets find their resolution in God's administration of law and covenant. In these provisions may be found ultimately the expectation of the Christ of the covenants, the lawkeeper for God's people, the lawgiver of God's people, who lives and dies to fulfill the demands of covenantal law and who embodies the heart of the covenant, which is Immanuel: God with us.

7 *(top right, chapter number)*

THE BIBLICAL-THEOLOGICAL SETTING OF ISRAEL'S LITERARY PROPHETS

In considering the biblical-theological setting of prophetism's development in redemptive history throughout the old covenant period, an awareness of contemporary trends in the analysis of prophetic materials may help to illuminate and accentuate the significance of the biblical testimony. In the end, the testimony of scripture itself alone can present a true picture of the unfolding revelation of God's redemptive purposes as expressed in Israel's writing prophets.

I. The tradition of multiple editors

For some decades, the assumption has been that the books of prophecy as they currently appear reached their present condition through the work of a multiple of editors across several generations.[1]

1. For an overview of the various critical approaches to the prophets, see Eissfeldt, "Prophetic Literature"; and Coggins et al., *Israel's Prophetic Tradition*. The various disciplines of literary criticism, form criticism, tradition criticism, redaction criticism, and rhetorical criticism have been applied to the prophetic books. As principal spokesman for a form-critical perspective on the writing prophets at the beginning of the twentieth century, see Gunkel, "Prophets as Writers and Poets." In a winning style, Gunkel proposes that the prophets were first speakers, and that only because of changing times did men like Amos and Isaiah begin to write. They first wrote only brief disjointed messages, which were altered, rearranged, and supplemented by many later editors, possibly over the next few centuries. Not until Ezekiel did a prophetic

One of the principle goals of the analysis of prophetic materials was to rescue the original words of the prophet from the many accretions that had built up through the long process of modification and editorializing. Primary worth was placed on the *ipsissima verba*, the very words of the prophet himself, in contrast with the secondary value attributed to added materials. But a more recent writer judges the effort at recovering the original and authentic words of the prophets to be "often a hopeless enterprise." Some comfort is taken in the conclusion that the tradition of prophetic utterances found in the prophetic books as we have them is "on the whole essentially reliable as a record of the ideas of the prophets." This assertion can be maintained because the writer additionally assumes that the "main intention" of the collectors of the various utterances of the prophets was "to preserve the divine words for posterity, and to adapt them to practical use."[2]

Some significant tension resides in this analysis of the work of the supposed editors and collectors of prophetic sayings. The words of the prophets were regarded by their collectors as "divine," which accords well with the biblical testimony that God put his words in the mouth of his prophets, communicating with them "mouth to mouth." Furthermore, it is asserted that these collectors of the prophetic words had as their "main intention" the preserving of the divine words for posterity, a conclusion also supported by scripture. If the prophetic words were God's very words, then they must be preserved exactly as they were received. Scripture never suggests that God communicated

---

author of a book of prophecy arise. As a consequence of this view, Gunkel affirms: "Sometimes these [the prophetic writings] contain many things that do not come from the old prophets, so that, for example, the Book of Isaiah can more accurately be termed an overview of Hebrew prophecy than a 'book of Isaiah'" (28). A significant change in the prevailing view of the prophets as writers of their own materials developed during the last half of the twentieth century. According to Eissfeldt, "*No countenance at all* will now be given to the theory that the prophets after whom the books are named themselves put down in writing their individual oracles or smaller collections of them" (117 [emphasis added]). But von Rad, *Old Testament Theology*, 2.40–45, presents evidence for the role of the prophets as writers, though he would nonetheless adopt the concept that many editors were the ultimate producers of the various prophetic books.

2. All quotations in this paragraph are from Lindblom, *Prophecy in Ancient Israel*, 279.

190

only vague ideas to his prophets. Always it was the word or words of God that came to the prophets, which would mean that as divine words they must be preserved. But then it is also proposed that the main intention of the collectors of these divine words included adapting this divine revelation to practical use. It would obviously be appropriate for disciples of the prophets to "apply" prior prophetic words to their contemporaries. But to "preserve" the words of the prophets and to "adapt" them in the sense of altering their original form and content are two entirely different things. This fact is made evident in the subsequent remark by this same author that these preservers of the "divine" words of the prophets made countless modifications, "which show that the text was not regarded as in any way sacrosanct."[3] In other words, although the words of the prophets are presented as "divine" words that must be preserved, they are at the same time represented as subject to "countless . . . additions, enlargements and comments" and not regarded as being "in any way sacrosanct."

This dizzying presentation of the character of the prophetic words is typical of the prevailing perspective. At one point Brueggemann critiques the contemporary treatment of the prophets by noting that historical criticism "operated with naturalistic assumptions, so that everything could and must be explained, without reference to any theological claim." The inevitable outcome was a "history of religion" that "resists any notion of Yahweh as an agent in Israel's life."[4] He complains that historical criticism produces "unhelpful philological comment, endless redactional explanations, and tedious comparisons with other materials," simply because it is "on the face of it, incongruent with the text itself." As he summarizes the problem: "Because the primal Subject of the text has been ruled out in principle, scholars are left to deal with these much less interesting questions."[5]

In his effort to determine the ultimate origin of this situation in the current treatment of Israel's prophets, Brueggemann strikes at the heart of the issue: "In much 'scientific' study of the Old Testament, it is generally assumed that skepticism is much more intellectually

3. Ibid.
4. Brueggemann, *Theology of the Old Testament*, 727.
5. Ibid., 104.

respectable than is fideism. . . . What passes for uncommitted objectivity in Old Testament study, moreover, is often a thinly veiled personal hostility to religious authority."[6]

This point is well taken, and the dilemma is not easily escaped. The prophetic word in Israel clearly presents itself as a divine revelation with all the authority of an utterance from almighty God, the one and only creator, sustainer, and redeemer of the universe. If it was received in the community of Israel with that perspective, then clearly it would have come initially to the nation with an inherent authority that defied anyone to tamper with its form and content. As a consequence, the modern academic community cannot with consistency treat the textual tradition of the prophets of Israel as pliable material subject to the manipulation of any number of groups and individuals, while at the same time affirming that its divine authority places it in a position above all human reorderings.

II. The search for an alternative

Where, then, is an alternative to this destructive atomization of the message of the Old Testament prophets to be found? How is the modern reader to avoid emptying the message of the prophets of any meaningful significance as a consequence of its being splintered into hopeless fragments that are only loosely related to one another? Walter Brueggemann offers one alternative solution, and Brevard Childs offers another.

A. Walter Brueggemann

According to Walter Brueggemann, postmodern man has finally escaped from "a cultural period that was dominated by objective positivism."[7] All common, universal assumptions have disappeared. Now we are left with only the "irascibly pluralistic character" of every biblical text.[8] Instead of analyzing the biblical text in terms of a process of ongoing editing or redaction, these contradictory elements must be

6. Ibid., 729.
7. Ibid., 61.
8. All of the following quotations by Brueggemann in this paragraph are from ibid., 64.

accepted for what they are, as the "ongoing work of adjudication, in which any settled point is reached only provisionally and is in turn subject to reconsideration." This process of constant modification and change applies not only to this or that subject, but defines "the very character of Yahweh, the God of Israel." The very essence of God himself is "pulled this way and that by the adjudicating rhetoric of Israel." Various texts of scripture that do not harmonize easily with one another must be regarded as bids for the truth that must live in the presence of other equally serious bids for being identified as truth. In other words, as an alternative to analyzing the text of scripture in terms of a series of editorializings, the reader must live with the reality of inner self-contradictions found in the text. To wish for more in terms of settled truth from the Old Testament, according to Brueggemann, is to wish for something that does not exist.

How radically different is the word that comes from the God of the prophets! He is to them the rock, the eternal, unchanging rock, and his word can be trusted through all the variables of human experience (Isa. 26:4; see also 8:14; 17:10; 30:29). There is none, no other rock, none to be known besides him (44:8). Even when mighty nations assemble as the instruments of God's judgment on Israel, he remains as the rock, their God, their holy one (Hab. 1:12). He is to them the same God who was hymned in the song of Moses: "The rock! Perfect are his works. For all his ways are just. A God of truth and without any wrongdoing, just and upright is he!" (Deut. 32:4).

This kind of God may seem strange to postmodern people. But he is undoubtedly the God of the prophets. As the creator and sustainer of the world, the redeemer of his people, he can be trusted to be true to his own unchanging essence. As embodying all that constitutes the essence of a rock, he is the same yesterday, today, and forever.

B. Brevard S. Childs

Another contemporary alternative to the older picture of prophetism grows out of the canonical approach to scripture made famous by Brevard Childs.[9] At one time it would have been regarded

---

9. See Childs's *Introduction to the Old Testament as Scripture*, 69–83; and *Biblical Theology of the Old and New Testaments*, 70–79.

as senseless to treat the various prophetic documents as though they were addressing the historical situation they proposed to confront. But with the birth of a canonical approach, it became legitimate to deal with the various prophetic books as they currently present themselves to the reader. The final form of the various documents, it is reasoned, was the shape in which they ultimately came to function as canon in Israel. Therefore some estimation must be made of the message of the various prophetic scriptures as it is reflected in this final form.

A short-term gain may be registered in the fresh theological insight uncovered when the prophets are treated "as though" they actually are what they present themselves to be. But eventually the piper who plays this new tune must be paid. For if the prophets did not actually deliver the message that their materials in the current form claim, then the integrity of their writings in terms of establishing a valid, trust-worthy theology must be forfeited.

An illustration of this approach may be seen in Childs's treatment of the prophecy of Isaiah. Childs acknowledges that "a strong case" may be made for regarding Isaiah 40–66 as originally addressed to the sixth-century exiles in Babylon. But in their present canonical shape, they have a very different setting. Now they belong to the ministry of eighth-century Isaiah of Jerusalem.[10]

The tragic aspect of perceiving the later prophecies of the book of Isaiah in their present literary circumstance as belonging to the eighth century B.C., while at the same time affirming that they actually arose in the sixth century B.C., is that the God of Isaiah is reduced to the level of the idols/gods he himself so famously mocks. All his ridicule of deaf and mute idols made of wood and stone falls ultimately on his own head. From a "canonical" perspective, the God of Isaiah cannot produce what he challenges the idols/gods to bring forth—a genuine long-term prediction of future historical events. The pretended predictions of the prophet eventually mock the god he proposes to serve.[11]

10. Childs, *Introduction to the Old Testament as Scripture*, 325.
11. Oswalt, *Isaiah*, 2.5, notes that while contemporary scholars are compelled to acknowledge the theological unity of the book of Isaiah, "their conception of the nature of prophecy still prevents them from taking the step that the book itself clearly asks its readers to take," which is to affirm the ability of the God of Israel to predict the future, just because he determines the course of nations.

III. The focus of the prophetic corpus

Whatever the perspective on the development of the prophetic corpus of the Old Testament, the writings of Israel's prophets eventually must be seen as centering primarily around two events of immeasurable significance: Israel's exile and restoration. The remarks of one commentator underscore the centrality of these two events for the prophetic ministry:

> The period of history which saw the golden age of the prophets had at its centre the immense crisis of the exile, which placed in jeopardy the entire life and faith of Israel. The prophetic interpretation of this disaster, and the promise of a renewal of divine grace, gave to Israel a spiritual insight which made it possible to accept this defeat and suffering as the will of Yahweh and to rise from it purified and spiritually strengthened.[12]

Purely from the perspective of historical significance, the exile of the nation looms large as the critical moment respecting Israel's termination or survival as a people with a viable identity among the nations of the world. Says Bright: "The destruction of Jerusalem and the subsequent exile mark the great watershed of Israel's history. . . . Israel was left for the moment an agglomeration of uprooted and beaten individuals. . . . The marvel is that her history did not end altogether."[13] As a consequence, the biblical-theological significance of these events in the life of Israel is crucial to a proper evaluation of the purposes of God regarding the redemption of his people.[14] It is through the ministry of the writing prophets that an understanding of these critical events is provided.

Israel was chosen uniquely as the servant of God. Abraham was called out of Ur of the Chaldees, even though his fathers worshiped idols on the "other side of the river" (Gen. 12:1; Josh. 24:2). The people

---

12. Clements, *Prophecy and Covenant*, 128.
13. Bright, *History of Israel*, 343.
14. Gowan is absolutely correct in attempting to shape the whole theology of Israel's prophets around the twin themes of exile and restoration as the biblical-theological equivalents of death and resurrection. His book *Theology of the Prophetic Books* is subtitled *The Death and Resurrection of Israel*.

were organized into a national entity by the covenantal revelation that came through Moses at Sinai. In time, the people were brought into the land that God promised them. It was a land flowing with milk and honey, comparable to the blessings of paradise restored. The possession of the land established this people as heirs of God's redemptive blessings. What then could banishment from the land mean to these people? What did exile signify for Israel? By the exile, God's people became "not my people" (Hos. 1:9). In forcing them to return to the land of their origins, the Lord seemed to indicate that the whole elective process had been reversed. What could be more drastic? Who could explain such an experience?

It should indeed be recognized that the message of the various prophets, even the preexilic prophets, includes the elements of both exile and restoration. A healthy turn in the prevailing perspective on prophetic interpretation recognizes prospective blessing and judgment in the message of prophetism before the exile.[15] The expectation of the prophets "directly concerned the experience of the exile and the hope of restoration which lay beyond."[16] In the concept of the covenant presented in scripture, judgment is regularly accompanied by the anticipation of restoration and deliverance. Accordingly, the "heart of the prophetic message" is to be found in the threat of judgment together with the hope of subsequent restoration.[17]

The events of Israel's exile and restoration had a multiplicity of meanings for the people of God. In many ways, these events were much more complex than the original call of Abraham out of Ur of the Chaldees. God's purposes of redemption originally focused on a single individual. But in exile and restoration, an entire nation was involved—

15. Contrast the earlier work of Mowinckel in his influential *Prophecy and Tradition*. Mowinckel presupposes that a prophet could not present both a message of disaster and a message of blessing simultaneously, for any good that might be accomplished by a threat of disaster would be canceled out by an accompanying message of blessing. In other words, declarations of coming judgment must be preexilic while words of blessing can be classified as postexilic.

16. Clements, *Prophecy and Covenant*, 114. Clements further states that according to the preexilic prophets, the people to whom they preached were "under the sentence of death." Yet beyond the judgment, Yahweh would "re-elect and re-establish his people" (113).

17. Ibid., 25.

a nation in which various members of its constituency responded to the challenges of these moments in widely differing ways. It is therefore understandable that a movement as significant as Israel's prophetic tradition would have arisen out of these momentous circumstances.

In the end, only God himself could explain the "why" and "wherefore" of Israel's exile and the restoration that followed, for these events had meaning not only for the contemporary Israelites. In accordance with the role of the major movements of the history recorded in the Old Testament, these events also were designed to communicate redemptive truth across the generations.

As a consequence, the anticipation of exile must not be viewed as "the same thing that had occurred hundreds of time in the ancient world" in which the worship of a particular god came to its conclusion with a destruction of its temple.[18] Neither should the great expectation of restoration be reduced to a situation in which "*Israel hoped beyond the hope or intention even of Yahweh, who had no such hope or intention for Israel.*"[19] Much to the contrary, by the Covenant LORD's own sovereign determination, the worship of this God would eventually broaden to encompass a worldwide community as a consequence of the nation's restoration after exile. In the prophetic vision, this restoration would expand so that it became universal in nature, embracing all the nations of humanity.[20]

From this perspective, the unfolding ministry of Israel's writing prophets may be perceived as being shaped around three key moments in the nation's experience:[21] the exile of the northern kingdom in 722 B.C.,

18. Westermann, *Prophetic Oracles of Salvation*, 268.

19. Brueggemann, *Theology of the Old Testament*, 439 (emphasis original).

20. Westermann, *Prophetic Oracles of Salvation*, 273. Westermann seriously restricts the long-term realization of this promise of restoration when he says that only the message of Deutero-Isaiah leads naturally to the New Testament, since only Deutero-Isaiah includes no defeat of enemies associated with the restoration (171). Although Westermann might assign Isa. 66 to the so-called Third Isaiah, his analysis contradicts the unified witness of the book of Isaiah and hardly fits with the teaching of Jesus when he quotes the concluding verse of Isaiah's prophecy: "They will go out and look upon the dead bodies of those who rebelled against me; their worm will not die, nor will their fire be quenched, and they will be loathsome to all mankind" (Isa. 66:24 NIV; Mark 9:47–48).

21. Gowan, *Theology of the Prophetic Books*, 9.

encompassing the ministries of Amos, Hosea, Isaiah, and Micah; the exile of the southern kingdom in 587 B.C., involving the continuing ministries of Isaiah and Micah and also including the ministry of Nahum, Habakkuk, Zephaniah, and Jeremiah; and the restoration of Israel from its exile beginning in 536 B.C., as addressed by the prophets Haggai, Zechariah, and Malachi. Ezekiel and Daniel are distinctive in that they performed their entire prophetic ministries while experiencing for themselves the reality of the nation's exile.[22] These three specific foci of 722 B.C., 587 B.C., and 536 B.C. should not be perceived as limiting the ministries of the various prophets to these moments in history, for each of the prophets ranges across the length and breadth of the themes of exile and restoration as these great events take shape in the prospects of redemptive history. But these specific historical points function as moments that dramatically affect the total message of the prophets.

This location of the main focus of the prophetic books in reference to exile and restoration might be viewed as merely one option among many. But these events appear to be something more than optional centers for their ministry. While the prophets regularly reflected on other great events of redemptive history (e.g., the call of Abraham, the exodus under Moses, and the kingdom established by David), the experience of exile and restoration was the unique experience of the prophets themselves. As a consequence, it was exile and restoration that provided the unique historical framework for the development of prophetism in Israel.

With this perspective in mind, the biblical-theological setting of the various prophets of Israel will be considered in the next five chapters. Accordingly, the progression of prophetic ministry may be analyzed as follows:

- prophetism prior to the nation's exile, encompassing the ministries of Amos, Hosea, Isaiah, Micah, and Jonah during the

---

22. This situating of the various prophets about these three historical foci includes all the prophetic books except Jonah, Joel, and Obadiah. Jonah, identified as preexilic by a reference in Kings, is unique in that his book centers on a message for non-Israelite people. Neither Joel nor Obadiah place themselves specifically in relation to external history, and both have been dated either quite early or quite late by various scholars.

eighth century B.C. and the ministries of Nahum, Habakkuk, Zephaniah, and Jeremiah during the seventh century B.C.

- prophetism during the nation's exile as experienced by Ezekiel and Daniel in the mid-sixth century B.C.
- prophetism at the time of the nation's restoration after exile, involving the ministries of Haggai, Zechariah, and Malachi during the last quarter of the sixth century B.C. and extending into the mid-fifth century B.C.

8

Prophetism prior to the Nation's Exile: The Eighth-Century Prophets

After Elijah's heroic purging of the Baal prophets of the northern kingdom in the ninth century B.C., the majority of Israel's remaining prophets apparently succumbed in a short time to the spirit of their age. "It would seem," says Bright, "that as a group they had sunk into the general corruption and become . . . professionals interested chiefly in their fees (Amos 7:12; Micah 3:5, 11)."[1] Yet the most impressive of all periods in the history of prophetism in Israel arose in the eighth century B.C. During this time God raised up prophets in both the northern and southern kingdoms who anticipated the awesome coming days of the exile as a consequence of Israel's sin, while offering consolation through the hope of a glorious restoration by the working of God's grace.

During this era, Hosea and Amos challenged the pollutions that infiltrated Israelite society in a period of unparalleled prosperity for the northern kingdom. At the same time, Isaiah and Micah addressed similar problems, concentrating their ministries primarily toward the southern kingdom of Judah. Israel's role as the elect nation of God also experienced a unique challenge as a consequence of Jonah's mission to Nineveh, the Assyrian capital to the north. The role of each of these prophets in relation to Israel's exile and restoration deserves special notice.

1. Bright, *History of Israel*, 261.

I. Hosea

Hosea locates his ministry during the reigns of kings Uzziah, Jotham, Ahaz, and Hezekiah of Judah and of King Jeroboam II of Israel, a period covering roughly the last three quarters of the eighth century B.C. (Hos. 1:1). This prophet's ministry would have been immediately understandable to his contemporaries from the outset. God commands Hosea to take an adulterous woman as his wife and to bear children of her as a way of vivifying the Lord's response to the nation's infidelity to him (1:2–3).[2] Having fallen into the sensual practices of contemporary Baal worship, Israel's apostasy led them to introduce cult prostitution into their sacred institutions.[3] This perversion of truth could not be ignored by the Covenant LORD.

Hosea's marriage provides a vivid picture of the Covenant LORD's relation to unfaithful Israel. Despite this chosen nation's having gone after other gods, gods that promised materialistic prosperity, God continues to love Israel even as he directs Hosea to love an unfaithful wife. But the Lord will bring Israel under the hand of his chastening judg-

2. Rowley, *Men of God*, 96, notes that several of Israel's prophets "perceived in germ the essence of the message with which they were charged" at the moment of their call. The initial command of the Lord that Hosea take a "wife of harlotry and have children of harlotry" (Hos. 1:2), encapsulates the essence of his message and ministry.

3. Did this prophet of the Lord actually enter into a marriage relationship with an adulterous woman? Or did this woman have only a potential for immorality? Or should this account be regarded as only an allegory of God's relation to Israel? While it might appear unwise under normal circumstances for a person to choose a spouse who had been engaged in immoral behavior, scripture does not seem to forbid this action. Leviticus 21:7, 13–15 forbids the marriage of a priest to a harlot or a divorced person, but this prohibition does not necessarily imply that no other office bearer in Israel could marry under these circumstances. For a full discussion, see Rowley, *Men of God*, 66–97. Young, *Introduction to the Old Testament*, 253, supports the view that the narrative is symbolic of Israel's apostasy, but that Hosea did not marry an adulterous woman. Wolff, after extensively describing the sexual immorality associated with the Baal cult in Israel, opts for a "metaphorical-ritual" interpretation, proposing that Hosea's bride had "taken part in the Canaanite bridal rite of initiation that had become customary" (*Hosea*, 15). Kidner, *Message of Hosea*, 19, insists that "whichever view we take, we should not soften it by making her a cult-prostitute, merely deluded and misused; for the Hebrew has a word for this (4:14), and it is not the word used here."

ments. In accord with the symbolic naming of Hosea's children, God will designate Israel as Lo-Ruhamah and Lo-Ammi, for he will "not have mercy" and they are "not my people" (1:6, 9). He will drive the nation back into the wilderness and strip her of all the material possessions that have meant so much to her (2:2–13). But in the end the Lord will return her to himself, to the land he has given them, and to a united monarchy under David (2:14–3:5). This return will involve a new exodus, a new wilderness wandering in a desert that has been transformed into a fruitful field, and a new conquest of the land, in which the previous bitter experience of defeat at Ai will now take on the form of a "door of hope" (2:15).

From this starting point, Hosea's prophecy returns regularly to these initial themes. The concept of God as "the marriage-Lord of Israel" shaped Hosea's presentation "at nearly every point." The people "ought to love the Lord supremely for His own sake, and should seek the external blessings only because in them His love expresses itself." But instead, "the people care only for the gifts and are indifferent to the Giver."[4] Their unfaithfulness to God explains the origin of Israel's social sins. A spirit of prostitution dominates the nation, and there is no knowledge of God in the land (4:1). As a natural consequence, there is only cursing, lying, murder, stealing, adultery, and bloodshed (4:2). Their spirit of prostitution leads them astray, so that their daughters are prostitutes and their daughters-in-law adulterers (4:12–14). Other allusions to a violated marriage relationship recur regularly in the book:

- The nation continues in its prostitution (4:18).
- Ephraim has turned to prostitution (5:3).
- A spirit of prostitution is in their heart (5:4).
- They are unfaithful to the Covenant LORD and have given birth to illegitimate children (5:7).
- They are all adulterers, burning like an oven (7:4).
- Ephraim has sold herself to her lovers (8:9).
- They love the wages of a prostitute (9:1).

4. The quotations in this paragraph are from Vos, *Biblical Theology*, 297.

- God will drive them out of his house and will no longer love them (9:15).

Hosea's major indictment against Israel grows out of his own tragic experience. The nation has been unfaithful to the Lord even as his wife has played the harlot.

The consequences of this infidelity is realized concretely in the expulsion of the people from the land. The Israelites will live many days without king or prince, without sacrifice or sacred stones, without ephod or idol (3:4). Ephraim will be laid waste in a day of reckoning (5:9). God will be like a lion to Ephraim, carrying them off with no one to rescue (5:14). Their calf-idol will be taken into exile, carried to Assyria (10:5–6). Samaria and its king will float away like a twig on the surface of the waters (10:7). Exile is inevitable.

Yet just as Hosea is directed to reclaim his unfaithful wife, so the Covenant LORD loves Israel to the point that he must bring her back to himself. Just as God promised in the covenant with the fathers, the Israelites will multiply until their number is like the sand on the seashore, which cannot be measured or counted (1:10). The people of Judah and Israel will be reunited, will appoint one leader, and will come up out of the land (1:11). They will return and seek the Lord and David their king (3:5).[5] After the Lord has dragged them off like a lion, he will go back to his place until they admit their guilt and seek his face (5:15). He will heal them, bind up their wounds, and come down on them like the refreshing rains (6:1–3). Though they have sold themselves among the nations, he will gather them together (8:10). "How can I give you up?" cries the Lord in his compassionate love for his people (11:8 NIV). He is God and not a man, and as a consequence he cannot dismiss them altogether (11:9b). His children will return to him in trembling when he roars. They will come like birds from Egypt, like doves from Assyria, and the Lord will settle them in their homes (11:10–11).

5. The genuineness of the reference to seeking David the king in this book of a prophet to the northern kingdom is frequently questioned. But as Andersen and Freedman, *Hosea*, 307, indicate: "We hardly know enough of Hosea's political thinking to rule out the restoration of the Davidic kingdom as an eschatological expectation."

The last of Hosea's messages of restoration returns to the imagery of fruitfulness. Baalism had promised this blessing to the Israelites. But the Lord is the only one who can actually make the land produce in abundance. The Lord himself will take the initiative, will heal their waywardness, and will love them freely (14:4). He will be like the dew to Israel, causing them to blossom abundantly (14:5). The restoration will be completed by a return to a fruitful land that they had ironically lost in the pursuit of their fertility gods. The people that had been judged as Lo-Ammi would now be known as sons of the living God.

Quite striking is the apostle Paul's application of the message of Hosea to the new covenant circumstance. God has made known the riches of his mercy to many people, "not only from the Jews but also from the Gentiles, *as he says in Hosea*: 'I will call them "my people" who are not my people; and I will call her "my loved one" who is not my loved one'" (Rom. 9:24–25). But how could this be? How could Paul legitimately apply a prophecy about the restoration of Israel to encompass the inclusion of Gentiles in the current gospel era? Has Paul twisted an old covenant prophecy to suit his own ends?

Not so! The apostle's development of the significance of this old covenant prophecy illumines several factors crucial to a proper under-standing of the message of the prophets. On the one hand, it indicates the radical significance of Israel's exile. Through this judgment of the Lord, Israel actually became Lo-Ammi, just as Hosea said. As the pronouncement of the prophet indicates, they were "not [God's] people" (Hos. 1:9). By the judgment of the exile, they were returned to the status they held before God's calling of Abraham their father. At the same time, this application of Hosea's prophecy by Paul to the influx of the Gentiles in the present day indicates the significance of the inclusion of Gentile peoples. They have become a legitimate part of the Israel of God. Believing Gentiles are God's people just as much as believing Jews have been and continue to be God's people. Still further, Paul's appeal to this passage indicates the precise time of Israel's "restoration." Their return is not to be viewed as though it were some movement that will occur among ethnic descendants of Abraham in the distant future. Instead, this "restoration" of "Israel" is already occurring as Jews and Gentiles together are reconciled to God by the working of his grace.[6]

Although the prophecy of Hosea arises out of a concrete historical circumstance in the history of the nation of Israel, it speaks directly to the redemptive events of the present day. Jew and Gentile together are being formed into the new covenant people of God, in fulfillment of the prophecy of Hosea.[7]

II. Amos

Amos addresses the northern kingdom of Israel during its days of greatest prosperity: the middle of the eighth century B.C.[8] This outspoken prophet underscores the universal character of the Covenant LORD's domain from the outset by announcing his coming judgment on all Israel's neighbors. He condemns the sin of Damascus to the northeast (1:3–5) and then turns diagonally across Israel to Gaza in the southwest (1:6–8). He moves up the coastland to Tyre in the northwest (1:9–10) and then crosses once more over Israel to Edom, Ammon, and Moab in the southeast and east (1:11–2:3). The prophet comes closer to home when he announces that not even Israel's sister-nation Judah can claim exemption from the Lord's judgments (2:4–5). Amos reaches the climax of this crisscross pattern of condemnation when he unleashes his most scathing judgments against the northern kingdom

6. The remark of Gowan, *Theology of the Prophetic Books*, 49–50, that Hosea's hopes of a return of the northern kingdom "did not come true" errs from failing to see the radical nature of the exile and the transforming character of the restoration. Exiled Israel became "not my people," and so the conversion of Gentile peoples actually fulfills this prediction far more gloriously than an ethnocentric return of the ten lost tribes would have done.

7. Fairbairn, *Interpretation of Prophecy*, 377, finds the consummate fulfillment of Israel's harlotry in an apostate church as depicted in the book of Revelation. On the one hand the apocalyptic vision sees a chaste virgin without spot or wrinkle, pure and glorious, clothed in the sun, and fit to be the Lamb's bride (Rev. 12:1–2; 21:2). On the other hand is Babylon the Great Harlot (17:3–6a; 18:3), representing "a church degenerate, faithless, sunk in the mire of worldliness and sin."

8. The prophet dates his ministry in the days of King Uzziah of Judah (approximately 779–740 B.C.) and Jeroboam II of Israel (approximately 783–743 B.C.) (Amos 1:1).

of Israel itself (2:6–16). God clearly does not intend to exempt his own people from his righteous dispensings.[9]

The tone of judgment in these first two chapters permeates the whole book of Amos, with the exception of the last few verses. The largest hope that may be given to Israel is an uncertain "perhaps": *perhaps* the Lord will respond in mercy if the people repent, for the Lord cannot be bound in a box (5:15).[10] The severity of the message of judgment becomes clearest at the time when Amos is commanded by the priest of Bethel to leave the land as a result of his pronouncement that King Jeroboam would experience a violent death and that the nation would go into exile (7:10–13). In recounting the experience of his call to the prophetic office in response to the challenge of the priest of Bethel, Amos essentially summarizes his whole prophetic message. No less than four times he declares that Israel will be dispossessed of its land and driven into captivity (7:17).[11] This message of certain exile is the thing that is new and different in contrast with the ministry of Israel's earlier nonliterary prophets.[12]

9. Wolff, *Joel and Amos*, 102, notes that at least two-thirds of the judgment passages in Amos specifically indicate that God himself is the one who executes justice.

10. Von Rad, *Old Testament Theology*, 2.134, speaks of "a faint-hearted 'perhaps'" as the only hope offered by Amos. The phrasing of von Rad has a poetic ring, but minimizes the sincerity and intensity of the prophet's plea for repentance.

11. Clements, *Old Testament Prophecy*, 32. While providing helpful insight into the heart of this message of Amos, Clements proceeds to express his own belief that these words cannot possibly be the genuine words of Amos. "We cannot doubt," says Clements, "that the author of the narrative knew of these tragic events [of Israel's exile] and has linked them directly with Amos' prophecy of Yahweh rising up in conflict against his people." Clements gives no reason as to why the narrative must be regarded as having been written after the fact of its fulfillment, rather than being a legitimate anticipation of the future. Under his reconstruction of the text, it is difficult to see how the material could avoid the accusation of an untrue representation of the originator of the prophetic word.

12. The declaration that Israel will go into exile is repeatedly pronounced by Amos in many different contexts (5:5, 27; 6:7, 8; 7:17). Clements, however, goes beyond the evidence of the text when he asserts that Amos declares the end of the covenant for Israel (*Prophecy and Covenant*, 40). Contrast the statement of Motyer, *Message of Amos*, 68: "Amos is declaring the vengeance which falls within the covenant; there is no such thing as a divine vengeance nullifying a covenant once made or revoking a promise once bestowed." It is true that God's covenantal dealings will take on a new form after the judgment of the exile, but the covenant as such does not come to an end, for God shall realize the purposes of his grace.

But why should the Lord bring such devastating judgment on this little nation that has finally reached a reasonable level of prosperity after so many years of struggle for survival? The prophet's penetrating answer to this question must have brought shock to those who heard it for the first time:

Hear this word the Covenant LORD has spoken against you, O people of Israel—against the whole family I brought up out of Egypt:

"You only have I chosen
    of all the families of the earth;
therefore I will punish you
    for all your sins." (3:1–2 NIV)

This rather startling statement expresses "one of the central themes of the whole book."[13] Because of Israel's special status, God has an even greater reason for punishing them for their disloyalty and disobedience. This special status, as the passage indicates, arises out of the historical event of the exodus by which the Lord established them uniquely as his covenant people.

The term *covenant* appears only once in the prophecy of Amos, and that in a context in which it does not clearly refer to a divine covenant (1:9). But it is equally true that the frame of reference in Amos presupposes both the covenant with the fathers and the covenant made through Moses.[14] This nation, these families alone of all the families of the earth, has been favored beyond all other peoples.[15] They are the ones the Lord brought out of Egypt by the exodus. For this reason of special privilege, they stand under special judgment. Because of the covenant they came to possess the land, and because of the

13. Andersen and Freedman, *Amos*, 382.
14. Bright, *Covenant and Promise*, 84, says that though Amos never uses the term *covenant* (which is not exactly accurate, unless the reference in Amos 1:9 is first removed), "it is clear that the crimes he attacks are infractions of covenant law."
15. Calvin, *Twelve Minor Prophets*, 2.202, takes the sting out of objections to the exclusiveness of God's electing grace by aptly remarking that if God had owed any other people anything, then surely he would have given it. But they deserved nothing of him.

covenant they will be exiled from the land. All the awesome judgments described so vividly in Amos's prophecy will fall on this nation just because they have been specially favored of the Lord.

Only in Amos's last words may be found a certain hope for the nation. Finally the prospect of restoration after exile is declared to be assured on the basis of God's covenants. This time it is the covenant with David that provides the sure hope, the expectation that God will raise up the "fallen booth of David" (9:11–12).[16] God's work of redemption shall go forward despite the incursion of sin into the hearts and lives of those who have been especially favored by the Lord's grace. Ultimately even the Edomites, the traditional adversaries of Israel, will have God's name implanted on them, symbolizing their sharing in the Lord's electing grace (9:12).

The final passage in Amos provides the framework for understanding the inclusion of Gentiles among the people of God in the context of the new covenant. At the great council of the church's leadership held at Jerusalem, the appeal by James to this prophecy of Amos decided the issue (Acts 15:15–19). The inspired words of the prophet

16. Many continue to regard the genuineness of Amos 9:11–15 as uncertain or unlikely. In his earlier *Prophecy and Covenant*, 111, Clements treats the passage as an authentic utterance of Amos. In his later *Prophecy and Tradition*, 46, he concludes that the message of hope in Amos must have arisen out of a later redaction. Then in his *Old Testament Prophecy*, 197, he concludes that these final words of Amos are not necessarily a postexilic addition. More recently, Gowan (*Theology of the Prophetic Books*, 36), says there is "no evidence" in Amos that a restoration might follow the exile. He affirms that it "seems unlikely" that any of the promises of Amos 9:11–15 originated from an eighth-century source. To his credit, Gowan provides some reasons for his conclusion, pointing to the absence of vocabulary and themes that fit the earlier portions of the book of Amos. Gowan says that the promises of restoration would have been meaningless before all was lost, which seems to involve a strange way of reasoning (i.e., why should not hope have a place before all is lost?). He then suggests that the place of these promises "in the final, canonical form of the book" makes good sense (37). But it may be asked, if offering promises before devastation made no sense in the original context of Amos, why would it make sense for a later editor to add them and make them appear to be words that Amos uttered before the devastation? From a different perspective, Andersen and Freedman, *Amos*, 917, assert that the idea of a restoration of the fallen booth of David must have arisen long before the exile. In fact, they affirm that this hope must have existed in Israel from the time of the disruption that separated the two kingdoms in the time of Solomon's son Rehoboam.

had anticipated the day in which the "fallen booth of David" would be restored. Amos had declared that even Israel's archenemies the Edomites would have God's covenant name set on them. By the resurrection and ascension of Christ, James declares to the Jerusalem council that David's throne has been restored and elevated to a new and more majestic position. From his location at the right hand of God as the Lord's anointed, Jesus has poured his Spirit on the Gentile nations. Nothing else could explain their massive conversion. It has now become plain that Gentiles may experience the ultimate blessing of being united with the God of the covenant without ever becoming Jews through the ritual of circumcision. The new day of the new people of God under the new covenant has come.[17]

III. Micah

The two grandest of Israel's prophets locate themselves in Judea and Jerusalem in the latter half of the eighth century B.C. Their prophetic visions came to them in the days of kings Uzziah, Jotham, Ahaz, and Hezekiah of Judah (Isa. 1:1; Mic. 1:1).[18] Both Isaiah and Micah lived through the traumatic days of the devastation of the northern kingdom and its exile at the brutal hands of the king of Assyria in 722 B.C., which is a fact too often overlooked. King Sennacherib ultimately pounded on the gates of Jerusalem itself and no doubt would have brought about its devastation if it had not been for direct divine intervention, just as Isaiah predicted. In greatest humiliation, the mighty Sennacherib eventually died in the temple of his god at the hands of his own sons (Isa. 37; 2 Kings 19:20–37; 2 Chron. 32:20–21).

The message of these prophetic twins, who spoke God's word during one of the great crises of Israel's history, is more easily grasped by first examining the patterns of Micah's message before turning to

17. For a fuller treatment of this passage and an analysis of the alternative interpretation in dispensational thinking, see Robertson, "Hermeneutics of Continuity."

18. Micah does not list King Uzziah among the kings that bracket the time of his ministry, suggesting that he may have begun his ministry some time after Isaiah. In turn, Micah alone mentions Samaria as the recipient of his ministry in his opening verse, while the text of Isaiah indicates that he spoke relevantly to both kingdoms.

Isaiah. While both these prophets clearly have their own distinctive emphases, several overlapping themes may be detected.

Though the term *covenant* does not appear in the book of Micah, the foundation of his message rests on the previous covenants that God established with his people. Condemnation comes to the nation because of its failure to respond properly to the blessings brought by the redemption from Egypt (Mic. 6:4–5). As a consequence, the Lord now brings his covenant-based lawsuit against them, calling on the earth and its peoples as witnesses (1:2; 6:1–2; see also Deut. 4:26; 30:19; 31:28; 32:1). Yet their only hope must be that God will display his wonders, just as he did when the nation came out of Egypt (Mic. 6:4–5; 7:15). Even more basically, their hope rests in the covenantal oath sworn to the fathers, to Abraham and Jacob (7:20). That expectation now finds its expanded expectation in the promise of a (Davidic) ruler from the clan of Judah who will come out of Bethlehem (5:2). His kingdom of peace eventually will reach to the ends of the earth (5:4–5).

In view of Israel's failure to meet its covenantal obligation, Micah prophesies devastation and exile for the capitols of both kingdoms: Samaria will be turned into "a heap of rubble" (1:6); Jerusalem "will be plowed like a field"; and the temple hill will resemble a "mound overgrown with thickets" (3:12 NIV). The authenticity of this precise prediction two hundred years before the actual occurrence is attested during Jeremiah's ministry, when people urged his execution for his similar prophecies of doom (Jer. 26:18).[19] More specifically, Micah announces that Babylon will be the destiny of those people who are expelled from the land (4:10).

Beyond the exile will be a restoration, a gathering of dispersed Israel (2:12; 4:6; 5:3). The whole nation will not return, but a remnant shall (2:12; 4:7; 5:7–8; 7:18). Once reestablished, this remnant shall multiply and flourish as they come to possess the wealth of the nations in the name of the Covenant LORD, and as the nations flow to the mountain of the Lord (2:12; 4:13c; 4:1–3). As the kingdom is restored, so the king will be restored, and paradise will be renewed.

---

19. The suggestion that Micah's words embodied a failed prophecy because Jerusalem's destruction did not occur in his lifetime ignores the constant biblical testimony of the longsuffering of Israel's God.

As Bethlehem was the birthplace of great King David, so Bethlehem will be the home of the greater than David, even though his origins have been from eternity (4:8; 2:13; 5:2–4).

IV. Isaiah

The book of Isaiah features the same dominant themes connected with exile and restoration as found in the prophecy of Micah. In a way similar to Hosea and Amos, the message of this prophet finds its summation at his initial call to office. Hosea's message is embodied in the initial commission from God that he marry a harlot. Amos's prophetic message of Israel's coming exile is repeated four times as he recounts his initial call to the prophetic office when accosted by Amaziah priest of Bethel (Amos 7:10–17). In a similar way, the essence of the message of Isaiah may be found in the vision that came at the time of his call to the office of prophet in Israel (Isa. 6). Consider the following key elements in Isaiah's call and then the critical reconstruction of Isaiah's message.

A. Key elements in Isaiah's call

1. The exaltation of the Lord as king

As his visionary experience begins, Isaiah sees the Lord seated on a throne, high and lifted up, with the train of his robe filling the temple (6:1). But simultaneously a note of sadness is struck: Isaiah saw his exalted vision of the Lord as king in the year that King Uzziah died. At the very beginning of his ministry, the contrast is set between God's rule and man's rule. Even the best of Israel's kings are sinners, men with feet of clay. But despite the rise and fall of human kings, the Lord continues uninterruptedly on his throne. This tension between Israel's needing a king even though the Lord himself remains as king carries over from the days of the judges.

The prophecies of Isaiah present the Lord in his exalted position as king throughout the various sections of the book. All other kings and potentates will be brought before the Covenant LORD for judgment, for he "rules on Mount Zion and in Jerusalem" (24:23). The righteous man "will see the king in his beauty," as did Isaiah (33:17

NIV), for the Covenant LORD is judge, lawgiver, and king (33:22). The king of Jacob effectively sets forth his case, in contrast with the inept mute idols (41:21). In a deliberate echo of Isaiah's initial vision of the Lord in his holiness, God declares himself to be "your Holy One, Israel's Creator, your King" (43:14–15 NIV). He is the king of Israel, who has heaven as his throne and earth as his footstool (44:6; 66:1).

Through Isaiah, the final resolution of the tension between the Lord's eternal kingship over Israel and the fallible, temporal kings of the nation is revealed more clearly than had been previously understood. Attention focuses on an ideal Davidic king. This theme unifies the first major section of the book (chaps. 2–11).[20] In the last days, many nations will flow to Jerusalem to hear the word of the Lord. As a consequence, a worldwide kingdom of peace will be established (2:1–4). The king of this great empire will be the promised descendant of David. As a consummate manifestation of the "God-with-us" principle, he shall be provided supernaturally, being born of a virgin (7:14).

The attempt to terminate the line of Davidic kings in the days of Isaiah must be appreciated for its full significance in providing a context for the announcement of a virgin birth. God's purpose for the world throughout the centuries to come was at stake. Syria and Ephraim, two powers much stronger than the little domain of Judah, formed an alliance with the express purpose of removing the descendant of David from the throne and replacing him with the "son of Tabeel" (7:5–6). The serious character of this threat provides the basis for understanding the extraordinary nature of the response. Isaiah the prophet is not content merely to reassure the descendant of David currently on the throne that he has nothing to worry about. Instead, he challenges faithless King Ahaz to ask for a miraculous sign. He may choose heaven or earth as the realm in which the miracle will occur, dispelling all possibilities of a concocted fakery (7:11). At the king's wish, this supernatural phenomenon can be manifested for all to see. When the king in pretended piety refuses Isaiah's spectacular offer, the prophet declares to the whole "house of David" that the Covenant LORD himself will

---

20. The theme of the coming Davidic king is not limited to the first eleven chapters of Isaiah. It recurs in 22:20–25 and 32:1–2.

provide a miraculous sign. This supernatural sign will be designed specifically to confirm the unshakable fact that the line of David cannot and will not be terminated. "Behold!" says the prophet. "Be amazed!" "The virgin will conceive and bear a son; and she shall designate him as 'Immanuel,'" meaning "God is with us!" (7:14).

Extraordinary efforts have been made to rid this passage of everything that sounds supernatural. But the whole context contradicts these efforts. The drastic design of the Syro-Ephraimite coalition is plain. These nations intend to nullify the solemn oath of the covenant that the Lord had made with David. The offer of a supernatural phenomenon in heaven or earth could hardly be fulfilled by the normal birth of an ordinary son to the king or the prophet. The miraculous nature of the "sign" that Isaiah was proposing may be compared to the subsequent case of Hezekiah's illness, when the sign provided by the prophet was that the sundial went backward ten steps (38:7–8).

A son born to the king or the prophet in the normal manner could hardly have the effect of guaranteeing the unbroken, perpetual continuation of the line of Davidic kings on the throne of Israel in accord with the divine oath to David. But a virgin with child, a virgin of the line of David with child—that indeed would be a spectacular sign worthy of meeting the challenge offered by this coalition of armies set against the Lord and against his Christ. The term chosen by Isaiah (*almah*) specifies not merely a "young woman," as the Revised Standard Version translates it. The word designates an "unmarried young woman" and in this case "virtuous" in character as the bearer of Immanuel. In the fullest sense, she is a "virtuous unmarried young woman," which is expressed more precisely by the word *virgin*.[21]

The supernatural sign of a child born of a virgin answers the challenge presented to the line of David in this context. Isaiah's introduction to his prophecy creates an unprecedented expectation for the miraculous, and the Septuagint translators rightly represented that expectation when they used the Greek term for "virgin" (*parthenos*) to describe the woman who would bear the child. Only the same unbe-

---

21. The alternative term available to Isaiah (*betulah*) means "virgin" in a more specific sense, but in some cases the word is used for a married woman (Joel 1:8).

lief that marred the response of King Ahaz to the message of the prophet will rationalize away the wonder of this word.[22]

Additional names characterizing the nature of this supernaturally provided child have the same striking quality as the designation *Immanuel*. He shall be known as "mighty God" and "everlasting Father" (9:6). The significance of these designations may be disputed, but a proper understanding of their meaning points out that this coming savior shall be a divine messiah, God himself among men.[23] He shall prove to be sufficient to his gigantic task only because of the unique nature of his person. This great savior-king of God's people shall reign on the throne of his father David forever (9:7). The Spirit of the Lord shall rest on him, and he shall rule in righteousness over all the nations (11:5, 10). The description of this mighty monarch sent by God breaks the bonds of anything else that has ever been seen among the human race.

So the first factor to be noted in Isaiah's commissioning vision is his emphasis on the kingship of God over his people. This divine lordship ultimately will be manifested redemptively in the person of the coming Davidic messiah.

2. Holiness as a defining characteristic of Isaiah's Lord

A second factor made explicit in Isaiah's commissioning vision is the Lord's holy character. "Holy, holy, holy" is the description of the essence of God as declared by the cherubim (6:3). Evenly divided between his two major sections is Isaiah's distinctive designation of God as the "holy one of Israel." The phrase occurs twelve times in Isa-

---

22. The idea of a double reference in this prophecy, both to a virgin-born child and to the son of the prophet or of the king, does not do justice to the commitment of the Lord in his covenant with David, to the meaning of *almah* as an unmarried young woman, or to the context of Isaiah's offer of a supernatural sign. The further reference to the youth of the child as a temporal measuring rod for the duration of the opposing kings (Isa. 7:16) does not require a contemporary birth, but only the span of time required for the child-yet-to-be-born to progress from birth to young infancy.

23. For a full discussion of this designation of messiah as "mighty God" in Isa. 9:6, see Warfield, *Christology and Criticism*, 28–39. The clear reference to God by the same designation in 10:21 strongly supports the conclusion that the intent in 9:6 is to affirm the deity of the promised messiah.

iah 1–39 (1:4; 5:19, 24; 10:20; 12:6; 17:7; 29:19; 30:11, 12, 15; 31:1; 37:23) and thirteen times in Isaiah 40–66 (41:14, 16, 20; 43:3, 14; 45:11; 47:4; 48:17; 49:7; 54:5; 55:5; 60:9, 14). The use of this distinctive characterization for God in Isaiah is even more striking when it is noted that it appears only twice in the entirety of the rest of the prophetic corpus (Jer. 50:29; 51:5). Clearly the initiating vision of the thrice-holy Lord affected the entirety of Isaiah's concept of God and his ministry to Israel.

This holy God will show himself to be holy by his righteous deeds (Isa. 5:16). He is the holy one, the holy one of Jacob, who must be regarded as holy (10:17; 29:23; 8:13). His name, his Spirit, his Sabbath day, and his arm (the symbol of his power in action) are holy (57:15; 63:10–11; 58:13; 52:10). As a consequence, the place of his dwelling is holy. Isaiah frequently refers to God's "holy mountain," which is identified as Jerusalem (11:9; 27:13; 56:7; 57:13; 65:11, 25; 66:20; see also 48:2; 52:1). The sanctuary, the house where he dwells, is also holy (63:18; 64:11). Even the road leading to Zion is characterized as a "highway of holiness" (35:8, 10). As a matter of fact, all the cities of his land may be called holy, and his people are holy as well (64:10; 4:3; 62:12; 63:18 NASB). At the same time, it must be recognized that heaven is his holy dwelling place (63:15).

So the whole of the message of Isaiah is affected by this identity of God as the holy one of Israel. As a consequence, all that is associated with this holy God takes on the characteristic of holiness.

3. The universal character of the Lord's domain

A third element central to Isaiah's ministry that emerges quite strongly at the time of his initial call is the universal character of the Lord's domain. This God must not be viewed as one more local deity among many, for "the whole earth is filled with his glory" (6:3). This universal sovereignty is clearly underscored throughout the book by the declarations of the Lord's control over all the nations. The Covenant LORD of Israel has a plan, a purpose for the nations that must stand. This plan encompasses the whole world, for his hand is stretched out over all nations (14:24, 26). More specifically, he plans to crush the mighty Assyrian nation even while they are invading Israel's land (14:25).

The universal character of his rule is rooted in the reality of his creating the whole world. The time will come when mankind (*haadam*) will look to their maker, who is none other than the holy one of Israel (17:7; see also 27:11). Israel's God is "the everlasting God, the Creator of the ends of the earth" (40:28 NIV). The Lord who made the earth, created mankind, and marshaled the starry host of heaven will raise up Cyrus the Medo-Persian emperor; and woe to him who quarrels with his maker (45:12–13; 9). Just as "all the earth" is filled with the glory of Israel's God (6:3), so Israel's maker is called "the God of all the earth" (54:5).

In a consummate sense, the Lord will display this sovereignty over all the earth when he removes the shroud of death that enfolds all peoples, that covers all the nations (25:7–8). Clearly at that point he will be manifested as the one true living God.

4. The sinfulness of God's own people

At the moment of his call to the prophetic office, Isaiah's first response to the manifestation of the Lord's holiness was a heartfelt "Woe is me!" (6:5). He and all his people must anticipate God's judgment as a consequence of sin's defilement. But the Lord graciously provides a way of cleansing by a coal taken from the altar of sacrifice. An additional major theme of Isaiah is thus established at the moment of his call. It is not merely that the nations surrounding Israel stand condemned in view of God's righteous judgments. The chosen people of the Lord themselves—even their prophetic mediators—manifest a defilement that disqualifies them from standing in the presence of the holy God. This holy, righteous God cannot be expected to compromise his holiness by simply passing over transgressions. Yet in his mercy, a provision for cleansing is provided at the altar of sacrifice.

Isaiah opens his prophetic message by addressing "a sinful nation, a people loaded with guilt" (1:4 NIV). These people draw sin along with cords of deceit (5:18). The nation has burdened the Lord with their sins (43:24). Their iniquities have separated them from their God; their sins have hidden his face from them (59:2). Perhaps most telling is the indictment of the nation in terms of its role as the Lord's chosen servant: "Who is blind but my servant, and deaf like the messenger I send? Who is blind like the one committed to me, blind like the servant of the LORD?" (42:19 NIV).

The prophet gladly announces that Jacob's sin is atoned for and that the sins of those who dwell in Zion will be forgiven (27:9; 33:24). The comforting news is that Israel's sins have been paid for and will never be remembered again (40:2; 43:25). Consistently it is indicated that these sins are not simply overlooked by the Lord. His righteousness will be maintained. As a consequence, a special servant of the Lord is crushed for the iniquities of his people as he bears in himself the guilt of their sin (53:5, 11).

5. The inability of the people to hear the word of the Lord

At the time of his call to the prophetic office, Isaiah receives his commission to go and speak to the people. But at this initial point in his ministry he is informed of the type of response he can expect: the people will see, but they will not perceive; they will hear, but they will not understand his message (6:9). The development of this theme is far more extensive and widespread throughout the book of Isaiah than might first be suspected.[24] God's judgment on Israel is that they will not see with their eyes, hear with their ears, or understand with their hearts the truth of God as it is made known to them (6:10). Isaiah has just seen the Lord as king in all his glory. But now the nation is doomed to spiritual blindness. From this beginning point, curse and blessing are repeatedly defined as a consequence of perceiving or not perceiving the truth about God that is being made available to them.

The Lord has sealed the eyes of the nation, which are their prophets (29:10). No one could be so blind as the Lord's servant (42:19). Israel gropes about like someone who has no eyes (59:10). Yet out of the gloom and darkness the eyes of the blind will see (29:18). Eventually their eyes will see the king in his beauty, just as did Isaiah at the time of his prophetic call (33:17). The servant of the Lord is given the special task of opening the eyes of the blind (42:7).

Two passages of special significance in Isaiah anticipate sight for the blind and light in the darkness as these two themes extend into the context of the new covenant. Zebulun and Naphtali, territories in the

24. See Clements, "Beyond Tradition-History."

northern portion of Israel known as "Galilee of the Gentiles," regularly received the brunt of assaults from invading nations. Normally they saw only fearful gloom and utter darkness (8:22). But the day will come when these people walking in darkness will see a great light, for the promise of a Davidic descendant who will establish righteousness forever will be fulfilled (9:2, 7). Eventually this Galilean territory was the recipient of the light of the good news of the gospel. When Jesus left Judah because of the arrest of John the Baptist to proclaim the coming of God's kingdom in Galilee, this promised light finally came to the darkened land of the Gentiles (Matt. 4:12–17). In a similar way, the promise that the eyes of the blind would be opened and the ears of the deaf unstopped finds its consummate realization in the healing ministry of Jesus according to the gospel of Matthew (Isa. 35:5; see also Matt. 11:5–6).

In any case, this permeating theme that first appears in the record of Isaiah's call regularly reappears throughout the book and binds its various sections together. It vividly depicts the justice and the grace of God in dealing with a sinful, hardened people.

6. The exile of the people and their restoration to the land

How long must the prophet continue to deliver his message to an unhearing people? This question is answered directly in the prophet's initial vision:

> Until the cities
>   lie ruined and without inhabitant,
> until the houses
>   are left deserted,
> and the fields
>   ruined and ravaged,
> until the Covenant LORD
>   has sent everyone far away
>   and the land is utterly forsaken. (6:11–12 NIV)

It is quite remarkable that this statement about the future exile of the nation emerges so clearly at the point of Isaiah's call to the prophetic office. Yet skepticism regarding its genuineness should be offset by the remembrance that this prophet actually lived through the awesome trauma of the exile of the northern kingdom and declared to King Hezekiah that the identical fate awaited the southern kingdom of Judah. The fact of exile for both the northern and the southern kingdoms was something that must have played on the prophet's mind all throughout his ministry.

Yet the promise of restoration after exile is also assured at this early point by the promise that a remnant seed shall be maintained:[25]

> But as the terebinth and oak
>   leave stumps when they are cut down,
> so the holy seed
>   will be the stump in the land. (6:13b NIV)

From this originating vision, the themes of exile and restoration serve as focal points throughout the book of Isaiah. The first explicit reference to exile actually appears in the introductory portion of the book, prior to the record of the prophet's commission. Because of their lack of respect for the work of the Lord, this people will "go into exile" (5:13).[26] But the early warnings of coming exile for Israel are only the beginnings of the prophet's message. Samaria, that "fading flower . . . set on the head of a fertile valley," will be like a fig ripe for harvest (28:1, 4 NIV). God himself will summon the king of Assyria as his hired razor to shave Israel's head, legs, and beard (7:17–20). All the wealth of Samaria will be carried off by this mighty king from beyond the river (8:4).

In the same way, the royal descendants of David will be deported to Babylon, where they will become eunuchs in the palace of the for-

25. In response to objections that both doom and restoration are found in this record of the call of Isaiah, the remarks of Lindblom are appropriate. He states that both elements "are absolutely inseparable and fundamental to the preaching of Isaiah from the beginning to the end." He continues: "It would be strange indeed if the idea of the saved remnant, so basic in Isaiah's preaching, had not been indicated already in the inaugural vision, in which the contents of his prophetic message were defined" (*Prophecy in Ancient Israel*, 188–89).

26. Since this reference occurs in the Hebrew perfect tense, it could describe the actual beginnings of captivity for the northern kingdom. See Seitz, *Isaiah 1–39*, 50.

eign king, unable to bring forth a royal seed for the future generations (39:6–7). God will speak to Jerusalem through the strange tongues of foreign invaders, annulling their covenant with death by an over-whelming flood that will carry them away (28:11, 18–19). Who is it that has turned Israel over to the plunderers except the Lord himself (42:24–25)? He is the one who will destine them for the sword (65:12). This uproar coming from Jerusalem's temple—what is it? It is the sound of the Lord repaying his enemies all they deserve (66:6).

The inevitability of exile for both the northern and the southern kingdoms of Israel is thus one of the constant themes of Isaiah that arise out of the prophet's initial call. But at the same time, restoration and return after exile are also major factors in his message. As a tree leaves a stump when it is cut down, so the "holy seed will be the stump in the land" (6:13b NIV).

The theme of restoration beyond exile plays a prominent role in the various sections of Isaiah. Even one of Isaiah's sons bears the sym-bolic name *Shear-Jashub*, meaning "a remnant shall return" (7:3). Though destruction is decreed for the whole land, a remnant shall return (10:20–23). The Lord will gather his remnant, the exiles of the northern kingdom of Israel as well as the scattered people of Judah, from Assyria, Egypt, and Babylon (11:11–12). Both the Egyptian Sea and the Euphrates River will be dried up in a way similar to the dry-ing of the sea at the time of the original exodus (11:15–16). The praises of Israel will sound again, exactly word for word as they did at the time of the deliverance at the Red Sea (12:2; see also Exod. 15:2).

With few exceptions, every chapter in the latter section of the book of Isaiah includes significant references to the restoration after exile. In considering the development of the idea of restoration after exile throughout the book of Isaiah, several points may be noted.

First, a difference appears in the development of the theme of restoration in the two major sections of the prophecy. In Isaiah 1–39, restoration is associated more specifically with the remnant idea (4:3; 10:20–22; 11:11, 16; 17:6; 24:6; 28:5; 37:4, 31–32; see also 46:3; 49:21), while in Isaiah 40–66, the concentration centers on the idea of the emergence of the seed (41:8; 43:5; 44:3; 45:19, 25; 48:18–19; 53:10; 54:3; 59:21; 61:9; 65:9, 23; 66:22; see also 6:13). A negatively critical perspective might seize on this distinction to support the idea of two different authors or traditions for the two sections of the book. One problem with this perspective is that many critics also propose that the same hand that composed the latter section of Isaiah in the sixth century B.C. must be responsible for inserting the references to a return from exile in the first section of the book. In terms of a more fruitful analysis, it would be quite fitting for the prophet to speak about a surviving remnant when struggling to adjust himself to the concept of an exilic experience. But then after the prophet has resolved himself to the inevitability of an exile that is sure to come, he might anticipate the bursting forth of a multiple seed of the preserved people of God in their restoration. In the expectation of the prophet, it is not the current generation of his contemporaries, but a future seed yet to be born that shall return from exile.

Second, the inclusion of the Gentiles as a vital part of a restored Israel appears as a major theme throughout the book of Isaiah. A sampling of passages underscores the strength of this point in the prophecy of Isaiah. From Isaiah 1–39:[27]

> Many peoples will come and say,
> "Come, let us go up to the mountain of the Covenant LORD." (2:3)
>
> The Root of Jesse will stand as a banner for the peoples;
>   the nations will rally to him. (11:10)
>
> Once again he will choose Israel
>   and will settle them in their own land.
> Aliens will join them
>   and unite with the house of Jacob. (14:1)
>
> Gifts will be brought to the Covenant LORD Almighty
>   from a people tall and smooth-skinned . . .
> to Mount Zion. (18:7)
>
> From the west they acclaim the Covenant LORD's majesty.
>   Therefore in the east give glory to the Covenant LORD. . . .

27. The following quotations are from the NIV.

From the ends of the earth we hear singing:
> "Glory to the Righteous One." (24:14–16)

On this mountain the Covenant LORD Almighty will prepare
> a feast of rich food for all peoples. . . .
He will destroy
> the shroud that enfolds all peoples. . . .
He will swallow up death forever. (25:6–8)

From Isaiah 40–66:

In the desert prepare the way for the Covenant LORD. . . .
And all mankind together will see it. (40:3, 5)

It is too small a thing for you to be my servant
> to restore the tribes of Jacob. . . .
I will also make you a light for the Gentiles,
> that you may bring my salvation to the ends of the earth. (49:6; see
>> also 42:6)

You will summon nations you know not,
> and nations that do not know you will hasten to you. (55:5)

I will bring [foreigners] to my holy mountain . . .
for my house will be called
> a house of prayer for all nations. . . .
> He who gathers the exiles of Israel [says]:
"I will gather still others." (56:7–8)

Nations will come to your light,
> and kings to the brightness of your dawn. . . .
Foreigners will rebuild your walls,
> and their kings will serve you. (60:3, 10)

I will send some of those who survive to the nations. . . . They will proclaim my glory among the nations. And they will bring all your brothers, from all the nations, to my holy mountain in Jerusalem. . . . They will bring them, as the Israelites bring their grain offerings. . . . And I will select some of them also to be priests and Levites. (66:19–21)

While the theme of the inclusion of Gentile nations may be found throughout the prophetic writings, nothing quite matches the extensive elaboration of the theme as it appears consistently throughout the book of Isaiah. The influx of the Gentiles, attached in Isaiah so regularly to the theme of the return from exile, represents a new phase in the development of the concept of Israel's restoration. This anticipated experience in the history of the nation will create a new era for God's people. By this process, the very idea of a people of God is redefined to include peoples from all the nations of the world.

Third, the restoration is represented ultimately in Isaiah not merely as a return to the former condition enjoyed by the nation before the exile. Instead, the expected restoration swells to the point of embracing the idea of a new cosmic creation:[28]

> The moon will shine like the sun, and the sunlight will be seven times brighter . . . when the Covenant LORD binds up the bruises of his people and heals the wounds he inflicted. (30:26)

> Behold, I will create
>   new heavens and a new earth. . . .
> For I will create Jerusalem to be a delight. . . .
> They will build houses and dwell in them. . . .
> The wolf and the lamb will feed together,
>   and the lion will eat straw like the ox. . . .
> They will neither harm nor destroy
>   on all my holy mountain. (65:17–18, 21, 25; see also 11:6–9)

> As the new heavens and the new earth that I make will endure before me . . . so will your name and descendants endure. . . . All mankind will come and bow down before me. (66:22–23)

It is not simply that the idea of a new creation developed on its own, apart from other theological considerations. Instead, the concept of a return from exile provided the womb out of which the expectation of a new world order has been born.

28. The following quotations are from the NIV.

Fourth, quite striking in the development of Isaiah's theology is the injection of a personified figure into the theme of exile and restoration. Only in the context of the nation's exile and restoration may the meaning of this unique person who embodies Israel be properly understood. He is brought low, very low, more humbled than any other person who has lived on the face of the earth. He has no beauty or majesty that would attract people to him (53:2b). His appearance is disfigured beyond that of any man, his form marred beyond human likeness (52:14). He is cut off from the land of the living and makes his grave with the wicked (53:8b–9). Yet by the will of the Lord he will see his seed and prolong his days (53:10). After the suffering of his soul he will see the light, he will be satisfied, and the Lord will give him a portion among the great (53:11–12). In the experience of this figure, exile and restoration mean humiliation and exaltation, death and resurrection. His exaltation is as a matter of fact so great that it can be described with the identical phraseology found in the original call of Isaiah depicting the exalted Lord himself. Initially the prophet saw the Lord "high and lifted up" (*ram wenissa*) (6:1); now he sees the servant of the Lord "high and lifted up" (*yarum wenissa*) (52:13). This combination of words is so distinctive that it could hardly be coincidental that the identical phrase is used to describe these two paramount figures in Isaiah: the Lord himself and his servant. The only other biblical use of this combination is a passage that designates the Lord himself as the "high and lifted-up [one]" (57:15).

With this background in the book of Isaiah in mind, it becomes understandable why the gospel writer is so bold as to combine quotations from Isaiah's introduction of the exalted servant of the Lord (Isa. 53:1) with his report of the vision of the exalted Lord himself (6:10) and affirm that Isaiah had seen "*Jesus'* glory" in these experiences (John 12:37–41, quoting both these verses from Isaiah). Jesus and Jesus alone is the Lord who experiences exaltation as a consequence of his role as servant of the Lord.

One great point of significance is the relation of this second major figure in Isaiah's prophecy to the ideal David of the first section. The Jews of Jesus' day did not understand the connection between these two figures. As a consequence, they joined with the Romans in fulfilling prophecy by crucifying their own messiah. The disciples of Jesus also had great difficulty understanding the connection, and so they looked for a glorious messianic kingdom, without being able to grasp the idea of a suffering messiah. For long periods in its history, the Christian church has not understood this union of the Davidic messiah with Isaiah's suffering servant, and so triumphalism has emerged regularly in its many different forms.

But the very first of the servant songs should have been enough to enable people to make the connection between the ideal Davidic messiah in the early chapters of Isaiah with the suffering servant of the Lord in the later section. In this first song it is noted that God "put his Spirit" on him (42:1), which is the same point made about the Davidic messiah (11:2). Three times it is stated that this servant of the Lord will establish justice in all the earth (42:1, 3–4), which is exactly the task assigned earlier to the Davidic messiah (9:7; 11:4–5). Despite his suffering, this servant will become the hope of men, even to the extremity of the farthermost islands (42:4); and in similar fashion it is noted that the Gentiles will be brought out of darkness by the Davidic messiah (9:1), for through his reign the earth will be filled with the knowledge of the Lord as the waters cover the sea (11:9). As great as may be the differences between these two figures, their overlapping ministries identify them as one and the same person. Two separate people could not fulfill roles that overlap so extensively. The suffering servant of the Lord is none other than the ideal Davidic messiah. The suffering one is the reigning one. While these profound perspectives become fully understandable only with the rejection, crucifixion, resurrection, and ascension of the one person, Jesus the Christ, the same concepts flow together in Isaiah's theology.

For Isaiah, the exile of Israel is a certainty. Already in his own lifetime he has witnessed the deportation of the northern kingdom. He understood that it would be only a matter of time before the southern kingdom experienced the same kind of devastation. Yet a divine messiah will set up a restored kingdom of God, and a distinctive servant of the Lord will bear the sins of God's people. The nation may therefore expect restoration that goes far beyond the replacement of what had been lost. Only a new creation in which the divine king reigns in righteousness can satisfy the expectations of these visions from the Lord.

In sum, three great connected mountain peaks provide the spinal backbone for Isaiah's prophecies: the coming of the ideal Davidic king, the sufferings of the anointed servant of the Lord, and the arrival of the days of God's eschatological kingdom. Efforts to divide the prophecies of Isaiah among several authors ignore the interlocking character of these themes. Failure to understand the relation of these themes to one another explains the inability of the Jews to recognize their messiah, the blindness of Jesus' disciples to the true character of his mission, and the confusion in the Christian church brought about by endless varieties of triumphalism. It is in this context that the question of the critical reconstruction of this greatest prophetic book may be considered.

B. Critical reconstruction of the book of Isaiah

For the past two centuries, prevailing opinion regarded the book of Isaiah as consisting of three (or sometimes two) major sections arising from three different ages and providing three diverse perspectives on the message of prophetism in Israel:[29] Isaiah 1–39 (preexilic), Isaiah 40–55 (exilic), and Isaiah 56–66 (postexilic).[30] This elemental division of the

29. For an analysis of the widespread influence of Bernhard Duhm in promoting the threefold division of the book of Isaiah, see Clements, *Century of Old Testament Study*, 51–56; Young, *Studies in Isaiah*, 39–72. Young notes (40 n. 7) that Duhm's development of three Isaiahs begins with a treatment of 2 Chron. 36:22–23, which Young characterizes as "nothing less than amazing." He observes that Duhm notes that the Chronicler indicates that in accordance with the word of the Lord through Jeremiah, the Lord stirred up the spirit of Cyrus. Even though it is clear from the context that the Chronicler was referring to the seventy-year duration of the exile as prophesied by Jeremiah, where Cyrus is not even mentioned, Duhm concludes that the Chronicler thought the Cyrus prophecy originated not with Isaiah but with Jeremiah. On that confused basis, he asserts that the book of Isaiah must have existed without the Cyrus prophecy and ended with Isa. 39 as late as the time of the writing of Chronicles! From this starting point, Duhm's whole development of a postexilic Trito-Isaiah had its beginning.

30. Supplementing the idea of a basic division of the book is the proposal of a school of Isaiah and of disciples who continually carried forward the prophet's original tradition into the next generation. This hypothesis is also being seriously questioned for its lack of objective evidence. Clements, *Old Testament Prophecy*, 146, says that the hypothesis "strains our credulity to an impossible extent, if we are required to believe that a body of Isaiah's disciples could have existed, as an identifiable and

book, with various modifications, has essentially dictated the dominant perspective on the historical development of Isaiah's theology.

Even conservative Old Testament introductions now promote the hypothesis of multiple authorship for the book of Isaiah, as seen in the work of Dillard and Longman.[31] In the context of an evangelical community, the attempt to justify multiple authorship for Isaiah is made by asserting that assigning Isaiah 40–66 to an author other than Isaiah is "not materially different" than recognizing that Moses was not the author of the record of his death as reported in Deuteronomy. In surveying the substance of Isaiah 40–66, they conclude that the background of these chapters "presumes an author living during the Exile." They further note that the prophet Isaiah is "not mentioned in the second half of the book."

While arguments have been made repeatedly for the distribution of materials in the book of Isaiah among the preexilic, exilic, and postexilic eras, the case made by Dillard and Longman is not particularly strong, especially given their premise regarding the divinely revealed character of the book. Paralleling the question regarding the authorship of Isaiah to the recording of Moses' death in Deuteronomy ignores the difference in genre between the two writings. The record of Moses' death comes as a historical epilogue dealing with matters of succession in a covenant-renewal document. As such, this material can be expected to conform to the scriptural conventions related to historical writings. For this elemental reason, it may be assumed that the Pentateuch did not intend to represent Moses as the person who recorded the circumstances of his own death and the ensuing funeral procedures, for historical writings do not as a standard rule describe events in advance of their occurrence. But Isaiah 40–66 appears as an entirely different literary genre. This material possesses all the characteristics of prophetic writings that anticipate events and circumstances of the future. In this case, it is quite natural to expect authorship to reside

functioning entity, through a period of almost four centuries, without leaving any proper record of their existence, save for the book in which they manage to preserve their cover of anonymity."

31. Dillard and Longman, *Introduction to the Old Testament*, 268–75. All quotations in this paragraph are from p. 275.

with someone who lives prior to the age being anticipated. For this reason, Isaiah ben Amoz would not be automatically eliminated from consideration as the author of this material as is Moses with respect to the historical record of his own decease.

The argument of Dillard and Longman then falls back on a presumption. In their judgment, the background of Isaiah 40–66 presumes an author living during the sixth-century Babylonian exile of the southern kingdom of Judah, which occurred at least one hundred years after the lifetime of Isaiah ben Amoz. For this reason, they conclude that the original Isaiah could not have been the author of these later chapters in the book.

In concession, exile may be part of the presumption of Isaiah 40–66. But it is too often forgotten that another exile occurred within Isaiah's own lifetime during the eighth century B.C. Isaiah witnessed the brutal invasion of the northern kingdom of Israel, the siege of the capitol city of Samaria, and the deportation of a significant portion of the population of the northern kingdom. He lived through the days in which Assyrian troops occupied Israelite territory to within eight or ten miles of Jerusalem. By divine revelation he was also informed that the kingdom of Judah would experience exactly the same trauma of exile. Should it then be surprising that the prophet would offer words of comfort to those already exiled, as well as to those who would experience exile at some point in the unknown future? Should it be presumed that the exiles of the northern kingdom had to live for 150 years without any word of divine comfort from the premier prophet of their day regarding the possibility of their restoration? Or should it be supposed that the exiles of the southern kingdom of Judah had to live through several decades in exile before a word of comfort from the Almighty was addressed to them?

When the author of Isaiah 40–66 is presumed to have lived during the Babylonian exile, good evidence must be given to overthrow the more firmly based conclusion, founded on the canonical context that connects these chapters to the ministry of eighth-century Isaiah. If appeal is made to the use of "Babylon" in Isaiah 40–66 to confirm the opinion that the author lived in Babylon, it should be noted that twice as many references to Babylon appear in the first thirty-nine chapters of Isaiah (nine references to Babylon in Isa. 1–39, versus four in Isa. 40–66). Among these references is the "oracle concerning Babylon that Isaiah son of Amoz saw" (13:1 NIV). If by divine revelation Isaiah could anticipate the fall of Babylon in the distant future, then certainly he could also anticipate the deliverance of Israel from Babylon by the same divine revelation.

The argument that the admonition to "leave Babylon" (48:20) assumes that the people are already in exile must take into account the context of this admonition. The prophet first anticipates the yet-future day when the Lord will bring down his purposed judgment on Babylon (48:14b). When that great day occurs, then Israel must take up its opportunity to leave Babylon. Since the purpose of God to judge Babylon was already announced by Isaiah ben Amoz in the first portion of the book (13:1), it would be wholly appropriate for this same Isaiah to admonish his people to leave Babylon when the moment of opportunity arose.[32]

It is argued that many passages anticipate an imminent redemption and return to Zion. Yet on a most basic level, the prophetic writings regularly treat matters of an uncertain future as imminent. The work of the servant of the Lord in bringing light to the Gentiles is listed among the imminent events of redemptive accomplishment.[33] Yet it could hardly be argued that the servant's work was imminent in the sense of being realized within the lifetime of the prophet (42:1–9; see also Matt. 12:15–21). If further appeal is made to passages in Isaiah 40–66 that presume the destruction of the city of Jerusalem, which historically would have occurred long after the lifetime of Isaiah, then those passages that address the city, its worship, and its corruptions as still continuing must also must be noted (57:5–7; 65:2–7, 11–12; 66:1–4, 6, 15–16).[34]

---

32. Dillard and Longman themselves note that shifting references to the Medes' destruction of Babylon from the eighth to the sixth centuries B.C. is an argument whose "circularity . . . is hard to miss" (ibid., 270 n. 2). Yet on the previous page they argue that references to Babylon in the second part of Isaiah must belong to the sixth century B.C. since "Babylon had not yet become a world empire, nor had it been the oppressor of Israel such that the Lord would take vengeance on Babylon."

33. Ibid., 269.

34. Dillard and Longman also note (ibid., 270) the reference to the watchman on the walls of Jerusalem in Isa. 62:6. Motyer, *Isaiah*, 529, says that the religious corruption described in these passages from Isa. 40–66 fits the "pre-exilic Canaanite cults." He then interacts with Foster, *Restoration of Israel*, 126, who offers his judgment that this material provides "a description of the corrupt popular religion that

In addition, a special problem exists for those who hold to a Babylonian origin for the words of comfort in Isaiah 40–66 (40:9; 41:27; 46:13; 51:16; 52:7–8).[35] If a prophet supposedly in Babylon speaks to exiles who also are in Babylon, how can he refer to them by saying, "You who bring good tidings *to Jerusalem*, lift up your voice . . . ; say *to the cities of Judah*, Behold your God" (40:9)? According to the restructuring of the book of Isaiah, the people being addressed in Isaiah 40–55 are not in Jerusalem or the cities of Judah; they are in Babylon! One supporter of the Deutero-Isaiah hypothesis acknowledges this mode of address to be remarkable and can only suppose that the theological significance of Jerusalem overrides its original geographical significance.[36] But then of course some explanation has to be given as to why these same people were so determined to return to the geographical Jerusalem if, as it is supposed, the theological significance of Jerusalem had overridden its geographical significance.

On the other hand, if someone in Jerusalem is offering comfort to those whom he has previously indicated will be going into exile (39:5–7), then he may legitimately address these people as Jerusalem, Zion, and the cities of Judah. His message is that her hard service will not go on forever; it will come to an end. Her sin will be paid for, and she will receive from the Lord's hand double for all her sins (40:1–2).[37] Clearly from no point of time in the old covenant could it be said that the sin of Israel had actually been atoned for. No animal sacrifices

---

existed in pre-exilic and doubtlessly in exilic and post-exilic times." But Foster provides no evidence for his assertion that these same corruptions doubtlessly existed in exilic and postexilic times. Says Motyer: "In so far as evidence extends, the pre-exilic apostasies and syncretisms were burned out by the fires of the exile." Westermann, *Isaiah 40–66*, 419, notes that the mention of the temple in 66:6 "only makes sense on the presumption that it had already been rebuilt." His conclusion accentuates the vividness of the language regarding a standing temple in Jerusalem, which would have been nonexistent during the days of Judah's exile. This passage is better understood as referring to the temple prior to the exile rather than after the exile, particularly since it anticipates devastation yet to be brought to the temple.

35. This problem is recognized by Clements, *Old Testament Prophecy*, 48.

36. Ibid.

37. Passages from the prophets translated into English with a past tense are often more properly understood as describing an action from the perspective of its being completed—irregardless of whether the event relates to past, present, or future time—rather than declaring that the event has already occurred.

could substitute for the punishment that human sin deserves, and nowhere is it indicated in scripture that human suffering had an atoning value. The prophet anticipates a future day in which atonement would be provided by the Lord himself for the sin of his people. As sin brought exile, so restoration from exile could come only with the removal of sin. No restoration could occur apart from proper atonement for transgression. In this context the concept of the atoning, substitutionary suffering of the servant of the Lord naturally arises in the later portion of Isaiah. But none of these accomplishments need necessarily to be viewed by the prophet as occurring within his own lifetime. No firm reason exists to deny the possibility of these words of comfort and anticipations of atonement as coming from Isaiah ben Amoz of the eighth century B.C.

Dillard and Longman further argue against the Isaianic authorship of Isaiah 40–66 by making the point that "Isaiah is not mentioned in the second half of the book."[38] But once more, the literary rationale related to the specific material under consideration must be taken into account. Prophets are mentioned by name in their literature essentially for two reasons: either for the purpose of attributing authorship, which uniformly though not exclusively occurs at the beginning of their material; or they are mentioned as a way of relating a specific incident in the life of the prophet to his message. As a consequence, the absence of the naming of any prophetic figure in Isaiah 40–66 argues more strongly for the Isaianic authorship of the material than against it. Although the observation is timeworn, it is nonetheless true: if a sixth-century prophet composed Isaiah 40–66, where is his name? Why should he break the established pattern of each and every one of the fifteen prophetic books in which the material is introduced by the identification of the prophet? Furthermore, if this unknown person ministered in the significant days of conquest by Cyrus and his subsequent decree that the people could return to their land, where is any reference to his historical experiences as a prophet? Isaiah we know well. We know of the experiences of Jeremiah as a prophet, even during his short stay as an exile in Egypt. Ezekiel left an extensive record of the

38. Dillard and Longman, *Introduction to the Old Testament*, 275.

significance of his prophetic life in Babylon. All these major prophets we know. But who is this Deutero-Isaiah? Was his career as perhaps the greatest of Israel's prophets so bland that we should know absolutely nothing about him?[39] On the other hand, since Isaiah of the eighth century B.C. did not himself undergo exile, it should not be surprising that no mention of his experience as a prophetic figure is to be found in connection with the latter half of his book. Contrary to the argument of Dillard and Longman, the very absence of reference to Isaiah in Isaiah 40–66 conforms more properly to the function of a prophet's name in prophetic literature if Isaiah actually was the author of this material.

Finally, the hypothetical proposal that a prophet "living later in the Exile foresaw through divine inspiration what God was about to do through Cyrus" appears as little more than a patchwork effort to salvage the prophecy from being regarded as a purely naturalistic production.[40] It furthermore reduces what is perhaps the most spectacularly framed prophecy in the Old Testament to little more than a keen political prognostication. The whole context of Isaiah 40–48 appears as a highly structured "challenge to prophecy" in which the one and only creator God and redeemer of his people does what no other supposed god can do: he predicts the future in a manner that only someone who controls the courses of nations could do. Any of the various gods of the nations might offer an impressive analysis of political prospects. In the latter days of Israel's sixth-century exile, just about anybody might have an inside line that Cyrus would reverse certain policies enacted by the Babylonians, which would result in Israel's return from exile. But what deaf and mute idol could match the climactic prediction of Isaiah, writing in the eighth century B.C., who names the conqueror of Babylon as the deliverer of his people 170 years before he appears on the scene of history! In the minds of many, not even God himself could have that kind of knowledge, much less

39. Westermann, *Isaiah 40–66*, 7, speaks of the "complete concealment of himself" in the shadow of the word of God. He observes that "we know practically nothing about Deutero-Isaiah himself, not even his name" (6), but finds nothing unusual about this fact.

40. Dillard and Longman, *Introduction to the Old Testament*, 275.

the necessary control of human history that could guarantee its occurrence. This distinctive prediction in its canonical context is actually the point at which the faith of many stumbles, leading to a denial of Isaianic authorship. Yet for an evangelical, this prophecy could hardly be regarded as more spectacular than Isaiah's anticipations of Jesus the messiah, his sufferings, and his glory, delivered seven hundred years before his birth.

No one in the contemporary scene should be so simplistic in their approach to this question as to suppose that Jesus and the apostles directly addressed matters of date and authorship for biblical books. Yet their inspired utterances and writings have unmistakable implications in these very areas. In quoting the second half of Isaiah, Luke introduces his reference with the phrase "the book of the words of Isaiah the prophet" (Luke 3:4 NIV). If he had said "the words of the book of Isaiah," then a case might be made for supposing that Luke was using only a conventional phrase to refer to a book known by Isaiah's name. But when he says "the book of the words of Isaiah the prophet," it becomes clear that he intends to attribute the origin of this material to the prophet Isaiah. Similarly, when the apostle John combines two quotations, one from the first part and one from the second part of Isaiah, and introduces both quotations with words that presume Isaianic authorship, his words must be heard with careful attention. In quoting Isaiah 53:1, John says, "This was to fulfill the word of Isaiah the prophet"; and in quoting 6:10 he says, "as Isaiah says elsewhere" (John 12:38–40 NIV). The apostle concludes his combined quotation by a remark that clearly sets both quotations within the life-experience of the eighth-century Isaiah: "Isaiah said these things [not "this," as NIV reads] because he saw Jesus' glory and spoke about him" (12:41). While these words must not be applied simplistically to matters of dating and authorship, they clearly should be given the weight they deserve in resolving issues related to the origin of the book of Isaiah.

Dillard and Longman may be correct in saying that "the question of the authorship of Isaiah probably should not be made a theological *shibboleth*."[41] For the issue is far more significant than a mat-

41. Ibid.

ter of alternative pronunciations of the same word by different communities. Their plea that this question not be made a test for orthodoxy must be considered with great care. It is not a light thing to recite the testimony of the Lord and his gospel writers and then to brush their uniform witness aside as though it were irrelevant to issues of faith and life today. Numerous ecclesiastical communities that have accepted negatively critical perspectives on questions such as the authorship of Isaiah have, within a generation or two, ended in bankruptcy regarding matters of faith and morals.

In the broader field of inquiry, the simple picture of two or three distinctive Isaiahs is becoming less and less credible.[42] More and more recognition is being given to manifestations of intertextuality within the one book of Isaiah. Comparable sections within this single prophetic book are being recognized so that a much greater unity of the materials is being acknowledged. One scholar affirms that because of their similarities, the materials commonly known as First Isaiah must have been deliberately rewritten to reflect the teachings of the later sections of the book.[43] In other words, the materials of Isaiah 1–39 are now being recognized as having such close correspondence to the prophecies of Isaiah 40–66 that a literary unity begins to emerge. A second scholar affirms that it is likely that Isaiah 40–66 "never circulated as a separate prophetic collection . . . and indeed that the only form we have of it is as it exists now: as the final chapters of a vision of Isaiah."[44] In other words, these later chapters of Isaiah are so closely integrated to the earlier chapters that they most likely never had a separate existence.

This acknowledgement of broad intertextual connections across the whole book of Isaiah by individuals who nonetheless continue to affirm that the book of Isaiah developed across two or more centuries has led to unusual lines of reasoning. Materials that clearly reflect the specific sins of preexilic Israel are acknowledged in Isaiah 56–57. The natural conclusion would be that these chapters must have actually addressed

42. Oswalt, Isaiah, 2.4, correctly notes that "at the present time, the idea of several independent books of Isaiah is in the eclipse."
43. Childs, Introduction to the Old Testament as Scripture, 333.
44. Seitz, "Isaiah 40–66," 320.

the preexilic community. But instead it is proposed that the supposed Third Isaiah used intertextual references to identify the evils of his day with descriptions relevant to the days of the supposed First Isaiah 170 years earlier.[45] Yet no effort is made to explain why the prophet would address the sins of his day in such a circuitous and irrelevant fashion.

Without question the book of Isaiah in its present form appears as a unified product of Isaiah ben Amoz in the eighth century B.C. Nothing in the text states any other alternative.[46] Assuming the integrity of this representation, many sections in Isaiah appear as prophetic predictions of the future. Some of those prophecies could not possibly find fulfillment until long after the time of the eighth century B.C. Still other prophecies anticipate circumstances that are yet future even from the perspective of the current age.

45. Childs, *Isaiah*, 462–63.

46. That the book of Isaiah in its present form appears as a literary unity and that this unified document is the only form in which any written record of the book exists should in itself provide adequate basis for the legitimacy of viewing the book as a unified product of Isaiah. Yet in responding to the work of Motyer, Clements states: "It has seemed to me a rather reactionary and unadventurous step therefore for recent commentary work on this so majestic prophetic writing to cling forlornly to the threadbare claims of an eighth-century date for Isaiah 1–39, and even of the whole book, when the very assumptions upon which such claims rested relate so poorly to the very nature of the text itself" (*Old Testament Prophecy*, 10). Yet Clements himself acknowledges the "many evident literary connections" between chaps. 1–39 and chaps. 40–66 (13) that would encourage the idea of a unified literary production dating in the eighth century. He provides what may be regarded as a brilliant development of the theme of Israel's blindness and deafness that connects chaps. 1–39 with chaps. 40–55 and concludes that there is a real unity, not just a superficial editorial unity, but a unity that belongs to the understanding of the book as a whole (83–86, 96). He also speaks in support of the idea that chaps. 56–66 are "closely related" to chaps. 40–55, even though it is "highly improbable" that they have the same author (98). One cannot help but wonder how much unity can be acknowledged without at least being open to the possibility that the book was produced by a single author. Clements provides a personal profile in which he explains that he has "reacted very negatively" to the tendency of some scholars who claim that one author wrote the book of Isaiah. He attributes this reactionary mode to his own background, which he describes as "strongly conservative and highly 'biblicist' in the best sense of the word" (12). It is somewhat surprising, given this self-testimony regarding his personal appreciation for the scriptures, that Clements would direct his most stringent criticisms against Motyer's work, which in time may prove to be the finest exposition of the book of Isaiah produced in the twentieth century.

What is at stake in the question of the origins of the various portions of Isaiah? Ultimately at stake is the integrity, the trustworthiness of the book. Is this prophecy to be treated as the unified whole that it presents itself to be? Or is the book to be divided among an assembly of divergent voices that represent a history of the development of prophetism in miniature? An acceptable analysis of the role of Isaiah in the progress of redemptive revelation hinges on this question of the overall reliability of the book as it presents itself.

If the integrity of the book of Isaiah is lost, any force of truth that might be felt from a legitimate unity of the book must inevitably be dissipated. How can the holy one of Israel expect truthfulness from his worshipers when a massive portion of the Isaianic material presents itself as predictions of the future arising in the eighth century B.C. when these so-called predictions actually appeared after the fact of their fulfillment in the sixth century B.C.? A God presented as consummating history by the restoration of primal blessedness loses his credibility when his message is announced by a prophet whose God cannot clearly demonstrate that he controls time-bound history by anticipating its future. No legitimate expectation can remain for the appearance of a predicted prince of peace who will establish righteousness in the earth or of a suffering servant of the Lord who will willingly suffer in himself the righteous judgments of the thrice-holy God in the place of his people if the prophet is denied the possibility of anticipating the future.

Some contemporaries seek renewed relevance for Isaiah's message in the birth of canonical criticism. This viewpoint momentarily pushes aside the "assured results" of negatively critical conclusions in order to view the book of Isaiah as the unified whole that it presents itself to be.[47] But always underlying this temporary suppression of neg-

---

47. In promoting a merger of concerns originating from widely differing theological perspectives, one scholar comments: "To put this another way, the gap between most modern critical commentaries and the pre-1700 literature . . . is now being bridged by the insights of modern stylistic and structural analysis. . . . It is not only the ancient scholars, precritical and fundamentalist, who ask questions about the meaning of the final form of the text: these are the questions that are being asked today by descriptive linguists" (Sawyer, "Change of Emphasis," 234). To illustrate his point, Sawyer provides several illustrations of similar phraseology taken from the traditional First and Second Isaiahs and employs these phrases to illuminate the message of the entire book (241).

atively critical judgments is the acceptance of what is assumed to be the real truth about the book. In one current analysis, the original setting of Isaiah 40–66 is judged as having been eliminated "almost entirely," and yet it is simultaneously affirmed that the material clearly belongs to the sixth century B.C. These later chapters of the book of Isaiah are regarded as connected to the circumstance of the eighth century B.C., and yet they are judged as being in a "non-historical setting." On the other hand, this new eighth-century setting of material that is supposed to have originally belonged to the sixth century B.C. is not to be disregarded as a "historical fiction."[48] At the same time, the first portion of Isaiah has been significantly modified "to assure that its message was interpreted in the light of Second Isaiah."[49]

Several questions arise in response to this canonical approach to the prophecy of Isaiah as the book now presents itself to the contemporary reader. First of all, if the authors/composers of Isaiah 40–66 wanted to express timeless theological truth that applied to any number of historical circumstances, why did he (or they) find it necessary or desirable to attach the material to Isaiah 1–39? Why would it not be better to simply issue their material anonymously in an undated fashion, so that it was clear from the beginning that he/they did not intend the material to be limited to any specific historical setting?

Second, if the motive for attaching this material to Isaiah 1–39 was to gain increased authority, what circumstance is to be imagined that would have given this individual or collective body the right to alter in such a drastic fashion the substance of materials already regarded as authoritative by reason of being attributed to the highly respected prophet Isaiah? Should it be assumed that this person (or these persons) had exclusive control of the only Isaiah scroll in existence at the time of the exile? Is it to be supposed that none but these certain individuals had any knowledge of what actually belonged in the Isaiah scroll, so that they were free to alter its contents or double its size without being questioned? If the writings of Isaiah had author-

48. Childs, *Introduction to the Old Testament as Scripture*, 325.
49. Ibid., 333.

238

ity, with whom did they have this authority? Since the producers of this additional material desired the authority that could be gained by associating their writings with the Isaiah materials, then clearly they were not the ones that injected this authority into Isaiah's materials. Otherwise they could have issued their additional materials on the basis of their own previously established authority. And is it to be supposed that the prophecies of Isaiah ben Amoz had existed for 170 years, from the eighth century B.C. through the entirety of the seventh century B.C., but in such a manner that no one knew exactly what existed in this material? No objective evidence whatsoever exists that might confirm these imagined circumstances. Yet it continues to be vigorously argued that an unknown individual or group of redactors of the sixth century B.C. could make major alterations to a respected document without raising objections from the community.

Third, if the new setting of Isaiah 40–66 is to be taken seriously as being interconnected with the words of Isaiah ben Amoz of the eighth century B.C., then the "challenge-to-prophecy" dimension of these chapters must be taken seriously. In this new eighth-century context, the appearance of Cyrus is still a matter of the distant future, and so all references to him must be seen as objects of prophetic prediction. While some may assert that Isaiah 40–66 has lost its historical context so that the material can be treated as though it fit right into the message of Isaiah 1–39, the historical circumstance of these latter chapters of Isaiah stands out boldly for all to read. The multiple references to King Cyrus of Persia in Isaiah 40–48 obviously contradict any suggestion that the material intends to be regarded as ahistorical. Far from being presented as a case of keen political prognistications, the context appears as one in which false gods are challenged to declare the future, which is something that only Israel's God can do.

In the end, this latest negatively critical procedure may be characterized as a "let's pretend" theology. The critical analysis of prophetic materials that has characterized the bulk of studies for over one hundred years is still regarded as having basic validity in its establishment of the genuine historical origins of the biblical materials. But in order to regain deeper appreciation for the biblical text as it now presents itself, this canonical approach *pretends* that the biblical prophecies actually are what they present themselves to be, while all the time expressing basic confidence in the modern critical conclusions that affirm exactly the opposite.

Yet the uniqueness of the prophetic witness, as well as the testimony of the scriptures as a whole, rests on the authentic historical rootedness of the biblical declarations. One noted critic summarized the uniqueness of the biblical witness some years before the development of the canonical approach: "The way in which the prophets give the exact time at which they received certain revelations, dating them by events in the historical and political world, and thereby emphasizing their character as real historical events, has no parallel in any other religion."[50]

In sum, believing any one of the various critical reconstructions intended to describe the process by which the book of Isaiah was formed requires a great deal of faith. As a matter of fact, to believe, without any supporting external evidence, in any one of these proposed processes that is supposed to have occurred over twenty-five hundred years ago, requires more faith, and a different kind of faith, than believing that the one and only God who created this world with a purpose revealed to his prophet a deliverance of Israel that was still 170 years in the future. To believe a reconstructed version of the originating process of the book of Isaiah requires a firm faith in one of the shifting opinions of modern schools of thought that depend essentially on the ability of naturalistic reasoning to explain all extraordinary phenomena related to the activity of the Covenant LORD of Israel. On the other hand, believing in the one true living God who created this world with a purpose, who has the capacity and the will to order human history so that it realizes his purpose, and who has chosen to reveal this purpose through certain individuals described by him as "my servants the prophets" leads quite naturally to a settled belief in the genuine integrity of the written, preserved, and highly respected material found in the book of Isaiah.

50. Von Rad, *Old Testament Theology*, 2.363.

V. Joel

Quite possibly the order of prophetic books among the collection of the twelve minor prophets is not based altogether on chronological judgments. Indeed, similarities of theme and phraseology very likely played their part in the Masoretic ordering. But these factors cannot be divorced altogether from the chronological. Similarity of theme and vocabulary naturally serve as principal factors indicating a united historical circumstance addressed by the various prophets. For this reason as well as for the antiquity of the tradition, the Masoretic order of the arrangement of the book of the twelve should be given significant weight. From this perspective, both Joel and Obadiah fall into the category of preexilic prophets, even though this ordering should not be regarded as originating by divine inspiration.

These two prophets are the most difficult to date, with proposals ranging from the ninth to the second centuries B.C.[51] Calvin notes that the consequences of difficulty in dating Joel are significantly less than they might be if, for instance, Hosea were equally difficult: "Not to know the time of Hosea would be to readers a great loss, for there are many parts which could not be explained without a knowledge of history; but as to Joel there is, as I have said, less need of this; for the import of his doctrine is evident though his time be obscure and uncertain."[52] Calvin's remarks are appropriate, so long as the extremely late dating into the second century B.C. is not given equal place with more appropriate possibilities.[53] With these considerations in mind, the message of these two small but significant books may be noted.

Building solidly on the unifying theme of the coming Day of the Lord, Joel's message moves dramatically toward its crescendo. First God's own people undergo a "scorched earth" judgment as a consequence of a devastating plague of locusts (1:4–2:11). But beyond the defoliation of the Lord's own land is nothing less than a miraculous

---

51. For a thorough discussion of dating prospects for these two small books, see Harrison, *Introduction to the Old Testament*, 876–79, 899–903. Compare Eissfeldt, *Old Testament*, 394–95, 402–3.

52. Calvin, *Twelve Minor Prophets*, 2.xv.

53. See Oesterley and Robinson, *Introduction to the Books of the Old Testament*, 362.

restoration, when the Lord returns all that the locusts have eaten (2:25). Yet the Lord's concern is not merely for his own Israel. It extends to all the nations. Just as the sky was blackened by the cloud of little creatures so that sun, moon, and stars were darkened, so the coming Day of the Lord will bring about a universal blackening of the skies above all the nations (2:10, 31; 3:15). Multitudes will be gathered in the Valley of Decision—not so that the peoples of the world may decide for or against God, but that God may render his judgment over all humanity (3:14). In that great and terrible coming Day of the Lord, a finalizing divine judgment will set the stage for the inauguration of a new age.

Despite this image of a universal judgment of the nations, Joel cannot be perceived as narrowly nationalistic in his attitude toward the peoples of the world. In connection with the promised restoration of Israel after its judgment, Joel declares that the supreme divine blessing will fall on all nations. God will "pour out [his] Spirit on all flesh" (2:28). Indiscriminately on men and women, young and old, Israelite and non-Israelite, God will abundantly pour out an effusion of his Spirit that will equip all peoples to bless others by their spiritual gifts (2:28b–29).

The description of the superabundant outpouring of God's Spirit on all human flesh makes this prophecy "one of the most 'universalistic' in the Old Testament."[54] This universalistic character is well proven by its consummate fulfillment. On the day of Pentecost when the original apostles of Jesus the Christ spoke all the languages of the world to representatives from all the peoples of the world, Joel's universalism came to significant fruition. Even though Jews and Jewish proselytes made up the crowd on the day of Pentecost, the multiple languages of the apostolic prophesying confirmed the universal significance of the Christian gospel. From that day until the present, the invitation of the Lord through his prophet Joel has extended to all mankind: "Whosoever will call on the name of the Lord shall be saved" (Joel 2:32; Acts 2:21).

54. Barton, *Joel and Obadiah*, 96. Barton observes that it cannot be supported from scripture that "all flesh" means all Israelites. Barton concludes, however, that this universalistic concept cannot fit into Joel's original framework, but must be a secondary addition.

But how is the drastic transition in the message of Joel from the destruction and restoration of plants and animals to the outpouring of God's Spirit on all human flesh to be justified? What precedent can explain this mature representation of salvation through the infusion of the divine Spirit? Should this development in the book be understood as a clear marker that two authors and two sources stand behind the text of Joel? Is it appropriate to speak of "Deutero-Joel"?[55] Two considerations that bind together the major sections of Joel argue against this bifurcation of the book: the role of the Spirit of God in the biblical record of creation and the place of the teacher of righteousness in Joel.

At creation, the Spirit of God brooded over a world that was "without form and void" (Gen. 1:2). After he had caused the earth to bring forth grasses, fruit trees, and animals, the creator turned to the making of a man (1:11, 24, 26). But in this case, many things were distinctly different. The Lord God took a personal interest by forming man of the dust of the earth and breathing into his nostrils the breath of life (2:7). In a unique sense the life of man depended on the Spirit of God. It should not be surprising then that after Joel's description of the restoration of plants, trees, and animals following the plague of locusts, the Spirit of God enters the picture with distinctive prominence in connection with the rejuvenation of man. Not just Israelite man, but "all flesh" experiences re-creation of life by the working of God's Spirit. From this perspective, the second portion of the prophecy of Joel (Joel 2:28–3:21) develops naturally out of the first (1:2–2:27).

The phrase *hammoreh litsedaqah* may be translated as either "teacher of righteousness" or "rain of righteousness" (2:23).[56] The context at first seems to support the idea of a righteous rain because of the reference to the "abundant showers" and the "autumn and spring rains"

55. This view is espoused by Barton, ibid., 31, who concludes that treating the book as a whole will not lead to "any useful conclusions about its message for the future." See Wolff, *Joel and Amos*, 7–8, who strongly contends for the unity of the book, even to the point of asserting that Joel's prophecy cannot be understood apart from its being regarded as coming from a single author. Wolff does not, however, exclude literary additions, which makes the case for single authorship more complicated to maintain.

56. A great deal of consideration is given to this small phrase. See the bibliography on the subject in Prinsloo, *Theology of the Book of Joel*, 66 n. 18.

in the latter half of the same verse (2:23b). But what is righteous rain? Rainfall obviously has no inherent moral qualities, and though various explanations are offered for the phrase, they are not altogether convincing.[57] After fuller consideration, the idea of the "teacher of righteousness" as a messianic figure serving in connection with the outpouring of God's Spirit as described a few verses later seems quite appropriate to the context. Support for this interpretation may be found in the distinctive connection in scripture between right teaching and the blessing of rain. At the dedication of the temple, Solomon prays that the Lord will "teach them the good way in which they should walk" and "send rain on Your land" (2 Chron. 6:27 NASB). The prophet Isaiah notes that the Lord promises that Israel will see and hear its teachers, "and he will give rain for your seed" (Isa. 30:20–23; see also Ps. 72:1–3, 6, 16; Hos. 10:12). The ideas of restoration of earth and renewal of man are regularly joined in scripture, appropriate to the biblical concept of a wholeness in the created order of things.[58]

As a consequence of these two considerations, the book of Joel can be read as a unity that anticipates several consecutive developments in God's working of salvation in a fallen world: (1) God's judgment falls on God's land and God's people; (2) God issues the call to repent and return; (3) the whole creation is supernaturally restored by the Lord's grace; and (4) all nations of the world are judged. The concept of the Day of the Lord binds together these various elements of the book. The coming of this great and terrible day darkens sun, moon, and stars in three different contexts throughout the book (1:10; 2:31; 3:15), but the dawning of that same day also brings about the earth's consummate restoration.

In considering the larger framework of the book, the best case for dating Joel may be made for an early preexilic setting.[59] The threat in

57. For the ways to understand the phrase *righteous rain*, see Robertson, *Prophet of the Coming Day of the Lord*, 72.

58. See the extensive treatment of the subject in Ahlström, *Joel and the Temple Cult*, 108. Ahlström notes the close connection between the blessing of rain and the person of the messianic king. The king is "like the rain" coming down to bless the earth (Ps. 72:6).

59. For a fuller discussion of the factors to consider in dating Joel, see Robertson, *Prophet of the Coming Day of the Lord*, 10–13.

Joel's prophecy is not exile, but a plague of locusts. Since neither Assyria nor Babylon are mentioned as the foreboding foes of God's people, it is quite possible that Joel may be the earliest of Israel's prophets and that most of the parallels with other prophetic works may be explained by regarding Joel as the source of quoted materials.[60]

In any case, Joel's place as the prophet who anticipated the new covenant Pentecost is firmly established (Acts 2:16–21; Joel 2:28–32). As a matter of fact, careful consideration of the connections between Pentecost and the outpouring of the Spirit may serve to further illuminate both Joel and Acts. The original Pentecost was a time for the consecration of the "bread of the firstfruits" of the harvest (Lev. 23:20; see also 23:15–17). On this festal occasion, the people were reminded of the renewal of the earth's fertility by the goodness of their God. Both Joel and the apostle Peter take this renewal one step further. Man by divine redemption is also renewed through the gracious outpouring of God's Spirit. The consummation of redemption cannot be complete without this full restoration of man remade in God's image. With this perspective in mind, the foundation is laid for Paul's further development of the total Spirit renewal that is yet to come by the transformation of the body of redeemed man so that it becomes a "pneumatic body," that is, a body wholly permeated by the Spirit of God (1 Cor. 15:44).

VI. Obadiah

Obadiah, the shortest prophetic book, has the briefest introduction, consisting in the original language of only two words: "Vision-of Obadiah" (Obad. 1). The book is all about Edom, the national embodiment of Esau. But who is Esau in the unfolding revelation of the prophets about the messiah and his coming kingdom, and what is the ongoing significance of the nation of Edom?

Two nations struggled in the womb of Rebekah according to the ancient prophetic declaration (Gen. 25:23). Jacob the "supplanter,"

---

60. For the complete listing of materials in other prophets paralleling Joel, see Crenshaw, *Joel*, 27–28.

the latter-born twin, embodies the principle of God's undeserved, unmerited grace in his work of redemption. Esau the firstborn represents the part of humanity that persists in rebellion against God. The continuing significance of this distinction is made evident by the appearance of the Jacob/Esau contrast in Malachi, the very last of Israel's prophetic voices (Mal. 1:2–5). Somewhere between the narrative of Genesis and the prophecy of Malachi is the message of Obadiah. In this brief prophecy, three prominent themes may be detected: the guilt of Edom, the judgment of Edom, and the consequences of Edom's judgment for God's people.

A. The guilt of Edom

Edom deserves divine punishment for exactly the same reasons that God's judgment must fall on various nations, as stressed repeatedly in the proclamation of the prophets (see chap. 6 §I.D). First on the list is their pride: "The pride of your heart has deceived you," declares the Lord (Obad. 3a NIV; see also Jer. 49:16a). They presumed to make their little nest among the stars (Obad. 4a) and boastfully declared, "Who can bring me down to the ground?" (3b NIV). With these arrogant words and proud presumptions, this little backwater people echoes the boasts of Babylon:

> I will ascend
> > to heaven;
> I will raise my throne
> > above the stars of God. (Isa. 14:13 NIV)

As a consequence, Edom must experience the same divine judgments, being cast down from heaven (Isa. 14:12; Obad. 4b). In this respect, both Babylon and Edom share the fate of Satan, their infamous forefather (Luke 10:18; Rev. 12:8–9).

The second cause of Edom's guilt is their mistreatment of God's people. They have abused no one less than their brother Jacob, which makes their wrongdoing only more heinous (Obad. 10). Neglect was a part of their guilt as they "stood aloof" while foreigners "cast lots" for Jerusalem (11). Invading nations offered up the Lord's holy city to the god of chance, and Edom shared in their crime by doing nothing about it.

If this indictment holds true against ancient Edom for their neglect of Jerusalem, how much more does it apply to men who dared to offer up the only possession of the sinless Son of God to this god of chance. All he owned were the clothes on his back. These garments were taken from him, ripped into quarters, and distributed among his tormentors. Then by the throw of the dice they determined the possessor of his seamless undergarment (John 19:23–24). Yet countless people across the ages remain unashamed of the wrongdoing done to God's son and so share in the guilt of their action.

Obadiah's fuller accusation comes in the form of a sevenfold reference to the day of Judah's misfortune, destruction, trouble, and disaster (Obad. 12–14). Edom personally contributed to these calamities by cutting down Israel's fugitives as they fled across their common border (14). The repeated reference to the day of devastation endured by God's people anticipates Obadiah's second major point: the just judgment of Edom will occur on the great Day of the Lord.

B. The judgment of Edom

At this point the prophet enlarges his spectrum to include all nations in the coming judgment of the Day of the Lord (Obad. 15a). Yet he never lets Edom out of his sights. The basis of God's universal judgment will be the lex talionis, "an eye for an eye, and a tooth for a tooth" (Exod. 21:24). Just as Edom did to Judah, so it will be done to Edom. "Your deeds will return upon your own head," is the Lord's pronouncement (Obad. 15b NIV). The extent of this judgment is seen in there being "no survivors from the house of Esau" (18 NIV). In the final judgment, the seed of Satan will be totally eliminated. None of them shall survive the scrutiny of God's final judgment.

But in this process of divine judgment on the coming Day of the Lord, how will God's own people fare? What shall be the consequences of Edom's judgment for God's people?

C. The consequences of Edom's judgment for God's people

The Lord's judgment of Edom will mean deliverance for Mount Zion. God's favored mountain will be called "holy" (Obad. 17). Throughout history, redemption for God's people has meant judgment on his enemies. In the case of Obadiah, a deliberate contrast is made between the exaltation of Mount Zion and the humiliation of Mount Esau. Obadiah consistently designates Zion as "Mount Zion" (17, 21), and only Obadiah in all scripture designates Edom or Esau as "Mount Esau" (8, 9, 21).[61] This deliverance will mean concretely that the whole land, including Edom, will be possessed by God's people. At this point, the prophet scans the limits of the territory that the Lord had promised: the southern coastland of Philistia (19b), the northern coastal area up to Sidon (20a), the Negev to the south (20b), Samaria and Ephraim to the north (19b), the southern Transjordan area of Edom (19a), and the northern Transjordan territory of Gilead (19c)— every portion of the land will belong to the people of the Lord.

More specifically, saviors will go up on Mount Zion to judge Mount Esau (Obad. 21). In this final phrasing of the prophecy, two prospects of hope for Edom may be detected, despite the devastations of divine judgment: saviors who will judge Mount Esau, and Obadiah's position in the canon of scripture. The idea of judges who save Israel occurs twice in programmatic texts in the book of Judges (Judg. 2:16, 18). After this introduction of the concept, this saving aspect of judgeship is applied to Othniel, Ehud, Shamgar, Gideon, Tola, Jephthah, and Samson—seven of Israel's judges (3:9, 15, 31; 6:15; 10:1; 12:2; 13:5). In Obadiah, the saving done by judges applies to Israel first. That these saviors on Mount Zion perform the task of "judging" Mount Esau suggests something more than merely conquering or destroying Edom. They judge Mount Esau, which hints strongly at the possibility that their judging will involve saving activity. In other words, Edom is the potential beneficiary of the judging by these saviors on Mount Zion.

61. The NIV obscures this deliberate contrast in Obadiah between Mount Zion and Mount Esau by translating the latter phrase as "the mountains of Esau" or "Esau's mountains."

The position of Obadiah within the book of the twelve minor prophets offers further support for this perspective.[62] The arrangement of the twelve clearly intends to follow a basic chronological pattern, moving consecutively through eighth-, seventh-, and sixth-century groupings of writings. Yet Joel and Obadiah do not specify a time for their prophecies. In both cases, thematic connections with adjacent books seem to have played a major part in their location within the twelve minor prophets. In this regard, it has been proposed that Obadiah may be perceived in toto as an explanation of a verse in the final chapter of Amos, which immediately precedes it.[63] According to Amos 9:11–12, God will restore the fallen booth of David, "so that they may *possess* the *remnant of Edom* and all the nations that have my name called upon them." Three times in verses 19–20, Obadiah notes that Israel will "possess" various portions of the promised land. In the first instance, people of Judah's Negev will possess Mount Esau, so that the connection with the ending of Amos is quite specific. But the consequence of this possession as spelled out in Amos is significant. The Covenant LORD lists Edom among the nations who "have my name called upon them," indicating that they have become the elect of the Lord. Just as Israel was marked as the chosen of the Lord because God's name was called upon them, so now Esau/Edom experiences that same privilege in connection with the reestablishment of the "fallen booth of David" (Deut. 28:9–10; Amos 9:11–12).

Despite the severity of the judgment pronounced on Edom/Esau by Obadiah, the hope of salvation is still theirs. God's raising up of saviors for Israel must eventuate climactically in the restoration of the fallen booth of David and the appearance of the long-awaited messiah. In the coming of this messiah is the hope for a restored cosmos that will include even the likes of a person like Esau and a nation like Edom. When he finally comes, "the kingdom will be the Covenant LORD's" (Obad. 21 NIV).

62. This position relates to the canon of the Hebrew Bible. The order in the Septuagint is different. See the discussion of Wolff, *Joel and Amos*, 3–4; Hubbard, *Joel and Amos*, 22–23; Barton, *Joel and Obadiah*, 4.

63. Allen, *Joel, Obadiah, Jonah, and Micah*, 129. See also Wolff, *Obadiah and Jonah*, 17; and Barton, *Joel and Obadiah*, 116.

VII. Jonah

Jonah distinguishes himself among the prophetic books from several perspectives. First of all, the book is given over almost exclusively to a narrative about the life of the prophet, rather than concentrating on the message from the Lord through his prophet. In this regard, Jonah resembles more the narratives about the prophets in the historical books of the Bible than the books that consist mainly of prophetic utterances. This fact in no wise minimizes the significance of the book, for the message is clearly communicated by the life of the prophet as well as by the few words originating with the Lord in the book. Jonah himself becomes a "sign" to the city of Nineveh that confirms the message he brings. As the Lord determined to be merciful to Jonah his disobedient servant and give him a second chance, so he may also choose to be merciful to a brutal city such as Nineveh if its people should repent.

Second, the book does not directly claim authorship, although Jonah is named as the composer of the poetic prayer in Jonah 2 (1:1; 2:1–2). The historical setting is clearly delineated by a reference in the book of Kings to "Jonah son of Amittai" who prophesied in the days of Jeroboam II (2 Kings 14:23–27).[64] As a consequence, the events of the book belong "in the context of the ancient Near Eastern world of the eighth century B.C., when Assyria was the rising world power and Nineveh was a great world city."[65] It was to this foreign city, the capitol of a massive empire, that God sent Jonah with his prophetic message.

Being commissioned to a foreign nation defines a further element of the uniqueness of Jonah among the prophetic books. Significantly, Jonah is reported in the book of Kings as prophesying the expansion of the kingdom of Israel in Nineveh's direction. But now he must go and preach to the cruel nation that threatened to bring this expanding kingdom of Israel to an unhappy end.

Questions about the literary genre of Jonah may legitimately be raised, but these questions must deal seriously with the historical nota-

64. The canonical location of the book among self-dating preexilic prophets of the eighth century B.C. supports this temporal setting.
65. Limburg, *Jonah*, 22.

tions that underpin the book.[66] Quite regularly the material in the book of Jonah has been described as a story. According to one interpreter, the advantage of the term *story* is that it is "neutral regarding the question of historicity."[67] Yet this supposed neutrality cannot be sustained for long, as the same author indicates: "The book of Jonah may be described as a fictional story developed around a historical figure for didactic purposes."[68] It becomes clear that designating the book of Jonah by the term *story* provides a basis for treating as historical only those elements in the book that each particular person wishes to believe might have happened.

The same effect is achieved when it is asserted that the question of the historical nature of the material is "irrelevant to the interpretation of the book."[69] If interpretation ultimately involves the object to which belief should be directed, then whether God brought Jonah back from the brink of death, or even from death itself, is certainly a matter of significance.[70] Obviously the framework of the entire book is set in a genuinely historical context. Jonah is identified as the prophetic figure that appears in the historical narrative of scripture as the "son of Amittai from Gath-hepher" who lived in the days of Jeroboam II (2 Kings 14:25). Joppa, Tarshish, and Nineveh all are historico-geographical places. When Jesus uses the account of Jonah as the principal model for his own three-day death and resurrection experience, the reality of Jonah's experience is clearly removed from the realm of nonhistorical irrelevance (Matt. 12:39–40; Luke 11:29–30). A closer look at the wording of Jesus regarding the relation of the experience of Jonah to his own should go a long way toward dispelling doubts

66. With respect to the question of the literary integrity of the book, the point made regarding the poem in Jon. 2 by Limburg, ibid., 32, is worth noting: "It is not necessary to prove that the psalm is part of the original book of Jonah; the burden of proof is on the side of those arguing in the other direction."

67. Ibid., 23.

68. Ibid., 24. Fretheim, *Message of Jonah*, 62, in seeking some historical reality for the book, states that "the book *is* historical at least in the sense in which it reflects the life and thought of the Jewish community."

69. Dillard and Longman, *Introduction to the Old Testament*, 393.

70. It is possible that Jonah actually died in the belly of the fish and was revived by the power of the creator God whom he confessed.

concerning the affirmation of Jesus regarding the historical reality of the events of the life of Jonah. The people of Jesus' day wanted a miraculous sign. The only sign promised them is not the message but the person of Jonah himself as provided to the Ninevites. The sign of Jonah for Jesus refers to the prophet's descent and revival as it anticipated his own death and resurrection. If Jonah's three-day descent into Sheol is to be regarded as "historical fiction," then the parallel with the experience of Jesus inevitably opens the door to regarding his three-day burial and subsequent resurrection as also fictional in character. If the people of Nineveh did in fact repent at the preaching of Jonah as Jesus affirmed, if a "last judgment" will actually occur in which the Ninevites of Jonah's generation will fare better than the unbelieving contemporaries of Jesus, if Jesus was buried and rose from the dead in three days after the pattern of Jonah's experience—then the most consistent way of viewing the record of Jonah's descent to the bottom of the sea and his rising again becomes quite clear.[71]

In attempting to establish that the book is a didactic story rather than didactic history, several commentators propose that the narrative represents the animals as participating in the repentance of the city.[72] It is true that Nineveh's king includes the animals in his command that no one eat or drink (3:7). Man and beast without exception must be covered with sackcloth (3:8a). But in terms of actual repentance, it is only and specifically man (*ish*) who is to call urgently on God and give up his evil ways (3:8b). Instead of being

71. See the citations from C. S. Lewis by Alexander, "Jonah and Genre," 35–36: "Scholars, as scholars, speak on [the miraculous] with no more authority than anyone else. The canon 'If miraculous, unhistorical' is one they bring to their study of the texts, not one they have learned from it." And again: "Whatever these men may be as Biblical critics, I distrust them as critics. They seem to me to lack literary judgment, to be imperceptive about the very quality of the texts they are reading. . . . These men ask me to believe they can read between the lines of the old texts; the evidence is their obvious inability to read (in any sense worth discussing) the lines themselves. They claim to see fern-seed and can't see an elephant ten yards away in broad daylight."

72. Note the section heading in Wolff, *Obadiah and Jonah*, 143: "Even the Cattle Repent." See Limburg, *Jonah*, 34; and Fretheim, *Message of Jonah*, 63. See also the reference to this view in Dillard and Longman, *Introduction to the Old Testament*, 392.

viewed as a didactic story, the book should be characterized as didactic history.[73]

Several themes common to other prophets appear in the book of Jonah. The Covenant LORD of Israel is the God of heaven who made the sea and the land (1:9).[74] He exercises continual control over all his creation, so that he raises a storm on the sea and calms it again (1:4, 15). He appoints a great fish, a shading vine, and a devouring worm (1:17; 4:6–7). He will bring devastating judgment on wicked people, but he may choose to spare those who turn to him (3:4, 10). He shows his mercy and grace not merely to Israel, but to the most wicked nation of the world.

The concepts of exile from the presence of the Lord and restoration to him take on broader significance than in other prophetic writings. For the disobedient prophet, being exiled from the presence of God means that he sinks to the bottom of the sea, wrapped in the cords of death. Separation from God can mean no less than the end of life. Correspondingly, restoration to God means resurrection to newness of life. This restored life means a second chance to serve the Covenant LORD, the God of Israel. In his restoration, the Lord graciously speaks to his servant "a second time," commissioning him to take the message of judgment and grace to Nineveh (3:1–2).

So Jonah is exiled to the abyss of Sheol and restored for service to the Gentile world.[75] While the other eighth-century prophets of Israel concern themselves with the darkening clouds of exile into Assyria, Jonah does his best to fend off the divine proposal that he preach in Nineveh, the capitol of the cruel kingdom that will exile his own people. In his resistance to this calling, Jonah goes down into a watery grave,

73. Limburg's view of Jonah as "didactic story" (*Jonah*, 26) may be contrasted with the perspective of Alexander, "Jonah and Genre," 59, who supports the idea of "didactic history."

74. Says Wolff, *Obadiah and Jonah*, 87: "What is important throughout the narrative is his theology of creation." He then refers to the storm, fish, plant, worm, and east wind—all made by Jonah's God. The Covenant LORD is the creator who orders all things to his own glory.

75. Fretheim, *Message of Jonah*, 22, underscores that the repentant sailors/Ninevites are Gentiles by noting the difference it would have made if these people had been Jews instead.

where he remains for three days. He cries out in desperation to God, and the Lord delivers him from the jaws of death. After that dramatic lesson, Jonah learns to appreciate God's determination to provide salvation for the cruelest nation in the world. Having experienced figurative death and resurrection, Jonah serves as God's instrument in bringing salvation to the Gentiles. In this case, the life-experience of Jonah prophetically anticipates the day in which restoration will mean the worldwide expansion of God's saving activity among all the nations of the world: "For as Jonah was three days and three nights in the belly of a huge fish, so the Son of Man will be three days and three nights in the heart of the earth" (Matt. 12:40 NIV). Having experienced exile from the Father in his death, Jesus rises in restoration to commission his disciples to go and make disciples of all the nations (28:18–20).

VIII. Conclusion

Israel's prophets of the eighth century B.C. uniformly anticipated exile and restoration. Both for the northern kingdom of Israel and the southern kingdom of Judah, exile was inevitable. This people that had begun with the call of Abraham from Ur of the Chaldees would be brought under the domain of a later form of the Chaldean Empire. Through the conquest of Assyria by Babylon, the survivors of the exile from both Jewish kingdoms would be brought under the same foreign domination.

Yet these eighth-century prophets did not speak as though the nation had no hope for the future. A new exodus would occur. The people would be enabled to return to their promised land. The covenanted kingdom of David would be reestablished, and foreign nations would fly to the uplifted banner of the restored empire.

But the awesomeness of the exilic experience still loomed before them. They must actually undergo the devastation and disorientation associated with being cast out of their land. It was the task of the prophets who arose in the next century to deal with this time of trauma in which the northern kingdom had been exiled by the Assyrian superpower and the Babylonian force would soon execute divine judgment on the kingdom of the south.

9

PROPHETISM PRIOR
TO THE NATION'S EXILE:
THE SEVENTH-CENTURY PROPHETS

During the seventh century B.C., prophetic activity was restricted to the southern kingdom of Judah since the tribes of the north had been taken into exile. But what happened to these northern tribes, the bulk of whom were carried into Assyria by Sennacherib in 722 B.C.?

A great deal of speculation has gone into the question of the eventual fate of the northern tribes. Scripture indicates that the king of Assyria imported foreign peoples into the land of Samaria, where they intermarried with the remnant of Jews living in the area (2 Kings 17:24–33). But little or nothing is known about the Jews taken into Assyria.[1] British Israelitism speculates that they ended up in England

1. Says Malamat, "Exile," 1035: "Notwithstanding the manifold legends fabricated about the exile of the so-called 'Ten Lost Tribes,' there is no certain information about the fate of the Israelite exiles in Mesopotamia during the Assyrian Empire or at a later period. Only a few extant allusions in the Bible and in epigraphic sources testify to their existence. Of the latter sources, the onomastic evidence from Mesopotamia contained in Assyrian documents dated to the end of the eighth and to the seventh centuries is of particular significance, since it presents names which are known from the Bible to be Israelite." But Malamat himself indicates the limitations associated with the criterion of names: "However, with the exception of personal names composed of the Israelite theophoric element *yau* (*Yhwh*), it is not always certain that the reference is to Israelite exiles, since these names are common Northwest Semitic ones and may also designate either Phoenicians or Arameans." The same caution is registered by Oded in a detailed study of mass deportations of the Neo-Assyrian Empire: "The use of the onomastic criterion in any research into deportations and

and bases its claim partly on spurious linguistic grounds. Since Hebrew *berit* means "covenant" and *ish* means "man," it is concluded that the word *British* must be a code word for "(Israelite) men of the covenant."[2] The supposed linguistic connection has no foundation in fact, as seen in the varied use of the *-ish* ending in the English language: Turkish, Polish, pinkish, finish, selfish. Various other theories locate the ten lost tribes in Africa, India, China, Persia, Kurdistan, and the United States.[3] But in a very real sense, it can be said that these ten tribes essentially "disappeared from the stage of history."[4]

If history lost contact with the ten tribes of the north, how then are the prophecies about the reunion of Judah and Israel to be understood? Does not Hosea predict a day in which the Israelites of the northern kingdom will live for many days without king or prince and

communities of deportees is also fraught with difficulties which necessitate a cautious approach and an awareness of the limitations of this method. . . . It is not always possible to determine a person's extraction from his name, since there are many commonly shared elements in the stock of names of the Semitic peoples" (*Mass Deportations and Deportees*, 12). Malamat further comments: "The striking of roots in Mesopotamian society by a large part of the descendants of the Israelite exiles resulted in their eventual absorption into the foreign milieu" ("Exile," 1036). He qualifies this conclusion by noting that part of the Israelite community "undoubtedly preserved its distinct national character and maintained connections with the homeland (2 Kings 17:28), later merging with the Judean exile." He further affirms that the return to Zion "apparently" included remnants of the ten tribes, as alluded to in Ezek. 37:16–22; Ezra 2:2; Neh. 7:7. The texts cited by Malamat do not, however, provide adequate proof of a continued identity of the ten tribes of the northern kingdom.

2. Silverman, "British Israelites," 1382. Silverman notes that Anglo-Israelism's first manifesto was issued by the Puritan member of Parliament John Sadler, author of *Rights of the Kingdom* (1649). He also calls attention to a best-selling book by Edward Hine entitled *Forty-seven Identifications of the British Nation with the Lost Ten Tribes of Israel* (1871).

3. Rabinowitz, "Ten Lost Tribes," 1006. Rabinowitz cites a case in which a traveler to South America in 1644 reported that he found Indians who greeted him by reciting the Shema.

4. Ibid., 1003. This conclusion finds partial confirmation in that the term *Jew*, which is generally taken to be inclusive of all the tribes of Israel, actually has its root in the term *Judahite*, alluding to the tribe of Judah. Wherever the word *Jew* appears in the English Bible, whether Old Testament or New Testament, it always translates the word *Judahite*. Descendants of the tribe of Levi might retain their identity because of their role as priests in Jerusalem. Some remnants of the tribe of Benjamin may maintain their identity because of the territorial connection with Judah. But virtually nothing is known of the remaining ten tribes of the north.

that they will then "return and seek the Covenant LORD" (Hos. 3:4–5 NIV)? Does not Jeremiah speak of a new covenant that will be made with the "house of Israel" and the "house of Judah" (Jer. 31:31)? Does not Ezekiel anticipate the day in which the two nations of Israel and Judah will be reunited under a single king (Ezek. 37:15–23)?

The fulfillment of these prophecies might be understood in two ways. It could be proposed on the one hand that although men may have lost track of the ten lost tribes, God has not lost them. So the day will come in which he shall sovereignly recover them.

But a second less speculative and more exegetical understanding of these passages gives fuller place to these prophecies anticipating a day of fulfillment in which prophetic images will pass beyond the shadowy stage of old covenant representations and enter into the realities of new covenant consummations. In this context, it is not simply the gathering of literal, physical descendants of each of the twelve tribes of Israel back to the land of the Bible that fulfills these prophecies. Rather, as Paul specifically explains, this prophecy finds its fulfillment in the present age, as the Lord calls people to salvation in Christ "not only from the Jews but also from the Gentiles" and so fulfills the prediction of Hosea (Rom. 9:24–26 NIV). While the words of Hosea anticipated the regathering of the dispersed ten tribes of the northern kingdom in accordance with the shadowy figures of the old covenant, they consummatively encompass the inflowing of people from all the nations of the world, including Jews as well as Gentiles. When the tribes of the north were banished from their homeland into the wide world of the Gentiles, they themselves became in effect Gentiles, "not my people." As a consequence, all who are gathered into Christ are identified as the Israel of God, whatever their ethnic background (Ezek. 37:24–28; Jer. 31:33; see also Heb. 10:15–18; Gal. 6:16).[5]

In terms of the ongoing prophetic ministry in Judah beyond the exile of the northern kingdom, the literary prophets of the seventh century B.C. may be identified as Nahum, Habakkuk, Zephaniah, and Jeremiah. Each in his own way interacts with the reality of actual exile that had already occurred for one portion of God's covenant people,

5. See Robertson, *Israel of God*, 38–46.

and the imminent exile awaiting the remaining portion. Consider the highlights of their message in the context of the nation's exile and restoration.

I. Nahum

The mighty world power of Assyria with its capitol city of Nineveh carried into exile a significant portion of the population of the northern kingdom of Israel in the previous century. How would the sovereign Lord respond to the excessive brutality of Assyria in its treatment of his own people, despite this nation's having been the Lord's appointed instrument of judgment? Nahum focuses his message exclusively on the Lord's coming work of destroying Assyria's capitol city of Nineveh. Throughout the three chapters of his prophecy, he drums the theme: Nineveh shall fall.

Since extrabiblical evidence indicates that Nineveh fell in 612 B.C., it may be assumed that Nahum prophesied before that date.[6] Still further, Nahum alludes to the collapse of the Egyptian capitol No-ammon (i.e., Thebes) in 664 B.C. as a way of taunting self-assured Assyria (3:8). Does Nineveh actually think its defenses are stronger than this ancient Egyptian fortification, which safely stood five hundred miles upstream at the convergence of the Blue and White Niles, flanked on either side by strong allies? Has Assyria forgotten that this ancient stronghold fell before its own advancing army? Is Nineveh so audacious as to think that it cannot fall?

The past fall of No-ammon and the future fall of Nineveh bracket the date for Nahum's composition.[7] Nahum's references suggest that the Assyrian capitol was still strong at the time of his prophecy, which implies that the book was written some years prior to the fall of Nineveh. In the face of a mighty world conqueror that has already devas-

6. See Wiseman, *Chronicles of the Chaldaean Kings*, 16–17.

7. On the dates of the fall of No-ammon and the conquest of Nineveh, see Bright, *History of Israel*, 311, 316; and Young, *Introduction to the Old Testament*, 270. For support of an earlier time within the period 644–612 B.C., see Roberts, *Nahum, Habakkuk, and Zephaniah*, 38–39.

tated the northern kingdom of Israel, Nahum dares to declare his prophetic message.

A note of triumphant exultation concludes the first chapter of the book: "How beautiful on the mountains are the feet of him who brings good tidings, who publishes peace" (1:15). It might be assumed that the good tidings to which Nahum refers anticipate the release of the captives of the northern kingdom from the oppressions of Assyria. But Nahum stops short of that desirable point. His good tidings center on nothing more and nothing less than the destruction of the wicked king of Assyria and his empire. The reason for rejoicing on the part of the people of God is the devastation of this brutal enemy.

Isaiah had earlier used these identical words to anticipate the future salvation for God's people. The beautiful feet on the mountains in Isaiah's vision belong not to those who declare the defeat of enemies, but to those who proclaim peace, announcing that Israel's God reigns (Isa. 52:7). It is appropriate that the same phrasing should introduce these diverse messages in Isaiah and Nahum. These two elements, the destruction of God's enemies and the salvation of God's people, must be combined if the kingdom of God is to be actually realized on earth. God's righteousness must be established, and his enemies must be overthrown. Apart from the defeat of God's enemies, no genuinely good news can be announced to God's people.

Appearing in a new covenant context, these joined prophecies of Nahum and Isaiah anticipate the worldwide proclamation of the gospel of Jesus the Christ. Climactically it may be said of those who bring the message of Christ's salvation to Jews and Gentiles: "How beautiful are the feet of those who bring good news of good things" (Rom. 10:15 NASB). The good news of the gospel contains the message that salvation has come for God's people. But it also underscores the fact that the "principalities and powers" under Satan's control have been despoiled by Christ on his cross (Col. 2:14–15). All the wickedness embodied in the brutal king of Nineveh finds its consummate expression in the powers of Satan that oppose the establishment of God's kingdom of righteousness and grace. But the cross of Christ dispelled these powers and openly displayed them as defeated.

259

II. Habakkuk

The book of Habakkuk is unique in that the reader is privileged to observe the prophet himself grow out of an attitude of rigorous complaint against God into a spirit of total submission.[8] He begins with an acrid tone of complaint: "How long?" (1:2). He challenges the consistency of the Lord's actions in light of his holy nature (1:12–13). He prepares to counter the Lord's rebuke with his own rebuttal (2:1). But in the end, he gives expression to the most beautiful spirit of submission found anywhere in scripture:

> Though the fig tree
>> does not bud
> and there are no grapes
>> on the vines,
> though the olive crop
>> fails
> and the fields
>> produce no food,
> though there are no sheep in the pen
>> and no cattle in the stalls,
> Yet I will rejoice
>> in the Covenant LORD,
> I will be joyful
>> in God my Savior. (3:17–18 NIV)

What brought about this radical change in the spirit of the prophet? The biblical-theological setting of the book explains the change.

The opening verses of Habakkuk provide no specific data regarding the book's historical setting. But the reference to the Kasdim or Chaldeans clearly places the ministry of this prophetic servant in the latter part of the seventh century B.C. (1:6).[9] Apparently at the time of

8. Roberts, *Nahum, Habakkuk, and Zephaniah*, 81, characterizes Habakkuk as being "unlike the typical prophetic book" in that the oracles appear as a "coherent, sequentially developed argument that extends through the whole book."

9. Some effort is made to identify the Kasdim with a people other than the Babylonians, but with little success. For other options, see Robertson, *Nahum, Habakkuk, and Zephaniah*, 34.

Habakkuk's prophecy Babylon had not yet reached its zenith of power, since the prophet refers to the Lord's "raising up" this fierce nation (1:6).

Living after the sobering experience of the northern kingdom's exile did not have much of a salutary effect on the moral behavior of God's covenant people in the southern kingdom of Judah. In dialogue with the Almighty, Habakkuk complains over the uncorrected misbehavior of God's own covenant people.[10] How long must he cry for help without receiving any response (1:2)? Violence is on every hand, and the torah is paralyzed (1:3–4). By this reference to the inability of the torah to function, the prophet makes it clear that he is dealing with the rampant sinfulness of God's own people.

It would not seem likely that this suffering of injustice without relief by the people of Israel would characterize the days of good King Josiah's righteous reign. The troubles that Habakkuk describes fit much better in the days of Josiah's son Jehoiakim, somewhere between the death of Josiah in 609 B.C. and the establishment of Babylon's dominance over Syria-Palestine at the battle of Carchemish in 605 B.C.

When the Lord responds to the prophet's complaint by announcing the coming devastation of Judah at the hands of the brutal Babylonians, it is quite a bit more than Habakkuk can comprehend. The Lord has given him far more than he had asked. He wanted only the correction of wrongdoing within the community of God's people. But now he learns that the inconceivable will come to pass. Judah and Jerusalem, like Israel and Samaria, will go into exile (1:5–11).

Now the prophet has a more serious problem. The Covenant LORD is the holy one, the rock who can do no wrong. But how can he remain silent when the wicked swallow up those more righteous than themselves (1:13)? Granted, the sinfulness of his own people is great, as he himself had argued. But will the Almighty allow an even more

---

10. This daring dialogue with the Almighty stands out as a distinctive aspect of Habakkuk's prophetic role. Baker describes Habakkuk as a prophet who was "calling God to account when his actions did not seem to correspond to those demanded by the covenant." He underscores this prophet's distinctiveness by contrasting his actions with the function of prophets in general: "The situation of a prophet was precarious enough when he confronted his people, but it is a very rare individual who will put himself completely on the line by confronting his God" (*Nahum, Habakkuk, and Zephaniah*, 43).

wicked nation to be his instrument for devastating his own people? Having boldly challenged the plans and purposes of the Almighty, Habakkuk steels himself for the rebuff that he is sure will come. Feisty fellow that he is, the prophet prepares to answer back in response to the Lord's rebuke (2:1).[11]

The Lord's next word catches the prophet totally off guard. The message is so significant that it must be chiseled on stone tablets like the Ten Commandments (2:2). It must be written so plainly that a person running may read it. This revelatory message will endure until the end and will not prove false (2:3). So what is this significant message?[12]

"The justified-by-faith shall live by his steadfast trust" (2:4).[13] Those who have been justified by their trust in the God of the covenant *shall live.* They shall survive God's judgments that bring about the collapse of one nation after another. Nations will crumble. God's own people will experience the severest chastening. After the Babylonians have fulfilled their divine commission, they in turn will undergo their own devastation by the hand of the Lord. Yet throughout this whole period of the shaking of empires, a word of hope rises above the rubble. The person who has been declared just by his trust in God alone shall continue to live through his steadfast trust. As a member of the faithful remnant who shall witness these cataclysmic events for himself, the prophet must continue to trust in the Lord through it all. The Lord will maintain his presence in his holy temple even in a time of the breaking up of nations. So all the earth must keep reverential silence before him (2:20).

The redemptive-historical problem confronted by Habakkuk anticipates the theological challenge faced by the apostle Paul and expressed in the book of Romans. Has God cast off his people? Because

11. The NIV's "what answer I am to give to this complaint" is too mild a rendering of the prophet's words. Habakkuk is actually saying that he is already preparing to answer back to the Almighty before his rebuke comes.

12. Roberts, *Nahum, Habakkuk, and Zephaniah,* 81, though providing an excellent summary of the progression in the argument of the book, fails to identify the key message of the prophet with the critical words of Hab. 2:4. He looks instead to the vision-theophany in Hab. 3.

13. For a fuller analysis of this crucial phrase in both its old covenant and new covenant contexts, see Robertson, *Nahum, Habakkuk, and Zephaniah,* 174–82.

in their unbelief they rejected their messiah, have they now been rejected by the Lord altogether (Rom. 11:1)? Habakkuk had asked the question centuries earlier. By delivering his people into the hands of the ruthless Babylonians, had God abandoned them altogether? No, for "the justified-by-faith *shall live*" (Hab. 2:4). Those who trusted him will survive. The apostle Paul faced essentially the same threat to the continuance of God's ancient people. The nation of Israel had rejected the Christ of God that had been sent to them. Had God in response rejected his people? Had he this time cast them off altogether? No, for once more: "The justified-by-faith shall live" (Rom. 11:1–2; 1:17). Paul himself is a living testimony to the fact that there remains a remnant according to the election of grace. This remnant shall survive by faith. They shall emerge with the vigors of new life in Christ as they continue to rely on him by faith alone.

Even today there remains a remnant of believing people according to the election of grace. Since his people are identified specifically as a people of faith, Jew and Gentile alike are included among those who live despite the severity of the Lord's continuing judgments. This gospel compelled Paul to go to the ends of the earth with the message that manifests the power of God unto salvation to the Jew first, but also to the Gentile. It is the same gospel that compels believers to go with the gospel today and to keep going until the Lord returns in glory.[14]

III. Zephaniah

Zephaniah alone among this first triad of seventh-century prophets specifically locates his ministry at a particular point in Israel's history. He indicates that he prophesied "during the reign of King Josiah son of Amon of Judah" (1:1), which locates his ministry between 640 and 609 B.C. That he addresses an oracle specifically to the king-

14. Roberts, *Nahum, Habakkuk, and Zephaniah*, 85, properly relates the overall message of Habakkuk to the experience of the Christian today: "The Christian lives after God's victory over evil in Jesus' death and resurrection but prior to his final victory at Jesus' second coming and the general resurrection. Thus it is no accident that Hab. 2:4 has become a key text in describing the Christian's eschatological lifestyle."

dom of Assyria furthermore indicates that his message came before the fall of Nineveh in 612 B.C. (2:13–15).

The other critical event in the days of Josiah's reign is the discovery of the lawbook in 622 B.C. This recovery of the covenant lawbook led to a thoroughgoing reform of the nation (2 Kings 22:1–13). If anything would save the nation of Judah from the disaster of exile that had come to the kingdom of the north, it was this reform according to the law of the Mosaic covenant.

Did Zephaniah compose his message before or after this last great reform movement in Judah's history? The close parallelism of expression between Zephaniah and Deuteronomy suggests that Zephaniah shaped his message on the basis of the newly discovered lawbook.[15] It hardly seems likely that Zephaniah would have anticipated this discovery by many phrases identical to the language of Deuteronomy. But it appears quite feasible that Zephaniah would have had a special role as prophet appointed by the Lord for the purpose of supporting the radical reforms of young King Josiah. Zephaniah thus based his message on the law of the Lord as it had been revealed to Moses and rediscovered by Josiah.[16]

Central to Zephaniah's prophecy is his announcement concerning the coming Day of the Lord. A century earlier, Amos had referred to the Day of the Lord in a way that indicated that the concept had been around for some time. Amos's contemporaries were longing for the Day of the Lord because they viewed it exclusively as a time of salvation and light. But he informed them that the coming day would bring darkness, not light, and judgment rather than salvation (Amos 5:18–20).

15. For illustrations of the parallels, see Robertson, *Nahum, Habakkuk, and Zephaniah*, 254–55.

16. There seems to be no good reason to attribute these parallels with the book of Deuteronomy to a later editor. Why should not the prophet who is himself on the scene be viewed as the natural person to make concrete application of the rediscovered lawbook to his contemporaries? Despite many helpful insights, Achtemeier appears inconsistent in evaluating the genuineness of the text. On the one hand, she notes "an organic wholeness about the book that argues against its overall arrangement by an editorial hand." But then she concludes that Zeph. 3:18–20 "represent[s] later Deuteronomic updatings of the work" (*Nahum–Malachi*, 62).

Distinctive to Zephaniah's development of the theology of the Day of the Lord is the connection made between this climactic day and God's ancient covenants. In his opening chapter, Zephaniah alludes to three successive covenants in Israel's history: the covenant with Noah, the covenant with Abraham, and the covenant with Moses. In each case, the language of covenantal curse anticipates the divine judgment of the future. Using the language associated with Noah's covenant, God declares that he will sweep away everything on the face of the earth, including men, animals, birds, and fish (Zeph. 1:2–3; Gen. 6:7). Employing imagery that compares closely with the description of the covenant-making ceremony in Abraham's day, the prophet indicates that the Lord has prepared a sacrifice in the form of victims who must undergo his judgment, having consecrated his guests for the coming banquet (Zeph. 1:7; Gen. 15:9–11). Echoing the circumstances surrounding the inauguration of the Mosaic covenant at Sinai, Zephaniah declares that the coming day of judgment will be a day of darkness and thick darkness, of cloud and thick cloud, of trumpet and battle cry (Zeph. 1:15–16; Exod. 20:21). These references center on the coming Day of the Lord that is declared by the prophet to be "near" (Zeph. 1:7). God's awesome presence that threatened judgment at the time of covenant inauguration in the past now anticipates the coming judgment of the great and awesome Day of the Lord. As the northern kingdom was swept away because of its persistence in violating covenantal stipulations, so the remaining kingdom of the south can expect an even more awesome devastation. Exile for the southern kingdom of Judah is now related directly to the coming day, the day in which the Covenant LORD will enforce all the sworn curses of the covenantal bond.

So in Zephaniah the Day of the Lord may be equated with the day of covenantal inauguration or enforcement. The day of the covenant is in a unique sense the "Lord's day," the day in which the Lord displays his sovereignty among the people of this world through the establishment and enforcement of his covenant. The Day of the Lord is that day in which God displays his lordship by sovereignly establishing or enforcing his covenantal bond.

265

No more terrifying picture of God's judgment can be found than that depicted in the first chapter of Zephaniah's prophecy: "On the day of the Covenant LORD's wrath . . . the whole world will be consumed, for he will make a sudden end of all who live in the earth" (1:18 NIV). But the picture of God's love also reaches a peak in the words of this prophet. It may appropriately be said that the Old Testament version of John 3:16 finds expression in the final chapter of Zephaniah, where the prophet declares: "The Covenant LORD your God . . . will take great delight in you, he will be quiet in his love, he will rejoice over you with singing" (Zeph. 3:17).[17] Who could imagine such a thing! The almighty God sinks into quiet contemplation over his love for his people. The Lord himself breaks out into singing because of his joy over those who are his own.

In terms of exile and restoration, Zephaniah goes well beyond the deportation of the people of Judah in his anticipations of the coming day of God's judgment. Now it is the whole world and all its inhabitants that will be swept away in the divine judgment. As in the case of Noah's flood, all living creatures will perish. But now in this coming cataclysmic judgment of the cosmos, even the "fish of the sea" will perish (1:3).

In similar fashion, restoration for Zephaniah goes well beyond the return of a remnant of Judah. Even the lips of foreign peoples will be purified, so that they call on the Lord for salvation (3:9). Beyond the rivers of Cush, deep in the heart of Africa, the Lord's worshipers will bring him their offerings (3:10).[18] At the same time, God's purifying work in relation to Jerusalem his holy hill will go forward (3:11, 14). He will gather those who have been scattered and bring them home from every land where they have been put to shame (3:19–20). Restoration to the land clearly plays a significant role in Zephaniah's anticipation of the future, but the dimensions of this restoration have been extended to embrace all humanity.

17. The intransitive character of the verb *harash* favors "be quiet" rather than NIV's "quiet you." Cf. Robertson, *Nahum, Habakkuk, and Zephaniah*, 340.

18. While it is possible to identify these worshipers beyond the rivers of Cush as returning Israelites, the context suggests instead that it is peoples of foreign nations who have become the Lord's people.

Interestingly, Zephaniah's prophecy contains very little in terms of expectation regarding a coming messianic king. Instead, it is God himself who will be the "mighty hero" who saves his people (3:17). Possibly disappointment over the kings who had ruled in Judah led this prophet to revert to the vision of the premonarchial days in which God himself was king and savior among his people. In one sense, this vision was correct, for only God himself could function as the savior of this sinful, fallen community.

IV. Jeremiah

Jeremiah is appropriately described as "a man of unflinching courage who never, so far as we know, tempered the word that his God had given him by the omission of so much as a syllable."[19] His courage, however, cannot be attributed to natural endowments, as the prophet himself readily acknowledges (1:6). Instead, Jeremiah was a man "driven by his calling to exhibit a strength that was not by nature his."[20] His fidelity to the word of the Lord is even more remarkable in view of the varied crises that he faced during his long career as prophet in Israel.

In the opening verses of his book, Jeremiah dates his divine call to the thirteenth year of King Josiah, or 627 B.C. (1:2).[21] He continued

19. Bright, *Jeremiah*, ci.
20. Ibid.
21. No compelling reason exists to question this opening statement concerning the time of Jeremiah's call, and yet this matter is generally regarded as one of the major controversial issues related to the book. Perdue, "Jeremiah in Modern Research," 1, lists the dating of Jeremiah's call among the key matters in current discussion. Yet he asserts that if a theological approach is taken to the question, the conclusion reached regarding this matter has little significance (4). Hyatt, "Jeremiah and Deuteronomy," 114, asserts that Jeremiah did not begin his prophetic work until about a decade after Josiah's reforms of 621 B.C. He concludes that the prophet actually opposed the reforms promoted by the Deuteronomistic theology. However, he asserts that the book as it now appears underwent major Deuteronomistic editing so that it looks as though Jeremiah favored the reforming movement. In his concluding remarks concerning the current state of discussions about the book of Jeremiah, Perdue observes: "The major frustration, of course, is the recognition that no dominant consensus has emerged in regard to any of the issues discussed" (31).

his ministry to a time beyond the exile of the southern kingdom, which occurred in 587 B.C. Even after being forced into Egypt by the still-rebellious Jewish leadership, he continued his prophetic ministry during those dark days of exile from his homeland (43:8–44:30). For over forty years Jeremiah lived with the burden of declaring the word of the Lord to a resistant people.

Jeremiah is distinctive among the prophetic books for the variety of material that his prophecies contain. Poetic sayings, biographical prose, and prose discourses are the three major types of literature in the book.[22] Especially noteworthy is the extent of biographical material contained in his prophecies. These expanded biographical notations are by no means extraneous to the message that the prophet brings to the people from the Lord.[23] As in the experience of many other prophets, Jeremiah's life embodies his message. Isaiah's sons were given to him as prophetic signs (Isa. 8:18). The death of Ezekiel's wife provided the opportunity for a large object lesson for the people of his day (Ezek. 24:15–18). Hosea's marriage to an adulterous woman vivified the unfaithfulness of Israel (Hos. 3). Jonah's descent into and deliverance from the belly of the great fish anticipated the only sign that Jesus would promise to his contemporaries (Matt. 12:40). In similar fashion, the opposition, sufferings, and rejection of God's prophet Jeremiah embodies the message concerning the servant of the Lord who suffers in connection with the redemption of his people.

As with Hosea, Amos, and Isaiah, the principal message of the prophet finds its summation at the time of his call to the prophetic office. In the case of Jeremiah, the extended report of his call includes *one key exhortation, two key visions,* and *six key words.*

The *single key exhortation* comes first. The Lord indicates that Jeremiah was appointed from the womb to be a "prophet to the

22. Bright, *Jeremiah,* lx. Bright notes the role of Bernhard Duhm in initiating this analysis of the material in Jeremiah. For an expanded treatment of the subject, see Seitz, *Theology in Conflict,* 1 n. 1.

23. The prose materials of the book are often represented as containing a theology contrary to the theology of the poetic sections and are thus denied to Jeremiah. See the comments regarding the conclusions of Duhm and Mowinckel by Hobbs, "Composition and Structure," 179.

nations" (Jer. 1:5, 10).[24] As a consequence, he must not fear, but must go to everyone the Lord sends him and speak whatever the Lord commands (1:7). According to the pattern of prophetism established through Moses, the Lord will put his words directly into the mouth of Jeremiah (1:9; see also Deut. 18:18).[25] The single key admonition for Jeremiah thus focuses on his inescapable responsibility to declare God's word not only to Israel, but as it affects the course of nations.

The *two key visions* connected with Jeremiah's call are the branch of an almond tree and the boiling cauldron tilting from the north (Jer. 1:11, 13). Both initiating visions encapsulate points of emphasis running throughout the book. The boiling cauldron tilting from the north is immediately linked to the next verse by the repeated phrase *from the north*. Disaster will be poured out on all people living in the land, anticipating the exile that will ultimately come through the northern nation of Babylon (1:14).[26] Common vocabulary links the allusion to the early-blooming almond tree (*shaqed*) to the Lord's watching (*shoqed*) to see

---

24. Calvin, *Jeremiah and the Lamentations*, 37, notes that Jeremiah's prophecies embraced all the nations who were "nigh and known to the Jews."

25. Says Thompson, *Jeremiah*, 148: "Probably no other account of a prophetic call in the OT resembles Deut. 18:18 so closely."

26. Extensive discussion surrounds the identity of this enemy from the north. Perdue, "Jeremiah in Modern Research," 6–10, identifies three views: (1) historical, where the enemy is either Scythian or Babylonian, (2) mythological-eschatological, and (3) fluid, in which the enemy first appears as historical in the genuine passages from Jeremiah, but then develops a transhistorical, apocalyptic character in the later sections of the book. This third alternative represents the view of Childs, "Enemy from the North." Childs (161) develops a neat progression from the preexilic (in which the enemy from the north remains on the plane of human history) to the early exilic (in which the enemy takes on superhuman characteristics described in language related to the chaos myth) to the late exilic and postexilic (in which the enemy invariably appears with the "great shaking" in a merging of these two traditions). This refined progression can be achieved by Childs only through relegating cosmic-shaking passages such as Isa. 13–14, Jer. 50–51 (but not 46–49), and Joel 2–3 to exilic or postexilic times. He also must assume that references to shaking the cosmos envision an event that is mythical in character rather than occurring in the actual realities of time and space. A saner though less spectacular analysis of the "enemy from the north" is found in Bright, *Jeremiah*, 7, who notes that the identity of the foe is "left vague" in the first chapter of the book, but later clearly identified with the Babylonians. A cataclysmic and eschatological element does seem to be an aspect of the prophetic perspective on this enemy from the north.

that his word is fulfilled (1:11–12).[27] As the Palestinian farmer diligently watches for the blossoming of the almond tree as the first sign of spring, so the Lord focuses his attention on his word as it goes forth. Consequently in the book of Jeremiah, attention is drawn repeatedly to the word of God that has been uttered, even to the point that the Lord's word appears to take on an entity in itself. It is a living word that has the inherent power to stand down kings and governors.[28]

The *six key words* grouped together in Jeremiah's call appear as six consecutive infinitives, four with negative and two with positive connotations: "to uproot and tear down, to destroy and overthrow, to build and plant" (1:10 NIV). While the significance of these terms in the message of Jeremiah is often recognized, their regular appearance at critical moments throughout the book is not generally noted.[29] Their prominent role at seven key points makes them deserving of more extensive consideration.

A. Jeremiah 1: the call of the prophet

The role of these six words in describing the commission of the prophet at the time of his call indicates their significance. By his prophetic word through Jeremiah, God will uproot and tear down, destroy and overthrow, build and plant nations and kingdoms. These specific words define the call and the commission of the prophet.

B. Jeremiah 11–12: God's covenant for Israel and the nations

A critical point in the ministry of Jeremiah occurred with the discovery of the lawbook in the days of Josiah, which gave strong impetus to the reform movement of the young king (2 Kings 22:8–23:3). A major part of the prophet's role was the concrete application of the covenantal lawbook to the lives of the people.

---

27. "There is no doubt that . . . the word association in the two verses is that of a true etymology, not of a folk etymology or simple word-play" (Holladay, *Jeremiah*, 1.37).

28. The permeating character of the concept of the "word" in Jeremiah is seen in the fact that the root occurs over three hundred times in the book.

29. For a bibliography of discussions on the role of these key words in Jeremiah, see Hermann, "Overcoming the Israelite Crisis," 301 n. 4.

In Jeremiah 11–12, the prophet receives the admonition to "listen to the terms of this covenant and tell them to the people of Judah" (11:2 NIV). The prophet then must pronounce the covenantal curses on all who will not abide by the terms of the covenant (11:3). Reference is twice made to the "planting" of Israel. But despite the Lord's having planted them, he has now decreed disaster because of their disobedience (11:17). The prophet acknowledges that the Lord planted them and that they have taken root and borne fruit (12:2a). Yet though the Lord is always on their lips, he remains far from their hearts (12:2b). As a consequence, the Lord will forsake his house, abandon his inheritance, and give over his land to many foreign shepherds who will ruin his vineyard (12:7, 10).

At this point Jeremiah's negative key words come into play. The Lord will "uproot" both the house of Judah and the foreign nations that have abused his people (12:14). As he had "planted" them by bringing them into the land he had promised, so now he will "uproot" them for their covenantal unfaithfulness.[30] But this uprooting is here broadened to include foreign nations that have violated his laws. These key words spoken by Jeremiah as a "prophet to the nations" have the inherent force necessary to determine the course of nations in the future.

Yet the comprehensive scope of these key words embraces even more than the planting and subsequent uprooting of peoples and nations. After God has uprooted them, he "will again have compassion and will bring each of them back to his own inheritance and his own country" (12:15 NIV). Beyond the uprooting of his people and their oppressors, the Lord will "build" them up again. This amazing restoration extends even to the point of causing foreign nations to be "built" in the midst of God's people if these nations will "learn well the ways of my people" (12:16 NIV).[31]

30. The harshness of these words of judgment seems to exclude all hope for the future. But the pronouncement of judgment was the only thing that could give hope. Says Bright: "Precisely in that Jeremiah's was a message of judgment, it was a saving message. By ruthlessly demolishing false hope, by ceaselessly asserting that the tragedy was Yahweh's doing, his righteous judgment on the nation for its sin, Jeremiah as it were drew the national disaster within the framework of faith, and thus prevented it from destroying faith" (*Jeremiah*, cxiv).

31. The NIV obscures the connection with the key words of Jeremiah's call by rendering the word as "be established" rather than "be built."

If a person is tempted to relegate this remarkable anticipation of international incorporation into the people of God to later editors, it must be remembered that Jeremiah's initial call anticipated exactly this development. He is designated not merely as a prophet "to Israel," but as a prophet "to the nations." The key words of his original commission specifically state that he is appointed "over nations and kingdoms" not only to uproot and tear down, but to build and plant.

These key words thus frame Jeremiah's prophetic ministry in terms of disaster and deliverance, of exile and restoration, according to the terms of God's covenant. Israel and its neighbors will be driven from their homeland. But they also will be brought back to the land of their origins.

C. Jeremiah 18–19: Jeremiah's visits to the potter

Jeremiah 18 and Jeremiah 19 are generally joined by commentators, partially because both begin with a visit to the potter by the prophet.[32] In Jeremiah's first visit, the potter determines to reshape a lump of clay marred in the process of molding. From this practice of the potter, the prophet learns a lesson about the ways of the Lord. Having first determined to "uproot," "tear down," and "destroy" a nation for its sin, the Lord may alter his purpose for a nation if the people repent. Hope remains for a nation even as it faces the prospect of imminent divine judgment. On the other hand, if the Lord announces that he intends to "build" and "plant" a nation and if that nation does evil, the Lord will reconsider the good he had intended to do for it (18:1–10).

In his second visit to the potter, the prophet purchases a clay pot, summons the elders of the people, and smashes the pot in the Valley of Ben Hinnom as a symbol of the imminent devastation of the nation of Judah. Progression beyond the previous potter incident may be seen

32. Says Drinkard: "In several ways chaps. 18 through 20 are connected literarily. On the level of theme, the potter theme as the basis for the message of chap. 18 is closely related to the potter's decanter that serves as the thematic center of chap. 19. These two themes are both similar and contrastive. In chap. 18 the vessel is remade according to the potter's wishes. But in chap. 19 the vessel is destroyed. While still plastic, clay can easily be remolded and shaped; once fired it becomes fixed and brittle. It can no longer be reshaped as the potter might wish, but it can be destroyed at its owner's hand!" (in Craigie, Kelley, and Drinkard, *Jeremiah*, 240).

in that now the handiwork of the potter is past the point of recovery. It must be smashed and discarded as a symbol of the devastation of the nation of Judah and the city of Jerusalem (Jer. 19). Though Jeremiah's key words are not present in this second chapter, their influence from the previous chapter is quite clear.

The message of the key words in connection with Jeremiah's visits to the potter symbolically seals the fate of the nation. They have rejected God by refusing to obey his commands. Even when given a second chance, they have refused to repent and amend their ways. Devastation is inevitable.

These words from Jeremiah come to fullest realization according to the new covenant scriptures with the payoff to Judas for his betrayal of Jesus by the leaders of Israel (Matt. 27:9–10). Matthew specifically cites "the words of Jeremiah the prophet" (27:9). Yet the wording of the Old Testament quotation comes quite evidently from a prophecy of Zechariah rather than Jeremiah (Zech. 11:11–13).[33] In both Matthew and *Zechariah* but *not in Jeremiah*, a payment of thirty shekels is made for the dismissal of the shepherd appointed by the Lord over Israel. How then is the reference by Matthew to the words of *Jeremiah* to be explained?

A critical element in Matthew's narrative missing from Zechariah is found in these chapters of Jeremiah. With their "blood money" the priests purchase the "Field of Blood" (Matt. 27:6–8). Judas in great contrition declares, "I have betrayed *the blood of the innocent*" (27:4). Despite their unfeeling disclaimer, the leaders of Israel are the guilty ones who by arranging for the death of Jesus "filled this place with *the blood of the innocent*," which echoes the phrase found in the second potter passage of Jeremiah (Jer. 19:4c NIV). Matthew speaks of betraying the "blood of the innocent," and Jeremiah says that the kings

---

33. Commentators struggle over the relation of Jer. 18–19 to this quotation in Matthew. For a presentation of the options, see Hagner, *Matthew*, 2.814–15. The resolution of the problem lies in the principles of conflation methodology and contextual primacy as predominant aspects of New Testament quotations from the Old Testament. It is not unusual for the New Testament to merge two or more Old Testament passages into a single quotation. The context in both the Old Testament source and the New Testament quotation is far more determinative than a verbatim representation of wording.

and people of Judah have filled Jerusalem with the "blood of the innocent." They have eliminated the possibility of a new course of action
by the Lord in their behalf, as symbolically represented during Jeremiah's first visit to the potter (18:1–10). The "uprooting," "tearing
down," and "destroying" of a nation that will not repent of its rejection of the Lord finds its fulfillment in the judgment on the nation of
Judah for the rejection of their shepherd/messiah (18:7). The clay jar,
symbolizing for Jeremiah and the elders of Israel their nation and city,
must now be smashed in the Valley of Slaughter (Jer. 19:1, 6–7, 11;
see also Matt. 27:8–10). Though the blood money and the Field of
Blood in Matthew apply directly to the fate of Judas, the consequences
for his collaborators who paid the betraying blood money and pur-
chased the blood field must also be included. Once more the six key
words of Jeremiah's call play a critical role in his ministry to a rebellious people.

D. Jeremiah 24: the vision of two baskets of figs

Jeremiah faced a new circumstance with the exile of King
Jehoiachin of Judah in 597 B.C. The prophet is at a critical juncture in
his ministry. He must deal with the situation of a people who have
been divided by the judgment of the Lord. In the case of the exile of
the northern kingdom of Israel, the monarchy came to its end with the
exile of 722 B.C. But how is this new circumstance to be interpreted,
in which one Judean king has been deported to Babylon, while a
replacement king continues to reign in Jerusalem?[34] How does the Lord
view these two groups of people, one element suffering exile, and the
other remaining in the land and continuing with the God-ordained
worship practices of the temple? What does the future hold for those
Jews who were carried into exile along with King Jehoiachin? How
should their fate be compared with the expectation of those who had
been left in the land by the conquering Babylonians?

Once more the key words of Jeremiah's call come into play to
define the issue between these two groups. In a memorable vision, Jeremiah sees two baskets, one containing good figs, and the other con-

34. Seitz, *Theology in Conflict*, 4–5, 30, 100–101, makes a strong case for seeing
the exile of 597 B.C. as being far more significant than is generally realized.

taining figs so bad that they cannot be eaten (24:2). Since these two baskets of figs are being compared to the two separated groups of Israelites, it might be assumed that the bad figs represent the people who have experienced the chastening judgment of the exile, while the good figs stand for those left in the land. But contrary to what might be expected, those Israelites exiled to Babylon are identified with the basket of good figs, while those who remain in the land are the rotten figs (24:5, 8).

The application of the key words of Jeremiah's call to the exiles in Babylon accents the difference between these two groups. The Lord declares that with regard to King Jehoiachin and the exiles, he will "build" them up and not "overthrow" them; he will "plant" them and not "uproot" them (24:6b). He will cause them to return to their own land (24:6a). In stark contrast, King Zedekiah and those left in the land will be banished once and for all from the land given to their fathers (24:9–10). Those remaining in the land will experience the Lord's righteous judgment by expulsion.

The radical nature of this religious reorientation for the people must not be overlooked. By his gracious mercy, the Lord will "build" and "plant" those who appear to be the least deserving. That the exiled peoples prove to be the favored ones underscores the gracious character of the Lord's dealings. Jeremiah's famous temple sermon had exposed the folly of those who put their trust in the external orderings of the faith, even though the directives for worship had come from the Lord. "The temple of the LORD, the temple of the LORD, the temple of the LORD is this" was their empty chant (7:4). But now the truth expressed earlier by Jeremiah takes on an even more dramatic form. Not those who remain in the land, attached to the worship rituals of the Jerusalem temple, but those under the chastening judgment of exile—they are the ones in whom the future hope of Israel resides.[35]

But what is it that should make the future hope of the nation reside in the already-exiled community, of all people? Do they not stand under the obvious judgment of God by their presence in exile? The Lord's word to Jeremiah makes the basis for this differentiation plain: "I will

35. See Clements, *Jeremiah*, 145–49.

give them a heart to know me, that I am the Covenant LORD. They will be my people, and I will be their God, for they will return to me with all their heart" (24:7 NIV). The priority of the Lord's grace is altogether evident in this formulation of the prophet. It is not that these chastened exiles first return to the Lord and then are given a new heart, for they would have no need of the gift of a new heart if they had already returned. Instead, the Lord will show his initiating grace to these undeserving, chastened people in giving them the new heart that they so desperately need. Then as a consequence, they will turn to him.[36]

Once again, exile and restoration are developed in the context of the key words of Jeremiah's call, but this time the message goes a step further. Restoration will be accomplished by means of a new covenant, as the phraseology of Jeremiah clearly shows. The Lord will give them a heart to know/love him, and *they will be his people and he will be their God*. This phrase summarizes the essence of the covenant relationship from Genesis to Revelation. While the exact designation *new covenant* does not appear in this passage in connection with the restoration of the exiles, the concept is clearly central throughout. The term *new covenant* itself becomes most prominent in the next passage to make use of the key words of Jeremiah's call.

E. Jeremiah 31: the prophecy of the new covenant

The most significant message of Jeremiah is generally acknowledged to be his prophecy concerning the new covenant.[37] But the connection of Jeremiah 31 with the total message of the book as a consequence of its being bracketed by strong references to the key words of Jeremiah is not often appreciated.[38] This larger context of the new

36. Says Kidner, *Message of Jeremiah*, 93: "While men's thoughts would dwell on politics and patriotism and on the puzzling distribution of suffering, God speaks of having *sent* the exiles to Chaldea (5), and of *regard[ing them] as good* (5), not in view of their merits but of what the New Testament would call his grace—that is, of the good which he planned to do for them (6) and, above all, within them (7)" (emphasis original).

37. Bright, *Jeremiah*, 287, refers to the new covenant passage as "deservedly famous," as "the high point of [Jeremiah's] theology," and as "one of the profoundest and most moving passages in the entire Bible."

38. Because of this failure to see the integrated position of the new covenant prophecy in the whole book of Jeremiah, the genuineness of this prophecy is often

covenant prophecy of Jeremiah places this section in a framework that in seed form anticipates the rejuvenation not merely of Judah but of the entire fallen universe.

In future days, the Lord will "plant" the house of Israel and the house of Judah "with the [seed] of men and of animals" (31:27 NIV). As he had once "watched" over them to "uproot" and to "tear down," to "overthrow" and to "destroy," so in the coming days he will "watch" over them to "build" and to "plant" (31:28). These verses are literally permeated with phrasing taken from the key words of the call of Jeremiah. All six original verbs appear in one verse, along with a double use of the verb *watch*, reflecting the opening vision of the almond tree (1:11–12).

The judgment of exile is inevitable. The words of God's prophets to this effect will surely be fulfilled, because the Lord is "watching" over his word. But beyond uprooting will be replanting. That this "planting" involves the "seed of men and of animals" hints at the prospect of a new cosmic beginning. Not just Israel, but the world will take on a different form.

But what ongoing hope could a people have when God has so clearly announced his intention to drive a rebellious nation out of their land? If disobedience had ruined them once, what would prevent the recurrence of the same tragedy again?[39] Jeremiah explains that as all redemptive history was structured in the past by divinely initiated covenants of grace, so the future expectations of God's people will rest in the establishment of a new covenant with even fuller manifestations of grace (31:31–34).

Even as the nation totters on the brink of devastation, this new covenant provides a future hope for Israel and involves points of continuity with past covenantal dealings as well as points of radical newness.[40] The torah of the Lord shall be in effect; but now this law shall be inscribed

---

denied. But as Bright says: "As regards its authenticity, one can only say that it ought never to have been questioned" (ibid.).

39. Clements, *Jeremiah*, 190.

40. For a fuller discussion of the precise relationship of Jeremiah's new covenant with the covenants established prior to Jeremiah's time, see Robertson, *Christ of the Covenants*, 280–86.

on the hearts of God's people rather than on cold stone tablets. Sins shall be removed, but apart from the repetitious offering of sacrifices. Knowledge of the Lord shall be the essence of the new covenant relation, but no teachers shall be needed to inculcate this knowledge.

The ultimate fulfillment of the prophecy concerning restoration according to the provisions of this new covenant cannot be satisfied by a purely physical return of Jewish peoples to the geographical territory of Palestine, such as that which occurred in the last half of the twentieth century. That type of return was accomplished at the end of Jeremiah's specified seventy years. But the rejuvenation of the heart along with the restoration of the entire earth by the replanting of the seed of man and beast can alone fulfill the expectations of the new covenant prophecy (31:27, 33–34).

At the same time, this expectation of the new covenant in Jeremiah comes to expression in the only way in which it could be presented under the shadowy forms of the old covenant era. In accordance with Jeremiah's key words, the city of Jerusalem will be "built" for the Lord "from the Tower of Hananel to the Corner Gate" (31:38 NIV). Even the places corrupted previously by dead bodies will be "holy to the Covenant LORD" (31:40a–b). In this revived state, the city will never again be "uprooted" or "overthrown" (31:40c).

Despite the old covenant form in which this prophecy comes to expression, this new covenant breaks the bonds of the old covenant in the progression of redemptive history by accomplishing a vital union with God through the work of the Holy Spirit on the basis of the redemptive work of Jesus Christ (Luke 22:20; Heb. 8:7–13). From this perspective, the formative impact of the new covenant across the span of human history since the time of Jesus can be appreciated. It is not by the events occurring in a single geopolitical entity of the globe during one historical moment that the new covenant finds its fulfillment. All across the stage of human history this radically new commitment of the Lord in the new covenant has accomplished a restoration that has shaped and continues to shape the origins and destinies of the peoples and nations of the world.

F. Jeremiah 42: a word to the surviving remnant

Even after the devastation of Judah and Jerusalem by the Babylonians in 587 B.C., Jeremiah's key words concerning "uprooting" and "planting" of nations continue to shape the course of history. In Jeremiah 42, the remnant that survived the Babylonian devastations pleads with Jeremiah for guidance from the Lord. A renegade of royal blood named Ishmael had murdered Babylon's appointed governor of Judah along with a contingency of Babylonian soldiers (41:1–3). Should the remnant of Jews risk remaining in the land, or should they flee to Egypt to avoid the retributive wrath of the Babylonians?

Jeremiah returns with his response from the Lord ten days later. His answer is framed in the language that by now should have been familiar to the people: "If you stay in this land, I will 'build you up' and not 'tear you down'; I will 'plant you' and not 'uproot you'" (42:10). Once more the fate of the people is cast in the language of Jeremiah's original call. Even though this remnant that survived the Babylonian devastations could hardly be called a nation or kingdom, the words of this prophet to the nations still apply. The Lord himself will build them up and not tear them down, plant them and not uproot them.

Over forty years have passed since Jeremiah's original commission. Yet the same wording that shaped his call as a young man defines the message he brings just before he himself is forced by these rebellious people to leave the land and share in their self-imposed exile. Throughout this entire period, the most crucial moments of his ministry have found him echoing the same key words that ushered him into the office of prophet.

G. Jeremiah 45: Baruch and the "saga of the scroll"

The word of the Lord in Jeremiah 45 is directed to Jeremiah's scribe Baruch, but it refers back to one of the most significant moments recorded in the book of Jeremiah. This dramatic incident might be called the "saga of the scroll" (Jer. 36). In the fourth year of the reign of King Jehoiakim of Judah, the Lord directs Jeremiah to inscribe all his prophetic words since his initial call twenty-three years earlier. The date of this commission to record his prophecies was 605 B.C., which would have been the same year that the Babylonians defeated the combined forces of Egypt and a weakened Assyria at Carchemish. From this critical moment, Babylon rather than Assyria or Egypt would dominate the landscape of the land of the Bible until Judah was taken into exile in 587 B.C. The only remaining hope for Judah was a genuine nationwide repentance that might be honored by the Lord.

The public presentation of this collection of Jeremiah's prophetic sayings came as much as a year later than their inscription, at a time when Judah had been summoned to a national fast (36:6, 9).[41] Because Jeremiah was "restricted," apparently from entering the temple area, his scribe Baruch was commissioned with the task of publicly reading the 23-year-long record of Jeremiah's prophetic messages (36:5–6).

The initial response of officialdom to Jeremiah's prophecies might have been encouraging to Baruch. After he had finished the reading, the people "looked at each other in fear" and concluded that King Jehoiakim himself must hear these words (36:16 NIV). But knowing the propensities of the king, the officials instructed Baruch and Jeremiah to go into hiding.

The scroll now takes on a life of its own. It is placed in a special room until the king can be informed of its existence. It is then brought before the king and his attendants in the royal palace. Because it is winter, the king is warming himself before a blazing firepot. As each new section of the scroll is read, the king slices off several columns with his knife and casts them into the fire until the entire scroll is consumed. He then gives orders to have Baruch and Jeremiah arrested (36:26). But because the Lord has hidden them, they escape with their lives.

Very possibly in response to Baruch's despair as he anticipates the king's negative reaction to Jeremiah's recorded prophecy, the prophetic word of the Lord comes specifically for Baruch. In his distress the scribe had exclaimed, "Woe to me! The Covenant LORD has added sorrow to my pain; I am worn out with groaning and find no rest" (45:3 NIV). Now the key words of Jeremiah's call are introduced once more. To Baruch the Lord says: "I will 'overthrow' what I have 'built' and 'uproot' what I have 'planted' throughout the land" (45:4). The Lord is in process

41. Bright, *Jeremiah*, ci, says that the public reading of this scroll of the prophecies of Jeremiah occurred "perhaps more than a year later."

of uprooting the nation that he himself has built up for the previous fifteen hundred years since the time of Abraham. Cataclysmic events leading to the termination of national existence for the people of God are in process. By the defeat of the combined forces of Egypt and Assyria at Carchemish, Babylon now has unimpeded access to the holy city of Jerusalem. Within twenty years the nation of Judah will no longer exist.

Is now the time for Baruch to seek "great things" for himself? The Lord admonishes, "Seek them not" (45:5a). Not enough is known about Baruch to determine the exact nature of the things he might have been seeking.[42] As a well-educated person with some position of prominence as Jeremiah's scribe, it would have been quite natural for him to expect some public recognition for his faithful service to the prophet. Perhaps he even entertained some hope that when he delivered the full message of Jeremiah to the people, they would be moved to repentance, and the nation would be saved. Or perhaps he was a more modest man, simply longing for some semblance of peace and quiet in contrast with his life as fugitive from the king.

In response to his complaint, the Lord admonishes Baruch to be content with escaping with his life (45:5). When entire nations are being dislodged all around him, what more might he expect? God's word of planting and uprooting, of building and tearing down has gone out to the nations. As a lone individual Baruch should not expect more than the survival that the Lord has promised.

H. Conclusion

From beginning to end, the critical moments in the book of Jeremiah focus on the key words that originally described his call and his commission. The entirety of the book finds a unity among its diverse elements through the employment of these six key words. Because these summarizing words embody the idea of exile and restoration for the nations, these same ideas must be seen as focal in the message of the book.[43]

42. See ibid., 185, for insightful suggestions regarding the possible aspirations of Baruch.

43. Some might propose that this structural unity was imposed on the diverse materials of the book of Jeremiah by a later editor. But it seems more appropriate to regard

In summary, all the seventh-century preexilic prophets in Judah carried out their ministries under the oppressive shadow of international superpowers. Knowing what had happened to Israel's northern kingdom, they faced the coming realities of inevitable devastation. In this context, they set their hopes more in the person of God himself than in the prospect of a coming messiah. He alone was capable of bringing these mighty empires to their knees. He alone could preserve a faithful remnant through the coming calamities. He alone could plant a new spirit in the hearts of the people, bring them back to their land, and reestablish a king and a kingdom that would reflect the righteousness of the Lord.

---

this unifying thread as the product of the prophet himself. He is the one who received so forcefully the initial call to the prophetic office in these terms. He is the one who personally went through all these various experiences. He is the one who dictated to his scribe Baruch what is often identified with the bulk of the first twenty chapters of the book. Jeremiah himself is the most natural person to have composed the record of his prophecies, using the same key words of his initial call to establish a unified perspective on his total ministry.

10

PROPHETISM DURING THE NATION'S EXILE: EZEKIEL

Prophetism's reaction to Israel's exile began in conjunction with the Assyrian captivity of the northern kingdom in 722 B.C. Hosea, Amos, Isaiah, and Micah all anticipated and interacted with the sad experience of the devastation of the kingdom of the ten tribes. But no evidence exists that any prophet was raised up by the Lord to live in the midst of these exiles in Assyria and declare his word among them. Nahum announced the future collapse of the city of Nineveh, and the Lord revealed to Habakkuk the rise of the Babylonian Empire, which would serve as God's instrument of judgment on Assyria. But these prophets functioned in a locale that was far removed from the captives scattered throughout the Assyrian Empire.

The situation was, however, significantly different with the exilic experience of the Judean kingdom of the south. Captives were taken to Babylon as a consequence of the incursions of Nebuchadnezzar into Palestine during the reigns of Jehoiakim, Jehoiachin, and Zedekiah, the last three kings of Judah. The initial deportations took place in 605 B.C., with further and more extensive captivities in 597 and 587 B.C.[1] From the earliest moments of Judean exile, the

1. Scriptural references to the earliest Babylonian deportation in the days of Jehoiakim are 2 Kings 24:1–2 and 2 Chron. 36:5–7. Daniel identifies his exile with this first deportation (Dan. 1:1–4), while Ezekiel dates his prophecies in relation to the exile under Jehoiachin (Ezek. 1:2; see also 2 Kings 24:10–17; 2 Chron. 36:9–10).

center of prophetic activity began to make a dramatic shift. Not in Israel, the land of God's people, but in Babylon, the land of Israel's conquerors, would come the word of the Lord through the prophets. Jeremiah had a limited prophetic ministry in Egypt due to the exile forced on him by fleeing Israelites (Jer. 43:4–13). But it was in Babylon, the nation's new overlord, that Ezekiel and Daniel fulfilled the ongoing role of bringing to the people the message of the Covenant LORD.

In analyzing this new phase in the ministry of Israel's prophets, note first something of the condition of the people during their exile. Then the distinctive message of the exilic prophets may be considered.

I. The condition of the people during their exile

A. Scant traces of the exiles

According to Bright, deciphering the history of the Israelite people in the period of the exile is "difficult to the extreme": "Our Biblical sources are at best inadequate. Of the exile itself, the Bible tells us virtually nothing save what can be learned indirectly from prophetic and other writings of the day."[2] Westermann agrees with this evaluation of the available evidence, observing that "our knowledge of Judah during the period of the exile, and of the fortunes of those taken to Babylon, is both scanty and uncertain."[3] In particular, the worship practices of the nation and the role that prophets might have had in this foreign context are wholly absent. Childs indicates that "information is lacking" by which to construct a clear picture of Jewish worship during Israel's captivity.[4] Was the Babylonian exile the point at which the synagogue system emerged? According to Ackroyd, a positive answer to this question is "without clear foundation."[5] Did the ritual practices of circumcision and Sabbath observance become more prominent in these days? Though many schol-

2. Bright, *History of Israel*, 343.
3. Westermann, *Isaiah 40–66*, 5.
4. Childs, *Biblical Theology of the Old and New Testaments*, 162.
5. Ackroyd, *Exile and Restoration*, 32.

ars posit this development, the available evidence does not provide a direct answer to the question.[6] Were the people planning to build a new temple in the land of their exile? Does the gathering of the elders before Ezekiel indicate a regular practice of assembling for worship? Answers to these questions are not forthcoming either by archeological evidence or from biblical sources. In some ways the exilic period of Israel's history may be characterized as a black hole, an era concerning which little can be known.[7]

6. Ibid., 36.

7. It is somewhat remarkable to note the confident assertions made by the majority of scholars today regarding the literary productivity of this period in the light of the meager knowledge that is actually available. Brueggemann comments: "It is now increasingly agreed that *the Old Testament in its final form is a product of and a response to the Babylonian exile*" (*Theology of the Old Testament*, 74, emphasis original). This hypothetical picture is quite amazing in light of the condition of the Israelite people during its relatively brief exile. A defeated people living as a small minority in a foreign land, scattered over a vast empire throughout cities, towns, villages, and even among ruined settlements, supposedly raises up a group of anonymous authors and editors who produce the most glorious body of religious literature found in human history. According to the generally accepted critical reconstruction, these exiles produced and/or edited the Deuteronomistic history, involving the shaping of the final forms of the book of Deuteronomy and of the historical books Joshua–2 Kings; essentially reworked the whole prophetic corpus; composed the glorious prophecies of Deutero-Isaiah, along with a thorough editing of the first portion of Isaiah so that it would conform with the message of Deutero-Isaiah; developed the cultic lawcodes of the priestly school, involving the collection and codification of the worship practices intended for the then-nonexistent Jerusalem temple and its priesthood; and integrated the priestly version of the narrative of Israel's most ancient history into the revered documents of the Pentateuch. All this work is affirmed to have been accomplished during Israel's exile, despite the absence of any objective evidence that might support the theory. Alt, *Essays on Old Testament History and Religion*, 85, asserts that the Deuteronomistic tradition could be kept alive under the governance of the Babylonians "only in secret." Bright, *History of Israel*, 350, states that "though the details are quite unknown, the process of collection which ultimately produced the prophetic books as we know them was carried forward" during this period of Israel's exile. Ackroyd, *Exile and Restoration*, 84, suggests a sixth- or fifth-century date for the Holiness Code, basing his conclusion on statements in Lev. 26, "which evidently envisage an exilic situation." He notes that the material of Lev. 26:33–39 depicts an exilic circumstance "in such a clear manner as to make the sixth-century dating for its final form quite evident" (86 n. 9). In this case, rejection of the possibility of precise predictive prophecy clearly functions as the ultimate criterion for judging the genuineness of a piece of biblical literature, despite the explicit claims of the biblical documents themselves to the contrary.

Yet on the basis of the widespread practice of deportation of peoples in the Middle East during the eighth through sixth centuries B.C., a generalized sketch of the life of Israel's deportees may be uncovered. This basic depiction of the life of peoples in exile may aid in understanding and appreciating the ministry of Israel's exilic prophets.

B. The experience of deportees

In terms of the numbers of people involved in deportations, the possibility of exaggeration and of figures that represent combined totals from several campaigns must be taken into account. Yet no available evidence contradicts the surviving records. Even assuming the impreciseness of figures, the number of deportees is stunning. One estimate indicates a total of four and a half million deportees by the Assyrian Empire over a period of about three centuries.[8] Sennacherib, in recounting his Judean campaign against Hezekiah in 701 B.C., indicates in an inscription that he deported "200,150 people, young and old, male and female."[9]

In the process of deportation across hundreds of miles, captives were generally cared for. Efforts were made to supply food and water. Apparently only the officials of a captive country were chained hand and foot.[10] Families were usually deported together, with the idea that they would be less inclined to escape and would be more productive.[11] Small children often rode on the backs of their parents. Even communities were kept together and resettled as "homogeneous small groups, as far as kinship, religion and culture were concerned."[12] Yet with the intent of keeping the captives subdued, the Assyrians would often deliberately place people from a mountainous region on the seacoast and vice versa.

By deportations, the Assyrians intended to minimize the possibility of uprisings. Some deportees became conscripts for the Assyrian army. Some became charioteers and cavalrymen, while others were

---

8. Oded, *Mass Deportations and Deportees*, 20. See his further exploration of the subject in "Settlements of the Israelite and Judean Exiles."
9. Pritchard, *Ancient Near Eastern Texts*, 288.
10. Oded, *Mass Deportations and Deportees*, 35–39.
11. Ibid., 24.
12. Ibid., 25.

joined to companies of archers and shield bearers. Some even served as personal bodyguards to the king. Others were employed as craftsmen and unskilled laborers.[13] Still others were used to repopulate abandoned or desolate regions.[14] State and legal documents indicate that "many foreigners, some of them deportees or their descendants, were serving as officials in the royal court, in the capitol, in Assyria proper and in the provinces."[15] Records also indicate that some captives were consecrated to the service of the Assyrian temples.[16]

Some evidence indicates that no basic social or legal distinction was made between deportees and the indigenous inhabitants of the same country. Both were taxed on the same basis and were equal before the law in the eyes of the Assyrian rulers.[17] But other evidence indicates that some captives were treated as booty and forced into tasks involving rigid manual labor. Some persons were not free, as attested by the sale contracts that included people living on the land along with the property.[18] As Oded observes, "the socio-economic and legal status of the deportees was not uniform and their conditions were not identical."[19] Their status differed greatly, as did their occupations and specific conditions.

It was to this scattered group of conquered, displaced people that the exilic prophets were sent.[20] In addition to their general state of dis-

13. Ibid., 53–54.
14. Ibid., 67.
15. Ibid., 104.
16. Ibid., 114–15.
17. Ibid., 84.
18. Ibid., 90, 96.
19. Ibid., 115.
20. Special attention has been paid to the Murashu documents, "a group of Babylonian legal documents compiled at Nippur during the last half of the 5th century B.C." (Stolper, "Murashû, Archive of," 927). This archive appears to be the most significant extrabiblical source of information about the Jews during the Babylonian captivity. Yet even here the evidence is limited primarily to the appearance of names that may indicate Jewish origin for the people mentioned. Stolper summarizes his observations: "Little can be said of [these bearers of Jewish names] that distinguishes them from other inhabitants of the region. . . . They have no special role in the texts, but figure as smallholders, as petty officials, or as witnesses" (928). Zadok, *Jews in Babylonia*, 48–49, notes that names associated with the Murashu family are typically Babylonian and that the assumption that the family was Jewish is "entirely

array, Israel's captives had to live with the message of the earlier prophets as well as their more ancient law ringing in their ears. The covenant law established through Moses had plainly announced that if they persisted in their sin, the Covenant LORD would not simply chastise them. He would drive them out of their land (Lev. 26:14–45; Deut. 28:15–68). They would "utterly perish from the land" (4:25–26). The Lord would scatter them among the peoples (4:27–28). In Joshua's farewell speech to the people, he warned that if they adopted the practices of the nations around them, they would "perish from this good land" that the Lord had given them (Josh. 23:13 NIV). The prophets repeatedly warned them of the same fate that awaited them if they continued in their sin (2 Kings 17:13). Even between the first major exile of Judah in 597 B.C. and their final expulsion in 587 B.C., the prophet Ezekiel had warned them. The Lord would bring them into "the wilderness of the peoples" just as he had brought their fathers into "the wilderness of the land of Egypt" (Ezek. 20:35–36 NASB). In that wilderness of chastening judgments, many of them would perish, far from their beloved homeland. But others would survive.

C. Response of the Israelites to exile

In the case of most other deported nationalities, the people and their distinctives disappeared from the records of subsequent history. Their gods perished with the people who worshiped them. Not so the people of Israel, and certainly not so their God. The Lord's sovereign grace kept this nation as a viable community, despite its widespread dispersion. Certainly their circumstance militated against their survival. As Bright vividly expresses the challenge: "With evidences of undreamed of wealth and power around them, with the magnificent temples of pagan gods on every hand, it must have occurred to many of them to wonder whether Yahweh, patron God of a petty state which he seemed powerless to protect, was really the supreme and only God after all."[21]

---

unfounded." He does, however, conclude that Jews resided in most of the districts surrounding Nippur and apparently held properties in as many as twenty-one settlements (50). It should be noted, however, that this material dates at least a century after the initial exile of the Jews (Ackroyd, *Exile and Restoration*, 32).

21. Bright, *History of Israel*, 348.

The continuance of this people was due, humanly speaking, to the ministry and the message of the prophets, both preexilic and exilic. Prior to the tragic events of the exile, the nation had been duly warned of the consequences of continuing in their rebellious ways. When the event occurred, they had a "coherent explanation" for their tragedies.[22] They also had a basis for hope that extended beyond the greatest devastation that any nation or people could undergo. Despite the judgments of the exile, they still were the elect people of God by which the Lord's purposes for all humanity would be fulfilled. If the words of their prophets could be trusted, restoration lay beyond exile. Beyond the abyss of death through banishment from the land would be resurrection by return to the land. Even before the event of the exile, Jeremiah had put this expectation into the form of a confession of faith for the nation, that the truth might remain deeply ingrained in their minds and hearts:

> The days are coming . . . when men will no longer say, "As surely as the Covenant LORD lives, who brought the Israelites up out of Egypt," but they will say, "As surely as the Covenant LORD lives, who brought the Israelites up out of the land of the north and out of all the countries where he had banished them." (Jer. 16:14–15 NIV; see also 23:7–8)

It now became the task of the prophets living among the people in exile to reinforce and expand on these great truths. In many ways, Ezekiel and Daniel were distinctive men "standing in the gap" who were commissioned to declare with boldness the complete collapse of the nation whose demise they were already beginning to experience. But they were also called to broaden the horizon of the future so that it embraced the servant role purposed for this nation from its beginning in realizing their God's worldwide program of redemption.

22. Ibid., 349.

II. Ezekiel's distinctive message

A. Introductory matters related to Ezekiel's prophecy

The opening of Ezekiel's book provides a specific location and a double dating for the beginning of his prophetic ministry. He was settled among the exiles from Judah situated in Babylon at Tel-aviv on the River Kebar (1:1). The first verses link Ezekiel's identification as a priest and "the thirtieth year" (likely a reference to his age),[23] which may indicate that his commissioning vision from God occurred in the very year in which he was inducted into the priestly office (1:1; see also Num. 4:30 and 8:24). Having been transplanted into unclean heathen soil, he was nonetheless favored with a spectacular vision of the exalted God.[24] Very possibly it was in part because of his priestly office that so much of Ezekiel's message centers around the temple and its priestly services.

The second date given in the opening verses of Ezekiel is the fifth year of the deportation of King Jehoiachin of Judah. Though ruling for only three months, Jehoiachin's reign was of great significance because he embodied the farthest genealogical point reached by the royal line of King David. His uncle Zedekiah succeeded him as ruler in Judah for eleven years, but the hopes of Israel continued to focus on Jehoiachin even after he was taken into captivity.[25] In 597 B.C., eighteen-year-old King Jehoiachin surrendered to Nebuchadnezzar of Babylon, who had overrun Judah and was besieging Jerusalem. The conquering monarch took the teenaged king back to Babylon along

23. Block, *Ezekiel*, 1.82, concludes that this ancient explanation by Origen "remains the most likely." Eichrodt, *Ezekiel*, 52, states that the number "most probably" indicates the age of the writer. Zimmerli, *Ezekiel*, 1.114, is more cautious, concluding that "we cannot obtain certainty on this point."

24. See Eichrodt, *Ezekiel*, 52.

25. The inscription on three jar handles that date to the time of Jehoiachin/Zedekiah reads, "Belonging to Eliakim, the servant of Jehoiachin." If this Jehoiachin is the same as the young king who reigned for only three months, the inscription may attest that some of the Judean population still regarded Jehoiachin, instead of his uncle Zedekiah, as their legitimate king, even though he remained a captive in Babylon. See Block, *Ezekiel*, 1.86. Note also the bold proclamation of the false prophet Hananiah, issued during Zedekiah's reign, that within two years the Lord would bring back King Jehoiachin along with all the treasures of the temple (Jer. 28:1–4).

with the queen mother, all his wives, his officials, and ten thousand leading men of the land, as well as all the golden treasures of the temple that Solomon had amassed four hundred years earlier (2 Kings 24:8–17).

Five years later, which would have been 592 B.C., the exiled Ezekiel received his fantastic vision of God's glory (Ezek. 1:2). At just about this time, King Zedekiah of Judah made his fatal mistake of daring to join other western nations in rebelling against the rule of the tyrannical Nebuchadnezzar. Very likely the armies of Babylon were marching westward to subdue this latest revolt. This time the mighty monarch was not so lenient. He totally destroyed Jerusalem, devastating its buildings, destroying the temple and its sacred articles, and demolishing the city's walls. He summoned rebellious King Zedekiah before him, murdered his sons before his eyes to reinforce the idea that he would have no successors, and then plunged the helpless king into perpetual darkness by putting out his eyes (2 Kings 25:6–21).

Ezekiel's prophecies center around the events of Israel's final exile and the anticipation of a future, glorious restoration. But the themes of exile and restoration are developed in a distinctive manner. Exile is presented specifically with a focus on the departure of God's glory from the temple in Jerusalem. Restoration reaches its climax in the vision of the return of God's glory to the temple. "The departing and returning glory" may thus serve as a summarizing theme for the message of this book of prophecy.

In terms of the formal arrangement of materials, the book of Ezekiel naturally divides into three major sections.[26] The first section

26. As in the case of virtually all the prophetic books, efforts are continually made to separate the genuine prophecies of Ezekiel from the secondary words that are presumed to have been introduced by later editors. However, the general tendency of late is to credit more of this prophetic book to Ezekiel himself than in the case of most other prophetic writings. According to Childs, "it is becoming increasingly clear that objective literary or historical criteria are missing by which to distinguish between primary and secondary levels" ("Enemy from the North," 159 n. 24). Deist describes the suggestion of a school of disciples that produced a significant amount of the prophet's materials as "a rather *ad hoc* invention for which there is neither firm (contemporary) textual nor sociological evidence" ("Prophets," 588). Whitney, *Exilic Age*, 87–93, goes to lengths to establish that Ezekiel's words most naturally belong to a Babylonian rather than a Palestinian locale and could be written only by "a contem-

presents prophecies uttered before the fall of Jerusalem and the final exile of the nation's inhabitants (Ezek. 1–24). Since Ezekiel experienced his initial vision and call to the office of prophet in 592 B.C. and the city of Jerusalem fell to Nebuchadnezzar in 587 B.C., the prophecies of these chapters would have been delivered during these six or seven years. A massive deportation of the peoples of Judah along with their king had already occurred in 597 B.C. Yet the false prophets were encouraging the people to trust that the sacred city would never fall. In this context, Ezekiel remained faithful in standing against the tide of popular sentiment by declaring God's word concerning the certainty of the fall of the city.

In the second major section of the prophecy, Ezekiel announces God's judgments against the nations (chaps. 25–32). Because many of the nations surrounding Judah mocked God's people at the time of their fall, they may expect God's righteous judgments in their turn (25:3, 6, 8, 12, 15; 26:2). A second basis for the condemnation of the nations is their lifting themselves up in pride (28:2, 5, 17; 29:3, 15; 31:10). The ultimate consequence of this judgment on the nations is repeated numerous times by Ezekiel: "Then they will know that I am the Covenant LORD" (25:7, 11, 17; 26:6; 28:22, 24, 26; 29:6, 16, 21; 30:8, 19, 25–26; 32:15). The one true God will make himself known among the nations by these judgments. But in addition, the way will be cleared for the restoration of God's people by this divine judgment on the nations. Quite remarkable is this declaration of Israel's restoration in the midst of the pronouncements of God's judgments on the nations. No more malicious neighbors will act as "painful briers and sharp thorns" for God's people (28:24 NIV). Instead, after inflicting his judgments on these neighboring nations who have maligned his people, the Lord will then gather them from all the nations where he has scattered them. They will live in safety in their own land, build houses, and plant vineyards. As a consequence, they will come to know in a fuller way that the Covenant LORD

---

porary of the historical scene" (89). He then asserts that if "any logical scheme" is to be attributed to the prophet, the passages giving hope to Judah and Jerusalem "must be regarded as being the interpolations of later hands" (93). To the contrary, the logic of hope based on the Lord's covenantal commitments would have no difficulty anticipating restoration after exile.

is their God (28:24–26). Even this declaration of judgment on the nations relates directly to the message of exile and restoration.

The third major section of the book of Ezekiel describes in vivid terms a vision of the restoration of Israel after its exile to Babylon, climaxing with the return of the glory to the restored temple (chaps. 33–48). After explaining the basic cause of Jerusalem's fall (chap. 33), the subsequent prophecies consist of three major sections: a vivid prediction of restoration (chaps. 34–37), the conflict with Gog and Magog (chaps. 38–39), and the return of the glory to the restored temple (chaps. 40–48).[27]

B. Critical moments in Ezekiel's prophecies

In considering the overall message of Ezekiel, concentration may be directed to three critical moments in the prophecies: the prophet's commissioning vision (Ezek. 1–3), the departure of the glory (Ezek. 8–11), and restoration beyond exile (Ezek. 34–48). As in the case of Isaiah and Jeremiah, the initial call of the prophet provides a summation of the heart of his message. In each of these key sections of the book, a visionary experience of the glory of God emerges as the central focus of the prophetic message.

1. Ezekiel's commissioning vision (Ezekiel 1–3)

Halfway between the two captivities of 597 and 586 B.C., Ezekiel the prophet, himself already an exile in the land of Babylon, experiences a vision of the exalted God of Israel. No other vision of God recorded in the old covenant scriptures is as glorious or as elaborately

27. The various prophecies are dated quite regularly throughout the book and are almost without exception arranged in chronological order. The fixed point for the dating of Ezekiel is the year that began King Jehoiachin's exile (597 B.C.). Specifics are as follows:

fifth year	593 B.C.	1:2
sixth year	592 B.C.	8:1
seventh year	591 B.C.	20:1
ninth year	589 B.C.	24:1
eleventh year	587 B.C.	26:1; 30:20; 31:1
tenth year	588 B.C.	29:1
twenty-seventh year	571 B.C.	29:17
twelfth year	586 B.C.	33:21
twenty-fifth year	574 B.C.	40:1

described as this one. Not even the vision of God experienced by Moses on the mountain can compare with God's self-revelation of his glory to Ezekiel. Perhaps the most striking aspect of this vision is that it occurs outside the holy land. As Block well states: "The prophet has witnessed the incredible—far away from the temple, among the exiles in the pagan land of Babylon, Yahweh has appeared to him!"[28]

Who could have imagined such a thing? Just at a moment in history when the people of God in Israel are relying heavily on the presence of their God in the temple of Jerusalem, this God manifests his glory far away from the holy place in the land of their conquerors. Most essential to the continuance of the theocracy was the special manifestation of the presence of God in the midst of his people. Yet now he appears in the greatest revelation of his glory seen by a human on earth in a setting far removed from the temple in Jerusalem. The first lesson to draw from this fact is the universal presence and sovereignty of the one true living God. He cannot be restricted to one part of the globe. He can display his sovereign power and glory in any place on earth. He will not be confined to a single locale.

Distinctive above all other elements in this vision is the presence of the wheels.[29] In the original imagery of the throne of God in the sanctuary of Israel, the cherubim were present (Exod. 25:17–22). But unique to this vision is the prominence given to the wheels, wheels within wheels (Ezek. 1:15–21). Wheels covered with eyes, wheels whirling, wheels in which abide the spirit of the living creatures, wheels moving like lightning in any direction, but always in perfect harmony with the living creatures. What are these wheels, and what is their significance?

The wheels represent a God who cannot be contained conveniently in a single place. This mobile sanctuary, this divine chariot-throne cannot be restrained so that it remains forever in Jerusalem. God's sovereignty can touch down on earth just as easily in Babylon as it can at Jerusalem. If the vision of God's glory as revealed to Ezekiel teaches

28. Block, *Ezekiel*, 1.105.
29. Eichrodt, *Ezekiel*, 118, asserts that the description of the wheels must be a later insertion. In so doing, he eliminates the most significant aspect of Ezekiel's commissioning vision.

anything, it communicates the truth that the presumption that God's presence can be restricted to one place must be forever abandoned.

This initial vision of God's glory becomes the centerpiece of Ezekiel's message. At the point of the prophet's commission (3:22–23), at the time of the departing of the glory from the temple in Jerusalem (8:4), and in the prophetic anticipation of the return of the glory (43:3), the original vision (1:4–28) returns to the prophet.

Only by exile from the promised land could the people of the old covenant comprehend the significance of a mobile sanctuary for their God. So long as the Jerusalem temple stood, with the presence of God's glory within the most holy place, no one could imagine that the glory of the Lord might be manifest anywhere else. But now the truth cannot be denied, particularly after the destruction of the temple and its sacred places. A hint of the mobile nature of God's throne might have been present during the construction of Solomon's temple (1 Chron. 28:18). But with the regular recurrence of the vision of wheels given to Ezekiel, the truth could not be denied. God's glory was not restricted to a single locale. He could, and would, manifest his presence at any place in the world he had made.

In response to this initial vision of the chariot-throne and its wheels, Ezekiel receives his commission to be a "watchman" for Israel. On two different occasions he is assigned the same task. At the conclusion of his initial call, he is commanded to be a watchman for Israel (3:16–21). Even though this same chariot he has just seen will assume the form of the Lord's war chariot, sowing coals of fire across the city of Jerusalem (10:6–7), Ezekiel is given the task of being a "watchman" for the nation.[30] Then subsequent to the fall of the city of Jerusalem, Ezekiel receives the charge to be a "watchman" once more, but this time publicly (33:1–20). Even after the city of Jerusalem has fallen and

30. In commenting on Ezekiel's charge as a watchman, Zimmerli, *Ezekiel*, 2.185, speaks of "the complete irrationality of the divine activity." He refers to God's first commissioning a foe against his people and then sending a watchman to warn them. "Such is divine logic!" says Zimmerli. This bold exclamation minimizes the justice of God in bringing judgment on the persistently wicked, the mercy of God in not taking pleasure in the death of the wicked (33:11), and the full responsibility of every human being for his own actions.

the nation has been carried into captivity, the same principles of justice remain. As a watchman, the prophet must bring each and every individual to account before God, for the Lord will judge each man according to his own ways (33:20).[31]

The prophet's commissioning vision thus serves as a critical moment in the book of Ezekiel. A new aspect of the reality of Israel's God manifests itself as a consequence of the exile of the nation. This God is universal in his sovereignty as well as in his saving activity and will not be contained within any specific locale.

2. The departure of the glory (Ezekiel 8–11)

A vision of the glory of God, like the first, but coming one year and two months after his initial commission, introduces the second critical moment in the prophecy of Ezekiel (8:1–4). This time the prophet sees the glory of God in what he might have assumed to be its proper context. Rather than having the glory appear to him in the plains of Babylon, he is transported in his vision to the temple of the Lord in Jerusalem (8:3). There he is led through a progression of corruptions that defile this most holy place, and there he witnesses a progressive withdrawal of the glory from this sacred sanctuary.

The cause of the Lord's departure is dramatically demonstrated in the prophet's visionary experience. At the entrance to the inner court of the sanctuary he is shown "the idol that provokes to jealousy" (8:3, 5 NIV). The Lord calls the prophet's attention to "the great abominations that the house of Israel is doing *here*!" (8:6). Right before the presence of the holy God they have erected an idol. But the prophet is informed that he will see even greater abominations. Ezekiel is then led through a hole in the wall into the inner court of the Lord's sanctuary. There he sees seventy elders of the house of Israel, each worshiping in the darkness at the shrine of his own idol (8:7–12). The leadership of the nation has gone far beyond the corruptions of Israel when they worshiped the golden calf at the foot of Mount Sinai. But the

31. The integrity of the two commissionings of Ezekiel as a watchman is defended by Klein, *Ezekiel*, 28–32. Klein argues that the first account is private and suitable to the time of the prophet's call, while the second account is public and suitable for the time after the fall of Jerusalem.

prophet will see still further abominations. At the entrance to the Lord's house, the women of Israel carry out their own cult worship (8:14). Yet still greater abominations await the prophet's vision. In the inner court of the holy house of the Lord he finds twenty-five men bowing to the sun with their backs to the temple of the Lord (8:16).[32]

The Lord underscores the dire consequences of these pollutions. These are the "things that will drive me far from my sanctuary" (8:6 NIV). He cannot abide these multiple corruptions of his holiness any longer. Ezekiel then witnesses one of the saddest moments in all human history. Four centuries of the distinctive blessing of the Lord must come to their end. The Shekinah, the glory of the Lord, will remove himself from his dwelling place in the sanctuary of Jerusalem. The prophet witnesses the step-by-step departure of the Lord's glorious presence. It was one thing for the captives in Babylon to contemplate the devastations of the promised land that had accompanied their own exile. It would be a wholly different thing for them to comprehend the abandonment of the temple by the Shekinah glory and the desecration of the sacred place where their Covenant LORD had promised to abide forever. Yet in his vision Ezekiel anticipates this very development.

First he sees the glory of the God of Israel rising above the cherubim in the most holy place, where it had resided since Solomon's dedicatory prayer (1 Kings 8:10–11), and moving to the threshold of the temple (Ezek. 9:3). Next, the glory of the Lord departs from the temple threshold and moves, along with the cherubim and the whirling wheels, to the east gate of the Lord's house (10:16–19). Finally, the glory of God, again with the cherubim and the wheels, rises above the city of Jerusalem and stops at the mountain east of it, the Mount of Olives (11:22–23). From this point on, the once-holy place stands openly exposed to the ravages of invading nations. The glory of the Lord is now positioned to witness the destruction of the once-holy city and temple.

It should not be regarded as purely coincidental that the noteworthy Olivet Discourse of Jesus took place on the same Mount of Olives as he overlooked the city of Jerusalem and declared its imminent fate

32. For a fuller development of this progression (or regression) of corruptions, see Block, *Ezekiel*, 1.283–300.

(Matt. 24:3; Luke 21:20–24). As the armies of Nebuchadnezzar would shortly surround the Jerusalem of Ezekiel's day, level it to the ground, and burn its remnants, so the holy city of Jesus' day would be surrounded by Roman armies that would not leave one stone on top of another.

Yet even in this darkest prophetic moment, the Lord does not leave his people without a glimmer of hope. These exiles already banished to Babylon, scorned by the judgmental residents of Jerusalem—they have a special role in the plan and purpose of God. "Your brothers, your brothers," they are called twice over to underscore their acceptance by the Lord as a part of the family of the redeemed (11:15). They are the true kinsmen of the prophet, to be regarded as "all the house of Israel, every remaining bit of it" (11:15). Most remarkably, before the final devastation of Jerusalem occurred, the Lord had already begun to prepare these exiles as a people for restoration. Even more astonishing is the Lord's declaration to his prophet concerning those who are in exile: "Although I have sent them far away among the nations and have scattered them across the lands, *yet I have been for them a sanctuary for a little in the lands where they have gone*" (11:16).

What is the Lord saying to his prophet? No more radical statement could be imagined. Scattered across obscure villages and diverse countries, living in small pockets as aliens, far from the sanctuary of the Lord's dwelling place—even in these distant places the Lord himself has become a sanctuary for them. As one commentator indicates, "They had, indeed, lost the outward temple (at Jerusalem); but the Lord Himself had become their temple."[33] Totally separated from the land and the place that had been designated as the Lord's dwelling on earth, not even assembled in a single place themselves, but scattered instead across numerous locales, these exiles were to understand that the Lord himself was their sanctuary. Even before the old temple in Jerusalem had been destroyed, a new, expansive temple for God's people had been erected.

Two radical concepts are now being introduced to the exiled people of God. First of all, the Covenant LORD himself is their sacred dwelling place. Not in buildings made with human hands, but in union with the Lord himself his people will experience the full realities of

33. Keil, *Ezekiel*, 1.151.

true worship. Second, any place on earth can be the locale for God's meeting with his people. These revolutionary concepts would never have been realized apart from the scattering of God's people, which provides new insight into the significance of the exile. Clearly Ezekiel as prophet of the exile realizes a new understanding of God's purposes for his people. The people of the Lord are not to limit their worship to a single locale on the face of the earth. Instead, because their God is everywhere as the Lord of all the nations, communion and fellowship with him can be maintained everywhere.

It is, of course, only a faint glimmer of the final light that God's exiled people now receive. This sanctuary is described specifically as "little," which could refer to its smallness in comparison with the Jerusalem temple. Or it may indicate its temporary character, describing something that ultimately must be replaced. In either case, centuries later a descendant of the displaced Samaritans receives from Jesus a clear development of the same line of thought. Neither in Jerusalem nor in Samaria is God to be worshiped. Wherever the Spirit and the truth are found, there the holy God will be present in all his glory (John 4:21–24).

This vision of Ezekiel is clearly set in the framework of old covenant images, while at the same time anticipating the radical differences of the new. Though the Lord established himself as the sanctuary of the exiled people, a fuller restoration is nonetheless anticipated. He will gather them from the lands where they have been scattered and will give back to them the land of Israel (Ezek. 11:17).[34] Then the Lord will give them an undivided heart, put a new spirit within them, and remove their heart of stone, giving them a heart of flesh (11:18–19). As a consequence, they will keep his laws. They will be his people, and he will be their God, obviously reflecting the heart of the covenant concept (11:20). A new exodus, a purified land, a single heart, a new spirit, and a new obedience fill out the picture of this restored people of the Lord.

---

34. Block, *Ezekiel*, 1.272–73, says that Ezek. 11:14–21 "seems totally oblivious to the vision account." But the contrast between the judgmental word for the corrupted inhabitants of Jerusalem and the encouraging word for the chastened deportees of the exile provide the framework for the unity of the chapter.

3. Restoration beyond exile (Ezekiel 34–48)

A significant factor in the overall structure of the book of Ezekiel is the report of Jerusalem's fall in Ezekiel 33:21. From this point on, the prophet concentrates his attention on the restoration that is sure to come.

Several themes dominate this final section of the book of Ezekiel. Most prominent are the following: the imagery of the divine Shepherd and the restored kingship of David; the revival of the dry bones; the reunification of the divided kingdoms of Judah and Israel; the consummation of the divine covenants; the final victory over all opposing powers; and the plan for the final temple of God. The unifying factor of all these themes is the expectation of restoration that now must follow the experience of exile.

a. Restoration by the divine shepherd and the Davidic king (Ezekiel 34)

The shepherd imagery, long a figure for the ideal king in Israel, is regularly applied to God himself as well as to the heirs of David's throne (Gen. 48:15; 49:24; Ps. 23:1). Because Israel's appointed shepherds failed so miserably in carrying out their responsibilities (Ezek. 34:1–10), the Covenant LORD himself shall take on the task of shepherding his sheep: "I myself will search for my sheep. . . . I will bring them out from the nations and gather them from the countries, and I will bring them into their own land. . . . I will search for the lost and bring back the strays" (34:11, 13, 16 NIV). At the same time, this shepherding responsibility will fall on the shoulders of God's servant David: "I will place over them one shepherd, my servant David, and he will tend them; he will tend them and be their shepherd. I the Covenant LORD will be their God, and my servant David will be prince among them" (34:23–24 NIV).

This merged imagery of God and David serving simultaneously as shepherd to a restored Israel anticipates the perfections of rule in the kingdom of redemption. A descendant of David who functions in the same way as God himself in the midst of his people resolves all the tensions felt throughout the old covenant theocracy. Eventually the Good Shepherd who gives his life for the sheep will appear as the sovereign Lord in their midst (John 10:11). In explaining his role as the one shepherd over the diversified flock that he will gather, Jesus says:

"I have other sheep [Gentile believers] that are not of this sheep pen [Jewish believers]. I must bring them also. They too will listen to my voice, and there shall be one flock and one shepherd" (10:16 NIV).

b. Restoration through the consummation of the divine covenants (Ezekiel 36:24–28; 37:24–28)

Integrally related to the restoration of the exiled people is the invoking of the various elements of the principal covenants that the Lord made with his people over the ages. In essentially duplicate paragraphs, Ezekiel casts the return from exile in terms of the Abrahamic, Mosaic, Davidic, and new covenants. His reconstituted people "will live in the land I gave to your forefathers" (36:28 NIV; 37:25, alluding to the Abrahamic covenant); they will follow his decrees and keep his laws (36:27; 37:24, alluding to the Mosaic covenant); David will be king over them, and they will all have one shepherd (37:24–25, alluding to the Davidic covenant); and they will be given a new heart and a new spirit and will enjoy the blessings of an eternal covenant of peace (36:26; 37:26, alluding to the new covenant). These consummative blessings of the various covenants will be experienced when the Lord gathers his people from all the nations and brings them back to their own land (36:24; 37:21).

While these descriptions are vividly presented in the garb of old covenant forms, the consummate realization of each of these covenants can ultimately be understood only in terms of their new covenant realities. Abraham eventually was weaned from his expectations of a topologically limited land and looked for a heavenly one, not enjoying the realization of the promises apart from new covenant believers (Heb. 11:9–10, 16). Moses experienced the limitations of the law by the perpetual reoffering of the sacrifices and so had to be delivered from divine condemnation by the look of faith (Lev. 23:4–8; Heb. 10:11; Num. 21:4–9). David saw corruption, but Christ his son overcame death by the resurrection (Ps. 16:10–11; Acts 2:24–33). Participants in the new covenant, whether Jews or Gentiles, celebrate their restoration to God every time they eat the bread and drink the cup of the new covenant, sealed by the blood of Jesus (Matt. 26:27–29; Luke 22:20).

c. Restoration by the revival of dry bones (Ezekiel 37:1–14)

The circumstance of Israel's restoration and return to the land is made most vivid in Ezekiel's vision of the valley of dry bones:

> This is what the Sovereign Covenant LORD says: O my people, I am going to open your graves and bring you up from them; I will bring you back to the land of Israel. Then you, my people, will know that I am the Covenant LORD, when I open your graves and bring you up from them. I will put my Spirit in you and you will live, and I will settle you in your own land. Then you will know that I the Covenant LORD have spoken, and I have done it, declares the Covenant LORD. (37:12–14 NIV)

Clearly Ezekiel is talking about a return to the land and a restoration of the people. But exactly what does his prophecy anticipate?

Many interpreters suggest that the prophet simply uses figurative language of bodily resurrection to anticipate nothing more than the return of Israel to the land.[35] But somehow the origin of this imagery must be explained. Where did Ezekiel get the idea of talking about a return from exile in terms of the opening of graves? Certainly he did not derive it from the cultic enactment of the myth of a dying and rising god, as some propose.[36]

Previous biblical references acknowledging the power of God to raise the dead support an understanding of the prophet's ultimate reference to go beyond merely a wondrous return of exiles to the promised land.[37] As one critical scholar notes: "That God by a miracle could

---

35. See Taylor, *Ezekiel*, 236, who is quite emphatic on this point. See also Eichrodt, *Ezekiel*, 509; and Zimmerli, *Ezekiel*, 2.264.

36. Taylor, *Ezekiel*, 236, citing the theory of H. Riesenfeld.

37. See the extensive treatment of Ezekiel's vision in Block, *Ezekiel*, 2.381–92, who takes note of Jewish and Christian interpretations that understand Ezekiel as describing an actual resurrection. Block discusses several scriptural passages predating Ezekiel that speak in terms of resurrection (386–87, esp. n. 97) and concludes: "In a new and dramatic way, the conviction that the grave need not be the end provided a powerful vehicle for announcing the full restoration of Israel. The curse would be lifted. Yahweh would bring his people back to life" (387).

restore the dead to life no devout Israelite ever doubted."[38] The skepticism of the New Testament Sadducees regarding the prospect of resurrection for the dead would require at least a modification of this all-embracing assertion (Matt. 22:23–32). Yet Jesus' response to this very skepticism indicates his assumption that testimony to bodily resurrection was a part of Old Testament teaching: "You are in error because you do not know the Scriptures or the power of God" (Matt. 22:29 NIV). Only a few cases of actual resurrection from the dead are recorded in the Old Testament (1 Kings 17:17–24; 2 Kings 4:18–37; 13:20–21). But additional testimony regarding the possibility of resurrection may be found scattered throughout the scriptures. Repeatedly the fulfillment of the land promise was associated with life beyond death, a prime example being the Lord's identifying himself as the God of Abraham, Isaac, and Jacob to Moses five hundred years after the patriarchs had died. He is, after all, the God of the living and not the dead; and so his promise of land to the patriarchs was still outstanding in the days of Moses (Exod. 3:6; Matt. 22:32). Somehow that personal promise to the patriarchs must be fulfilled.[39]

38. John Skinner, as cited in Taylor, *Ezekiel*, 236. Taylor and others feel that Skinner is quite wrong in this assessment.

39. It is not indicated specifically that Moses himself fully grasped all the implications of God's self-revelation at the burning bush. Nonetheless he heard the Covenant LORD identify himself as the God of Abraham despite the patriarch's having been dead for almost five hundred years. This hint of resurrection from the dead may be detected at other points in the Genesis narrative. In reasoning about the relation of Isaac's role in God's promise to the divine command to sacrifice his son, Abraham declared to his servant, "*We* will worship and then *we will come back* to you" (Gen. 22:5 NIV, emphasis added). According to the New Testament, Abraham concluded that, if necessary, God could raise Isaac from the dead (Heb. 11:19). Rather than despairing as he grew older without possessing the promise of the land, Abraham began to look for a city "whose architect and builder" was God and for a "better country" that had the characteristics of heavenly realities (Heb. 11:10, 16). Joseph showed his confidence in the upcoming exodus by giving a commandment concerning the disposition of his bones (Gen. 50:25; see also Heb. 11:22). Joseph might have expressed concern that his bones be transported to the promised land for purely sentimental reasons. On the other hand, his determination in this matter may indicate that he expected to personally participate in the possession of the land that had been promised. If Abraham had progressed in his faith to the point of looking for a heavenlike, eternal realization of the land promise (Heb. 11:10, 16), then almost certainly this expectation would have been passed on to later generations that would have included Joseph (Gen. 18:17–19).

The word of the Lord to Ezekiel fits squarely into this expectation.[40] At a minimum, Ezekiel's prophecy of the return to the land involves God's putting his Spirit in people so that they "come alive" (Ezek. 37:14a). This description of *new life* generated by God's Spirit is the most likely scripture that Jesus expected Nicodemus to understand as they discussed the necessity of being "*born* of water and the Spirit" (John 3:5, 10 NIV). But the specificity of Ezekiel's language regarding the uncovering of graves and the context of dry, dead bones coming to life further suggests the expectation of bodily resurrection. Upon the opening of graves and the coming alive of the dead, a return to the land shall be effected in its fullest sense.[41]

From this perspective on Ezekiel's prophecy, the minimalistic return from exile that occurred shortly after Ezekiel's own day could not be regarded as the consummate fulfillment of expectations created by his prophecy. Israel's return at that time, as significant for redemptive history as it might have been, served in its turn to point to a greater restoration in accord with the provisions of the new covenant.[42]

40. In spite of serious questioning by many regarding the presence of resurrection faith in the Old Testament, additional passages deserving careful consideration include Ps. 16:9–11 (Acts 2:24–32); Ps. 17:15 (1 John 3:2); Isa. 25:6–8 (Rev. 21:4); Isa. 26:19; Dan. 12:2–3 (John 5:28–29). It is significant that Paul's summation of the essence of the gospel that he had received and that he also passed on includes the affirmation that Christ "was raised on the third day according to the Scriptures" (1 Cor. 15:4 NIV).

41. Feinberg, *Prophecy of Ezekiel*, 214, emphasizes the two stages involved in the process of resurrection described by Ezekiel. First the bones and sinews come together, and then the Spirit of God breathes life. It is proposed that the two phases represent Israel's return to the land without the vitality of new spiritual life from God, followed by a second stage involving the revival of true faith in the coming messiah. But the obvious parallel with the creation account in Gen. 2:7 makes it plain that this return to life, though in two stages, must be viewed as a single event. God first formed man of the dust of the earth, and then he breathed into his nostrils the breath of life. Only after this second action of the creator was man declared a "living being." In a similar fashion, the skeleton formed by the coming together of the bones in Ezekiel was a totally lifeless being still lying at the foot of the valley. Only after the breath of life from God entered the skeleton did it come to life.

42. A similar analysis of the significance of Israel's restored-temple vision may be found in Walker, *Jesus and the Holy City*, 313. In light of references to the temple prophecy of Ezekiel in the New Testament, Walker concludes that New Testament writers "were presumably not expecting Ezekiel's prophecy to be fulfilled literally at some future point in a physical Temple. Instead this prophecy became a brilliant way

For similar reasons, the return of the Jews to the land in the twentieth century, eventuating in the formation of the modern state of Israel in 1948, cannot fulfill this prophecy of Ezekiel. Their re-formation involved no opening of graves, no resurrection of the body, no inpouring of the Spirit of God, and no affirmation of Jesus as the Christ of the new covenant. However the restoration of the state of Israel may be viewed, it does not fulfill the expectation of Ezekiel as described in this vivid prophecy.

d. Restoration accomplishing the reunification of the divided kingdoms (Ezekiel 37:15–28)

The last of a long line of prophetic enactments by Ezekiel is the only one that communicates salvation rather than judgment.[43] Ezekiel is instructed to write "Belonging to Judah" on one stick and "Belonging to Joseph" on another. Then the two sticks are to be joined, symbolizing the merger of the northern and southern kingdoms at the time of their restoration (37:16–17, 22).[44] The Lord will "take the Israelites out of the nations where they have gone" and "make them one nation in the land" so that "they will never again . . . be divided into two kingdoms" (37:21–22 NIV).

The message of national reunification as an aspect of Israel's restoration is quite clear. But how is its fulfillment to be envisioned? It is suggested that nothing but an ethnic reunion of the various tribes of Israel could fulfill the prophecy of Ezekiel. Since he speaks so specifically of the northern kingdom, representatives of the ten lost tribes must be included in this reunion.[45]

---

of speaking pictorially of what God had now achieved in and through Jesus. Paradoxically, therefore, although Ezekiel's vision had focused so much upon the Temple, it found its ultimate fulfilment in that city where there was 'no Temple,' because 'its Temple is the Lord God Almighty and the Lamb' (Rev. 21:22)."

43. For analysis of prophetic signs in relation to the word of the prophet, see Block, *Ezekiel*, 1.164–67.

44. For a summary of the discussion concerning the nature of the sticks and their inscriptions, see Block, *Ezekiel*, 2.397–406; and Zimmerli, *Ezekiel*, 2.273.

45. See for this view, Block, *Ezekiel*, 2.410, who states that "the prophet's ethnic focus" is highlighted by the expression *sons or descendants of Israel*. But this assertion is difficult to prove in view of the multiethnic character of Abraham's seed from the initial point of the identification of those who would inherit the Abrahamic prom-

The problem with this perspective is of course that the ten lost tribes have no continuing ethnic identity (see introduction to chap. 9). No record remains of the various tribes of the northern kingdom. This reality is attested, among other things, by the fact that the term *Jew* in both Testaments (Hebrew *yehudi* and Greek *ioudaios*) "originally applied to members of the tribe of Judah." But after the destruction of Israel, the term *Jew* designated any Israelite, irrespective of his tribal status.[46] In other words, this term identified all the surviving members of the ancient Israelite community, since tribal identities of the northern nation had been lost.

It could, of course, be proposed that God has maintained for himself an identity of each of the ten northern tribes and that these tribes all will be represented in the reconstitution of Israel when Ezekiel's prophecy is fulfilled. Block states: "The reconciliation [of the northern and southern tribes] envisioned by Ezekiel could no more be achieved by their own initiative than the Judeans could perform their own heart transplant (36:26–27), or the dead bones could of themselves come back to life (37:1–14). Every phase of the restoration required direct and miraculous divine intervention."[47] However, the apostle Paul provides a more substantial resolution of this problem than appeal to a miraculous reconstitution of the ten lost tribes might offer. As noted earlier, in explaining the fulfillment of Hosea's prophecy concerning the restoration of the northern kingdom from its exile, Paul says the transfer from the status of "not my people" to "my people" refers to the divine calling of the objects of God's mercy "not only from the Jews but also from the Gentiles" (Rom. 9:23–25 NIV). By the exile, the tribes of the northern kingdom became "not my people," just as the Lord declared. They were absorbed into the Gentile mass, living without God and without hope in the world. But God in his grace transformed people from this Gentile world into being his favored people by the work of his Spirit. In this manner, the ten tribes lost to the Gentile world have been and are being restored.

---

ises. From the beginning, any Gentile could become a full-fledged Jew by undergoing ritual circumcision, while ethnic descendants might be totally excluded. See Gen. 17:12–14; Exod. 12:48.

46. Grintz, "Jew," 21–22.

47. Block, *Ezekiel*, 2.412.

e. Restoration involving the final victory over all opposing powers (Ezekiel 38–39)

Multitudinous have been the interpretations offered of the famous Gog and Magog passage in Ezekiel. The various views may be categorized as referring either to secular nations threatening a renewed Jewish state at some future point in time or to an idealized enemy standing opposed to the people of God throughout the ages.

Concrete references to the "mountains of Israel" (38:8; 39:2, 4, 17), "my people Israel" (38:14, 16; 39:7), "my [God's] land" (38:16), "the land of Israel" (38:18–19), "my [God's] mountains" (38:21), "the towns of Israel" (39:9), "the house of Israel" (39:12, 22, 29), and "the people of Israel" (39:23, 25) seem to favor treating the passage in purely geopolitical terms.

Yet several considerations favor a more broadly eschatological understanding of the passage. First, the names of the nations attacking Israel derive from the ancient table of nations in Genesis 10. Magog, Meshech, Tubal, Gomer, and Togarmah (Ezek. 38:2, 6) are listed as descendants of Japheth (Gen. 10:2–3). Cush, Put, Sheba, and Dedan (Ezek. 38:5, 13) appear as descendants of Ham (Gen. 10:6–8). None of the names in Ezekiel appears as descendants of Shem, except Meshech and Sheba, who are also found in the list of Japhethites and Hamites. The conflict in Ezekiel thus mirrors a broader struggle of the descendants of Japheth and Ham with the descendants of Shem over the matter of participation in redemption, as depicted earlier in Noah's blessing for Shem and his curse over Ham's son Canaan (Gen. 9:24–27). Yet a tracing of these lines of descent (as far as they are indicated in scripture) does not favor seeing this struggle across the ages as basically an ethnico-political conflict. Instead, scripture points to a redemptive-historical context, for not all Shemites were favored with redemption, as the classic conflict between the Shemite twins Esau and Jacob indicates (Mal. 1:2–3). Similarly, the descendants of Rahab the Canaanite can enjoy the full benefits of divine redemption, even to the point of having their descendancy registered in David's regal line (Matt. 1:5).[48] Thus the allusion to this age-old conflict by Ezekiel does not

48. For a fuller development of this perspective, see Robertson, "Current Critical Questions."

promote the idea of a climactic struggle among humanity's races. It alludes instead to the warfare between the "seed of the woman" and the "seed of Satan" in terms of God's redemptive purposes, which crisscross all ethnic considerations (Gal. 6:15–16; Rom. 16:20).

Second, the "foe from the north" mentioned in Ezekiel 38–39 ultimately becomes a biblical type of the great forces that oppose God's people, without reference to political or geographical specifics (Ezek. 38:15; 39:2; Isa. 14:31; Jer. 1:14; 4:6; 6:1, 22; 10:22; 13:20; 25:9; 46:20, 24; 47:2; 50:41; see also Rev. 17:5–6; 18:1–24; 20:8).

Third, the conflict reaches eschatological proportions, involving a "great earthquake," having an impact comparable to Noah's flood, that terrorizes the "fish of the sea, the birds of the air, the beasts of the field, every creature that moves along the ground, and all the people on the face of the earth" (Ezek. 38:19–20 NIV). This conflict climaxes with the people of Israel sitting down at a "great sacrifice on the mountains of Israel" in which they "eat the flesh of mighty men and drink the blood of the princes of the earth" (39:17–18 NIV). There at God's table they eat their fill of horses and riders, mighty men and soldiers of every kind (39:20). While this vivid language appropriately depicts covenantal curses symbolically in an eschatological framework (Rev. 19:17–18), it hardly can be read in a way that presumes their occurrence in the events of normal human history.

These chapters describing the struggle with Gog and Magog basically confirm that God's people will never again be totally overcome by the nations, as was Israel by its exile.[49] No superpower will arise in the future to altogether overpower the restored people of God. As Jesus said, "The gates of hell will not prevail against it" (Matt. 16:18).

f. Restoration including a plan for the final temple (Ezekiel 40–48)

(1) Setting of the vision

Now comes the "enormous final vision" of the prophet.[50] Ezekiel's prophecy would not have been complete without this final vision of the glory returning to a restored temple. This priest/prophet had first

49. Klein, *Ezekiel*, 166.
50. The phrase is from Zimmerli, *Ezekiel*, 2.327.

envisioned the exile in terms of the departure of the glory from the temple. Although his previous descriptions of a renewed covenant relationship and a return to the land were glorious, the missing, unmentioned element was the return of the glory to a restored temple. Since the time of Moses, all through the periods of Joshua, Judges, and Kings, the Shekinah served as the focus of Israel's worship, marking out this people to be God's own in a unique way. The imagery of Ezekiel must conclude climactically with the return of the glory that had departed from Solomon's temple according to the prophet's own earlier reports.

This final vision of the restored temple counterbalances the departure of the glory recorded in Ezekiel 8–11. The glory had abandoned the temple of Jerusalem because of the people's pollutions. But now because of the permanent purification of the people through the gift of the new heart, the glory will return, never to depart again. This vision of the restored temple is also linked to the restoration described in Ezekiel 34–37, which climaxes with the declaration that God will put his sanctuary among them forever. His dwelling place will be with them, and his sanctuary will remain among them forever (37:26–28).

In accordance with the pattern set throughout the book, this vision of the restored temple is dated by reference to the year of King Jehoiachin's exile.[51] The twenty-fifth year of his exile would be 572 B.C., meaning that the last monarch in the line of David, who had been brought to Babylon as a teenager, was now well advanced into his middle years.

This "twenty-fifth" year has been seen to have significance in that it represents exactly one-half of the fifty-year period of Israel's Jubilee.[52] In the Jubilee, each person would return to his family property and to his family clan (Lev. 25:10). The captives in exile could now rejoice that they were passing the halfway mark of their loss of land. This view receives some support by scriptural indications that the exile would be measured in terms of making up the Jubilee years that had been ignored by the nation (Lev. 26:34; 2 Chron. 36:21). The prophet Isaiah also

51. A second date for this vision given by Ezekiel is the fourteenth year after the fall of Jerusalem, which corresponds exactly with the twenty-fifth year of Jehoiachin's exile (from 597 B.C. to 572 B.C.).

52. See Zimmerli, *Ezekiel*, 2.346; and Block, *Ezekiel*, 2.495, 512.

anticipated release from exile's enslavements in terms of the Jubilee, the great year of release (Isa. 61:1). Ezekiel shows some awareness of the Jubilee principle in this section by his reference to the reversion of property rights in the "year of freedom" (Ezek. 46:17). If this understanding of the reference to the twenty-fifth year is correct, it enforces the symbolic character of the prophecy, since the next twenty-five years would fall short of the actual end of Israel's exile by a decade.[53]

(2) Substance of the vision

At the outset, it should be remembered that this message comes to Ezekiel in the form of "visions of God" (40:2). Many elements in these chapters enforce the idea that it is indeed through the medium of vision and not simply by direct revelation that Ezekiel is shown the pattern of a restored temple. In this regard, the revelation to Ezekiel on this occasion is by its very nature of a different character than the detailed instructions given to Moses concerning the tabernacle in the wilderness. In Moses' experience, directions regarding the construction of the tabernacle were very specific: "Be sure that you make it according to the pattern shown you in the mount" (Exod. 25:40; see also Heb. 8:5). Significantly, the nation is never given explicit directions that they should construct this visionary temple of Ezekiel.

Several elements of the temple complex revealed to Ezekiel deserve further consideration:

- The temple itself: In a manner similar to the earlier experience in which Ezekiel witnessed the departure of the glory from the temple, the prophet is transported in the visions of God to the land of Israel and situated on a "very high mountain" (40:2). It may be assumed that the environs of Jerusalem are the intended locale, though it is significant that the city itself is nowhere mentioned in these chapters.[54] At any rate, Ezekiel is shown a vision of a restored temple in the land of Israel.

53. Jehoiachin's exile began in 597 B.C., so the twenty-fifth year is 572 B.C. An additional twenty-five years of captivity reaches to 547 B.C., at least ten years short of a 536 B.C. date for the return from exile.

54. Jerusalem is mentioned by name twenty-six times in Ezekiel, but never in chaps. 40–48.

- The priesthood: The priests of this new temple are specified as "the sons of Zadok, who are the only Levites who may draw near to the Covenant LORD to minister before him" (40:46; 43:19).
- The altar and sacrifices: To consecrate this altar, a young bull is to be sacrificed for a sin offering, along with daily offerings of a male goat, a young bull, and a ram for seven days. After this initial consecration, the priests are to present burnt offerings and fellowship offerings on the altar (43:18–27).
- The river flowing from the temple: In his vision, Ezekiel sees a river emerging from under the temple, flowing eastward. This river gets ever deeper as it progresses from the temple. When it enters the Dead Sea, the salty waters are instantly converted into fresh water, so that fishermen are able to catch fish of many kinds in the waters that previously had been uninhabitable by fish of any sort. Along the banks of this river are trees having leaves that never wither, bearing fruit every month of the year (47:1–12).
- The redivision of the land: In a new arrangement, seven tribes will inhabit strips of territory running east and west, north of Jerusalem. The remaining five tribes will possess strips of territory running east and west, south of Jerusalem (48:1–29).
- The territory for the temple: Disagreement concerning the precise dimension of the area measured in 42:15–20 goes back to the oldest preserved forms of the text itself. Hebrew manuscripts favor a reading of 500 rods, while the Septuagint favors 500 cubits.[55] A rod is 6 cubits (40:5), so that 500 rods equals

55. The Kethib (the written text) in the Hebrew manuscripts reads "he measured 5 cubits [*khamesh-emot*] rods by the measuring rod" (Ezek. 42:16), which makes no sense. The ancient Hebrew scribes, restraining themselves from modifying the written text, nonetheless indicated in the Qere (the text that was read) that the original wording of the text should be "he measured 500 [*khamesh-meot*] rods by the measuring rod." Quite obviously the written form of the Hebrew text in this verse represents an ancient scribal error, since the temple area must be many times larger than five cubits, and to say "5 cubits rods" is doubly confusing. In the judgment of many interpreters, ancient and modern, 500 rods (at 6 cubits to the rod or roughly 4,500 feet) seems far too large. The Septuagint represents the text as simply "500 by the measuring rod," but this apparent modification of the text then requires the elimina-

3,000 cubits. At 1.5 feet to a cubit, the total distance of each side of this square would equal 4,500 feet. As a consequence, this temple area would stretch far beyond the limits of Mount Zion. It would, in fact, reach westward from the Mount of Olives to a point beyond Jerusalem on the far side of the Tyropean Valley. Some conclude from this observation that the text must refer to 500 cubits rather than 500 rods.[56] Only with this reduction in size could Ezekiel's temple area fit on Mount Zion.

However, given the other larger-than-life aspects of Ezekiel's temple complex—the stream flowing from Mount Zion that rapidly increases in depth so that it cannot easily be crossed, the miraculous power of this stream to heal the waters of the Dead Sea, and the capacity of trees growing along this stream to bear fruit every month with leaves that never wither—it appears perfectly reasonable that the dimensions of the temple area should stretch beyond the confines of Jerusalem's topography. All these elements underscore the fact that Ezekiel, as he himself indicates, is reporting a vision, not a factual description of a temple model that Israel's reconstituted people are expected to construct. In this context, the enlarged size of the temple area suits quite well the visionary character of the prophecy. As Fairbairn states: The size of the temple area as represented in Ezekiel's vision "is an incontrovertible evidence that the prophet had something else in his eye than the masonry of stone and lime erections, and was labouring with

tion of "500 rods" from the next three verses, implying that the measurement was in cubits. In support of the reading "500 rods" is the observation that the phrase *according to the measuring rod* communicates the same meaning even without the presence of the additional appearance of the word *rods*. Keil, *Ezekiel*, 2.269, concludes that "according to one cubit" in 40:21 functions in the same manner as "according to the rod" in 42:16. If the measurement had been in cubits, the text of 42:16 should read "according to the cubit" rather than "according to the rod." For Keil's full discussion of the issue, see 269–73. The reading "500 rods" in 42:16 is also strongly supported by the consistent reading three times in the following three verses: "500 rods according to the measuring rod" (42:17–19).

56. See the discussion of Zimmerli, *Ezekiel*, 2.402. For an alternative interpretation that nonetheless favors cubits, see Block, *Ezekiel*, 2.568 n. 161.

conceptions which could find their embodiment only in the high realities of God's everlasting kingdom."[57]

In other words, the temple envisioned by Ezekiel was never intended to be built, much less built on Mount Zion. Its massive dimensions should be viewed as expressive of the expansive outreaches of the kingdom of God in its future form. A similar circumstance may be seen in the dimensions of the new Jerusalem in the book of Revelation. In this later case, the measurements of the cubical city cause its dimensions to stretch from Jerusalem to Rome and an equal distance upward (Rev. 21:16).

- The returning glory: Central to Ezekiel's vision is the return of the glory that he had seen depart in his earlier vision (43:1–5). The prophet indicates that this vision was "like" the vision he had seen when the Lord came to destroy the temple and "like" the vision he had seen at the time of his initial call by the Kebar River (43:3). The glory of God enters this new temple through the east gate and then fills the temple (43:4–5; 44:4). As a consequence, the Lord declares, "This is the place of my throne and the place for the soles of my feet. This is where I will live among the Israelites forever" (43:7 NIV).

So these various elements constitute the major aspects of Ezekiel's final temple vision. But what is its precise significance?

(3) Significance of the vision

The final vision of Ezekiel has many significances, which arise out of the various perspectives from which it may be viewed. Several of these perspectives may be considered.

How would this concluding vision be viewed by the exiles who had been brought to Babylon by Nebuchadnezzar? Certainly Ezekiel's final message would have given them hope. By this time, some of the exiles, along with their king and their prophet, had resided in this foreign land for twenty-five years or more. This last vision of Ezekiel should have revived in their minds and hearts the expectation of a return at the end of the prescribed seventy years. God was keeping

57. Fairbairn, *Ezekiel*, 470.

time, and he would restore his people to a condition of even greater glory than before, just as he had promised.

How did those who returned from exile at the decree of Cyrus in 536 B.C., some thirty-five years after its revelation to the prophet, view the temple vision of Ezekiel? Did they determine to model their restored temple according to the plan provided by Ezekiel? Did they even make an attempt to reflect the prophet's model? The available evidence offers no suggestion whatsoever that the people who returned from exile reflected in any way the temple plan of Ezekiel when they built their new temple in Jerusalem.[58]

This fact raises the question whether Ezekiel ever intended that a temple be built according to the model described in his vision. Several factors support the presumption that he did not have this intention. The river flowing from under the temple indicates that a geophysical realization of this vision could not be experienced in the present world order. In addition, the imagery of reconstituted tribes of Israel after the loss of their distinctive identity and the division of the land in its new form of parallel plots suggests something other than an actual fulfillment according to the plan of Ezekiel. Furthermore, if the earlier conclusion is correct regarding the size of the temple area, the envisioned temple complex simply could not fit on Mount Zion. As a consequence of these considerations, it appears that Ezekiel never intended his temple to be built after Israel had returned to its land.

But what about the relation of Ezekiel's temple to the provisions of the new covenant anticipated by the prophet himself? How is this temple structure related to the day in which God will give his people a new heart and a new spirit? Could a future day arise in which the ethnic descendants of the twelve tribes of Israel reassemble in the land of their fathers and activate the temple orderings of Ezekiel?

Before an affirmative answer is offered to this question, the consequences of such a conclusion must be carefully weighed. First of all, it must be recognized that though he is now acknowledged as great high priest of the new Israel of God, Jesus Christ could not serve as priest in any such reconstituted temple. Ezekiel's vision gives no recog-

---

58. In the judgment of Block, *Ezekiel*, 2.503, "the postexilic community appears not to have made any effort to implement Ezekiel's program."

nition to a new priesthood "according to the order of Melchizedek" that has replaced the old priestly order. According to his vision, only Levites of a specific family would be able to serve in this temple.

Furthermore, Jesus Christ's self-sacrifice would not have ended blood offerings for sin if this vision becomes reality at some time in the future. Renewed daily and seasonal sacrifices would naturally become the focal center of worship in this new temple. The effort to explain the renewal of sacrifices in terms of memorials looking back to the sacrifice of Christ ignores the fact that the offering of these animals would cost the offerer dearly. In effect, he would have "paid" for the forgiveness of his sins by sacrifice. The idea of memorial sacrifices ignores the explicit declaration that "there remains no more sacrifice for sin" (Heb. 10:18).

These same principles resist even more forcefully the idea that these renewed sacrifices actually would offer temporal cleansing and forgiveness to the offerer and so guarantee protection from physical and temporal punishment.[59] Because the period of anticipating the offering of a coming Christ is now past, no return to the older forms of worship can be accepted to supplement the perfections of the sacrifice of the Christ.

How then is the vision of Ezekiel's temple to come to its fulfillment? Four levels of realization of this consummate vision of the prophet may be noted:

- With regard to the essential concept of a restored temple, this vision of Ezekiel found its realization in the return after exile in 536 B.C. The people of Israel returned to their land, rebuilt the temple, and reinstituted priesthood and sacrifices. Though by the admission of their own prophets, the "greater glory" of the temple was yet to come, God partially displayed his glory in the temple of Israel's restoration.
- In terms of the actual coming of the messiah, John's gospel indicates that in the person of the word incarnate "we beheld his *glory*" (John 1:14 King James Version). Jesus identified

59. See the description of this view in Block, ibid., 503.

himself as the temple that would be destroyed but then revived in greater glory (2:19). He cried out that "springs of living water" would flow from the belly of everyone who believed in him, thereby identifying himself as the source of living water: "'Whoever believes in me, as the Scripture has said, streams of living water will flow from within him.' By this he meant the Spirit, whom those who believed in him were later to receive. Up to that time the Spirit had not been given, since Jesus had not yet been glorified" (7:38–39 NIV).

• A further fulfillment of Ezekiel's temple vision may be seen in individual believers under the new covenant becoming temples, residences of the deity (1 Cor. 6:19). Corporate communities in Christ as well may be described as living temples of God (3:16–17).[60]

• From the perspective of consummative eschatology, it seems difficult to sever the relationship between Ezekiel's vision of the temple and the vision of the apostle John on the isle of Patmos. Granted, no "temple" appears in John's vision. But all that the temple symbolized across the centuries finds its full manifestation in the Lord God Almighty and the person of the Lamb, who have replaced the temple (Rev. 21:22; John 2:19–22). The river of life appears in Revelation together with its trees bearing fruit for every month of the year.[61] In Revela-

60. Block, ibid., 505, expresses well the view of many contemporary Christians when he says that it would be "inconceivable" for Ezekiel to envision a full restoration of his people without a literal fulfillment of a restored Davidic dynasty and a permanent residence of God in the midst of a restored ethnic Jewish community. Yet he instantly comments: "Nevertheless, in view of the considerations cited above, it seems best to interpret ch. 40–48 ideationally." He rejects an eschatological interpretation of the temple vision, but affirms that by this vision Ezekiel "lays the foundation for the Pauline spiritualization of the temple" (506). Block sees no inconsistency in these divergent views.

61. For development of the paradisiacal origins of Ezekiel's river, see Zimmerli, *Ezekiel*, 2.510. In referring to Gen. 2:10–14, Zimmerli says: "All the great rivers of the world come down from this place, which must therefore be thought to be on a high mountain. The inhabited world lives on the surplus of the riches of paradise." This motif of the river of paradise "has been clearly at work in the formation of Ezek 47:1–12 alongside the bare natural phenomena of Palestine." The same imagery recurs in Ps. 46:4, which refers to the "streams that make glad the city of God." See also Isa.

tion's consummative vision, however, the nonwithering leaves are for the healing of the nations (Rev. 22:1–2).[62] Indeed, Ezekiel's temple was never intended to function in a narrowly provincial manner, for he specifically states that residential aliens will receive the identical heritage as the native born (Ezek. 47:22–23). Yet the consummate realization of the heavenly city clearly and properly appears as much more expansive in embracing all the nations of the earth.[63]

In summary, Ezekiel's final vision of the restored temple with the returned glory embodies a fitting conclusion to his message for Israel's exiles as well as for the generations that would follow. Clearly he reached beyond the conceptions of the preexilic prophets that went before him, even though he follows in their train.

8:6–7, where the small stream of Jerusalem is presented as having more potency than the great waters of Assyria.

62. Block, *Ezekiel*, 2.503 n. 26, goes to great lengths to establish that Ezekiel's temple does not correspond to the vision of Rev. 21–22. But the various parallels to which he calls attention are more supportive of a comparison than discouraging to it. Block suggests as a contrast that the "holy city" of Ezekiel remains unnamed, while the city in Revelation is Jerusalem. Yet it might be proposed that the very reason the city remains unnamed in Ezekiel is because he did not intend that it be identified precisely with the contemporary city of Jerusalem. But in the case of John's exalted vision, his city ran no risk of being mistaken for the earthly city. Block also notes that Ezekiel's city is square while John's city is cubical. But does not the movement from shadow to reality involve exactly this kind of enlargement of vision?

63. For extensive discussion of hermeneutical considerations relative to the interpretation of Ezekiel's temple vision, see Fairbairn, *Ezekiel*, 260–68, 431–50. Among other salient points, Fairbairn indicates that the interpreter must begin by noting that the form of the material comes in a visionary form, that modern literalistic Christian interpreters use exactly the same principles as traditionally literalistic Jewish interpreters, and that this method of interpretation, if followed consistently, will lead to the rejection of Jesus the Christ.

11

PROPHETISM DURING THE NATION'S EXILE: DANIEL

Ezekiel views the history of Israel's experience of exile and restoration from the perspective of a priest. He centers his attention on the defilement, devastation, and perfected restoration of the temple. Daniel, on the other hand, views the history of Israel's experience of exile and restoration from an entirely different perspective. He perceives the nation's exile and restoration as a person serving as an official of state on behalf of emperors that rule the world.[1] According to the book's narrative, Daniel was taken captive during one of Nebuchadnezzar's earliest conquering excursions into the west.[2] Having finished off the remnants of the Assyrian army as well as the prime troops of the pharaoh of Egypt at the battle of Carchemish in 605 B.C., the king of Babylon was in supreme control of all territory west of

1. It is often suggested that Daniel's place among the writings rather than among the prophets in the Jewish canon indicates that the book was written after the collection of canonical prophetic books had been completed. But the role of Daniel as a statesman rather than a prophet provides a better rationale for his placement in the canon. Though Daniel had the gift of the prophet in terms of foretelling the future, he never held the office of prophet. According to Harrison, *Introduction to the Old Testament*, 284, "Daniel was a statesman rather than a classic mediator between God and a theocratic nation. His position in the third division of the canon was apparently justified by the fact that works in the K^ethubhim were deemed to have been written by individuals who were not prophets in the strictest sense of the word, but who nevertheless wrote under divine inspiration." See Young, *Prophecy of Daniel*, 20.

2. The opening narrative of Daniel concludes by indicating that Daniel remained in Babylon until the first year of Cyrus (1:21). In other words, he was present during the entire seventy years of Judah's captivity, from 605 to 536 B.C.

the Euphrates down to the border of Egypt.[3] Scripture indicates that "the king of Egypt did not march out from his own country again, because the king of Babylon had taken all his territory, from the Wadi of Egypt to the Euphrates River" (2 Kings 24:7 NIV). Apparently at the same time, this mighty king swept into Judah and took back with him a select number of choice young men so that he could educate them for service in the Babylonian court (2 Kings 24:1; 2 Chron. 36:5–7; Dan. 1:1–4).

The experience of exile and the prospect of restoration obviously had critical significance for Israel. But these events also had clear implications for other nations of the world. The message of the book of Daniel centers on the impact of the dispersal of God's people on the world's empires and the ultimate outcome of the chosen nation's dispersal.

I. A permeating theme: the universal domain of the kingdom of God

Daniel and Ezekiel alone of Israel's prophets make use of a striking image depicting the worldwide character of the kingdoms that are the subjects of their prophesying. This imagery compares the world's empires to a large, spreading tree in which the birds of the air come to nest. According to Ezekiel, the nation of Assyria was once like a cedar in Lebanon, towering above all the other trees of the field. All the birds of the air nested in its boughs, the beasts gave birth under its branches, and other great nations lived in its shade (Ezek. 31:3, 5–6). But because of its pride and wickedness, the Lord handed Assyria over to the most ruthless of foreign nations, which cut it down (31:10–12). Ezekiel then applies the same imagery to the pharaoh of Egypt: "You, too, will be brought down with the trees of Eden to the earth below" (31:18 NIV).

3. According to the Babylonian Chronicle, after defeating Pharaoh Necho at Carchemish, Nebuchadnezzar "conquered the whole area of the Hatti-country," referring to all Syria and Palestine (Wiseman, *Chronicles of the Chaldaean Kings*, 69, line 8; see also 25). Wiseman notes that the effect on Judah "was that king Jehoiakim, a vassal of Necho, submitted voluntarily to Nebuchadrezzar, and some Jews, including the prophet Daniel, were taken as captives or hostages to Babylon" (26).

Even the future, restored kingdom of Israel is depicted by Ezekiel with the same imagery. The prophet first describes the uprooting of a vine as symbolic of the exile of Judah's last king by Nebuchadnezzar (17:1–21). But then the Lord himself declares that he will take a shoot from the very top of a cedar and plant it on the mountain heights of Israel. This tender shoot will become a splendid cedar. Birds of every kind will nest in this tree and will find shelter in the shade of its branches (17:22–23). By this imagery Ezekiel anticipates the future restoration of the Israelite monarchy after its Babylonian exile. Inherent in this imagery is the expectation of a glorious rebirth of the kingdom of God on earth.

In the book of Daniel, the imagery of a spreading tree that provides a safe nesting place for the birds of the air depicts King Nebuchadnezzar of Babylon. The king reports to Daniel his dream of an enormous tree: "The tree . . . was visible to the ends of the earth. Its leaves were beautiful, its fruit abundant, and on it was food for all. Under it the beasts of the field found shelter, and the birds of the air lived in its branches; from it every creature was fed" (4:11–12 NIV). Nebuchadnezzar is puzzled over the significance of this magnificent tree and the decree from heaven that it must be cut down. Daniel explains the vision: "You, O king, are that tree!" (4:22 NIV). His empire has stretched across the breadth of the earth, but he will be humbled under the God of heaven. After his restoration, the king acknowledges the Most High, recognizing that the greatness of the domain represented by the spreading tree actually belongs to Daniel's God. The dominion of God is eternal, and he does as he pleases with the powers of heaven and the peoples on earth (4:34–35). The vast domain of this earthly monarch can function only under the universal dominion of the God of Daniel.

The same concept of the universal, everlasting dominion of the God of heaven recurs as a permeating theme throughout the book. In his interpretation of Nebuchadnezzar's initial vision of the colossus, Daniel declares: "In the time of those kings, the God of heaven will set up a kingdom that will never be destroyed, nor will it be left to another people. It will crush all those kingdoms and bring them to an end, but it will itself endure forever" (2:44 NIV).

After Daniel's deliverance in the den of lions, the theme of the everlasting character of the Lord's kingdom reappears. The king declares: "I issue a decree that in every part of my kingdom people must fear and reverence the God of Daniel. For he is the living God and he endures forever; his kingdom will not be destroyed, his dominion will never end" (6:26 NIV).

Once again, in his own vision of the four beasts that correspond to the four sections of Nebuchadnezzar's colossus, Daniel sees one like a Son of Man approaching the Ancient of Days. This human figure of divine origin receives special honor: "He was given authority, glory and sovereign power; all people, nations and men of every language worshiped him. His dominion is an everlasting dominion that will not pass away, and his kingdom is one that will never be destroyed" (7:14 NIV).

The subsequent interpretation of this vision reaches the same conclusion. Though the powers that oppose the Ancient of Days may triumph at points in their struggle against the saints, their partial victory cannot last forever (7:21–22). The end shall witness the establishment of the eternal kingdom of God: "Then the sovereignty, power and greatness of the kingdoms under the whole heaven will be handed over to the saints, the people of the Most High. His kingdom will be an everlasting kingdom, and all rulers will worship and obey him" (7:27 NIV).

This imagery of the spreading tree shared by Ezekiel and Daniel, Israel's two exilic prophets, appears nowhere else in the written records of either the preexilic or the postexilic prophets of Israel. Their own personal experience of exile, their life under the dominion of the great monarchs of the sixth century B.C., made this imagery especially suitable for them. In a sense they too were as the birds of the air nesting in the branches of these great empires. With all the pain these potentates brought to humanity, they also bestowed blessing on the inhabitants of their land, whether native-born citizens or deportees from other peoples. Jeremiah anticipated this condition when he provided counsel to Israel's captives:

Build houses and settle down; plant gardens and eat what they produce. Marry and have sons and daughters; find wives for your sons and give your daughters in marriage, so that they too may have sons and daughters. Increase in number there; do not decrease. Also, seek the peace and prosperity of the city to which I have carried you into exile. Pray to the Covenant LORD for it, because if it prospers, you too will prosper. (Jer. 29:5–7 NIV)

Seeing these kingdoms prosper in their vast domains must have aided these two exilic prophets in their understanding of what might be expected from the ultimate realization of the universal kingdom of the one true God. The idea of an expansive kingdom, with its center on a high mountain in the land of Israel, is clearly present in the prophecies of Ezekiel (Ezek. 17:23). The picture painted by Daniel stretches to even broader dimensions, though working in the same framework. His concept of the coming kingdom of God broke the bonds of Jewish provincialism and embraced the whole created universe. None of the representations of this vast kingdom of God in Daniel are restricted or even specifically related to Israel's land or nation. This eternal kingdom of God as he saw it embraces equally all the nations of the world.

The imagery of a spreading tree representing the kingdom of God finds its consummate development in the teaching of Jesus. He compares the kingdom of God to a mustard seed, the smallest seed when planted in the ground. Once planted, it "becomes a tree, so that the birds of the air come and perch in its branches" (Matt. 13:32; Mark 4:32; Luke 13:18–19 NIV). The prophets of Israel's exile, living far from their homeland, were the first and only people of the old covenant who spoke with these expansive figures. Jesus, in anticipating the full restoration of the people of God in the kingdom of the messiah, makes use of the same imagery. Peoples from all ages and nations of the world have been blessed with the coming of this kingdom of the Christ and shall continue to be blessed until the consummation.

The whole book of Daniel works from this perspective of a prophesied coming kingdom of God that shall supersede all the earthly kingdoms of this world. The assumption of the book is that God has a plan that will consummate in his kingdom, replacing all earthly, temporal powers. Daniel as God's representative in the kingdom of Babylon appears as the inspired presenter of this universal divine plan.

II. Five critical points

In examining this permeating theme of the book of Daniel, five critical points deserve closer consideration: (1) the colossus of Nebuchadnezzar (2:31–45); (2) the stone cut out without hands (2:34–35); (3) the four beasts, the "little horn," and the Son of Man (7:2–28); (4) the "seventy sevens" (9:24–27); and (5) the "stern-faced king" who "magnifies himself above every god" (8:23; 11:36).

A. The colossus of Nebuchadnezzar (Daniel 2:31–45)

The enormous statue with a head of gold, chest and arms of silver, belly and thighs of bronze, legs of iron, and feet partly of iron and partly of clay appeared to King Nebuchadnezzar in a revelatory dream. According to Daniel, the king's dream originated with the "revealer of mysteries" and unveiled "things to come," anticipating "what is yet to happen" (2:29). The dream made known "what will take place in the future" (2:45). As a consequence, Nebuchadnezzar acknowledges that Daniel's God is the God of gods and the Lord of kings (2:47).[4]

The four different elements of the colossus represent four successive world kingdoms (2:37–40). But what are these kingdoms?

The head of gold is specifically identified by Daniel as Nebuchadnezzar's Babylonian kingdom (2:37–38), but the remaining portions of the statue are not explicitly connected with any subsequent empires. If the declaration is taken seriously that this dream revealed the course of history to Nebuchadnezzar in the sixth century B.C.,

---

4. Nebuchadnezzar acknowledges that Daniel's God is the supreme God because of his ability to anticipate the future. If the God of Daniel does not in actuality predict the future, then the inevitable conclusion must be exactly the reverse: he is not the "God of gods and the Lord of kings."

identification of the subsequent kingdoms is not difficult. Medo-Persia smashed Babylon, Greece overran Medo-Persia, and Rome succeeded Greece as the greatest of ancient empires. As a consequence, this remarkable passage anticipates the broad lines of human history across the subsequent five hundred years. The consummate goal of this history is seen in the establishment of a kingdom by the God of heaven that will never end. This divine kingdom will crush all previous kingdoms and will endure forever (2:44). Noteworthy is the fact that Daniel never foresees a distinctly Israelite kingdom as the consummate realization of God's purposes in human history. Having progressed beyond that point, he sees instead a worldwide kingdom of God that shall encompass all the other kingdoms of the world.

Alternative identifications of the four successive kingdoms generally view the vision of Nebuchadnezzar not as a prediction of future events among the nations of the world that climaxes with the coming of God's kingdom on earth. Instead, these alternative viewpoints see this narrative as a report of history that already has occurred, which is only *presented* as though it were describing future events. Having presupposed that the prediction of future events, particularly on this large scale, is not possible, some other explanation must make sense of Nebuchadnezzar's vision.[5] Since existing manuscripts of the

---

5. See Collins, *Daniel*, 166, who indicates his reason for rejecting the order of Daniel's four kingdoms as being Babylon, Medo-Persia, Greece, and Rome: "Within the chronological restraints of the Book of Daniel, the fourth kingdom can be no later than that of Greece (despite the longstanding tradition that identified it with Rome, beginning with Josephus)." Though he does not elaborate on the nature of these "chronological restraints," he apparently works with the assumption that predictive prophecy cannot function as a legitimate aspect in the analysis of Daniel, despite the book's clear claims to anticipate the future by virtue of divine revelation. In explaining the shift in the identification of the fourth kingdom among commentators, Keil, *Daniel*, 245–46, indicates that "when faith in the supernatural origin and character of biblical prophecy was shaken by Deism and Rationalism, then as a consequence, with the rejection of the genuineness of the book of Daniel the reference of the fourth kingdom to the Roman world-monarchy was also denied." Note also more recently the incisive remark of Baldwin, *Daniel*, 184–85: "With regard to prophecy as foretelling, the church has lost its nerve. An earthbound, rationalistic humanism has so invaded Christian thinking as to tinge with faint ridicule all claims to see in the Bible anything more than the vaguest references to future events. Human thought, enthroned, has judged a chapter such as Daniel 11 to be history written after the event, whereas God enthroned, the one who was present at the

book of Daniel date back to only the second century B.C.[6] and since the final chapters in the book are generally regarded as describing in significant detail the career of Antiochus IV Epiphanes (175–163 B.C.), it is concluded that the narrative sections of Daniel cannot extend beyond events of the second century B.C. As a consequence, the four portions of the statue are identified with a succession of nations that extends only to the second century B.C., thereby leaving Rome (and the coming of Jesus Christ) as outside the scope of Daniel's purview.[7] This perspective yields a suggested sequence of Babylon, Media, Persia, and Greece.[8]

The result of this reassignment puts the author of Daniel in a rather bad light, since the kingdom of Media separate from Persia never replaced Babylon or ruled over the Jews.[9] To speak of a kingdom of Media that conquered Babylon, which in turn was overrun by Persia is to commit a basic historical error. This smirch on the reputation of the author of Daniel, whoever he might be, is still further compounded, for if this material actually originated in the second century B.C., the author is guilty of a subterfuge by pretending that his writings actually predicted future events centuries before they

---

beginning of time and will be present when time is no more, may surely claim with justification to 'announce from of old the things to come' (Is. 44:7)."

6. Collins, *Daniel*, 2.

7. Rome's conquest of Palestine did not occur until 63 B.C. See Bright, *History of Israel*, 458.

8. See Eissfeldt, *Old Testament*, 520. More recently, Goldingay, *Daniel*, 51, limits the span of the four kingdoms to "the period from Nebuchadnezzar to Cyrus." He deduces that "there is no hint of timing in Daniel's revelation" (59) and concludes, without providing a basis for his conclusion, that the vision "implies that history can be divinely foreknown, but not that it is divinely foreordained."

9. Collins, *Daniel*, 166 says: "The inclusion of Media in the succession of world empires appears odd because Media never ruled over the Jews." He then notes that according to some ancient traditions Assyria was succeeded by Media and concludes: "It is clear that the sequence of kingdoms that we find in Daniel is based on the traditional sequence of Assyria, Media, and Persia, which was of Persian origin but was widely known throughout the Near East. Daniel substituted Babylon for Assyria for reasons obvious in the context of Jewish history" (168). However, it is not merely a matter so simple as the substitution of the name *Babylon* for *Assyria* in Daniel. Nebuchadnezzar and his kingdom play a central role in the whole metanarrative of the book.

occurred.[10] The author of Daniel thus appears as a good liar and a bad historian.[11]

Of course, this perspective must ignore the fact that the book of Daniel subsequently identifies the Medo-Persian Empire as a united entity. Daniel later sees a ram with two horns. This two-horned ram is specifically identified as "the kings of Media and Persia" (8:20). This

10. The effort to shield Daniel's reputation by identifying the genre of the book as apocalyptic is not very effective. Collins, *Daniel*, 57, feels compelled to provide "suggestive . . . ways in which departures from literal truth might be morally justified." He refers to Plato's explanation that rulers might find "a considerable dose of falsehood and deceit necessary for the good of their subjects"—as necessary, in fact, as the use of medicine. This representation of the moral character of Daniel stands in stark contrast with the integrity of the same Daniel depicted in the book. This Daniel will in no wise resort to pretense in interpreting the dream of Nebuchadnezzar, contrary to the habit of the king's magicians. According to Collins, the "great achievement of two centuries of historical criticism of the Book of Daniel has been to clarify the genre of the book" (123). Yet a great diversity of opinion still surrounds this very question. While some characteristics generally associated with apocalyptic literature appear in Daniel, the book simply does not fit neatly into a stereotypical apocalyptic genre. In the continuum between prophetic and apocalyptic, Daniel belongs as much to the prophetic form as to the apocalyptic. In commenting on Daniel's development of the kingdom concept, Goldingay, *Daniel*, 59–60, says that Daniel's "understanding of this kingdom is more like the prophetic idea of the Day of Yahweh than that of some later apocalypses." Baldwin, *Daniel*, 46, says that there is "little that strikes the reader as apocalyptic in style or in content in the first six chapters." In a similar vein, Keil, *Daniel*, 27, comments: "Accordingly, the prophecies of Daniel are not distinguished even in their apocalyptic form from the whole body of prophecy in nature, but only in degree." Noting that Daniel does not conform exactly to the apocalyptic model, Collins, *Daniel*, 58, indicates that Daniel is one of the earliest in apocalyptic genre and that its "combination of tales and visions does not conform to any clear precedent and, indeed, does not become a recurrent feature of the genre." He further notes that if Daniel were not presumed to be pseudonymous and therefore containing prophecy *ex eventu*, "the affinities with the apocalypses would be greatly diminished." Collins concludes that its pseudonymous character "has long been established beyond reasonable doubt" (56). But presumed to be pseudonymous is not the same as established as pseudonymous. It is difficult to see how Daniel can be established as a pseudonymous second-century document apart from the presupposition that the possibility of predictive prophecy cannot be considered as a valid alternative.

11. Collins, *Daniel*, 123, judges that "Daniel is not a reliable source of factual information about either the past or the future." He explains that this deficiency is apparent from the "notorious problems" of the references to Darius the Mede and to the period of madness for Nebuchadnezzar, neither of which are attested in external documents. This type of argument from silence should be treated with caution, particularly in view of the long tradition of confident affirmation that Daniel's reference to Belshazzar as

united empire is then attacked by a "shaggy goat," identified as "the king of Greece" (8:21). Daniel thus shows clear evidence of understanding that the Medo-Persian Empire is a single entity and is not to be regarded in his visions as successive empires.

When the later picture of various nations in Daniel 8 is compared with the sequence of four empires in Daniel 2, it leads to the conclusion that from Daniel's perspective the kingdom succeeding Babylon must be Medo-Persia, followed by Greece. With this order in mind, the fourth kingdom must be identified with Rome, and the "stone made without hands" that expands into a worldwide empire should be connected with the birth of Christianity. If the book is taken as it presents itself, the sovereign purpose of the God of redemption across the ages becomes quite apparent.[12]

B. The stone made without hands (Daniel 2:34–35)

The stone cut out without human hands in Nebuchadnezzar's vision requires further consideration. This stone smashes the colossus at its feet and then grows into a "huge mountain" that "fill[s] the whole earth" (2:35). The stone is identified with the kingdom set up by the God of heaven that will never be destroyed (2:44). But can anything be said about the origin of this image of the stone that might aid in its precise identification?

Prior to Israel's exile, Isaiah the prophet had identified the Lord of Israel's covenant as a sanctuary for his people, but also as "a *stone* that causes men to stumble and a rock that makes them fall" for both

---

king of Babylon was unhistorical. This point was asserted as an error in Daniel for many years, until reference to Belshazzar was discovered in the Babylonian Chronicle. A more modest response to the question of the identification of Darius the Mede may be found in the comment of Young, *Prophecy of Daniel*, 183: "Who this individual was, we do not know." Collins also asserts that the inaccuracy of the book is proven by the "unhistorical claim that the book recounts the visions of a Jew in the Exile," a point that may be assumed but is yet to be proven.

12. Since portions of Daniel are found among the Qumran documents, any dating of the book of Daniel that recognizes this sequence is forced to recognize the prophetic anticipation of the events of human history by the God of Daniel. For analysis of the significance of the Qumran material for critical questions regarding the book of Daniel, see Harrison, *Introduction to the Old Testament*, 1118.

houses of Israel (Isa. 8:14 NIV). At the time of Isaiah's prophecy, the nation of Judah along with its king was trembling because of its unbelief as it faced the Syro-Ephraimite military coalition. Though the Covenant LORD is Israel's God, he is no respecter of persons. If the nation will not believe in Immanuel, they will be judged just as severely as the heathen nations. So the Lord manifests himself to them as a stone that makes them stumble and a rock that makes them fall.

As a solid "stone," the Lord does not alter his purpose to execute righteous judgment on his own servants or on the nations of the world. In Daniel the stone imagery serves as a symbolic instrument of God's righteous judgment on the nations of the world. This stone crushes the nations at its coming and then expands to become a kingdom that rules over all peoples. But just as King Nebuchadnezzar himself served as symbolic embodiment of earthly power, so this stone in the king's dream functions as an image of the regal head of God's kingdom on earth. This "stone" is not merely an inanimate power, an "it." Instead, the "stone" should be perceived as a person, a sovereign that embodies the kingdom of God in himself and supersedes all other earthly monarchs.

From the perspective of new covenant scriptures, Jesus Christ is the sovereign stone who appeared in the days of Daniel's fourth kingdom and who exercises authority over all the kings of the earth. Though rejected by the Jewish people who were commissioned to rebuild the holy temple of God in the midst of a depraved world, Jesus became the chief cornerstone of the kingdom of God on earth (Mark 12:10; Ps. 118:22). He is the "stone that causes men to stumble" and the "rock that causes offense" (1 Pet. 2:8, quoting Isa. 8:14). He has become the single great point of judgment for all men and nations, for "everyone who falls on that stone will be broken to pieces, but he on whom it falls will be crushed" (Luke 20:18 NIV).

C. The four beasts, the little horn, and the Son of Man (Daniel 7:2–28)

Daniel's own personal vision of the four great beasts arising out of the tumultuous sea (7:2–3) raises the question of the structure of the book. A great temptation exists to simplify the book's structure by dividing between Daniel 1–6, which presents historical experiences and revelations arising from contact with the rulers of Babylon, and Daniel 7–12, which records the dreams and visions of Daniel himself. A more convincing division is the following:[13]

- Daniel 1 (Hebrew) describes the historical setting of the book.
- Daniel 2–7 (Aramaic) begins and ends with visions of the four kingdoms that stretch into the future.[14]
- Daniel 8–12 (Hebrew) deals with visions and events related to Daniel's second and third kingdoms, leading up to the final consummation.

This structural analysis of the book underscores the close connection between the four kingdoms of Daniel 2 and the four beasts of Daniel 7. This connection in turn suggests a relationship between the stone cut without hands in Daniel 2 and the Son of Man in Daniel 7.[15]

13. In support of this analysis of the structure of the book, see Keil, *Daniel*, 15.

14. For the impact of the Aramaic portions of Daniel on fixing a date for the book, see the discussion of Baldwin, *Daniel*, 30–35. After citing discussions of H. H. Rowley, K. A. Kitchen, and E. Y. Kutscher, Baldwin concludes: "It is becoming an accepted fact that the date of Daniel cannot be decided on linguistic grounds, and that the increasing evidence does not favour a second-century, western origin" (34–35).

15. For a strong argument supporting the unity of the book based significantly on the pivotal role of Dan. 7, see Rowley, *Servant of the Lord*, 250–60. In concluding his treatment, Rowley says: "The onus of proof lies upon those who would dissect a work. Here, however, nothing that can be seriously called proof of compositeness has been produced. On the other hand, evidence for the unity of the work that in its totality amounts to a demonstration is available" (268). Rowley's case for the unity of Daniel effectively sets aside proposals for a split-level approach that dates chaps. 7–12 in the second century B.C. during the time of the Maccabees, while assigning chaps. 1–6 to some uncertain occasion in a previous century. Having established so convincingly the book's unity and integrity, Rowley himself is compelled to make a choice. Either he must regard the whole book of Daniel for what it presents itself to be, as a sixth-century message of comfort and reassurance from the sovereign Lord of all nations to Israel's exiles in Babylon; or he must treat the book as one massive literary charade composed in the second century B.C., while presenting itself under the consistently held pretense that it arose in the sixth century B.C. Rowley dates the book in the Maccabean era and, as might be expected, presents an imaginative case for turning the stories of the first six chapters into tales that suit the age of the Maccabees (264–66). His argument that these same narratives would have no significance "before the second century B.C." fails to consider the consistent min-

In seeking to understand the vision of Daniel 7, three elements prove to be of great significance: the four beasts, the "little horn," and the Son of Man.

1. The four beasts

Inherent in the description of the four beasts in Daniel 7 are many factors that confirm their identity as the same four kingdoms represented by the various portions of the colossus in Daniel 2: Babylon, Medo-Persia, Greece, and Rome:

- The first beast is "like a lion" but has the wings of an eagle. The wings of this beast are torn off, and it is given the heart of a man (7:4). This description fits King Nebuchadnezzar, identified in the first vision as the head of gold. The torn-off wings and the heart of a man represent his humbling experience at the hands of the Almighty (4:31–33).
- The second beast is "raised up on one of its sides," making apparent that it has two sides and establishing a correspondence with the two-horned ram in Daniel 8, which is identified as the kingdom of Medo-Persia (7:5; 8:3, 20).
- The third beast appears as a leopard with four wings. The rapid conquest of this kingdom is underscored by its comparison to a leopard, particularly a leopard equipped with four wings (7:6a). This characteristic of speed complies well with the conquests of Alexander the Great and connects with the vision of the single-horned goat coming from the west that crosses the whole earth without touching the ground, which is identified as Greece (8:5, 21). This beast has four heads, anticipating the fourfold division of Alexander's empire (7:6b; see also 8:8).
- The form of the fourth beast is not identified with any particular member of the animal kingdom. Instead, his terrifying countenance, large iron teeth, and ten horns underscore

---

istry of Israel's prophets to the nation by assuring them of their God's long-term redemptive plans for the future.

the beastly aspect of this creature and remind the reader that all these images appeared as beasts. Something noble might be associated with the gold and silver portions of the colossus in Daniel 2. But these beasts rising from the tumultuous sea are all carnivorous creatures, deadly threats to the life of a human.

The four beasts of Daniel 7 thus correspond quite closely to the four elements of the colossus of Daniel 2. In Daniel 7 the dominant powers of the coming ages are seen as beasts that threaten the life of the people of God. Rising out of the tumultuous sea, they represent the disorder created by the corrupt kingdoms of a fallen world (Isa. 17:12–14; Jer. 46:7–8; Rev. 13:1). If the kingdom of God is to be restored on earth, it will face great opposition from these beastly authorities.

2. The little horn

Climactically, the ten horns of the fourth creature are superseded by a little horn. Though an embodiment of the force that belongs to the fourth beast, this horn had "the eyes of a man and a mouth that spoke boastfully," which immediately places him in a sinister role (7:8 NIV). This little horn reappears in the interpretation of the vision provided to Daniel. In accord with his boastful speaking, this embodiment of human power will "speak against the Most High," will "oppress the saints," and will "try to change the set times and the laws" (7:25). Surprisingly, "the saints will be handed over to him" for a specified period ("time, times, and half a time"; 7:25), but eventually God will bring this oppression of his people to a halt. He will take away all power that is subversive to his righteous rule, and the "sovereignty, power and greatness of the kingdoms . . . will be handed over to the saints, the people of the Most High" (7:26–27 NIV).

Who is this little horn? From Daniel's perspective, he represents an embodiment of governmental powers arising as a late manifestation of the fourth empire. If the sequence of the four kingdoms is rightly identified, he arises as part of the Romanish manifestation of earthly powers and represents the epitome of human authority in opposition to the kingdom of God.[16]

Quite remarkable is the extent of the parallelism between this little horn of the fourth beast of Daniel and the beast described in Revelation 13. This beast comes out of the sea, has ten horns, and resembles in its various parts a leopard, a bear, and a lion (Rev. 13:1–2; Dan. 7:4–6). This beast utters blasphemies and exercises his authority for forty-two months, the equivalent of Daniel's "time, times, and half a time" or 3.5 years (Rev. 13:5; Dan. 7:25). He is given power to war against the saints "and to conquer them" (Rev. 13:7; Dan. 7:21). The saints who are conquered by the beast are described in Revelation as those who "go into captivity," indicating that the exilic experience of Israel now has taken on eschatological significance (Rev. 13:10). From a New Testament consummative perspective, this little horn of the fourth beast in Daniel 7 appears to find its ultimate embodiment in Paul's depiction of the "man of lawlessness." According to the expectation of the apostle, "He will oppose and will exalt himself over everything that is called God or is worshiped, so that he sets himself up in God's temple, proclaiming himself to be God" (2 Thess. 2:4 NIV).

The final outcome of this conflict with the various manifestations of the beast will be a sure victory of the saints. At an earlier point, one of the three heads of this beast received what appeared to be a fatal wound, but the wound healed (Rev. 13:3). Eventually the one who made the heaven, earth, and sea shall be properly worshiped by his creation (14:7). In that day, one "like a Son of Man" will appear on a white cloud with a crown of gold on his head and a sharp sickle in his hand (14:14). This one shall preside over the righteous judgment that all created beings must undergo (Dan. 7:11–14, 22, 26–27). This Son of Man is the third element that requires further consideration in the vision of Daniel 7.

16. Young, *Prophecy of Daniel*, 147, does not interpret the ten horns of this fourth beast as operating simultaneously. Instead, these ten horns are understood as representing an indefinite number of empires after the Romanish style of Western culture.

3. The Son of Man

In one of the most discussed passages of all scripture, Daniel describes his vision of one like a Son of Man who comes with the clouds of heaven to the Ancient of Days. This Son of Man is depicted in the most exalted terms imaginable: "He was given authority, glory and sovereign power; all peoples, nations and men of every language worshiped him. His dominion is an everlasting dominion that will not pass away, and his kingdom is one that will never be destroyed" (7:14 NIV).

Several factors may be affirmed about this Son of Man. First of all, he is a man, a person, a human being in sharp contrast with the previously described beasts. As man, he bears the image of the creator God and possesses the potential to rule over all creation (Gen. 1:27–28). Second, he comes in the clouds to the Ancient of Days for an occasion of investiture. This coming in the clouds indicates his divine origin, since in scripture only God himself comes in the clouds.[17] Third, this Son of Man receives from the Ancient of Days a kingdom that is both universal and eternal. All peoples of all nations worship him, and his dominion over all endures forever. In other words, he is king of kings and lord of lords. This kingdom, as expansive as God's domain, reaches far beyond the boundaries of a restored Jewish empire restricted to the land of the Bible.

This glorious Son of Man cannot be properly located in the hall of Jewish heroes of the second century B.C. As Jerome in his fourth-century commentary insisted on pointing out, by the greatest stretch of the imagination this Son of Man in Daniel cannot be identified with Judas Maccabees, for that man obviously never came with the clouds in glory to rule eternally over all nations.[18] The whole imagery of

17. The clouds serve as the chariot on which God comes from heaven to execute judgment, which fits well the context of Dan. 7. See Pss. 18:10–11; 97:2–4; 104:3; Isa. 19:1; Nah. 1:3.

18. Jerome's remarks are worth quoting in full as a no-nonsense response to the first unbelieving, rationalistic commentary on Daniel: "Let Porphyry answer the query of whom out of all mankind this language might apply to, or who this person might be who was so powerful as to break and smash to pieces the little horn, whom he interprets to be Antiochus? If he replies that the princes of Antiochus were defeated by Judas Maccabeus, then he must explain how Judas could be said to come with the clouds of heaven like unto the Son of Man, and to be brought unto the Ancient of Days, and how it could be said that authority and royal power was bestowed upon him, and that all

Daniel's vision breaks the bonds of the limited conquests of the Maccabean resistance to Seleucid rule.

Neither should this Son of Man be defined as a corporate personality, as only a symbol for the saints of the Most High. It is true that later in this chapter the sovereignty of earthly kingdoms is handed over to the saints, the people of the Most High (7:27a). But the point is immediately made that the kingdom belongs to the Most High and that all rulers will worship and obey him (7:27b). The worship of all nations also belongs to the Son of Man, but never to the saints (7:14).[19]

Interestingly, this Son of Man is never identified by Daniel as a son of David or as an heir to David's throne. This kind of notation might have been expected if the book of Daniel had its origin in the days of the Maccabees.[20] The absence of this sort of connection further indicates the authenticity of this passage in the context of the historical Daniel, who spent his entire adult life at the highest level of the court officials of the Babylonian Empire. Daniel had the special task of interpreting the significance of Israel's exile for the nations of the world in which he lived. The kingdom of God that he portrayed never took on the form of a restored kingdom of Israel. It was instead a worldwide kingdom that embraced equally all the nations of the world.

At the same time, though not related specifically to the expectation of a restored Davidic kingdom, this Son of Man represents a natural extension of the idea of a coming Davidic messiah. The figure of the Son of Man in Daniel 7 parallels the image of the stone cut out without human hands in Daniel 2. This earlier image in Daniel develops out of the previous description of the stone found in Psalm 118:22–23 and Isaiah 8:14; 28:16. In Daniel 7, however, this mes-

---

peoples and tribes and language groups served him, and that his power is eternal and not terminated by any conclusion" (*Daniel*, 80–81).

19. Collins, *Daniel*, 309, rejects the corporate interpretation of Son of Man. He identifies the saints as angels and the Son of Man as Michael, the leader of the heavenly host (318). But this view has special difficulties when it is noted that the Son of Man receives worship and is made Lord over all the nations in a way that reflects the authority of God himself (Dan. 7:14).

20. According to Fischer, the rule of the Maccabees "was regarded as the fulfillment of prophecy and even as the re-establishment of the empires of David and Solomon" ("Maccabees," 441).

sianic stone imagery is expanded in a manner that makes it suitable to the enlarged vision of the kingdom of God as developed in Daniel.

This perspective on the Son of Man in Daniel finds explicit confirmation in the term's being the principle mode of self-identification by Jesus. According to the testimony of the gospels, Jesus rarely if ever referred to himself by the term *messiah*, and on only a few occasions was he addressed with that title by others. But he constantly spoke of himself as the Son of Man. The reason for these choices on Jesus' part seems to be that while the designation *messiah* was overloaded with popular conceptions involving strong political overtones, the term *Son of Man* could function for Jesus as a self-designation with a more moldable character. Though certain Old Testament scriptures made use of the phrase, it apparently had not penetrated deeply into the parlance of the day.[21] As a consequence, Jesus could freely use the term in reference to himself without stirring up strong political connotations in the minds of his hearers. He was even able to shape the definition of the term, which he did by depicting the Son of Man in basically two frameworks: as one who would suffer abuse (Matt. 17:22–23) and as one who would come in glory as judge (24:30–31).

The climax of Jesus' use of the term *Son of Man* as a self-designation emerges at the end of his life when he deliberately and unquestionably places himself in the role of Daniel's glorious Son of Man. This use of the term by Jesus bursts into center stage at the dramatic moment of his cross-examination by the high priest of Israel: "Are you the Christ, the Son of the Blessed One?" the high priest enquires of Jesus. "'I am,' said Jesus. 'And you will see the Son of Man sitting at the right hand of the Mighty One and coming on the clouds of heaven'" (Mark 14:61–62 NIV). "With this verse we come to the christological climax of the gospel," says France.[22] He further comments:

21. See Goldingay, *Daniel*, 167, who says the term comes to be a title in *1 Enoch* 37–71, *4 Ezra* 13, the New Testament, and rabbinic writings, but "even here it is doubtful whether we should think in terms of a 'Son of man concept' in Judaism. Still less is there evidence that in the second century B.C. the phrase is used as a title or alludes to a well-known concept."

22. France, *Mark*, 610.

[Jesus'] use of that [Son of Man] title here in place of the high priest's "the Christ" serves to emphasise the contrast between this vision and the connotations which the term Christ might have evoked for most Jews at the time. He is the Messiah [*ego eimi*], but his messianic vision is on a different level altogether from what the high priest may have been implying. Any concept of the Messiah as a nationalistic deliverer at a political level has been left far behind: Jesus' "triumph" is to be at the right hand of God. Even though the charge brought before Pilate will resuscitate the more political connotations of the term *Christos*, Jesus has in this climactic declaration again distanced himself decisively from any such understanding of his mission.[23]

The high priest needs no further testimony. Filled with pious indignation, he rips apart his clothing and pronounces Jesus guilty of blasphemy. All those with him agree that the man uttering this statement must die.

Because Jesus placed himself in the role of the Son of Man depicted by Daniel, he is judged to be claiming deity for himself. If he depicts himself as sitting enthroned at God's right hand and coming from heaven enveloped in clouds, he must be assuming God's prerogative as sovereign and judge. While Jesus had previously used this Son of Man terminology to identify himself many times, he now clearly sets himself in the context of Daniel's glorified image of the Son of Man, thus claiming deity as well as humanity. People may choose to acknowledge or to repudiate this declaration of Jesus about himself, but the claim is apparent. He is the God-man, worthy of the worship of all men and nations. In this regard, the concept of a coming messianic ruler is carried a significant step beyond the limiting idea of a descendant of David who restores a distinctively Jewish kingdom in the land promised to the fathers. Now the coming king unites a divine origin with his human manifestation. Rather than depicting restoration after exile as simply a return of Jewish people to their ancient homeland, the realm of this kingdom now encompasses all peoples of all nationalities in an eternal kingdom with universal dimensions.

23. Ibid., 613.

D. The seventy sevens (Daniel 9:24–27)

One of the few passages in the prophets that actually uses the term *messiah* is found in the prophecy of Daniel concerning the seventy sevens (9:24–27). This passage has been called the "dismal swamp of Old Testament criticism," and yet it is one of the most glorious of prophecies found in the old covenant scriptures.[24] However the passage is interpreted, the main point of the revelation to Daniel is plain: "A definite time has been decreed by God for the accomplishment of all that which is necessary for the true restoration of God's people from bondage."[25] Several pieces that make up this exegetical puzzle must be fit together to make sense of the prophecy.

1. The context

The immediate, intermediate, and full biblical-theological contexts all have significant bearing on the interpretation of this passage. Starting with the intermediate range that encompasses the whole book of Daniel, the place of the seventy sevens has special significance. Nebuchadnezzar's dream of the image in Daniel 2 had anticipated successive earthly kingdoms beginning with Babylon and continuing through Medo-Persia, Greece, and Rome. This sequence climaxed with the triumph of the eternal, worldwide kingdom of God over all earthly domains as the "stone made without hands" expanded to fill the whole earth. Daniel's own vision of the four beasts in Daniel 7 climaxed with the awarding of all these kingdoms to one like the Son of Man, coming in the clouds as he approached the Ancient of Days. In a similar way, the "seventy sevens" of Daniel 9 spans the time from the contemporary kingdom of Medo-Persia to the arrival of the anointed one, the prince. In each of the three instances of prophetic vision recorded in Daniel 2, 7, and 9, the time span stretches from the period contemporary with the prophet to the coming of the messiah in the glories of his ever-enduring kingdom.

24. Montgomery, as cited in Young, *Prophecy of Daniel*, 191. Montgomery also speaks of the "trackless wilderness of assumptions and theories" that attempt to determine an exact chronology for the seventy weeks that fits the history of redemption; Montgomery, *Daniel*, 401.

25. Young, *Prophecy of Daniel*, 194.

The immediate context within Daniel 9 itself connects the opening reference to the "seventy years" of Israel's captivity, as predicted by Jeremiah, to the "seventy sevens" that anticipate future days (9:2, 24). The relationship between these two seventies leads naturally to the fuller biblical-theological context of the prophecy as it relates to the old covenant scriptures. "Seventy" was not simply a random number that determined the length of Israel's years in captivity. As the inspired historian of Israel indicated, their captivity lasted for seventy years because of Israel's neglect of the sabbatical-year principle (2 Chron. 36:21). This analysis of the seventy years of Israel's captivity finds its root even more deeply in redemptive history, going back to the witness of the Pentateuch. The threat of the covenantal curse for Israel's disobedience was that they would be expelled from the land of their inheritance, so that "the land will have the rest it did not have during the sabbaths you lived in it" (Lev. 26:35 NIV). "Then the land will enjoy its sabbath years all the time that it lies desolate" (26:34 NIV). This fuller consideration of the context of the concluding verses in Daniel 9 provides the proper framework for understanding the nature of the seventy sevens.

2. The nature of the seventy sevens

It might be presumed that the seventy sevens of Daniel 9 should be regarded purely from a figurative perspective, in light of the broader scriptural role of the Sabbath concept in redemptive history. Indeed, the symbolic character of the number seven as an aspect of the Sabbath concept must not be ignored. The perfection of sevens as embodied in the "seventy sevens" speak of the movement toward the final climax of the Covenant LORD's redemptive work in the world. The Sabbath rest that remains for the people of God must be seen as the ultimate goal of the seventy sevens (Heb. 4:9).

At the same time, the context in which Daniel's prophecy is found inevitably points to an actual chronological ordering in the purposes of God. Jeremiah did not predict Israel's banishment from the land to be, for example, twenty-three years or forty-one years in length—he predicted seventy years. While the overscrupulous may bicker about the precise beginning and ending of the seventy years, the span still stands quite definitively. Seventy years prior to 536 B.C. takes us back

339

to approximately 605 B.C., which served as Jeremiah's marker for the beginning of the seventy years of exile (Jer. 25:1–3, 11).

If a specific chronological ordering is manifest in the seventy years of Israel's captivity as predicted by Jeremiah, and if this principle of seventy in the earlier portion of Daniel 9 has a significant connection with the seventy of the latter portion of the same chapter, it seems likely that the "seventy sevens" also have some chronological significance.[26] In addition, some reason must be given for the breakdown of Daniel's seventy sevens into three periods consisting of seven sevens, sixty-two sevens, and one seven. A purely figurative analysis is totally at a loss to explain this subdivision of the sevens; and yet the breakdown clearly has significance in Daniel's vision.

Resolution of the question concerning the nature of the seventy sevens may be found in an inclusion of the symbolic in the chrono-

---

26. The proverbial horns of a dilemma are evident in this question of whether the seventy sevens should be understood chronologically or symbolically. It is true that Dan. 9 refers several times to the rebuilding of the city of Jerusalem and not merely the temple in its references to Cyrus's decree (Isa. 44:28); that the context of Dan. 9 flows naturally toward an expectation that the prophesied seventy weeks will begin as the seventy years of captivity conclude in 536 B.C.; and that the decree of Artaxerxes (as an alternative date for the beginning of the seventy sevens) was unknown to the age contemporary with Daniel (Poythress, "Hermeneutical Factors"). These observations favor a purely symbolic understanding of the seventy weeks. At the same time, it is also true that a distinction is specifically made in Ezra and Nehemiah between the historic decree of Cyrus to rebuild the temple and the decree of Artaxerxes to rebuild the city; that the actual decree of Cyrus as recorded in the Cyrus Cylinder (Pritchard, *Ancient Near Eastern Texts*, 316) authorizes the rebuilding of temples of foreign gods (not cities); that the connection with the clearly chronological seventy years of Daniel favors a chronological dimension to the seventy weeks; and that many prophetic elements, particularly in subsequent chapters of Daniel, remain altogether unknown to the prophet, as Daniel himself acknowledges (12:8–9). These considerations favor a chronological/symbolical understanding of the passage. Still further, support "after the fact" may be found in the closeness with which the period designated by the seventy weeks approximates the actual historical chronology between the decree of Artaxerxes and the ministry of Jesus Christ. Insistence on absolute precision in dating should not be allowed to detract from the remarkable character of the prediction. On balance, the chronological/symbolical understanding of the passage is to be favored, with the decree of Artaxerxes serving as the beginning point of the seventy weeks. Though not supporting the chronological nature of the seventy sevens, Kline binds the two seventies of Dan. 9 together by noting their joint connection with the sabbatical-year principle of Lev. 25 ("Covenant of the Seventieth Week," 459).

logical. The larger picture of movement through history toward the climax of God's redemptive purposes in the rest, the Sabbath that remains for the people of God, must not be forgotten. At the same time, some effort must be made to determine the intentional chronological ordering of the ages.

3. The chronological limits of the seventy sevens

The supposition that the initiation point of the seventy sevens must begin at 536 B.C. with the decree of Cyrus makes any chronological rendering of the passage untenable. The seventy "sevens" of Daniel quite clearly intend to echo the seventy years of Israel's exile mentioned earlier in the same chapter. Since the seventy years of captivity represent seventy Sabbath years that have been neglected by Israel (2 Chron. 36:21; Lev. 25:1–7), Daniel's seventy "sevens" are best understood as involving seventy "weeks" of years, or 490 years. If these 490 years begin at 536 B.C., they reach to only 47 B.C., a date with no special significance. Closer adherence to the text itself indicates that the starting point of the seventy weeks of years is not the initial return of the Jews in response to the 536 B.C. decree of Cyrus, but the subsequent return under Nehemiah in approximately 445 B.C. The going forth of the decree for the "rebuilding of Jerusalem," not simply the return of the people to the land, marks the beginning of the chronological clock of the seventy weeks (Dan. 9:25). The distinction between these two royal proclamations is made apparent in the historical description of the two events in the books of Ezra and Nehemiah. The 536 B.C. decree of Cyrus was directed toward the rebuilding of the temple, while the 445 B.C. decree of Artaxerxes commissioned the rebuilding of the city (Ezra 1:2–4; Neh. 1:1, 3; 2:3, 5, 8, 17).[27]

With this starting point for the seventy sevens or 490 years, the subdivision of the seventy weeks of years is as remarkable as the

27. See the specific nature of the decree of Cyrus as found in the Cyrus Cylinder: "I returned to (these) sacred cities on the other side of the Tigris, the sanctuaries of which have been ruins for a long time, the images which (used) to live therein and established for them permanent sanctuaries. I (also) gathered all their (former) inhabitants and returned (to them) their habitations" (Pritchard, *Ancient Near Eastern Texts*, 316). The objection of Baldwin, *Daniel*, 176, is not supported by the statements of the texts in Ezra and Nehemiah.

prophecy of Jeremiah concerning the seventy-year length of Israel's captivity. The first unit of seven weeks, or 49 years, extends from the decree of Artaxerxes to approximately 400 B.C., which corresponds to the time at which old covenant revelation came to its conclusion. The next unit of sixty-two weeks, or 434 years, comes down to approximately A.D. 30, the time of the life, ministry, death, and resurrection of Jesus the anointed one. The final single week of years has its own distinctive significance, which also must be determined in the framework of a full biblical-theological context.

Obviously this kind of detailed anticipation of the course of human history cannot be entertained for one instant by modern negative criticism. In the contemporary context in which the idea that God has a plan for this world is totally denied, the inevitable conclusion must be that to the degree that this material describes the actual course of human history, it must have been composed after the event. But taken in the form in which it actually appears as a detailed, long-term prediction of the course of human events as they relate to God's purposes of redemption, the prophecy of Daniel concerning the seventy sevens is indeed remarkable. It by no means stands alone among biblical anticipations regarding the work of the coming messiah. But it should call forth a firm, well-grounded faith in the God who orders the course of history so that it serves his greater redemptive purposes.

4. The accomplishment of redemption within the seventy sevens

Six noteworthy redemptive purposes are realized within the context of these seventy weeks, three of them referring to the removal of sin and three describing the establishment of righteousness. First of all, this period is determined by God as a time to "finish transgression, to put an end to sin, and to atone for wickedness" (9:24a NIV). These first three items clearly reflect the divine response to the acknowledgement of sin made ten times over by Daniel in the first half of the chapter (9:5, 6, 7, 8, 9, 10, 11, 14, 15, 16). This threefold description of the removal of sin places at the center of God's purposes in human history the removal of offenses that separate people from their creator God. Transgression, sin, and iniquity will be atoned for, ended, and finished. This reference to the removing of human sin by atonement anticipates no other event than the sacrifice of the innocent lamb of God for the sin of his people. By his death on the cross and by his death alone can the liability for transgression of God's law be removed. No other event of the past or the future can possibly repeat what the death of Jesus Christ accomplished. At the same time, the complete removal of actual sin and transgression must await the consummative return of the Christ. At that time he shall put away iniquity with absolute finality.

In addition, this period of seventy sevens is appointed by God "to bring in everlasting righteousness, to seal up vision and prophecy and to anoint the most holy [place]" (9:24b). The righteousness that Jesus Christ established by his life and death will never pass away, for the sinner who has once been declared just by faith will possess forever all the righteousness of the Son of God that has been imputed to him. Upon the completion of his work on the cross, the resurrected, ascended, and exalted Lord Jesus Christ anointed the heavenly most holy place with his blood (Heb. 9:12). As the final, the consummate word from God to men, Jesus sealed up vision and prophecy. Once his redemptive work was properly interpreted and transcribed by the apostles and prophets of the New Testament era, no need remained for additional vision and prophecy.

The six items accomplished by the conclusion of the seventy weeks all focus on the life, death, resurrection, and entering into glory of the Lord Jesus Christ, the anointed one, the prince of his people. The previous world-history visions of the earlier chapters of Daniel confirm this point, for in each case they climax with Christ's coming into the world and the spread of his kingdom until the end of the age. In Daniel 2, he is the stone cut out without human hands that crushes all earthly empires and then expands to fill all the earth. In Daniel 7, he is the glorious Son of Man who approaches the Ancient of Days, brings an end to sin, and receives from him power over all the kingdoms of the world. The seventy sevens of Daniel's vision, therefore, focus on the two great advents of the Christ. In this vision, all human history is dramatically depicted. It is in this context that the uniqueness of the seventieth week must be understood.

5. The uniqueness of the seventieth week

The setting apart of the seventieth week from the other sixty-nine weeks inherently implies the uniqueness of the last week. But what specifically is the nature of this uniqueness? Why is it set apart from the other sevens? Many answers to this question have been proposed. Two rather different answers may be contrasted with one another.

First, some students of the Bible find the temporal placement of this seventieth week to be unique. According to this hypothesis, regularly designated as the "gap theory," the seventieth week is distinctive in that it is chronologically separated from the other sixty-nine weeks. According to this view, the presence of a gap in the seventy weeks is proven by the destruction of Jerusalem almost forty years after the death of Christ, which represents too long a period for the seventieth seven.[28] As a consequence, an initial gap appeared in the seventy weeks. In the meantime, the whole contemporary age of the church has developed. The past two thousand years, from the time of Christ until the present, represent a gap in the prophesied weeks of Daniel. This gap could continue into the indefinite future and will continue until the end of the unforeseen church age, the establishment of a revived Roman Empire, and the beginning of the Jewish millennial kingdom.

Two rather obvious considerations argue against this gap theory regarding the seventieth week of Daniel. First and foremost, the complete absence of any hint of a gap in the passage itself argues against the theory. Nothing in Daniel 9:24–27 even implies, much less establishes, this kind of gap in the progress of the seventy sevens. Kaiser proposes that the phrase *after the sixty-two sevens* "seems to suggest a gap."[29] But the minute exegetical possibility resting on an unusual interpretation of the common word *after* appears as a rather precarious base for establishing a two-thousand-year-long gap in world history. Everything in the context suggests a normal succession of the seventieth week following the sixty-ninth. It is somewhat difficult to imagine how the writer might have indicated that the seventieth week

---

28. Walvoord, *Daniel*, 230.
29. Kaiser, *Messiah in the Old Testament*, 203.

followed the completion of the sixty-ninth week without saying that the seventieth week came "after" the previous weeks.

A second perspective on the question of the distinctive nature of the seventieth week appears to be more firmly rooted in the context of Daniel as well as in the larger biblical-theological framework of scripture. This final week, unlike all the previous weeks, is divided into two halves: "In the midst of the seven [i.e., at the halfway point of the seven; *khatsi*], he will cause sacrifice and offering to cease" (9:27). This cessation of sacrifice corresponds with the atoning of iniquity and the bringing in of eternal righteousness (9:24) accomplished earlier in the seventy sevens. Once iniquity has been covered by a proper atonement, there can be "no more sacrifice for sin" (Heb. 10:26). This climactic event, according to Daniel 9:27, is to occur at the halfway point of the seventieth week of seven years, or 3.5 years into the last week.

The figure of 3.5 years receives further development in the final chapter of the book of Daniel and even more extensively in the book of Revelation. In his final interview with the revealing person, Daniel overhears the question, "How long will it be before these astonishing things are fulfilled?" (Dan. 12:6 NIV). The man clothed in linen takes a solemn oath that the period will be "for a time, times, and half a time," reflecting the same earlier measurement of the time that the saints will suffer at the hands of the little horn of the fourth beast of Daniel 7 (12:7; see also 7:25). This same measurement recurs in the form of 1,290 (or 1,335) days that are to expire between the time that the daily sacrifice is abolished and the abomination that causes desolation is set up (12:11–12).

The various ways in which this last half of the final week is designated in Daniel suggest that the time measurement has been modified from the chronological/symbolical to the purely symbolical. The book of Revelation reflects the same diversity in referring to an identical period as a symbolical device: 1,260 days, 42 months, and "time, times, and half a time" (Rev. 11:2–3; 12:6, 14; 13:5). The last half of the seventieth week of Daniel may thus be regarded as a different form of time measurement. This last half-week symbolically represents a longer period of time, indefinite in length, which extends from the ending of sacrifice until the destruction of the antichrist at the consummation of the present age. During this last epoch of time, if the book of Revelation is allowed to provide some insight, the true people of God will be persecuted relentlessly as they bear witness throughout the world. But they will also be protected by the providential orderings of the Lord (11:2–3; 12:6, 14; 13:5). At the end, all enemies of the Lord will be destroyed at his coming.[30]

This section in Daniel should be viewed as one of the significant passages anticipating the coming of the messiah and his kingdom into this fallen world. By his appearance, sin will be overcome, eternal righteousness brought in, and the powers of darkness embodied in the work of Satan and manifested through earthly world powers will be destroyed. The coming of Jesus the Christ, the offering of his body as a sacrifice, and the subsequent spread of his kingdom through all ages to the ends of the earth should encourage the believer to look forward with great anticipation to the final defeat of all his and our enemies. Even though the saints must endure a prolonged period of persecution, their ultimate deliverance will be glorious.

E. The stern-faced king (Daniel 8:23; 11:36)

If a person accepts the reality of predictive prophecy in the old covenant scriptures, no principle problem should exist in regarding

---

30. Several other points of exegetical difficulty appear in these verses in addition to the question of the significance of the seventy sevens: (1) The "cutting" of the anointed one (Dan. 9:26a) possibly alludes to his substitutionary death, particularly in view of the regular use of the verb *cut* as a description of the covenant-making process, which anticipates the ultimate curse of the covenant. (2) The destruction of the city and the sanctuary by the people of the ruler who will come (9:26b) could anticipate the destruction of Jerusalem by the army of Titus in A.D. 70. But in the flow of the passage, it more likely refers to the destruction worked by the people of God's true messianic prince, who had just been mentioned, since judgment regularly accompanies redemption in scripture (Kline, "Covenant of the Seventieth Week," 463). (3) "Making [a covenant] to prevail" with "many" in one seven by an "anointed one" (9:27a) does not introduce a different "anointed one" in addition to the one mentioned in the previous verse. Instead, the same anointed one strengthens his covenant with his people. Kline comments: "Gabriel here assures Daniel that the cutting off of the anointed one (vs. 26) would not mean the failure of His mission but, on the contrary, its accomplishment" (ibid., 463). (4) The "abomination of desolation" set up in the temple (9:27c) could refer to the defamation of the temple by the Romans. But ultimately it anticipates the consummate defamation of the true worship of God by the antichrist.

the first nine chapters of Daniel as anticipating the redemptive history that will develop from the time of the Babylonian Empire until the appearance of Christ. As the history of the old covenant era approached its end, it might even have been expected that the days to come would have been anticipated. At the time of the formalizing of the Abrahamic covenant, God informed the patriarch of the course of history that would affect his people for the next four hundred years. They would experience enslavement in a country not their own. But then they would return to possess the promises made to the patriarch (Gen. 15:13, 16). Similarly, prior to their exile to the land of Babylon, the Lord informed the nation that their captivity would last for seventy years (Jer. 25:12; 29:10; Dan. 9:1–2). Now, as the people of God are about to enter another period of four hundred years in which they would be subjected to the kings and kingdoms of this world, it might have been expected that the Lord would make known in broad outline the plan and purpose he had for the coming epochs, just as he had done previously. According to the perspective of scripture, the history of rising and falling nations focuses on the redemptive purposes of the God of all creation. For these reasons, no great difficulty should remain in accepting these first nine chapters of the book of Daniel to be what they present themselves to be: a prophetic anticipation of the divine plan and purpose for the epochs between the kingdom of Babylon and the kingdom of Christ.

The last three chapters of Daniel are generally perceived to be of a different character. Particularly with reference to Daniel 11, the question in virtually every reader's mind is: Should the material of this chapter be viewed as history written after the described events transpired? Or should this material be understood as prophecy, as the prediction of events yet to occur? In short, did this material arise in the sixth century B.C. or in the second century B.C.?

It must be readily admitted that the extensive detail found in Daniel 11 encourages the view that the chapter records historical events that have already occurred. Nowhere else in the prophetic material of the Old Testament can so many details be found about events that are yet future. Furthermore, these happenings generally seem to be far removed from any redemptive purposes of God as they might affect his people.

According to this prophecy, successive kings of Persia will assault the kingdom of Greece (11:2). Then a mighty king will appear whose kingdom will be divided fourfold, but not among his descendants (11:3–4).[31] The king of the south, identified with Egypt, will seek an alliance with the king of the north through his daughter, but will not succeed (11:6; 11:8).[32] A subsequent king of the south will then attack the king of the north (11:7–8). Then the king of the north and his succeeding sons will counterattack with assaults against the king of the south (11:9–10). This struggle between the two kingdoms and their successors is represented as continuing for many years (11:11–32, 40–45).

The question naturally arises: What is the relation of these detailed accounts to the ongoing redemptive purposes of God? Why should the specific details of history outside the redemptive events of scripture be the objects of specific predictive prophecy? Does not this section of Daniel appear to be more like a report of history that has already transpired than as predictive prophecy?

On the other side of the question is the report of Daniel's reaction to these revelations. In his earlier experience as interpreter of Nebuchadnezzar's dreams, Daniel appeared quite calm in his faith that the God of revelation had made known to him truth concerning empires yet to come. But this later vision, though not nearly so sweeping in its revelations of future history, totally overwhelms the prophet. Even the men with him are so terrorized "that they fled and hid themselves" (10:7). Daniel himself was left without strength. His face turned deathly pale; he was totally helpless and fell into a deep sleep with his face to the ground (10:9). As the experience of the vision progresses, he is overcome with anguish. All his strength is gone so that he can hardly breathe (10:16–17).

In further contrast with the earlier visions, Daniel remains puzzled at the conclusion of the vision. He does not understand. He over-

31. This mighty king appears to be Alexander, whose kingdom was divided into four parts, but not among his sons.

32. This king of the south appears to be one of the Ptolemies of Egypt, who were prominent among the heirs of Alexander's kingdom. The corresponding king of the north represents descendants of the Seleucid empire of Syria, the second powerful line of Alexander's divided empire.

348

hears two figures in the vision asking, "How long will it be before these astonishing things are fulfilled?" (12:6 NIV). This query receives a cryptic answer: "It will be for a time, times, and half a time" (12:7). Daniel then notes that he had heard the response to the question, but did not understand. So he asks a further question: "My lord, what will the outcome of all this be?" (12:8). At that point, the interpreting angel abruptly cuts off the discussion. "Go your way, Daniel, because the words are closed up and sealed until the time of the end" (12:9 NIV).

With this contextual framework in mind, the original question may be asked once more. Is this vision presented as a recounting of history that already has occurred or does it involve prophetic anticipations?

From the perspective of Daniel as reported in the narrative, the answer to this question seems quite clear. If Daniel could grasp so calmly and clearly the significance of Nebuchadnezzar's dreams that anticipated the rise and fall of nations across the centuries to come, why should he be so overwhelmed if he were simply being informed about events that had already transpired in contemporary history? If Daniel could comprehend so clearly the course of future events through a divine revelation that interpreted for him the obscure dreams of Nebuchadnezzar, why would he be so totally baffled over a message about historical events that had already taken place?

In light of these considerations, it appears that the intended framework for these later chapters in Daniel is no different than the framework of the former material of the book. Daniel is not receiving messages about current events of the second century B.C. Instead, as a person living during the days of the Medo-Persian Empire (10:1), he receives divine revelations concerning the end. Noteworthy is the fact that references to the end occur six times in the last two chapters of the book (11:35, 40; 12:4, 9, 13 [twice]). It could be proposed that this perspective is only assumed by the creator(s) of the book of Daniel and that the actual perspective is one in which historical events that already had occurred are placed in a setting in which they appear to be in the distant future. From this perspective, Daniel's fainting spells would then become part and parcel of a literary device to give the impression to the reader that a spectacular revelation came to him. This perspective, however, can be maintained only at the expense of the integrity of the book, and no appeal to literary genre can adequately recover this loss.[33]

How then does this closing vision of Daniel fit into the history of redemption? Since these events are represented as transpiring after the fourfold division of the kingdom of Greece has occurred, the various kings of the north would refer to the rulers of the Seleucid Empire, while the kings of the south refer to the Ptolemies of Egypt. But in what sense are details of the struggle between the Ptolemies and the Seleucids during the third and second centuries B.C. relevant to God's ongoing purpose of redeeming a people to himself? It might be enough to simply observe that earlier portions of the book of Daniel provided information about the other three kingdoms as they related to the kingdom of God's people. Babylon, the first kingdom, was the nation that brought God's people into exile. Medo-Persia, Daniel's second kingdom, empowered the restoration of his people. Rome, the fourth kingdom, was identified as the realm that the stone cut out without hands would crush. Yet to this point nothing has been said about the relation of this third realm to the coming kingdom of God. In these last chapters of Daniel, it is explained that this third kingdom will be the great oppressor of God's people, thereby anticipating the last great persecution that would come at some future date. This perspective appears to provide adequate rationale for the extended treatment of the period embracing the third of Daniel's kingdoms.

But further reasons are ready at hand in the text itself to explain Daniel's concern for the events related to this third kingdom in the

---

33. Although not telling the whole tale, Keil, *Daniel*, 28, is essentially correct when he notes that "all critics who reject miracles and supernatural prophecy hold its spuriousness as an undoubted principle of criticism." He observes that in antiquity "no one doubted its genuineness except the well-known enemy of Christianity, the Neo-Platonist Porphyry." Collins, *Daniel*, 26, states that conservatives "argued that the critical position rests on a dogmatic, rationalistic denial of the possibility of predictive prophecy." He affirms, instead, that for the critical scholar "the issue is one of probability." It must be remembered, however, that Collins himself speaks of the "chronological restraints" of the book, which dictate for him a second-century date, despite the book's consistent representation of itself as arising in the sixth century B.C. (166). It seems inevitable that on the basis of dogmatic and rationalistic considerations, Collins must reject the repeated claims of divine revelation as the source of Daniel's insight into the course and the significance of future events.

sequence that leads from Babylon to Rome. First, it should be noted that the king of the north and the king of the south occupy territories adjacent to the land of Israel. Allusions to the "beautiful land," the "people who know their God," and the abolishing of daily sacrifices in the temple suggest the significance of these incursions for the people of God and the land of Palestine (8:9, 11, 13–14, 24; 10:14; 11:16, 31–35, 41, 45). These successors to the Grecian empire of Alexander march from north and south against one another through the land promised to the patriarchs. As a consequence, the progress of their struggle had clear implications for the realization of God's program of redemption within the land of Palestine. Humanly speaking, these two earthly powers, Egypt and Syria, were going to determine the future for the region, for in the second century B.C., they were the "two great world powers" that between them had "a monopoly of political and military strength."[34] But the message of Daniel 11, "which reiterates that of the whole book, is that, however mighty the rulers of the earth, they 'stumble and fall, and shall not be found' (11:19)."[35] This third in the sequence of world powers is dealt with more specifically, not because the author knew it firsthand by being contemporary with the events, but because the struggle within this nation became the greatest threat to the people of God in the land of the Bible prior to the appearance of the messiah.

Second, the utter defilement of the temple in Jerusalem by Antiochus IV Epiphanes, the most prominent of the Seleucid kings, had implications that stretched far beyond the days of the Maccabees. Dubbed Epimanes (Madman) rather than his self-exalting title of Epiphanes ([God] Manifest), the empirical aspirations of Antiochus suffered severe humiliation at the hands of the Romans. When invading Egypt, he was met outside Alexandria by the Roman Popilius Laenas, who issued an ultimatum that Antiochus abandon his incursions into Egypt once and for all. When Antiochus replied that he needed time to think it over, Popilius instantly drew a circle around him in the sand and demanded that he decide before he step out of the circle.[36]

34. Baldwin, *Daniel*, 41.
35. Ibid., 41–42.
36. See Whitehorne, "Antiochus," 270.

Infuriated at this humiliation, Antiochus returned to Palestine and embarked on even more stringent steps to complete the Hellenization of his entire domain. Eventually he ordered his chief tax collector to launch an attack against Jerusalem on the Sabbath. Most men of the city were killed, and most women and children enslaved. The Jerusalem temple was dedicated to Olympian Zeus, and pagan sacrifice was offered on an altar to Zeus erected over the altar of burnt offering in the temple.[37] A monthly check was instituted, and any Jew found with a copy of the torah or any child who had been circumcised was put to death. Antiochus was trying his best to force the Jewish community to conform to his efforts to impose Greek worship and lifestyle as the unifying factor of his empire. If he had succeeded, no place and no people would have remained for the planting of the seed of the kingdom of God that was destined to grow into the great tree that would fill the earth.

The "abomination that causes desolation" as described in Daniel's vision seems very likely to have anticipated this utter defilement of the temple of God by Antiochus IV Epiphanes (11:31–32; 8:23–25). Antiochus could therefore be identified as the "stern-faced king" (8:23) who "magnif[ies] himself above every god" (11:36 NIV). Yet this rigid opposition to the worship of the true God simultaneously introduced a model that would recur at the time of the end.[38] At the end time, a period of distress for God's people would develop "such as has not happened from the beginning of nations until then" (12:1 NIV). Yet God's people, whose names have been written in the book of life, would be preserved (12:1–4).

Third and even more important, this final vision of Daniel appears as the climactic cycle of historical movements progressing

37. Ibid.

38. Baldwin, *Daniel*, 201, concludes that "the prediction was to be applied to Antiochus as the first of many oppressors." She further elaborates: Human pride leads governors to make themselves their own final authority. This self-exalted human authority finds a scapegoat on whom to vent its bitterness "and sets in motion all the weapons of war, psychological as well as material, against the people of God." This cycle repeats itself throughout human history, but "the escalation of opposition will culminate in a final onslaught in which evil will appear to triumph, and only the intervention of God will prove the contrary."

toward the consummation of God's redemptive activity. In the book of Daniel, three historical cycles of redemptive history move through phases of devastation and deliverance, of persecution and praise, of exile and restoration. Wickedness increases, empires are overthrown, a consummate struggle occurs, the ultimate enemy is defeated, and God's holy, elect people are preserved and restored. The first cycle is measured by the seventy years of Israel's exile. It begins with the initial taking of Judean captives by Nebuchadnezzar and ends with the decree of Cyrus that the exiles are free to return to their homeland (9:2). The second cycle encompasses the seventy weeks that stretch from the issuing of the decree to restore and rebuild Jerusalem to the coming of the anointed one (9:24–27). The third and final cycle as described in Daniel 8 and 10–12 corresponds in principle closely to these previous cycles of the book. The first cycle of seventy years brought the progress of redemption up to the decree of Cyrus that the Jews return to the land they had lost. The second cycle of seventy sevens climaxed with the coming of the messiah and the restoration that could come only with a full atonement that removed all transgression, sin, and iniquity. The final cycle of redemptive history begins when the daily sacrifice is abolished and "the abomination that causes desolation" appears (12:11).[39] From this starting point, which is related directly to the first coming of Christ by the abolishment of sacrifice, the climax is reached in the final restoration of God's people by their resurrection from the dead (12:13). This cycle of measured time consists of "time, times, and half a time" or 3.5 "weeks" or 1,290 days (12:1–3, 7, 11–12). Once more, the use of these deliberately cryptic time measurements depicts a period of uncertain length. On this occasion, the measured period stretches from the time of the atoning work of Christ to the complete restoration of all things when the dead are finally raised (Dan. 12:2–3; Acts 3:21; 1 Cor. 15:22–25).

For Daniel, the coming persecution of God's people under the rule of the stern-faced king is characterized as a "time of wrath" (8:19). The same concept is used earlier by Isaiah to describe Assyria as the

39. In this case, the abomination of desolation may be extended to include the defilement of the Jerusalem temple area by the Romans, which in turn anticipates the final abomination at the end of the age (Matt. 24:3, 15).

"rod of [God's] wrath" (Isa. 10:5). The exile of Israel thus manifested God's righteous wrath against sin, which anticipated the final wrath that was yet to come.

But beyond the exile was restoration. This restoration, in terms similar to the expectation of Ezekiel, would come by the resurrection of the dead and the renewal of the whole earth. Daniel has moved significantly beyond the anticipations of the preexilic prophets by the extent to which he viewed the restoration in terms of this renewal of the earth. This distinctive perspective of Daniel is well stated: "Prophecy had looked towards a goal, but it was usually limited to the fulfilment within history of the promises to Israel. Daniel's wider perspective applied the promise-fulfillment theme to all nations, as indeed the writer of Genesis 12:3 had done, and looked on to the end-time and the completion of God's purpose for the world He created."[40]

III. The theological significance of Israel's exile

The ministry of Israel's writing prophets centers primarily around the events of Israel's exile and restoration. From the eighth century B.C. with Hosea and Amos in the northern kingdom and Isaiah and Micah in the southern kingdom, the nation's exile and its prospect of restoration dominated the prophetic horizon. In the seventh century B.C. with Nahum, Habakkuk, Zephaniah, and Jeremiah, the theme still predominated. For Ezekiel and Daniel as exiles themselves in the sixth century B.C., the great concern was the inevitable expulsion of the remnant from Judah, the destruction of Jerusalem and its temple, and the prospect of restoration that lay ahead for the devastated nation. An understanding of the biblical-theological significance of these events in the life of Israel is crucial to evaluating the ministry of the writing prophets.

Before considering the message of Israel's restoration prophets as the final chapter of the nation's prophetic movement, some effort may be made to analyze the theological significance of the event of Israel's

40. Baldwin, *Daniel*, 14.

354

exile as presented by the prophets ministering prior to and during the nation's experience of exile.

Israel had been chosen uniquely to be God's servant to the nations. Abraham had been called out of Ur of the Chaldees, even though his fathers worshiped idols on the "other side of the river" (Gen. 12:1; Josh. 24:2). The people were organized into a national entity by Moses as they came out of the land. The prophetic revelation that came through Moses at Sinai provided the foundation for the birth of the nation. In time, the people were brought into the land that God had promised them. It was a land flowing with milk and honey, comparable to the blessings of paradise restored. The possession of the land sealed for the people their position as heirs of God's blessings.

But what then could banishment from the land mean to the people? What did exile signify for Israel? By the exile, God's people became "not my people" (Hos. 1:9). In forcing them to return to the land of their origins, the Lord indicated that the blessings of the nation had been removed. What could be more drastic? Who could explain such an experience?

The whole prophetic movement was raised up to deal with this crucial issue. Only God himself could explain the "why" and the "wherefore" of Israel's exile, for the exile had meaning not only for the contemporary Israelites. In accordance with the role of the major movements of the history of redemption, this event was also designed by the Lord to communicate redemptive truth across the generations. The exodus had communicated the concept of redemption from the guilt of sin by the blood of the Passover lamb (Exod. 12:13, 23; 1 Cor. 5:7–8). The possession of Canaan had anticipated the eschatological entry into the rest that remained for the people of God (Ps. 95:10–11; Heb. 4:3, 9–11). The monarchy had embodied the principle of messiah's lordship over his people in the eschatological kingdom that was to come (Ps. 2:2, 8–9; Acts 2:29–36).

The nation's exile, on the other hand, seemed to fall in a different category than all other phases of redemptive history. Rather than moving the nation's experience of redemption forward, expulsion from the land appeared to cancel out all the gains made up to that point. In this sense, the exile created a theological crisis for the nation. So how did the prophets respond to this crisis? What message from the Covenant LORD could answer this challenge to ongoing faith?

The prophetic answer to this dilemma was multifaceted, as might be expected. The problem of understanding the exile was large, and the answer of the prophets was complex. Several leading elements in the response of the prophets may be noted. These various elements relate to the differing categories of people that can be identified among the exiles of the nation.

A. For apostates

Exile had a specific significance for those who formally confessed the God of Israel but showed their disbelief through syncretism or through actually worshiping other gods. Zephaniah describes these people as those who "swear to the Covenant LORD while swearing by Milcom" (Zeph. 1:5).[41] Jeremiah identifies them as "bad figs" too rotten to be eaten (Jer. 24:3). This category of people has always lived in the midst of God's elect nation. But by the exile, the final fate of the apostate is vivified. They have fallen under the ultimate curse of God. In accordance with the law of the covenant, those who worship other gods must be cut off, for they had broken the covenant. For these people, exile depicted eternal banishment from the presence of the Lord.

B. For compromising, disobedient believers

The exile communicated a particular redemptive truth for believers in the God of Israel who compromised their faith by walking in disobedience. It taught once and for all that the Lord would severely chasten his own people if they persisted in their disobedient ways. In his prayer of confession on the eve before the return from exile, Daniel confesses the sin of the people that made them deserving of this chastening judgment of the exile: "All Israel has transgressed your law and turned away, refusing to obey you. Therefore the curses and sworn judgments written in the Law of Moses, the servant of God, have been poured out on us, because we have sinned against you" (Dan. 9:11 NIV). It is a lesson to be learned in every generation. "Whom the Lord

41. The telling distinction in Zephaniah is obscured by the NIV, as previously noted.

loves, he chastens" (Heb. 12:6). These chastening actions of the Lord against his own people may be severe at times. Yet, it must be remembered that the worst chastening judgment in this life is always less than the punishment that every sin deserves. Only by this acknowledgment will God's chastening judgments lead to true repentance rather than to resentful rebellion.

C. For Israel as the typological embodiment of the "servant of the Lord"

Despite the common practice of popular orators, it is wholly inappropriate to make specific application of the prophecy of Isaiah concerning the vicarious sin-bearing servant of the Lord to anyone other than the innocent, sinless lamb of God, whose sufferings atoned for the sins of his people. Yet in the limited sense associated with other old covenant types, Israel in its exile anticipated the vicarious sufferings of the singular servant of the Lord. It was not an accident that the theology of the suffering servant developed in a context that anticipated Israel's exile. Nor was it accidental that an interchange developed between the concept of the nation as God's servant and a singular suffering servant of the Lord. The sentence of judgment on the one anticipated the abandonment by God of the other. Clearly none of Israel's sufferings may be regarded as atoning in substitution for the guilt of others, since no Israelite has ever existed who has not himself sinned. Yet this imagery of Israel's sufferings found its fulfillment when Jesus Christ as the true Israel of God became "not my people" on behalf of his people in the "exile" of his crucifixion. In his unique role as servant of the Lord, he suffered banishment "outside the camp," the innocent for the guilty (Heb. 13:11–13; 1 Pet. 2:22–25).

D. For the faithful remnant

Jeremiah, Ezekiel, and Daniel along with other faithful worshipers of the true God were transported into foreign countries in the company of the rebellious sinners of the nation. Although these prophets and others like them remained true to their trust in the Lord, they suffered exile alongside the rebellious and disobedient. In their banishment they saw visions of the worldwide expansion of God's kingdom.

357

The provincialism of Israel was broken by the very act of divine judgment that scattered these faithful ones among the nations. As a consequence, the door was opened in a new way for participation in God's kingdom by all the peoples of the earth. This principle finds consummate manifestation in the sufferings of the disciples of Jesus today as they "fill up what is lacking in the sufferings of Christ" for the sake of the spread of the gospel to the ends of the earth (Col. 1:24).

The event of the exile thus had a multiplicity of meanings for the people of God. In many ways, the exile was a much more complex event in redemptive history than the original call of Abraham out of Ur of the Chaldees. God's purposes of redemption had first focused on a single individual. But in the exile, an entire nation was involved—a nation in which its various members responded to the challenges of faith in widely differing ways. It is therefore understandable that a movement as significant as Israel's prophetic tradition would have arisen out of these momentous circumstances.

12

Prophets of
the Restoration

Equally as significant as exile for Israel's experience of redemption is their restoration after exile. The history of the restoration spans a period of approximately 150 years (536–400 B.C.). Three key events mark the progress of this period:

- the first return and the beginning of the rebuilding (536 B.C.)
- the restart of the rebuilding (520 B.C.)
- the second return under Ezra (458 B.C.) and Nehemiah (445 B.C.)

The prophets of the restoration communicated God's word to the people during the last two phases of this restoration history. Haggai and Zechariah prophesy as contemporaries during the restart of the rebuilding, and Malachi prophesies during the time of the second return under the leadership of Ezra and Nehemiah. Though no prophetic activity in the promised land is mentioned during the first return in 536 B.C., an awareness of the principal events associated with this initial return is essential for understanding exactly what God was doing with his people at this new stage in the progress of redemption.

How amazing in itself was the fact of Israel's return! Who ever heard of such a thing! Who could have anticipated that an empire would arise of the same gigantic proportions as the great Babylonian Empire, which would then reverse international policy toward conquered nations that had prevailed for over two hundred years? Yet the prophets of Israel who so solemnly declared the inevitability of their nation's exile were the very ones who promised national restoration. Amos could have lost his life for declaring, "Israel will surely go into exile, away from their native land" (Amos 7:11, 17c NIV; see also 5:27; 6:7). Yet he also announced, "I will restore David's fallen tent," "bring back my exiled people," and "plant Israel in their own land, never again to be uprooted" (9:11, 14–15 NIV). Micah had declared: "Zion will be plowed like a field, Jerusalem will become a heap of rubble" (Mic. 3:12 NIV). But he also reported the Lord's word of restoration: "I will gather the lame; I will assemble the exiles and those I have brought to grief. . . . The Covenant LORD will rule over them in Mount Zion from that day and forever" (4:6–7 NIV). Even more specifically, Jeremiah designated seventy years as the length of Judah's exile (Jer. 25:11–12; 29:10), and Isaiah identified Cyrus by name as the Lord's servant who would be his instrument for accomplishing this grand restoration (Isa. 44:28; 45:1).

At the appointed time in the plan of the Almighty, this great event of return from exile occurred. Daniel, who was among the first of Judah's exiles seventy years earlier, witnessed the collapse of Babylon and anticipated the decree of the return issued by the Medo-Persian Cyrus (Dan. 9:2). The God of Israel was true to his word. Israel would return to its land.

Immediately on their return to Palestine in 536 B.C., the people of Israel began to restore their center of worship in Jerusalem. As a first priority, the altar at the site of the Solomonic temple was restored (Ezra 3:1–3). In April of the next year, work began on the temple itself (3:8–13). As a consequence of rigid Samaritan opposition, the work on the temple ceased later that same year (4:24) and would not to start up again for another fifteen years.

Shortly after the accession of Darius I as Medo-Persian emperor (522 B.C.), the prophet Haggai began to urge the renewal of efforts for the rebuilding of the temple (Hag. 1:1). Approximately two months later, Zechariah began his ministry by calling the people to repentance (Zech. 1:1). Due to the urgings of these two prophets, the restored temple was completed in about four years (516 B.C.; Ezra 6:14–15). One of the most moving descriptions in scripture captures the drama of the moment. Shouts of joy so mingled with wails of disillusionment that the one could not be distinguished from the other. The younger generation rejoiced without inhibition as they witnessed the laying of the foundation for the new temple. The older generation that remembered the glories of Solomon's magnificent edifice convulsed with weeping.

This dramatic scene encapsulates the actual state of events during the days of Israel's restoration. Great expectations of grandeur existed side by side with the realities of a "day of little things" (Zech. 4:10). Israel's restoration prophets spoke directly to both situations. Yes, the days of grandeur eventually would come—days far greater than anything that could be remembered from the past. But in the meantime, the little things of the present moment must not be despised. God's chosen people must be warned about resorting to their own devices as a way of compensating for the frustrations they so keenly felt.

During the next seventy-five years, the events of the book of Esther took place in the distant land of Persia. It should be remembered that the vast majority of exilic captives remained in the land of their deportation rather than returning to Palestine. Near the end of this period, Ezra led the second return to Jerusalem in about 458 B.C. (Ezra 7:6–10).[1] The ministry of Malachi occurred in conjunction with the circumstances developing out of this second return. Although the prophecy of Malachi is not specifically dated, the circumstances described in the book parallel rather closely the situation associated with this second return. The temple evidently had been completed and sacrifices restored (Mal. 1:7–10; 3:8), but the levitical priesthood was in serious need of purification, and mixed marriages between Israelites and worshipers of other gods were common practice (3:2–4; 2:10–12). Similar abuses characterized the days of Ezra and Nehemiah (Neh. 13:23–31). Malachi warns against the corruptions of his day and anticipates the sudden return of the Lord to his restored temple. In declar-

1. For discussion of current issues related to the dating of Ezra's return, see Bright, *History of Israel*, 391–402. Bright must rely on an emendation of Ezra 7:7–8 to maintain that Nehemiah preceded Ezra. This conclusion is questioned by William P. Brown, the editor of the fourth edition of Bright's *History of Israel*. In support of the date of 458 B.C. for Ezra's return, see Merrill, *Kingdom of Priests*, 502–6.

ing the last words of the old covenant era, Malachi anticipates the early events that will herald the dawning day of the new covenant.

In analyzing the distinctive message of these three prophets, first the ministries of Haggai and Zechariah as the early restoration prophets may be considered. Then as the last of the prophetic spokesmen for the age of the old covenant, the message of Malachi may be noted.

I. The early restoration prophets: Haggai and Zechariah

In considering the message of these early restoration prophets, three matters of principal concern emerge: the state of the people who were restored to their land, the state of the nations surrounding them, and the anticipations of the future as it was revealed to Haggai and Zechariah.

A. The state of the people

The first factor that surfaces in analyzing the period of Israel's restoration is the meager character of Israel's return. In no way did the nation even approximate the glories of their former days. They were not restored to their earlier glory. The group that came out from Egypt under Moses numbered over 600,000 males, which would have involved as many as three million people when women and children are considered (Num. 1:46). But the total number of men coming out of Babylon was a mere 49,697 (Ezra 2:64). Rather than enjoying the expansive dimensions of Solomon's kingdom in its glory days, the people of the restoration were confined to a small area surrounding Jerusalem. Just to the north were the hostile Samaritans, and blocking their expansion to the south was the Negev and the wilderness of Sinai. In the political and religious realm, the people who returned from Babylon were severely restricted. Except for some relative independence during the revolt of the Maccabees, the Jews never governed themselves, a condition that prevailed for the next twenty-five hundred years. The laying of the foundation of the new temple inspired only convulsive weeping on the part of those who remembered the magnificence of Solomon's temple.

362

As radical as the following assertion may appear, the restoration of the Jews in the second half of the sixth century B.C. can only barely be called a restoration. In fact, this period of Israel's history saw no true restoration of the Israelite community as constituted under the provisions of God's covenant with Moses and David. The shell was there, but the substance was sadly absent.

This assertion is based on the inability of any functioning monarchy in the restored community to constitute the people as a nation. Though Zerubbabel their governor was a descendant of David, his powers extended only so far as the Persian governmental authority would allow. Furthermore, even though a levitical priesthood existed and sacrificial offerings were reinstituted, the highest moment of sacrifice could never be realized. All available evidence indicates that the most holy place of the restored temple never contained a reconstituted ark of the covenant. In the spot where the ark should have stood, a "stone of foundation" three fingers high was placed, according to Jewish tradition.[2] Josephus enumerates the various sacred objects taken from the temple when the Roman general Pompey forced his way into the temple in 64 B.C., but he makes no mention of the ark of the covenant.[3] Presumably the ark had been lost during the destruction of Jerusalem by the Babylonians and was never reconstructed for the restored temple.[4]

Critical for understanding the state of Israel from the time of its exile is the significance of this absence of the ark. Never since the destruction of the temple in 586 B.C. has it been possible for the Day of Atonement to be properly observed in Judaism, as the procedures of the day are prescribed in the law of Moses. With no ark, there can be no mercy seat (Lev. 16:11–17 [NIV: "atonement cover"]; Exod. 25:17–22; Lev. 23:26–32). Without a mercy seat, there can be no sprinkling of the atoning blood of the substitutionary sacrifice. Without the sprinkling of the atoning blood on the Day of Atonement, there can be no annual covering for the guilt of sin. Without the covering for sin

2. Seow, "Ark of the Covenant," 391.
3. Ibid., who cites Josephus, *Antiquities* 14.71–72; *Jewish War* 1.152–53.
4. See Kitchen, "Ark of the Covenant," 111, who cites Josephus as indicating that there was no ark in the Second Temple (Josephus, *Jewish War* 5.219).

363

by the sprinkled blood, there can be no forgiveness. Without forgiveness there can be no peace with God. Without this objective establishment of peace with God, there can be no legitimate claim by anyone that he is a part of the true Israel of God.

Lacking these two essentials of the Mosaic theocracy—the kingship and the properly functioning priesthood—the people of the restoration could not legitimately claim that the Mosaic theocracy had been reconstituted.[5] They may have returned to the land. They may have rebuilt the temple. But nothing indicates that the Shekinah glory returned to reconstitute these people as the continuing covenant nation. Though the prophets of the restoration assured the people that the Lord was with them, his presence was not manifested in the way in which it had been evident in the past.

So, why such a meager restoration? Why any restoration at all? Had not God indicated his disgust with Israel's corruptions by withdrawing his glory from the temple in Jerusalem? Had not the Lord displayed to Ezekiel in dramatic terms that his glory was as mobile as a chariot and could be manifest in the foreign land of Babylon just as easily as at the temple site in Jerusalem? As strange as these questions may appear, they serve to highlight the actual significance of Israel's restoration.

From the outset, the proposal that Israel's restoration came in such a small way because the people merited no more glorious experience in their return must be rejected.[6] Daniel's extensive confession

5. See the discussion of this point in Keil, *Daniel*, 8–10: "The restoration of the Jewish state after the exile was not a re-establishment of the Old Testament kingdom of God" (8). He notes that even those who returned "were not set free from subjection to the heathen world-power." Though the city and the temple were rebuilt, the glory was not present. Because there was no ark of the covenant, "the high priest could no longer go before God's throne of grace in the holy of holies to sprinkle the atoning blood of the sacrifice" (8–9).

6. This view is expressed by Kline, "How Long [I]?" 27. This conclusion rests on Kline's presumption that the Mosaic covenant was a "covenant of works" in the typological realm, so that the nation of Israel had to merit its temporal blessings. Kline himself, however, has difficulty maintaining this view with consistency, for he subsequently indicates on the same page that Israel's restoration was a gift of grace (27). But an event cannot be a matter of "grace" and based on "meritorious works" at the same time. Kline's view of the Mosaic covenant as a "covenant of works" is fundamentally flawed

of sin on the eve of Israel's return makes it quite plain that the nation merited absolutely nothing in terms of the blessings of restoration (Dan. 9:1–19). Even the meager renewal that they experienced came as a manifestation of the undeserved grace of God. More to the point, by the restoration God was intent on displaying before the world his unswerving commitment to realize his purposes of redemption among a fallen humanity. Apart from the restoration of the nation of Israel to the promised land, the line of continuity with the past purposes of God would be lost.

Interconnected with this intent of displaying continuity in redemptive purpose was the commitment of the Lord to maintain his redemptive intentions among the nations of the world. In anticipating Israel's restoration, the prophet Ezekiel declared, "The nations will know that I the Covenant LORD sanctify Israel, when my sanctuary is in the midst of them for evermore" (Ezek. 37:28). While this reason may seem somewhat secondary at first consideration, it properly suits the reality that all true beneficence among humanity will arise only through a proper honoring of the one true God. Rightly understood as a unique action of the divine creator, Israel's restoration effectively promotes God's uniqueness among all other supposed gods of this world. Only Israel's God anticipated their nation's exile and return. To him alone belongs the glory for ordering the course of human history.

---

at several points. He bases his case on the assumption that in God's redemptive covenants a distinction can be made between the basis of temporal benefits and salvific benefits. But in scripture these two aspects of redemption are both matters of grace. He must also assume that a difference in the basis for operation may be made between the typological experience of Israel and the redemptive experience. But Vos effectively makes the point that the typological can communicate in its essence nothing different than the symbolized reality it portrays (*Biblical Theology*, 145–46). Kline's definition of the Mosaic covenant as a covenant of meritorious works is also flawed by its effort to make a radical distinction between the basic nature of the Abrahamic and Davidic covenants in comparison with the Mosaic covenant. The same typological images present in the Abrahamic and Davidic covenants may be found in the Mosaic, and the same type of law condition in relation to promise is found in all three covenants. David admonishes his son/successor Solomon to "keep [God's] decrees and commands, his laws and requirements, as written in the Law of Moses, so that . . . the Covenant LORD may keep his promise to me" (1 Kings 2:3–4 NIV). David obviously saw his covenant relation to the Lord as an extension of the Mosaic covenant and had no problem joining commandments to promises.

But why should the restoration from exile be realized on such a small scale? If the display of God's glory is an essential point in the restoration of the nation, why should not this glory be manifest to the fullest possible degree? The message of the restoration prophets concerning the greater glory of the restored temple combined with revelations regarding the role of the coming royal priest holds the key to answering this question. This coming anointed one of the restoration prophets is to appear in a state of humiliation so that he might fulfill the previously described role of the suffering servant of the Lord. He is to manifest the presence of God's redemptive kingdom in himself, first in humiliation and only afterward in glory. But if a Davidic successor were already reigning in Israel over a gloriously restored kingdom, the proper setting would not be in place for the humble character of the coming one who was to suffer before his exaltation.[7]

Three elements characterize the state of the people themselves who made up this restored community. First of all, these people of the restoration were living in self-centeredness, while neglecting the house of the Lord. No listing of gross sins on the part of these people is found in the messages of the prophets Haggai and Zechariah, though it may be inferred that they were guilty of lying, swearing falsely, and cheating one another by the use of false measurements (Zech. 5:1–11). Some evidence indicates that idolatry still remained among them, and resorting to diviners may have been practiced (10:2). Corrupt leadership apparently is depicted in Zechariah's exposure of the bad shepherds, and it may be inferred that false prophets were still a problem for the people (11:15–17; 13:2–6). But the great sin of this people was complacency over lack of progress in the building of God's kingdom in their day. They had time and resources to invest in the improvement of their own living conditions, which indicates that they had significant freedom even though continuing under Persian rule (Hag. 1:4, 9). They had come to resent the regimen of fasting four times a month in remembrance of the sad days of Jerusalem's fall (Zech. 7:3, 5; 8:19).

7. See Kline, "How Long [I]?" 27. Despite my rejection of Kline's analysis of the role of the Mosaic covenant, a hearty appreciation must be expressed for the numerous stimulating insights provided by his work on the prophets of the restoration.

Yet while the house of the Lord remained in ruins, they were thoroughly enjoying their own paneled residences (Hag. 1:4).

These returnees represent the few exiles who made the great effort to return to this devastated land of their fathers. How is the distress of their economic problem to be explained? They work hard to plant much, but they harvest little. They earn a good wage, but it is as though their purses are filled with holes (Hag. 1:6). Are these disturbing developments to be attributed merely to the natural ebb and flow of good days followed by bad? By no means! The Covenant LORD of the heavenly hosts himself declares the reason for this distressing circumstance: "Because of my house, which remains a ruin, while each of you is busy with his own house" (1:9 NIV)! Their self-centered lifestyle has brought down the chastening hand of the Lord on them and all they possess. As a consequence of their long continuance in the sin of complacency, the Lord's corrections continue. They may not yet be driven again into exile, but they must learn well the lesson of their past expulsion from the land. God's impartial hand brings judgment on all who do not acknowledge him to be supreme over all life. They must put the Covenant LORD first at all costs. They must concretely display their devotion by rebuilding the house of the Lord, the place where he will be worshiped as he dwells in their midst.

Yet beyond the chastening currently being experienced by the community despite their restoration, a greater threat looms. It is an unthinkable prospect. They may be carried into exile once more. Devastation and repetition of their exile are live options for even the people who have returned from Babylon. A massive flying scroll with writing on both sides enters the house of thieves and false swearers, consuming both wood and stone (Zech. 5:1–4). In the second part of this vision of prospective destruction, a woman portraying wickedness is stuffed into a measuring basket with a lead weight covering its opening. This basket with its lid, symbolizing the regular use of deceptive weights and measures by the Israelites, is then transported by two huge unclean birds to the land of Shinar, the ancient designation for Babylon. There it is situated permanently on its base (5:5–11). The Lord through his prophets makes the message quite plain: a restored people cannot assume that they will forever occupy the place of God's blessing. Continuation in unrepentant sin will eventuate in a repetition of the awesome judgment of exile that they have already experienced. From this second exile there can be no expectation of return.

These people are not, however, consigned to a hopeless future. Despite their failings, they nonetheless manifest a true readiness to repent and change their ways. Their previous experience of exile has not been altogether in vain. One positive effect of God's work of grace through Israel's exile may be seen in the repentance manifested by the restoration community. The response of repentance is registered first with the two primary leaders of the people, Zerubbabel the governor and Joshua the high priest (Hag. 1:12a). But then the "whole remnant of the people" join their leaders in this singular act of obedient repentance (1:12b). Together they take up the task of building the house of the Lord.

The reason for the effectiveness of Haggai's summons to repentance is clearly delineated: "Because the Covenant LORD their God had sent him" (1:12b NIV). Of course, the Lord had previously sent his prophets during the preexilic and exilic periods. But Haggai, the first prophetic voice to speak since the time of the nation's restoration, explicitly indicates the source of their true repentance. The Lord "stirred up the spirit" of leaders and people, and so they came and began to work on the house of the Covenant LORD of hosts their God (1:14). The priority of divine grace in working repentance in the hearts of his people is made explicit.

This priority of grace in the people's repentance is made even more obvious in the expectation of a further, deeper repentance on the part of the people of God in a future day. At that time the Lord will "pour out on the house of David and the inhabitants of Jerusalem a spirit of grace and supplication" (Zech. 12:10a NIV). As a consequence of this ultimate manifestation of divine grace toward the chiefs of sinners, "they will look on me, the one they have pierced, and they will mourn for him as one mourns for an only child, and grieve bitterly for him as one grieves for a firstborn son" (12:10b NIV).

The great puzzle associated with the interpretation of this prophecy is suggestive of its profoundness. Who is the "me" for whom they mourn? The solution to this mystery is to be found in the plain meaning of the words. The "me" whom they have pierced is none other than the very one who poured out the spirit of grace and supplication on them, so that now they gaze on him and break down with bitterest weeping. God's own people, the ones who were granted the privilege of returning to their beloved city and rebuilding their revered temple—they are the ones who pierced the source of all grace. This superabundant grace is climactically displayed when on that very day, a "fountain . . . to cleanse them from sin and impurity" will be opened for the very same people who have pierced the one who is the source of all grace (13:1 NIV). Both the leadership and the citizens of Jerusalem will experience the cleansing power of this opened fountain.

From the perspective of consummate fulfillment, these prophetic descriptions anticipate exactly the circumstances of the agonizing death and the glorious restoration of the one who is the source of all grace. At the time of his piercing by crucifixion, they looked on him. The one who pierced the side of Jesus with his spear saw a fountain opened, "a sudden flow of blood and water" (John 19:34 NIV). The one who saw it testifies, and his testimony is true. He offers his witness "so that you also may believe." These things happened so that the scripture would be fulfilled: "They will look on the one they have pierced" (John 19:37 NIV, quoting Zech. 12:10). The gracious one who loved us and freed us from our sins by the fountain of his blood shall be seen once more: "Look, he is coming with the clouds, and every eye will see him, even those who pierced him; and all the people of the earth will mourn because of him. So shall it be! Amen" (Rev. 1:7 NIV).

So the state of the people who have been restored from their exile is made quite explicit. They are living in self-centeredness, neglecting the house of the Lord; they remain subject to the chastening hand of God, even to the point of facing a second, more permanent exile; and yet they may experience by God's grace the gift of repentance leading to salvation.

B. The state of the nations

As a small subjugated people in a vulnerable territory under the domination of foreign powers, the people of the restoration were fully aware of the significance of the mighty nations of the world for their own ongoing existence. Given this humbled circumstance, Israel in the days of its restoration after exile could serve as a picture of God's true people throughout the ages in the midst of alien forces. How then were these nations of the world viewed by the prophets of the restoration? Two aspects of these worldly nations come to the fore: they are at rest despite their participation in the decimation of God's people, and they will inevitably experience divine judgment.

In the first of a series of visions, the prophet Zechariah overhears a report of divinely commissioned horsemen who have gone to and fro throughout the whole earth (Zech. 1:8–11). As a result of their reconnaissance mission, they inform the angel of the Lord as their "commanding officer" that they have found the whole world to be "peaceful and quiet" (NASB) or, more literally, "sitting while undisturbed" (1:11c). This circumstance appears at first to be most encouraging. But the immediate response registered by the angel of the Lord requires careful analysis of this global situation. "Covenant LORD Almighty, how long will you withhold mercy from Jerusalem and from the towns of Judah?" he implores (1:12 NIV).

Something is terribly wrong about the state of the world. After having devastated God's covenant people, the nations have not a care about their depressed circumstance. They trip along on their own way, blithely unaffected by the ruin of Judah and Jerusalem. In the estimation of the Lord of heaven and earth, this is no small offense, for unconcern about the affairs of God's people must be equated with secularistic unbelief. This "how long?" of the appointed mediator and head of God's people anticipates martyrdom for some saints as they struggle to survive in the midst of a secularized world (Rev. 6:10). But the powerful intercession of the angel of the Lord receives a definitive answer. The response to the prayer in Zechariah's first vision comes by way of two subsequent visions of the prophet. In these two visions it becomes clear that the nations will be judged and devastated for their abuse of God's people.

First is the vision of four horns and four craftsmen (Zech. 1:18–21). The horns symbolize the raw power of the secular nations of the world. The number four represents an inclusion of all the world's nations, even as the four winds of heaven symbolize universality (2:6).

These four horns have done two things: they have lifted themselves up in a show of pride, and they have mercilessly scattered the people of God. These nations have presumed that in their own power they have scattered God's people, not properly realizing that they were only instruments of divine justice. Apart from the Lord's appointment, they never could have overcome the people protected by God's gracious covenant of redemption. The prophet Jeremiah indicated earlier the proper perspective that nations contemporary to Judah should have: "See, I am beginning to bring disaster on the city that bears my Name, and will you indeed go unpunished? You will not go unpunished, for I am calling down a sword upon all who live on the earth, declares the Covenant LORD Almighty" (Jer. 25:29 NIV). Let all the nations of the world, both past and present, learn this lesson. It was not the power of the nations themselves that brought Israel into exile. The sovereign Lord of heaven and earth brought about this disastrous experience of his own people. Should any nation of the world think that by its own power it can preserve itself from similar devastations? By no means! The cup of God's wrath eventually shall come around to them all.

Zechariah's vision also reveals four craftsmen, skilled workers who know their trade well. These "craftsmen" possess the special skill required for toppling dictators, governments, authorities. These four masters of destruction correspond in number to the four horns, indicating that they will always be sufficient for the task of bringing down each and every secularistic power that arises.

If this vision of the four horns and the four craftsmen symbolizes the fate of all nations that oppress the true people of God throughout the various epochs of human history, the final vision of Zechariah indicates the consummate end of this judgmental process. The images shown to the prophet progress from temporal judgment to eschatological judgment. In the end he sees four war chariots emerging from between two mountains of bronze (6:1–8). The significance of these bronze mountains is explicitly indicated by the statement that the chariots emerge from "standing before the Lord of all the earth" (6:5 NASB).[8]

8. These bronze mountains housing the presence of the Lord may reflect the prominent bronze pillars of Solomon's temple (1 Kings 7:13–22).

God's chariots of wrathful judgment appear elsewhere in scripture. The Almighty has millions of war chariots (Ps. 68:17) with which he can "scatter the nations who delight in war" (68:30 NIV). The Lord will come with his chariots, bringing down his fury like a whirlwind on all mankind (Isa. 66:15–16). From the divine throne issue forth these chariots of wrath that bring final judgment on the nations of the world.

The first and most central object of the judgment brought about by these chariots of the Lord is the "land of the north" (Zech. 6:6, 8). In an earlier vision of Zechariah, this land of the north is identified as Babylon (2:6–7). But even by the days of Zechariah, Babylon has assumed a symbolic value, since the Babylonian Empire had been in ruins for a generation. This nation served as the appropriate symbol of political opposition to the kingdom of God for many reasons. Babylon had destroyed the Lord's chosen city of Jerusalem, burning it to the ground. Babylon had terminated the four hundred years of Davidic succession to the throne of Israel, displaying its readiness to bring an end to God's covenant promises. Babylon had displaced God's own people from the land that had been promised them. Because of this determination to destroy the whole redemptive purpose of God in the world, Babylon serves as a most suitable image for the visible and invisible powers set against God.

The ultimate consequence of this launching of divine war chariots against a nation that epitomizes enmity against God's redemptive purposes is *rest*. More specifically, God's Spirit *rests* in the land of the north (6:8). He has taken over the very territory that has opposed his purposes and is now seated triumphantly on his undisputed throne. Throughout their wandering in the wilderness, the people of God were set in motion by the setting out of the ark that symbolized God's throne. "Rise up, O Covenant LORD! May your enemies be scattered," was the cry of Moses (Num. 10:35 NIV). But when the ark would come to rest, Moses would cry, "Return, O Covenant LORD, to the countless thousands of Israel" (10:36 NIV). Now in the eschatological perspective of Zechariah, final rest is realized in the defeat of God's ultimate enemy. As the parallel passage in the final chapter of Zechariah's prophecy indicates, the definitive destruction of the Lord's enemies means that the Lord is established as "king over the whole earth" (Zech. 14:9 NIV).

In view of this final divine judgment on the land of the north, the urgency of the imperative to flee Babylon can be fully understood, even though that nation no longer existed in the days of Zechariah (2:7). Unless God's people distance themselves from reliance on raw political power, they will be consumed in the coming conflagration, just as was Lot's wife, whose fate is to be well remembered by every generation (Gen. 19:26; Luke 17:32).

C. Anticipations of the future

As in the case of all Israel's prophets, the concern of the restoration prophets was not merely with the circumstances of their own day. Contrary to the idea that the prophets focused narrowly on current needs for social reform, the vision of the prophets regularly expanded to embrace both the nearer and the more distant future that might be expected for God's people. In this regard, five elements of future significance may be noted in these early restoration prophets.

1. Jerusalem and the temple will be rebuilt

Even a cursory reading of the prophets of the restoration makes it quite evident that the rebuilding of Jerusalem and the reconstruction of the temple were central features in their expectation of the future. But why? Had not Ezekiel experienced the manifestation of the Shekinah glory in Babylon, indicating no need for a temple in Jerusalem (Ezek. 1)? Had not the Lord revealed that he himself would be a sanctuary for his people across the scattered realms of their exile (11:16)? Had not Ezekiel's final vision shown him a prospective temple that broke the bounds of geographical limitations (chaps. 40–48)? Surely, "there must have been a more fundamental reason for the rebuilding of the Temple than resumption of the ritual."[9]

This more fundamental reason for the restoration to the land and the rebuilding of the temple was the witness these events would give to the Lord's ongoing purposes of redemption. "When my sanctuary is in the midst of them for evermore," said Ezekiel, "then the nations

9. Baldwin, *Haggai, Zechariah, Malachi*, 19.

will know that I the Covenant LORD sanctify Israel" (Ezek. 37:28). The divine intention to provide a way of reconciliation between sinners and himself did not come to an end with the exile. Though Haggai and Zechariah witnessed only a limited restoration of the temple in their own day, they envisioned a time in which the glory would be greater in this Second Temple than that of the original temple built by Solomon. Eventually the wealth of all the nations would flow to Jerusalem for the rebuilding of this great and glorious final temple (Hag. 2:6–9). A cosmic shaking of all the nations would cause their most desirable things—their silver and gold—to flow to Jerusalem.[10]

The short-term fulfillment of this prophecy concerning the flow of the wealth of nations toward the project of completing the temple in Jerusalem occurs almost instantly. Darius as new king of Medo-Persia orders the officialdom in Palestine that had protested the rebuilding of the temple to provide the cost of its reconstruction (Ezra 6:8–12). Within a matter of four years, the temple of the restoration was completed.

But the language of the prophet presses for a long-term realization of the prediction. Greater glory than the former temple was not by any stretch of the imagination realized in this small Second Temple. Yet Haggai's prophecy must mean something. In similar fashion, Zechariah describes the rebuilt city of Jerusalem through a vision of the eschaton. The city is so expansive that it cannot be measured by man or limited by a wall. Yet a wall of fire surrounds it, and the glory dwells in its midst (Zech. 2:4–5). Herod's Temple in the days of Jesus Christ was indeed a magnificent structure. But his edifice could hardly match up to the expectation of these prophets. The glory was absent from its inner sanctuary, and the nations of the world did not pour their wealth into its coffers.

---

10. The older traditional identification of the expected messiah with the "desire of all things" is misdirected. Calvin, *Twelve Minor Prophets*, 4.360, considers it possible that the text may refer to Christ as the desire of the nations, but concludes that the reference is to riches of the nations that will be brought to the restored temple. Though the subject is singular, the verb *shall come* is plural. The immediately following statement in Hag. 2:8, "mine is the silver, and mine the gold," supports the idea that it is the wealth of the nations rather than the Christ that shall come. In the fuller context of scripture it is to the Christ as saving sovereign that the nations will present their wealth.

Ultimately, in referring to himself, Jesus makes a startling statement: "One greater than the temple is here" (Matt. 12:6 NIV). The drastic nature of this self-assertion tempts the reader of the gospel to ask the question, "Did he really make this claim? Did he actually state that he himself was greater than even God's most holy place on earth?" The resurrection of his body from the dead provides the only adequate response to this query. His body was the temple of God. In him the fullness of the Godhead resided. Though this "living temple" of his body was destroyed at his crucifixion, it could not be held by death, so his body was raised up in his resurrection (John 2:19).

The people of the exile had to return to the land and the temple had to be rebuilt in order to provide a sanctified theater in which the great acts of divine redemption could be brought to completion. By these significant events of the sixth century B.C., the groundwork was laid for the climax of redemptive history at the appearance of Jesus the Christ.

2. God himself will return to live with them

The deepest tragedy of Israel's exile from their land is well summarized in the following words: "The real tragedy of the exile was not the removal of the people nor even the utter destruction of the city and temple. It was the departure of their God from their midst, an absence symbolized in one of Ezekiel's visions by the movement of the Shekinah from the temple to the summit of the Mount of Olives (Ezek. 11:23)."[11]

The departure of the Lord's presence as reported so dramatically by Ezekiel opened the floodgates of devastation to be poured out on the temple in Jerusalem, the land, and its people. Contrariwise, the return of the Lord himself to his place in their midst was critical to the nation's restoration, for "apart from God's Presence there is no restoration, no holy land, no holy city, no holy temple, for it is this Presence alone that sanctifies."[12] Zechariah's first vision of the mysterious man among the myrtles in the valley indicates that the Lord will return to Jerusalem, where his house will be built and the city restored (Zech. 1:16). This encouraging word is confirmed by none other than the

11. Merrill, *Kingdom of Priests*, 470.
12. Kline, "How Long [II]?" 27.

Covenant LORD of hosts, a designation of God repeated three times in this prophet's first word to the people: "Thus says the Covenant LORD of hosts: 'Return to me,' says the Covenant LORD of hosts, 'and I will return to you,' says the Covenant LORD of hosts" (1:3). Fifty years of prophetic silence in the promised land is first broken by the prophet Haggai with the same self-identification of the deity: "Thus says the Covenant LORD of hosts" (Hag. 1:2).[13] While promising that he will yet return to his people, the Lord by speaking again in the land of their fathers indicates that he has already begun his return. The people must not be discouraged by their lowly condition or despise the "day of little things," for the Covenant LORD of hosts has sent his messenger among them (Zech. 4:9–10).

The reality of restoration, though associated directly with the return to the land and the rebuilding of the temple, finds its distinctive confirmation according to the prophets of the restoration through the abiding presence of the Holy Spirit among his people. Exile in the sense of banishment from the Lord did not end with the return of the people to the land or even with the rebuilding of the temple. It could be said to end only with the return of the Lord to his people. Haggai interprets the traditional covenant phrase "I am with you" to mean "My Spirit remains among you" (Hag. 2:4c, 5). For Zechariah, the consummate restoration of the temple appears in the visionary form of two massive olive trees within the most holy place that provide an uninterrupted flow of oil for a complex, redesigned golden menorah. The interpretation of the vision leaves no doubt regarding its significance: "This is the word of the Covenant LORD to Zerubbabel: 'Not by might nor by power, but by my Spirit,' says the Covenant LORD Almighty" (Zech.

13. The distinctive designation of God as "the Covenant LORD of hosts" (NIV: LORD Almighty) never occurs in the Pentateuch, but elsewhere in the Old Testament about 300 times. According to Baldwin, *Haggai, Zechariah, Malachi*, 44, it occurs predominantly in the prophets (247 times) and quite frequently in the prophets of the restoration (Haggai, 14 times; Zechariah, 53 times; and Malachi, 14 times). Baldwin notes that the designation is probably related first to Israel's worship and thus refers to the angelic hosts. The phrase first appears when Elkanah went to sacrifice to the Covenant LORD of hosts in Shiloh (1 Sam. 1:3). See also 1 Sam. 4:4; 2 Sam. 6:18; 7:26; Isa. 6:1–6 for use of the term in worship contexts.

4:6 NIV). Even the physical act of reconstructing the temple can be accomplished only by the abiding presence of the Lord's Spirit (4:7–9).

Indications of the role of the Spirit of God among his people were present in earlier days. God's Spirit had been among the people at the exodus and had guided them through the wilderness to their rest (Isa. 63:11c, 14; Neh. 9:20). The Spirit that had rested on Moses was distributed among the seventy elders, enabling them to prophesy (Num. 11:17). The tabernacle as the place of God's dwelling could be constructed only by a person "filled . . . with the Spirit of God" (Exod. 35:30–31 NIV). But for these prophets of the restoration, the Spirit of God takes on greater prominence as the one by whom the light of life is maintained among his people, as seen in the symbolism of the perpetual provision of oil for the lampstand, and through whom power is granted for overcoming enemies in the work of building the house of the Lord.

The new covenant counterpart to this dependence of God's people on his Spirit in the days of the restoration is found in the role of the Spirit in building the temple of the Lord with living stones. This whole structure of God's new covenant people "is joined together and rises to become a holy temple in the Lord . . . being built together to become a dwelling in which God lives by his Spirit" (Eph. 2:21–22 NIV). The ascended Christ has given gifts of the Spirit to men "so that the body of Christ may be built up" (4:7–13 NIV). Believers in the Christ, "like living stones, are being built into a spiritual house . . . offering spiritual sacrifices acceptable to God through Jesus Christ" (1 Pet. 2:5 NIV). The shadow of the restored temple under the old covenant anticipates a far more glorious dwelling, animated by God's own abiding Spirit.

3. Many more people will return

While from one perspective the restoration of the people to their land is viewed as an accomplished fact, the frequently repeated expectation of prophecy during the restoration is that many more will join them in the return. Quite remarkable is the announcement that the Lord will yet in the future gather his people from the land of Assyria, a country that had been nonexistent for one hundred years by

377

Zechariah's day (Zech. 10:10). The prophet also issues a summons to the captives of the land of the north, identified as Babylon (2:6–7). Since Babylon was no longer existent in the days of the restoration, the prophet must be speaking of a more general return of the people to the land. This fact is clearly indicated by the simultaneous reference to a gathering from "the four winds of heaven" (2:6). He "will save [his] people from the countries of the east and the west [and] bring them back to live in Jerusalem" (8:7–8 NIV). Several references are made to the restoration of those from Ephraim, representing the lost tribes of the northern kingdom (9:10, 13; 10:7; see also 10:6), who will return to Gilead and Lebanon, representative of the eastern and western extremities of the northern kingdom (10:10a). These further returnees will be so numerous that "there will not be room enough for them" (10:10b NIV).

Perhaps most remarkable is the repeated expectation that Gentile nations will also join in this future, fuller restoration. Haggai encourages the people who are in such a lowly condition with the announcement that the future wealth of the nation will not be dependent on the resources they themselves can generate. Instead, the Lord will shake all the nations of the world, so that the desired things of all nations will fill the restored temple with glory. The silver and gold of all nations belong to the Lord, which means that he can guarantee that this Second Temple will radiate with far greater glory than Solomon's edifice (Hag. 2:7–9). But if the nations come laden with treasured gifts for Israel's God, then they too must acknowledge him to be the deity that he is.

This perspective is confirmed by Zechariah. At the heart of the expanding city of Jerusalem will be "many nations" that will be "joined with the Covenant LORD" and will become his people (Zech. 2:11). These Gentile nations will not come merely in a formalistic manner, paying a courtesy call and dropping off their tributes. Even though they are "far away," they will "come and help build the temple of the Covenant LORD" (6:15 NIV). In concluding the first major section of the book, Zechariah announces climactically that many peoples and powerful nations will come to Jerusalem to seek the Covenant LORD of Israel (8:22). More specifically, those who are left in Philistia will

378

belong to the Lord and will become "leaders in Judah" (9:7b). The final portion of the second half of Zechariah's prophecy also indicates that the survivors of all the nations that attacked Jerusalem in the past "will go up year after year to worship the King, the Covenant LORD Almighty" (14:16 NIV).

While the future inclusion of Gentile nations on a massive scale is a regular theme of the prophets, the mystery about their inclusion was kept hidden until the fullness of time. This mystery has proven to be one of the most difficult truths to be grasped through the ages, even though its nature is clearly spelled out. The mystery does not consist in the fact of the inclusion of the Gentiles, for this coming reality is announced regularly by virtually all the prophets. Instead, the apostle Paul indicates the precise nature of this mystery: "This mystery is that through the gospel the Gentiles are *heirs together* with Israel, *members together* of one body, and *sharers together* in the promise in Christ Jesus" (Eph. 3:6 NIV). Gentiles are not simply participants, but equal participants of all the promises of God's covenants; not merely sharers in the inheritance, but equal heirs with Israel in all God's promises; not only strangers who have been welcomed, but members together in a single body with Jewish believers—this is the mystery associated with Gentile participation in the salvation of Israel. This mystery has now been made known, but it is regularly denied. This mystery has the potential of changing the total perspective on the Lord's ongoing work of redemption among the nations of the world and of bringing the church of Christ to its full maturity.

4. Sin will be removed

Both major sections of the book of Zechariah provide vivid descriptions of the removal of sin as a part of restoration from exile. If sin was the root cause of the people's banishment from the land and the temple's destruction, then the removal of sin's defilements must be an essential part of restoration from exile. As a matter of fact, it may be concluded that apart from provision for cleansing from sin, genuine restoration from exile could not occur.

The Mosaic legislation had ample representations of the removal of sin through the rituals of the sacrificial system. But obviously these

379

procedures had not been effective in the fullest sense, or the exile would never have occurred. That the offering of the Day of Atonement recurred annually indicated that the blood of animals was not sufficiently effective to remove sin once and for all.

The centerpiece of Zechariah's visions anticipates the resolution of this ongoing problem of sin and its inevitable liability to punishment. The symbolism associated with the trial of Israel's high priest communicates the way of finally setting aside sin (3:1–10). This passage serves as the central scene of Zechariah's series of visions and functions as the linchpin of this first section of the book.[14] Its centrality is also seen in narrowing of the visions from their beginning and their ending to this critical point. The first vision describes reconnoitering horsemen who have gone throughout the world, while the last vision depicts war chariots of God bringing judgment on the four corners of the earth. But now the central point narrows to the most holy place in the temple of Jerusalem.[15]

In this central vision of Zechariah, the angel of the Lord is again prominent and functions in the same two ways in which he was manifest in the first vision. At that point he functioned as sovereign over divine emissaries, receiving and assessing the reports of the angelic scouts sent throughout the earth (1:11). But he also filled the role of mediator for his people, interceding for them (1:12). Now in this fourth vision, the angel of the Lord is presented even more clearly as judge of his people and as the one who mediates cleansing from sin (3:1–2, 4). Joshua represents the nation of Israel, guilty before the divine tribunal. He is also identified as a "brand plucked out of the fire," the fire of God's judgment by exile.

14. See Kline, "Servant and the Serpent [I]," 21; and idem, "Anathema," 3–4. Kline argues that the two parts of Zech. 5 actually constitute a single vision. In the first scene, a flying scroll brings devastating judgment on all lawbreakers, which represents the first stage of exile (5:1–4). The second scene depicts a woman personifying wickedness being carried to Babylon in a measuring basket (5:5–11) and completes the imagery of exile begun in the first. The symmetry created by seven visions with the vision of the high priest in the holy place as the fourth is attractive. But even if the balancing feature is somewhat lost by counting eight instead of seven visions, the third chapter still remains as the central point of this first section of Zechariah.

15. See Kline, "Servant and the Serpent [I]," 21, for significant insights into the structure of these night visions.

At this critical point, Satan emerges as the great adversary of the kingdom of God.[16] His name means "the Accuser," and his activity corresponds to his name. At the outset of this confrontation, Satan seems clearly to have the upper hand. Joshua's filthy clothes represent the permeating corruptions of the community even after the chastening judgments of the exile. But the divinely appointed judge, the angel of the Lord, casts Satan out of the court, strips filthy garments from the high priest, and clothes him with festal attire (3:2–4). Joshua is then informed that he along with his associates serve as symbols for the future, for the Lord is bringing forth his servant the Branch (3:8). By this reference to the Servant-Branch in the context of the role of Joshua the high priest as a prophetic sign, a distinctive combining of the offices of priest and king has been effected. In this context, the Lord indicates that through this priestly Servant-Branch he will remove the sin of the land "in one day" (3:9). By this phrase, the prophet alludes to the annual cleansing of the nation's sin in the Day of Atonement.

The second half of Zechariah's prophecy also underscores the provision of future cleansing. A "fountain for cleansing" "will be opened to the house of David and the inhabitants of Jerusalem, to cleanse them from sin and impurity" (13:1 NIV). Both king and people will find cleansing from sin in this opened fountain. This cleansing flow appears to arise from the piercing of one who causes mourning comparable to the grief that arose with the death of King Josiah, the last of the godly monarchs of Israel, in the plains of Megiddo (Zech. 12:10–11; see also Luke 23:27–28; John 19:34–37). Thus, in conjunction with the two offices of high priest and king, a way for the forgiveness of sin will be provided at some point in the future. Only with these developments can it be said that Israel's restoration after exile will be complete.

5. The Lord's priestly servant-messiah will come

Despite contrary opinions currently held by many in the academic community, the expectation of a singular saving hero who would defeat

16. Regarding the place of a personal Satan in scripture, see Kline, ibid., 24: "We are not dealing with the evolution of a metaphysical notion in the Israelite mind but with the progressive divine revelation of a specific historical entity."

God's archenemy even as he himself received a painful wound goes back to man's first fall into sin.[17] At that critical point, the word of God promised that a singular seed of the woman would crush the head of the serpent, even as the serpent crushed his heel (Gen. 3:15). Testimony to the messianic significance of these words may be found as early as the third century B.C. in the Septuagint. Instead of rendering in Greek the critical phrase "*it* [the gender-neutral seed of the woman in Hebrew] shall crush the head of the serpent," the pre-Christian Jewish translators chose to read the text as "*he* [a singular saving hero sent by God] shall crush the head of the serpent."[18] This expectation of the removal of the divine curse on creation may be traced throughout the biblical testimony, from the hope of Noah's father that his son would be the one to give rest from the toil of the earth (Gen. 5:28–29) to the triumph of Daniel's Son of Man over the beast (Dan. 7:11–14).

Prophetism prior to Israel's exile concentrated on the prospect of an ideal Davidic king as the nation's deliverer, with an enlarged realization that the consistent failure of earthly monarchs meant that only a divine intervener could rectify the disorders created by sin (Isa. 7:14; 9:6–7; 11:1–10). During Israel's exile, the hope of a future king and kingdom expanded to larger dimensions, while retaining a relationship of continuity with the past. The people of God would be restored. They would leave the place of their exile and return to the promised land, where the temple of the future would break the bonds of geographical limitations (Ezek. 40–48) and the singular saving hero would be a Son of Man, a son of humanity as a whole, not narrowly a son of Jacob. He would be invested with universal sovereignty (Dan. 7:11–14).

With this background in mind, what is the hope concerning a singular saving hero who is to come according to the prophets of the restoration? What particular emphases may be detected in Haggai and Zechariah concerning the one by whom their deliverance would come?

First, these restoration prophets continued to expect the emergence of a God-appointed king of the Davidic line. In this regard, their

17. See Robertson, *Christ of the Covenants*, 93–103.
18. See Martin, "Earliest Messianic Interpretation of Genesis 3:15"; and Woudstra, "Recent Translations of Genesis 3:15."

anticipations reflect connections and continuity with the past. This element in their messianic expectation is seen in that both Haggai and Zechariah focus a great deal of attention on Zerubbabel, the prominent descendant of David in their day. In his last recorded prophetic word, Haggai envisions a cataclysmic day involving the shaking of heaven and earth, the overturning of royal thrones and foreign kingdoms. In that very day, the Covenant LORD of hosts will take Zerubbabel his servant and make him his signet ring, for he is the chosen one (Hag. 2:20–23).

This reference of Haggai to a shaking of the cosmos and kingdoms as a part of his final prophetic word must be connected to his prior reference to shaking the heaven and earth that would cause the nations to bring their glory to the restored house of the Lord (2:6–7). This second shaking presses into prominence a single Davidic descendant who will be empowered to act with divine authority over all the nations. Just as God's temple and David's throne merged on Mount Zion with the bringing of the ark to Jerusalem, so the prophet anticipates a future glorious unification of divine worship and dominion through a restored Davidic monarch.

Haggai's three designations of Zerubbabel as God's "servant," "signet ring," and "chosen one" all point to messianic expectations. Isaiah's first servant song introduces this messianic figure as "my servant, whom I uphold, my chosen one in whom I delight" (Isa. 42:1 NIV). The Lord vigorously rejected Jehoiachin, the last scion of the Davidic line prior to Judah's exile: "Even if you . . . were a signet ring on my right hand, I would still pull you off" (Jer. 22:24 NIV). But Zerubbabel is now singled out as the one who will be God's signet ring, bearing in himself the full designated authority of the Lord himself (1 Kings 21:8). Because of the breadth of the connotations of these messianic designations as applied to Zerubbabel, it seems highly unlikely that Haggai's contemporaries anticipated a realization of these expectations within the person of Zerubbabel himself. This conclusion is supported by Haggai's prophetic contemporary Zechariah, who also casts not only Zerubbabel but also the high priest Joshua into a messianic role.

In Zechariah's case, Zerubbabel fulfills the role of regal temple builder and fits into a long-standing pattern associated with Israel's rulers.[19] At the earliest stage of the nation's history, the plan of God's tabernacle was entrusted to Moses as the shepherd-king of the nation (Exod. 25:1–8; 40:33; Num. 12:7). King David later expressed his desire to replace the mobile tabernacle with a permanent house for the Lord, but the honor went instead to his son Solomon (2 Sam. 7:11b–13). Now at the critical moment of the restoration of the temple after the devastations of the exile, David's descendant Zerubbabel becomes the designated builder. The word of the Lord comes specifically to Zerubbabel that the temple will be built "not by might nor by power, but by [God's] Spirit" (Zech. 4:6 NIV). A mountain of opposition to completing the project will instantly be transformed into a plain before Zerubbabel (4:7). The word of the Lord makes quite clear the pivotal role of Zerubbabel in this rebuilding of the Lord's house: "The hands of Zerubbabel have laid the foundation of this temple; his hands will also complete it" (4:9 NIV).

This regal messianic figure of the prophet Zechariah appears once more in the second half of the book, where he takes on a form that is both more glorious and more humble. Designated specifically as Zion's king, this future figure comes to establish righteousness, but appears in humility (9:9). He rules over all nations. His kingdom stretches from sea to sea and from the river to the ends of the earth, just as the psalmist anticipated (Zech. 9:10c; Ps. 72:8). His power is made evident by his ability to rid Ephraim and Jerusalem of their weapons of war and to proclaim peace to the nations (Zech. 9:10a–b).[20]

19. For this perspective on the role of the king as temple builder, see Kline, "By My Spirit [II]," 9.

20. Petersen, *Zechariah 9–14 and Malachi*, 58, refers to evidence from second-millennium B.C. texts that depict a king riding on a donkey, which presents no suggestion of lowliness on the part of the monarch. He views this passage in Zechariah as the "sole exception of this pervasively royal imagery" by the introduction of the term *humble*, "which is used here to redefine the character of the divine king" (58). McComiskey, "Zechariah," 1166, states that the donkey "stands out in this text as a deliberate rejection" of a warhorse as a "symbol of arrogant trust in human might." He continues: "We must view Jerusalem's king in contrast to Alexander the Great and the other proud conquerors of history. The reference to his riding a beast of burden, not a white charger, underscores this sense of the word ʿānî. Jerusalem's king is of humble mien, yet victorious, and so it has always been that the church does not effectively spread the gospel by sword or by arrogance, but by mirroring the humble

The combination of humility and sovereignty in the coming messiah receives even further development in the imagery of the abused shepherd-king. Anticipating a distressing day in the future, the Lord instructs his prophet: "Shepherd the flock marked for slaughter" (11:4). But this recalcitrant flock detests their shepherd and dismisses him with the paltry payment of thirty pieces of silver, the restitutional price of a slave that had been gored (Exod. 21:32). Yet in his abused state of being dismissed by his thankless flock, this humble shepherd retains authority by his possession of the shepherd's staffs. The humbled shepherd breaks these staffs, symbolically called "Favor" and "Union," indicating the termination of the covenantal bond between the Lord and all nations and between Judah and Israel (Zech. 11:7, 10, 14).

But the worst is yet to come for this humble shepherd-king. The Lord himself calls for the executioner's sword to smite his favored companion, his own divinely appointed shepherd (13:7). The only viable explanation of this attack on the Good Shepherd initiated by the Lord himself is that the shepherd-king also fulfills the role of priestly sacrifice—or, as he may be properly perceived—the sacrificial priest. As a consequence of his being smitten, the sheep will be scattered, chastised, purged, purified. The larger portion of the flock will be lost forever, while a remnant will be further refined. But eventually the sufferings of the humble shepherd-king on behalf of his flock will accomplish the Lord's ultimate end: "They will call on my name and I will answer them; I will say, 'They are my people,' and they will say, 'The Covenant LORD is our God'" (13:9 NIV).

The appearance of the various elements of Zechariah's royal-shepherd imagery in the passion narratives of the gospel records cannot be missed. The last week of Jesus' life begins with the people's hailing him as their king as he rides into Jerusalem on a donkey (Matt. 21:4–5, quoting Zech. 9:9). The dismissal by Israel of their God-appointed shepherd for the "handsome price" of thirty pieces of silver comes to realization when the temple's officialdom pays Judas for his betrayal (Matt. 26:14–16; 27:9, quoting Zech.

---

spirit of its king and savior." In either view of the significance of the donkey, the text explicitly affirms this humble character of the coming messianic king.

11:12–13).[21] In the third citation from this section of Zechariah, Jesus himself modifies the form of the Old Testament's wording to underscore the fact that God himself originates the deathblow to the Good Shepherd: "*I* will smite the shepherd, and the sheep will be scattered" (Matt. 26:31, quoting Zech. 13:7). The gentle king of his people has become the priest sacrificed at the hands of the Lord himself. Only in this manner could actual redemption be accomplished.

The second major element of a messianic message in the postexilic prophets is seen in this merger of the offices of priest and king. The uniting of the two offices in a single figure underscores the most significant development in the messianic idea of Zechariah as the premier prophet of the restoration period. Throughout Zechariah's prophecy, the union of the two offices of priest and king in a single figure takes on a prominence not found elsewhere in the previous prophets. In his first vision, Zechariah sees a mysterious man on a red horse, subsequently identified as the "angel of the Lord" (1:8, 11). This angel of the Lord receives the report of the divine messengers and responds as judge over the world's nations (1:11).[22] At the same time, he intercedes on behalf of the suffering saints of Judah and Jerusalem (1:12). In this way, he is "cast in the dual role of judge of the nations and advocate of the Israel of God."[23] He thus possesses regal as well as priestly elements.

The messianic significance of this dual role of the angel of the Lord finds further development in subsequent representations of Joshua

21. Though the quotation is attributed to Jeremiah as the more prominent of the two prophets being cited, the place of Zechariah's wording is clearly evident.

22. This angel of the Covenant LORD appears at significant points in earlier episodes of redemptive history and is regularly brought into a close relationship with the deity himself. The angel/messenger of the Covenant LORD is equated with God as he confirms the covenant with Abraham by divine oath (Gen. 22:15–18). The same angel of the Covenant LORD appears to Moses in the burning bush, revealing himself to be the God who is the eternal "I am" (Exod. 3:2, 5, 14). This same angel of the Covenant LORD later identifies himself as the one who brought Israel out of Egypt (Judg. 2:1). He thus appears repeatedly in a way that brings him into the closest possible relationship with the deity, while at the same time having an existence separate from the deity. As a consequence of this regular representation of the angel of the Covenant LORD, he may be regarded from the perspective of the greater light of the new covenant as a preincarnate manifestation of the second person of the trinity.

23. Kline, "How Long [I]?" 29.

as a priest who is crowned king. Joshua is specifically identified as a person symbolic of things to come. He is designated as "my servant the Branch," a title previously used by the prophets to identify the expected messianic king of David's line (Zech. 3:5–6, 8; Isa. 11:1; 4:2; Jer. 23:5–6; 33:14–17; Ezek. 17:22–24; cf. Ps. 132:16–17). The stone or engraved golden plate on the face of Joshua's crowning turban becomes the focal point of the "seven eyes" of God (Zech. 3:9). "Holiness to the Lord" was engraved on this golden plate, which depicted the perfected holiness of God's kingdom of priests (Exod. 28:36–38). As a consequence of the work of this priest-king in Zechariah, the sin of the land will be removed in one day (3:9). The high priest Joshua thus serves as "a prophetic type of the coming one."[24]

The sequence of visions in the first half of Zechariah consummates by a real-life enactment of prophetic significance that once more merges the offices of priest and king in a messianic context. The high priest Joshua is designated with the messianic title *Branch* (6:12). But now in this nonvisionary setting, a dramatic action of prophetic significance takes place. At the command of the Lord, Zechariah takes silver and gold that has been brought back from Babylon by the exiles. With these treasures extracted from other nations of the world, the prophet is directed to "make a crown and set it on the head of Joshua the high priest" (6:11). The astounding character of this action is fully confirmed by the stream of biblical critics who deny that it could have happened. From the days of Wellhausen on, it has been regularly objected that a priest in Israel could not be crowned as king. Critics propose that the text of scripture must be corrupt and assert that the passage originally indicated that Zerubbabel the governor rather than Joshua the priest was recipient of the symbolic crowning, even though no manuscript evidence supports this hypothesis.[25]

This imaginary rewriting of the ancient text completely misses the point. Just because this action of crowning the high priest cannot be fitted into previous patterns of the biblical testimony, it must be appreciated for its uniqueness. Since this placing of a royal crown on

24. Kline, "Servant and the Serpent [II]," 23.
25. See Baldwin, *Haggai, Zechariah, Malachi*, 134 n. 1, who lists many commentators who adopt this view.

a priest runs contrary to the political expectations of the postexilic period, the action must be seen for its prophetic value. The passage is clearly messianic in its intent.

The uniqueness of Zechariah's particular messianism is dramatized in this merger of kingly and priestly roles. This fact is underscored by the crowning of Joshua the priest rather than Zerubbabel the descendant of David. If Zerubbabel had been the person crowned, no merger of the two offices would have been represented. The crowning of the priest makes the point as vividly as possible. The intent to exalt the priest to the office of king is reinforced by the statement that explains the significance of the symbolic action: "[The priest] will be clothed with majesty and will sit and rule on his throne" (6:13 NIV). The prophesied priest-to-come will rule as king on his throne. This statement naturally raises many questions. What is a priest doing on a throne? Whose throne is he occupying? Since a priest in Israel had no legitimate throne of his own, he must be seated on another person's throne. What precisely is meant by the statement that he shall sit and rule on "his" throne?

In this case, the throne appears to be God's throne. This priest-king shall "build the temple of the Covenant LORD . . . and will sit and rule on his [God's] throne" (6:13 NIV).[26] The most holy place in the temple was the throne room of God. In that place he sat as king over his people. Once a year the high priest of Israel was allowed into the throne room to sprinkle the mercy seat with atoning blood. But now the future priest who is also messianic king enters the most holy place and is seated permanently on God's throne in this most sacred place. When the prophet indicates that the "counsel of peace will be between them both" (6:13), he refers to the peace between the Lord himself and the priest-king who rules with him.[27] Sharing in God's own throne, the messianic priest-king must be in perfect harmony with the Lord himself.

26. For the development of this concept, see Kline, "Structure of the Book of Zechariah," 182. Kline finds the background for the merger of messiah's throne with God's throne in 1 Chron. 29:23, where the throne of Solomon is called the "throne of Yahweh." In addition, he notes that this passage merges the ideas of temple building with royal succession, as does the passage in Zechariah.

27. Ibid., 182.

The regal function of this exalted high priest is further underscored by the repeated declaration that he "will build the temple of the Covenant LORD" (6:12–13). Normally the building of a temple for the deity is a special privilege reserved to the king.[28] But in this case, Joshua the high priest of Israel will be the one to "build the temple of the Covenant LORD" (6:13). Bearing the messianic title *Branch*, this priest on the throne shares with Zerubbabel the distinctive honor of building the Lord's temple (6:12). But of course the high priest Joshua cannot actually assume regal sovereignty over the people of Israel. The pitiful state of the restored people of Israel is underscored by their remaining subject to secular authorities. The Persian overlord would not allow the Jews to establish their own sovereign, so the symbolic crown is removed and placed in the temple as a prophetic memorial (6:14).

The final expectation created by this memorial action is a glorious one. One day "those far away" will come and join with this exalted messianic priest-king in the building of the temple of the Lord (6:15). This expectation may refer to Jews yet to return from their exile. But it also could point to Gentiles, those who have been far removed from the proper worship of God and who one day will become an integral part of the Israel of God.

The great advance in the prophets of the restoration concerning man's redemption may be found in this fuller understanding of the role of the coming messiah. He will be an anointed king of the line of David, while at the same time serving as a priest. He will in fact serve as a sacrificial priestly king on his throne. Rather than entering the throne room of the Lord only once a year, he will remain permanently seated with God on his throne. By the combined authority invested in him as Israel's high priest and reigning king, he will build the temple of the Lord.

II. Old covenant prophetism's final word: Malachi

By the time of Malachi in the mid-fifth century B.C., Zerubbabel the Davidic prince and Joshua the high priest of Israel's restoration

---

28. See Kline, "By My Spirit [II]," 8–9; and idem, "Exaltation of Christ," 5–6, who notes biblical as well as extrabiblical sources in this regard.

had died. They had been represented to the people of their day as symbolic men, embodying the hope of the nation's future. Zerubbabel was to complete the restoration of the temple by overcoming all resistance through the power of God's Spirit (Zech. 4:6, 9). Joshua the high priest had been crowned king over the nation, but only in a symbolically prophetic manner (6:11–12).

The day of these two symbolic figures had now come and gone. Though the temple had been rebuilt, none of the greater glory prophesied by Haggai had been realized. The royal line of David had not risen to the position of sovereignty over the land, and the high priest of the nation certainly was not seated on a throne.

Seventy-five years after the ministry of these early restoration prophets, Malachi appeared on the scene.[29] The circumstances of his day were entirely different than the initial state of things at the time of Israel's restoration. A priesthood was now actively functioning in offering sacrifices regularly at the restored temple. The people who had returned from exile with such high hopes had settled down to a humdrum routine. Elements of the lifestyle of the non-Israelite community had been absorbed by the people. Even complaints about the inactivity of their God were being voiced.[30]

So what then was the message of this last prophet of the old covenant era? What distinctive word did he bring from the Lord to the people of the restoration?

29. The name *Malachi* means "my messenger" and is treated by some interpreters as a symbolic designation rather than as the name of an actual person. The Septuagint renders the Hebrew name as "his messenger," which could indicate its support of this conclusion. None of the arguments against treating the designation as a title rather than a person have convincing force. After reviewing the pros and cons of the issue, Verhoef, *Haggai and Malachi*, 156, concludes that in the absence of compelling arguments to the contrary, the designation *Malachi* should be regarded as the name of the prophet.

30. Parallels with the situation in the days of Ezra and Nehemiah provide strong substantiation for dating Malachi to the middle of the fifth century B.C. In addition to evidence that the restoration temple was completed, intermarriage with non-Israelites appears as a major problem of the day (Mal. 2:10–11; see also Ezra 9:1–2; Neh. 13:1–3, 23–24). Failure in the presentation of the proper tithes also indicates similar circumstances (Mal. 3:8–12; see also Neh. 10:35–40; 13:10–12).

In terms of literary form, the book of Malachi is distinctive in its use of the "disputation" mode. The prophet poses a series of queries or assertions directed by the people to their God that encapsulate their attitude (1:2, 6c, 7, 12–13; 2:14, 17; 3:7c, 8, 13–14). The Lord and his prophet respond with their own series of questions (1:2c, 6, 8–9, 13; 2:10, 15; 3:2, 8). Though the precise nature of these interchanges is debated, their permeating presence supports the literary unity of the book.[31]

Malachi is often denigrated as a second-rate piece of prophetic literature.[32] But the masterful development of an overarching thematic structure within the book is generally overlooked. In response to the deteriorating situation among God's people at the end of the long movement toward the accomplishment of redemption, Malachi founds his prophetic appeal on the three great mandates of creation and covenant: the worship mandate, the marriage mandate, and the labor mandate.

A. The worship mandate

At creation, the Lord sanctified the seventh day and made it holy (Gen. 2:3). By this action, he summoned all he had made, but mankind in particular, to consecrate all their endeavors to him as their benefi- cent creator. In the processes of redemptive revelation, the Lord repeat- edly refocused the attention of his people on the centrality of worship. First he placed the tabernacle and then the temple at the center of their corporate life (Exod. 25:30; 40:34–38; Num. 10:36; 1 Kings 6–8; 2 Chron. 2–7). The divine establishment of priests, sacrifices, and holy convocations underscored this centrality of worship directed toward their creator and redeemer. The restoration remnant displayed their perception of the importance of this aspect of their life through the urgency placed on the rebuilding of the sacrificial altar and the tem-

31. Petersen, *Zechariah 9–14 and Malachi*, 31, characterizes the work as a Hel- lenistic "diatribe," which he describes as being similar to a dialogue, except that only one party speaks, though often impersonating a second party. In either case, the per- meating character of the form underscores the inherent unity of the work.

32. C. Kuhl, *Prophets of Israel*, 169, characterizes Malachi as "simply a precur- sor of later Judaism." See references to other negative evaluations in Baldwin, *Hag- gai, Zechariah, Malachi*, 216 n. 1.

ple. Before anything else was done, this tiny struggling community, with the urgings of their prophets ever behind them, set a priority on the task of reconstituting their worship center as the focal point of their communal life (Ezra 3:1–4).

Seventy-five years had now passed since the completion of the nation's Second Temple. As two, even three generations widened the gap between the original zeal of the restoration community and the realities of hard life in the land, both priest and people turned their focus away from the "first love" of their Lord to their own personal aggrandizement.

In response to this downgrade situation, the prophet Malachi forces the people to stand before their God and anticipate the coming day of their final reckoning in his presence. Forty-seven of the fifty-five verses in Malachi report a first-person address of the Lord to his people. As a consequence, the prophet creates "a vivid encounter between God and the people, unsurpassed in the prophetic books."[33] Far from being an inferior work among the prophets, this concluding witness to the centrality of God in the life of his people appropriately summarizes the overriding message from the Lord that had been repeatedly declared by the prophets.

In reacting more specifically to the worship situation that prevailed in his day, Malachi first describes the God who is to be worshiped. He has displayed the unchanging character of his electing love by the restoration of Israel to an area within its original borders, which is reinforced by the contrary treatment of the neighboring nation of Edom (1:2–5). The people of Israel presume to ask how the Lord has demonstrated his love to them, even as their priests weary of bringing regular sacrifices (1:13). It even appears irrelevant to the people whether they do good or evil (2:17), and it seems futile to serve the Lord (3:14). The Lord responds by directing the attention of the people across the border to their brotherly relative. Edom had been devastated by divine judgment. In their brazenness, they had declared, "We will rebuild" (1:4). They had determined to reestablish their ruined cities. But the restoration of a nation is not a thing that can be accom-

33. Baldwin, *Haggai, Zechariah, Malachi*, 216.

plished by the human will, however determined it might be. Despite its mightiest efforts, the Lord declares that Edom will remain a ruin.

God's love assures the restoration of Israel. All their prophets had announced the certainty of that fact. Though their national restoration was not at this point as glorious as they might have wished, they could not deny its actuality. They had returned to their homeland. They had restored their sacrifices and their temple. God displayed his special love for them in these events, which stood in stark contrast with the fate of their Edomite neighbors.

But the restored nation totally failed to register a proper worshipful response to this manifestation of God's special love toward them. God affirms himself to be both the fostering father of Israel and their sovereign king. Yet he receives neither the honor deserved by a father nor the respect due to a king (1:6, 14). They bring blind, maimed, and diseased animals as their tribute to him, gifts they would not dare present to their earthly governor (1:8, 13b, 14a). Despite all the effort that the people had put into the restoration of the temple, the Lord now wants its doors slammed shut (1:10).

No more radical statement could be imagined. Yet "a closed temple, however terrible this may be, is preferable to the perpetuating of worthless worship."[34] As one commentator notes: "It is better to be speechless than to blaspheme. It is preferable to experience the agony of being far away from God than to deceive oneself by assuming that God will listen to the appeals of a hypocrite."[35]

The community in Jerusalem may have been favored by their return to the land, but their polluted sacrifices are cursed. This curse pronounced over half-hearted worshipers is directed particularly to the practices of the priests. Malachi provides the most beautiful description of the role of the priest in all scripture. God established a covenant of life and peace with Levi.[36] The priest of Israel walked with God, provided true instruction to the people, and turned many from sin

34. Verhoef, *Haggai and Malachi*, 220.
35. Ibid., quoting H. Brandenburg.
36. A covenant with Levi is nowhere specifically mentioned in the narratives of scripture, but it is implied in Exod. 32:26–29, since the Levites obeyed Moses' command by not sparing their own brothers.

(2:5–6). He was even designated as the "messenger of the Covenant LORD of hosts" (2:7). But now God has cursed the blessings of Israel's priests because of their insincerity of heart (2:2). As the priest pronounces the Aaronic benediction over the people (Num. 6:24–27), the intended blessing becomes a curse. "The Covenant LORD bless you and keep you" has the effect of declaring "The Covenant LORD curse you and destroy you." "The Covenant LORD make his face shine on you and be gracious unto you" becomes "The Covenant LORD turn his face away from you and show you no mercy." Instead of "The Covenant LORD lift up his countenance upon you and give you peace," the priest's benediction becomes "The Covenant LORD hide himself from you and burden you with unending strife."

This divine curse surfaces once more at the conclusion of Malachi's prophecy. Unless the people respond properly to the call for repentance, the Lord will come and "strike the land with a curse" (Mal. 4:6). An exile worse than their previous experience will overtake them. Just as Canaan was once placed under the ban, so now this land of false priests and worshipers will experience the same calamitous, all-consuming curse. Yet despite this chastening judgment from the hand of the Lord, the priestly covenant with Levi will somehow be maintained. These strong judgments fall on the priests "so that my covenant with Levi may continue" (2:4). In the end, the Lord shall receive the proper worship due to him by a restored creation. A proper priesthood shall function with holiness and purity.

In contrast with this exposure of Israel's failed worship, Malachi prophetically anticipates a radical reorientation of worship throughout the world. Though the doors of the temple in Jerusalem may close, proper offerings will be brought in the name of the Covenant LORD from all the nations of the world. Though the sacrifices of Israel's restoration community are rejected, the offerings of the world's nations will be accepted by him (1:11).

Some propose that by this statement Malachi breaks out of a narrow, exclusivistic perspective and acknowledges the acceptability of all religions by the Lord. According to Driver, the text seems to be saying that when "the heathen in his blindness bows down to wood and stone," his adoration is "worship of the Lord, simply because it is worship in sincerity, though not in truth."[37] But this interpretation totally ignores the clear statement of the text. The Lord indicates that this worship by all the nations of the world will be acceptable only because it is offered "in my name," because "'my name will be great among the nations,' says the Covenant LORD Almighty" (1:11c NIV). By the repetition of the name of God and the specification of that name as the Covenant LORD of Israel, the point is made obvious. Worship of each and every concept of the deity is not acceptable to the Lord. Only worship that treats the Covenant LORD in his uniqueness will be pleasing to him.

How radical this statement is! The phrases "in every place" and "from the rising to the setting of the sun" stand in stark contrast with "in Jerusalem" and "on Mount Zion." Still further, "the nations" contrast with "Israel." The idea of offerings presented by the nations is not unique to Malachi (see Isa. 66:18–21; Zech. 14:21). The distinctiveness of Malachi's proclamation is that this worldwide worship "would not be dependent on the levitical sacrifices offered in Jerusalem."[38] Rather than having all nations flowing to Mount Zion, a global activity of pure worship will replace the centrality of the single city of Jerusalem. People and places from all over the world will be regarded as the proper domain of pure worship.

All these various elements regarding worship as presented in Malachi come into focus when viewed through a new covenant perspective. It might be asked, When will the nations present to the Lord proper sacrifices in their own locales apart from a centralized worship center in the city of Jerusalem? The immediate and obvious answer is, "Now, in this age!" From the days of the ministry of Jesus and his apostles until the present, nations scattered across the globe have offered proper sacrifices in the name of the only true God. At the same time, the nation of Israel was placed under the ban, driven out of its land. Even its reconstitution as a nation in Palestine during the twentieth century has not materially altered the prophetic picture. Indeed,

37. Verhoef, *Haggai and Malachi*, 226, quoting Driver in Driver and Sanday, *Christianity and Other Religions*, 31–46, as summarized in *Expository Times* 20 (1909): 151–52.
38. Baldwin, *Haggai, Zechariah, Malachi*, 230.

many Jews have joined with Gentiles in worshiping the one true God revealed in the person of Jesus the Christ by the power of the Holy Spirit. But the doors of the temple in Jerusalem have remained closed for the past two thousand years. Even if Jewish bloody sacrifices should be renewed in Jerusalem, they would be regarded as an abomination by the Covenant LORD, for he has declared "it is finished" by the unsupplementable sacrifice of his Son. Only in and through his self-offering can mankind, both Jews and Gentiles, be restored to a proper frame of heart that will lead them to consecrate all they are and have as a supreme act of worship to the only creator and redeemer.

Malachi's denunciation of the worship practices of the priests finds its counterpart in his condemnation of the polluted offerings presented by the people. They robbed God in their tithes and offerings, and so they are placed under the curse (Mal. 3:8). They spoke harsh words against the Almighty. They blasphemed him by saying it is futile to serve God, implying that nothing is gained by keeping his requirements (3:13–14).

Yet once more, the grace of God is manifested beyond the consuming devastations of the curse. A faithful remnant will remain, and they will belong to the Lord as his "treasured possession" (3:16–17). The concept of the treasured possession first appeared at Sinai, when the Lord claimed the people of the covenant as his own (Exod. 19:5–6). The same concept is renewed in the plains of Moab after the forty years of wandering in the wilderness (Deut. 7:6; 14:2; 26:18–19) and still later reiterated by the psalmist (Ps. 135:4). The Septuagint rendering of the term provides the linguistic link of this rich theological concept to the new covenant documents. Believers in Jesus the Christ are God's "treasured possession," providing a direct line of fulfillment from the old covenant shadows into new covenant realities (Eph. 1:14; 1 Pet. 2:9). The treasured possession of the Lord has become a royal priesthood that offers the true worship of sacrificial praise to the one true, living God (1 Pet. 2:9).

B. The creational ordinance of marriage

It is often suggested that the book of Malachi consists of a disjointed patchwork of homilies with no nuclear focus or coherent development. Despite its obvious unity through the permeating form of the dialogue, the prophecy is generally divided among many supposed editors and redactors.

The larger concepts of creational institutions provide the key to discovering the unifying themes of this book. Genesis offers a panoramic picture of creational order by setting forth the basic ordinances of Sabbath worship, marriage, and labor. Malachi concludes the final chapter of the old covenant narrative by returning to these identical themes. In this light, the treatment of marriage and divorce in Malachi should not be regarded as a redactional imposition on the text, but as an integral aspect of the development of his central themes.

Neither should this treatment of the hallowed subject of marriage be denigrated to the point of regarding it as a parabolic polemic against pagan worship. One commentator supposes that rather than dealing with marriage and divorce in human relationships, the prophet presents Yahweh as the "female spouse" and Israel as the "male spouse."[39] This commentator concludes that Malachi expresses in parabolic form his concern over the "improper veneration of a male deity at a Yahwistic shrine" and at the same time critiques the veneration of a female deity in Israel.[40]

In order to maintain this viewpoint, this commentator must assume, without supporting textual evidence, that a later scribe added the key phrase "let no one act faithlessly with the wife of his youth," which clearly refers to the marriage relationship (Mal. 2:15b). The commentator also declares: "What had been language directed toward Judeans, the personified Israel, becomes language directed to individual Israelites."[41] Treating this passage as a redactional gloss without supporting textual or manuscript evidence can be done only by circular argument in assuming what he has set out to prove.

Much more convincingly, Malachi may be read as treating with all solemnity the creational institution of marriage. The passage begins with the affirmation that one God "created us," using the term for creation found in Genesis 1:1 (Mal. 2:10). From that basis, the prophet

39. Petersen, *Zechariah 9–14 and Malachi*, 203.
40. Ibid., 202.
41. Ibid., 204.

concludes that Judah profaned the covenant and defiled the sanctuary "by marrying the daughter of a foreign god" (2:10–11). The solemnity of the marriage relationship is further underscored by "the Covenant LORD . . . acting as the witness between you and the wife of your youth" (2:14a NIV). The people generally are guilty of breaking faith with the original wife of their marriage covenant (2:14b).

No higher view of the institution of marriage may be found anywhere in scripture than in Malachi's prophecy. Rooted in creation, founded on God's redemptive covenant, solemnized by the Lord himself acting as covenantal witness, marriage is lifted far above the concerns of human convenience. No full restoration of his people from the captivity brought about by sin can be complete apart from the proper reverence directed toward this God-ordained institution of marriage.

Stated negatively, no action can arouse the displeasure of the Almighty more than an abuse of the order of marriage. "I hate divorce" (2:16) is the most natural reading of the biblical text and underscores with emphasis the reaction of the Lord to the violation of his act in uniting male and female. From the most ancient times, repeated efforts have been made to blunt the directness of this assertion. Though leaving the consonants of the text intact, the Masoretes supplied vowels that turned the verb into a third-person indicative form: "'He hates divorce,' says the Covenant LORD God of Israel," which makes little sense in the context. The Septuagint offers an interpretative translation of the passage that provides a justification of divorce: "If one hates, [let him] send away." More in conformity with both the context of the passage and the social circumstance of the day, the phrase is best read as a strong affirmation: "I am hating the sending away."[42]

In view of ancient efforts to read the text as other than a direct condemnation of divorce, the attitude expressed by Jesus' disciples is understandable. They were stunned by the teaching of Jesus concerning the inviolability of marriage (Matt. 19:9–10). But Jesus offers them no easy out from the original intent of the ordinance at creation. What God has joined together no man should put asunder (19:6).

---

42. A present participle with an understood subject is followed by a piel infinitive construct. The verb used here means "to send away" and is also used for divorce in Isa. 50:1 and Deut. 22:19.

Although the law of Moses graciously provided legislative control over what the Lord knew would inevitably occur, the purpose was never to nullify the creator's intent regarding marriage. At the end of the old covenant period, this word from the Lord is sounded loudly and clearly. If restoration to paradise is the goal of redemption, marriage must be regarded as inviolable.

C. The institution of labor

Because of man's original sin, the ground was cursed beneath him. Thorns and thistles became its inevitable crop (Gen. 3:17–19). As a consequence, the original commission of God for man to "subdue the earth" became a burdensome chore. More labor would always be required for the fruit that would be produced. Man would eat bread, but only in the sweat of his brow (3:19a). Now at the conclusion of redemptive history under the old covenant, this curse is reiterated once more. "You are under a curse—the whole nation of you," declares the prophet (Mal. 3:9b NIV). The curse from which the people need relief is spelled out quite specifically. Pests devour their crops, and vines cast their fruit (3:11). Their daily labor has become a burdensome chore that could be rightly characterized as "frustration of frustrations, all is frustration" (Eccl. 1:2).

These people are supposedly the redeemed of the Lord, those who were delivered from the curse. They have responded to the challenge of returning to the land. Why then must they be the ones to undergo this disciplinary chastening at the Lord's hand? The prophet's straightforward answer gets to the heart of the problem. God has come to them in judgment, testifying against those who defraud laborers of their wages, oppress the widows and the fatherless, and deprive aliens of justice (Mal. 3:5). The Lord has not failed to fulfill the promises of the covenant. Instead, the people have brought this curse on themselves. Employers cheat their workers of a fair wage. Society's well-positioned oppress the defenseless. As a consequence, God has placed this curse on a merciless, greedy people.

Yet despite the Lord's judgment, hope for the future rests with "those who feared the Covenant LORD" and "talked with each other" (3:16a NIV). A remnant of the people could not rest content with the

399

prevailing corruptions. As a consequence, the Lord maintained a "book of remembrance," where he recorded the deeds of the faithful (3:16b–17).

The transformation expected of those who participate in the consummation of God's covenants stands in stark contrast with the behavior of Malachi's contemporaries. The apostle Paul admonishes the early Christian community: "Let him that stole steal no more, but rather let him labor, performing with his own hands what is good, so that he will have something to share with one who has need" (Eph. 4:28). Not only is it assumed that the believer in Jesus the Christ will be diligent in his labor to the glory of God. Beyond that essential aspect of the redeemed life, he is expected to have as his goal in work the providing of life's necessities for those in need. In this magnificent way, the fullness of the redemption accomplished in Christ will be realized.

D. Consummate expectations, exhortations, and realizations

Beyond his emphasis on the creational order of the past is Malachi's consummate expectation regarding the future. The prophet's message concerning the ultimate end of this world has nothing to do with a dreamy, unrealistic perspective on future prospects. He speaks instead in sobering terms that anticipate historical realities. As the last of the prophetic voices of the old covenant, his words ultimately find their fulfilling echo in the early developments of the new covenant era.

In accord with the permeating form of assumed dialogue between God and the people, an accusatory question directed at the Lord by the people provokes a divine response that looks to a coming day that will inaugurate a state of finality. The divine response to the people's question, "Where is the God of justice?" (2:17 NIV), indicates that the query should be read as equivalent to asking, "Will the covenantal promise of a Spirit-anointed king who will establish justice in the land ever be realized?"[43] The nation's restoration brought many disap-

---

43. The chapter break between Mal. 2:17 and 3:1 is particularly unfortunate. The answer to the people's query helps in understanding the implications of the question regarding messianic expectations.

pointments, and chief among them was the absence of a messianic figure in accord with the covenantal promise made to David. As a consequence of this absence of a divine representative with authority to subdue evil, many people in the nation continually suffered from the prevalence of injustice. So the accusing question arose, "Where is the God of justice?"

The divine response to this bold accusation is introduced with an attention-demanding "Behold!" (3:1; see also 4:1). The people had asked, "Where is God, the God of justice?" The divine response declares, "The Lord you are seeking *will come*." Without any doubt, he will fulfill his word by sending his messianic representative who will establish justice in the land. The parallelism of expression supports the identity of the Lord himself with a unique designation found only in Malachi:

> Then suddenly he will come to his temple—
>> the Lord
>>> whom you are seeking,
>> even the messenger of the covenant
>>> whom you are desiring—
> Behold, he comes! (3:1b)

The sought-after Lord is the same as the desired-for messenger of the covenant. In response to the disappointment of the people regarding the apparent failure of the Covenant LORD's promise concerning a messiah who would establish justice, the Lord assures them that he will certainly come. Though the identity of God as the messenger of the covenant is unique to this passage in Malachi, it draws on the older reference to the "messenger" from the Lord who preceded Israel in the wilderness as he led them to their eschatological rest (Exod. 23:20–23). In this earlier instance, the text easily moves from the "messenger" to the "Lord" himself, so that the one is identical with the other. God's name is in this messenger, he has the authority to forgive sins, and the messenger says what the Lord commands. While distinctive in its designation of the Lord, this messenger of the covenant is the Lord. Though sent by the Lord, he is the Lord.

The complaint of the people regarding the absence of the "God of justice" receives an answer with clear directness. Their messianic expectations will not be disappointed. The Lord himself will come in the person of the messenger of the covenant to establish the justice they crave.

His coming will occur "suddenly" (3:1b). Yet it will be preceded by another messenger: "See, I will send my messenger, who will prepare the way before me" (3:1a NIV).[44] This declaration does not envision a series of messengers similar to the stream of prophets that had brought the word of the Lord in previous generations. Instead, it anticipates a single individual who will prepare the way for the coming of the Lord himself. By this phraseology, Malachi echoes the language of Isaiah concerning the voice that was to prepare the way for the Lord as the exiled nation returned to its land (Isa. 40:3). But now that the initial postexilic restoration anticipated by Isaiah had been accomplished, Malachi anticipates another restoration that shall be realized with the coming of the Lord himself.

When the Lord appears, he will come to his temple (Mal. 3:1). In this reference, the community of the restoration could take heart. Their labors in reconstructing the temple in Jerusalem have not been in vain. This restored temple will serve as the focal point of the Lord's coming visitation.

Just as the contemporaries of Amos got more than they anticipated with their desire for the coming of the Day of the Lord (Amos 5:18–20), so the people of Malachi's day may expect that the coming of the Lord will bring startling surprises in its wake. "Who can endure the day of his coming, and who can remain upright in his presence?" Their priests will have to undergo intense purification, even as gold and silver are refined by fire. But in the end the offerings of the people will be presented in righteousness (Mal. 3:3–4). The Lord of the covenant will himself offer testimony against all covenant breakers,

---

44. Noting the complexity created by the various personages, Petersen, *Zechariah 9–14 and Malachi*, 209, concludes that these verses are "the product of a complex process of growth." He recognizes original material at the beginning and end of the section, but discovers editorial insertions in the middle, even though he finds an eschatological perspective in both portions of the passage (212). This type of analysis represents a convenient way to resolve an exegetical problem, but does not explain why a supposed editor would make a clear passage more difficult to understand.

including adulterers and those who oppress widows, orphans, and strangers (3:5; see also Deut. 24:14–17). Once and for all the accusation that the God of justice is absent will be put to rest.

A further complaint against God evokes a final eschatological pronouncement. The people spoke harsh words against the Lord (Mal. 3:13). Though they deny the charge, the Lord insists. They have concluded that it is futile to serve God (3:14).

The day is coming in which it will become completely clear that refusing to serve the Lord has far-reaching consequences. The people will clearly see the distinction between the righteous and the wicked, between those who serve God and those who do not serve him (3:18). God maintains a "book of remembrance" (Pss. 69:28; 87:6; 139:16; Rev. 20:12; see also Isa. 4:3; Ezek. 13:9), and those who serve him will be displayed as his "treasured possession" (3:16–17). This image of a treasured possession first appeared at Mount Sinai, when the Lord declared that the nation in covenant with him is to be regarded as his "treasured possession" (Exod. 19:5–6; Deut. 7:6; 14:2; 26:18–19; Ps. 135:4).

The coming day of judgment will thus make plain the distinction between the righteous and the wicked. All the presumptuous along with everyone who practices evil will be set on fire. Neither a root nor a branch will remain to maintain their rebellion against the Lord (Mal. 4:1).[45] For those who fear the Lord, the sun of righteousness will rise with healing in its wings. Just as the rays of the sun bathe the earth with healing and purification, so the establishment of righteousness will bring blessing to God's true people (4:2).[46]

The final message of Malachi begins with a sharp admonition to "remember" (4:4). In light of the announced eschatological distinctions that will be made between the righteous and the wicked, the people have a grave responsibility to "remember." This charge does not simply mean that the people should recall these things in their

45. Once more, the chapter division is unfortunate. While some commentators support a disjunctive function of "for behold" at Mal. 4:1, the phrase is better understood as connecting with the previous thought.

46. Petersen, *Zechariah 9–14 and Malachi*, 225, traces this idea to the imagery of the deities in ancient Mesopotamia and Egypt. While the relationship is possible, it is not necessary. The universal awareness of sunlight's balming effect serves as a sufficient source for the idea.

minds. In preparation for this great coming day of judgment, they must put into practice all that has been revealed to them throughout all redemptive history. This passage alludes to the various segments of the divine revelation to Israel: "torah of Moses" refers to the Pentateuch, the reference to Elijah alludes to the former prophets, and the "great and terrible Day of the Lord" quotes Joel 2:11 as representative of the message of the latter prophets (Mal. 4:4–5). They must be careful to observe *all* the statutes and commandments given to Israel that define the basis of their covenantal relationship (4:4).

Before the arrival of that "great and terrible day of the Covenant LORD," God will send to them the prophet Elijah (4:5). He will declare a message of repentance, causing the hearts of young and old to turn sympathetically toward one another as they return to the Lord (4:6a). Just as the first Elijah confronted an apostate society with the call to repentance, so this second Elijah will summon the people to turn in their hearts. If they do not heed his message, the Lord himself will come and strike the land with the ban (*kherem*) (4:6b). An all-consuming divine anathema will be pronounced over the people.

So who is this Elijah who is to come, and how is the fulfillment of this prophecy to be understood? In the immediate context of Malachi's prophecies about the consummation, this Elijah should be identified with the messenger previously indicated as the individual who would precede the coming of the Lord (3:1a). He is the consummate fulfillment of Isaiah's prophecy concerning a voice crying in the wilderness that anticipates Israel's return from exile (Isa. 40:3).

Does Malachi's reference to Elijah's return demand an actual reincarnation of the ancient prophet? Will the old Elijah who ascended to heaven in a fiery chariot return to earth as the consummate forerunner of the coming of the Lord? Nothing in the historical experience of the old covenant scriptures anticipates such a development. At other points the prophets predict a day in which David will return as king in Israel (Hos. 3:5; Ezek. 34:23; 37:24). Yet the expectation is not that a reincarnated David will return to rule over Israel, thereby superseding the dominion of the promised messiah who was to be greater than David. Instead, these prophecies anticipate the coming of a king with the mind and the spirit of David who will reign over God's universal people.

404

PROPHETS OF THE RESTORATION

It is in this framework that the new covenant identification of John the Baptist as "Elijah" is to be understood. The disciples ask Jesus why their teachers of the law say that Elijah must come before the messiah appears (Matt. 17:10). The point of reference is clearly Malachi's prophecy concerning God's sending of his servant Elijah (Mal. 4:5–6). Jesus replies that the teachers of the law are correct: "Elijah comes and will restore all things. But," says Jesus, "Elijah has already come, and they did not recognize him, but have done to him everything they wished" (Matt. 17:12 NIV). As a result of Jesus' explanation, the disciples understood that he was referring to John the Baptist. By his ministry, John fulfilled Malachi's prophecy concerning the return of Elijah.

But how is this explanation of Jesus to be understood? Was John the Baptist literally Elijah? Did Jesus intend to affirm faith in reincarnation? A wooden interpretation of the words of the prophecy point in this direction, for elsewhere Jesus is quite explicit: "If you are willing to accept it, he is the Elijah who was to come" (Matt. 11:14 NIV). But if scripture is allowed to interpret scripture, another conclusion must be reached. The gospel of Luke indicates that John the Baptist will come "in the *power* and *spirit* of Elijah" (Luke 1:17). He is not literally Elijah in the sense of being a reincarnation of the old prophet. But he is a literal fulfillment of Malachi's prophecy about Elijah in that he is the flesh-and-blood fulfillment of the promise concerning a messenger who would precede the coming of the messiah in the "spirit" and "power" of Elijah. Jesus was speaking perfectly in accord with the message of Malachi when he identified John the Baptist as the fulfillment of the prophet's word, and yet the forerunner of the Christ was not a reincarnation of the ancient prophet.[47]

So the last words of the long movement of prophetism under the old covenant fittingly anticipate the inaugurating events of the new covenant era. The message of John the Baptist brought participation

47. The suggestion of a second literal return of Elijah in terms of a reincarnational event in the future must be rejected outright. This kind of proposal implies that Jesus was in error in his application of the passage to John the Baptist. Many other connections in scripture between the old covenant promises and the new covenant fulfillments related to John the Baptist provide strong support for Jesus' understanding of Malachi's prophecy.

in the blessings of the messianic kingdom to all who would heed his summons to repentance. But for those who would not hear, the ban came into effect.

The witness of the New Testament scriptures to the ministry of John the Baptist as the fulfillment of Malachi's prophecy is a testimony that must be reckoned with. His ministry fits exactly the description provided by Malachi. As a consequence, the identity of Jesus as the God-sent messenger of the covenant who is the Lord himself must be fully appreciated for its perpetual significance. Jesus is the Lord for whom John the Baptist prepared the way. He is at the same time the messenger of the covenant who brought the "message of the covenant," the word concerning the new covenant in his blood that was poured out for the remission of the sin of many. By his coming, a proper restoration of the true Israel of God at last has come to pass.

13

Prediction
in Prophecy

Prediction of future events excites people. Churches can always count
on drawing large crowds to a well-advertised prophecy conference.
Yet from a biblical perspective, prediction is not the essence of
prophecy. Prophecy is represented in scripture as a speaking forth of
the very word of God, regardless of whether prediction of the future
is involved. The distinguishing element of biblical prophecy is the characteristic of its being a revelation from God. The laws delivered by
Moses at Sinai provide the foundational example of prophecy in scripture, and yet little in the way of futuristic prediction may be found in
the Ten Commandments. Prediction of the future, then, is incidental
to the essence of prophecy.

Yet indisputably prediction of future events is a distinctive characteristic of the prophetic declarations of the Bible. Significant portions of every prophetic book in the Old Testament are given over to
predictions regarding the future. Accurate prediction of future events
is held up in scripture as one of the major criteria for distinguishing
between true and false prophecy (Deut. 18:21–22). In the present chapter, several aspects of prediction in prophecy will be considered.

I. Critical perspectives on prediction in prophecy

The repeated and often spectacular claims found throughout the
old covenant prophetic literature respecting the prediction of future

events create more tensions for negative, unbelieving criticism than does any other aspect of biblical prophecy. Critics not prepared to accept the full self-testimony of scripture regarding prophecy may sound rapturous notes in praise of the "high ethical monotheism" that characterizes the prophets of Israel. But the constant affirmations that permeate the writings of Israel's prophets regarding predictions of the future pose large problems for the negatively critical mindset.

Reaction to this problematic aspect of prediction in prophecy is registered in a variety of ways. On the one hand, something of a "conspiracy of silence" seeks to avoid the problem by simply ignoring this aspect of prophetic literature.[1] The vast majority of studies in biblical prophecy cover matters regarding the origins of prophecy, its historical setting, the literary form, the theological substance of the material. But prediction of the future by the prophets is a subject that often remains unrecognized, untouched, and unexplored.

On the other hand, the tension felt over the presence of prediction in biblical prophecy leads various individuals to express themselves in ways that seemingly affirm the presence of prediction in prophecy while at the same time seriously qualifying if not contradicting these very affirmations. Eichrodt states that prediction is "the invaluable method by which the nation is guided along God's paths through the enigmas of history, and it thus retains its inner truth even when it is not literally fulfilled."[2] Eichrodt finds it an easy matter to cast aspersions on prediction in biblical prophecy by denigrating the straw man of literal fulfillment. But he does not supply convincing criteria for discovering what he calls the "inner truth" in a biblical prediction in distinction from its specific assertions. When Jeremiah declares that his false-prophet adversary will die within the year (Jer. 28:15–17), he risks his prophetic credibility before the watching world,

1. Albright, *From the Stone Age to Christianity*, 17, acknowledges that he, along with a majority of biblical scholars, underestimated the predictive element in prophecy. Rowley, *Servant of the Lord*, 125–26, also observes that the role of prediction in biblical prophecy is wrongly minimized. See Barr, *Concept of Biblical Theology*, 20, who states with respect to modern perspectives on biblical theology: "In the prophetic books, the mystery of verbal prediction seemed to have gone, and it was not necessary to bring it back."

2. Eichrodt, *Theology of the Old Testament*, 1.505 n. 1.

not on his awareness of Hananiah's general mortality, but on his divinely revealed knowledge of the maximum number of months that will pass before the false prophet's demise. Even greater tension arising from the subject of prediction appears in the dialectic approach of von Rad. On the one hand, von Rad declares that "the Lord of history is he who can allow the future to be told in advance" and "the power to foretell proves his [God's] specific difference from them [idols]."[3] Yet he also asserts that "not one of all his [Isaiah's] great sayings about Zion came true . . . Jahweh did not protect his city."[4] Simultaneously maintaining these two assertions means either that a person must live with theological self-contradiction or that the God of Israel actually is no better than the idols that Isaiah mocks so effectively.

This resident tension in the treatment of prediction in prophecy is continued in recent works. Clements acknowledges the uniqueness of Old Testament prophecy by affirming that "no comparable non-biblical works from the ancient world are to be found," which means that the biblical material must be studied "inductively, from within the evidence of the surviving scroll itself."[5] He even goes so far as to attribute the writings of the prophets to the work of the Holy Spirit, who inspired both the prophets and the revisionists.[6] Yet in describing the redactor of Amos's prophecy, Clements asserts that a revisionist incorporated into the prediction of the prophet "historical information *post eventum*."[7] That is, Amos anticipated God's judgment of Israel only in general terms, but the redactor then inserted subsequent historical facts as though they were a part of the original prediction. As a consequence, the impression is given to the reader that these specific historical facts were also predicted by Amos, even though they actually were not. "Yet," judges Clements, "this was in no way a falsifying of prophecy, or a fabricating of its truthfulness, but rather a way of drawing out its fuller meaning."[8]

3. Von Rad, *Old Testament Theology*, 2.242.
4. Ibid., 167.
5. Clements, *Old Testament Prophecy*, 7.
6. Clements, *Prophecy and Covenant*, 128.
7. Clements, *Old Testament Prophecy*, 33.
8. Ibid., 34. While the genre of literature would be quite different, one wonders if Clements would offer the same evaluation of a student who, after writing an exami-

The tension inherent in Clements's treatment is quite obvious. He wishes to attribute significant religious value to the utterances of the prophets even to the point of tracing their origin to the inspiration of the Holy Spirit. Yet the prophetic claims of prediction create a special problem. Either the specifics of insight into future historical events must have originated with direct revelations from the God who controls the future or, despite Clements's disclaimers, the supposed redactor must be charged with subterfuge.

In similar fashion, Gowan claims that God was involved in Israel's history "both at the level of communication with certain chosen individuals, and at the level of actual participation in the events of world history."[9] At the same time, he asserts that Isaiah "no more knew exactly what the future will be like than any other human (inspired or not)" and that he predicted "many things that did not come true."[10] If the prophet Isaiah presumed to present as divine messages numerous supposed predictions even though he knew no more about the future than any other human being, one can only wonder about the trustworthiness of the communication that he supposedly received from God.

Still other perspectives on the problem of prediction in the prophets are suggested. Fohrer proposes that the prophets often announced in their predictions events that were "already on the point of coming to pass." They had "just enough time" to point out what was happening, and so they could help the people reach the proper conclusions about the significance of the "prophesied" event.[11] As an alternative to proposing that a well-meaning redactor added subsequent historical details to a generalized prophecy, Sawyer suggests that some redactors invented events that never actually happened as a way of confirming the fulfillment of a prophetic prediction: "An event could be invented or at least elaborately embroidered to match a well-documented prophecy that was already in existence."[12] Sawyer cites

nation in rather general terms, should somehow gain access to his paper after it had been submitted and then add extensive details to his earlier generalizations.

9. Gowan, *Theology of the Prophetic Books*, 9.
10. Ibid., 161–62.
11. Fohrer, *Introduction to the Old Testament*, 352.
12. Sawyer, "Prophecy and Interpretation," 564.

a passage from the book of Ezra to illustrate "the power of prophecy to create its own fulfillment in spite of the evidence."[13]

Perhaps one of the most straightforward rejections of the biblical testimony regarding prediction in prophecy may be found in Carroll's belief in the impossibility of the prophets' ability to accurately predict the future:

> The kinds of arguments used in some theological circles to secure the authenticity of prophecy as genuinely predictive and also as incapable of being wrong need not concern the argument here. They are based on a number of dogmatic positions that are not open for critical discussion. These positions include the notions that God knows the future, he reveals it to the prophets and as such the revealed word cannot be wrong. These archaic metaphors belong to a discarded form of theological discourse and raise far more problems than solutions for the understanding of prophecy. To equate *simpliciter* the words of men with the word of God is to saddle the deity with the errors of men. Talk about God knowing the future is unnecessary even for theological thought as process theology makes so clear. The hermeneutical gymnastics required to give any coherence to the notion of God knowing and revealing the future in the form of predictions to the prophets does no religious community any credit. Furthermore the account of prophecy produced in such circles is banal beyond belief and on a footing with astrological charts and other such diversions of irrationalism.[14]

From one perspective, it is helpful to have this negatively critical perspective expressed so blatantly. No one can miss the point. Even God does not know the future, so there is no possibility of anyone else possessing that knowledge. This position allows for no halting opinions. A universe closed to the direct intervention of God forbids any acknowledgment of the validity of the repeated claims of prophets to predict the future. This world-and-life view simply excludes the possibility that anyone, even God himself, could actually know what will happen in the future, much less reveal it to others.

13. Ibid., 565.
14. Carroll, *When Prophecy Failed*, 34–35.

At the same time, it is quite astounding to read such bold, raw statements about what God can and cannot do. Elsewhere Carroll speaks positively of the value of process theology in "rescuing God."[15] But the self-contained, self-sufficient deity that actually is God hardly needs to be rescued by men. On what ground does a mere human being stand in order to affirm that it is impossible for the almighty, eternal creator to know the future? In response to a person making these kinds of assertions, it simply must be said, "Your God is too small." The God who revealed himself in scripture has no trouble knowing, controlling, and predicting the future. As Daniel said to a baffled King Nebuchadnezzar, "No wise man . . . can explain to the king the mystery . . . but there is a God in heaven who reveals mysteries. He has shown [you] what will happen in days to come" (Dan. 2:27–28 NIV).

II. The biblical concept of prediction in prophecy

Many factors contribute to a full-orbed view of prediction in prophecy according to the scriptures. First and foremost is the prediction of the future as altogether a supernatural work of almighty God. Repeatedly the prophets contrast their reception of divine revelation respecting the future course of events with the machinations of the human mind displayed by the lying prophets (Jer. 28:2–4, 10–17). The deity's involvement in the prediction of the future clearly indicates that the miraculous, the supernatural, provides the only feasible framework for a legitimate concept of predictive prophecy.

This miraculous dimension of prediction in prophecy may be compared with the emphasis on miraculous actions in the historical

15. Ibid., 227 n. 47. Carroll cites Hartshorne, *Reality as Social Process*, 161–62: "Even God's anticipation would have reference to action as choice among probabilities. He would not see what 'is to happen,' but the range of possible things among which what happens will be a selection. And he will see that a higher percentage of some kinds of things will happen than others, that is, he will see in terms of probabilities. This seems to be the only view of God's knowledge that does not make human freedom impossible, or that does not destroy the religious idea of God as perfect in goodness and wisdom." Once more, it is quite amazing that a person would presume to know so precisely the way in which God views the future.

books. The dividing of the Red Sea, the provision of manna in the wilderness, the collapse of the walls of Jericho—all manifested the supernatural, miraculous actions of God in the realm of redemptive history. In the case of the prophets, the supernatural comes to expression in the formation of the prophetic word. These predictions of the future are equally as miraculous as the wondrous deeds of the Lord in delivering his people from bondage and sin under the leadership of Moses. But now through the ministry of the prophets, the people experience what Vos calls "the wonders of prediction."[16]

In this light, it is no wonder that any person who comes to the writings of the prophets with a naturalistic perspective will find it difficult—no, impossible—to accept the records of predictive prophecies at face value. Somehow declarations that take the form of predictions of the future must be explained in naturalistic rather than supernaturalistic terms. It must therefore be proposed that either the text was altered to make it appear as though a prediction were involved or the historical facts must have been altered to suit the details of the prediction. Only as a person acknowledges the role of the one and only all-powerful, all-knowing God in predictive prophecy can the genuine phenomenon as represented in scripture be appreciated.

A second essential factor in genuine predictive prophecy is the recognition of a divine creation of this world with a purpose. The prophets of Israel continually espouse this very perspective. The prophetic self-testimony to the role of divine creation as the ultimate origin of prophetism was noted above (see chap. 1 §II). He who forms the mountains declares his thoughts to men (Amos 4:13). The Covenant LORD who lays the foundation of the earth makes his declaration concerning Jerusalem (Zech. 12:1–2). The maker of all things brings to pass the word of his servant (Isa. 44:24–26).

Jeremiah also underscores the connection between prediction in prophecy and divine creative activity. Five nations surrounding Jerusalem sent envoys to King Zedekiah, apparently with the intent of staging a united revolt against King Nebuchadnezzar of Babylon (Jer. 27:1–3). God sent a message from his prophet Jeremiah to these

16. Vos, *Biblical Theology*, 251.

various nations through their appointed envoys: "With my great power and outstretched arm I made the earth and its people and the animals that are on it, and I give it to anyone I please" (27:5 NIV). The Lord of creation determined to hand over these nations to his servant Nebuchadnezzar, making "even the wild animals subject to him" (27:6 NIV). Because he made all these things, their present and future dispensation will be according to his will. Even the mighty monarch of Babylon is the servant of creation's God, which will be clearly displayed in time when his turn rolls around and he is subjugated by "many nations and great kings" (27:7 NIV).

In this case, the prophet rests the certainty of his very specific predictions about the rise and fall of nations on the sure foundation of the Lord's power as manifested in creation. He boldly predicts that the coalition's revolt against Babylon will fail. And in its appointed time, Babylon will in turn be overrun by a more powerful coalition of nations. While these predictions could be attributed to Jeremiah's personal political acumen, such a conclusion flies in the face of the stated origin of this declaration. God the creator of men and animals decreed it, and on that sure foundation the prophet can confidently send his message through these national emissaries.

Still further, prediction in prophecy presumes not only that the one true God created this world, but that he did his wondrous work of creation with a clear purpose in mind. In this regard, the question might be posed this way: Why would the Almighty do his work of creation without having any purpose for the world that he made? If he had a purpose in creation, then it may be assumed that he has followed with great interest the course of events that have developed over the years. Even more, with a distinctive purpose for his creation in view, it may be assumed that this creator God has been intimately involved in the course of the world's history to see that his divine purpose in creation shall be realized.

Consequently, the idea of a purposeful creation is underscored by two closely related ideas: the purpose of the Lord and the counsel of the Lord. God declares that Cyrus the Medo-Persian ruler "will fulfill all my purpose" in defeating Babylon and restoring Israel (Isa. 44:28). While the exact circumstance of the recording of this prophetic utterance is regularly debated, the time at which the Lord determined his purpose most naturally refers to eternity past. Consonant with the character of the eternal creator God is the eternity of his redemptive purposes. For this reason, the Lord can reveal his purpose to his prophets long before the event occurs.

This perspective on God's purpose as it relates to prediction in prophecy finds full development in the Lord's pronouncement of coming judgment on Assyria:

> Surely as I have planned,
>   so it will be,
> and as I have purposed,
>   so it will stand.
> I will crush the Assyrian
>   in my land;
>   on my mountains
> I will trample him down. . . .
> This is the plan determined
>   for the whole world;
> this is the hand stretched out
>   over all nations.
> For the Covenant LORD Almighty has purposed,
>   and who can thwart him?
> His hand is stretched out,
>   and who can turn it back? (Isa. 14:24–27 NIV)

According to this text, the plan of the Lord is not narrowly directed to counteract problems that arise with the activities of a single nation. Instead, the whole world and all nations have their courses set in accordance with his plan.

The immediate connection between the eternal plan of God for the nations of the world and the predictive utterances of his prophets is found in references to the council of the Lord. In confronting the lying prophets, the Lord declares, "Which of them has stood in the council of the Covenant LORD to see or to hear his word?" (Jer. 23:18 NIV). These lying prophets pretended that they received their prophetic word from God himself. "But," says the Lord, "if they had stood in my council, they would have proclaimed my words to my people and would have turned them from their evil ways" (23:22 NIV).

These references to the council of the Lord do not mean that, because of inherent limitations, God must seek counsel from his own creatures, whether earthly or heavenly. Instead, the Lord chooses as he will to reveal the wonders of his plan to his servants, both angelic and prophetic. The prophet Micaiah's depiction of a scene in which the Lord appears to seek counsel regarding the way to accomplish the destruction of King Ahab should be viewed as a stylized dramatization (1 Kings 22:19–23). That God himself orders the course of subsequent events is clearly communicated by the narrator's description of an arrow that finds its way to the joint in Ahab's armor as he rides his chariot into the battle, thereby fulfilling the prediction of his prophet (22:34).

This council of the Lord represents that point at which the true prophet was initiated into God's secret purposes. The nations do not know the plans of the Lord and have no access to his counsel (Mic. 4:12). But the true prophet of the Lord has the privilege of hearing for himself the Lord's plans for the nations. Only on the basis of his initiation into the council of the Lord is he able to predict the future.

A third element in predictive prophecy underscores the fact that the Lord's prophets predict divine redemptive activities. Contrary to all pseudoprophetism, ancient and modern, biblical predictions never appear as isolated prognostications about secularized political or personal eventualities. The predictions of the prophets always relate to God's ongoing purposes to redeem a people to himself, beginning with Israel and reaching ultimately to all the nations of the world. The curse on creation will be removed, sin will be forgiven and rooted out, universal justice will be established, and peace will be restored between God and men, between men and men, and between men and creation. God's ongoing purpose for the "restoration of all things" (Acts 3:21 NASB) provides the purposeful framework in which all biblical predictions operate.

A fourth element in predictive prophecy as presented in scripture has to do with the interconnection of successive generations in the redemptive purposes of God. In anticipation of the destruction of Sodom and Gomorrah, the Lord says regarding Abraham: "Shall I hide from

416

Abraham what I am about to do? . . . For I have chosen him, so that he will direct his children and his household after him to keep the way of the Covenant LORD . . . so that the Covenant LORD will bring about for Abraham what he has promised him" (Gen. 18:17, 19 NIV).

At the very essence of the divine covenants of redemption is this factor of generational commitments. Noah with his whole house must go into the ark (Gen. 7:1). God's promise to Abraham embraces a thousand generations (Ps. 105:8–9; see also Gen. 17:10). The covenant at Sinai included generations not yet born (Deut. 5:2–3; 29:14–15). David's sons will sit on the throne after him (2 Sam. 7:12). God initiates his new covenant with the house of Israel and the house of Judah (Jer. 31:31). Because the word of the covenant stretches far beyond the current generation, it inevitably embraces events of the future.

This foundational principle of covenantal commitment across the generations lies at the base of prophetic anticipations of the future. It is not by some freak of mystic insight that the prophet predicts what will transpire in future days. Instead, he can be absolutely certain of the future's outcome from generation to generation because of the solemn, divine oath of the covenant. The sovereign Lord of heaven and earth has sworn how things will work themselves out for his people in the generations to come, and it shall occur in just that way.

A fifth element of predictive prophecy in scripture is its character as ongoing miracle in written form. Prophetic predictions preserved *in writing* represent a unique evidence of supernatural intervention in the realm of human experience. A major purpose for the writing of these prophecies is that they may function as *ongoing, ever-present* attestations of the Covenant LORD's gracious working of redemption for a fallen world. Who but an almighty God, the creator, preserver, and only redeemer of this world could anticipate the future as comprehensively as is witnessed by the writings of Israel's prophets? If the self-representation of the prophets in these predictions is true, then clearly there can be no other God, for only God could control the course of men and nations to the degree that would be necessary for the prophets to write out their predictions.

Many passages in the prophets make specific reference to their commission from the Lord to write their predictions. Early in his prophetic ministry, Isaiah is commanded by God to write on a large scroll, "The spoil speeds, the prey hastens" (Isa. 8:1). These written words anticipate the destruction of the northern kingdom of Israel along with Syria by the king of Assyria (8:4). The written word of the prophet provided a permanent record of his prediction. On another occasion, the Lord commands Isaiah to write on a scroll his prediction concerning the fall of the southern kingdom of Judah (30:8). In this case, the prophet anticipates an event that is over one hundred years away. The reason for the writing of the prophecy is made quite explicit:

> Go now, write it
>   on a tablet for them,
> inscribe it
>   on a scroll,
> that for the days to come
>   it may be an everlasting witness. (Isa. 30:8 NIV)[17]

The very purpose of the writing is so that all future generations may confirm the truthfulness of God's word as it was transmitted by his appointed prophet. In this way, the true God of this universe will clearly identify himself.

An additional reference to the "scroll of the Covenant LORD" by Isaiah underscores the prophet's awareness of the divine inspiration of his writings (34:16). His recorded judgment on Edom is not his own inventive prognostication. It is instead a written document that has its origin in God himself.

Indicators of more comprehensive writings that predicted the course of future events appear in the book of Jeremiah. In the drama that may be called the "saga of the scroll," the Lord commands Jeremiah to record "all the words I have spoken to you concerning Israel, Judah and all the other nations from the time I began speaking to you . . . till now" (Jer. 36:2 NIV). This prophetic writing would embrace

17. Von Rad, *Old Testament Theology*, 2.40–45, goes well beyond previous critical traditions in his assertions concerning the writing activity of the prophets. But his conclusion that in this passage Isaiah is being dismissed from his prophetic office goes beyond the exegetical evidence.

over twenty years of prophetic declarations. It may be safely presumed that enough material from this original writing has been preserved in the current book of Jeremiah to indicate that a great deal of these prophecies involved both short-term and long-term predictions. The purpose of these writings, and their relation to the future course of the nation, is made explicit: "Perhaps when the people of Judah hear about every disaster I plan to inflict on them, each of them will turn from his wicked way; then I will forgive their wickedness and their sin" (36:3 NIV). In the good purposes of the Lord, this extensive record of predictions of future disaster for Judah had the intent of making possible their deliverance from the calamity that the Lord had ordered for them. When King Jehoiakim burned this prophetic scroll, the Lord commanded Jeremiah to write an even fuller version of his prophecies (36:28). Now, however, the purpose of the writing was altered: it now serves as the death knoll for the rebellious king and his people. Their future has been set by the declaration of God's written word of judgment (36:30–31).

On yet another occasion a further purpose lies behind the written word of the prophet. Jeremiah is told: "Write in a book all the words I have spoken to you" (30:2 NIV). The prophet is then instructed to record predictions of the return of both Israel and Judah from the land of their exile (30:3). This introductory statement presumably includes the prediction of the new covenant recorded in the next chapter of Jeremiah (31:31–34). If the new covenant scriptures are to be believed, Jeremiah's writings now embrace events that came to pass some six hundred years after their writing.

All these records of prophetic predictions, taken in their integrity, openly display before the whole world an ongoing miracle. Nothing less than divine supernatural intervention could originate these writings. It is for this reason that current critical deconstruction of the prophetic writings has such a faith-destroying impact. The prophetic writings regularly claim to predict the future. If they cannot be trusted to be what they represent themselves as being, then they cannot be trusted at all.

The sixth and climactic element of prediction in prophecy arises naturally in connection with the Lord's final goal for history. God's purposes do not exist without a consummative goal. The very element of the miraculous in predictive prophecy serves as a harbinger of the final, consummative miracle that will transform the entire universe.[18] The present world order will not come to its end by a process of natural degeneration, and not by its inherent powers of revitalization will this world be restored again. Only by the consummative miracle of the return of the resurrected Christ of glory will every enemy of righteousness be consumed. Only by the divine release of the same supernatural power that raised Jesus from the dead will the universe experience its necessary transformation. The admittedly miraculous dimension in predictive prophecy will find its final expression in this supernatural transformation of the entire universe.

The supernatural work of God in the purposeful creation of this world, along with its assured consummation, is intimately connected with the phenomenon of prediction in prophecy. The Lord's redemptive purposes across human generations as predicted in advance by his servants the prophets must be viewed as the focal point of divine revelation in the scriptures.

In many senses, attempts to explain away prediction in prophecy may be compared to earlier efforts of the older liberal theology to discount the miracles of Jesus. The appearance of his walking on the water was explained as having been made possible only because of a sandbar just beneath the surface of the lake. The miraculous feeding of the five thousand was explained as occurring because the little lad's unselfish generosity inspired others to share their lunches. Once naturalistic explanations are endorsed, no reason exists for affirming predictions about the coming Christ or his substitutionary sacrificial death for sinners who live in constant denial of their creator.

But the testimony of scripture is uniform. Over a period lasting for more than two hundred years, the prophets of Israel made their claims of divine inspiration for their predictions of future events. As a consequence, the message and ministry of Israel's whole prophetic movement can be properly understood and appreciated only when the element of prophetic prediction is given its proper place. Affirm the

18. See Vos, *Biblical Theology*, 251.

420

ongoing miracle of predictive prophecy in accord with the self-testimony of scripture, and faith in all the supernatural wonders of creation, redemption, and consummation will be confirmed. Rationalize away the reality of prophetic prediction, and a corresponding decline in faith that affirms divine supernatural intervention as the hope of a fallen world will inevitably follow.

III. Categories of prophetic prediction

Because the true prophets of the only Lord of heaven and earth knew that their prophetic word came to them by divine revelation, they had a certain inherent confidence in the predictions regarding the future that they so boldly proclaimed. Despite their knowledge that the death penalty hovered over the heads of anyone who presumed to predict the future incorrectly, the true prophets regularly dared to anticipate the future with both long-term and short-term predictions. Sometimes they reinforced their prophecies by dramatic enactments. Sometimes they provided conditions that determined the ultimate outcome of their prophetic anticipations. Sometimes they spoke quite boldly concerning the fate of the nations small and great that surrounded them. Sometimes they spoke in cataclysmic terms of the climactic realization of God's ultimate purposes in the long-term future. But always their predictions regarding the future related ultimately to the redemptive purposes of the Lord.

In attempting to comprehend the scope and focus of the futuristic predictions of the prophets, it should prove useful to consider their anticipations in terms of certain major categories. These categories of prediction include the following: short-term predictions, conditional predictions, predictions regarding the nations, and long-term predictions.

A. Short-term predictions

In a very real sense, the true prophets of the Lord often laid their lives on the line by short-term predictions that could be readily verified within their own lifetime. Mosaic legislation indicated that the lying prophet who made up his own failed predictions must be put to

421

death (Deut. 18:20–22). Amos was given fair warning that he should stop predicting that Israel would go into exile and that King Jeroboam would die by the sword (Amos 7:11–16). Jeremiah regularly had to endure confrontations with contemporary lying prophets on the basis of whose predictive word would be fulfilled (Jer. 28). Short-term predictions thus regularly proved to be the testing ground of Israel's prophets.

The people's expectation concerning short-term predictions that could verify the credentials of a prophet comes to full expression in Ezekiel's day through a popular taunt: "The days go by and every vision comes to nothing" (Ezek. 12:22 NIV). Apparently this proverb arose because many false visions and flattering divinations were being uttered by pretending prophets to avoid the scrutiny of a test of fulfillment because of their vague and long-term characteristics (12:24). As a consequence of this abuse of the prophetic role in the nation, God's true prophet also suffered from the sting of this mockery. But the Lord would not tolerate this situation for long. Instead of this old proverb, a new saying will take its place: "The days are near when every vision will be fulfilled" (12:23 NIV).[19] The people's complaint apparently focused on visions that would come to pass only in the distant future (12:27). But the Lord will now give them more than they asked for: "None of my words will be delayed any longer; whatever I say will be fulfilled" (12:28 NIV). The nation failed to appreciate the grace involved with the delay in fulfillment of the prophet's predictions, but now every judgment spoken against this rebellious house would be fulfilled without delay (12:25).

This expectation of predictions clear enough to have recognizable fulfillments in the near future was legitimately grounded in the original establishment of the prophetic office in Israel and continued throughout the nation's history. If a prophet's words did not come to pass, then the Lord had not spoken through that person (Deut. 18:22). The distinctiveness of young Samuel was that the Lord did not let any "of his words *fall to the ground*." As a consequence, all Israel heard that "Samuel was established as a prophet of the Covenant LORD"

19. A very slight alteration of the Hebrew text makes the difference between the two proverbs, which makes the point of the change even more pungently.

(1 Sam. 3:19–20). In the heat of his conflict with the lying prophet Hananiah, Jeremiah appeals to the long-established tradition of the test for true prophets. A prophet can be recognized as truly from the Lord "only if his prediction comes true" (Jer. 28:9 NIV). In similar fashion, Ezekiel hangs his reputation on the fulfillment of his prediction concerning the devastation of the land of Israel: "When all this comes true—and it surely will—then they will know that a prophet has been among them" (Ezek. 33:33 NIV).

The short-term predictions of the true prophets of the Lord thus served a vital purpose: they confirmed the truthfulness of the words of the prophet and provided a basis for confident faith on the part of the people. In a similar fashion, the many fulfilled predictions retained in written form in the scriptures serve to confirm the truthfulness of the moral and redemptive messages found in scripture, while also laying a firm foundation for faith in the long-term predictions of the prophets. Only by denying the integrity of the written word of God can these conclusions be avoided, to the great loss of the unbeliever.

In considering more particularly the short-term predictions of the prophets in scripture, it should first be recognized that the attention of prophetic predictions is never directed toward incidental matters that are not directly related to the Lord's ongoing purposes of redemption. Biblical prophets do not predict which horse will win a race, which team will prevail in an athletic contest, or which investment will yield the greatest return. Instead, their concern always focuses on the plan of God made from eternity past to redeem a people to himself. This specific perspective leads the prophets to anticipate near and distant future circumstances.

1. The course of the nation of Israel

As shall be considered in the next chapter, the prophetic anticipation of Israel's experience of exile and restoration deserves special consideration on its own. But several examples of short-term predictive prophecy related to this subject may be helpful at this point.

Though prophesying in the days of the northern kingdom's greatest glory, Hosea predicts in no uncertain terms that God will put an end to the kingdom of Israel, but will show special love to the house

423

of Judah (Hos. 1:4b, 7). More specifically, he declares that the calf-idol of Beth-aven (Bethel) will be carried away to Assyria as tribute to the "great king" (10:5–6). This prediction found its fulfillment within the space of approximately thirty years.

Shortly thereafter, Isaiah predicted that the "mighty floodwaters" of the king of Assyria would overflow its channels, sweep into Judah, and swirl "up to the neck" (Isa. 8:5–8). Though the nation was warned that the Assyrian army would "shake their fist at the mount of the Daughter of Zion" (10:32 NIV), they were encouraged not to fear this invading force (10:24). In offering a word of comfort to harassed King Hezekiah, the prophet predicted that though the king of Assyria already stood outside Jerusalem's gates, he would not enter the city. By the way he came he would return, for the Lord would defend Jerusalem for his own sake as well as for David's sake (37:33–35). In all three of these prophecies, Isaiah recognizes the seriousness of the Assyrian threat. But he also indicates that their army would not succeed in over-running the chosen city of Jerusalem. Having witnessed the fall of Samaria to the same Assyrian troops, Isaiah could have known the outcome of this threat to Jerusalem only by divine revelation.

A century later, Jeremiah prophecies early in the reign of Zedekiah that unless the nation willingly submits, Judah and all the surrounding nations will be subjected to the brutality of King Nebuchadnezzar of Babylon (Jer. 27:1–15). As much as ten years before the city fell, and even in the face of contradictory predictions by other so-called prophets, Jeremiah declared unequivocally that the holy city will fall. While his foresight might be attributed to political acumen, the past experience of the nation pointed in a different direction. Had not God entered into an eternal covenant with David that guaranteed the preservation of the city? Had not Jerusalem proved impregnable when assaulted by the equally powerful army of the Assyrians? Why then should anything else but divine deliverance be forecast for this select city?

Divine revelation made certain the imminent fall of Jerusalem. God's prophet knew in advance that chastening judgments of the Lord would be administered at the hand of God's servant Nebuchadnezzar. He predicted with sadness, yet with confidence, the tragedy that would befall the nation.

These short-term predictions all found their fulfillment within the lifetime of the prophet and his contemporaries. Though people then were as capable of rationalizations as scholars of today, the written records of scripture point to divine revelations of the future course of events that inevitably manifested the true nature of a sovereign, gracious, and righteous redeemer.

2. The rise and fall of the nation's kings

Because the kings of Judah and Israel embodied the idea of a coming messiah, the lives of these kings naturally became a primary subject of the predictions of the prophets. Due to their inherent imperfections, these lesser anointed ones often demonstrated a pattern of life that was just the opposite of what might be expected of the anointed savior of God's people.

Amos predicted that with his sword the Lord would rise against the "house" of Jeroboam (Amos 7:9). Amaziah the priest of the illegitimate, idolatrous worship center at Bethel twisted Amos's words and accused him of prophesying that Jeroboam himself would die by the sword (7:11; see also 2 Kings 14:29). But it was Jeroboam's son Zechariah who experienced a violent death by the sword of Shallum, exactly as Jeremiah had predicted (15:8–10).

As the monarchy of the southern kingdom of Judah began to come to its close, Jeremiah offered a series of predictions about their last kings. Jehoiachin along with his mother would be hurled into exile never to return, and none of his sons would succeed him on the throne (Jer. 22:24–30; 2 Kings 24:8, 12, 15). Even though lying prophets contradicted him by promising the return of Jehoiachin from Babylon, Jeremiah's prophecy proved true (Jer. 28:4).

Because of his arrogant destruction of the treasured scroll that recorded all the Lord's messages to Jeremiah the prophet, a special word of judgment was spoken over King Jehoiakim of Judah. He had shown utter contempt for the word of the Lord by slicing and burning the scroll. Therefore his body would be thrown out, with none of his descendants allowed to sit on the throne of David (Jer. 36:30–31). This prediction creates difficulties in two respects. On the one hand, the book of Chronicles indicates that Jehoiakim was taken to Babylon, not buried outside the gates of Jerusalem (2 Chron. 36:6; Ezek. 19:9). In addition, Jehoiachin the son of Jehoiakim succeeded him on the throne of Judah (2 Kings 24:6).

In considering the second problem first, it should be noted that Jeremiah later indicates that Zedekiah was made king by Nebuchadnezzar "in place of Jehoiachin son of Jehoiakim" (Jer. 37:1 NIV). Jeremiah was fully aware that a son of Jehoiakim succeeded him on the throne of Judah, but apparently did not regard this fact as a contradiction of his previous prediction. Very possibly Jeremiah is taking into consideration that Jehoiachin ruled in Judah for only three months and was then snatched from the throne by Nebuchadnezzar. This brief interlude might well be regarded as not "sitting on the throne" in a normal sense of the term.

With respect to Jehoiakim's dishonorable burial, the text says his body shall be "thrown outside the gates of Jerusalem." The phrase indicates a burial in disgrace, though not specifying the concrete circumstances of the final disposition of his body. Whatever the case, the king did not receive the normal honors associated with the expiration of a monarch.

At a dramatic moment during the final siege of Jerusalem, Nebuchadnezzar and his forces were distracted by an incursion of the army of Egypt (Jer. 37:5). Naturally this interruption of the Babylonian assault on the holy city spurred hopes of a divine deliverance like that previously experienced in the days of Hezekiah. But Jeremiah had already predicted that the city would fall to Nebuchadnezzar and that King Zedekiah would be taken to Babylon (32:1–5; 34:1–7). He now further declares that the pharaoh with his army will return to Egypt and that the Babylonians will reinstitute their siege and eventually burn Jerusalem to the ground (37:6–10). When King Zedekiah arranged for a private session with Jeremiah, the message of the prophet was the same: the king would be turned over to Nebuchadnezzar (37:17).

Simultaneously in Babylon, the prophet Ezekiel was enacting his own prophecy concerning the siege of Jerusalem and the capture of King Zedekiah. At the command of the Lord, he packed his belongings for exile, and as night fell he slipped through a hole he had dug in the wall (Ezek. 12:3–7). The Lord then provided an interpretation of the prophet's symbolic action, so that even the blindest people could understand: "The prince . . . will put his things on his shoulder at dusk and leave, and a hole will be dug in the wall for him. . . . He will cover his face so that he cannot see the land. . . . I will bring him to Babylonia, . . . but he will not see it, and there he will die. I will scatter to the winds . . . his staff and all his troops" (12:12–14 NIV).

The details of Ezekiel's prophecy are substantiated by Jeremiah's subsequent narrative. The Babylonians eventually effected a breach in the walls of Jerusalem. The king and his army fled through the wall under cover of darkness. All his soldiers were separated from him, and he was captured. Zedekiah was then brought before Nebuchadnezzar, who murdered his sons before his eyes, blinded him, and led him away to Babylon where he remained in prison until his death (Jer. 52:4–11; see also 2 Kings 25:4, 7). Just as Ezekiel predicted, the king fled through the wall at dusk, his men were separated from him, he was captured and brought to Babylon but never saw it, and there he died.

Who could possibly anticipate these details in advance of their occurrence except the God who himself orders the course of history! While rationalizations may explain away the predictions of the prophet, the obvious integrity of the text of both Jeremiah and Ezekiel testify to something else. If this prophecy alone is allowed to stand, then it becomes clear that there can be only one God, the God who orders the course of kings to the glory of his justice and mercy.

3. The personal lives of God's prophets

Predictions regarding the personal lives of God's special servants, the prophets themselves, do not appear apart from an intimate connection with God's ongoing program of redemption. Even as the Babylonian siege is in full swing and Jeremiah remains under house arrest, the word of the Lord informs him that his uncle will come to ask that he purchase a piece of real estate (Jer. 32:6–7). When the uncle shows up and makes his proposal, Jeremiah is confirmed in the fact that his uncle's request must come as the word of the Lord (32:8). Who but the Lord would direct someone to respond positively to a proposal that he purchase a piece of real estate in the very territory currently occupied by an invading force, while at the same time revealing the circumstances of the proposal before it occurs?

427

Jeremiah must do what the Lord instructs, but he cannot help but wonder at the incongruity of these directions. Why should he, a poor preacher under house arrest, buy land when the whole territory of Judah is just now in the process of falling into the hands of the Babylonians? The Lord answers his prophet's legitimate query by disclosing his purposes for the future: "This is what the Covenant LORD says: As I have brought all this great calamity on this people, so I will give them all the prosperity I have promised them. Once more fields will be bought in this land. . . . Fields will be bought for silver, and deeds will be signed, sealed and witnessed in the territory of Benjamin . . . because I will restore their fortunes, declares the Covenant LORD" (Jer. 32:42–44 NIV).

This chapter in the prophet's life becomes a prophetic symbol, a sign of hope for the future. Jeremiah was given the solemn responsibility of declaring the inevitability of Jerusalem's being burned to the ground by the Babylonians, in direct contradiction of many other prophets who insisted that the holy city could never fall. And now his action of investing his sparse resources in Judean land even while the final siege is in process declares loudly and clearly a message of hope. His enacted prediction anticipates the truly inconceivable: after exile, Israel shall return to its land and repossess its properties.

A similar predictive incident occurs in the life of Ezekiel. While living in Babylon, he is told in advance that his wife, the "delight of his eyes," will die. But he must not participate in any of the customary rituals of mourning. The very next evening his wife dies. Yet according to the directions of the Lord, the prophet restrains himself from participation in any of the customary rituals of mourning (Ezek. 24:15–18). The Lord then tells his prophet to instruct the people regarding the significance of these events. The Lord is about to desecrate his sanctuary in Jerusalem, the "delight of their eyes." But the people will be so stricken with grief that they will follow Ezekiel's example. They will perform none of the customary rituals of mourning, and they will eat none of the customary foods. By this prophetic anticipation of the chief of all imaginable tragedies, Ezekiel becomes a sign, and the people come to know that their God is indeed the one and only God, the Covenant LORD (24:20–27).

428

While these predictions in connection with the life-experience of the prophets are quite significant, the largest grouping of prophecies associated with the prophets' lives has to do with the conflict that arose as a consequence of their predictions. Amos received rigid opposition because of his predictions regarding the fall of the northern kingdom to the armies of Assyria. But in response to the opposition of Amaziah the priest of Bethel, Amos offers a further prophecy containing no less than five specific predictions: Amaziah's wife will become a prostitute in the city, his sons and daughters will die by the sword, his land will be divided as spoil, the priest himself will die in a pagan country, and Israel will go into exile (Amos 7:17). Only the last of these predictions can be verified as historical fact, but the very preservation of the other predictions supports the assumption that they also found fulfillment.

Three incidents of Jeremiah's conflict with pretentious prophets evoke three additional predictions of a short-term nature. First, Hananiah dramatically smashes the symbolic yoke around Jeremiah's neck, declaring that within two years Nebuchadnezzar's power will be broken and the exiles returned (Jer. 28:3–4, 10–11). Jeremiah hails the prediction as a fond hope of all, but then prophesies that because of his rebellion against the true word of the Lord, Hananiah will die within the year. By the seventh month Jeremiah's prophecy is fulfilled; the false prophet dies (28:16–17). In a second incident, Jeremiah predicts that the lying, immoral prophets Ahab and Zedekiah will be captured by Nebuchadnezzar and burned to death in the fire (29:20–23). In still a third case, a lying prophet named Shemaiah widely distributed a letter in Jerusalem that he wrote while in Babylon. In the letter he accused Jeremiah of posing as a prophet and denounced Jeremiah's word that the people in Babylon should settle down for the long captivity ahead of them. He urged the priests of Jerusalem to regard Jeremiah as a madman and put him in stocks and neck irons (29:24–28). Jeremiah responds with a prophecy that Shemaiah will never see the good things the Lord will do for his captive people and that none of his offspring will survive (29:29–32).

These stern predictions spoken against the people who contradict the Lord's true prophets should not be regarded as manifestations

429

of personal vindictiveness. Instead, these declarative judgments about the future course of events could originate only with the God who controls the future. As a consequence, they underscore the seriousness of contradicting the very word of the living God. To speak against the word of God's true prophet is to speak against God himself.

In this context, the blatant manner in which many current studies treat the written word of the living God is rather astonishing. If these pronouncements of judgment against the lying prophets of ancient days represent true revelations from God, "how shall we escape if we ignore such a great salvation . . . , which was first announced by the Lord" and then "confirmed to us by those who heard him, God also testif[ying] to it by signs, wonders and various miracles, and gifts of the Holy Spirit?" (Heb. 2:3–4 NIV).

The short-term predictions of the prophets thus had a significant role to play. Particularly as a way of confirming the truthfulness of the prophet's words, these divine revelations of specifics regarding the future were and continue to be an important aspect of the prophetic ministry. Since the spectacular theophanies associated with the revelation of God's truth at Sinai are not to be expected in the present age, the confirmed word of the humble prophet of old in the writings of scripture has vital significance for the people of God today.

B. Conditional predictions

The imagery of a watchman as presented by the prophet Ezekiel epitomizes the idea of conditional predictions in the message of Israel's prophets.[20] The watchman had the responsibility of warning a nation in the event of an impending assault. He must blow the trumpet to offer clear warning of the threat approaching the city. Though the watchman would not be held responsible for the people's reaction to his warnings, he would be guilty for any bloodshed if he failed to sound his alarm (Ezek. 33:1–6).

The Lord applies this principle to Ezekiel as his appointed prophet. He must warn the wicked of the consequences of his ways. If the wicked responds in faith and repentance to the summons of the

20. For a balanced treatment of questions related to conditional predictions, see Pratt, "Historical Contingencies."

430

prophet, his life will be spared. But if he continues in his same sinful patterns, divine judgment will inevitably fall. If, however, the prophet fails to warn the wicked of his ways, the Lord will hold him accountable for the blood of the wicked (Ezek. 3:17–21; 33:7–9).

So the predictions of personal and national devastation by Israel's prophets may or may not come to pass, depending on the response of the people who are addressed. Of course, the purposes and determinations of the Lord remain forever unchanged. But in the dispensings of the Lord's mercy, guilty sinners may be spared even after a coming judgment has been announced by the prophet if they turn in repentance and faith.

Yet an immediate problem arises with the unequivocal character of some of the declarations by the prophets that have no explicit conditions attached. Within forty days Nineveh shall be destroyed, according to Jonah's pronouncement (Jon. 3:4). He says nothing about the possibility of divine mercy in the eventuality of the city's repentance. Yet in the end the mourning city is spared. In a similar manner, the prophet Isaiah makes an unequivocal declaration to King Hezekiah at the time of his illness: "This is what the Covenant LORD says: Put your house in order, because you are going to die; you will not recover" (Isa. 38:1 NIV). The word of the prophet is certain. The king's illness will be fatal. Yet in response to the king's prayers, the Lord adds another fifteen years to Hezekiah's life (38:5). The prophet Micah offers an unequivocal prediction about Jerusalem's future: "Zion will be plowed like a field, Jerusalem will become a heap of rubble, and the temple hill a mound overgrown with thickets" (Mic. 3:12 NIV). Yet the city was spared from destruction by the invading Assyrians and remained intact for another 150 years.

In each of these prophecies, no hint of conditionality may be detected. The declaration is unequivocal: these things shall happen. Since they do not happen it might be suggested that on occasion the predictions of the Lord's true prophets failed. Their prophecies regarding the future did not come to pass.

The conclusion that the Lord's prophets failed in their predictions manifests a very low view of the attributes of God.[21] A central

21. See the discussion on this point in Fairbairn, *Interpretation of Prophecy*, 58–82.

aspect of the nature of the one true God as revealed in scripture is that he graciously provides a way for receiving sinners who repent. In this regard, his character never changes. Jonah himself explains the supposed dilemma regarding Nineveh's survival despite his prediction of its destruction: "That is why I was so quick to flee to Tarshish. I knew that you are a gracious and compassionate God, slow to anger and abounding in love, a God who relents from sending calamity" (Jon. 4:2 NIV). Because Jonah himself knew the unchanging character of God, he expected all along that a repentant Nineveh would be spared divine judgment. The same conclusion may be reached regarding Micah's so-called failed prophecy concerning the destruction of Jerusalem. A century later certain elders in the time of Jeremiah quote Micah's prediction (Jer. 26:18), but the purpose of their quotation is not to show that Micah erred in his prophecy or to indict Micah as a false prophet. Instead, they quote his prophecy "to argue that, as a result of Micah's prophecy, the king [Hezekiah] and the people repented, and hence Yahweh forgave them and spared the city."[22]

Ezekiel makes the same point. The people were complaining that the ways of the Lord were unjust because he punished the righteous and spared the wicked. But the Lord responds by noting that when a righteous man turns from his righteousness, he will be punished; and when a wicked man repents of his sin, he will be spared. God is not unjust in the essence of his being, and so he will not act unjustly. Even if unexpressed at the time a prophecy is uttered, the Lord's essential character will be manifest in the consequences that follow the predictions of his prophets.

A mere human being cannot presume to know when the Lord in his justice will conclude that certain individuals shall be spared his declared judgments and when they have gone beyond the point of no return. "Return to the Covenant LORD," pleads Joel, for "who knows? He may turn and have pity" (Joel 2:13–14 NIV). "Hate evil, love good," admonishes Amos, for "*perhaps* the Covenant LORD God Almighty will have mercy" (Amos 5:15 NIV). As a consequence, presumption never has a proper place in the face of God's announced judgments.

22. Freedman, "Between God and Man," 61–62.

On the other hand, because of the Lord's mercy it may never be too late. Even in the fourth year of King Jehoiakim, just as the first captives of Judah such as Daniel were being carried away to Babylon, the scroll that contained all Jeremiah's prophecies was publicly presented with the hope that perhaps the people would turn from their wicked ways and bring their petitions before the Lord (Jer. 36:7). Despite their persistence in sin, they still may be saved. In a similar way, even after King Nebuchadnezzar experienced the revelatory dream of his coming humiliation, Daniel advised the monarch to renounce his sins by being kind to the oppressed, for "it may be that then your prosperity will continue" (Dan. 4:27 NIV). The king continued in his prideful ways, however, and so ended up grazing on grass like a beast of the field.

According to Jeremiah, the promise of restoration to the land after seventy years of exile hinges on the fulfillment of certain conditions. The people must call on the Lord, pray to him, and seek him with all their heart. Then and only then will he bring them back from their captivity (Jer. 29:12–14). Indeed, the gracious plan of the Lord guarantees that these conditions will be fulfilled when the seventy-year period has elapsed (29:10–11). Yet the conditions for fulfillment are very real.

The predictions of future blessing and cursing by the prophets are thus clearly conditioned on the reaction of the people. Human beings are treated as responsible people who must give account to the Lord for their actions. At the same time, the redemptive purposes of the Lord shall inevitably move forward to their consummate goal, as anticipated by the prophets.

C. Predictions concerning the nations

It would be quite remarkable if a person in the modern world could even approximate the message of the prophets of Israel with respect to the nations that surrounded them. Several distinctive elements constitute the proclamations of Israel's prophets concerning neighboring nations: (1) the nations will be judged by God, particularly for their sins of brutality, idolatry, and pride; (2) the nations will be treated by God in accordance with their treatment of the nation of

Israel (see chap. 6 §I.D); and (3) the nations eventually will share in the redemption provided for Israel. In the message of the prophets, the Lord's interaction with the nations regularly appears in the form of predictions respecting the future.

Several prophetic books include sections devoted to prophecies regarding the nations surrounding Israel. The scope of these predictions is quite extensive:

- Ammon (Jer. 49:1–6; Ezek. 21:28–32; 25:1–7; Amos 1:13–15; Zeph. 2:8–11)
- Assyria (Isa. 10:5–19; 14:24–27; Nahum; Zeph. 2:13–15)
- Babylon (Isa. 13; 14:3–23; 21:1–10; 47; Jer. 50–51; Hab. 2:4–20)
- Cush (Isa. 18; 20:3–6; Zeph. 2:12)
- Damascus (Isa. 17:1–3; Jer. 49:23–27; Amos 1:2–5; Zech. 9:1–4)
- Edom (Isa. 21:11–12; 34:5–15; Jer. 49:7–22; Ezek. 25:12–14; 35; Amos 1:11–12; Obadiah)
- Egypt (Isa. 19; 20:3–6; Jer. 46:2–26; Ezek. 29–30; 32)
- Moab (Isa. 15–16; Jer. 48; Ezek. 25:8–11; Amos 2:1–3; Zeph. 2:8–11)
- Philistia (Isa. 14:28–32; Jer. 47; Ezek. 25:15–17; Joel 3:4–8; Amos 1:6–8; Zeph. 2:4–7; Zech. 9:5–8)
- Tyre and Sidon (Isa. 23; Ezek. 26–28; Joel 3:4–8; Amos 1:9–10; Zech. 9:2–4)

In fitting fashion, focus centers particularly on Babylon as the epitome of animosity against God's people (Isa. 13:1–22; 14:3–23; 21:1–10; 47:1–15; Jer. 50:1–46; 51:1–64; Hab. 2:4–20). But perhaps most remarkable is the consistency of prediction concerning the ultimate salvation that these nations will share along with Israel. The extent of this element in the prophetic anticipation regarding the future is often overlooked. But rightly perceiving this aspect of the prophetic message is essential for understanding the prophetic picture of the future. Despite the constant mistreatment and devastation that the nations brought on Israel, the message comes through clearly at every new stage in the nation's history. The nations of the world will share in the redemption and the restoration promised to Israel. This aspect of prophetic prediction may be considered from a preexilic, an exilic, and a postexilic perspective.

1. Gentile inclusion from a preexilic perspective

Quite amazingly, even in the midst of repeatedly announcing the devastation that neighboring nations will bring on Israel, the preexilic prophets regularly proclaim the blessings from God that will come to these same nations. In Jonah's case, every instinct of national loyalty forbids him to go to Nineveh, the capitol of the Assyrian kingdom that will ultimately devastate Israel's northern tribes. Yet as a consequence of his preaching, the whole city repents, and the Lord shows his mercy by sparing its people (Jon. 3:6–10). Hosea describes Israel's severest judgment in terms of their being turned back to their original Gentile state. They will become *Lo-Ammi* (not my people) (Hos. 1:9). But then God in his sovereign grace will transform these newly made Gentiles back again into *Ammi* (my people) (2:1, 23). When this declaration of transformation from Israelite to Gentile to Israelite again is taken seriously, then it becomes understandable that this prophecy of Hosea properly functions as a basis for Paul's ministry to the Gentile nations. The ten tribes that constituted the northern kingdom were swallowed up, assimilated into the vast world of the Gentiles. But by Christ's calling Gentile peoples to himself, the promised restoration of the Israel of God is being accomplished (Rom. 9:24–26). Amos mercilessly pounds Israel with the message of God's coming judgment on them. But in the end he predicts the restoration of the fallen booth of David and the conversion of alien Edom into people on whom the name of God is called, making them participants in God's electing grace in the same way as was Israel (Amos 9:12; see also Deut. 28:9–10, where the identical phrase indicates Israel's election). This declaration of Gentile inclusion proclaimed by Amos ultimately provides the church of the new covenant with a basis for resolving the question regarding how Gentiles who have received the Holy Spirit are to be received into the community of the new covenant (Acts 15:15–19).

435

The most glorious description of the inclusion of the Gentile world among the pre-exilic prophets comes from Isaiah. From all the various sections of the book the grand expanse of the coming kingdom of God incorporates the teeming multitudes of the Gentile nations. Early in the first portion of his prophecy, Isaiah declares that "in the last days," "many peoples will come . . . to the mountain of the Covenant LORD." He will "judge between the nations and will settle disputes for many peoples," turning "their swords into plowshares and their spears into pruning hooks" (Isa. 2:2–4).[23] The second half of the book opens with the announcement that at the time of the new exodus, "the glory of the Covenant LORD will be revealed, and *all mankind* together will see it" (40:5). The messianic king of David's line will serve as light for the darkened land of the *Gentiles* (9:1–2) and "will stand as a banner for *the peoples*" (11:10). *The nations* will rally to him, for he will gather not only the exiles of Israel; he will also "raise a banner for *the nations*" (11:12; see also Matt. 4:12–17). The second great figure of Isaiah that stands alongside the restored Davidic ruler is made known through the servant songs. This servant of the Lord will not only restore the people of Israel; he will also serve the Gentile world. He "will bring justice to the nations," and "in his law the islands will put their hope" (Isa. 42:1, 4). If it appears to be "too small a thing" for this select servant "to restore the tribes of Jacob," he will have an even larger task to perform. God will make him "a light for the Gentiles" that he "may bring [God's] salvation to the ends of the earth" (49:6). Despite his being brought so low, "he will be . . . highly exalted" (52:13), so that he will "sprinkle many nations, and kings will shut their mouths because of him" (52:15). These servant songs bear testimony to the universalistic dimension of God's intention in restoring a fallen world and are regularly cited for this very reason by various portions of the new covenant documents (Matt. 12:13–21; Acts 8:32–35; 13:46–48).

And yet there is more. This visionary prophet looks squarely at Egypt and Assyria, the prime national enemies of his day to the south and the north, and dares to place them alongside his own nation of Israel as belonging to the Lord! Can you imagine it! "An altar to the

23. All biblical quotations in this paragraph are from the NIV.

Covenant LORD of Israel in the heart of Egypt" (Isa. 19:19). A highway running directly from Egypt to Assyria, so that these two enemies of Israel conveniently travel back and forth, bypassing Jerusalem, to worship the Covenant LORD together in their own countries (19:23). As a consequence, "Israel will be the third, along with Egypt and Assyria, a blessing on the earth. The Covenant LORD Almighty will bless them, saying, 'Blessed be Egypt my people, Assyria my handiwork, and Israel my inheritance'" (19:24–25 NIV).

Still further confirmation of this universalistic dimension of the futuristic expectation of Isaiah is found in his declaration that God's house will be called "a house of prayer for all nations" (Isa. 56:7b NIV; see also Mark 11:17). No foreigner will ever be excluded from belonging to his people. God himself will take the initiative in bringing to his house all foreigners who love his name and will give them joy in his house of prayer (Isa. 56:6–7a).

That these predictions of the wholehearted inclusion of Gentile nations with his people should be offered in the very days in which the brutal nation of Assyria was invading the land of Israel is nothing less than astounding. Yet it would not be appropriate to arbitrarily assign these predictions of the inclusion of the Gentiles to a subsequent era of Israelite history. In any event, these passages from the different portions of Isaiah offer strong testimony to the genuine expectation of Israel's prophets regarding the future inclusion of the Gentile world into the very heart of the chosen nation's worship and life.[24]

This tradition of Gentile inclusion in the Lord's future blessings is continued unbroken in the testimony of the seventh-century preexilic prophets. The kingdom of Judah is now on the brink of exile. Because the nation in its hour of deepest distress became the object of Moab's ridicule, Jeremiah pronounces the Lord's woe over that nation (Jer. 48:27–46). Yet after forty-six verses of severe condemnation, a sudden turn of perspective introduces the prediction that the Lord will restore the fortunes of Moab in days to come (48:47). The same star-

24. The passages explicitly discussed from Isaiah by no means exhaust his predictions concerning Gentile inclusion. Other passages include Isa. 14:1; 17:7–8; 18:7; 23:18; 24:14–16; 25:6–8; 27:6; 60:3–16; 66:19–21.

tling projected turn in the future appears in the Lord's word concerning Ammon and Elam (49:6, 39).

The concept of the Lord's restoring the fortunes of non-Israelite nations is all the more remarkable in view of Jeremiah's regularly using the same expression to describe the restoration of his people Israel (30:18; 32:44; 33:11; 33:25–26). Whatever blessings of restoration belong to the nation of Israel, the Lord offers equally and exactly to every other nation and people that come into existence across the history of the world.

The anticipation of God's restoring the fortunes of non-Israelite nations is not restricted to these specific cases, but finds programmatic expression. Jeremiah applies his key term *uproot* to all the "wicked neighbors who seize" Israel's land: "But," says the Covenant LORD, "after I uproot them, I will again have compassion and will bring each of them back to his own inheritance and his own country. And if they learn well the ways of my people and swear by my name, . . . then they will be established among my people" (12:15–16 NIV).

How amazing is this perspective on the future by the prophet Jeremiah! Unequivocally offered to all nations without discrimination is the opportunity to be restored to God's favor and established among his elect people. Those nations that have sinned most heinously in their brutal treatment of God's people in their hour of greatest need are declared to be the recipients of these promises of restoration. Still further, the Lord announces that if at any time any nation or kingdom repents of its evil, then the Lord will not inflict on it the disaster he had planned (18:7–8). These people were altogether worthy of destruction at the hand of the Lord, but in his compassion he stood ready to forgive them if they would only repent of their evil. Jeremiah personally witnessed their ruthless treatment of God's own people, and yet in the Lord's name he offers them the same salvation as he offers to Israel.

Nothing in terms of this promise of restoration for the nations of the world is found in Nahum and Habakkuk. But in a fashion similar to Jeremiah, his contemporary, Zephaniah, predicts that the Lord's judgment will fall on Moab and Ammon. Yet he concludes that "the nations on every shore will worship him, every one in its own land" (Zeph. 2:11b NIV). Looking even further to the most distant horizons, this prophet anticipates the day in which after the purging judgments of the Lord, the lips of the peoples will be purified, "that all of them may call on the name of the Covenant LORD and serve him shoulder to shoulder" (3:9 NIV). Deep into the continent of Africa, "beyond the rivers of Cush," the Lord's true worshipers will present to him their offerings (3:10).

Despite their certain experience and expectation of the devastations heaped on God's people by brutal neighboring nations, the preexilic prophets uniformly testify to the grace of God in ordering restoration for these same nations. Israel will by no means be the only people restored after divine judgment. This promise and this hope is available to all the nations of the world, even the cruelest of peoples.

2. Gentile inclusion from an exilic perspective

Ezekiel and Daniel, Israel's prophets who personally participated in the nation's exile, obviously view the nations of the world from a different perspective than do the preexilic prophets. Rather than looking at the world's nations from within the borders of the promised land, these two servants of the Lord fulfill their prophetic ministry while living within the territory of a non-Israelite nation. They have, as it were, been swallowed up in the vast regions of the great world empires of their day. How then do they view the inclusion of nations that are many times larger and much more powerful than their own nation of Israel?

As do the preexilic prophets, Ezekiel anticipates a future for Egypt that involves scattering and gathering, exile and restoration, in a way similar to Israel's experience. Because of their blasphemous declaration, "The Nile is mine, I made it" (Ezek. 29:9 NIV), the Egyptians will be dispersed among the nations and scattered through the countries (29:12). But after forty years, the Egyptians will be gathered again to their own land (29:13–14). Yet Egypt will remain forever a "lowly kingdom . . . and will never again exalt itself above the other nations" (29:14–15). As a consequence, Egypt will never again be a source of confidence for the people of Israel and will be a reminder of the nation's sin in looking to human powers rather than to God (29:16).

The exile and restoration of Egypt in a way similar to the Lord's treatment of Israel anticipates Ezekiel's final vision of a new temple with a correspondingly new land allotment for God's people. But now the visionary apportionments of the land must include equal treatment of foreigners within Israel. The land must be allotted as an inheritance for the Israelites "and for the aliens who have settled among you and who have children" (47:22a NIV). Not merely as a temporary measure, but for the generations to come, Gentiles will share in Israel's inheritance. Even more specifically, "you are to consider them as native-born Israelites; along with you they are to be allotted an inheritance among the tribes of Israel" (47:22b NIV). Not in some sort of Gentile ghetto, but "in whatever tribe the alien settles, there you are to give him his inheritance" (47:23 NIV). The foreigner is not simply to be tolerated among the restored people of God. Instead, he is to have equal inheritance alongside a restored Israel.

According to Ezekiel, the final state of things will see the inclusion of Gentiles alongside Israel. His prediction of the future, though cast in the only mold he knew—the mold of old covenant types—strains to break out into the totally different mold of new covenant realities. Tension between the inclusion of Gentiles and the exclusiveness of old covenant Israel becomes apparent by comparing Ezekiel's earlier vision of the glory of God manifesting itself within the territory of Babylon (1:1–2) with the final vision of the return of the glory to the restored temple, which cannot be contained within the confining space of Jerusalem's Mount Zion (42:15–19). The exilic prophecy of Ezekiel may thus be seen as playing a transitional role between the continuation of Israel's old covenant exclusivism and the coming of God's restorative blessing on the Gentile world.

The word *beastly* suits the description that Daniel gave to the concentrations of human despotism that he experienced as an exile within the massive empire of Babylon. In his dream he sees four great beasts, each different from the others, coming up out of the sea (Dan. 7:3). These beasts depict earthly power, manifesting the speed of a leopard and an eagle, along with the ferocity of a bear and a lion (7:4–6). These beasts terrify and frighten, crush and devour (7:7). But the Ancient of Days takes his sovereign seat, the court goes into session, the beasts are stripped of all authority, and their ultimate representative figure is slain, with its body thrown into a blazing fire (7:9–12). Then one comparable to the first Adam ("one like a Son of Man") comes in the splendor of heaven's clouds (7:13). He is triumphantly led into the presence of the Ancient of Days, and "he was given authority, glory, and sovereign power; all peoples, nations and men of every language worshiped him. His dominion is an everlasting dominion that will not pass away, and his kingdom is one that will never be destroyed" (7:14 NIV).

What exactly is it that exiled Daniel foresees in terms of the future of the nations of the world? He predicts days in which governmental powers will crush, devour, and trample underfoot other nations of the world, while at the same time waging war against the saints of God and defeating them (7:19, 21). These suffering saints will be handed over to the beast "for a time, times, and half a time" (7:25). But in the end, the sovereignty, power, and greatness of all these kingdoms will be taken from them and handed over to the saints, the people of the Most High (7:26–27a). This climactic kingdom will endure forever, and all rulers will worship and obey the Most High God (7:27b).

Like the book of Revelation, Daniel anticipates a succession of beastly governmental powers arising out of the mass of humanity that war against the people of God across the ages and conquer them (Rev. 13:7). Yet in the end, the indestructible kingdom of God prevails, and peoples from all nations are brought in submission to one comparable to the first Adam ("one like a Son of Man") (14:14). Eventually the nations walk by the light that is identified with the Lamb of God, and kings of the earth bring their splendor to his temple (21:22–24).

3. Gentile inclusion from a postexilic perspective

"Little things" may serve as an apt description of the nation, temple, and people of the restoration period (Zech. 4:10). The nation was confined to a very small portion of the previous empire of Judah; the tiny dimensions of the restored temple brought tears to eyes that had seen the magnificence of Solomon's; and the people numbered only slightly more than forty-nine thousand total. This struggling community, which had displayed the willingness to risk returning to their devastated land, had no choice but to remain a puppet government under the thumb of Persian, then Greek, then Roman dominance. The revolt under the leadership of the Maccabees was only a brief blip in the screen of their ongoing subjection. Survival with a distinctive identity was about all they could reasonably strive for. What was the attitude, expectation, and prediction of the prophets of the restoration era at the beginning of this six-hundred-year period, which ended in the destruction of Jerusalem by the Romans in A.D. 70?

The remainder of Zechariah's famous statement about little things sets the tone. The people of the restoration must not despise the day of little things (4:10). Instead, the daughter of Zion must "shout and rejoice," for the Lord is coming. As a consequence, "many nations will be joined with the Covenant LORD and will become [God's] people" (2:10–11 NIV). "Those who are far away," most likely referring to Gentile peoples, "will come and help to build the temple of the Covenant LORD" (6:15 NIV). As Haggai, Zechariah's contemporary explains, God will cause a cataclysmic shaking of all nations, and the wealth of the nations will fill the Lord's house in Jerusalem with glory (Hag. 2:7).

What audacity! What a bold anticipation of the future by these prophets who lived in the postexilic days of little things. Living in the midst of continued dominance by the world's superpowers, the prediction of these prophets is that nations throughout the world will concretely pledge their allegiance to Israel's God so that they will become his people alongside the Jews. Yet Malachi as the last prophetic voice of the old covenant era reinforces the same message, though with a distinctive twist. The name of the Covenant LORD of Israel "will be great among the nations, from the rising to the setting of the sun." In every place in the world, not simply in Jerusalem, "pure offerings will be brought" in the name of the Covenant LORD, "because my name will be great among the nations" (Mal. 1:11 NIV).

Did these prophets of the restoration overstep their bounds? Did they speak in extravagant terms that never could find fulfillment? Certainly if politico-ethnic-geographic realization of these prophecies is demanded, history over the past twenty-five hundred years will have to draw a blank. But if it is allowed that the shadowy form of the kingdom of God finds its proper fulfillment in the realities of the new covenant kingdom as defined by Jesus the Christ of God, then every age since his coming has seen an increased realization of that predicted expansion of the kingdom of God's covenants. A new heart, a Spirit poured out on all flesh, a purified people full of good works has sprung up in virtually every corner of this universe. From the time of the apostles' ministry to the known world of their day until the present hour, people from essentially every nationality have worshiped the Covenant LORD of Israel as he came to be known in the person of Jesus Christ.

In further reflection on this overview of the inclusion of the Gentile nations at Israel's redemption and restoration, the legitimate question may be asked: What then is the mystery about Gentile inclusion to which Paul refers (Eph. 3:3–4)? This apostle to the Gentiles plainly states that what was happening in his day regarding the inclusion of the Gentiles "was not made known to men in other generations" (3:5 NIV). Yet clearly the prophets of the old covenant at every new stage of Israel's history continually predicted a wondrous inclusion of Gentile nations. So what is the mystery to which Paul refers? Obviously it was not a mystery to the prophets that the Gentiles would be redeemed and restored along with Israel.

Paul himself spells out the nature of this mystery unknown to the prophets by a threefold repetition of the same concept. His own explanation of the mystery is that Gentile believers have become "heirs *together* with Israel, members *together* of one body, and sharers *together* in the promise" of God (Eph. 3:6 NIV)—not in any sense partial participants in the promises to Israel, but fully, equally, altogether one as sharers with Jewish believers in all the promises of God. This was the truth that the old prophets could not perceive, even though the seed of the future reality was inherent in their predictions. It proved to be the most difficult doctrine of the new covenant for even the apostles of Jesus themselves to grasp. Even today the church has great difficulty understanding the full implications of this fact of the spread of the gospel throughout the Gentile world. Every promise made to Israel now belongs equally to every Gentile believer grafted into Christ. Nothing in terms of redemptive and restorative promises remains the exclusive possession of the Jewish people. Anything in the future that belongs to Jewish believers belongs equally and altogether to Gentile believers.

Even today readers of Paul's words have difficulty assimilating their full significance, despite two thousand years that have verified their truthfulness. The church has for so long assumed that some special dispensation belongs distinctively to the Israelite people that it continues to propagate this erroneous idea. Yet the declarations of the inspired apostle are plain: Gentiles are *fellow* inheritors, *fellow* participants, *fellow* possessors of the promises of God along with Jewish believers (Eph. 3:6). This is the mystery that needs to be fully comprehended by the church today if it is to properly communicate to the nations of the world the great gospel of the new covenant.

The extravagant description of the inclusion of the Gentiles leads naturally to the final category of predictive prophecy among the prophets, the matter of long-term predictions.

D. Long-term predictions

The concern of Israel's prophets with respect to the future was by no means restricted to their own contemporary circumstances. Contrary to the old idea that the prophets were exclusively men of their times, these visionaries for the Lord regularly anticipated events that were to unfold at an unspecified time in the future. It is rather short-sighted to suggest that anticipations of the unspecified, though possibly distant future must be viewed as basic irrelevancies with respect to the practical, day-to-day lives of people. Every person's conscience alerts him that at some unknown day in the future he may have to give account for everything he has done, whether good or bad. A person may choose to ignore these inherent warnings of his psyche. That this day of reckoning may become reality at some time in the unknown future hardly makes the prospective coming of the day irrelevant. Roman governor Felix trembled before his prisoner Paul when he spoke of righteousness, self-control, and the judgment to come (Acts 24:25). Even though the Christian message of accountability before God leaves the precise time of God's judgment as an event of the undefined future, the concept of that critical day can have a powerful effect on people's everyday behavior. Still further, the matter of imminence with respect to human accountability must also be taken into account. From the prophetic perspective, no one knows the hour or the day when the chain of events related to the last days will begin to unfold. As a matter of fact, the drama of the end time has already begun (Heb. 1:2; 9:26; 1 Pet. 1:20). The prospect of the termination of time is an ever-present factor to be reckoned with. For this reason, predictions with respect to the unknown, possibly long-term future will be relevant in every generation, even as they were in the days of Israel's prophets.

These predictions of the prophets about the unspecified, possibly long-term future are by no means restricted to the latter days of Old Testament prophecy. The idea of a late-developing apocalyptic genre that replaces more traditional prophetic forms simply does not fit the evidence of the prophets themselves. Early on, Amos envisioned the sun going down at noon and the darkening of the earth in broad daylight (Amos 8:9); Isaiah depicted the stars of heaven dissolving and the sky being rolled up like a scroll on the day that God judges all the nations (Isa. 34:4); and Joel anticipated blood, fire, and smoke in connection with the day when God pours out his Spirit on all flesh (Joel 2:28–30). These cataclysmic predictions speak of the undefined future of God's redemptive working in the world. Though distributed widely throughout the entire two hundred years of Israel's literary prophetic activity, the long-term predictions of Israel's prophets share many characteristics.

First, these prophetic anticipations of the unspecified, possibly distant future are regularly eschatological, terminal, and often cataclysmic in nature. They involve supernatural transformations of the world as it is currently known. One recurring feature in these prophecies is the disturbance of heavenly bodies. Sun, moon, and stars cease to shine (Amos 8:9; Isa. 13:10, 13 [see also Matt. 24:29; Mark 13:24–25]; Isa. 24:23; 30:26; 34:4; 60:19–20; Joel 2:31; 3:15; Ezek. 32:7–8; [see also 2 Pet. 3:10; Rev. 21:23]). Simultaneously, the earth shakes as it undergoes cataclysmic transformations (Isa. 2:19c, 21c; 5:25b; Joel 2:10; Hag. 2:6–7; 21–22; Zech. 14:4–6). The fertility of the earth increases so that it produces immeasurable quantities. The harvest is so great that the reaper does not have adequate time to gather his abundant harvest before the plowman begins to break soil for the next season of planting (Amos 9:13). The deserts of Palestine are transformed so that trees, plants, and animals flourish where once only barrenness prevailed (Isa. 35:1–2, 6–7). Mount Zion ascends from its lowly altitude so that it towers above surrounding mountains, while the Mount of Olives splits in half, opening a valley from Jerusalem that leads to the Dead Sea (Isa. 2:2; Zech. 14:4–5, 10). A stream flows from the temple in Jerusalem, expands to the largest imaginable dimensions in the Judean desert, and purifies the Salt Sea so that the once-dead body of water teems with every possible species of fish (Ezek. 47:1–12; Zech. 14:8).

While the term *apocalyptic* is regularly used to identify prophecy of this sort, the word *cataclysmic* may function as a better descriptive term. The idea of apocalyptic has taken on something of an unreal aura that does not properly suit the genuine expectations of the biblical prophets.[25] While many factors indicate that the prophets did not expect their poetic images of the future to undergo literal fulfillment, enough indicators of anticipated reality permeate these prophecies to require that they be taken as indicating genuine expectations of a cataclysmic nature. Joel may not have expected that the moon would actually turn from rock to blood, but he did anticipate genuine cosmic revolution (Joel 2:31). Ezekiel may have never thought that his plan for a restored temple would be carried out according to the preciseness of his details, but he did expect that in the future God would dwell in the midst of his people in a dramatically different way than he had done at any time in the past (Ezek. 48:35). These predictions of the prophets pointed to real supernatural events that could be accomplished only by direct divine intervention in ways similar to the Almighty's activity during his original creation of the universe (2 Pet. 3:10, 13).

The prophetic expectation of the Day of the Lord may be properly evaluated in this context. Origins of the concept of the Day of the

25. The relation between prophetic and apocalyptic is difficult to define. Childs, *Biblical Theology of the Old and New Testaments*, 182, discusses the recent efforts "to trace the historical growth from exilic prophecy, through proto-apocalyptic writings, to full-blown apocalypticism." He concludes: "In sum, the biblical tradition itself does not provide the needed information by which to trace precisely the growth from prophecy to apocalyptic" (183). For a bibliography of apocalyptic literature in general, see VanGemeren, *Interpreting the Prophetic Word*, 410–11, 523 n. 32.

Lord continue to be debated, although a good case may be made for tracing its roots not specifically to the imagery of God as a warrior but more precisely to God as covenant maker and covenant enforcer.[26] Man, beast, bird, fish, and the whole inanimate creation are bound to the Almighty by the covenants he has established across the ages (Hos. 2:18–23; Zeph. 1:2–3). These covenantal commitments began with creation and will find their consummate realization in the Day of the Lord in which he renews the earth and brings all mankind under the edicts of his final judgment. This day will be realized, not as a twenty-four-hour period, but as both an era and a point in time in which the Lord enforces the blessings and the curses of his covenant.[27]

The unknown future of humanity and the universe will thus find its consummate realization by the cataclysmic, supernatural intervention of the almighty creator God when he finally brings to fulfillment his eternal purposes. The prophets consistently looked for an extraordinary manifestation of divine involvement in the course of this world at the climax of the ages.

Second, this prophetic anticipation of a total transformation of the world's order is at the same time firmly rooted in history and the previous framework of God's redemptive working. Ezekiel and Daniel had witnessed for themselves through dream and vision the Lord's intention to work out his redemptive purposes in the broader realm of the Gentile empires. Yet their expectation of the future eventually

26. See von Rad, "Origin of the Concept of the Day of Yahweh." Von Rad's proposal to find the origin of the Day of the Lord in the imagery of God as a warrior cannot encompass all the universe-transforming aspects of the Day of the Lord. For the suggestion that the covenant in its moments of inauguration and enforcement provides the source of the Day of the Lord, see Robertson, *Nahum, Habakkuk, and Zephaniah*, 266–69. The Day of the Lord is that time when he declares and enforces his lordship, which is equivalent to the day in which he inaugurates and enforces his covenantal relationship with his people, humanity, and the world.

27. Principal passages from the old covenant scriptures dealing with the Day of the Lord appear regularly across the centuries: Amos 5:18–20 and Isa. 2:12–21 in the eighth century; Zeph. 1:7, 14–18 in the seventh century; and Mal. 4 in the fifth century. Joel's references (1:15; 2:1–17) may be dated as the earliest or the latest prophet, though an earlier date is to be preferred. Reference in the new covenant scriptures includes Acts 2:17–21 (quoting Joel 2:28–32); 1 Thess. 5:2; 2 Thess. 2:2; 1 Cor. 1:8; 5:5; 2 Cor. 1:14; 2 Tim. 4:8; 2 Pet. 2:9; 3:10.

turns back to Israel as a land and a people. Ezekiel's visionary temple is located on a very high mountain in the land of Israel (Ezek. 40:2). Daniel's climactic vision of the seventy weeks that anticipates the whole course of human history begins with his awareness that the seventy years of Israel's exile as predicted by Jeremiah is about to come to an end, so that the captive people are about to return to their own promised land. This orientation toward Israel as land and people is regularly reflected in the writings of the prophets as they anticipate the cosmic events affecting the future. The Lord's supernatural, cataclysmic intervention in the future will occur within time and history and in close connection with his past relations with the seed of Abraham, the descendants of David, the city of Jerusalem, and the land of Israel.

How could the prophets of old have framed their expectations of the future in any other way? They spoke about the unknown future in accordance with what they knew from the past. The God of their past would in the future carry forward his original purposes to their consummate realization. It could be assumed that these divine goals would be realized in a similar fashion as the nation's experience of redemption in the past. The prophets could not and should not be expected to speak apart from the context of the old covenant shadows that were their complete frame of reference, for the more precise language of new covenant realities was not yet known to them.

At the same time, their expectations of the future broke the bonds of the old covenant. Ezekiel's temple cannot fit on the peak of Mount Zion, but spills across the Kidron and the Tyropean valleys because of its mammoth size (Ezek. 42:15–19; see chap. 10 §II.B.3.f.(2)). Zechariah both depicts the future Jerusalem as a city without walls because of the number of its inhabitants and simultaneously describes a wall of fire that surrounds it (Zech. 2:2–5). This very way of expressing themselves with respect to the consummate future meant that, while anchoring their expectations in the traditional pattern of God's previous redemptive workings, these prophets also understood that something greater and larger than their past was ahead of them. The tension between the limited character of the "already" and the boundless expectations of the "not yet" did not first occur with the arrival of

448

new covenant eschatology. Its roots are firmly grounded in the end-time expectations of the prophets of the old covenant.

A third element of the long-term expectations of Israel's prophets is that they themselves were not capable of totally grasping the scope of their own messages. At the conclusion of receiving his revelation concerning the restoration of Israel after their exile, the prophet Jeremiah is informed: "In days to come you will understand this" (Jer. 30:24c NIV). This statement clearly implies that the prophet's full apprehension of his own prediction would have to await its fulfillment. On a short-term basis, Jeremiah displays his bafflement over the significance of the Lord's word to him regarding the purchase of his uncle's property even as the Babylonians are about to take Jerusalem as the last of Judah's strongholds. He puzzles over the rationale for the Lord's illogical command: "Though [as you have decreed] the city will be handed over to the Babylonians, you, O Sovereign Covenant LORD, say to me, 'Buy the field with silver and have the transaction witnessed'" (32:25 NIV). Jeremiah has no doubt that this instruction comes from the Lord. But he cannot understand it. As a prophet presently under house arrest, why should he invest the little silver he has, when at this very moment the nation's entire land is being taken over by the Babylonians, with its inhabitants being shipped to foreign countries! He does not comprehend the point of his own prophecy.

Understanding for Jeremiah comes only later. The Lord speaks again and explains that, though the people will be driven from their land, they will eventually return. They will possess land again. Properties will be bought and sold once more (32:42–44). Eventually Jeremiah understands his purchase to be a symbolic action anticipating the future restoration of Israel's fortunes. But the prophet himself did not at first grasp the significance of his own prophetic action.

This rather domestic incident in the life of one prophet serves to illustrate the larger picture. The predictions of the future that anticipated the consummation of divine purposes were not always understood by the prophet himself. This principle shows itself to be at work in several of the long-term prophecies of Daniel. Though even as a youth he was especially gifted with wisdom, Daniel had serious difficulty comprehending his own messages about the end time. After his vision of the four beasts, the Ancient of Days, and the Son of Man, Daniel admits that he was "troubled in spirit," and his visions disturbed him. He was bold enough to inquire about the true meaning of this vision (Dan. 7:15–16). After further explanation, he still wanted to know the true meaning of additional aspects of his vision (7:19–20). At the end of the process, he remained deeply troubled by his thoughts, and his face turned pale (7:28).

Again, at the end of his vision of the two-horned ram and the goat, Daniel receives assurance that the vision is true. He is then instructed to "seal up the vision, for it concerns the distant future" (8:26 NIV). In response, Daniel remains overwhelmed for several days. He subsequently testifies that he was "appalled by the vision," for "it was beyond understanding" (8:27 NIV). In this case, his vision of the distant future is not clear to him. He is furthermore instructed to seal up the vision, implying that it had significance for the future that could not be grasped in his own day.

At the end of his book, Daniel is instructed to "close up and seal the words of the scroll until the time of the end" (12:4 NIV). Many search here and there to come to a proper understanding of this revelation regarding the future. Overhearing the message that these "astonishing things" would be fulfilled in "time, times, and half a time," Daniel indicates that he "heard, but . . . did not understand" (12:7–8 NIV). In response to a further clarifying question, Daniel is told that "the words are closed up and sealed until the time of the end" (12:9 NIV). Yet he is assured that even though none of the wicked would be able to comprehend his message, the wise would understand (12:10).

The long-term predictions about the future thus take on a peculiar characteristic. By divine design, they will not be fully comprehended until they are actually in the process of being fulfilled. The general thrust of the prophetic message may be understood, but the details will remain sealed until the time has come. This perspective on eschatological prophecy is confirmed by the comment in the new covenant scriptures that the prophets "searched intently and with the greatest care, trying to find out the time and circumstances to which the Spirit of Christ in them was pointing when he predicted the sufferings of Christ and the glories that would follow" (1 Pet. 1:10–11 NIV).

450

While this aspect of predictive prophecy concerning the end time must be a factor to be recognized, it never should serve as an excuse for dismissing selected prophetic utterances as incomprehensible. Some basic aspects of the revelatory vision will always be understandable and applicable.

What precisely is the central message of the prophets concerning the long-term future? What is it that captures the bulk of their predictions? Analysis of this aspect of the predictive message of the prophets leads to the central focus of predictive prophecy: messiah together with his people will undergo devastation and restoration through exile and return. Of all the topics treated in predictive prophecy, exile and restoration of messiah and his people is by far the most permeating, the most far-reaching, and the most significant.

14

THE CORE EVENT
OF ISRAEL'S
PROPHETIC MOVEMENT

Exile and restoration provided the focal moment in history for Israel's prophetic movement. The nation's exile and restoration, involving the devastation and restoration of their messianic king together with his people, were as significant as the events surrounding the original formation of the elect people: the call of Abraham, the exodus, and the inauguration of the covenant at Sinai. Through exile and return, Israel's anointed king—their messiah together with his people—experienced devastation and restoration.

What could be more radical! What could it all mean? The gigantic task of the prophets was to anticipate the exile by predictive declarations and thus prepare the people for this unimaginable shock. At the same time, their task was to maintain hope in the Covenant LORD's long-term redemptive purposes by predicting a return from the abyss of the exile. These two great events of exile and restoration therefore became the focal point of the predictions of the prophets.

I. The significance of prophecies concerning exile and restoration

The sheer number of predictions about exile and restoration in the prophets may serve as a fair indicator of their importance. By way of comparison, no more than twenty-five specific prophecies about the coming messiah may be clearly identified throughout the writings of Israel's prophets. On the other hand, almost two hundred predictions about Israel's coming exile and restoration occur in the same body of prophetic literature. These predictions are dispersed from Isaiah through Daniel, from Hosea through Malachi. Hardly a prophetic book fails to include some anticipation of exile and restoration.[1]

The permeating character of these predictions about exile and restoration is underscored by the extensive use of reinforcing prophetic actions and figures of speech. On one occasion Jeremiah smashes the clay jar of a potter at the Valley of Ben Hinnom and declares to the people: "This is what the Covenant LORD Almighty says: I will smash this nation and this city just as this potter's jar is smashed and cannot be repaired" (Jer. 19:11 NIV). The public smashing of the clay jar as a visible accompaniment to the message of exile must have made a vivid impression on its witnesses. God would indeed bring about the captivity of his own people despite their false security, rooted in the presumption that God's presence would always remain among them in the holy temple of Jerusalem.

In a similar way, the Lord commanded Jeremiah to buy a linen belt and put it around his waist to display it before the people. Later he was commanded to go to Perath (possibly the Euphrates) and hide the belt in a crevice of a rock. Many days later he received a third command: he must return and retrieve his belt. By this time the belt was ruined and completely useless (13:1–7). Presumably the people had seen this handsome belt when Jeremiah first put it around his waist. They now saw the rotted remains of the same belt after it had been abandoned in "exile." This prophetic enactment depicted Judah's deportation from their land. Just as the prophet bound this handsome linen belt around his waist, so the Covenant LORD had "bound the whole house of Israel and the whole house of Judah" to himself (13:11 NIV). They were his people for renown and praise. But now he would "ruin the pride of Judah and the great pride of Jerusalem" because

---

1. A cursory overview of the prophets shows 83 units predicting exile and 91 predicting restoration, for a total of 174. Jonah and Malachi appear to be the only prophetic books without a prediction concerning exile or restoration, but their particular situations provide adequate explanations for their omission.

they had gone after other gods (13:9–10 NIV). They would be like Jeremiah's spoiled belt—utterly useless.

A third instance of prophetic enactment solidifying predictions about Israel's exile and restoration was Jeremiah's purchase of land just when King Nebuchadnezzar of Babylon was pounding on the gates of Jerusalem (32:1–2, 6–12). The poor prophet puzzles over the Lord's intention in having him purchase land at this inopportune moment. The Lord's answer is not long coming: "This is what the Covenant LORD Almighty, the God of Israel, says: Houses, fields and vineyards will again be bought in this land" (32:15 NIV). At just about the same time, King Zedekiah was quizzing the prophet concerning his predictions of coming judgment. Jeremiah's prophetic action of purchasing property communicated better than words the expectation of restoration for Israel, even if not for the king. The prophet's investment in Judean real estate visibly demonstrated that he fully believed that his message of restoration after exile had come from the Lord and not from himself.

Further reinforcement of the centrality of the prophecies concerning exile and restoration is found in the vivid figures of speech used to communicate the message. God shall cause the land to revert to the state of precreation chaos: "I looked at the earth, and it was formless and empty; and at the heavens, and their light was gone. I looked at the mountains, and they were quaking; all the hills were swaying. I looked, and there were no people; every bird in the sky had flown away. I looked, and the fruitful land was a desert; all its towns lay in ruins before the Covenant LORD, before his fierce anger" (4:23–26 NIV).

In addition, the Lord declares that he shall hurl the people out of the land, using the imagery of a sling (10:18). God shall scatter Israel like chaff driven by the desert wind (13:24). He shall send fishermen and hunters, and they shall treat Judah as game to be captured (16:16). God shall bring such a disaster that it will make people's ears tingle (19:3). The people set for permanent captivity are like bad figs, rotten and putrid (24:8). But those who will return to the land may be compared to good figs (24:5). The expectation of exile and restoration impregnated Jeremiah's mind with these various images.

Ezekiel's treatment of exile and restoration also makes extensive use of symbolism and figures of speech that are marked by both variety and vividness. In terms of figures of speech, Ezekiel says that just as God designed the twisted wood of the vine to be good for nothing except for burning, so Jerusalem is to be regarded as "fuel for the fire" (Ezek. 15:1–6). At another time he declares that Jerusalem is a cooking pot filled with pieces of meat (24:3–14). Still more dramatically, he reports the Lord as saying: "As men gather silver, copper, iron, lead and tin into a furnace to melt it with a fiery blast, so will I gather you in my anger and my wrath and put you inside the city and melt you" (22:20 NIV). Suddenly the holy city of Jerusalem has become a blast furnace for the melting down of its inhabitants so that they can be purified of all their iniquity.

In two vivid sections, Ezekiel compares Israel and Judah to adulterous women (chaps. 16, 23). Because of their life of adultery in pursuing other gods, the Lord will take drastic action: "I will sentence you to the punishment of women who commit adultery. . . . I will hand you over to your lovers, and they will . . . strip you of your clothes and take your fine jewelry and leave you naked and bare. They will bring a mob against you, who will stone you and hack you to pieces with their swords" (16:38–40 NIV). The Lord "will put an end to lewdness in the land, that all the women [of the world] may take warning and not imitate" Israel in its sin (23:48 NIV).

Beyond these figures of speech, Ezekiel's extensive use of symbolism permeates the book from start to finish. These symbols come in the form of prophetic enactments as well as prophetic visions. Ezekiel's prophecy opens with a mysterious vision of wheels within wheels associated with the manifestation of God's glory (1:4–28). Although the vision is perhaps the best-known section of Ezekiel's prophecy, it may also be the least understood. Its significance is made plain subsequently in the book when the Shekinah glory makes a step-by-step departure from the temple in Jerusalem (chaps. 10–11). The significance of the wheels in the opening vision now becomes plain. God's presence cannot be permanently localized by human design. The glory of God is mobile; and after that glory has departed from Jerusalem's temple, the once-holy place becomes commonplace, just as subject to the devastation of human armies as any other religious shrine. The centerpiece vision of Ezekiel thus relates directly to the theme of exile.

Next God commands the prophet to make a clay tablet with a picture of Jerusalem carved into its surface. Ezekiel must lie on his side for over a year, anticipating a siege of the city by the symbolic drawing on the tablet (chap. 4). Still later the prophet is commanded to shave his head and beard. One-third of the hair must be burned, one-third struck with a sword, and one-third thrown to the wind. These symbolic actions also involve an enacted prediction of Israel's coming exile (chap. 5). Next the prophet is instructed to pack his belongings in the presence of all the people, dig a hole in the wall at dusk, and enact a flight from the city (12:1–20). Finally, the prophet is told that he must prepare to lose his wife, the delight of his eyes. But the prophet must not shed a tear. This experience embodies a prediction of the traumatized state of the exiles of Jerusalem (24:15–27).

In addition to these enacted prophecies, Ezekiel receives a series of visions dramatizing the message of exile and restoration. Visions of the two eagles (Ezek. 17), of the king of Babylon at the fork in the road (21:18–23), of the two sticks united into one (37:15–28), of the valley of dry bones (37:1–14), and of the restored temple (chaps. 40–48)— all these visions serve to communicate the certainty of the message of judgment related to exile and hope related to restoration. Together they vivify the message of future expectation that arose out of the divine plan of redemption that continues even until the present day.

The prophetic enactments, figures of speech, vivid visions, and simple statistics of manifold reference all combine to underscore the central significance of prophetic predictions regarding exile and restoration. No other topic compares with this single concern in the prophetic literature. Its importance cannot be overemphasized. Further analysis may underscore key concepts related to predictions about Israel's exile and restoration.

II. Key concepts related to predictions about exile and restoration

A. Exile and restoration are intertwined

The prophets regularly unite the ideas of exile and restoration, so that they cannot easily be separated from one another. Exile is not

457

the end of the road for Israel. The prospect of restoration is consistently held out as a hope even as the judgment of exile is being announced.

Virtually the whole book of Hosea is given over to the prediction of the two events of exile and restoration. His prophecies repeatedly join together these two themes. God shall soon punish the house of Jehu, the current dynasty of the northern kingdom (Hos. 1:4). Yet Israel and Judah shall be restored in unity and rebuilt under the direction of a single leader (1:11). The Covenant LORD will punish Israel for the days she burned incense to the Baals (2:2–13). Yet in driving her into the wilderness he shall speak lovingly to her and bring her back into the promised land (2:14–23). Israel shall live many days without king and sacrifice; but then the nation will return and seek the Lord their God and David their king (3:4–5). Because Ephraim will not repent, they cannot remain in the Lord's land, but will return to Egypt (9:3; 11:5). Yet the Covenant LORD's compassion will not let him give them up altogether. Eventually

> They will come trembling
>   like birds from Egypt,
>   like doves from Assyria. (11:11 NIV)

The people of Samaria must bear their guilt and fall by the sword. Yet the Lord will heal their waywardness, love them freely, and make them grow in the land like a cedar of Lebanon (13:16; 14:4–8). While negative criticism often denies the possibility of uniting predictions of judgment with predictions of blessing, the intertwining of these themes throughout the prophecy of Hosea supports the idea that both elements were anticipated by this single prophet.

Quite noteworthy is the fact that even the prophetic commission that thrust Isaiah into his role as prophet centers on the theme of exile and restoration. In response to the prophetic call that came in connection with his vision of the thrice-holy God, the young prophet asks, "How long?" How long must he declare God's message of coming judgment to a recalcitrant people? The Lord's answer is disturbing to say the least:

Until the cities
>lie ruined and without inhabitant,
until the houses
>are left deserted
and the fields
>ruined and ravaged,
until the Covenant LORD
>has sent everyone far away
and the land
>is utterly forsaken.
And though a tenth remains in the land,
>it will again be laid waste.
But as the terebinth and oak
>leave stumps when they are cut down,
so the holy seed
>will be the stump in the land. (Isa. 6:11–13 NIV)

This programmatic text, anticipating as it does the entire ministry of the prophet Isaiah, predicts the exile as a consequence of the stubbornness of the people's hearts. But it also predicts restoration as a consequence of God's redemptive grace. By the Lord's mercies, a holy seed will fill the role of the remnant, the stump in the land.

The permeating character of predictions regarding exile and restoration in Jeremiah can hardly be overestimated. With only two or three exceptions, every one of the first thirty-eight chapters of the book includes explicit predictions of exile and restoration. The predictive nature of these prophecies is emphasized by the explicit command given to Jeremiah by the Lord that he write his prophecies about these anticipated events (Jer. 30:2). The final chapters of the book present the actual history of the fall of Jerusalem and its aftermath (chaps. 39–45; 52), combined with predictions concerning the surrounding nations (chaps. 46–51). These predictions about exile and restoration began around 627 B.C., forty years before the actual exile of Judah (1:2). They continued through the period in which the Babylonians actually besieged and took the city of Jerusalem in 587 B.C. (39:1–3). The central role of these predictions in Jeremiah's ministry is dramatized in the theme verses summarizing the commission of the prophet:

"See, today I appoint you over nations and kingdoms to uproot and tear down, to destroy and overthrow, to build and to plant. . . . For I am watching to see that my word is fulfilled" (1:10, 12 NIV).

This description of Jeremiah's prophetic ministry includes both uprooting and planting, both tearing down and building up. These terms summarizing the commission of the prophet concentrate on both ideas: exile and restoration. In addition, this commission extends beyond Israel itself to include nations and kingdoms beyond the bounds of God's covenant people. The Covenant LORD subsequently declares that by the word of the prophet he will uproot all Israel's wicked neighbors from their lands and also uproot the house of Judah from among them (12:14). Yet in his compassion he will restore these same nations and establish them among his people (12:15–16). But any nation that refuses to listen to the Covenant LORD will be uprooted and destroyed completely (12:17). Subsequently, when the emphasis of the prophet falls on predictions of restoration for Israel, the terminology of the theme verses reappears: "'The days are coming,' declares the Covenant LORD, 'when I will plant the house of Israel and the house of Judah with the offspring of men and of animals. Just as I watched over them to uproot and tear down, and to overthrow, destroy and bring disaster, so I will watch over them to build and to plant,' declares the Covenant LORD" (31:27–28 NIV).

Most wondrous is the declaration by the Lord himself that he will be wholeheartedly committed to this restoration of his people: "I will rejoice in doing them good and will assuredly plant them in this land with all my heart and soul" (32:41 NIV). That the almighty God would take such delight in the restoration of his people is indeed good news. This determination to restore his people after their devastation should not be regarded as the development of a subsequent prophetic school that formulates these ideas some time after the actual event of the exile of the nation. Instead, the testimony of the introductory theme that weaves together the whole fabric of the book affirms from the beginning that not only exile but also restoration plays a central role in the plans and purposes of the Lord.[2] Hope beyond divine judgments is integral to the message of the prophets.

2. Other passages in the prophets confirm the combination of exile and restoration. Hosea labels the day of Israel's exile as "Jezreel" (Hos. 1:4) because of the mas-

B. Exile and restoration occur for different reasons

The reasons given for exile and restoration are drastically different from one another. Exile occurs because Israel sinned. The nation violated the commands of their God (Jer. 9:1–11). Because Israel refused to repent, it went into exile (Hos. 11:5c). Exile for Judah is not simply a meaningless happening in the course of human history that occurred without reason. The sin of the people caused their devastation. To vivify this message, Ezekiel is commanded to lie on his side for 390 days, corresponding to the "years of their sin" (Ezek. 4:5). Even those who escape exile shall moan like doves of the valleys, "each because of his sins" (7:16). The prophet is transported to Jerusalem in a vision, and there he witnesses one abomination after another, including a detestable idol that resided within the temple directly in front of the manifestation of God's glory (8:3–5). This defilement can have no other effect than to drive the Lord from his own sanctuary (8:6).[3] The present rebellions of Judah against the Lord are just as serious as the sins committed in Egypt and during the nation's wilderness wanderings (20:1–29). Perhaps more than any other prophet, Ezekiel makes use of the Ten Commandments as a base for identifying the particulars of Judah's sins (22:6–12). This exposure of the sin of the people provides the basis for the predictions of the prophet concerning the inevitability of Judah's exile.

Perhaps some of the saddest words found in the book of Jeremiah are those that anticipate the reaction of many other nations to the devastation of Jerusalem. They know full well the reason for the nation's exile to a foreign country: "People from many nations will pass by this city and will ask one another, 'Why has the Covenant LORD done such a thing to this great city?' And the answer will be: 'Because

---

sacre committed at Jezreel by Jehu (2 Kings 10:1–14). Since the term *Jezreel* means "God sows," it contains the inherent idea of a harvest to follow. Hosea also announces that the people of Judah and Israel will be reunited and will come up out of the land of their exile, for "great will be the day of Jezreel" (Hos. 1:11). In other words, sowing (i.e., exile) results in reaping (restoration) what was sown. In this case, the two expectations of exile and restoration are merged in the single term *Jezreel*. See also Jer. 33:2–9; Ezek. 16.

3. Elaboration of this defilement and its consequences is found in Ezek. 8:7–9:11.

they have forsaken the covenant of the LORD their God and have worshiped and served other gods'" (Jer. 22:8–9 NIV). It will be evident not only to Judah that this horror of exile has come on them because of their violation of the covenant; even the heathen nations will know the reason for their calamity.

In sharp contrast with the reasons for the exile, the banished nation could never experience restoration because of renewed merits in the eyes of God. Not even the Lord's compassion for their sufferings provides the reason of their return. Instead, they will be restored because of the honor of God's name. Ezekiel says: "It is not for your sake, O house of Israel, that I am going to do these things, but for the sake of my holy name, which you have profaned among the nations where you have gone. I will show the holiness of my great name. . . . Then the nations will know that I am the Covenant LORD. . . . For I will take you out of the nations; I will gather you from all the countries and bring you back into your own land" (Ezek. 36:22–24 NIV).

Such an exalted concept of God and his centrality to all the affairs of men will seem extremely strange in the modern context, where little if any thought is given to the place of God in the course of the world. But since God is truly God, he deserves to be given first consideration at all times. When he is properly honored, all other affairs of human existence fall in their proper places. When he is perceived as the holy God who defines the nature of true justice and then maintains that righteousness among men, when he is understood to be forever faithful to the covenant commitments he himself voluntarily made, then health, happiness, and wholeness will abound among humanity. Yet even at this level, the well-being of mankind must not be perceived as the ultimate good, so that God is perceived as existing for man's sake. Instead, the first place of honor must remain with the honoring of God, which is exactly what Israel's restoration intends to accomplish.

C. Exile and restoration are connected to the exodus, wilderness, and conquest

The themes of exile and restoration are developed interconnectedly with the ancient traditions of exodus, wilderness, and conquest.

The significance of this fact can hardly be overestimated, for relating exile and restoration to the older redemptive events has the effect of placing these later historical occurrences in the same category as those earlier historical moments that embody redemptive revelation. If the only way of man's redemption from the blameworthiness of sin is found in the shedding of the lamb's blood on the night of the Passover, if believers in the Christ today are "in the wilderness" and on the way to the promised land as communicated by the ancient experience of Israel, and if the events of exile and restoration are presented as recapitulations of Israel's previous redemptive experience, then these later events of exile and restoration must also have been designed by God to communicate redemptive truth.

The crucial role of the new exodus, new wilderness wandering, and new conquest in the prophetic development of exile and restoration is regularly recognized.[4] In particular, the prophets Hosea and Isaiah develop these themes. Because the northern kingdom of Israel was swallowed up in the materialism integral to Baal worship, God will lead them back into the wilderness and strip them of all their material possessions. Then the "Valley of Achor," where Israel suffered their first serious defeat in the early days of their conquest, will become a "door of hope" (Hos. 2:15 NIV). God will punish Israel for its sin by making them return to the bondage of Egypt (8:13c; 9:3). In addition to returning to Egypt, Assyria will rule over them (11:5). Yet because the Lord loves Israel, he cannot give them up to utter devastation:

> They will come trembling
> like birds from Egypt,
> like doves from Assyria.
> I will settle them in their homes,
> declares the Covenant Lord. (Hos. 11:11 NIV)

Using the device of prophetic recapitulation, Isaiah predicts that the Covenant Lord will cause his people to experience a new exodus and a new wilderness experience. They shall undergo a dramatic deliv-

4. See Anderson, "Exodus Typology in Second Isaiah"; and Mauser, *Christ in the Wilderness*.

erance from enslavement by their enemies: "Forget the former things; do not dwell on the past. See, I am doing a new thing! Now it springs up; do you not perceive it? I am making a way in the desert and streams in the wasteland" (Isa. 43:18–19 NIV). In anticipating the restoration of both kingdoms, Isaiah resorts to the imagery of a new exodus-wilderness-conquest experience. The Lord will dry up the Egyptian sea and sweep his hand over the Euphrates River so that people can cross it in sandals (11:15–16). The eyes of the blind will be opened and the ears of the deaf unstopped as water gushes forth in the wilderness, for the ransomed will return, entering Zion with singing (35:5–10). A voice cries out in the wilderness because a new exodus is taking place (40:2–3). The Lord who once before made a way through the sea even as he devastated the chariots, horses, and army of Egypt will do it again (43:14–17; see also 41:18–20; 49:9–12; 55:12–13; Jer. 16:14, 15; 23:7–8).

Most significantly, these end-time events of Israel's history—the nation's exile and restoration—are intimately linked to the heart and core of past redemptive interventions of the Lord. If exodus, wilderness, and conquest can embody redemptive truths about deliverance from sin's guilt and oppression, about divine preservation through years of wandering in the wilderness, about final entry into the perfections of a restored paradise, then the critical experiences of exile and restoration may also be understood as conveying truths of a redemptive nature. These truths clearly have a connection to the redemptive realities conveyed through exodus-wilderness-conquest. But because of the later hour in redemptive history, they can be expected to convey a distinctive perspective on the way of God's working redemption for his people.

D. Exile and restoration are connected to the termination of Israel's monarchy and the appearance of the coming messiah

Exile and restoration in predictive prophecy are intimately connected with the termination of Israel's current monarchies and their replacement by a new descendant of the Davidic line. The prophets make extensive use of the history of Israel's monarchy as a means of depicting exile and restoration. According to the prophets, the evil

464

kings of Israel will be violently removed from their position of honor by being driven into exile. At the same time, hope for the future resides in the restoration of a king faithful to the Lord in accordance with the covenant made with David.

As he anticipates the northern kingdom's banishment from their land, Hosea declares that "the Israelites will live many days without king or prince" (Hos. 3:4 NIV). In his anger God gave them a king, and in his wrath he will take him away (13:11). A major consequence of the exile according to this prophet is the destruction of the monarchy in Israel.

Both Hosea and Amos pull no punches as they present the hope of restoration for the northern kingdom. The people must seek David their king for the restoration of the northern kingdom. The rebuilding of the fallen booth of David constitutes the hope of Israel in the north (Hos. 3:5; Amos 9:11). The northern kingdom had its beginning in a massive revolt against the rule of the Davidic line, which involved a rejection of the covenant with David (1 Kings 12:16). By maintaining the restoration of the Davidic line as the hope for the devastated northern kingdom, these prophets place the expectation of restoration squarely in the center of the covenant promises to David.

At two particularly critical points in Judah's history, the kings of the nation appear as key persons in Isaiah's message. The prophet is sent specifically to King Ahaz at the time of the threat by Syria and Ephraim (Isa. 7:1–3), yet the prophet's message takes the plural form, since he addresses the "house of David" threatened by this coalition of nations: "If you [plural] do not stand firm in your faith, you [plural] will not stand at all" (7:9b NIV).[5] Though speaking to King Ahaz in particular, the prophet's warning encompasses the whole house of David that the enemy intends to terminate (7:6b). Although Ahaz lacks the faith required of the Lord, the prophet's message indicates that if necessary even a virgin will bring forth a son to maintain the Davidic line (7:14). Though devastation of the royal line may occur, the Lord will remain faithful to his promise by restoring a descendant of David to the throne in accord with the promises of his covenant.

5. The NIV reflects the original play on the word *believe*.

In a second confrontation with the reigning king of Judah, Isaiah again anticipates a coming exile for the nation. King Hezekiah errs seriously by displaying the wealth of his nation to a visiting delegation from Babylon. As a consequence, the prophet announces that everything of value in the royal palace will be carried into exile. More significantly, the royal line of David will be removed from the throne: "Some of your descendants, your own flesh and blood who will be born to you, will be taken away, and they will become eunuchs in the palace of the king of Babylon" (Isa. 39:7 NIV). The previous prophecies offered by Isaiah regarding the permanent reign of a coming messianic king exclude the possibility of a total end to the line of David and offer a promise of restoration in the future (7:14; 9:6–7; 11:1–10). Yet clearly the prophet anticipates a period in which the descendants of David will be exiled from their land and removed from their throne.

Jeremiah's predictions of a coming messianic king relate directly to the expectation of restoration after exile. The prophet issues a series of condemning judgments aimed at the various kings ruling over Judah in the days immediately preceding their national exile. These kings failed in their solemn responsibility as mediators of God's covenant with David and so shall experience devastation:[6]

- King Jehoahaz (Shallum) will die in exile and never have the privilege of seeing the promised land again (Jer. 22:11–12). He shall experience this fate even though Jeremiah promised him that if he would obey God's commands, "then kings who sit on David's throne will come through the gates of this place, riding in chariots and on horses, accompanied by their officials and their people" (22:1–2, 4 NIV).
- King Jehoiakim will have the burial of a donkey, being dragged away and thrown outside the gates of Jerusalem (22:19).
- King Jehoiachin will be handed over to King Nebuchadnezzar of Babylon, hurled into a foreign country, and never return to the promised land. None of his offspring will sit on the throne of David (22:24–27, 30).

6. Three of these kings (Jehoahaz, Jehoiakim, and Zedekiah) were sons of Josiah, and one (Jehoiachin) was his grandson.

- King Zedekiah sends for Jeremiah even as Nebuchadnezzar assaults Jerusalem, hoping that he will predict miraculous interventions similar to past deliverances (21:2). The prophet instead predicts exile for the king and his surviving people, denouncing the royal house of Judah, the house of David (21:7, 11–12).

The prophet then pronounces a general woe over the shepherd-kings of Judah who have scattered the sheep. Because they have completely failed, the Lord himself will take the initiative in bringing the people back from exile and will "place shepherds over them who will tend them" (23:1–4 NIV).

In the context of these prophecies concerning the failure of Judah's kings, the prediction is made concerning a singular Davidic descendant who will rule in righteousness over his people. God had earlier promised to give them "shepherds after my own heart," anticipating kingly figures who could be compared to the original David (Jer. 3:15 NIV; 1 Sam. 16:7). But now the Lord declares: "The days are coming . . . when I will raise up to David a righteous Branch, a King who will reign wisely and do what is just and right in the land. In his days Judah will be saved and Israel will live in safety. This is the name by which he will be called: The Covenant LORD Our Righteousness" (Jer. 23:5–6 NIV).

Jeremiah did not originate this concept of a singular descendant of David who would fulfill all the expectations created by the establishment of the reign of God on earth through the kingdom of Israel. King David himself had symbolically merged his own throne with the throne of God by bringing the ark representing God's throne into his royal city of Jerusalem (2 Sam. 6:12–15, 17). Jeremiah built on this merger of God's throne with David's throne when he indicated that the old ark of the covenant would one day be superseded by the throne of the Covenant LORD in Jerusalem:

> "In those days, when your numbers have increased greatly in the land," declares the Covenant LORD, "men will no longer say, 'The ark of the covenant of the LORD.' It will never enter their minds or be remembered; it will not be missed, nor will another one be made. At that time they will call Jerusalem The Throne of the Covenant LORD, and all nations

467

will gather in Jerusalem to honor the name of the Covenant LORD. No longer will they follow the stubbornness of their evil hearts." (Jer. 3:16–17 NIV)

A century earlier, Isaiah gave expression to his expectations of a righteous Branch from the line of David (Isa. 4:2; 9:7; 11:1). But now as the kingdom of Judah is about to be swallowed up in its exile to Babylon, this older expectation emerges once more. Restoration after exile will occur in conjunction with the appearance of a descendant of David, who will have none of the faults of his predecessors.

Unique to this scion of David's line is the fact that the righteousness necessary for God's people to be acceptable before the Almighty will be found in him. As Jeremiah says, his name will be called "the Covenant LORD Our Righteousness" (Jer. 23:6 NIV). Not only will he be different from the reigning kings in Judah by being righteous in himself in sharp contrast with their unrighteousness, but he himself will be the righteousness of his people.

In further anticipating Judah's restoration, Jeremiah returns to this figure, using virtually the same words: "In those days and at that time I will make a righteous Branch sprout from David's line; he will do what is just and right in the land. In those days Judah will be saved and Jerusalem will live in safety. This is the name by which it will be called: The Covenant LORD Our Righteousness" (Jer. 33:15–16). In explaining this prophecy, Jeremiah indicates that after this righteous Branch appears, David will never fail to have a man sit on the throne of the house of Israel (33:17). Just as surely as day and night are fixed by the covenant word of the Lord, so the permanence of a descendant of David on the throne of God's kingdom is determined (33:20–21, 25–26).

The final reference in Jeremiah to the maintenance of the Davidic line in connection with the restoration of Israel appears in the closing verses of the book. On this occasion, the message comes as the report of a historical event rather than as a predictive prophecy. Yet this event anticipates the same ultimate exaltation of the descendant of David as did the earlier prophetic words of Jeremiah. A new king in Babylon rises to the throne and releases King Jehoiachin of Judah from prison. He does not send him back to Judah, which would have contradicted the specific prediction of Jeremiah (Jer. 22:27). He gives Jehoiachin, grandson of Josiah and representative of the furthermost genealogical reach of the line of David, "a seat of honor higher than those of the other kings who were with him in Babylon" (52:32 NIV).

It might be suggested that nothing special is indicated in this final observation by Jeremiah. Yet in the context of his predictions concerning the restoration of David's line as the hope of exiled Israel, something significant may be observed in this brief concluding narrative.[7] Jehoiachin embodies the future hope of the messianic line of David. His favorable treatment by the king of Babylon hints that God's promise regarding the restoration of David's line will not fail.

So it should not be surprising to find in the genealogy of Jesus recorded in the gospel of Matthew the name Jeconiah, also called Coniah or Jehoiachin, who received favorable treatment at the hands of the Babylonian king (Matt. 1:11–12). From this exiled line of descendants came the restored line of David that eventually led to Jesus the Christ. Not without reason did Jeremiah connect exile and restoration in Judah closely to the fortunes of the line of David, for it is through this line that the chosen messiah ultimately would come. With the birth, life, death, resurrection, and ascension of Jesus the Christ, this righteous Branch of the line of David has finally appeared. Today he sits at the right hand of power on the throne of God, which is to be identified with the throne of David. From that throne he never shall be removed.

Messianic predictions also arise out of a theology of exile and restoration in Ezekiel's parable regarding an eagle (Nebuchadnezzar) who carries the top of a cedar (most likely Zedekiah) to a land of merchants (Babylon) (Ezek. 17:2–4). After this word of anticipated judgment, the prophet declares that the Lord himself will take another shoot from the very top of a cedar and plant it on the mountain heights of Israel. In the limbs of this tree the birds of the air will find shelter and shade (17:22–24). While the allusion is somewhat veiled, the central message is clear: the Lord himself will establish a king to rule in Israel

---

7. See the treatment of this question by Provan, "Messiah in the Books of Kings."

after its own kings have been exiled. A further prediction regarding this God-appointed replacement of the corrupted kings of Judah declares:

> O profane and wicked prince of Israel, whose day has come, whose time of punishment has reached its climax, this is what the Sovereign Covenant LORD says: Take off the turban, remove the crown. It will not be as it was: The lowly will be exalted and the exalted will be brought low. A ruin! A ruin! I will make it a ruin! It will not be restored *until he comes to whom it rightfully belongs; to him* I will give it. (Ezek. 21:25–27 NIV, emphasis added)

The ruination of the wicked prince of Israel thus provides the framework for a prediction concerning the rightful possessor of the nation's throne that will appear in the future.

Other predictions in Ezekiel concerning a coming messianic figure follow more closely on the expressions of hope found in the earlier prophets. God will place one shepherd over his restored flock, who is designated as his servant David. This shepherd will be a prince among them and will continue forever (Ezek. 37:23–25).[8]

So future expectation of a messiah in Ezekiel is closely related to predictions regarding exile and restoration. This expected messianic figure was not himself present at the time of Ezekiel's prophecy. That

8. Not quite so clear is Ezekiel's prediction regarding the "prince" mentioned repeatedly in connection with the vision of the restored temple. The term *nasi* appears 37 times in Ezekiel and most often serves as a synonym for "king" (12:10, 12; 19:1; 21:12, 25; etc.). In chaps. 44–48, it occurs 17 times in association with the vision of the reestablished temple. This prince is the only person allowed to eat in the presence of the Lord (44:3) and has special land allotted to him adjoining the sacred district of the city (45:7). In addition, he has the duty of making sacrifice (45:17) and is warned not to take any property belonging to the people (46:18). The term also appears occasionally in the plural (45:8–9). These references may include predictions of a messianic figure, but they appear in a shadowy form that is not so clear in intent as other messianic predictions in Ezekiel. Keil, *Ezekiel*, 2.300, appears to be correct when he states that this prince "is neither the high priest [of Israel] . . . nor a collective term for the civil authorities of the people of Israel in the Messianic times." Instead, this "prince" is the messianic "David" who is earlier designated "prince" in 34:23–24. Keil explains the problem of the transmission of properties by this prince to his sons (46:16) as arising because, from Ezekiel's perspective, this prince is thought of in terms of a king after the fashion of the previous kings of Israel, so that the limitations of the old covenant type are reflected in predictions regarding the new covenant fulfillment (431).

470

Israel was restored to her land cannot be doubted. That a messianic figure descended from David has come to reign over God's people is the central claim of the new covenant writings.

Prophets of Israel who actually experienced the restoration from Babylon after Israel's exile somewhat surprisingly continue to predict further restoration and exile in the future. By reference to an eschatological shaking, Haggai predicts the reestablishment of the Davidic line (Hag. 2:21–22). In a special message to Zerubbabel the appointed governor of the nation's restoration, the Lord declares that he will make him his personal signet ring (2:20–23). This Zerubbabel is elsewhere identified as a direct descendant of Jehoiachin and so represents the continuation of the royal line of David (1 Chron. 3:18–19; Ezra 5:2). As God's designated leader, he will be invested with the authority of the Almighty, so that what he orders will have the insignia of God's authority stamped on it. Even though the Davidic monarchy was never reinstated in Israel, this symbolic pronouncement concerning Zerubbabel was of great significance for the people of the restoration. This prophetic declaration anticipated the appearance of a future son of David who would arise to rule some day in the future. The connection from David through Zerubbabel to Jesus Christ is clearly established in Matthew's gospel, where Zerubbabel is listed in the genealogy that leads to the consummate restoration of the throne of David among God's people (Matt. 1:12).

The expectation of further exile and restoration continues into the final section of the book of Zechariah. In Zechariah 9–14, Zion's king is yet to come in righteousness and humility. When he finally arrives, he will proclaim peace to the nations and will rule "from sea to sea and from the River to the ends of the earth" (9:9–10 NIV). In light of this expectation, the "prisoners of hope" are urged to return, for the Lord now announces that he will "restore twice as much" to them (9:12). In that day, the Lord will fight for his people, and they will "sparkle in his land like jewels in a crown" (9:14–17 NIV). Even though the restoration had already begun in Zechariah's day, the Lord promises that he will yet bring them back from Assyria and Egypt, so that they will be as though he had never rejected them (chap. 10).

With all this anticipated blessing, the prophet predicts that because of the evil nature of the nation's shepherds, the people will be

471

handed over to their neighboring nations once more. By choosing to pay off their one Good Shepherd for the "handsome price" of thirty pieces of silver, the nation will find itself in the clutches of worthless shepherds (11:4–17) who will "eat the meat of the choice sheep" (11:16 NIV). While no Good Shepherd-king arose in days contemporary with the restoration prophets, one Good Shepherd eventually did appear among the people (John 10:1). This Good Shepherd was rejected by the people and of his own accord gave up his life for the sheep (Matt. 27:9–10; John 10:11). In this way, the prediction of the prophet concerning the smitten shepherd found its consummate fulfillment.

E. Exile and restoration are predicted in spectacular fashion

The significance of predictions about Israel's exile and restoration is seen in the spectacular nature of their prediction in the old covenant scriptures. Among the several hundred predictions of the future in the old covenant scriptures, two sections in the prophets stand out as the most spectacular: the challenge to prophecy in Isaiah and the prediction specifying seventy years as the time of Israel's exile in Jeremiah. Both these spectacular predictions are related to Israel's exile and restoration, and both deserve further consideration.

1. Isaiah's challenge to prophecy

The high ethical monotheism of the later chapters in Isaiah is generally recognized on all sides. The prophet mocks lifeless idols, contrasting their incapacity to act with the greatness of the one true living God. But the major feature of this mockery is often overlooked: the idols are mute; they cannot speak. This incapacity to speak is dramatized by the prophet's challenge that they predict the future:[9]

> Bring in your idols to tell us
>> what is going to happen. . . .
> Declare to us the things to come,
>> tell us what the future holds,
>> so we may know that you are gods. (41:22–23)

9. The following quotations are from the NIV.

472

Lead out those who have eyes but are blind. . . .
Which of them foretold this
    and proclaimed to us the former things? (43:8–9)

Who then is like me? Let him proclaim it.
    Let him declare and lay out before me . . .
    what is yet to come—
    yes, let him foretell what will come. (44:7)

Declare what is to be, present it. . . .
Who foretold this long ago,
    who declared it from the distant past? (45:21)

Let your astrologers come forward,
    those stargazers who make predictions month by month,
    let them save you from what is coming upon you. . . .
Each of them goes on in his error;
    there is not one that can save you. (47:13, 15)

Neither with respect to predictions made in the past nor concerning prospects for predicting the future can the mute idols speak. They cannot point to previous occasions in which they predicted accurately, and they cannot foretell the future—not only because they cannot speak, but more basically because they have no power to control the future.[10] The god who predicts the future must also have the power to determine the future.

10. It is generally agreed that Isa. 40–48 repeatedly presents idolatrous gods with a challenge to predict the future; that the Covenant LORD of Israel accepts his own challenge; that past predictions already fulfilled are a part of the challenge; and that the deliverance to be brought about by Cyrus represents the climactic prediction of the Lord through his prophet. According to von Rad, *Old Testament Theology*, 2.248, "the new as well as the old had been foretold long ago. This gave his message its legitimation: it was legitimised by the continuity of prediction." He further notes that it is of "great importance . . . that the events of this [saving] history were all foretold, and came to pass accordingly" (246–47). Significant disagreement surfaces when the effort is made to identify precisely the "former things," the things "of old" that the Covenant LORD has already predicted and brought to pass. The temporal perspective from which the prophet offers his challenge to prophecy also plays a significant role in the debate. North, "Former Things," concludes that the prophet speaks from an exilic perspective and that the "former things" include the early conquests of Cyrus up to the fall of Sardis in 547 B.C. The

The failure of the idolatrous gods of the heathen nations to respond to the challenge that they predict the future provides the occasion for the one true God, the Covenant LORD of Israel, to display his power to predict. In contrast with all other so-called gods, he has the power to control the future. The God of Israel takes up his own challenge. He speaks specifically of a dramatic event yet coming in the life of Israel that encompasses the course of the mightiest nations on earth. Specifically, he predicts three things: (1) the return of Israel from their exile, (2) the naming of Cyrus as Israel's deliverer, and (3) the coming of the suffering servant of the Covenant LORD.

a. The return of Israel from exile

Using the device of prophetic recapitulation of past saving events as a way of anticipating redemption in the future, Isaiah predicts that the Covenant LORD will cause his people to experience a new exodus

---

"latter things" would then be the defeat of Babylon and the decree that captive peoples are free to return home, which means that the prophet is located in the narrow space of time between 547 B.C. and 536 B.C. North's analysis runs into certain exegetical difficulties. Why would these predictions about the early conquests of Cyrus be directed by an exilic prophet to "Zion" and "Jerusalem," when virtually no Israelite community existed there during the early days of Cyrus (41:27)? Why would the "former things" be designated as ancient (43:18; 44:7; 48:3–8) if they referred to events or predictions that occurred just a few years earlier, assuming the prophet speaks between 547 B.C. and 536 B.C.? The explanations of North regarding these difficulties cannot overcome their cumulative effect to the contrary. Childs, *Isaiah*, 322, notes the problem felt by many commentators of "no apparent prophecy in Second Isaiah in which Yahweh had indeed predicted the coming of Cyrus," since Cyrus was by then supposedly already on the scene. He offers a solution based on canonical criticism, in which the book of Isaiah is viewed from the perspective of its final form. From this perspective, the "prediction" concerning Cyrus is supplied by a redactional entry in Isa. 13 that describes the fall of Babylon, presumably to Cyrus. On the basis of this redaction, Isa. 41 can argue that God "foretold the coming of Cyrus, which is now being fulfilled for all to see." In this reconstruction, the whole case made on behalf of the God of Israel ends up being based on a farce. From this viewpoint no prophecy actually occurred. As a consequence, the argument based on predictive prophecy found in Isaiah ends up proving that Isaiah's own God is a no-god, for as Childs correctly observes, the force of Isaiah's argument is that "the claim to true divinity rests on the ability not only to control the course of future events, but also to have predicted the events before they occurred" (321).

and a new wilderness experience. They shall be delivered from the exilic enslavement to their enemies:[11]

> Forget the former things;
>> do not dwell on the past.
> See, I am doing a new thing!
>> Now it springs up; do you not perceive it?
> I am making a way in the desert
>> and streams in the wasteland. (43:18–19)

> Do not tremble, do not be afraid.
>> Did I not proclaim this and foretell it long ago?
> You are my witnesses. (44:8)

> I am the Covenant LORD . . .
>> who carries out the words of his servants
>> and fulfills the predictions of his messengers,
> who says of Jerusalem, "It shall be inhabited,"
>> of the towns of Judah, "They shall be built,"
>> and of their ruins, "I will restore them." (44:24, 26)

> I make known the end from the beginning,
>> from ancient times, what is still to come. (46:10)

> I foretold the former things long ago,
>> my mouth announced them and I made them known;
>> then suddenly I acted, and they came to pass. . . .
> Therefore I told you these things long ago;
>> before they happened I announced them to you. (48:3, 5)

The intention of these and other statements permeating this section of Isaiah is quite clear. Isaiah's God accepts for himself the challenge to prediction that he issued to the idolatrous gods. What they could not do, he is capable of doing. Because he and he alone is God, he and he alone can predict the future.

11. The following quotations are from the NIV.

At the heart of the Lord's prediction is the announcement that Israel shall be restored from exile. Viewing the words of the prophet as though they were composed after the fact totally negates the impact intended by this prediction. Consideration of the circumstances required for this prophesied event to actually occur uncovers its remarkable character. First, the Babylonian Empire had to be conquered by a yet unknown foreign power. Then this foreign power had to reverse the policy of deportation of conquered peoples practiced by the Babylonians. And finally, the Israelite people must be willing to return, despite the comfortable lifestyle they had acquired in Babylon during their exile. Yet "in the fullness of time," the Medo-Persian Empire arose. Immediately after his conquest of Babylon, Cyrus their leader issued his decree that deported peoples should be assisted in returning to their homeland. Although only a small number of Jewish exiles responded, the predicted return did occur, and the people of Israel were reestablished in the promised land.

This description of restoration in a context of predictive prophecy over a hundred years before the event occurred may be treated in one of two ways. On the one hand, the material could be shifted down the corridors of history so that the events under consideration are viewed as already taking shape at the time of Isaiah's so-called prediction. As a consequence, Isaiah's apparent prediction of future happenings would end up being only a clever political analysis by someone contemporary to the events. On the other hand, the material could be treated as it actually presents itself, meaning that divinely inspired predictions of significant future events were actually recorded in these portions of the prophecy of Isaiah.

The major problem with understanding these verses as actually presenting predictions of the future is related to the contradiction it presents to a naturalistic approach to human history and experience. If supernatural interventions of God are excluded from the arena of human history, then the inevitable presumption is that it must be altogether impossible for any human being to have accurate knowledge of future events. But the view that denies the truly predictive nature of these words eventually has the largest number of problems, particularly if a person professes to have faith in the God that presents himself in the scriptures of the old covenant. In the first place, some explanation must be given for the numerous other anticipations of exile and restoration found in the preexilic prophets, including Isaiah, as previously noted. At some point the convenient shifting of material to suit a preconceived theory based on the impossibility of prediction loses something of its convincing power. Perhaps even more tellingly, the consequence of a "pretense" of predictive prophecy in Isaiah must be considered. If no genuine predictions of the future were forthcoming by Isaiah himself, then the God of Israel becomes the supreme object of his own sarcastic ridicule. The idols cannot predict the future because they cannot speak; but Israel's God, according to this theory, issued a challenge concerning prediction that he himself could not fulfill.

A far more consistent perspective on this material gives glory to the God of time and eternity, the God who from the beginning had a redemptive purpose spanning the ages. If this Lord of all creation made the world with a purpose, does he have no knowledge and no control over the outworking of the significant events that will determine the realization of that purpose? Is not the uniform testimony of scripture that the smallest as well as the largest events in this world are under his direction, even as he himself assures that the people of the world continually make meaningful decisions? This God of the scriptures is truly worthy of the designation *God*.

b. The naming of Cyrus as Israel's deliverer

The more specific concern of those who deny the truly predictive nature of these prophecies in Isaiah centers on the naming of Cyrus as Israel's deliverer well over one hundred years before he arrived on the scene of history. Even if it is granted that an omniscient, omnipotent God could make this kind of prediction, the question remains, Why would he make such a precise prediction of the future?

Once more, this stupendous prediction must not be read in isolation from the larger picture of God's redemptive purposes presented in the book of Isaiah. The naming of the person who would be God's chosen instrument to return his people to their homeland does not occur as a single isolated phenomenon. At several points, his person

477

and work as God's chosen instrument to advance the larger plan for the redemption of his people comes to the fore:[12]

> I have stirred up one from the north, and he comes—
>   one from the rising sun who calls on my name.
> He treads on rulers as if they were mortar,
>   as if he were a potter treading the clay. (41:25)

> I am the Covenant LORD,
> who has made all things . . .
>   who fulfills the predictions of his messengers . . .
> who says of Cyrus, "He is my shepherd
>   and will accomplish all that I please;
>   he will say of Jerusalem, 'Let it be rebuilt,'
>   and of the temple, 'Let its foundations be laid.'" (44:24, 26, 28)

> This is what the Covenant LORD says to his anointed,
>   to Cyrus, . . .
> I will go before you . . .
> so that you may know that I am the Covenant LORD,
>   the God of Israel, who summons you by name.
> For the sake of Jacob my servant,
>   of Israel my chosen,
> I summon you by name
>   and bestow on you a title of honor,
>   though you do not acknowledge me. (45:1–4)

> From the east I summon a bird of prey;
>   from a far-off land, a man to fulfill my purpose.
> What I have said, that will I bring about;
>   what I have planned, that will I do. (46:11)

It is not merely a matter of prognostication of a future event that might make people marvel with open mouth.[13] This prediction about

---

12. The following quotations are from the NIV.

13. For a full development of the predictive dimension of these passages, see Allis, *Unity of Isaiah*, 51–80. Allis convincingly shows how the poetic structure of the phrasing climaxes with the naming of Cyrus.

the one assigned by God to deliver his people from exile fits into the larger scheme of God's ongoing purposes of redemption. Cyrus was appointed by God to serve his revealed purposes in redeeming a people for himself, and the return of Israel to the promised land was an integral part of that process. By predicting this event before it happened, the Covenant LORD established that the events of redemptive history were not simply chance occurrences. Instead, they were sovereignly directed by God the creator and redeemer.

This connection of the predictions concerning Cyrus to the redemptive purposes of God is underscored by the simultaneous introduction of a second series of predictions about the suffering servant of the Lord. Woven into this section of Isaiah's prophecy, these prophecies are actually more spectacular than the predictions about Cyrus and focus even more precisely on the heart and core of God's redemptive working in the world. It is quite remarkable to note that some scholars vigorously defend the propriety of this second set of predictions as true anticipations of the future while at the same time offering rationalistic explanations of the prophecies about Israel's restoration and the naming of Cyrus. This additional set of predictions focuses on a second distinctive figure now well known as the "suffering servant of the Lord."

c. The coming of the suffering servant of the Lord

Predictions concerning the sufferings and exaltations of the servant of the Lord, which are introduced in the same chapters of Isaiah that contain the Cyrus prophecy, should not be isolated from the larger picture of exile and restoration being developed simultaneously by the prophet. *The very process that the elect nation must undergo in exile and restoration finds its personalized expression in the sufferings and exaltations of this distinctive servant of the Lord.* As a matter of fact, the prophetic values of Israel's exile and restoration find their consummate realization in the sufferings and exaltations of the servant, while the sufferings and exaltations of the servant find their ultimate significance in their vicarious, substitutionary nature in behalf of the elect nation.

This interconnection between the corporate body of the elect nation and the individualized servant of the Lord is confirmed not only by the similarity of experiences of the two personalities. It also finds vivid manifestation in the ease with which the term *servant* is applied first to the elect nation and then to the servant as an individual (42:19; 44:1–2, 21; 42:1; 49:3; 52:13). The experience of the one foreshadows the experience of the other; the sufferings and exaltation of the singular servant serve vicariously to achieve redemption for the multiple servants. Both the elect nation and the individual servant undergo the trauma of devastation and rejection by men and nations, the one by national exile and the other by personal assault. They are a people plundered and looted, with God's wrath poured out on them (42:22, 25); and he is "despised and rejected by men" (53:3 NIV), ultimately because it was the Lord's will to cause him to suffer (53:10). Both the nation and the individual servant experience the exhilaration of honor and prominence, the one by national restoration and the other by personal exaltation. The Lord says that Jerusalem and the towns of Judah "shall be built," for he shall restore their ruins (44:26); and he declares that his servant will be made very high (52:13) and enjoy a portion among the great (53:12).

This integrated understanding of the relation of the elect nation to the individual servant provides a framework for understanding the predictive nature of these utterances. As Isaiah envisions the situation, the vicarious work of suffering is not yet accomplished. Even though much of the language in a passage like Isaiah 53 appears in the grammatical form that seems to indicate completed action, the servant's humiliation and exaltation must be understood in context as events of the future. "He was wounded for our transgressions" does not mean that the wounding had been completed at the time these words were written. Instead, the language speaks of future events in the most vivid manner available, as though the events were already accomplished. These prophetic words about the sufferings and exaltations of the individual servant are predictive in nature, anticipating events in history that from the perspective of the prophet himself are yet to occur.

At the same time, despite their future realization, how vivid is their description:[14]

14. The following quotations are from the NIV.

480

I offered my back to those who beat me. . . .
I did not hide my face
   from mocking and spitting. (50:6)

Surely he took our infirmities
   and carried our sicknesses. (53:4)

He was led like a lamb to the slaughter. (53:7)

He had done no violence,
   nor was any deceit in his mouth. (53:9)

He bore the sin of many,
   and made intercession for the transgressors. (53:12)

I will also make you a light for the Gentiles. (49:6)

He will be raised and lifted up and highly exalted. (52:13)

In his law the islands will put their hope. (42:4)

The natural question about these predictions is, "Of whom does the prophet speak? Of himself or of someone else?" (Acts 8:34). The question is not so much, "About what does the prophet speak?"—for that message is plain for all to read. Instead, the question has always been, "Of *whom* does the prophet speak?"

Clearly this individualized servant cannot be identified with national Israel, since at several points his ministry is to and for Israel (Isa. 49:5–6; 53:4–5). The records of human history can be searched across the centuries. No one can be found whose person and life matches all the various aspects of this prediction concerning the individual servant of the Lord—with one exception. In Jesus, the man of Jewish descent who lived in Palestine two thousand years ago, all these predictions find their focus. He was not believed by the great majority of his own people of the Jewish nation and is still not generally believed by them (Isa. 53:1; John 12:38). His method in ministry was to bear patiently with those opposing him, avoiding conflict wherever possible (Isa. 42:3; Matt. 12:14–21). He absorbed into himself the fatal sicknesses and diseases of others, that they might experience healing (Isa. 53:4; Matt. 8:17). He let himself be abused and mistreated, receiving at the hand of his tormenters spitting, beating, and mockery (Isa. 50:6; Matt. 27:30; 26:67). He was led like a lamb to the slaughter in the process of his trial, not opening his mouth in self-defense (Isa. 53:7; Matt. 27:12–14). He did no violence to others, nor was any deceit ever found coming out of his mouth (Isa. 53:9; 1 Pet. 2:23). He suffered not for his own sins but for the sins of others (Isa. 53:12; 1 Pet. 2:24). As a consequence of his faithful service, his name has been lifted higher than any other name (Isa. 52:13; Phil. 2:7, 9–11). Today he has become a light to the Gentile nations, and the most distant portions of the earth put their hope in him (Isa. 42:4; 49:6; Acts 13:47).

It might be supposed, as certain negative critics are inclined to do, that all these parallels between the individual servant of Isaiah and the person of Jesus are a fabrication of the early Christian church. Quite strikingly, by following this procedure they themselves fulfill predictions about the servant of the Lord through their unbelieving rejection of him (Isa. 53:1). It may be acknowledged that the writers of the documents of the new covenant had the possibility of manipulating their own recordings. But quite obviously they could not manipulate the documents of the old covenant scriptures. As a consequence, the question of the Ethiopian eunuch still begs response: "Of whom does the prophet speak? Of himself or of someone else?" And if he speaks of someone other than Jesus Christ, who is it that even approximates the details of this description? Is there no one else in the history of humanity who can fulfill these expectations?

The vacuous answer to this question naturally leads to the response of Philip to the query of the eunuch: "Beginning with that scripture, he preached to him the good news of Jesus" (Acts 8:35). Without even considering other predictions of the documents of the old covenant to which the life and ministry of Jesus correspond, the relationship of his person and work to the predictions about the individual servant in the book of Isaiah is remarkable enough for the world to take note.

In this light, the matter of predictions concerning Cyrus must be reconsidered. Most believers who call themselves evangelicals are quite happy to insist on the predictive nature of the words about this individual servant of Isaiah and their fulfillment in the person of Jesus. The amazingly predictive nature of this material applies whether a person treats this section of Isaiah as having originated in the eighth century B.C. (seven hundred years before the birth of Jesus) or the sixth century B.C. (five hundred years before the birth of Jesus). These particular predictions are of such a nature that it is impossible to speak of a nearer and a more distant fulfillment, since the ministry of this individual servant is to bear the sins of his people, and only Jesus, who was himself sinless, could fulfill that expectation. Evangelicals in general are quite insistent that these particular words predict the life and ministry of the person of Jesus.

Why, then, it might be asked, should predictions about the life and ministry of Cyrus prove to be such a stumbling block to evangelicals, not to speak of the rejection of its authentic nature by negative, unbelieving critics? Clearly the material regarding Israel's exile and its glorious restoration, as well as the identification of Cyrus as the nation's designated deliverer, is set in a context of predictive prophecy. The material speaks of things that Cyrus as God's servant is yet to do and of a deliverance from exile that is still in the future from the perspective of the prophet. No extant manuscript evidence indicates that this material had an existence separated from the book of Isaiah as a whole. The entire challenge-to-prediction framework of the Cyrus material becomes a legitimate basis for having Isaiah's mockery of the idols fall on his own head if the predictive nature of the words about Cyrus is denied. The suggestion that the author of this material, whoever he might be, was simply an acute political prognosticator living in the days of Cyrus almost two hundred years after the eighth-century Isaiah ben Amoz hardly suits the context of these multiple predictions.

In the end, the most coherent case may be made for seeing the words about Cyrus as an apex of predictive prophecy in the old covenant documents, suitably designed as a framework for the consummate predictions about the coming servant of the Lord. The predicted deliverance by the one servant becomes the framework for comprehending the greater deliverance mediated by the consummate servant of the Lord.

It may be noted at this point that the canonical approach being recommended so highly in many circles has the effect of cutting the jugular vein of these predictive prophecies. If the major concern of biblical interpretation rests with the final form of any particular portion of scripture, then the idea of a prediction regarding the exile and restoration of Israel runs the risk of having no authentic significance at all, since it is assumed that the prophecy actually took shape only after the pretended prediction had occurred. If the material that appears in Isaiah as a prediction of the future actually took on this form only after the events of exile and restoration had occurred, or were at least imminent, then the prediction is no prediction at all. Even worse, the final form must also be understood as a farce, a "prediction" flying under false colors. Worse than being mute about the future, as were the idols of the heathen gods, would be a pretense to predict the future when all along the material came into this form after the events had already occurred. It is not surprising that the more astute subscribers to the older critical approaches regarding the Old Testament documents wonder why their comrades should be upset about canonical criticism. Properly understood, no premises of the older criticisms have been surrendered by the canonical criticism of more recent days.

2. Jeremiah's prediction of seventy years for the exile

The most distinctive prediction of Jeremiah with respect to exile and restoration is found in his declaration that Israel would remain in captivity for seventy years. On the one hand, he states that the captured nation will serve Babylon for seventy years (Jer. 25:11). On the other hand, he states that Israel will return to its own land after seventy years (29:10). The two ideas are not exactly identical since it is conceivable that after seventy years the Babylonian Empire would disintegrate without Israel returning to the promised land. These two specific prophecies combine to affirm the significance in God's purposes for both the exile and the restoration of Israel.

Calculating the date of this seventy-year period is done in a variety of ways.[15] The most straightforward handling of the subject begins by noting that Jeremiah dates this particular word from the Lord as

15. See Thompson, *Jeremiah*, 513–14.

having come to him twenty-three years after the thirteenth year of the reign of Josiah (Jer. 25:3). Josiah began his reign in approximately 640 B.C., so his thirteenth year is approximately 627 B.C.. If the dating is reckoned inclusively, twenty-three years from that date is 605 B.C., which corresponds with the date of the first of Judah's deportations by Nebuchadnezzar (2 Kings 24:1–2; 2 Chron. 36:5–7; Dan. 1:1–6). Seventy years later would be 536 B.C., which corresponds precisely with the date of Cyrus's decree that the peoples brought into exile by the Babylonians should be allowed to return to their homelands.[16]

How is a prediction of this sort to be handled? Should it be supposed that this specification of seventy years for the length of Israel's exile demonstrates Jeremiah's political acumen? Hardly so, since no political sense could have determined seventy to be the precise number of years for Israel's exile. Is, then, this prediction to be perceived as a classic case of *vaticinium ex eventu*, of a pretended prediction that actually arose only after the event occurred? The rationalistic mind that automatically excludes all interventions of God into the present world order is forced to reach this conclusion. But this brings into question the whole larger framework of the book of Jeremiah, since the uniting theme of the book focuses on prediction of an exile and restoration of Israel that was yet future. Certainly a person is free to denigrate the integrity of the entire prophecy of Jeremiah, but not without also questioning the whole presentation of redemption by a designated savior as a consequence of its connection with the same themes of exile and restoration. It hardly seems feasible that the divine message of salvation by God would be delivered by means of a fabricated, corrupted ancient text that pretends to predict what it could not possibly know.

There is of course a different option. Considering the integrity of the text as a whole, the idea of precisely seventy years of exile for Israel fits not only with the objective historical facts of the day but also accords with the ancient theology of the sabbatical year. As indicated in the book of Chronicles, the seventy years of Israel's exile were deter-

16. As in all cases with biblical dating, dates cannot be substantiated with absolute finality. Yet on any calculation, these figures are indeed remarkable.

485

mined by God because this length of time equaled the period needed for the fulfillment of Israel's neglected Sabbaths (2 Chron. 36:21; see also Lev. 26:34–35).[17] The wholeness of the biblical testimony encourages faith in all its various parts. The unified message of this book elicits trust, and its ability to release divine power into the human realm is repeatedly demonstrated.

III. The biblical-theological significance of Israel's restoration

The significance of Israel's exile from their land has already been evaluated (see chap. 11 §III). But now consideration must be given to the significance of the redemptive event of Israel's restoration from exile. Four aspects of significance regarding restoration may be noted: Israel's restoration includes the forgiveness of sins; it involves the new life of grace; it includes the Gentile nations; and it involves the rejuvenation of the earth, culminating in resurrection from the dead.

A. Israel's restoration involves the forgiveness of sins

Never in the writings of the prophets is the return of Israel to the land treated as a purely mechanical event. Just as in the exodus from Egypt the sin of the people was removed through the blood of the Passover lamb, so the forgiveness of sins by the vicarious work of the suffering servant was a vital part of restoration after exile. If sin brought about the nation's exile, then cleansing from sin must be integral to restoration.

The prophet Micah is careful to relate the experience of restoration after exile to the pardon of sin. In concluding his prophecy, he declares:

17. With these texts in mind, it becomes quite clear why negative critics find themselves obligated to deny the Mosaic authorship of the Pentateuch. From a naturalistic perspective, it is absolutely impossible that the exile of Israel could have been anticipated by Moses eight hundred years before the event. At the same time, it should not be supposed that the proposals of canonical criticism offer a better alternative. To talk about the theology arising out of a "final form" of these predictions concerning a seventy-year exile without affirming the truly predictive character of these statements is to fall into the clutches of a postmodern perspective that denies the significance of objective truth. If God did not reveal to Jeremiah these perimeters of Israel's exile and restoration as the prophet claims, then the integrity of the book must be regarded as fatally damaged.

As in the days when you came out of Egypt,
    I will show them my wonders. . . .
Who is a God like you,
    who pardons sin and forgives the transgression
    of the remnant of his inheritance?
You do not stay angry forever
    but delight to show mercy.
You will again have compassion on us;
    you will tread our sins underfoot
    and hurl all our iniquities into the depths of the sea.
You will be true to Jacob,
    and show mercy to Abraham,
as you pledged on oath to our fathers
    in days long ago. (Mic. 7:15, 18–20 NIV)

Emphasizing this aspect of Israel's restoration, Jeremiah says the Babylonians will fill the city of Jerusalem with dead bodies because of all its wickedness (Jer. 33:5). But then he will bring Israel back from its exile and will "cleanse them from all the sin they have committed against me and will forgive all their sins of rebellion against me" (33:8 NIV). Jeremiah notes that Assyria was the first to devour Israel and that Nebuchadnezzar of Babylon will be the last to crush her bones. But now he promises that he will punish the king of Babylon as he punished the king of Assyria when he brings Israel back to his own pasture:

"In those days, at that time,"
    declares the Covenant LORD,
"search will be made for Israel's guilt
    but there will be none,
and for the sins of Judah,
    but none will be found,
    for I will forgive the remnant I spare." (Jer. 50:20 NIV)

When Daniel recognizes that the seventy years of captivity predicted by Jeremiah are finally coming to their end, he immediately launches into an extended prayer of confession (Dan. 9:2, 4–19). In conclusion, he pleads for the restoration of their sanctuary and city, exclaiming: "We do not make requests of you because we are righteous, but because of your great mercy. O Lord, listen! O Lord, forgive! O Lord, hear and act!" (9:18–19 NIV). In similar fashion, Ezekiel notes that on the day that the Lord cleanses them from all their sins, then he will resettle their towns, and their ruins will be rebuilt (Ezek. 36:33).

How could it be otherwise? If sin and its accompanying guilt were the cause of Israel's exile, then the forgiveness of sin and the removal of guilt are essential to restoration after exile's judgment. But how shall this forgiveness of sins be accomplished? How can this forgiveness of sins be different from the previous provisions of the Lord in this regard?

Jeremiah specifically answers these critical questions by his teaching regarding the establishment of the new covenant. Once more in a context of restoration after exile, the prophet points to an entirely new covenant relationship in the future that will not be according to the older covenant made at Sinai when God brought his people out of Egypt. In this new covenant, the people will be granted a new heart, for their sins will be wholly forgiven, and God will remember their sins no more (Jer. 31:33–34). A perpetual reminder of the people's continuing sinfulness was inherent in the older sacrificial system. Year after year, even as they presented their sacrifices on the Day of Atonement, they were at the same time being reminded that their outstanding sins still needed to be forgiven. Now under this new covenant there will never again be any remembrance of sin.

How is this new covenant to be realized? When will adequate sacrifice for the once-for-all removal of sin be provided? This consummative covenant finds its historical inauguration when Jesus Christ symbolically and then really substituted the sacrifice of his own body and blood in place of the offering of the Passover lamb (Luke 22:20). His shed blood that atones for the sins of his people once and for all is the inaugurating blood of the new covenant (Heb. 9:25–28). By this sacrifice, a full and complete restoration of his people is accomplished. Because of its uniqueness, no restoration of the sinner to his God is possible apart from the removal of sins through this sacrifice.

488

B. Israel's restoration involves a new life of grace

That the experience of restoration should be regarded as a matter of unmerited favor from the hands of a gracious God is vividly depicted by Jeremiah's vision of the two baskets of figs (Jer. 24). According to the vision, which came shortly after King Jehoiachin and key leaders had been taken into exile, one basket contains very good figs, and the other contains figs so bad that they cannot be eaten. The basket of good figs represents Jehoiachin and the people already taken into exile. Despite the sin that caused these people to be banished from the promised land, the Lord will watch over them for their good and will eventually bring them back to the land. He will build them up and not tear them down; he will plant them and not uproot them; he will give them a heart to know him (Jer. 24:5–7, using extensive phrasing taken from the book's theme verse: 1:10).

Clearly nothing but the Lord's grace can explain this treatment of these exiles. Already they have been shown to be objects deserving God's wrath by his exiling them from the land. Yet now the Lord commits himself to prospering them with blessings and eventually restoring them to the land. The gracious, undeserved character of this benediction is underscored by the Lord taking the initiative in giving them a heart to know him. Prior to this sovereign act of mercy, these people did not manifest a proper love for him. The characterization of these figs as good does not refer to some inherent quality of goodness. Instead, this goodness owes its origin to the sovereign initiative of the Lord that transforms the corrupted hearts of these people. Some day in the future, a regeneration of their inmost beings will occur—but only by the grace of God.

The bad figs, on the other hand, receive nothing more and nothing less than they deserve. These bad figs represent Zedekiah and the Israelites still remaining in the land. Like the first basket of figs, they deserve the Lord's wrath and judgment for their evil ways and evil hearts, and in the divine administration of justice that is exactly what they shall receive (Jer. 24:8–10). In the mystery of God's saving grace, the mystery of divine election and reprobation, some vessels were prepared for glory,

489

and others for destruction (Rom. 9:22–23). The exile and restoration of Israel displays in large letters these eternal principles.

As a manifestation of God's grace, the restoration of Israel after exile will surpass even the saving event of the exodus:

> "The days are coming," declares the Covenant LORD, "when people will no longer say, 'As surely as the Covenant LORD lives, who brought the Israelites up out of Egypt,' but they will say, 'As surely as the Covenant LORD lives, who brought the descendants of Israel up out of the land of the north and out of all the countries where he had banished them.' Then they will live in their own land." (Jer. 23:7–8 NIV)

Israel's restoration from exile thus embodies a redemptive event that pales even the exodus in its significance. The gracious working of God's electing purposes will be even more evident, for Israel and Judah will not be forsaken by their God, "though their land is full of guilt before the Holy One of Israel" (51:5 NIV). God in his grace and mercy has chosen this people and will bring them to Mount Zion (3:14).

This restoration will not, however, be without Israel's own involvement, for "they will come with weeping, they will pray as I bring them back" (Jer. 31:9 NIV). The Lord hears Ephraim moaning:

> After I strayed,
> I repented;
> after I came to understand,
> I beat my breast.
> I was ashamed and humiliated
> because I bore the disgrace of my youth. (Jer. 31:19 NIV)

Soul-searching repentance and sorrow for sin must accompany deliverance from divine judgment. In anticipation of these deep-seated agonies, the prophet predicts the remorse that shall characterize the return after exile. As the nation returns, the people of Israel and Judah "will go in tears to seek the Covenant LORD their God" (Jer. 50:4 NIV). These tears will not, however, last forever. One of the great consequences of restoration will be the return of joy and gladness:

The Covenant LORD will . . .
> redeem [Jacob] from the hand of those stronger than they.
They will come and shout for joy on the heights of Zion;
> they will rejoice in the bounty of the Covenant LORD—
the grain, the new wine and the oil,
> the young of the flocks and herds.
They will be like a well-watered garden,
> and they will sorrow no more.
Then maidens will dance and be glad,
> young men and old as well.
I will turn their mourning into gladness;
> I will give them comfort and joy instead of sorrow. (Jer. 31:11–13
> NIV)

In their restored state, "there will be heard once more the sounds of joy and gladness, the voices of bride and bridegroom, and the voices of those who bring thank offerings to the house of the Covenant LORD, saying, 'Give thanks to the Covenant LORD Almighty, for the Covenant LORD is good; his love endures forever.' For I will restore the fortunes of the land as they were before, says the Covenant LORD" (33:10c–11 NIV).

By citing this well-known phrase from the psalms concerning the enduring character of God's love, Jeremiah places the restoration from exile alongside the mighty acts of God in creation and redemption (Ps. 136:1; 1 Chron. 16:34). By this final great saving event, the Lord has brought everlasting joy to his people. But how is the fulfillment of this promise of grace in restoration to be identified? Did the people return to their ancient land with a renewed heart as the prophet anticipated after the seventy years of Jeremiah had transpired?

The evidence of the postexilic prophets indicates that in some cases the grace of God was clearly at work in the hearts of the people as they returned from Babylon. After Haggai's exhortations, the spirits of the people were so moved that they began rebuilding the temple (Hag. 1:14). Yet the imperfection of their response indicated the need for further fulfillment of this working of grace in restoration (Zech. 5:3–4; Mal. 1:6, 8, 13–14; 2:2; 3:8).

According to the new covenant scriptures, the coming of Jesus together with the ministry of his apostles heralded the arrival of the day of restoration by God's grace. Jesus began his ministry in Nazareth by proclaiming the "acceptable year of the Lord" (Luke 4:18–21). It is by grace that people came to believe the good news as it was shared with them (Acts 18:27; 13:48; 16:14; 20:24, 32; Eph. 2:8–9). The whole establishment of the new covenant, beginning with the choice of the originating twelve and rapidly expanding into the vast Gentile realm, indicates the broad dimensions in which this restoration by the infusion of divine grace worked—and continues to work until the present day. The inclusion of Gentiles may itself be considered a primary aspect of restoration by grace as depicted by the prophets.

C. Israel's restoration includes Gentile nations

The inclusion of the Gentiles as a significant aspect of predictive prophecy was noted above (see chap. 13 §III.C). It is also important to recognize that Israel can never regard itself as being properly and scripturally "restored" apart from the full inclusion of the Gentile peoples. *Reconstitution of Israel in the land that underscores Jewish nationalism and builds walls of separation between them and Gentile peoples cannot possibly qualify as the restoration depicted in the writings of the prophets.*

Both Hosea and Amos as prophets to the kingdom of the north provided foundational statements that served well in resolving the problem of Gentile inclusion in the early Christian church. At the height of the debate in Jerusalem, James as presiding officer appeals to the statement of Amos that Gentile peoples would have God's name placed on them, indicating their election to salvation exactly as was Israel (Acts 15:14–18). The "setting of the name" of the Lord on a person encapsulates a biblical concept laden with the idea of sovereign electing grace. This experience had once set Israel apart as God's own people (Deut. 28:9–10). But now the same phraseology is used both in the quotation from Amos and in the introductory comments of James (Amos 9:11–12; Acts 15:14c, 17c). In a similar way, Paul cites the reference in Hosea that describes the transformation of "not my people" into the people of God to explain the inclusion of Gentiles (Rom. 9:24–25). According to the conjoined testimony of prophets and apostles, restoration from exile inherently involves inclusion of Gentile peoples.

By use of a startling imagery, Paul further describes his mission to the Gentiles in terms reminiscent of the language of the prophet Isaiah. He has received the special grace of God "to be a minister of Christ Jesus to the Gentiles." In this capacity, he has a "priestly duty" of presenting the Gentiles as "an offering acceptable to God, sanctified by the Holy Spirit" (Rom. 15:15–16). The apostle thus sees his missionary efforts to the Gentiles as a new covenant priestly duty. Through the preaching of the gospel to the Gentiles, he is enabled to present them to God as a sanctified sacrifice that will be acceptable to him.

Paul's imagery parallels exactly the concluding message of the book of Isaiah. God will commission some of those who survive the catastrophe of the exile with a special task. They will proclaim God's glory among the nations (Isa. 66:19). As a consequence, just as the Israelites bring their grain offerings, so these specially commissioned messengers will bring Gentile "brothers from all the nations" to God's holy mountain in Jerusalem as an offering to the Lord (66:20). Some of these Gentiles who participate in Israel's restoration will then be selected as "priests and Levites" to offer sacrificial service to the Lord (66:21).

No more radical mode of expression could be imagined! Gentiles designated as brothers, purified before the Lord in Jerusalem, and selected by God himself to serve as priests and Levites in the most sacred functions before the Lord. Yet both the old covenant and the new covenant scriptures confirm the fact. No true restoration of God's people can be legitimized without the intimate inclusion of peoples from the various Gentile nations. Paul's point, as is stressed numerous times throughout the scriptures of the new covenant, is that this restoration through the inclusion of the Gentiles is accomplished by his preaching of the gospel of Jesus the Christ. Here and now in the present age, the restoration of the Israel of God has become reality.

D. Israel's restoration rejuvenates the earth, climaxing with the resurrection of the dead

The prediction of restoration in the prophets goes far beyond the simple fact of the return of a remnant of Jewish people from Babylon to Palestine. The prophets perceived a restoration with far-reaching consequences that would involve the rejuvenation of the earth, climaxing with the resurrection of the dead.

The cosmic renewal associated with the nation's restoration in the vision of the prophets counterbalances the cataclysmic destruction of the earth connected with Israel's exile. Jeremiah reports that the Lord weeps and wails for the mountains and pastures that were desolated by the exile (Jer. 9:10, 16). The earth has returned to its original state of being "without form and void," with the mountains quaking, the hills swaying, and every bird of the sky having flown away (Jer. 4:23–25; cf. Gen. 1:2). The prophet Zephaniah depicts Israel's coming judgment in terms reminiscent of the cosmic destruction at the time of Noah's flood. The Lord declares that he "will sweep away everything from the face of the earth," including men, animals, birds, and fish (Zeph. 1:3 NIV; Gen. 6:7, 17; 7:21–23). He will assemble all nations and kingdoms, for the whole world will be consumed by the fire of his jealous anger (Zeph. 3:8).

Fair treatment of these texts does not allow simple relegation to the realm of the hyperbolic. As the prophets contemplated the coming exile of their nation, they saw in it a microcosmic image of the great judgment of the nations of the world that was yet to come. If God should treat his own people with upright justice in accord with the terms of curse in the covenant, then the remainder of the nations of the world must expect that eventually they will receive a similar just treatment (Isa. 24:1, 4–6, 19–23; Jer. 25:30–33; Joel 3:1–3, 12–16).

The nations of the world today would do well to study the implications of Israel's exile for their own future. If the one and only creator and sustainer of the universe should bring devastating judgments on his favored nation, should they actually expect less for themselves?

In the prophetic predictions regarding future cosmic judgment associated with Israel's exile may be found a framework for evaluating the prophetic anticipations of future cosmic rejuvenation. Obviously figurative language is used at points to depict the extravagance of blessing that may be expected in the future. Mountains dripping new wine and hills flowing with milk provide images that depict fruitful vineyards and productive cattle (Joel 3:18). Comparison of the restored land with the garden of Eden suggests an idyllic renewal, but at the same time points to a consummate expectation that parallels the original state of creation

(Isa. 51:3; Ezek. 36:35). "Every man under his own vine and fig tree" portrays paradise restored as a picture of the nation's future hoped-for condition (Mic. 4:4; Zech. 3:10; 1 Kings 4:25; Isa. 36:16).

Yet within and around these images, the prophets spoke with all seriousness about the transformation of their land in connection with their restoration. After taking away Israel's grain, wine, and wool through the process of exile, the Lord would give back her fruitful vineyards (Hos. 2:9, 15). He would respond to the plea of the skies, the skies would respond to the plea of the earth, and the earth would respond to the plea of grain, wine, and oil (2:21–22). Along with a new heart and new spirit, the Lord would give his restored people fruitful trees and bountiful crops (Ezek. 36:26, 29–30). To round off the testimony of preexilic Hosea and exilic Ezekiel, the witness of postexilic Zechariah may be cited: "The seed will grow well, the vine will yield its fruit, the ground will produce its crops, and the heavens will drop their dew. I will give all these things as an inheritance to the remnant of this people" (Zech. 8:12 NIV). Clearly no platonic idealism dictated the expectations of restoration for Israel. A modern-day culture that purchases the earth's produce in bottles, bags, and cans tends to take these essentials of life for granted. Yet the prophetic predictions regarding the age of restoration should be seen as finding fulfillment in the grace of God as it is displayed currently in the age of the new covenant.

Yet there is more. According to Isaiah's prophecies regarding the days to come, Israel will bud and blossom, filling all the world with its fruit (Isa. 27:6). The desert will burst into bloom, and rivers will flow in the barren heights (35:1–7; 41:18–20). "The food that comes from the land will be rich and plentiful," oxen and donkeys will have abundance of fodder, "the moon will shine like the sun, and the sunlight will be seven times brighter, . . . when the Covenant LORD binds up the bruises of his people and heals the wounds he inflicted" (30:23–26 NIV). When the Spirit is poured out from on high, then the desert will become a fertile field, and the fertile field will seem like a forest (32:15).

In this continuum stretching from the renewal of the raw earth to the transformation of heavenly bodies and consummating in the outpouring of the divine Spirit, it is difficult to determine where reality ends and pictorial language begins. Yet the biblical emphasis on the indis-

495

soluble unity of the physical with the spiritual encourages caution in minimizing the expectation of a final cosmic transformation that will remove every remnant of the curse that originated with the fall. This is exactly what the prophet predicts in terms of the consummate state of things. "The wolf will live with the lamb, . . . a little child shall lead them, . . . [and] the earth will be full of the knowledge of the Covenant LORD as the waters cover the sea" (Isa. 11:6–9 NIV). The Lord will create a new heaven and a new earth, and (once more—this time in the second section of Isaiah's prophecy), the wolf and the lamb will feed together (65:17, 25; 66:22). Nothing in the language of these passages suggests anything other than an actual transformation of the earth in connection with the broader dimensions of a final restoration of all things.

In this framework the ultimate renewal of God's people by restoration from the dead may be comprehended. As the earth is rejuvenated, so his people will be resurrected. Hosea's declaration that the Lord will make alive the very ones he has injured could be regarded as only a veiled reference to the prospect of resurrection from the dead (Hos. 6:1–2).[18] But the affirmations in Isaiah regarding resurrection from the dead are so clear that they evoke an almost universal opinion from negative biblical critics that they must be later insertions:

> On this mountain he will destroy
> > the shroud that enfolds all peoples,
> the sheet that covers all nations;
> > he will swallow up death forever.
> The Sovereign Covenant LORD will wipe away the tears
> > from all faces. (Isa. 25:7–8 NIV)

> But your dead will live;
> > their bodies will rise.
> You who dwell in the dust,
> > wake up and shout for joy.
> Your dew is like the dew of the morning;
> > the earth will give birth to her dead. (Isa. 26:19 NIV)

18. Context indicates that the reference in Hos. 13:14 to ransoming from the power of the grave is best interpreted not as an affirmation of hope in the resurrection but as a question expecting a negative answer: "Shall I ransom them from the power of the

This perspective on resurrection from the dead is substantiated in predictions respecting the future by both Ezekiel and Daniel. Ezekiel's vision of the valley filled with dead, dry bones provides the occasion for the prediction of renewal of life in connection with restoration of the exiles. The Lord declares through his prophet: "O my people, I am going to open your graves and bring you up from them; I will bring you back to the land of Israel. Then you, my people, will know that I am the Covenant LORD, when I open your graves and bring you up from them. I will put my Spirit in you and you will live, and I will settle you in your own land" (Ezek. 37:12–14 NIV). Some commentators insist that Ezekiel speaks only of the return from exile by the imagery of resurrection from the dead.[19] But the presence of resurrection hope even in the days of the patriarchs suggests that Ezekiel was only extending the same concept to the expectation of restoration after exile.[20]

Daniel is quite explicit in his affirmation concerning a general resurrection of the dead: "Multitudes who sleep in the dust of the earth will awake: some to everlasting life, others to shame and everlasting contempt" (Dan. 12:2 NIV). If the expectations of a new heaven and new earth are a legitimate part of Israel's anticipations concerning their restoration after exile, then humanity also must be newly equipped to live in this new environment. A resurrected body infused with the life-

---

grave?" No. "Shall I redeem them from death?" No. See Vos, *Biblical Theology*, 290. The defeat of death and the removal of the curse of the law by the death and resurrection of Jesus Christ provides adequate rationale for Paul's employment of the same text to inspire resurrection hope (1 Cor. 15:55–56).

19. See Taylor, *Ezekiel*, 236 (who is quite emphatic on this point); Eichrodt, *Ezekiel*, 509; and Zimmerli, *Ezekiel*, 2.264.

20. See the implicit affirmation of the presence of resurrection faith in the old covenant scriptures in Jesus' rebuttal of the Sadducees because of their skepticism regarding the resurrection of the dead: "You are in error because you do not know the Scriptures or the power of God" (Matt. 22:29 NIV). With respect to this passage in Ezekiel, note the extensive treatment of the question in Block, *Ezekiel*, 2.381–92. Block takes note of Jewish and Christian interpretations that understand Ezekiel as describing an actual resurrection. He discusses several scriptural passages predating Ezekiel that speak in terms of resurrection (386–87, esp. n. 97) and concludes: "In a new and dramatic way, the conviction that the grave need not be the end provided a powerful vehicle for announcing the full restoration of Israel. The curse would be lifted. Yahweh would bring his people back to life" (387). For additional discussion, see Robertson, *Israel of God*, 21–25.

giving power of God's Holy Spirit provides a suitable framework for mankind's new, holy, and perfected habitation. The rejuvenation of the earth along with the resurrection of the body provides a climactic dimension to prophetic predictions about the return after exile. Nothing less than the renewal of creation will suit the prophet's anticipation of the future.

This holistic perspective on restoration after exile corresponds precisely to the expectation voiced by the apostle Peter in his sermon after the healing of the lame beggar at the temple. He admonishes the people to repent so that sins may be wiped out (an integral part of the prophetic perspective on Israel's restoration). Then times of refreshing will come from the Lord (a further dimension of the old covenant concept of the restoration). Finally God will again send the Christ, who must remain in heaven "until the times come for the *restoration of all things*, concerning which the Lord spoke through the mouth of his holy prophets long ago" (Acts 3:19–21). In other words, when the prophets spoke of restoration, they were referring ultimately to the rejuvenation of the whole earth that would occur in conjunction with the consummate coming of the promised messiah.

CONCLUSION

Despite repeated warnings by the prophets, it must have been extremely difficult for the people of Israel to accept the fact that the unbelievable event of banishment into exile would actually occur. The Lord was longsuffering toward his wayward people across the decades and the centuries. But a time eventually came in which he would delay no longer. The hour for the fulfillment of all warnings concerning exile finally arrived.

It fell to Ezekiel among the prophets to underscore this fact of the imminence of exile. In order to drive home the reality regarding the arrival of the hour of Jerusalem's destruction, the prophet emphatically repeats himself: "The end! The end has come upon the four corners of the land. The end is now upon you. . . . An unheard-of disaster is coming. The end has come! The end has come! . . . It has come! Doom has come upon you—you who dwell in the land. The time has come, the day is near" (Ezek. 7:2–3, 5–7 NIV).

After long delays, after many prophetic warnings, the time for Judah's final devastation had come. The Lord directed his prophet, "Record this date, this very date, because the king of Babylon has laid siege to Jerusalem this very day" (24:2 NIV). Invading armies had come in and out of the land of Israel in the past, but now the real thing was happening. The predictions of the prophets were being fulfilled. As the Lord declared: "The time has come for me to act. I will not hold back; I will not have pity, nor will I relent. You will be judged according to your conduct and your actions, declares the Sovereign Covenant LORD" (24:14 NIV). For many years the Lord had shown his patience.

But finally the time had come when he would act. In his righteousness he would bring just judgment against his own people.

Most difficult to comprehend was the fact that both the righteous and the wicked would suffer in this disaster. An invading Babylonian army would put no value on righteousness and wickedness among those who would experience devastation. As a consequence, the prophet groaned with a broken heart and bitter grief, for the Lord had affirmed, "It is coming! It will surely take place" (21:3, 6–7 NIV).

In a similar way, people in every generation since the days of Jesus Christ have had a difficult time believing in the imminence of his return. Even to the very last days, scoffers will say, "Where is this 'coming' he promised? . . . Everything goes on as it has since the beginning of creation" (2 Pet. 3:4 NIV). The current generation is no different. It too cannot believe in the imminence of his coming. Yet he will come at the very time when people do not expect him.

In summarizing the prophetic focus on exile and restoration, the following emphases may be noted:

- Both the city of Jerusalem and the person of the messiah play a major role in the restoration of the nation. The significance attached to city and messiah is understandable in light of their distinctive place in the promises of the Davidic covenant.[1] This last covenant in the history of Israel centers around two promises: the maintenance of the city of Jerusalem and the continuation of the line of David. While nothing in Israel's secular history since the time of the restoration fulfills these expectations, the coming of Jesus the Christ and the establishment of his throne in the heavenly Jerusalem introduces the final stage that fulfills the expectations created by the predictions of the prophets.
- Israel's exile and restoration have a significant impact on all the nations of the world. Both in judgment and in restoration, the nations have their future defined by reference to this one nation's experience. As God's own nation ultimately under-

1. See the discussion of the promise regarding the city of Jerusalem and the person of messiah in the Davidic covenant in Robertson, *Christ of the Covenants*, 236–43.

went righteous judgment, so all peoples will eventually undergo the Lord's judgments. Even as Israel experienced restoration after exile, so all those who repent and call on the name of the Lord will be saved.

- The history of Israel in exile and restoration becomes a basis for projection into the future. Just as recapitulation eschatology in terms of a renewed experience of the exodus dominated the futuristic projections of prophets like Isaiah and Hosea, so also the experience of Israel's exile and restoration provides the basis for prophetic prediction of the future. In this way, the prophetically typological nature of redemptive history under the old covenant receives reinforcement both at the beginning and the end of the chosen nation's history. As exodus, wilderness wandering, and conquest of the land embodied principles of God's redemptive working, so also exile and restoration communicate truths regarding judgment and deliverance.

The permeating character of the themes of exile and restoration throughout the ministry of Israel's prophets may provide some guidelines for understanding the consummate fulfillment of prophecy in the present age. This fulfillment finds its focal point in the person of Jesus Christ. As the suffering servant of the Lord, he has gone into the abyss of exile from the presence of God. He has also experienced restoration by his resurrection from the dead and ascension to the right hand of the Father. All who are united to him by faith have died with him and have been raised again.

At the same time, the people of God await the final restoration that will come with the return of Jesus Christ. The blending of eschatological expectations in the prophets with the imagery of restoration after exile leads naturally to the uniting of these same themes under the expectations of the new covenant. The rejuvenation of the world that will come with the final establishment of messiah's reign represents the consummation of expectations imbedded in the prophetic predictions of restoration after exile.

The transferal of the values of exile and restoration into the new covenant era establishes the permanent worth of these prophetic predictions. The understanding of the sufferings and death of Christ are enriched by viewing them in terms of a theology of exile. The appreciation of his triumphant victory in resurrection and ascension is multiplied by perceiving it as a restoration after divine judgment. He triumphed in his resurrection so as to lay the foundation for the restoration of all things, which will be accomplished at his glorious return (Acts 3:21).

BIBLIOGRAPHY

Achtemeier, Elizabeth. *Nahum–Malachi.* Interpretation. Atlanta: John Knox, 1986.

Ackroyd, Peter R. *Exile and Restoration: A Study of Hebrew Thought of the Sixth Century B.C.* London: SCM, 1968.

Ahlström, Gösta W. *Joel and the Temple Cult of Jerusalem.* Vetus Testamentum Supplement 21. Leiden: Brill, 1971.

Albright, W. F. *From the Stone Age to Christianity: Monotheism and the Historical Process.* New York: Doubleday, 1957.

Alexander, J. A. *Isaiah: Translated and Explained.* 2 vols. Philadelphia: Presbyterian Board, 1851.

Alexander, T. Desmond. "Jonah and Genre." *Tyndale Bulletin* 36 (1985): 35–59.

Allen, Leslie C. *The Books of Joel, Obadiah, Jonah, and Micah.* New International Commentary on the Old Testament. Grand Rapids: Eerdmans, 1976.

Allis, O. T. *The Unity of Isaiah.* Philadelphia: Presbyterian & Reformed, 1955.

Alt, Albrecht. *Essays on Old Testament History and Religion.* Oxford: Blackwell, 1966.

Andersen, Francis I., and David Noel Freedman. *Amos: A New Translation with Introduction and Commentary.* Anchor Bible 24A. New York: Doubleday, 1989.

———. *Hosea: A New Translation with Introduction and Commentary.* Anchor Bible 24. Garden City: Doubleday, 1980.

Anderson, Bernhard W. "Exodus Typology in Second Isaiah." Pp. 177–95 in *Israel's Prophetic Heritage: Essays in Honor of James Muilenburg.* Edited by Bernhard W. Anderson and Walter Harrelson. New York: Harper, 1962.

Ashley, Timothy R. *The Book of Numbers*. New International Commentary on the Old Testament. Grand Rapids: Eerdmans, 1993.

Baker, David W. *Nahum, Habakkuk, and Zephaniah: An Introduction and Commentary*. Leicester: Inter-Varsity, 1988.

Baldwin, Joyce G. *Daniel: An Introduction and Commentary*. Tyndale Old Testament Commentaries. Leicester: Inter-Varsity, 1978.

———. *Haggai, Zechariah, Malachi: An Introduction and Commentary*. Tyndale Old Testament Commentaries. London: Tyndale, 1972.

Baltzer, Klaus. "Considerations regarding the Office and Calling of the Prophets." *Harvard Theological Review* 61 (1968): 567–81.

Barr, James. *The Concept of Biblical Theology: An Old Testament Perspective*. London: SCM, 1999.

Barton, John. "Ethics in Isaiah of Jerusalem." Pp. 80–97 in *The Place Is Too Small for Us*. Edited by Robert P. Gordon. Winona Lake, Ind.: Eisenbrauns, 1995.

———. *Joel and Obadiah: A Commentary*. Old Testament Library. Louisville: Westminster John Knox, 2001.

———. *Oracles of God: Perceptions of Ancient Prophecy in Israel after the Exile*. London: Darton, Longman & Todd, 1986.

Blenkinsopp, Joseph. *Ezekiel*. Interpretation. Louisville: John Knox, 1990.

———. *A History of Prophecy in Israel*. Revised edition. Louisville: Westminster John Knox, 1996.

———. "Introduction to the Pentateuch." Vol. 1 / pp. 305–18 in *The New Interpreter's Bible*. Edited by Leander E. Keck et al. Nashville: Abingdon, 1994.

———. *Isaiah: A New Translation with Introduction and Commentary*. 3 vols. Anchor Bible 19. New York: Doubleday, 2000–2003.

Block, Daniel I. *The Book of Ezekiel*. 2 vols. New International Commentary on the Old Testament. Grand Rapids: Eerdmans, 1997–98.

Bright, John. *Covenant and Promise*. London: SCM, 1977.

———. *A History of Israel*. 4th edition. Louisville: Westminster John Knox, 2000.

———. *Jeremiah: A New Translation with Introduction and Commentary*. Anchor Bible 21. Garden City: Doubleday, 1965.

Brownlee, William H. *Ezekiel 1–19*. Word Biblical Commentary 28. Waco: Word, 1986.

Brueggemann, Walter. *A Commentary on Jeremiah: Exile and Homecoming*. Grand Rapids: Eerdmans, 1998.

————. *Isaiah*. 2 vols. Westminster Bible Companion. Louisville: Westminster John Knox, 1998.

————. *Theology of the Old Testament: Testimony, Dispute, Advocacy*. Minneapolis: Fortress, 1997.

Calvin, John. *Commentaries on the Book of the Prophet Jeremiah and the Lamentations*. Reprinted Grand Rapids: Baker, 1993.

————. *Commentaries on the Four Last Books of Moses Arranged in the Form of a Harmony*. 4 vols. Edinburgh: Calvin Tract Society, 1852.

————. *Commentaries on the Twelve Minor Prophets*. 5 vols. Reprinted Grand Rapids: Baker, 1993.

————. *Commentary on the Book of the Prophet Isaiah*. Edinburgh: Calvin Tract Society, 1850.

————. *Ezekiel*, vol. 1: *Chapters 1–12*. Grand Rapids: Eerdmans, 1994.

Carroll, Robert P. *When Prophecy Failed: Reactions and Responses to Failure in the Old Testament Prophetic Traditions*. London: SCM, 1979.

Carson, D. A. (ed.). *From Sabbath to Lord's Day: A Biblical, Historical, and Theological Investigation*. Grand Rapids: Zondervan, 1982.

Childs, Brevard S. *Biblical Theology of the Old and New Testaments: Theological Reflections on the Christian Bible*. London: SCM, 1992.

————. "The Enemy from the North and the Chaos Tradition." Pp. 151–61 in *A Prophet to the Nations: Essays in Jeremiah Studies*. Edited by Leo G. Perdue and Brian W. Kovacs. Winona Lake, Ind.: Eisenbrauns, 1984.

————. *Introduction to the Old Testament as Scripture*. London: SCM, 1979.

————. *Isaiah*. Old Testament Library. Louisville: Westminster John Knox, 2001.

————. *Old Testament Theology in a Canonical Context*. London: SCM, 1985.

Clements, Ronald E. "Beyond Tradition-History: Deutero-Isaianic Development of First Isaiah's Themes." *Journal for the Study of the Old Testament* 31 (1985): 95–113.

————. "The Book of Deuteronomy: Introduction, Commentary, and Reflections." Vol. 2 / pp. 269–90 in *The New Interpreter's Bible*. Edited by Leander E. Keck et al. Nashville: Abingdon, 1998.

————. *A Century of Old Testament Study*. London: Lutterworth, 1976.

————. *Ezekiel*. Louisville: Westminster John Knox, 1996.

————. *Jeremiah*. Interpretation. Atlanta: John Knox, 1988.

————. *Old Testament Prophecy: From Oracles to Canon*. Louisville: Westminster John Knox, 1996.

————. *Prophecy and Covenant*. London: SCM, 1965.

————. *Prophecy and Tradition*. Oxford: Blackwell, 1978.

Coggins, Richard J. "Prophecy—True and False." Pp. 80–94 in *Of Prophets' Visions and the Wisdom of Sages: Essays in Honour of R. Norman Whybray on His 70th Birthday*. Edited by Heather A. McKay and David J. A. Clines. Sheffield: Sheffield Academic Press, 1993.

Coggins, Richard, Anthony Phillips, and Michael Knibb (eds.). *Israel's Prophetic Tradition: Essays in Honour of Peter R. Ackroyd*. Cambridge: Cambridge University Press, 1982.

Collins, John J. *Daniel: A Commentary on the Book of Daniel*. Hermeneia. Minneapolis: Fortress, 1993.

Craigie, Peter C., Page H. Kelley, and Joel F. Drinkard Jr. *Jeremiah 1–25*. Word Biblical Commentary 26. Dallas: Word, 1991.

Crenshaw, James L. *Joel: A New Translation with Introduction and Commentary*. Anchor Bible 24C. New York: Doubleday, 1995.

————. *Prophetic Conflict: Its Effect upon Israelite Religion*. Berlin: de Gruyter, 1971.

Cullmann, Oscar. *The Christology of the New Testament*. London: SCM, 1959.

Dahood, Mitchell. *Psalms: Introduction, Translation, and Notes*. 3 vols. Anchor Bible 16–17A. New York: Doubleday, 1965–70.

Deist, Ferdinand E. "The Prophets: Are We Heading for a Paradigm Switch?" Pp. 582–99 in *The Place Is Too Small for Us*. Edited by Robert P. Gordon. Winona Lake, Ind.: Eisenbrauns, 1995.

Dillard, Raymond B., and Tremper Longman III. *An Introduction to the Old Testament*. Leicester: Apollos, 1995.

Driver, S. R. *A Critical and Exegetical Commentary on Deuteronomy*. International Critical Commentary. Third edition. Edinburgh: Clark, 1902.

Driver, S. R., and W. Sanday. *Christianity and Other Religions: Three Short Sermons*. London: Longmans, Green, 1908.

Durand, Jean-Marie. *Archives epistolaires de Mari*, vol. 1.1. Archives royales de Mari 26. Paris: Recherche sur les Civilizations, 1988.

Eichrodt, Walther. *Ezekiel: A Commentary*. Translated by Cosslett Quinn. Old Testament Library. London: SCM, 1970.

————. *Theology of the Old Testament*. Translated by J. A. Baker. 2 vols. Old Testament Library. London: SCM, 1961–67.

Eissfeldt, Otto. *The Old Testament: An Introduction*. Translated by Peter R. Ackroyd. Oxford: Blackwell, 1965.

————. "The Prophetic Literature." Pp. 115–61 in *The Old Testament and Modern Study: A Generation of Discovery and Research*. Edited by H. H. Rowley. Oxford: Clarendon, 1951.

Fairbairn, Patrick. *Ezekiel and the Book of His Prophecy: An Exposition*. Edinburgh: Clark, 1963.

————. *The Interpretation of Prophecy*. London: Banner of Truth, 1964.

————. *The Typology of Scripture*, vol. 1. Edinburgh: Clark, 1870.

Feinberg, Charles Lee. *The Prophecy of Ezekiel*. Chicago: Moody, 1969.

Fischer, Thomas. "Maccabees, Books of." Translated by Frederick Cryer. Vol. 4 / pp. 439–50 in *The Anchor Bible Dictionary*. Edited by David Noel Freedman et al. New York: Doubleday, 1992.

Fohrer, Georg. *Introduction to the Old Testament*. Translated by David E. Green. London: SPCK, 1970.

Foster, R. S. *The Restoration of Israel*. London: Darton, Longman & Todd, 1970.

France, R. T. *The Gospel of Mark: A Commentary on the Greek Text*. Grand Rapids: Eerdmans, 2002.

Freedman, David Noel. "Between God and Man: Prophets in Ancient Israel." Pp. 57–87 in *Prophecy and Prophets: The Diversity of Contemporary Issues in Scholarship*. Edited by Yehoshua Gitay. Atlanta: Scholars Press, 1997.

————. *Pottery, Poetry, and Prophecy: Studies in Early Hebrew Poetry*. Winona Lake, Ind.: Eisenbrauns, 1980.

Fretheim, Terence E. *The Message of Jonah: A Theological Commentary*. Minneapolis: Augsburg, 1977.

Gesenius, Wilhelm. *Hebrew Grammar*. Edited by E. Kautzsch. Translated by A. E. Cowley. 2d edition. Oxford: Clarendon, 1910.

Goldingay, John E. *Approaches to Old Testament Interpretation*. Leicester: Apollos, 1990.

————. *Daniel*. Word Biblical Commentary 30. Dallas: Word, 1989.

Goldsworthy, Graeme. *Gospel and Kingdom: A Christian Interpretation of the Old Testament*. Exeter: Paternoster, 1981.

Gordon, Robert P. "From Mari to Moses: Prophecy at Mari and in Ancient Israel." Pp. 63–79 in *Of Prophets' Visions and the Wisdom of Sages: Essays in Honour of R. Norman Whybray on His 70th Birthday*. Edited by Heather A. McKay and David J. A. Clines. Sheffield: Sheffield Academic Press, 1993.

507

Gowan, Donald E. *Theology of the Prophetic Books: The Death and Resurrection of Israel*. Louisville: Westminster John Knox, 1998.

Grintz, Yehoshua M. "Jew." Vol. 10 / pp. 21–23 in *Encyclopaedia Judaica*. Jerusalem: Keter, 1972.

Grudem, Wayne. *The Gift of Prophecy in the New Testament and Today*. Eastbourne: Kingsway, 1988.

Gunkel, Hermann. "The Prophets as Writers and Poets." Translated by James L. Schaaf. Pp. 22–73 in *Prophecy in Israel*. Edited by David L. Petersen. Philadelphia: Fortress, 1987.

Habel, Norman. "The Form and Significance of the Call Narratives," *Zeitschrift für die Alttestamentliche Wissenschaft* 77 (1965): 297–323.

Hagner, Donald A. *Matthew*. 2 vols. Word Biblical Commentary 33A–B. Dallas: Word, 1993–95.

Harrison, R. K. *Introduction to the Old Testament*. London: Tyndale, 1970.

Hartshorne, C. *Reality as Social Process: Studies in Metaphysics and Religion*. New York: Hafner, 1971.

Hengstenberg, E. W. *Christology of the Old Testament*. 2 vols. 1854. Translated by Reuel Keith. Reprinted MacDill AFB, Fla.: MacDonald, 1972.

Hermann, Siegfried. "Overcoming the Israelite Crisis: Remarks on the Interpretation of the Book of Jeremiah." Translated by Leo G. Perdue. Pp. 299–312 in *A Prophet to the Nations: Essays in Jeremiah Studies*. Edited by Leo G. Perdue and Brian W. Kovacs. Winona Lake, Ind.: Eisenbrauns, 1984.

Hobbs, T. R. "Some Remarks on the Composition and Structure of the Book of Jeremiah." Pp. 175–91 in *A Prophet to the Nations: Essays in Jeremiah Studies*. Edited by Leo G. Perdue and Brian W. Kovacs. Winona Lake, Ind.: Eisenbrauns, 1984.

Holladay, William L. *Jeremiah: A Commentary on the Book of the Prophet Jeremiah*. 2 vols. Hermeneia. Philadelphia: Fortress, 1986–89.

Hubbard, David Allan. *Joel and Amos: An Introduction and Commentary*. Leicester: Inter-Varsity, 1989.

Huffmon, Herbert B. "A Company of Prophets: Mari, Assyria, Israel." Pp. 47–70 in *Prophecy in Its Ancient Near Eastern Context: Mesopotamian, Biblical, and Arabian Perspectives*. Edited by Martti Nissinen. Atlanta: Society of Biblical Literature, 2000.

———. "The Origins of Prophecy." Pp. 171–86 in *Magnalia Dei, the Mighty Acts of God: Essays on the Bible and Archaeology in Memory of*

G. *Ernest Wright*. Edited by Frank Moore Cross, Werner E. Lemke, and Patrick D. Miller Jr. Garden City, N.Y.: Doubleday, 1976.

Hyatt, J. Philip. "Jeremiah and Deuteronomy." Pp. 113–27 in *A Prophet to the Nations: Essays in Jeremiah Studies*. Edited by Leo G. Perdue and Brian W. Kovacs. Winona Lake, Ind.: Eisenbrauns, 1984.

Jerome. *Commentary on Daniel*. Translated by Gleason L. Archer Jr. Grand Rapids: Baker, 1958.

Johnson, A. R. *The Cultic Prophet in Ancient Israel*. Cardiff: University of Wales Press, 1962.

Kaiser, Walter C., Jr. *The Messiah in the Old Testament*. Grand Rapids: Zondervan, 1995.

Keil, C. F. *Biblical Commentary on the Prophecies of Ezekiel*. Translated by James Martin. 2 vols. Edinburgh: Clark, 1876.

———. *Biblical Commentary on the Twelve Minor Prophets*. Translated by James Martin. 2 vols. Edinburgh: Clark, 1871.

———. *The Book of the Prophet Daniel*. Translated by M. G. Easton. Edinburgh: Clark, 1872.

———. *The Books of the Chronicles*. Translated by Andrew Harper. Edinburgh: Clark, 1872.

———. *Introduction to the Old Testament*. Translated by G. C. M. Douglas. Reprint Peabody, Mass.: Hendrickson, 1988.

Kidner, Derek. *The Message of Hosea: Love to the Loveless*. Leicester: Inter-Varsity, 1981.

———. *The Message of Jeremiah: Against Wind and Tide*. Leicester: Inter-Varsity, 1986.

Kitchen, Kenneth A. *Ancient Orient and the Old Testament*. London: Tyndale, 1966.

———. "Ark of the Covenant." Vol. 1 / pp. 110–11 in *The Illustrated Bible Dictionary*. Edited by J. D. Douglas et al. Leicester: Inter-Varsity, 1980.

Klein, Ralph W. *Ezekiel: The Prophet and His Message*. Columbia: University of South Carolina Press, 1988.

Kline, Meredith G. "Anathema." *Kerux* 10.3 (Dec. 1995): 3–30.

———. "By My Spirit [II]." *Kerux* 9.2 (Sept. 1994): 3–22.

———. "The Covenant of the Seventieth Week." Pp. 452–69 in *The Law and the Prophets*. Edited by John H. Skilton. Nutley, N.J.: Presbyterian & Reformed, 1974.

———. "Evangel of the Messianic Angel [I]." *Kerux* 7.2 (Sept. 1992): 15–25.

———. "Evangel of the Messianic Angel [II]." *Kerux* 7.3 (Dec. 1992): 39–61.

———. "The Exaltation of Christ." *Kerux* 12.3 (Dec. 1997): 3–29.

———. "How Long [I]?" *Kerux* 6.1 (May 1991): 16–31.

———. "How Long [II]?" *Kerux* 6.2 (Sept. 1991): 23–42.

———. "Marana tha." *Kerux* 11.3 (Sept. 1996): 10–28.

———. "Messianic Avenger." *Kerux* 7.1 (May 1992): 20–36.

———. "The Rider of the Red Horse [I]." *Kerux* 5.2 (Sept. 1990): 2–20.

———. "The Rider of the Red Horse [II]." *Kerux* 5.3 (Dec. 1990): 9–28.

———. "The Servant and the Serpent [I]." *Kerux* 8.1 (May 1993): 20–37.

———. "The Servant and the Serpent [II]." *Kerux* 8.2 (Sept. 1993): 10–34.

———. "The Structure of the Book of Zechariah." *Journal of the Evangelical Theological Society* 34.2 (June 1991): 179–93.

———. *Treaty of the Great King*. Grand Rapids: Eerdmans, 1963.

Kraus, Hans-Joachim. *Psalms: A Commentary*. Translated by Hilton C. Oswald. 2 vols. Minneapolis: Augsburg, 1988–93.

Kuhl, Curt. *The Prophets of Israel*. Edinburgh: Oliver & Boyd, 1960.

Limburg, James. *Jonah: A Commentary*. Louisville: Westminster/John Knox, 1993.

Lincoln, A. T. "From Sabbath to Lord's Day: A Biblical and Theological Perspective." Pp. 343–412 in *From Sabbath to Lord's Day: A Biblical, Historical, and Theological Investigation*. Edited by D. A. Carson. Grand Rapids: Zondervan, 1982.

Lindblom, Johannes. *Prophecy in Ancient Israel*. Oxford: Blackwell, 1962.

Malamat, Abraham. "Exile, Assyrian." Vol. 6 / pp. 1034–36 in *Encyclopaedia Judaica*. Jerusalem: Keter, 1972.

———. "A Forerunner of Biblical Prophecy: The Mari Documents." Pp. 33–52 in *Ancient Israelite Religion: Essays in Honor of Frank Moore Cross*. Edited by Patrick D. Miller Jr., Paul D. Hanson, and S. Dean McBride. Philadelphia: Fortress, 1987.

———. "Prophecy at Mari." Pp. 50–73 in *The Place Is Too Small for Us*. Edited by Robert P. Gordon. Winona Lake, Ind.: Eisenbrauns, 1995.

Martin, R. L. "The Earliest Messianic Interpretation of Genesis 3:15." *Journal of Biblical Literature* 84 (1965): 425–27.

Mauser, Ulrich W. *Christ in the Wilderness*. Naperville: Allenson, 1963.

McComiskey, Thomas E. "Zechariah." Vol. 3 / pp. 1003–1244 in *The Minor Prophets: An Exegetical and Expository Commentary*. Edited by Thomas Edward McComiskey. Grand Rapids: Baker, 1998.

McConville, J. Gordon. *Law and Theology in Deuteronomy*. Sheffield: JSOT Press, 1984.

McNeile, A. H. *The Book of Numbers*. Cambridge: Cambridge University Press, 1911.

Mendenhall, George E. "Ancient Oriental and Biblical Law." *Biblical Archaeologist* 17 (1954): 26–46.

Merrill, Eugene H. *Kingdom of Priests: A History of Old Testament Israel*. Grand Rapids: Baker, 1987.

Montgomery, James A. *A Critical and Exegetical Commentary on the Book of Daniel*. International Critical Commentary. Edinburgh: Clark, 1927.

Motyer, J. Alec. *The Message of Amos: The Day of the Lion*. Downers Grove, Ill.: InterVarsity, 1974.

———. *The Prophecy of Isaiah: An Introduction and Commentary*. Downers Grove, Ill.: InterVarsity, 1993.

Mowinckel, Sigmund. *Prophecy and Tradition: The Prophetic Books in the Light of the Study of the Growth and History of the Traditions*. Oslo: Dybwad, 1946.

———. "The 'Spirit' and the 'Word' in the Pre-exilic Reforming Prophets." *Journal of Biblical Literature* 53 (1934): 199–227.

Murray, John. *Principles of Conduct: Aspects of Biblical Ethics*. London: Tyndale, 1957.

Nicol, T. "Molech, Moloch." Vol. 3 / pp. 2074–75 in *The International Standard Bible Encyclopedia*. Edited by James Orr. Grand Rapids: Eerdmans, 1939.

Niehaus, Jeff. "Amos." Vol. 1 / pp. 315–494 in *The Minor Prophets: An Exegetical and Expository Commentary*. Edited by Thomas Edward McComiskey. Grand Rapids: Baker, 1992.

Nissinen, Martti. "The Socioreligious Role of the Neo-Assyrian Prophets." Pp. 89–114 in *Prophecy in Its Ancient Near Eastern Context: Mesopotamian, Biblical, and Arabian Perspectives*. Edited by Martti Nissinen. Atlanta: Society of Biblical Literature, 2000.

——— (ed.). *Prophecy in Its Ancient Near Eastern Context: Mesopotamian, Biblical, and Arabian Perspectives*. Atlanta: Society of Biblical Literature, 2000.

North, C. R. "The 'Former Things' and the 'New Things' in Deutero-Isaiah." Pp. 111–26 in *Studies in Old Testament Prophecy Presented to Professor Theodore H. Robinson*. Edited by H. H. Rowley. Edinburgh: Clark, 1950.

Noth, Martin. *The Deuteronomistic History*. Journal for the Study of the Old Testament Supplement 155. Sheffield: JSOT Press, 1981.

511

Oded, Bustenay. *Mass Deportations and Deportees in the Neo-Assyrian Empire.* Wiesbaden: Reichert, 1979.

———. "The Settlements of the Israelite and Judean Exiles in Mesopotamia in the 8th–6th Centuries BCE." Pp. 91–103 in *Studies in Historical Geography and Biblical Historiography.* Edited by Gershon Galil and Moshe Weinfeld. Leiden: Brill, 2000.

Oehler, Gustav F. *Theology of the Old Testament.* Translated by Sophia Taylor. 2 vols. Edinburgh: Clark, 1874–75.

Oesterley, W. O. E., and Theodore H. Robinson. *An Introduction to the Books of the Old Testament.* London: SPCK, 1934.

Oswalt, John N. *The Book of Isaiah.* 2 vols. New International Commentary on the Old Testament. Grand Rapids: Eerdmans, 1986–98.

Parker, Simon B. "Official Attitudes toward Prophecy at Mari and in Israel." *Vetus Testamentum* 43 (1993): 50–68.

Parpola, Simo. *Assyrian Prophecies.* State Archives of Assyria 9. Helsinki: Helsinki University Press, 1997.

Perdue, Leo G. "Jeremiah in Modern Research: Approaches and Issues." Pp. 1–32 in *A Prophet to the Nations: Essays in Jeremiah Studies.* Edited by Leo G. Perdue and Brian W. Kovacs. Winona Lake, Ind.: Eisenbrauns, 1984.

Perdue, Leo G., and Brian W. Kovacs (eds.). *A Prophet to the Nations: Essays in Jeremiah Studies.* Winona Lake, Ind.: Eisenbrauns, 1984.

Petersen, David L. "Defining Prophecy and Prophetic Literature." Pp. 33–44 in *Prophecy in Its Ancient Near Eastern Context: Mesopotamian, Biblical, and Arabian Perspectives.* Edited by Martti Nissinen. Atlanta: Society of Biblical Literature, 2000.

———. "Introduction to Prophetic Literature." Vol. 6 / pp. 1–23 in *The New Interpreter's Bible.* Edited by Leander E. Keck et al. Nashville: Abingdon, 2001.

———. *Zechariah 9–14 and Malachi: A Commentary.* Old Testament Library. London: SCM, 1995.

Phillips, Anthony. "Prophecy and Law." Pp. 217–32 in *Israel's Prophetic Tradition: Essays in Honour of Peter R. Ackroyd.* Edited by Richard Coggins, Anthony Phillips, and Michael Knibb. Cambridge: Cambridge University Press, 1982.

Porter, J. R. "The Origins of Prophecy in Israel." Pp. 12–31 in *Israel's Prophetic Tradition: Essays in Honour of Peter R. Ackroyd.* Edited by

Richard Coggins, Anthony Phillips, and Michael Knibb. Cambridge: Cambridge University Press, 1982.

Poythress, Vern Sheridan. "Hermeneutical Factors in Determining the Beginning of the Seventy Weeks (Daniel 9:25)." *Trinity Journal* n.s. 6 (1985): 131–49.

Pratt, Richard L., Jr. "Historical Contingencies and Biblical Predictions." Pp. 180–203 in *The Way of Wisdom: Essays in Honor of Bruce K. Waltke*. Edited by J. I. Packer and Sven K. Soderlund. Grand Rapids: Zondervan, 2000.

Prinsloo, Willem S. *The Theology of the Book of Joel*. Berlin: de Gruyter, 1985.

Pritchard, James B. (ed.). *Ancient Near Eastern Texts Related to the Old Testament*. 3rd edition. Princeton: Princeton University Press, 1969.

Provan, Iain W. "The Messiah in the Books of Kings." Pp. 67–85 in *The Lord's Anointed: Interpretation of Old Testament Messianic Texts*. Edited by Philip E. Satterthwaite, Richard S. Hess, and Gordon J. Wenham. Carlisle: Paternoster, 1995.

Rabinowitz, Louis Isaac. "Ten Lost Tribes." Vol. 15 / pp. 1003–6 in *Encyclopaedia Judaica*. Jerusalem: Keter, 1972.

Rad, Gerhard von. *Deuteronomy: A Commentary*. Translated by Dorothea Barton. Old Testament Library. London: SCM, 1966.

———. *Genesis: A Commentary*. Translated by John H. Marks. Revised edition. Old Testament Library. London: SCM, 1963.

———. *Old Testament Theology*, vol. 2: *The Theology of Israel's Prophetic Traditions*. Translated by David M. G. Stalker. Edinburgh: Oliver & Boyd, 1965.

———. "The Origin of the Concept of the Day of Yahweh." *Journal of Semitic Studies* 4 (1959): 97–108.

———. *Studies in Deuteronomy*. Translated by David M. G. Stalker. Studies in Biblical Theology 9. London: SCM, 1953.

Roberts, J. J. M. *Nahum, Habakkuk, and Zephaniah: A Commentary*. Louisville: Westminster/John Knox, 1991.

Robertson, O. Palmer. *The Books of Nahum, Habakkuk, and Zephaniah*. New International Commentary on the Old Testament. Grand Rapids: Eerdmans, 1990.

———. *The Christ of the Covenants*. Phillipsburg, N.J.: P&R, 1980.

———. "Current Critical Questions concerning the 'Curse of Ham' (Gen. 9:20–27)." *Journal of the Evangelical Theological Society* 41.2 (June 1998): 177–88.

———. *The Final Word: A Biblical Response to the Case for Tongues and Prophecy Today*. Edinburgh: Banner of Truth Trust, 1993.

———. "Hermeneutics of Continuity." Pp. 89–108 in *Continuity and Discontinuity: Perspectives on the Relationship between the Old and New Testaments: Essays in Honor of S. Lewis Johnson Jr*. Edited by John S. Feinberg. Westchester, Ill.: Crossway, 1988.

———. *The Israel of God: Yesterday, Today, and Tomorrow*. Phillipsburg, N.J.: P&R, 2000.

———. "A People of the Wilderness: The Concept of the Church in the Epistle to the Hebrews." Doctoral dissertation, Union Theological Seminary, Richmond, Va., 1966.

———. *Prophet of the Coming Day of the Lord: The Message of Joel*. Durham: Evangelical Press, 1995.

Rowley, H. H. *Men of God: Studies in Old Testament History and Prophecy*. London: Nelson, 1963.

———. *The Servant of the Lord and Other Essays on the Old Testament*. London: Lutterworth, 1952.

——— (ed.) *Studies in Old Testament Prophecy Presented to Professor Theodore H. Robinson*. Edinburgh: Clark, 1950.

Sanders, James A. "Hermeneutics in True and False Prophecy." Pp. 21–41 in *Canon and Authority: Essays in Old Testament Religion and Theology*. Edited by George W. Coats and Burke O. Long. Philadelphia: Fortress, 1977.

Sawyer, John F. A. "A Change of Emphasis in the Study of the Prophets." Pp. 233–49 in *Israel's Prophetic Tradition: Essays in Honour of Peter R. Ackroyd*. Edited by Richard Coggins, Anthony Phillips, and Michael Knibb. Cambridge: Cambridge University Press, 1982.

———. "Prophecy and Interpretation." Pp. 563–75 in *The Place Is Too Small for Us*. Edited by Robert P. Gordon. Winona Lake, Ind.: Eisenbrauns, 1995.

Seitz, Christopher R. "The Book of Isaiah 40–66: Introduction, Commentary, and Reflections." Vol. 6 / pp. 307–552 in *The New Interpreter's Bible*. Edited by Leander E. Keck et al. Nashville: Abingdon, 2001.

———. *Isaiah 1–39*. Interpretation. Louisville: John Knox, 1993.

———. *Theology in Conflict: Reactions to the Exile in the Book of Jeremiah*. Berlin: de Gruyter, 1989.

Seow, C. L. "Ark of the Covenant." Vol. 1 / pp. 386–93 in *The Anchor Bible Dictionary*. Edited by David Noel Freedman et al. New York: Doubleday, 1992.

Silverman, Godfrey Edmond. "British Israelites." Vol. 4 / pp. 1381–82 in *Encyclopaedia Judaica*. Jerusalem: Keter, 1972.

Stolper, Matthew W. "Murashû, Archive of." Vol. 4 / pp. 927–28 in *The Anchor Bible Dictionary*. Edited by David Noel Freedman et al. New York: Doubleday, 1992.

Taylor, John B. *Ezekiel: An Introduction and Commentary*. Leicester: Inter-Varsity, 1969.

Thompson, J. A. *The Book of Jeremiah*. New International Commentary on the Old Testament. Grand Rapids: Eerdmans, 1980.

VanGemeren, Willem A. *Interpreting the Prophetic Word*. Grand Rapids: Zondervan, 1990.

Vawter, Bruce. "Introduction to Prophetic Literature." Pp. 186–200 in *The New Jerome Biblical Commentary*. Edited by Raymond E. Brown, Joseph A. Fitzmyer, and Roland E. Murphy. London: Chapman, 1989.

Verhoef, Pieter A. *The Books of Haggai and Malachi*. New International Commentary on the Old Testament. Grand Rapids: Eerdmans, 1987.

Vos, Geerhardus. *Biblical Theology: Old and New Testaments*. Grand Rapids: Eerdmans, 1948.

Walker, Peter. *Jesus and the Holy City: New Testament Perspectives on Jerusalem*. Grand Rapids: Eerdmans, 1996.

Walvoord, John F. *Daniel, the Key to Prophetic Revelation: A Commentary*. Chicago: Moody, 1971.

Warfield, Benjamin Breckinridge. *Christology and Criticism*. New York: Oxford University Press, 1929.

Watts, John D. W. *Isaiah*. 2 vols. Word Biblical Commentary 24–25. Waco: Word, 1985–87.

Weinfeld, Moshe. "Deuteronomy: The Present State of Inquiry." Pp. 21–35 in *A Song of Power and the Power of Song: Essays on the Book of Deuteronomy*. Edited by Duane L. Christensen. Winona Lake, Ind.: Eisenbrauns, 1993.

Weiser, Artur. *The Psalms: A Commentary*. Translated by Herbert Hartwell. Old Testament Library. London: SCM, 1962.

Wellhausen, Julius. *Prolegomena to the History of Israel.* Translated by John S. Black and Allan Menzies. Edinburgh: Black, 1885.

Wenham, Gordon J. *Numbers: An Introduction and Commentary.* Tyndale Old Testament Commentaries. Leicester: Inter-Varsity, 1981.

Westermann, Claus. *Isaiah 40–66: A Commentary.* Translated by David M. G. Stalker. Old Testament Library. Philadelphia: Westminster, 1966.

———. *Prophetic Oracles of Salvation in the Old Testament.* Edinburgh: Clark, 1991.

Whitehorne, John. "Antiochus (person)." Vol. 1 / pp. 269–72 in *The Anchor Bible Dictionary.* Edited by David Noel Freedman et al. New York: Doubleday, 1992.

Whitney, Charles Francis. *The Exilic Age.* London: Longmans, Green, 1957.

Wildberger, Hans. *Isaiah: A Commentary.* Translated by Thomas H. Trapp. 3 vols. Minneapolis: Fortress, 1991–2002.

Williamson, H. G. M. *King, Messiah, and Servant in the Book of Isaiah.* Carlisle: Paternoster, 1998.

Wilson, Robert R. *Prophecy and Society in Ancient Israel.* Philadelphia: Fortress, 1980.

———. *Sociological Approaches to the Old Testament.* Philadelphia: Fortress, 1984.

Wiseman, D. J. *Chronicles of the Chaldaean Kings (626–556 B.C.) in the British Museum.* London: British Museum, 1956.

Wolff, Hans Walter. *Hosea: A Commentary on the Book of the Prophet Hosea.* Translated by Gary Stansell. Hermeneia. Philadelphia: Fortress, 1974.

———. *Joel and Amos: A Commentary on the Books of the Prophets Joel and Amos.* Translated by Waldemar Janzen, S. Dean McBride Jr., and Charles A. Muenchow. Hermeneia. Philadelphia: Fortress, 1977.

———. *Obadiah and Jonah: A Commentary.* Translated by Margaret Kohl. Hermeneia. Minneapolis: Augsburg, 1986.

Woude, A. S. van der. "Micah in Dispute with the Pseudo-prophets." *Vetus Testamentum* 19 (1969): 244–60.

Woudstra, Martin. "Recent Translations of Genesis 3:15." *Calvin Theological Journal* 6 (1971): 194–203.

Wright, Christopher J. H. *The Message of Ezekiel: A New Heart and a New Spirit.* Leicester: Inter-Varsity, 2001.

Young, E. J. *The Book of Isaiah.* 3 vols. New International Commentary on the Old Testament. Grand Rapids: Eerdmans, 1965–72.

516

———. "Daniel's Vision of the Son of Man." Pp. 425–51 in *The Law and the Prophets*. Edited by John H. Skilton. Nutley, N.J.: Presbyterian & Reformed, 1974.

———. *An Introduction to the Old Testament*. London: Tyndale, 1964.

———. *My Servants the Prophets*. Grand Rapids: Eerdmans, 1952.

———. *The Prophecy of Daniel: A Commentary*. Grand Rapids: Eerdmans, 1949.

———. *Studies in Isaiah*. London: Tyndale, 1954.

Zadok, Ran. *The Jews in Babylonia during the Chaldean and Achaemenian Periods according to the Babylonian Sources*. Haifa: University of Haifa Press, 1979.

Zimmerli, Walther. *Ezekiel: A Commentary on the Book of the Prophet Ezekiel*. Translated by Ronald E. Clements and James D. Martin. Hermeneia. Philadelphia: Fortress, 1979–83.

———. "From Prophetic Word to Prophetic Book." Pp. 419–42 in *The Place Is Too Small for Us*. Edited by Robert P. Gordon. Winona Lake, Ind.: Eisenbrauns, 1995.

———. *The Law and the Prophets: A Study of the Meaning of the Old Testament*. Oxford: Blackwell, 1965.

INDEX OF SCRIPTURE
AND ANCIENT TEXTS

25:4—427
25:6–21—291
25:7—427

1 Chronicles

3:18–19—471
16:34—491
25:1—12n.7
25:3—12n.7
28:18—295
29:22–23—75
29:23—388n.26

2 Chronicles

2–7—391
6:27—244
20:1–30—172
20:14—12n.7
24:20—12n.7
26:16–21—72
29:30 —12n.7
32:20–21—210
34:3–7—73
35:15 —12n.7
36:5–7—283n.1, 320, 485
36:6—426
36:9–10—283n.1
36:21—309, 339, 341, 486
36:22–23—227n.29

Ezra

1:2–4—341
2:2—256n.1
2:63—35
2:64—362
3:1–3—360
3:1–4—392
3:8–13—360
4:24—360
5:2—471
6:14–15—360
7:6–10—361
7:7–8—361n.1
9:1–2—390n.30

Nehemiah

1:1—341
1:3—341
2:3—341
2:5—341
2:8—341
2:17—341
7:7—256n.1
7:65—35
9:20—377
10:35–40—390n.30
13:2–3—390n.30
13:10–12—390n.30
13:23–24—390n.30

Psalms

2—4, 20
2:2—355
2:8–9—355
16:9–11—304n.40
16:10–11—301
17:15—304n.40
18:10–11—334n.17
23:1—300
46:4—316n.61
51:7—83
68:17—372
68:18—57
68:30—372
69:28—403
71:22—77n.22
72—20
72:1–3—244
72:1–17—3
72:6—244
72:8—384
72:16—244
78:41—77n.22
78:67–72—181
80:15—62n.18
87:6—403
89:18—77n.22
89:19–37—3
95:10–11—355
97:2–4—334n.17

104:3—334n.17
105:8–9—417
115:4–8 —49
118:22–23—335
118:32—329
132:1–18—3
132:16–17—387
135:4—396, 403
136:1—491
139:16—403

Ecclesiastes

1:2—399

Isaiah

1–39—77, 216, 221, 222, 227, 229, 235, 236n.46, 238, 239
1:1—44, 71n.12, 210
1:4—216, 217
1:16–17—185
1:17—163
1:19—185
1:23—156, 167
2–11—213
2:1—44
2:1–4—213
2:2—446
2:2–3—181
2:2–4—436
2:3—222
2:12–21—447n.27
2:19c—445
2:21c—445
4:2—387, 468
4:3—216, 221, 403
4:3–5—181
5:6—175
5:13—220
5:16—77, 216
5:18—217
5:19—216
5:20—93
5:24—216
5:25b—445
6—68, 72n.12, 212

522

42—279
42:10—279
43:4-13—284
43:8-44:30—268
44:10—147
44:15—150n.9
45—98, 279
45:3—280
45:4—280
45:5—281
45:5a—281
46-49—269n.26
46-51—459
46:2-26—434
46:7-8—332
46:20—308
46:24—308
46:27—178
47—434
47:2—308
48:27-46—437
48:47—437
49:1-6—434
49:6—438
49:7-22—434
49:16a—246
49:23-27—434
49:39—438
50-51—269n.26, 434
50:1-46—434
50:4—490
50:4-5—183n.36
50:17-18—171
50:20—487
50:29—77, 171, 216
50:41—308
51:1-64—434
51:5—77, 216, 490
51:24—171
52—459
52:4-11—427
52:32—469
54:23-25—494

Lamentations
2:14—116

Ezekiel
1—373
1-3—293
1-24—292
1:1—74n.17, 290
1:1-2—440
1:2—283n.1, 291
1:2-3—74
1:4-28—295, 456
1:4-2:8—78
1:4-3:11—68
1:15-21—294
2:3—79
3:4—79
3:7—84
3:15—10, 75, 82
3:16-21—84, 295
3:17—80
3:17-21—431
3:18—83
3:22-23—295
3:26-28—309
4—457
4:5—461
5:5-7—148
5:8—148
6:8-12—374
7:2-3—499
7:5-7—499
7:16—461
8-11—293, 296, 309
8:1-4—296
8:3—296
8:3-5—461
8:4—295
8:5—296
8:6—296, 297, 461
8:7-12—296
8:7-9:11—461n.3
8:14—297
8:16—297
9:3—77, 297
10-11—456
10:6-7—295
10:13—77

10:16-19—297
11:12—148
11:14-21—299n.34
11:15—298
11:16—298, 373
11:17—299
11:18-19—299
11:20—299
11:22-23—77, 297
11:23—148, 375
12:1-20—457
12:3-7—426
12:10—470n.8
12:12—470n.8
12:12-14—427
12:22—422
12:23—422
12:24—422
12:25—422
12:28—422
13:8-9—117
13:9—403
13:15-16—117
13:19—95, 115
13:22—115
14:3-4—137
14:7—137
15:1-6—456
16—456, 461n.2
16:38-40—456
16:59-63—183n.36
17—457
17:1-21—321
17:2-4—469
17:22-23—321
17:22-24—387, 469
17:23—323
18-19—77
19:1—470n.8
19:9—426
20:1-29—461
20:5—178
20:12—152
20:13—147
20:16—147

528

530

537

Index of Subjects and Names